THE COMPLETE LIVES OF CAMP PEOPLE

THEORY IN FORMS
A Series Edited by Nancy Rose Hunt and Achille Mbembe

DUKE UNIVERSITY PRESS · DURHAM AND LONDON · 2020

THE COMPLETE LIVES OF CAMP PEOPLE

COLONIALISM, FASCISM, CONCENTRATED MODERNITY

RUDOLF MRÁZEK

© 2020 DUKE UNIVERSITY PRESS
All rights reserved
Designed by Matthew Tauch
Typeset in Warnock Pro by Westchester Publishing Services.

Library of Congress Cataloging-in-Publication Data
Names: Mrázek, Rudolf, author.
Title: The complete lives of camp people : colonialism, fascism, concentrated modernity / Rudolf Mrázek.
Description: Durham : Duke University Press, 2019. | Series: Theory in forms
Identifiers: LCCN 2019013464 (print) | LCCN 2019016276 (ebook)
ISBN 9781478007364 (ebook)
ISBN 9781478005773 (hardcover)
ISBN 9781478006671 (pbk.)
Subjects: LCSH: Boven Digoel (Concentration camp) | Concentration camps—Indonesia—Boven Digoel. | Political prisoners—Indonesia—Boven Digoel.
Classification: LCC HV8964.B86 (ebook) | LCC HV8964.B86 M739 2019 (print) | DDC 365/.4509516—dc23
LC record available at https://lccn.loc.gov/2019013464

Cover art: Photo by FlamingPumpkin / Getty.

Duke University Press gratefully acknowledges the support of the University of Michigan Department of History, which provided funds toward the publication of this book.

For Jan

výborný je zadák

CONTENTS

Introduction 1

9 .... PART I. FASHION

1. Clothes 11
2. Beauty Spots 27
3. Pink Bodies 43
4. Sport 72

81 .... PART II. SOUND

5. Noise 83
6. Voice 91
7. Music 104
8. Radio 119

141 .... PART III. LIGHT

9. Clearing 143
10. Enlightenment 169
11. Limelight 189

209	PART IV. CITY	12. Blocks 211
		13. Streets 239
		14. Suburbs 265
295	PART V. SCATTERING	15. Nausea 297
		16. Escape 319
		17. Dust, or Memory 349

Notes 379
Bibliography 451
Index 469

INTRODUCTION

In the late 1980s and early 1990s, forty years after the end of World War II and as "the Communism was finally defeated," the "Heidegger affair" burst into the European philosophy. Martin Heidegger (1889–1976), since the 1920s widely recognized as a major and perhaps the greatest philosopher of the twentieth century, became the subject of a painful and often fratricidal debate. Heidegger's membership in the Nazi party in Hitler's time, and some of his pro-Nazi speeches from that time, had long been known. But now, a number of new documents came to light, and this at a moment when the world feverishly searched for a new identity. The "Heidegger question" became urgent as a question why a man at the pinnacle of modern thought kept silent about the camps.

The French philosopher Jean-François Lyotard in his intervention in the debate assumed a position that I found close to what I tried to do in this book. Lyotard equaled Heidegger's silence with the spirit of the time—of our time. Instead of writing "the Jews," Lyotard wrote "the jews" with a lowercase "j." "The jews," he wrote, are both "Jews and non-Jews." "The jews," in the spirit of the time, are those "exiled from the inside."[1] One becomes "a jew" when his or her being becomes uncomfortable to the spirit of the time, when he or she stands out, uncomfortably to the rest, as "a witness to what cannot be represented."[2]

Minorities, refugees, misery—"this servitude to that which remains unfinished"[3]—are "the jews." "The so-called avant-garde," Lyotard wrote, is "the jews"—as long as it stands firm and thus "asks unanswerable questions." Even after they are "exiled from the inside," "the jews" as a specter haunt the spirit, and here the reference is clear. Even after exiled, "the jews" haunt the culture and the civilization from which they had been exiled. "Indeed," wrote Lyotard, "it is not 'by chance' that 'the jews' have been made the object of the final solution."[4]

Both camps that inspired this book were camps for "the jews." Theresienstadt (1942–45) was a "ghetto" for the Jews with a capital "J," in the center of Europe, in the western part of Nazi-occupied Czechoslovakia. Boven Digoel (1927–43) was an "isolation camp" in the Dutch East Indies, in Southeast Asia, for "the so-called avant-garde," the Indonesian rebels who, in late 1926 and early 1927, attempted to overthrow the colonial order. There were non-Jews in Boven Digoel, and many of them were Muslims.

Neither Theresienstadt nor Boven Digoel was Auschwitz—they were not Auschwitz yet. In Auschwitz, all norms of a civilization as it was known, lived, and believed in for centuries had imploded. Unlike the people in Auschwitz, "the jews" of Theresienstadt and Boven Digoel were allowed to live, "privileged until further notice," in a Potemkin village, a reader might think so—but let him or her imagine!

Trial and length of imprisonment were not a part of the decision to send people to Boven Digoel and Theresienstadt. The people going to the two camps were never allowed to know the trajectory of their lives from the point of their deportation on. They did not know how and whether their "as yet" might end. In Theresienstadt, much closer, intimately close, to Auschwitz, they, often with the greatest effort, rather would not know. In their not-knowing, the camp people of Boven Digoel and Theresienstadt came closer than any other people in modern history to an awe-inspiring closure of everything—that is to say, in Europe as in Asia, closure of the modern.

The people driven to both of the camps were educated, urbanized, and "Westernized," on the whole, high above the level of the society from which they had been exiled. It was indeed because of their being so (uncomfortably) modern that they were exiled. Neither of the two camps was the *nuit et brouillard* [night and fog]. The modernity did not ebb away in the two camps. Rather, the two camps became a space of the modern crushed into sharp pieces.

Many of the pieces of the broken modern, which "for the time being" were left to the people in the camps, had been merely everyday and often negligible parts of the people's lives before the camps. In the camps, however, under a possibility of the ultimate implosion of everything, the pieces became untimely. Even trifles became potent and, indeed, the *Wunderkabinetts* of the trivial now determined the camp people's lives and the camps as operative communities. It now became vital and could become fatal—how one wore a cap, how one held a spoon, and how one played an étude by Chopin, or recalled it playing. The trivial always has a high rate of surviving existential and historical changes of modern times. Under the unprecedented pressure of the narrow space and time of the camps, the trivial, and the trivial in particular, was "frightened" into an unprecedented import and, indeed, beauty. One could hardly call it a resistance. Rather, the camps became a space of a trivial-sublime.[5]

There were never more than 2,000 internees in Boven Digoel, while as many as 140,000 internees passed through Theresienstadt. Theresienstadt lasted three and a half years, while Boven Digoel continued for fifteen.

Boven Digoel was a camp for people interned for their politics. Theresienstadt was a camp for people interned on the basis of their "race." Theresienstadt was surrounded by walls. Boven Digoel was a clearing in a jungle, at the end of the world; just one step, the people said, and you will fall out. Theresienstadt was set up in an eighteenth-century rococo town, sixty kilometers from Prague, in the middle of the orchards, a weekend destination before the war, especially when the fruit trees were in blossom.

Except for their camp-ness, the two camps had barely anything in common. A comparative study would make little sense. However, the fragments of the broken modern disturb the sense of the time, of our time, and should be studied. They made the two *cosmically* different camps into one sign, one constellation, possibly enlightening and certainly warning.

....

Even the story of Hansel and Gretel, and even in the Grimms' most gruesome first edition, has a happy ending: the witch is punished, father and children sit around the table at home again (the bad mother has died), and everything about the little house in the forest is forgotten. Ludwig Wittgenstein thought that "something must be taught to us as foundation," but he immediately added that then "doubt gradually loses its sense."[6] When the past is bound by representation, the specter of "the jews" might not haunt us anymore.

Unlike on the way to Auschwitz, the people in these two camps were allowed to take "stuff" with them—fifty kilograms to Theresienstadt, and whatever a particular ship captain permitted to Boven Digoel. People could take their comforters to Theresienstadt, and some internees brought sewing machines to Boven Digoel. People packed the familiar, useful, and useless, in the inhuman haste, having no knowledge of what was ahead of them—under a possibility of the absolute disaster. In the very process of packing, the moment they pushed down the lid of a suitcase, they became camp people as no one in known history before them—"modern," in the meaning at the root of the word that comes from the Latin *modernus, modo*, which translates as "just now."

"The murder," Theodor Adorno wrote after the war (by "the murder" he meant Auschwitz, but he might as well have written "the auschwitz" with a lowercase "*a*," and he might simply write "the camps"), "the murder," he wrote, "has not happened once, sometime ago, . . . it is happening now," in the time in which we live, "where '*Immergleiche*', the 'forever same' endlessly repeats itself."[7] As I wrote, I felt that Adorno was right, except that he stopped in the middle. As the rabbi in Isaac Bashevis Singer's story says, "Abraham Moshe, it's worse than you think."[8] I became convinced that, instead of "Immergleiche," Adorno should write "trajectory," or still better, "progress."

"When I start looking at walls," Samuel Beckett wrote in a letter, "I begin to see the writing. From which even my own is a relief."[9] Every attempt to explain the camps presents an ethical challenge, in the face of which, eventually, a historian has to fail. Writing about the camps can perhaps be justified only when it is "frightened into existence."[10] The most one can do, to say with Beckett again, is to resist "the arrogance of pity," resist subjecting the lives (and deaths) of "the jews" to "metaphysical simplification," resist "describing a tree as a bad shadow."[11]

Writing about the camps can be justified only when conceived of as a "fugitive analysis,"[12] out of breath, looking over a shoulder. In a moment of panic, one might perhaps get a little close to the camp people and the camp lives that were also (at best) on the run.

I might have met some "survivors" of a type Elias Canetti described: "The moment of survival is the moment of power. . . . The dead man lies on the ground while the survivor stands."[13] If I ever met the type, I did not notice. The survivors I met had unsteady memories and unsteady hands. Naturally. They were all late in their lives when I reached them, and life had not always been nice to them, even after the camps let them go. As we talked, I even felt the topic of my research moving toward that of the aging of memory. I became aware that what I was learning was formed very much by my entering a stage of fogginess myself. "We see only what looks at us," Walter Benjamin wrote.[14]

Inevitably, I spent more of my time with the survivors' children and even grandchildren. It neither was less breathtaking or disturbing nor forced me to look less often over my shoulder. As I listened to them, the camps increasingly were being bound by representation. With an increasing anxiety and skill, the specters were being kept away, sometimes by forgetting, other times by mourning. The "études by Chopin" were still in the air, "the jews," now mostly an immortal community of dead people, were still with us. The camps were still with us, and all around us in fact. In their immensity, and this was new, they sprawled like suburbs: the memory aged in reverse, growing younger, ever more architectural, straight, permitting easy traffic.

....

I made an effort to learn about Theresienstadt and Boven Digoel in as much detail as possible. In Prague, Theresienstadt (now again Terezín), in Jakarta, Jerusalem, Tel Aviv, or Boven Digoel, I interviewed as many "camp people" as I could still find. I consulted the archive of Boven Digoel, now in Jakarta. Nazis managed to burn most of the Theresienstadt archive in the last days of the war. I went through the public libraries and was given access to some family libraries, even etuis of letters and empty envelopes with stamps often cut away for other collections.

My lifelong career of teaching and writing, mostly on Southeast Asia, as well as my experience of Prague, where I was born and spent forty-five years of my life, appeared in a new perspective as I went on writing about the camps. Always, writers, musicians, and philosophers were precious to me, as I believed they were precious to the civilization in which I lived or wished to live—Franz Kafka, Gustav Mahler, Joseph Roth, Walter Benjamin, Jean-Luc Nancy, Pramoedya Ananta Toer, Mas Marco, Tan Malaka. They also appeared to me in a new and unexpected light. They often looked and spoke, and ran, as the camp people did or wished to do—including Heidegger, who became locked in silence by his philosophy as much as his fear.

In the end, this project turned out to be a history of "concentrated modernity," an unprecedented energy and ethos that emerged in the camps, and radiated out of the camps, like the wise rabbi said, changing our world.

....

I feel deep gratitude to three anonymous readers for the press, and to the press editors for their uncommon understanding of, and patience with, the unwieldy manuscript.

I have tried my ideas of the camps on teachers and students at Michigan in Ann Arbor; Northwestern in Evanston; Berkeley in San Francisco; Columbia and New School in New York; Komunitas Utan Kayu [the Jungle Community] in Jakarta; KITLV, The Royal Institute of Anthropology, in Leiden; and Tokyo and Waseda Universities in Japan. If only the book may be as good, as gracious and helpful, as the people at these renowned places have been!

....

Nothing with the camps is "merely technical," neither naming nor spelling. Theresienstadt was called a "ghetto" as often as it was called a "Jewish settlement," a "camp," or a "concentration camp." "Ghetto" in particular was a name forced on the Jews by the Nazis, suggesting the medieval, a place where a still-living Jew might wait until the final solution. The more neutral (kind of) "camp" is used throughout the book, except where other terms are parts of a direct quote. The Czech-speaking internees called the camp Terezín, as the town had been called before it became a camp and as it is called today. The internees from the other language regions, however, generally used the German "Theresienstadt," which was also the camp's official designation. "Theresienstadt" is used in the book, except when "Terezín" appears in direct quote.

In 1972, the Indonesian government decreed a language reform, substituting "u" for "oe," "c" for "tj," "j" for "dj," and "y" between vocals for "j." Like the military, right-wing and oppressive government was unpopular and resisted, so many people, including virtually all the Boven Digoel people, kept their names with their pre-1972 spellings. This is the way their names are spelled in this book, except when the new spelling is used in direct quote. The local names are given in the new spelling for the comfort of current maps users especially.

Boven Digoel was called a "camp," an "isolation camp," and also a "concentration camp," until about 1940, when the last term was deemed by the Dutch officials to be too discredited. "Tanah Merah" was also often used, meaning "red soil," not "The Red Land" or even "The Land of the Reds," as might seem logical or even natural. "Boven Digoel" is used with few exceptions in the book, and in the old spelling, as it appears almost universally in documents and memories. "Boven Digoel" is still today the official name of the place where the camp stood.

Some of the Theresienstadt people started to use Hebrew names after the experience of the camps: Eva became Chava; Vlasta became Nava; Jindra became Avri. The immensity of this change, like that of the others, could not be adequately conveyed, only respectfully transcribed.

I

FASHION

Before falling asleep yesterday I had an image of drawing.... The two distinct pairs of lines that outlined his legs crossed and softly merged with the lines outlining his body. His pale, colored clothes lay heaped up between these lines with feeble corporeality. In astonishment at this beautiful drawing...

—KAFKA, *Diaries*

ONE

Clothes

The Jews (as Hitler defined the Jews) were registered and called up to the camp. Each man, woman, and child was permitted a fifty-kilo piece of luggage and a handbag or a backpack, a carry-on. Everything was to be chosen with a care unprecedented in modern times. The things of the life before were to be squeezed into trunks, handbags, and backpacks, and into pockets, too. All the modernity (as far as the modern had developed at the time and at the moment of each Jew's life) had to be stomped, crammed in. Clothes for all seasons. Emigrant luggage, but as never before.

"One stuffs in," Mrs. Thea Höchster, going to Theresienstadt, wrote later in her camp diary, "and there is so little time. Woolens sure, but what about shoes, and comb! All is too little, and all is too much when in a wink, one has to go."[1]

The German authorities calling up the Jewish women in the Netherlands to get ready for Theresienstadt advised them to take shoes "that would stand up to country walks."[2] Never before had vestment—clothes, shoes, and hats—mattered so much. Etty Hillesum, one of the Dutch women about to go (and die), wrote in her diary on August 23, 1941, still waiting in Amsterdam,

"Yesterday afternoon when I went to buy S.'s cheese and as I walked through the beautiful South Amsterdam, I felt like an old Jewess, wrapped up tightly in a cloud. . . . I felt so warm, protected, and safe."[3]

What Ms. Hillesum meant by "cloud" was the shroud of the moment and for the season: "The first time a little boy goes to school," according to a Jewish tradition in some places, "he is carried entirely swathed in his father's *tallit* to prevent him from seeing impure things."[4]

At the camps, the manner of dress continued to evolve as it had through the centuries. However, dress became, perhaps finally, perhaps ultimately, but certainly as never before, "the most energetic of all symbols."[5] Truly modern and dynamic. "Why are you so untidy?" became an essential and often fatal question.[6]

The Jews on their way to the camps and thus to Theresienstadt, to save a space in their luggage, "wrapped themselves" (Hillesum's words) in three, even four layers of clothes, be it winter or be it summer. "Men dragged themselves with their *lumpen* of clothes,"[7] and they were "dressed 'for the road.'"[8] "The Jews always have the best clothes," was the white anti-Semitic wisdom of Europe since as soon as the Jews began to wear modern clothing.[9]

"Everything new I had, I put on myself"; Petr Ginz, a fourteen-year-old "half-Jewish" boy, recalled packing "three pairs of socks, two shirts, a sweater, two pairs of trousers, and a winter coat."[10] "I'm telling you," a man advised his friends on the night before going, "you should take your best clothes and the best underwear, so that they'll last."[11]

Theresienstadt did not have a direct rail connection in the first months of its existence.[12] It was three kilometers from the nearest train station in Bohušovice, and the Jews had to walk, "topped by heavy winter coats, carrying knapsacks on their backs and suitcases in their hands."[13] They were watched by the Czech inhabitants of a little village they were passing on their way. "A man's mind," Honoré de Balzac wrote a century before, "can be known by the manner in which he carries his walking stick."[14]

Younger women taken to Theresienstadt watched the elderly women going. Nava Shean, one of the younger ones who later became a famous actress in Israel, recalled, "Their [the older women's] clothes, expensive and old-fashioned, looked like for a masked ball on the morning after. Hats with ostrich feathers falling sideways—and umbrellas! Long fanciful umbrellas with ruffles." After a few days in the camps, she added, "Now, the umbrellas are used to drive away flies."[15]

The crucial moment was that of stomping in, squeezing, closing the lid, concentration, and this is no pun. Franz Kafka, a writer and a Prague Jew, escaped the Nazis only because he died before they got to him; he would surely have gone to Theresienstadt. Yet, without having to go, he knew as much about the camps as anyone. In a diary entry of October 28, 1911, he described a dream he had had the night before about himself; his best friend, Max Brod; and Max's brother Otto (Otto later went to Theresienstadt and perished in Auschwitz). The three men in Kafka's dream were about to board a train: "I dreamed that Max, Otto, and I had the habit of packing our trunks only when we reached the railroad station. There we were, carrying our shirts, for example, through the main hall to our distant trunks. Although this seemed to be a general custom, it was not a good one in our case, especially since we had begun to pack only shortly before the arrival of the train. Then we were naturally excited and had hardly any hope of still catching the train, let alone getting good seats."[16]

....

In the Dutch Indies, a camp called Boven Digoel was newly designed in 1926, in a panic, for the Indonesian rebels who had attempted a Communist revolution.

The Boven Digoel camp was as far from Europe as one could imagine, especially at the time. It was even endlessly far from Java and Sumatra, where the rebellion happened and from which most of the internees came. The camp was set up in Dutch New Guinea. The journey from Java by ship took four weeks, and the internees, if they so desired, could take their families with them. They were less restricted than the Theresienstadt people would be, but their turn came as a rule on very short notice, too, often after spending months in prison in the place where they were arrested. As they packed their stuff, they also knew next to nothing about where they were going, and they did not know at all how long they would be gone or if they would ever come back.

Like the Jews of Theresienstadt, the camp people of the Indies had to pack "for all seasons." Many were Communists and many were Muslims, and the vestments they packed became, of a sort, their *tallit*. They, too, readied their clothes to maintain their bearing. According to one of the ships' records, now in the Boven Digoel archives in Jakarta, internee Toepin's "trunk no. 8" contained "clothes and other stuff," and "trunk no. 9" "clothes, sarongs, and shawls."[17] Internee Ngalimoen, traveling on the same ship, traveled with "trunk no. 12: clothes and other personal items."[18]

Krarup Nielsen was a Danish journalist and travel-adventure writer who somehow managed to convince the Dutch authorities to let him travel with the first ship that took the Boven Digoel internees to the camp. The people he went with endured the four weeks on the sea, squeezed in—stomped in—the airless, hot, and often widely swaying hold of the ship, or on the open deck, sundeck it might be called, exposed to tropical heat and rains. Nielsen described the internees as they reached the camp, and mainly through their clothes

> They embark from the ship. More than half of the men are clothed the European way, and certainly in what they suppose are city clothes. They have slack, felt, or straw hats on, some wear black silk bonnets as Muslims now do, and I could see many wearing Western shoes. As a whole, they make a contrast with the dull-brownish-yellow fatigues of the Dutch soldiers who watch over the embankment. The internees walk down on the plank from the ship. In the boat that will take them from the ship to shore, they are seated next to each other, each holding a small trunk or a briefcase on his lap; some even have an umbrella stuck under their arm. The guards lean on the ship railing and gaze down at the scene in silence.[19]

Even to a seasoned journalist and adventure writer this was clearly a significant story, and there was much of the camp already in it.

The description stuck. Still after seven years, by which time the camp was already well established, another author, Dr. Schoonheyt, a medical officer assigned to Boven Digoel, recalled the same scene as it evidently reached him through the chain of memory. Again, but even more so, the internees presented themselves and were seen "dressed to the nines." Through the years, they became more of camp people, and their clothes, in the doctor's description, more significant. The internee's "cloud and shroud" became more garish. Dr. Schoonheyt's description even betrays some of the unease of the observer. "They were clothed impeccably European," Dr. Schoonheyt amplified what Krarup Nielsen wrote:

> They flashed socks with shouting stripes, neat half-shoes, and their hats were definitely knock-out and worn as conspicuously as possible. Of course, the briefcases, the penholders, and the razor-sharp pencils in the breast pockets of their jackets were impossible to overlook; they were no doubt indispensable to the camp. The penholders especially made a glaring presence as the Communists put their feet on the land to engage in a battle with the primeval forest.[20]

Neither Theresienstadt nor Boven Digoel was Auschwitz or any of the other Nazi camps of death, and neither was the Devil's Island of Cayenne, the notorious penal colony of the French colonial empire. The Jews in Theresienstadt and the Communists in Boven Digoel, for one thing, could keep and wear the clothes they managed to bring in with them. Through the camps' existence, the clothes in the camp remained as precious as when packed, and gained even more value with the years in the camps. With each passing day in the camp, the clothes became a little more of a fashion and of the season, more concentrated, more sublime, more than normally insistent on keeping and heightening form, in spite of everything adverse to it, and because of everything, more of a cloud and shroud—in exposing nakedness.

Philip Mechanicus was a Dutch Jewish journalist who wrote a diary in the transit camp of Westerbork waiting for transport either to Theresienstadt or to Auschwitz: "One of my neighbors has brought a wardrobe fit for a world tour; it hides three bedsteads. Three or four suits and a few coats hang neatly on coat hangers from the bar of the topmost bed, just as if they were in a wardrobe. When I climb into my bed and get down from it one of the suits or coats always falls to the floor."[21]

When internee Djaidin, alias Mardjoen, died in Boven Digoel, the authorities of the camp recorded what he left behind: "One rattan trunk (old) containing one neck scarf, one red hat (old), three head scarfs, one sarong (black), one sarong (of Pekalongan style), one batik headdress, two woman's jackets, one man's jacket with buttons (old), one chintz undershirt (old), one white cotton undershirt (old), one long batik undershirt (old), one napkin (torn), one handkerchief white, one belt (new)."[22] When internee Soewita, alias Soeparman, died in Boven Digoel, he left behind "two open jackets (no buttons), three pairs of pajamas trousers, one pair of shorts, one pair of white trousers, two shirts, one neck scarf, one sarong, two handkerchiefs."[23]

The Boven Digoel authorities recruited some internees for a special camp police, Rust en Orde Bewaarders, ROB [Calm and Order Guards]. It was the duty of the ROB agents to walk through the camp three times a day, and in a special police book record everything significant. On Sunday, May 23, 1937, at 10:15 in the morning, ROB agent Zainoeddin, for instance, wrote down a list of items reported as stolen from an internee: "One dressy shirt, one ordinary shirt, two sport socks, two pairs of shorts (one with stripes, one black)."[24]

In Yad Vashem, the Holocaust Museum and Memorial in Jerusalem, I saw a photograph of a Theresienstadt street from the time of the camp. There is clearly visible a sign, like those used on shops in Central Europe through the 1920s and 1930s, *Herrenbekleidung* [Gent's Clothes].[25] This particular sign might have been a fake installed specifically for a visit of a high official on inspection—a Potemkin village site. But the internees were buying clothes in

Theresienstadt, and there were Herrenbekleidung stores and ladies clothes, too, and also shop windows. Only, one could never pass by the clothes shop windows in the camp as one might a store in the outside before.

"Nobody walks here in clogs," wrote an elderly Dutch Jewish internee, Gabriel Italie, in his Theresienstadt diary on September 7, 1944.[26] On December 22, 1944, Italie noted, "On the ninth of this month... I 'bought' a set of suit and a pair of working shoes. The suit is not new, of course, but is quite decent."[27] Pavel Weiner, a thirteen-year-old boy from Prague, wrote in his Theresienstadt diary, "*Sunday, January 14, 1945* . . . We stand in line in the freezing weather to get some gloves. We have to stand outside, and I don't care for it a bit. I bang at the door and it is a miracle that I don't get into a fight with the saleswoman. My mother is angry at me for my poor behavior."[28] Philipp Manes, an older Theresienstadt internee, wrote in his diary, "A distribution site was opened in the fall of 1943. One can get there mainly the clothes left by the deceased.... From time to time there is also stuff available from confiscations or from the shops on the outside that was bought and brought into the camp by the ss."[29]

The best clothes of those left by the dead were being sent to "the needy" in Germany. Nevertheless, "the rest remained in the camp."[30] The "distribution centers," and the "clothing stores" in the camp (a special camp currency was issued for the purpose), like the trunks packed by the people as they were leaving for the camps, were concentrated modern. They could bring as never before the thrilling experience of luck: "When one was lucky to lay his hand on an ordinary working-man overall, he considered himself one who hit the bank."[31]

There was a clothing market in Boven Digoel as well, which, like the one in Theresienstadt, was exclusive by its being of a camp. *Nieuws van den Dag voor Nederlandsch-Indië*, a white-colonial daily, published an article about Boven Digoel on January 15, 1931, reporting, "All clothes in the camp are exceedingly expensive."[32] As in Theresienstadt, what had been brought in was cared about at the greatest cost, and what might be left behind by the dead could be put up for sale. The items left behind after the death of Mohamad Saleh, alias Marip, were sold on credit on October 16, 1937: "One can buy (or get on credit): one jacket (khaki-drill) for *f* [florin] 0.50; ... one jacket (white) for *f*0.80; one jacket (*tricot*) for *f*0.80; three shirts (short sleeves) for *f*0.70; one jacket (for home) for *f*0.30; two sarongs for *f*1.76; one night cap for *f*0.50."[33]

Clothes might be sent to the camps by a relative or a friend, with some restrictions, and stuff could even be mail-ordered to Boven Digoel. *Keng Po*, a Chinese newspaper in the Indies, published "A Letter from Boven Digoel" in its issue of October 4, 1927, in which internee Kartoatmodjo is quoted "asking his family to send him a pair of shorts."³⁴ Few internees could afford better. Soetan Sjahrir, who came to Boven Digoel in the eighth year of its existence and stayed there just for a year (after 1945 he became the first prime minister of the independent Indonesia), wrote from the camp to his wife who lived in Holland,

> Mieske, I need underwear.... And a pair of pajamas. I have only two sets now, and both are completely worn out. Besides, they are too coarse. I have not many more clothes left on the whole, just one pair of green cotton trousers and another pair of trousers of some sort, rather ancient. I could well use some of the white suits of Tjammie [Sjahrir's brother Sjahsam, living in Holland at the time]. But, to tell you the truth, not really, because most of the time I stay in the house, and then only in pajamas.³⁵

In the tropical Indies camp, in the middle of the humid and hot New Guinea jungle, each piece of modern, which meant Western, fashion was sublime, and flagrantly so. A pair of shoes and a jacket was a statement much louder than it ever could have been in modern Europe and modern colony. In the camp, the stakes were higher and the efforts more strenuous. Internee Mohamad Sanoesi sent a mail order to "Shoes Magazine, The New York Company, Weltevreden, Batavia, Java," and to "Shop Singapore, Soerabaja, Java." Internee Mas Soewigno even ordered some pieces of clothing from "Bros. Gerzens Mode" and "Magazine De Bijenkorp, Amsterdam."³⁶ Internee Kadimin ordered a pair of shoes from "Hen Son Than Shoemaker in Sigli, Aceh, North Sumatra."³⁷

There were tailors in Boven Digoel; some of them had practiced their craft before, but few learned it in the camp. Putting patches on trousers, everyday repairing jackets, skirts, blouses, or underwear could easily be made by the internees themselves. Tailors were for custom-made clothes. Internee Partoredjo was registered in the camp as "gentlemen's tailor."³⁸ Internee Ibing "used to be an agent propagandist for the Communist Party" and "used his tailor shop as a hotbed for agitation."³⁹ Now he was listed as "working as a tailor." Internee Roejani is on record as a "tailor from Serang, Banten, Java."⁴⁰ "Uncle Prawito," Mr. Trikoyo, who was a boy in Boven Digoel at the time, told me, "worked in the camp as a specialist in clothes." "Men's tailor, I mean," Trikoyo added.⁴¹

There were shoemakers in Boven Digoel, repairing as well as sewing up new shoes for the authorities as well as the internees. Under the date September 11, 1936, at eight o'clock in the morning, a Boven Digoel ROB police book records that agent Sanoesi "left the ROB station to bring the repaired shoes to *toean wedana* [camp's district chief]."⁴²

There were sarongs, a traditional garment, a piece of cloth wrapped around the lower body, worn by both women and men; no tailor needed. But a significant and certainly striking number of the camp inhabitants, male and female, wore the modern "on the go and in the know."⁴³ The daughter of the first Dutch chief civilian administrator of the camp, Mrs. Ottow, recalled in an interview long after Boven Digoel how she "herself came often to the camp and gave the women advice on their sewing." She also gave the internees' wives, mothers, and daughters sewing patterns and fashion magazine cuttings. "They could," Mrs. Ottow added, "order what stuff they needed, sewing matter and even sewing machines themselves."⁴⁴

Some rebels sent to Boven Digoel managed to pack a sewing machine and sewing matter on the ship as they went to the camp; others, as Mrs. Otto suggested, mail-ordered a machine with the spare parts and thread. The list of what the internees were able to take on the ship and what they sent for reads like an avant-garde poem: "Lamp, shoes, and a sewing machine."⁴⁵

Mr. Trikoyo, who was brought as a baby to Boven Digoel and who was eighty when I spoke with him, recalled his first set of clothes ever, *celana monyet*, a children's playsuit, trousers and shirt in one piece. His mother, he said, had made it out of fabric cut from a discarded mattress—"*on a sewing machine*," he added with an emphasis.⁴⁶ Mrs. Sumono Widayasih, a friend of Trikoyo in Boven Digoel, told me fifty years after her camp experience: "My mother spent most of the evenings under an oil lamp, sewing skirts and blouses for my older sister, Darsini, and for me. At first, she had to do everything by hand. But then we had a sewing machine, and I still can see it, she made a dress for me. Complete, poplin, white, collar embroidered with a blue thread."⁴⁷ I tried to be clever and, recalling my own childhood and my mother at the foot-pedaled machine, said "Singer." "No!" she cried back: "Pfaff!"

The second journalist allowed into Boven Digoel, a year after Krarup Nielsen, was a reporter for *Nieuwe Rotterdamsche Courant*, Dr. Marcus van Blankenstein. He was of a liberal persuasion, and after visiting Boven Digoel wrote a series of sensational articles in Dutch and Indies papers painting a scathing picture of the camp. Yet fashion was very much part of his story. "To be a tailor in Boven Digoel," he wrote, "is not a bad profession to have. If just out of habit, the internees like to walk around smartly dressed."⁴⁸ On special occasions, when a ship bringing a new group of internees was announced, all internees would put on their very best—not sarong or batik but hats and shoes, white trousers, jackets, shirts, *hagelwitte*, van Blankenstein might have said, "white-as-snow," "all-white," modern-colonial.[49]

The police books of Boven Digoel, the voluminous records of the ROB police-internee agents walking through the camps and reporting on the life, often, entry after entry, read like fashion notes. An internee is described as "clothed completely in the new,"[50] another as wearing "his best," and yet another as "clothed neatly today."[51] On May 1, as could be expected, on the day of the international proletariat, an ROB agent saw the camp at its fashion-wise best. The internees were reported as "truly clothed," "sharp," and, naturally, "with a red tie."[52]

It could not have been otherwise, if only because of the eagerness of the packing. If there were to be flâneurs anywhere in the modern world, it had to be in the camp. Mrs. Widayasih let me read the handwritten memoirs of her girlhood in the camp. One of the particularly memorable figures in the camp and in her memoirs was internee Thomas Najoan. He became famous, truly mythical, by trying to escape three times; twice he was brought back, and the third time he disappeared in the jungle. As Mrs. Widayasih recalled him, "Uncle Najoan was small and stocky. His walk was energetic and you would meet him everywhere in the camp. His clothes were always perfect, all-white, even shoes were white; white shorts, white shirt, with long sleeves, a pith helmet, and a walking stick. And how he ended! His corpse, they say, was found floating in the river!"[53]

As known and as important in the camp as Najoan was Aliarcham, the ex-chairman of the Indonesian Communist Party, the man perhaps most responsible for the party decision to rise in rebellion. A fellow internee and writer Mas Marco Kartodikromo described Aliarcham in the camp as "wearing a yellow jacket open at the neck, black shirt with a flower design, sarong, and a batik scarf."[54] ("Jacket open at the neck" signaled that it was not a traditional Javanese jacket nor a Dutch officials' jacket; both buttoned up to the chin.)

The people interned in Boven Digoel had grown up in a fast-developing colony of the early twentieth century, at the edge of the modern. Now, on the ship, in the camp, and in the middle of the jungle, they moved as on a catwalk. The native people of the forest, the Papuans Kaja-Kaja, as the Catholic missionaries called them, meaning "friends," were the first to appear to the camp people as the internees traveled up the Digoel River. Appropriately to the newcomers from the other world, they appeared originary, as "naked figures."[55] As the camp was settling down, the Kaja-Kaja came closer day by day, and then even "visited" the camp. In the process, some clothes were "put on them." The doctor who was quoted above making "funny" comments about the rebels' attire as they embarked from the ship, took and published at least one "equally funny" photograph of a young Papua woman, in just a thigh-short grass skirt, and wrote a caption under the photograph, "A dashing prima ballerina on the settlement."[56]

Other times, Kaja-Kaja were seen in their boats on the river: "Three of the rowers in the long proa were naked and the fourth wore a pajama jacket with wide stripes, a present evidently from someone in the camp."[57] Western norms were being proved and progress measured in the camp by the savages' dishabille. "One Kaja-Kaja makes rounds in the camp wearing a blue soldier's kepi and a very tired pair of flannels. Another one appears in a corset that he must have been given by a camp soldier's wife."[58]

For the internees, as Mrs. Widayasih wrote in her memoirs, the clothes of the Papuans were "still traditional."[59] Mrs. Zakaria, another girl of Boven Digoel, told me much later about "her" Papuan. Her father, an internee, hired the young man to help the family around the house and to watch over his little daughter. "He followed me everywhere," Mrs. Zakaria recalled. "He kept an eye on me.... Sometimes, however, the desire to visit his people back in the forest was too much for him. He asked my mother for permission, and then he took off the shirt and the shorts we had given him—you know," Mrs. Zakaria pointed to her lap and blushed a little. "He left the shorts and shirt with us and ran home naked as he was. When he came back, he put the shirt and the shorts on again."[60] As the time of the camps went on, the clothes brought from home, like the people wearing them, were becoming tired but also more camplike. In Theresienstadt, Ruth Bondy, a former internee and major Israeli writer after the war, recalled the clothes becoming "too big because we all lost weight."[61] Like the people, the clothes became more pathetic with each day, that is, their pathos more concentrated and more profound. People and clothes, looking for cloud and shroud, became "more elegant." The life acquired a radically more powerful fashion appeal. A "Persian lamb coat and a string of pearls" that before the war only some affluent Jewesses wore on special occasions in Prague, Vienna, Berlin, or Amsterdam, were now remembered in the camp, became "typical wear," "a must" for every woman, in camp dreams.[62]

The camps, in all their misery, became the sites of a heightened sense of fashion. "Daddy gave me his best shirts and a thick jacket, his ski boots, and all sorts of things," Petr Ginz wrote in his diary about leaving for Theresienstadt.[63] He was forced to the camp as a *Mischling* [mixed-blood Jew]. His father, who was not a Jew, did not have to go according to the law of the moment.

Another Mischling, Peter Demetz, who later became a prominent Germanist in the United States and the editor of Walter Benjamin's *Reflections*, also did not have to go in the first roundups. But his Jewish mother did. After many years, Professor Demetz recalled his (final) parting with his mother, again as a moment of fashion. Before the war, he wrote, his mother regularly spent her winter holidays in Semmering, an upper-middle-class Austrian hill resort near Vienna: "A group of elegant ladies often went for healthy walks up the Pinkenkogel, an unheroic hill near the hotel, and my mother would don firm shoes and woolen stockings for the occasion. I noted eight years later that she put on the same shoes and stockings when she had to join her transport to the ghetto of Theresienstadt."[64]

It should be emphasized again that neither Boven Digoel nor Theresienstadt were camps of the Auschwitz type. One can train oneself to see nuances. In Theresienstadt, the SS authorities wished the camp to be a "passable," to use a fashion word. The first SS commandant of Theresienstadt issued a special order on July 23, 1942: "It is forbidden to dress in mourning garb."[65] To use a fashion phrase, "black was out."

In 1944, two years into the camp's existence, a delegation of the International Red Cross was allowed to "inspect" the camp. Dr. Maurice Rossel of the delegation wrote a report to the Geneva Red Cross headquarters: "The people we met on the streets were dressed correctly [*korrekt gekleidet*]. There were elegant women to be seen on the street who wore silk stockings, hats, shawls, and modish handbags. Young people were generally well clothed, too, and we even met 'zazou' [zoot-suit] types."[66]

Dr. Rossel might have been duped; the camp was made ready for his visit. But many of the Theresienstadt diaries and the postwar memories of those who survived do give a picture not much different from Dr. Rossel's, uncomfortably so.

Mrs. Käthe Goldschmidt, a German Jewish ex-internee of Theresienstadt, recalled the style of wear and the manners of wearing one reads about in Dr. Rossel's shocking report, as a part of the camp's everyday—at the moment of inspection or not. In a letter to a relative written in the first days after the camp liberation, she describes a friend of hers, Mr. Hugo Friedmann. It happened in the last months of the camp, just hours before Hugo Friedmann was taken on transport to Auschwitz (and to his death). "He wore a long black leather coat," Mrs. Goldschmidt wrote, "and a striking hat. He looked so smart. Oh, my god! His shorts were still at the tailor and he had no time to collect them. I even do not know if the tailor is still alive."[67]

Another Theresienstadt prisoner, Ab Caransa, an elderly man who was taken to Theresienstadt from the Netherlands in 1944, recalled his first impressions of the camp. They were, as manner of dress goes, not too different from those of Dr. Rossel: "It was a splendid summer day," Mr. Caransa wrote about his passing through a gate into the Theresienstadt camp. "We saw Jews wearing shorts and shirts with an open neck. It just could not be so serious here!"[68] Another internee, Dr. Saron, recalled "many young men and women in impeccable clothes and of the best of manners."[69]

A Czech Jew and Communist (so he might have gone to Boven Digoel had he been born in the Indies instead of Czechoslovakia), Josef Taussig, in his late twenties, wrote several short stories while in Theresienstadt. Some of them (unlike him) survived and are available in the Jewish Museum in Prague. In one of them, a young man walks through the camp: "All the girls who are passing by! Their skin is either tanned or white like milk. Some are slender and tall, others are fleshy. Some wear glasses and have a look of an intellectual, the eyes of others are romantically clouded. Some walk around in stylish overalls others in chic suits." "Was macht der Herr Vater? [How is your father doing?]," Taussig's young hero is asked when stopped "by a little elderly man in a blue ski cap."[70]

Mr. Manes, who came to the camp from Berlin, and was much older than Taussig, wrote in his Theresienstadt diary, "The women walk around in slacks. The young men and women, both, wear shorts of a kind that makes one think of swimming trunks, except that these here are even shorter." "It is a summer day," Mr. Manes wrote, "and women do not wear stockings. On the whole, they prefer bright colors and light materials, cheerful scarves, and flowing blouses."[71]

It is often assumed that fashion, as a frivolous matter, and as a matter of ornament, disappears in times of need. The camps show, however, that, in times of need, manner of dress becomes ever more important, that the aspiration to hold on to humanity and to avoid death is linked to a special investment in fashion and not at all to its demise. The camps, dramatically, yet with profound historical significance, became the catwalks of the world.

An advance team of George S. Patton's victorious Third Army reached Theresienstadt in the first days after it had been liberated in May 1945. One of the three soldiers on the team happened to be a Jew, a recent emigrant to America. He looked for his mother, who did not escape with him and who, there was some faint hope, might even be in Theresienstadt. I did not learn from the documents whether he found his mother. But I have the team's report to the army headquarters, and it appears that the soldiers could hardly believe their eyes.

The camp to all intents and purposes was still closed to the outside world when the US team arrived. The people were not allowed to leave because there had been an outbreak of spotted typhus in the camp in the last days of the war. The soldiers reported meeting "walking skeletons" in Theresienstadt. These were the prisoners who, as the German fronts collapsed and the Red Army pushed in, began to be moved in panic and disorder away from the Red Army and from Auschwitz and the other truly horrific camps in the east to Theresienstadt. These new arrivals probably brought the epidemic to Theresienstadt. "This is one kind of population you find here," the US soldier wrote about the half-dead new arrivals, "and then you have the best dressed women and men running around . . . as if in a summer resort. No women without lipstick, the men wear the best tailored suits, nice patterned ties, etc."[72]

Fashion, Gilles Lipovetsky wrote, is "dressing modern democracy" and at the same time "cascades of 'little nothings,'" of infinitely fine "variations in an understood sequence."[73] Walter Benjamin, long before Lipovetsky, perhaps not yet having the camps fully on his mind but already deep into the time of the camps and as if he knew the camps, wrote that "fashion mocks death."[74]

"Fashion," Benjamin wrote, "has opened the business of dialectical exchange between . . . carnal pleasure and the corpse. . . . Fashion was never anything other than the parody of the motley cadaver, provocation of death . . . bitter colloquy with decay."[75] Roland Barthes, in his own study of fashion, spoke of "neomania," a phenomenon of unproductive change, "which probably appeared in our civilization with the birth of capitalism."[76] Benjamin might rather call it necromania: "Every fashion," he wrote, "stands in opposition to the organic. Every fashion couples the living body to the inorganic world. To the living, fashion defends the rights of the corpse."[77]

Neither Boven Digoel nor Theresienstadt, again, were death camps. They were "toward death." Fashion in these two camps was deadly frivolous. Honoré de Balzac's not yet fully articulated flâneurish truth of the nineteenth century in the camps became a full-fledged and uncompromising truth of the twentieth century: *"A rip is a misfortune, a stain is a vice,"* Balzac wrote.[78] To the people of fashion, Balzac wrote too, "cruelty is the most natural."[79] A century after Balzac, and already knowing intimately well about the camps, Georges Perec held to the same unshakable truth: "Fashion," he wrote, "is entirely on the side of violence."[80]

The uniform is the truth of fashion. Nothing can make "the cascade of little nothings" into a matter of power more truly than the uniform. The uniform is the form of dress most fashionable, most flâneurish, most trivial, most ranking and ordering, and closest to cruelty, violence, and death. In the camps, the uniform became what, across a couple of modern centuries, fashion had increasingly been aspiring to be.

The guards and the people of authority in Boven Digoel and Theresienstadt wore uniforms. The SS officers in Theresienstadt, famously, notoriously, and ostentatiously dressed themselves up in the sharpest manner: a black jacket, an image of skull and bones on each button, spit-and-shined black boots, a white shirt, and a black tie: "I see them advancing," Winston Churchill memorably said at the beginning of the war, "the Nazi war machine, with its clanking, heel-clicking, dandified."[81] "There's nothing more powerful than a uniform," Fyodor Dostoyevsky wrote in *Demons*. "After that," he added, "the second most powerful force is, of course, sentimentality."[82] The first SS commandant of Theresienstadt, SS-Hauptsturmführer Dr. Siegfried Seidl, as internee Zdeněk Lederer recalled after the war, "was always immaculately dressed, kept hounds, and spoke in *staccato* sentences."[83]

It was hot and humid in Boven Digoel throughout the year, and everything in the camp soon got soaked and crumpled—including uniforms. Still, all the guards in the camp, and the civilian authorities, too, neatly and assertively as possible, wore uniforms: cascades of significance, from the top down. The Moluccan and Ambonese "native" lower-rank soldiers and guards wore uniforms that were not exactly tip-top but were still uniforms. The Dutch, the white middle- and high-ranking officers, both military and civilian, "set the tone," made the whole system of fashion and power work— no rip, no stain, no misfortune.

To prove the system, there had to be less and decidedly even less sophisticated uniforms, on the brink of what might become, speaking like a fashion magazine, *impossible* or even *passé*. There were, in both camps, uniforms, subuniforms, and sub-subuniforms.

In Theresienstadt, to make their job easier and for matters of appearance, the SS administration of the camp set up a twelve-man Jewish so-called Council of the Elders. It was made up of selected, distinguished, and willing, or not able to resist, internees. On special occasions, the head of the Council of the Elders wore a uniform, or a sort of uniform. One such occasion was when the Red Cross delegation visited the camp in 1944. The head of the council at the time, Dr. Edelstein, welcomed the team ceremoniously, on the main square of the camp, and he wore a uniform. Historian and ex-internee of the camp Hans Günther Adler described the scene. The SS commandant of the camp at the time, SS-Obersturmführer Karl Rahm, "a few days before gave a punch to the Elder, and the man, as he stepped forward to welcome the guests, still had a blue stain over his eye. Nevertheless, he wore an elegant tails and a half-top hat, like a true mayor."[84]

In Boven Digoel, likewise, a "self-governing authority" was put together by the Dutch authorities from among the internees. These people, distinguished, forced or willing, as well as in Theresienstadt, wore a kind of uniform. Or, certainly, they were expected to. When a Dutch high official reported on one of his inspection visits to the camp, writing to the still higher authorities, he complained, "In spite of the clear horn signal my ship gave, which had to make everybody in the camp aware of my arrival, and which gave enough time for everybody to get ready, a *wedana* failed to put on his official uniform [*ambachtskostuum*]."[85]

Camps were the high point of uniform fashion. At the moment of the camps in modern history, perhaps ultimately, life and death on one side, and keeping up appearances, being smart on the other side, became one. Mr. Boedisoetjitro, one of the top leaders of the rebellion, because he was still thought to enjoy respect among the internees, was appointed by the Dutch administrator to head the Boven Digoel "self-governing authority," a kind of Council of the Elders in Theresienstadt. A fellow internee wrote about Boedisoetjitro then, "in the service," as he was seen walking through the camp: "We recognized him by a white jacket, white trousers, complete, with the *lars* jungle boots and tropical helmet."[86]

In both camps, the internees selected to serve in the auxiliary camp police wore uniforms. A Dutch official wrote on another visit to Boven Digoel and his encounter with the ROB corps (and one can hear a chuckle), "They are attired in the most extraordinary way, sort of a *cowboy uniform*."[87] Still, old photographs show the ROB agents in striking all white. In Theresienstadt, the Jews' police, the *Ghettowache*, deep below the SS men and even the Czech gendarmes, also wore uniforms. And, an internee also recalled, they were given uniforms that were "deliberately ridiculous."[88] In another Theresienstadt description, the uniform included "a cap like that the tram-conductors used to wear before the war, but with three yellow stripes. On the chest the policemen had a metal plaque with the agent's number and letters 'G' and 'W' for *Ghettowache*."[89]

The uniforms were there, ranking the camp, from the moment one first stepped into it. Some uniforms might seem to make matters ambiguous, but everyone knew the essential meaning. At the train station, as the people arrived at Bohušovice, and before they embarked on their march toward Theresienstadt, one of the new arrivals recalled, "We were greeted by a group of well-dressed youth. They all had leather jackets and they strutted around like the ss people. We did not know whether they were Jews or whether they were not Jews."[90]

As this was fashion, there were incessant modifications made to the uniforms—slight, trivial, and frivolous but always designed to make a uniform more of a uniform. On Thursday, August 3, 1944, Pavel Weiner, a boy in Theresienstadt, wrote, "The *Ghettowache* have now changed their uniforms."[91] Mr. Philipp Manes wrote, "*Ghettowache* now got a new uniform again, new blouse, gray-green, and jacket with pockets—an elegant piece of clothing."[92] In one of the few photographs from the camp that survived, of another of the camp Jewish-staffed and authorities-approved corps, the firefighter brigade, a firefighter stands next to a fire engine. He wears a firefighter uniform, a dark jacket buttoned to the neck, with a visible Jewish star on the chest.[93]

Fashion might envelop people and by its tactility bring a sense of suppleness. A man as concerned with the sublime as Martin Heidegger could logically also write, "Being can reveal itself through touch."[94] During one of the parades that the Theresienstadt Jewish police performed regularly in the main square of the camp, the head of the Council of the Elders at the time, Jakob Edelstein, commanded the corps. He was known to have been a traveling salesman in textiles in one of his former lives. Now, as the parade was at its best, Jacob Edelstein—was it a joke or a gesture of a philosopher?—"went over to one of the policemen, all of whom were wearing new gray uniforms made of old dyed bed sheets, fingered the material like a textile merchant does and said: 'Very nice, very nice.'"[95]

TWO

Beauty Spots

The Mosaic law forbids tattoos.[1] According to the covenant, nothing can be "inscribed in the flesh."[2] Blushes, birthmarks, stigmata, or indeed tattoos have always been considered much more than just "marks that slide along."[3] They always more or less "inscribe and excribe the body."[4] Like a vestment, they always more than just covered the body, and now, in the time of the camps, they became more of a cloud and a shroud. Like clothes, skin has always been a matter of fashion; in the camps it became ultimately so.

Neither Boven Digoel nor Theresienstadt were Auschwitz. Neither in Boven Digoel nor in Theresienstadt were the bodies of the victims tattooed Auschwitz-style, and even less were internees burned—on the arms, chests, cheeks, and foreheads—as Dostoyevsky described in the Tsarist camp of just before his time.[5] In Boven Digoel and in Theresienstadt the internees were allowed to keep their own clothes; and their skin, too, baring accidents, was left intact.

Still, fashion in Boven Digoel and in Theresienstadt reached unprecedentedly close to the skin, so close that a skin might feel like clothes and clothes like a skin. There is a most excellent Prussian officer in one of

Hermann Broch's novels of the early twentieth century: "He could almost have wished that the uniform was a direct emanation of his skin."[6] The camp people might or might not have wished for this, but their sense of wearing clothes and wearing their skin now reached as high on the scale of sensing.

In both Theresienstadt and Boven Digoel, people went through "harsh stripping—checking for lice," "searching one's clothes, for scabies, for sharp things, for golden ornaments, and precious stones."[7] Yet there was, neither in Boven Digoel nor in Theresienstadt, the Auschwitz-like "shaving off of all one's hair, . . . face and body."[8]

There were, according to Hans Günther Adler's history of Theresienstadt, "nine hairstyle salons" in the camp, plus a number of "barbers" and one evidently more exclusive "women's hair studio."[9] In the previously quoted short story by Josef Taussig, the young man on his walk through the camp "stopped at a large group of people in front of a barber's shop display window."[10] In Boven Digoel, too, there were, if not hair salons, then certainly barbers, for the authorities as well as the internees and by the internees. In the lists of the newly arriving internees one finds, for instance, "thirty years old barber, formerly the chairman of a local Communist section," and "internee Kartomidjojo, the barber."[11]

The internees who were barbers in their former lives were allowed to take their tools to Boven Digoel; they just had to deposit them with the ship's captain for the length of the journey. This is why we know about them. In the case of internee Kartomidjojo, his etui contained "one straight razor, sixteen safety razors, one razor holder, one razor strop, one badger shaving brush, and one hand mirror."[12]

As was the case with the tailors, some Boven Digoel internees learned the barber trade in the camp. Thus, there were several barbershops in Boven Digoel, of a tropical kind—sometimes just a couple of chairs or just a cleared space at the side of the road, and there were barbers going from house to house, serving internees as well as the Ambon and Moluccans guards and Dutch officials. Camp police watched and reported on them, too.

> SUNDAY, JUNE 23, 1940. MORNING: 10:47 . . . Soeganda is at the house of internees Gaos and Soeleman; also Ngadiman is there, getting a haircut.[13]

> FRIDAY, JUNE 21, 1935 . . . AFTERNOON: . . . 3:55. Karsosoemarto, barber, passes by the police station. He carries his tools and says he is on the way to the administration section. Agent Soedirman inquires further and Karsosoemarto says that he is going to do a haircut at the Lieutenant's house.[14]

"Our heads," Dostoyevsky wrote about his early modern Tsarist Russia camp, "were shaved in different ways; some of us had half the head shaven lengthwise, others across."[15] The Boven Digoel women were described by Krarup Nielsen as "wearing their hair in a very attractive traditional style." "Most of the men in the camp," wrote the Dane, "walk around with hairstyles irreproachably European."[16]

Initially, the ss commander of Theresienstadt issued a haircut order for men to "wear their hair no longer than three millimeters" and for women to wear a *Herrenschnitt* [men's haircut].[17] The order, according to the internees themselves, was never really enforced, and eventually it was to all intents and purposes forgotten.[18] Nevertheless, the internees might accept the order and its vacillation, lightly or not, the stronger ones with a wink, like a true fashion change or like another case of Etty Hillesum's shroud. For a modern man in Europe of the time just before the camps, through the 1930s, very short hair was a fashion, and *Herrenschnitt* was a Josephine Baker rage. They might feel as if they were locked in a fashion world, and so they were, in the camp more than in the outside before.

"There is hardly another article of dress," Walter Benjamin noticed at the time just before the camps, "that can give expression to such divergent erotic tendencies, and that has so much latitude to disguise them, as a woman's hat."[19] And nowhere did hats, female and male, caps and scarves, close to flesh, skin, and hair, and of erotic tendencies, appear to matter more than in the camps. Jiří Bruml wrote for a magazine of and by the Jewish boys in Theresienstadt about the importance of hats and caps in the camp. Women's hats were not exactly the young Bruml's cup of tea, but about the male hats and caps he wrote as an expert, "A high-peak cap with a badge and two yellow stripes indicates that its owner is a ghetto cop. We know who is a firefighter from his hunters' cap. Do you meet a man in a white cap? If the man is fat, he is a cook. If he is not fat, he is a corpse bearer."[20]

ss-Sturmbannführer Hans Günther (internee and later historian Adler hated to use his name in full because it so closely resonated with the ss man's), one of the high-level officers in Berlin supervising Theresienstadt, was rumored among the internees to deeply engage himself and "ask to see several possible proposed models of a police cap."[21] When internee Philipp Manes saw the approved new police cap, he recorded the event in his camp diary with excitement: "Now the men are given to wear blue-and-white stripes as bordering of their caps. Finally. *Blue and white . . . Shalom! Shalom!*"[22]

Gabriel Italie, an elderly man like Mr. Manes, one of the practicing Jews in the camp (far from all Jews interned in the camp were practicing or orthodox), wrote on October 12, 1944, "I failed to bring my hat to Theresienstadt and so I had to manage with the ancient cap from Westerbork. Mercifully, after some weeks, a junior rabbi in the camp Ernst Lieben let me to have a nice soft black hat of his. So now, I have something to wear on Shabbat and on Yom Tov."[23] Two months later, on December 12, 1944, Mr. Italie wrote in his diary, "Today is the second day of Hanukkah.... I am going to get a new hat: Let's go shopping!"[24]

Honoré de Balzac, the nineteenth-century expert on elegance, in his imaginary *My Journey from Paris to Java*, told a strange story about hats as heads and indeed souls. "I got to know the priest of the crocodiles and had the perilous honor of seeing these horrible creatures," Balzac spoke through the mouth of his hero-traveler about Javanese crocodiles. "There are vague similarities between the stupid cruelty of their faces and that of revolutionaries; their overlapping carapaces, their dirty yellow bellies are the very image of insurrectional clothing—they lacked only the red bonnet to make them a symbol of 1793."[25]

The rebels, not the Balzac crocodiles, French, not Balzac Javanese, sang a hat song during the next Paris revolution after the one that Balzac talked about: "Hats off before the cap! On your knees before the workman!"[26] Those in power as well as those powerless, in France, in the Indies, as in Germany, knew well the significance of this frivolous piece of clothing, not just of female hats. One of the very first laws that helped to establish the new Nazi order in occupied Europe was a prohibition in 1940 against "selling hats to Jews—men or boys."[27] In Theresienstadt the Jews were allowed to wear their caps, hats, and scarves if they managed to get some in the camp. The rule, particularly sublime and cruel in when and where it was applied.

In Boven Digoel, the internees wore hats rather than caps—straw hats, soft felt hats, even Borsalino hats were mentioned.[28] There was at least one professional hat maker in Boven Digoel, a "thirty-year-old, born in Solo," Central Java, learning his trade before and practicing it in the camp.[29]

The *helmhoed*, a tropical or pith helmet, also a part of the military's "real" uniform since the early twentieth century, was the epitome of modern colonial. Among the progressive Indonesians it was considered a "new style." Substituting sometimes for the hat, the helmhoed became the chic wear of the camp. Often the helmet figures on the list of internees' belongings, even those who clearly had not much else to be listed.[30]

By hats, caps, scarves, and helmets, as never before, a person and his place among other persons in the camp was recognized. Without a hat, a cap, a scarf, or a helmet, or with a hat, a cap, or a scarf worn incorrectly or on the wrong occasion, for the wrong season, in the camp, one became, to use a German expression that came into wide use at the time, *entwürdigen* [deprived of dignity]³¹—something like clothless. A *Grüßflicht* [an order to give a greeting] was issued in Theresienstadt very early on, on December 21, 1942. According to it, "every one of the camp population, when encountered by an ss officer, a Czech gendarme, or anyone of authority in uniform" (the subuniforms of Jews were not included), "must give a greeting. Jews marching to work in columns must take off their caps. Every man must take his head cover off, every woman must curtsy."³²

The two men of authority who took Josef K. to his execution in Kafka's *The Trial*, a novel written twenty years before Theresienstadt, are described as wearing "frock coats . . . with top hats that were apparently irremovable."³³ Peachum, the paragon of capitalist high modernity in Bertolt Brecht's *Threepenny Opera*, "always keeps his hat on, since he expects the roof to fall in at any moment."³⁴ Walter Benjamin described Charlie Chaplin, a citizen of the same epoch as the camp people, as one who "looks to men's fashion. He does this in order to take the master caste at its word. His cane is the rod around which the parasite creeps (the vagabond is no less a parasite than the gent), and his bowler hat, which no longer sits so securely on his head, betrays the fact that the rule of the bourgeoisie is tottering."³⁵

There were fashion faces in the camps, under the hats and caps and in the scarves, of an unprecedentedly concentrated multitude of shapes and colors. In Theresienstadt, they were faces of the peoples brought from Central and Western Europe, Czech lands and Moravia, Austria, Germany, Holland and Denmark, and much less but also "from as far as Biska in Balkans," "from "the East," from Poland up to the Soviet borders, "packed in a hurry." "From a white Negress," Bernhard Kold wrote in his Theresienstadt camp diary, "through the people with Gypsy, Hungarian, Slovenian, and Rumanian-Italian blood to blond people, some almost white-blond, and also a few albinos, from the slender and tall West-European ladies—From a Mongolian-Russian face to . . . a strikingly elegant woman face with lipstick and with hair dyed."³⁶

Boven Digoel was no less varied. Most of the internees in this camp had come from the western parts of the huge Indonesian-Malay archipelago, from the islands of Java and Sumatra, where the real and only fighting of the rebellion of 1926 and 1927 took place. But there were also Madurese packed in, Borneans, Menadonese, Ambonese, Timorese, Chinese, Dutch-Indonesians, and, of course, the people on the camp staff, whose faces were "white."

In both camps, fashion-wise, there were faces differing in a cascade of little nothings, faces as models for the season, as well as faces *"definitely passé*." In Theresienstadt, there was, most flagrantly ("loudly"), a "Jewish face." In Boven Digoel, also a sign of the time, there was a "Communist face." Browsing the illustrated magazines of the time, German as well as Dutch, one could easily find them both. There was also easily to be found, in the magazines of the Netherlands and Dutch Indies, a "Boven Digoel face," and it was thus named in the captions.

Krarup Nielsen closely observed the faces of the internees already on the ship to Boven Digoel: "There were the most various types among them," he wrote. "Some look at you unfriendly with a gross and arrogant face. Others look so decent and peaceful that they make one wonder how they ever got here."[37] The "Boven Digoel face" was a face to put on. "Those brutal mugs," the Boven Digoel camp doctor wrote about ten years after the journalist.[38] In the camp doctor's memoirs, there is a photograph of a Boven Digoel internee with a caption that reads, "*The Sumatran Communist Mohamed Jatim*. During the rebellion of 1926 he attempted to throw a bomb at an official. The bomb exploded in his hand and Jatim lost right eye, his right hand was shattered, and he suffered deep wounds on his left arm and chest."[39] As an aside: Jatim looks at me from the photograph, and I can see a beautiful face.

Face in the camps was a thing to wear and thus a thing to point at and to show. Another internee with his face marked—and marking—is remembered by Mr. Trikoyo. "During a skirmish in the 1926 uprising," Mr. Trikoyo recalled, "Uncle Zainal Abidin's face was badly wounded. It was cut open by a sword of a Dutch soldier. Uncle Abidin used to show his face to us children in the camp. The scars, he told us, were brought about by colonialism."[40]

In Theresienstadt, the predictable, ready-to-wear, was "the Jewish face," a *Stockjude* face.[41] It was put on people and in the fashion of the camp people put it on themselves as well. The Stockjude face of Moses, "with earlocks and a crooked nose," became the face put on *Ghettokronen* [Ghetto crowns], the banknotes issued at a moment as the camp currency. This face inevitably became the most "popular" graphic of Theresienstadt in the time of camp.[42] This was how it was clearly intended by the SS rulers of the camp, and the Jews understood it instantly: "The Kohn's face it was called," a Theresienstadt internee wrote.[43] The bills were technically very well produced, and they were designed by a young Jewish painter and poet, Theresienstadt internee Peter Kien. Like real money, they were printed on paper with a watermark.[44]

There were many things in which the camps brought about a culmination. Like a jacket, a hat, or a skin, one was now expected, to try at least, to put a nose on or to take it off. Possibly the most generally well-liked person in the Theresienstadt camp was Freddy Hirsch, a German Jew in his twenties. He was an excellent gymnast, an enthusiast, and a great organizer. He was thought of and was remembered by the other internees most affectionately, and was sometimes called, as we read in the camp memoirs, as almost perfect, "Apollo with a Jewish nose."[45]

In a "Jewish survivor report" on Theresienstadt written in March 1946, Mr. Jacobson, an ex-internee, recalled, "One could see many young people in the camp, fine strapping youth with good physiques. Hardly anyone among them would have fitted in the physiognomic scheme of Streicher's *Stürmer*."[46] *Stürmer* was a virulently anti-Semitic Nazi paper with crude caricatures describing the Jewish physiognomy in particular (the rest, the bodies, would come logically) as—passé. Otto Bernstein, another internee, wrote about the Theresienstadt Jews that they "were, and I say it in these words, 'a beautiful race' [*schöne Rasse*]." They could be, Bernstein wrote, "mistaken for the Germanic [*germanisch*] people."[47]

Mr. Manes (who did not survive) wrote in his camp diary about the Theresienstadt children, "They are the most beautiful children—I would not find ten among hundreds of an explicitly Jewish type."[48]

True to the power of the little cascade of nothings, color and even a shade of color mattered in the camps, as before and more than ever before. Through the centuries, the Jews were seen as dark or even black and sometimes yellow "like of the Mongolian East." The "natives" in the Indies, of course, were "natives" because they were "dark." One may hear people in Indonesia still today say that their child is "beautiful like an Arab," meaning of light complexion (and, for instance, of a narrow-at-root and straight nose). Some may talk about "an ancestor with blue eyes."[49]

Face wearing in Europe became increasingly significant as the time of the camps approached. Siegfried Kracauer, a contemporary of Benjamin, wrote about Germany of the 1920s, "With the huge supply of labor, a certain physical 'selection' inevitably occurs." Kracauer visited an employment agency in Berlin. An official in the place explained to him, "We have to do things the same way as the Americans do. The man must have a friendly face." Kracauer asked what "friendly" meant. Was it "pleasant—saucy or pretty?" "Not exactly pretty," the official said. "What's far more crucial is—oh, you know, a morally pink complexion."[50] (Heinrich Himmler, the architect of the Nazi camps, a few years after Kracauer had written this, gave a speech in which he expressed his worries about the character of the members of the SS. In the speech, Himmler insisted on the importance of "desirable faces."[51] He could have said "pink.")

As history was coming close to the moment of the camps, fashion raged. Peter Demetz wrote about the increasing attraction of makeup in Prague, after it was occupied by the Nazi forces and as many people were getting ready for the camps. Czech women in Prague, Demetz wrote, began to put especially bright tones of rouge on their lips and faces, "like the young women in French and American movies, in symbolic opposition."[52] Opposition against the Germans, that is. "Only rarely," Demetz added, a German woman—and there was an increasing number of them in Prague, arriving with the German armies—could be seen walking around with "rebellious traces of rouge on her lips."[53]

In Theresienstadt, the SS command repeatedly issued prohibitions against using makeup and cosmetics. However, judging just from how repeatedly the prohibitions were being issued, there evidently had to be equally frequent disregard of the orders.[54] "Rumors have it," Gonda Redlich wrote in his camp diary in July 1943, "that SS man Burger is going to prohibit lipstick for the women again."[55] "Many women," wrote Adler, "put makeup on, they were quite insistent on cosmetics and they could not care less about what the SS thought."[56]

"I saw skeletons walking around on sticks," the American soldier quoted in the previous chapter as being surprised about how nicely some people were dressed in the camp, added, among other confusing things he saw, "No woman without lipstick."[57] Theresienstadt might even have brought to his mind a dictionary rare definition of the word "camp," "*camp* (of manner): heavily made up."

Charles Baudelaire, a dandy and a prophet of the modern, in his nineteenth-century *In Praise of Cosmetics* proclaimed perfume to be a "symptom of the taste for the ideal."[58] One hundred years later, Rem Koolhaas, a Dutch architect and in many ways Baudelaire's heir, found one of the main characteristics of the space we live in now to be the fact of the space being filled with "more and more insistent perfumes."[59] Koolhaas called this space a "Junkspace" but he might have called it a postcamp space or even a camp space.

There were "more and more insistent perfumes" in Boven Digoel, too. According to a "shopping list" among the papers of the camp government commissary, "Internee Darmoprawiro [bought] two cans of coffee for $fo.90$, one bottle of vinegar for $fo.40$, 1¼ pounds of mung beans for $fo.90$, and one flacon of eau de cologne for $fo.75$."[60] In a popular Indies novel about Boven Digoel published in Batavia at the time, a young heroine is just about to be deported with her Communist father to the camp. She is described as "made up, with the powders and the creams, and there is a smell of eau de cologne around her." In addition, "she smokes a cigarette and she does not care in the least about that the people are watching."[61]

....

Other fashion accessories made their rarely seen presence in the camps—the *spécialité*, the novelties, the trivialities worn on clothes, close to the skin or even on the naked skin. They could almost make clothes into skin and skin into clothes. The fashion accessories were the hit in the camps, as dandy as hardly ever before, even if often by virtue of their scarcity—"ribbons, diadems, beauty marks," the "ever-new creations of bow and frill," the "*bandeaux* in women's hair," the "*chignons*."

There were several—few and the more so exclusive and desirable—*Galanterieladen*, thread-and-needle shops, in Theresienstadt, which, if one was lucky and came at the right moment, might offer "thimbles, ribbons, pieces of lace, ... brooches, chains, and colorful frippery."[62] There were golden ornaments, precious stones, and trinkets in the camp, of radically increased significance in their presence or absence, "strings of pearls" that the Jewish women left or imagined they had left behind when sent to the camp, which could not be squeezed into the trunk or sewed into a coat as they packed.[63] No jewels, gems, or gold could be brought into the camp except wedding rings; it was the ss rule.[64] Still, there were women wandering about the camp wearing "the most beautiful necklaces, rings, and bracelets."[65]

An elderly lady, a former diva of the Berlin Opera, was fondly remembered after the war as appearing in the camp with a "veil on her face and a feather boa around her neck."[66] Could it be, I wonder as I write this book about two camps, that this was one of the boas made of the feathers of birds of paradise, indeed the most exquisite kind and style of boa at the time of the lady's best years? Dutch New Guinea, particularly the area along the Digoel River, where the camp was to be built thirty years later, was one of the very few spots of the world where the birds of paradise were found and "harvested."

Jewels, gold, and silver, as well as fake doubles, precious and "precious" stuff, were packed and brought by the Communist internees all the way to Boven Digoel. Lists of the items collected from the internees for safekeeping by the captain of the HMS *Jawa* to Boven Digoel in January 1927 included:

Soetaslekan: one golden watch, one golden chain, one wallet.
Nawai: one golden ring.
Soekindar: two golden rings, one knife ...

> Kadarisman: two golden rings, one knife, one post stamp in value of f1.50 (dirty).
> Padmosoesastro: one watch that plays a melody, one golden chain, two golden rings . . .
> Soendoro: one watch with a chain and charivari.
> Djoefri: one wallet, two stones . . .
> Hartadi, alias Koesmo: one nickel watch with a chain, and one pack of nails.[67]

One very special "specialty" in both camps, a particular "manifestation of preciosity,"[68] were armbands and patches. A power as well as a fashion statement, these armbands and patches were of carefully selected shapes and sizes and of carefully selected materials and colors; they were attached, buttoned or sewed on, or pinned to, the clothes, or they might be hung around the neck. They were a *novelty* in the camp, but not new. Only in the camps, suddenly and radically, they became so profound, a must to have.

"At the arrival to Theresienstadt," Jehuda Bacon, a boy at the time, recalled later, "a completely new and foreign world had been unveiled before me. Sometimes, we children found the scene actually comical, . . . so many people with armbands."[69] Mr. Manes, who was charged in the camp with organizing a Jewish Orientation Section of the Jewish police, as if responding to the boy Bacon's impressions, wrote in his own diary, "We simply have to wear armbands, otherwise we would not appear to be official persons at all."[70] "Armbands," Adler wrote, "were a camp fashion . . . the police yellow . . . the order orientation service blue . . . blind and disabled people yellow with black points."[71]

"Everything was very well organized," Kafka wrote in his *Nature Theatre of Oklahoma*, again, as if knowing it was coming. Karl, the hero of the novel, is not a Jew, at least it is stated nowhere in the novel. At a gathering point from which the people are to be taken to the wonderful Theater of Oklahoma, he is asked about his race and profession. At a loss, he gives his identity (logically?) as "Negro" and "technical worker." To his amazement, when a while later he was "met by a servant who put an armband around his arm," when he "lifted his arm to see what was on the band, it was, quite rightly, 'Negro, the technical worker.'"[72]

In the spring of 1935, Benjamin noticed, "Something new appeared in women's fashions, medium-sized embossed metal plaquettes which were worn on jumpers or overcoats and which displayed the initial letters of the bearer's first name."[73] The novelty, Benjamin thought, "profited from the vogue for badges, which had arisen among men in the wake of the patriotic leagues."[74] At the moment of Benjamin's writing, the novelty was already getting ahead of itself, to where it would weight most heavily, in the camps. This was in Berlin, and roughly at the time when Benjamin noticed the plaquettes. A Jewish woman, an emigrant to the US, recalled the scene decades later, "I was beginning to look a little bit like a woman and was walking on a Berlin street, when an SS man approached me and asked me if he could accompany me home. It was winter time, and I had to open my coat in order to hold up a small gold Star of David I had begun to wear on a little chain around my neck."[75]

In a copy of the magazine *Vedem* [We Are in the Lead], which a group of boys in Theresienstadt wrote for themselves, an article appeared in September 1943, already deep in the time of the camps. There was a watercolor by one of the boys of a Jewish policeman in the camp. "A ghetto cop is of the male sex," the caption read. "He has a patch of cloth with a letter 'W' [like *Wache*, "Watch"] and a number stuck to the shoulder on his coat. He has the same letter and number inscribed on a badge that shines on his chest."[76] Josef Taussig similarly described "a strange figure" appearing before the hero of his short story. "The man wears a heavy winter coat across which there is a wide ordinance belt. Above all and distinguishing the figure from all others, swings a copper medal. The man has a face of a valiant soldier—a Theresienstadt policeman."[77]

There were medals, patches, and pendants in Theresienstadt, in all sizes and models and worn in all manner of ways. There were several Jews in the camp who had fought for Wilhelmian Germany or Habsburg Austria in World War I, and had received medals for their service. There were some, even, who had received the most coveted German award, "Iron Cross." Yet "it was forbidden to the Jews to wear any medal or order from the time before the camps."[78] Of course! But these medals had to be the more powerful, and present, in their status of not being permitted to be worn.

Many medals in the camp were powerful in their presence. "A chase after the titles in the camp grew into an orgy," Emil Utitz wrote about Theresienstadt after the war. Easily he might say "rage." Utitz was Kafka's schoolmate as a young man, then he taught at the university in Prague, and then spent more than three years in the camp: "A little medal, and even an usher armband on the sleeve," he wrote about the camp, "became a goal to be desired."[79]

As it has always been in the matters of fashion, shame was an important part of the camps. To signify authority (or subauthority in this case), the Boven Digoel selected willing internees who entered the camp ROB police corps, and who got plaquettes and patches, quite fancy ones, in fact, to distinguish them but also to help them feel less degraded in the eyes of their comrades who did not join. "So that they were not embarrassed as they were walking on duty through the camp," an internee remembered, "they got uniforms with cockades pinned on their chests, a blue disk with the letters ROB in white."[80]

Why try to explain everything? In Theresienstadt, among the last belongings of an elderly Jewish woman who died alone in the camp, they found a pendant on the woman's dead body, under the blouse, on her skin. Gonda Redlich, a fellow internee, wrote in his diary on June 24, 1943, without a comment, "They found a swastika."[81]

Georg Simmel argued (namely for Germany, in the early twentieth century) that it is hardness and deadness, the "nature of stone and metal," that makes adornment precious and powerful.[82]

Fancy penholders and superbly sharpened pencils in the breast pockets were worn close to heart as the Boven Digoel internees disembarked for the camp. Little books in hard cardboard red covers, Communist Party membership cards, in the breast pockets, too, were carried by the internees all the way to Boven Digoel with an equal sense of significance. The Dutch guards strip-searching the internees on arrival, as wrote Dr. Schoonheyt, found the cards on the body of almost every one of the internees.[83]

"Accessories make the spring," Roland Barthes in his *The Fashion System* quoted repeatedly from a haute couture magazine.[84] Adornments make the spring—and all the seasons, and the world in change, and the people—by cliché, through clichés into the real. A man who survived the Theresienstadt camp, and Auschwitz, too, told Elena Makarova, in Jerusalem, after the war: "You know, in Theresienstadt there was an epidemic of making medallions and inserting photos of your loved ones. For quite obvious reasons, I and Zdenka [his wife] had medallions, too. I managed to carry mine through Auschwitz, and through all the camps. I remember hiding my medallion in a boot, under my underwear—but how could I keep it, if I had to be naked for all selections? Well, I must have found a way, if it's here, at home."[85]

Chains—tiny chains made of gold or less precious metal, watch chains showing from the vest pocket, were a fashion in the 1930s as in the decades before. Delicate thin chains, short or long, were worn over the neck or as a bracelet with miniature charms. Big chains and shackles were something else, but not completely; they were still stone-hard and stone-dead, they too were worn close to the skin, so close, sometimes, wrote Dostoyevsky, that "they rubbed the skin into sores."[86] Chains became ornaments, the small and the big. They were accessories concentrating people into their symbolism, and hardening the traces of the people's desire. They made the chained people into who they were.

In Theresienstadt, the big chains were rarely worn. But they were present, heavy on people's minds in their possibility. Putting a Jew in chains in Theresienstadt was rather rare a punishment, applied only "when a Jew did something wrong." Then he or she was taken to the basement of the local Gestapo office on the main square of the camp, to be chained, invisible, but for all the others to know.

The big chains were not the everyday in Boven Digoel, either. As in Theresienstadt, they were a possibility, for special occasions. When an internee attempted to escape from Boven Digoel, for instance, and was caught and brought back, or sometimes on the ship during a transport to the camp, one was made to wear the chain. Internee Marsudi, who went to Boven Digoel on the ship *Rumphius*, recalled that, in his case, five men were chained by one long chain. When any one of the five needed to go to the toilet, all five had to go.[87]

Only in the camps, and so late in the history, with the sense of the grave irony implied, it becomes possible to see the chains, big and small, as a fashion. They fitted the season and defined the people, humiliated them one moment and the other built their dignity, shamed them and made them shine. Like all items of fashion, in the final analysis, they were a commodity. They appeared in various models, responded to demand, light or heavy, long or short, state of the art or used. They could also be mail-ordered. There were "American models of chains." The military commander of Tandjong Priuk harbor in Batavia recorded, "The commanding officer of the government steamer WEGA on the way to Boven Digoel confirms with his signature below that he received from the harbor commissar of the police for transport to Boven Digoel twenty-five pairs of American handcuffs."[88]

Eventually everything was absorbed into and constrained within the chains, as it should in a perfect accessory—novelty, cruelty, flair, and also mourning. When Fyodor Dostoyevky, one of the pre-Theresienstadt and pre–Boven Digoel camp people, died in Saint Petersburg in 1881, the students of the city insisted, in a gesture that became prophetic with hindsight (but they were not permitted in the end), on carrying "his chains" behind the coffin.[89]

....

One accessory was missing in Boven Digoel. It was exclusively European, truly a *spécialité*. Like medallions and penholders, it was also to be worn close to the heart, but its hardness was in spirit, not in the stuff it was made from. The Jewish star was a patch, a piece of cloth, that most radically and completely was supposed to make a person wearing it into what the patch was supposed to signify. By the way of the camps, too, it was also supposed to make Europe what the patch signified, and the world, as it was and as it is. "It felt as if we were being branded," Eva Benda recalled about going to Theresienstadt with a star, "and in a way we were."[90]

The star, again, was not wholly a novelty. It was, in fact, older than modernity itself, yet, again, it did not become fully modern until the time of the camps. Honoré de Balzac, the French nineteenth-century fashion expert (among other things), wrote of a man on a Paris street shouting at another man, "Do you have a yellow wheel by way of decoration on your surcot?" Balzac records this exchange in his *Treatise on Elegant Living*. "Move on, outcast of Christianity!—Jew, go back to your hole at curfew or be punished by a fine."[91]

Even before Balzac, multiple decrees, all of them fashion decrees in their core and execution, codified the Jews and the European order. Some required "Jews to wear badges or conspicuous garments, such as special headgear or footwear," others prohibited the Jews "from wearing certain fabrics or colors."[92] In some locations and times, "earrings were imposed on Jewish women, suggesting an association with prostitutes."[93] In the time of the camps, to make the idea ultimately pure and ultimately powerful, the cut, the color, and the manner of wearing the thing got finally settled.

The marking of the Jews by the Nazis was first proposed by the SS-Obergruppenführer Reinhard Heydrich on November 12, 1938. It is recorded that as Heydrich tabled his proposal, Hermann Göring, a fellow Nazi who was known as Nazi business conscious and who was also notorious as a Nazi dandy, exclaimed excitedly, "A uniform?" But Heydrich did not plan for wind being taken from his sails, and retorted, "An insignia."[94]

The decree as eventually issued, first on September 1, 1941, for Germany, ordered "Jews six years or over to appear in public only when wearing the Jewish star." The star had to be "as large as the palm of a hand." Its color had to be black, the background yellow, and for the center of the star the decree prescribed the black inscription "*Jude*." The Jews were "to sew the star tightly on their clothing, left on the chest."[95]

People, wrote Philip Roth, an Austrian Jewish writer and journalist, "with a bit of yellow material were tagged as Jews."[96] In most cases, the stars were ready-made. In Germany itself, they were manufactured and distributed by Geitel and Co., the Berlin Flag Factory.[97] They were a commodity. In

Prague, one paid "one Czechoslovak crown for one star made of fine prewar material." For the poor Jews, the stars were distributed free.[98]

Custom-made stars were possible. It was permitted to cut one's own star, and some, wrote Imre Kertész, "gave the matter an innovative twist . . . they have the material stretched over some cardboard base, so that way, of course, it looked more attractive, plus the arms of the stars weren't cut in such a ludicrously clumsy fashion as some of the homemade ones that were to be seen."[99] Ruth Bondy recalled, "Good Jewish housewives sat and padded the stars with black cloth to make them sturdier, and then carefully sewed them onto coats and jackets using a meticulous blind stitch."[100] "One afternoon," a Jewish girl living in Amsterdam at the time and getting ready for the camp, too, later remembered: "Papa comes home and all of us stand around the table looking at sheets of yellow cloth. The cloth has stars with black borders and black letters in the center. They are made to look a little like Hebrew but they don't at all, really. They say '*Jood*' [the Dutch for "Jew"]. Papa says, 'Well, they aren't too awful.' No one answers him."[101]

The young Jews in Europe, in despair no doubt, but also with all the energy of the time, unprecedented energy, made the star into a "rage" of their own. Their generation grew up on the American Western films and cowboy lore, and so now, as they had to wear the star, they began to call each other "Sheriff."[102] In Paris, the centers for the distribution of Jewish stars began to be called "*Place de l'Etoile.*"[103]

Peter Demetz recalled his mother in Prague, getting ready for Theresienstadt (and death): "Mother took needle and thread, which she handled so well, and sewed the stars to two blouses and a dress, as the decree required. Immediately the star made it impossible for her to move freely through the city, since all parks, gardens, and many streets were forbidden to Jews."[104] Yet Mrs. Demetz insisted on keeping on her walks through Prague, and how I understand her! Peter remembered the way his mother did it. She grabbed, so he wrote, her "elegant handbag, square, black, and shiny, a little Hollywoodish à la Claudette Colbert," and she got out on the streets, holding the Colbert bag close to her heart, where the star was.[105]

As the time of the camps approached, the world increasingly became a part of the camps, and, increasingly, everything became a matter of fashion. Etty Hillesum waited for her transport to the camp at the same time as Mrs. Demetz. In her diary, Hillesum described the day the decree had been announced that the Jews in Amsterdam had also to wear the star: "You can really tell, what the history books will leave out. That man in Beethovenstraat this afternoon won't get a mention in them."

She was losing faith, but then she was struck by something extraordinary: "I looked at him as one might at the first crocus in spring, with pure enchantment. He was wearing a huge golden star, wearing it triumphantly on his chest. He was a procession and a demonstration all by himself as he cycled along so happily. And all that yellow—I suddenly had a poetic vision of the sun rising above him, so radiant and smiling did he look."[106]

On overcoats, jackets, shirts, and blouses the Jews wore a star, and, of course, on uniforms. "The Jewish policemen," Mrs. Mayer-Kattenburg recalled as she was already in Theresienstadt, "they all walked around with a great yellow star."[107] In hot summers, waivers were issued for the "men working in the open without shirts to attach their star on their pants and wear it there until they put on their shirt and jacket again."[108] "So now I have three stars," wrote Petr Ginz in his camp diary on April 16, 1942, "one on top of the other, on my shirt, on my jacket, and on my overcoat."[109] "I did have a white spot on my breast," another Jewish man wrote, "because we worked just in shorts, in the sun, with the stars hanging around our necks."[110]

To use another one of the fashion magazines, expressions Barthes analyzed so exhaustively, "One just would not go out" without a star. There were weeks in Theresienstadt when "there was a great shortage of stars, and they had often to be unraveled and re-sewed." The Jewish camp police had to make sure that each internee wore a star all the time. "One saw people startled on the street," Adler wrote, "'Oh, I have lost my star!' Or one might be stopped: 'Where is your star?!'"[111]

THREE

Pink Bodies

Aliarcham (*far right*), the former chairman of the Communist Party of the Indies, with his family in Boven Digoel, ca. 1931. With permission of the National Library, Jakarta.

In the camps, more than ever before, fashion became an accessory, an extension of the body, and more. All the squeezing and packing of the vestments and jewels for the camps, all the stuff's compacting, concentration, and sublimation, reached an unprecedented new stage. Walter Benjamin, at the outset of the time of the camps, again wrote as if he were writing about the camp and from within the camp: "Fashion invents an artificial humanity."[1] The camp bodies became accessories of the camp clothes and camp jewels. Bodies were worthy of being as long as they were fashionable.

The camp bodies were fashioned with a cruelty and concentrated care. Like the camp clothes, the camp bodies were cut for the season. An unhealthy body meant a body passé and thus discardable. Healthy meant "pink," which meant fit for the camp.

In 1894, in Vienna, the already well-established Secession painter Gustav Klimt had been commissioned to decorate the ceilings in the new assembly hall of Vienna University. He was asked to paint allegories of Philosophy, Jurisprudence, and Medicine. Medicine Klimt conceived as "personifications of pain, disease, and death." The sketches he made were "images of naked men, women, and children, old people and pregnant women." His designs caused a scandal lasting years, and a parliamentary inquiry, and in the end the university rejected the project, "sexual" children, "sensual" death, "open" bodies, and all the other "perversions."[2]

According to Martin Heidegger, "freeing is taking care of," "we work on it, improve it, destroy it."[3] In contrast to Gustav Klimt, Martin Heidegger's approach to the human body was easily moving between sublime and instrumental, and thus, also in this case, he signaled the camps.

Dr. Erich Springer was a successful medical practitioner before the war. After he was sent to Theresienstadt as a Jew, the Jewish Council of the Elders with ss approval appointed him to serve as the acting chief of the whole health system that was being established in the camp. Dr. Springer survived and, shortly after the war, wrote a long and detailed report on Theresienstadt medical care: "The first surgery we did," Dr. Springer wrote, "was a small gynecological intervention. The next was an amputation of a leg under the knee.... Soon, quite complicated surgeries were performed in a new surgery, which was already equipped with good ventilation that offset much of the heat produced by the five old theater reflectors above the operating table."[4]

An exception was allowed for the Jewish physicians transported to Theresienstadt. They were permitted to take medical equipment from their prewar offices to the camp beyond the limit on luggage allowed to the others.

Larger or more complicated equipment was moved into Theresienstadt with SS permission from the now-closed Jewish hospitals all over Nazi-occupied Europe. "We had some historical pieces in the camp," Dr. Springer reported, "some of it almost useless, but we also had some state-of-the-art instruments and machines, several x-rays, a number of ultraviolet lamps, diathermy equipment..."[5] At one point, Hans Günther Adler describes Theresienstadt medicine as *übermechanisiert* [overmechanized].[6]

According to Heidegger, "The everyday interpretation of the self" always has "the tendency to understand itself in terms of the 'world taken care of.'"[7] "*Letting things be relevant,*" Heidegger wrote (and the emphasis is his), "*constitutes the existential structure of taking care.*"[8] It seemed logical to him, and it seemed logical in the camps—and this is why Heidegger sounds to me in this case more like a Nazi than like a philosopher—that "things that cannot be used, a tool that would not work... something like damage to the tool... something unhandy... something unsuited for," what does not pass "'inspection,'" or is deemed "deficient" in the process of the care, inevitably, *caringly* (here the emphasis is mine), is subject to "removal."[9]

"The oldest patient operated on in Theresienstadt," wrote Adler, "was a case of hernia, and he was a man of ninety." Abdominal laparotomies, Adler also wrote (and I do not know what Abdominal laparotomies means), were operated upon in the camp, and there "appeared no postoperative thrombosis or embolis." "In treating bone fractures," Adler wrote, "a bloodless method was attempted with satisfactory results. These treatments, in almost all cases, resulted in full recovery."[10] Ruth Bondy mentions at least one successful mastectomy.[11]

The teeth of the Jews in Theresienstadt (and one has to think of Auschwitz and what happened to the Jews there) were plumbed in the camp "with silver amalgam or cement. Larger oral surgeries, however, in the dental offices of the camp health system were being done only with difficulties and they often had unsatisfactory results." Similarly, "One had to wait for decent glasses six months and even longer in spite of the fact that all the glasses of the dead and the glasses of the internees that were not necessary, have been either confiscated or collected at the time of death, and then given to the optician['s] office."[12]

This was, to use Heidegger's words, "the existential structure of taking care." Mr. Gabriel Italie, who was forty-nine years old at the time, wrote on November 12, 1944, in his Theresienstadt diary, "Today, I was auscultated at the doctor's office, weighed (57.5 kg), measured (1.69 m), and my blood pressure was checked."[13] Gonda Redlich, in his camp diary, on October 28,

1942, wrote, "I was x-rayed and checked for tuberculosis. Thanks G-d, nothing bad turned up."[14]

From the beginning of the nineteenth century and into the 1930s in Europe, "Doctor was said to be a Jewish first name."[15] My mother, with the "nonlethal" anti-Semitism that was never missing in her generation, used to say that the Jews were the best doctors there were. Many of "the best doctors there were," indeed, went to Theresienstadt. At least Dr. Springer testified in that sense: "The Health Office in Theresienstadt, in spite of all the difficulties, provided exemplary services. Many great cities in Europe at the time might have learned from the Jewish camp."[16]

....

"The very moment Boven Digoel was decided upon as a place of political isolation," the retired captain of the Indies colonial army, L. Th. Becking, the first commandant-administrator of the camp, laid "foundations for military barracks, hospital, radio station, and post office."[17] In one of the first telegraph messages from Batavia to what was still a largely untouched jungle, it was stated: "Needed immediately—stop—two military brigades under a captain—stop—hospital with staff and equipment."[18] In a matter of days, the staff and first pieces of equipment were there, and in a matter of weeks the Wilhelmina Ziekenhuis, WZH, the Queen Wilhelmina Hospital, stood in the camp. In a description by an ex-internee, I. F. M. Salim, who came with the earliest groups of internees, as one embarked from the ship and entered the camp, "the first thing one noticed to one's left was the Wilhelmina Hospital built of stone." "It was intended for us," Salim added.[19]

Still in Salim's description, as one entered the hospital itself, to one's right, there was an ambulance "properly equipped." Next was a dark room for eye, nose, throat, and ear examination, a pharmacy "well stocked," a delivery room, two small isolation rooms for infectious diseases, and a women's general hall. To the left of the main entrance "was another examination room, a laboratory, an isolation room for tuberculosis patients, and a large men's yard. Next to the entrance, too, there were two offices, one for the doctor and the other for the chief nurse. There were several outbuildings belonging to the hospital. Altogether, this gave an impression of a modern institution."[20]

This soon, like the notorious camp itself, became known throughout the colony, through the Dutch reporting, but through the internees' letters home as well. "General Hospital" signified Boven Digoel.[21] Krarup Nielsen, who arrived at Boven Digoel with the very first ship of internees, already reported "a well-ordered hospital barrack, in fact better equipped than many hospitals in the Indies."[22] The official reports sent from Boven Digoel regularly to the higher authorities, and even often more critical internal reports, repeated almost as a mantra, "The state of health care in the camp can be considered good, even better than in most of the other native quarters elsewhere in the Indies."[23] Dr. Schoonheyt, in charge of the Wilhelmina Hospital for two years, even threw his hands up at the "incongruity" of the situation and in his memoirs expressed angry disbelief: "The fact that we are unable to build a modern hospital for the military and civilian authorities in the camp, can perhaps be understood. But how may one comprehend that, in the same place, a very fine hospital of stone was built for the enemies of state?"[24] The doctor returned to the matter a hundred pages further on: "The internees in the camp, people who, before, in their homes in Java or elsewhere in the Indies had to walk hours in order to get a medical care, are now getting help next door. It makes one wonder how they achieved such privilege!"[25]

Dr. Schoonheyt was an impulsive man. Somehow, the system "knew" what it was doing. Even the liberal Dutch voices in the Indies, which otherwise might criticize the very idea of the camp, isolation and incarceration, approved the camp medical care. They only wished for more of it. Marcus van Blankenstein, who belonged to the liberals, wrote after his visit to the camp, "Section D of the camp, for instance, is located four kilometers from the hospital and the roads are bad; even bicycle is of no use. For efficient care, it is too much of a distance."[26]

Except for the chief doctor, who, throughout the camp's existence was Dutch or European-trained, the entire staff of the Boven Digoel hospital, as in Theresienstadt, was made up of the internees themselves. They appear on the payroll in an archival file as "laboratory technician," "pharmacist," "secretary," "male nurse," "assistant male nurses," "female nurses," "scribe," "messengers," "cooks," "gardeners," "scrubbers," and "firefighter."[27]

Several of the chief medical officers serving in Boven Digoel belonged among the best the Indies could offer, and all were very good professionals—"the best doctors there were," my mother might say. Doctors, it appears, were selected to serve in the camp based on their expertise, namely in treating and research into the "famous" Boven Digoel malaria. Some of the most serious cases of disease, which might be beyond the capacities of the camp hospital, such as black-water malaria or insanity, might be transported by ship to Amboina, one of the largest hospitals in the eastern archipelago.[28]

In the case of malaria in particular, the concentrated camp medical care, as well as Heidegger's notion of caring, came to its own. "All internees are required," an official internal document of Boven Digoel reported, "to submit themselves to intensive medical examination."[29] "A special malaria team," wrote ex-internee Salim, who, by the way, had worked in the hospital for several of the years he was in the camp, "distributed quinine, artebrine[?], or plasmochine[?] to the adults, and euchinine[?] to the children. . . . Blood samples were collected from all the internees and brought to the hospital laboratory where they were microscopically analyzed."[30]

The Boven Digoel ROB camp police made up of the internees, as they walked through the camp, checked up on the antimalarial procedure every day and dutifully recorded their findings:

> FRIDAY, APRIL 9, 1937 . . . AFTERNOON: . . . 5:30. . . . There are still persons who did not take the pill: Karioredjo, Aminkoesasi, and Raswin . . . 6:00 Agent Hamid goes back. Nothing out of ordinary. Only Aminkoesasi refuses to take the pill.[31]
>
> TUESDAY, APRIL 13, 1937 . . . AFTERNOON: . . . 5:30. . . . Nothing out of ordinary. Only Sentot pretends he is deaf and does not want to take the pill. After the agent insists, Sentot submits.[32]
>
> SATURDAY, MAY 1, 1937 . . . AFTERNOON: . . . 4:30. Agent Soedirman watches over prophylaxis . . .[33]
>
> SUNDAY, MAY 28, 1939 . . . AFTERNOON: . . . 4:20. Agent Djoko watches over the pill-taking.[34]
>
> TUESDAY, JUNE 16, 1940 . . . AFTERNOON: 4:23. Agent A. B. Siregar goes to the hospital to watch over prophylaxis. . . . He returns and reports all as usual.[35]

People's daily doses were exactly prescribed by the chief medical officer and meticulously recorded. These are among the bulkiest files to be found in the camp archives. "The pill" pervades and dominates Boven Digoel memories, and like anything else makes them "accurate." "Accurately" the number of pills a day is recalled: "Everybody took quinine, two pieces three times a day."[36] "We had to take quinine tablets, six pieces a week."[37] "I felt sick with *tertian malaria* and each day I have to take quinine, six pills a day."[38] In the recollection of Mrs. Widayasih, who was in her early teens at the time, "Each late afternoon all people had to present themselves in front of the hospital to take the pill. (I caught malaria anyway.) If there were people permitted to take the pills with them home, they might forget or decide not to drink them at all; we did not have much discipline. I also might have taken the pill under my tongue and spit it out later. This is why Uncle Surgeb, the nurse, demanded that we show him our tongue."[39]

"The pills were red and white," Mr. Bangun Topo, another Boven Digoel child, told me.[40] "I lost hearing in my left ear," Mohammad Bondan, an ex-internee, wrote in his memoirs, "so strong was the medicine."[41] "Many internees," according to a postwar Indonesian report based on several interviews, "became hard of hearing or completely deaf. Children taking *artebrine* got yellowish eyes. They also became tired as if from lack of sleep. The older people became forgetful."[42]

In this sense, Boven Digoel became, if not a city on the hill, then certainly a catwalk. The people of the forest surrounded the camp. Not certainly the "civilized" Czechs surrounding Theresienstadt, but, even according to the accepted views of anthropologists and missionaries at the time, "the most primitive people on the earth," and a curious folk, too. The Papuans, first through the trees and then, as they were coming closer to the camp and into the camp, were being clothed, and also cared for, in a new way. By the power of the camp, attraction of the camp, they were getting "freed." Ever more of them, in widening circles around the camp, they were being tested and cared for.

TUESDAY, SEPTEMBER 25, 1934 ... AFTERNOON: ... 3:35 Agent Soedirman is sent to bring a group of Kaja-Kaja to the hospital for blood draw.[43]

MONDAY, OCTOBER 20, 1934. MORNING: ... 10:30: Agent Soedirman is sent to get Kinop (a Kaja-Kaja working for internee Djamal) and Endong (a Kaja-Kaja working for internee Mohammad Isa) and to bring them to the hospital for examination (as requested by the nurse). ... *11:55:* Telephone from the hospital: Kanop ran away during the examination; Soedirman sent to look for him. *12:00:* Soedirman returns to the post: the Kaja-Kaja was not found.[44]

THURSDAY, JULY 28, 1936 ... NIGHT: ... 10:00: The ROB leaves to look for a mad Kaja-Kaja who ran from the hospital. Not found.[45]

SUNDAY, OCTOBER 15, 1939. MORNING 7:50. A Kaja-Kaja comes to the station and says that his younger brother died in the hospital.[46]

In Theresienstadt, there were flies, fleas, and bedbugs rather than mosquitoes. Jacob Jacobson recalled, "Barracks and smaller houses alike swarmed with rats and smaller vermin, mainly fleas. ... The insects were the eleventh plague."[47] In the heat of summer "armies of bedbugs ... nested in the bunks more than usual, and the women would sleep on the ground in the courtyard."[48] Else Dormitzer, another ex-internee, remembered bedbugs in particular "in unimaginable masses." "I myself," she wrote, "killed 103 of them in my bed one night; each morning I found forty to fifty on the wall."[49] Bugs were getting through clothes to the skin. It was truer than Balzac in his essay on fashion could imagine: "*a stain is a vice.*"

Elderly women, Nava Shean recalled of Theresienstadt, were being watched by the younger ones, their clothes expensive as they were old-fashioned, like costumes for a masked ball of a long time ago. Their hats were slipping askew, and they had umbrellas, "long fanciful umbrellas with ruffles." After just a few weeks in the camps, "the umbrellas were used to drive away flies."[50] Infectious illnesses, "scarlet fever, measles, mumps, or chickenpox," were common and often just an uncomfortable part of life in the Europe of the 1930s. Now, like the people and most other things, they were concentrated in the camp and became deadly.[51]

The care, again, was concentrated as well. On Tuesday, July 18, 1944, Pavel Weiner wrote, "I cannot make it to the boy-group meeting because I have to get my shots against whooping cough."[52] New arrivals to the camp, at their very first moment in the camp, "at the gate," were cared for. "Our luggage was searched and we ourselves had to undergo an examination by a medic, and inoculation."[53] Signs of epidemics were closely watched for and registered. Typhoid appeared in the camp for the first time in January 1943. Measures were taken: "SS-Obersturmbannführer Eichmann ordered the typhus epidemics stopped." "All residents under sixty-five were inoculated," wrote Ruth Bondy, "three injections at one-week intervals."[54]

A special category of physicians had been established and became a fixture of the Theresienstadt camp—the *Läusedoktor* [lice physician]."[55] "At the turn of 1942 and 1943 the struggle turned especially against clothes lice. . . . The clothes were removed from the living quarters and both the clothes and the living quarters were treated with Ventox and later Zyklon B. . . . A delousing station was set up, with a bath."[56] In a story written by internee Otto Weiss in Theresienstadt, the people are described (and his daughter draws a picture of them in the manuscript) "tying their clothes into a bundle for the gas chamber."[57]

On Wednesday, June 14, 1944, Pavel Weiner wrote, "The lice doctor arrived. He concluded that my hair is dirty."[58] As the news of a possible visit of the International Red Cross delegation spread through the camp, "the inmates joked that they were going to paint the fleas with phosphorus, so the delegation would think they were fireflies."[59] Care of clothes, skin, and body became indistinguishable from manner of dress and appearance. "Send me a comb with fine teeth," a young woman wrote to a friend still outside the camp, "against lice" she added.⁶⁰

In Theresienstadt, people spent hours standing in line for a water faucet or for a place in a toilet.⁶¹ A *Pisskolone*, or "piss column," appears (merrily) in one of Josef Taussig's short stories—the young women marching and singing "every-night on their way to the latrines."⁶² "Gentlemen, dress up yourself in the outside," special latrine volunteers demanded, "the line is to the courtyard."⁶³ Theresienstadt children called latrines *havaj* [Hawaii].⁶⁴ "The news comes that a wagon of toilet paper is on its way," wrote Pavel Weiner in his diary on December 20, 1944. "Everything turns upside down." And, late in the same afternoon, "I still help to store the paper."⁶⁵

The camps were places of concentration in the most material and existential senses of the word. Under medical, intensive, concentrated camp care, people were dying like flies. Or, as van Blankenstein put it 1928, writing in the *Nieuwe Rotterdamsche Courant* about Boven Digoel, "like rats during a plague."⁶⁶

The medical records were intensive and concentrated, no less. The data containing the tests taken and deaths were burned by the Nazis in Theresienstadt during the last days of the camp and the smoke, it is remembered, covered the whole camp. For Boven Digoel, data still can be found in the archives in Jakarta, the causes of death, "pneumonia, beriberi, tuberculosis, mental illness, tumor, black-water malaria, asthma, skin disease . . . gorged by a crocodile, killed in the forest, drowned, suicide,"⁶⁷ "tetanus, cerebral syphilis, hemiplegia, spasms . . . valvulae mitralis cordis, pulminary tuberculosis."⁶⁸

Tuberculosis patients were called "Koch patients," or simply KP, in Boven Digoel.⁶⁹ Next, in the Indies, as in Europe, there were seasonal epidemics. In 1933, an epidemic of measles, starting from a few cases among the internee children in the camp, spread into the jungle and ravaged an unknown number of the Kaja-Kaja people.⁷⁰ Malaria was still the main cause of death in Boven Digoel. People remembered how they did not dare to get out from under their bed covers at night, "not a hand, not a finger."⁷¹ The Boven Digoel authorities provided the camp people with free mosquito nets, recalled Salim, in "orange, white, and blue," the Dutch national colors.⁷²

Gustav Klimt's images of bodies, unwholesome, unpink, and unclean, were banned from the university hall in Vienna. A possible rupture, but equally a possible pollution of body, of norm and of fashion, "a stain is a vice," became less permissible, as the world moved deeper into the twentieth century. An increasingly prone-to-be-polluted order required, among other things, increasingly progressive preventive hygiene-based care. The camps, again, became the models—of cleanliness.

Even before the foundation for the hospital in Boven Digoel had been laid, a "government hygienic report" was commissioned to check the suitability of the place. The camp was not finally decided upon until the report was done, until one Dr. Kalthofen, its author, found "nothing unfavorable about the spot."[73] Afterward, and throughout, as the first order of the day, the authorities did everything to keep the camp clean, or *net* and *rapi* [neat], as the Dutch and Malay terms were used interchangeably with "clean." "Wholesome" might be another word referring to the un-Klimt—no wounds visible, no guts hanging out, pink.

> MONDAY, SEPTEMBER 3, 1934 . . . AFTERNOON . . . 4:00 Abd. Hamid of the health department makes rounds through the camp; he brings an order to the internees to clean front yards and backyards.[74]
>
> WEDNESDAY, MAY 8, 1935. MORNING: . . . 8:00. The ROB brings an order to the internees to clean the ditches around their houses.[75]
>
> SATURDAY, MAY 11, 1935 . . . AFTERNOON: . . . 12:33 Agent Nawawi makes rounds through the camp and informs the internees about the newly issued order concerning neatness . . . *2:30* Agent Soeleman walks through the camp and brings additional instructions about neatness and order. . . . *3:20* . . . A report is written in the station on order of neatness. . . . There are nine internees in section C of the camp whose yards are still dirty.[76]

It did not take long, internees recall, and there stood a camp "neat and clean." The camp exuded cleanliness and neatness, the same thing.

> THURSDAY, MAY 9, 1935 . . . 7:00. Agent H. Sanoesi is sent to look for a Kaja-Kaja who understands Malay so that he can translate to his people. Tomorrow at six o'clock in the morning, Kaja-Kaja will be taken to the hospital and checked for cleanliness.[77]

"We gave clothes to Kaja-Kaja," wrote an anonymous Boven Digoel internee, "and we made them take a bath twice a day, once in the morning and once in the afternoon, so that their bodies at least look clean and they do not smell so much."[78]

In spite of whatever filth might still be found there, the camps were aiming toward what Ernst Bloch, reflecting all the sadness of the age, called "the spirit of utopia." "The bathroom and the toilet," Bloch wrote in his book on utopia, "became the most indisputable and original accomplishments of our time, just as Rococo furniture and Gothic cathedrals represent structures that define every other art object of their respective epochs. Now *lavatoriality* dominates the wizardry of modern sanitation."[79]

There might be lines at the latrines in Theresienstadt, and mud everywhere in Boven Digoel when it rained, but Bloch meant a *vision* of the bathroom and the toilet, the *wizardry*. In those, the camps became—as no human community ever before—the sites of the supermodern, most energetic social will and commitment. "Commitment," Theodor Adorno wrote in *The Jargon of Authenticity*, "is the current word for the unreasonable demand of discipline." And "commitments," he added, "are classed under mental hygiene."[80]

Mr. Trikoyo recalled for me a day of his childhood in Boven Digoel: "Father finished his midday prayer. He nodded to me and we left our house. We took a narrow path toward the house where Uncle Isa lived. There was a large metal barrel in the house garden and, first, my father went in. Then it was my turn, I got into the barrel and Uncle Isa brought a bar of LUX soap. I soaped myself, all over my body, with the Uncle Isa's LUX soap."[81]

In Theresienstadt, three words expressed the camp's order, style, and indeed its *esprit* completely: "*Gesundheit und Hygiene*" (in German of course), "health and hygiene."[82] Dr. Adolph Metz, a Theresienstadt ex-internee, explained in a letter to a Jewish agency in New York after the war, "A group of physicians had one specific duty, to check on the living quarters, each room, and to ascertain the *Sauberkeit*, airing, state of the toilets, and so on, and, when needed, to bring matters to order as quickly as possible."[83] "*Sauberkeit*" is another camp/German word for "cleanliness," or, more absolutely as it became the truth in the camps, for "health" and "healing."

Throughout the Theresienstadt camp's existence, and with an increasing urgency, it seems, posters appeared on the walls of the camp. Ruth Bondy recalled, "On January 1943, signs are being posted throughout the ghetto reading;

> After going.
> Before eating,
> Do not forget your hands' cleaning![84]

Or,

> Latrine—Cleanness—Order—Comradeship![85]

Or,

> Show me how you left the toilet and I will tell you who you are![86]

Leo Haas, a Jewish artist from Prague, was "commissioned" by the SS authorities to produce such posters. A little boy eats with dirty hands, the doors to the toilets can be seen behind him; "Sweetie," the big letters shout, "this you should not do!"

Other posters are described in *Šalom na pátek* [Shalom for Friday], a magazine the internees in one of the barracks wrote for themselves. Two of the posters read, "Be clean, clean, and again clean!" and "Washing yourself is being yourself!"[87]

Medicine, in the camps, ahead of time became a medicine of fear of what might come and of fear for the sake of the social order. Logically, in Theresienstadt, it was the duty of the camp police to watch over "order and cleanliness."[88] "Our camp police," a boys' magazine, *Vedem*, wrote, "supervise toilets and pumps."[89] Each room's, hall's, and barracks' "elder," an internee responsible for an order in his sector, "will be sentenced to eight days of prison if the place is found dirty."[90]

It was a stern order, and it penetrated and overwhelmed the camp. "In our dormitory," Jehuda Bacon recalled, "ruled order and cleanliness." Bacon was in his teens when he was in the camp. "Everything was tidied," he said. "The place was not just to be stuffed like that; nothing was to impair an impression of an orderly place."[91] Pavel Weiner, also a boy at the time, wrote on June 21, 1944, "During the roll call, I got into trouble because my shoes were dirty."[92] Another day, he wrote, "Franta [the youth leader; Franta is a pet form of František] even inspects our ears, and we are punished when he is not satisfied."[93]

In the summer of 1944, an amendment to the "General Order of the Jewish Self-Government" had been issued, with its paragraph thirteen stating, "The streets, courtyards, and alleys must be kept punctiliously clean. The camp inhabitants are under the order, whenever they happen upon a piece of paper or speck of dirt on the ground, to pick it up immediately, without waiting for a command, and to deposit it in a place designed."[94]

Internee Gonda Redlich wrote that the matters that could push the camp commander, SS-Hauptsturmführer Dr. Siegfried Seidl, into fits of the most explosive anger more than anything were "shreds of paper [on the ground] and spitting."[95] According to a postwar testimony of Theresienstadt ex-internee Max Berger, in November 1942, for instance, as punishment for people spitting on the streets and throwing paper on the ground, everyone in the whole camp was forbidden to leave the barracks for four weeks, and the electric light was switched off in the living quarters for almost the same period of time.[96]

The rules of hygiene in the camp were whipped up to a limit of and in fact beyond what was actually possible. The rules' and those under their control had a certain feverish alertness, alertness in the line that began as far back as in the nineteenth century, as norms and manners of the bourgeois society tightened, with a Baudelairian dandy as an epitome. A dandy was also aware that any little misstep, any wrong shade of color, one button more or less, rip or stain, would make him ridiculous—or, in the camps, truly and fatally "impossible."

Jiří Grünbaum wrote in the Theresienstadt *Vedem* magazine, "After I obtain a red or white ticket with the letter M or J, I take my soap and towel and go to Vrchlabí barracks. . . . The *Zentralbad* has two shower rooms and one pool where people are rarely allowed in. In each room a boy on duty turns on the water: this is done twice at seven-minute intervals. In between you have to soap yourself down. When the bath is over cold water is let in."[97]

For better or worse, the camp people of Theresienstadt, according to all signs, until the last weeks of the camp (except, perhaps, for the members of the Council of the Elders) did not really know what was really happening "in the east," in the death camps, in the lavatorial order beyond the extreme— "the same procedure of waiting, stripping, and giving up their belongings." The people in Theresienstadt did not know, for better or for worse, that "in the east," the camp people like them "were led into a bathhouse, but instead of steam and water, poison gas was infiltrated into the chamber."[98]

....

To spend some time of the year at spas or hot springs had been a longstanding tradition, a habit, and certainly a fashion, of the "good society," including the Jewish people, of course. It was a middle class joie de vivre, initially European, but since the late nineteenth century spreading beyond Europe to the distant corners of the world. *In de Bergen een koude neus halen* [to cool one's nose in the hills] became a custom and fashion in the Dutch Indies as well, a gesture of elegant "whiteness," but soon of being modern more generally. In the early twentieth century and on into the 1930s, whoever could afford it, and people were falling in debt to afford it, in Europe or in the Indies, once a year at least, one tried to "take waters," "recuperate," get clean and healthy, "pink," we may say. In proper spa attire— and fashion magazines were full of spa collections, for women, men, and children—people went "to meet people like us."

Because of their concentrated fashion and sense of hygiene, both Boven Digoel and Theresienstadt, at one moment or another, got a hot-spring and spa or hill-resort label, a travel-tag attached to them, as a joke perhaps, or a sneer, in the style of the moment.

Repeatedly, the internees being described as people carrying "superbly sharp pencils" and "loudly colored socks," Boven Digoel was also called a "sanatorium," or, to make it more local, a "primitive jungle sanatorium."[99] And Theresienstadt was not just once called *Reichsaltersheim* [Reich Retirement Home], or *Theresienbad* [Theresian Baths], or *Kurort Theresienstadt* [Theresienstadt Spa].[100] I found nothing about how the Boven Digoel internees took to the tag or the idea or the sneer. Some Jews, however, in particular the older ones arriving from Germany, at least according to Adler, the historian and ex-internee, when they had been called up for the transport to Theresienstadt, "made themselves to imagine friendly villas and hotel pensions." It was their way into the open, and they simply had to imagine something to go on living. "They have packed their clothes for the trip," Adler wrote about some of them, "like for a seasonal time out."[101]

....

Legal families—wives, husbands in the few cases of female internees, children from legal wedlock, and legal grandparents—legal according to the modern Western bourgeois code, were allowed to accompany the rebels to Boven Digoel. That is, if they so wished. The Dutch Indies government even helped to cover the costs of the legal trip—one way.[102] So they went, the families, on one ship after another.

In June 1927, several family members who were to accompany the internees to the camp on the ship *Melchior Treub* from the port of Medan, on the east coast of Sumatra, decided at the last moment that they did not wish to go.

1. Siti, the wife of Adoel Moenir with her two children;
2. Asan, a youngest child of Toepin;
3. Oemi, the wife of Said Ali, because, in her own statement, she is in fact not a lawful wife of Said Ali and, moreover, is under a standing order to appear before the Resident of Sumatra's West Coast; she expects to be sent to Boven Digoel as an internee on her own;
4. Wife of Aboesmah with her just born baby; she disappeared and her whereabouts could not be established by the time of departure.

> N. B. Seran, mother of Ngalimoen, will travel and stay in the camp at her own expense; she will be supported by her son. She would be left here without any family and this is why I have permitted her to go.
> *Signed: Governor of the East Coast of Sumatra*[103]

On this particular ship, thirty-three persons were being taken to Boven Digoel—fifteen internees, eight wives or other female relatives, and ten children, as the document had it, "age three, five, seven, seven, eight, eight, ten, twelve, fourteen, and fifteen."[104] "Every fashion," Benjamin wrote, "is to some extent a bitter satire on love; in every fashion, perversities are suggested by the most ruthless means."[105] In this sense, the camps' families, too, the camps' children, and the camps' love to that effect, were fashionable, like every fashion, and more.

Throughout the existence of Boven Digoel, only one man in the camp is on record as having more than one wife, something that was otherwise still quite common in the not-quite-yet-so-modern colonized indigenous society of the Indies at the time (and still is). The man with two wives in Boven Digoel, moreover, was a guard, not an internee, and his manner of marriage was ridiculed by the internee population of the camp as that of someone still living in the past.

New marriages among the internees happened in Boven Digoel, but they were not registered in the civilian camp main office. They were known as *perkawinan ala Digoel* [marriages à la Digoel].[106] They were officiated, sometimes by an Islamic *kijaji*, and sometimes by a respected comrade, in a truly progressive way. The people in both cases considered themselves legally married, or divorced for that matter. Both marriages and divorces mattered greatly, and both, according to Islam and colonial law, were real in the camp. The Boven Digoel police, for instance, might report:

> SATURDAY, JULY 6, 1940 . . . NIGHT . . . 9:10: Soemotaroeno is giving away his daughter to Kasban, and the wedding celebration is attended by ten internees.[107]

Mrs. Widayasih's parents were married in Boven Digoel, and this is how she "legally à la Boven Digoel" came into this world.[108]

Like everything else, marriages and divorces in Boven Digoel were modern and modern concentrated. To become and in particular to remain a legal family in Boven Digoel was radically more energy-requiring than to become and remain a legal family in the Indies outside of the camp. The legal marriage in the camp, like elsewhere, was a life and a statement, performance and manner of bearing oneself. But in the camp it all was always on the precipice of the proper, and most open to ridicule and pain in the case of the smallest misstep. It was a dandy serious thing. In the middle of the jungle, in a space closely watched by guards and fellow internees, it was risky, like donning hats or carrying umbrellas.

Throughout Boven Digoel's existence, there was a cruel disproportion, sensual to pornographic in its effect (*porné* means "prostitute"), between the number of men and women. In 1935, for instance, 475 men were listed, as compared to 65 women. "Given the ratio," a Boven Digoel official wrote in a report, "there is a great demand for women."[109] Marriage in Boven Digoel was not only precarious, it was fantasized about, and often just the fantasy of marriage remained. In many cases, wives declined to follow their husbands or for other reasons failed to accompany them to the camp. Ex-internee Salim recalls fellow "internees writing letters home, painting rosy pictures of Boven Digoel. The men wrote to women whom they happened to know before the camp, to lure them into coming."[110]

"Especially in the early years," writes Dr. Schoonheyt with a sneer again, "a number of single 'beauties' traveled to Boven Digoel." Some young women even did so, encouraged by the authorities, and almost all went at the government's expense. The "women of a harbor quality," the doctor wrote, were generously represented.[111] Internees, the prospective husbands, waited at the Boven Digoel landing for the ship's arrival. They were nervous, never having seen the woman before.[112]

In a novel about Boven Digoel, *Darah dan Aer-Mata* [Blood and Tears], published at the time of the camp and most probably written by a former internee, the main male character, Soegiri, is to be sent to Boven Digoel, and he succeeds in convincing his young wife to travel with him. They arrive and spend their first night in the camp. "She has just sat up in the bed. Soegiri can see in her face, that she has not slept at all through the night." The young woman looks at her husband and starts to cry, "again, and again." "The only thing she asks is to be returned to Java."[113]

There are letters in the Boven Digoel archives, not fiction, written by the internees' wives begging the camp authorities to be permitted to leave. The wife of internee Moerwoto "asks to be let go because of persistent malaria."[114] Others wish to go "because of illness and on the recommendation of the doctor," or "because of a desire to see her parents again," or "because her only child has died," or "because she cannot stand it anymore," or "because of [the] infectious disease of her husband."[115]

There were too many single men in the camp, flâneurs of the moment, moving around under the compulsion, or call it freedom, of the camps. The "legal marriages," most intimately felt and most desperately guarded in the camp, were most intensely challenged.

SATURDAY, JUNE 22, 1940 . . . NIGHT, 9:57 . . . The two children of internee Panjokoesoemo (they are still little) are heard crying in Panjokoesoemo's house. Panjokoesoemo tells the ROB that his wife *pigi djalan* (took off) with internee Padmosoedarmo.[116]

Soetan Sjahrir, like so many others, was a young man when he was sent to Boven Digoel. Even though he had recently married a woman living in Holland, he evidently felt like he was single and felt even more so, evidently, in the camp. Salim, who was Sjahrir's cousin, recalled years later, "We have called Sjahrir a *vrolijke zwerver* (cheerful rambler). He was in his twenties and not cold to a female beauty. The opposite!"[117]

In another novel about Boven Digoel from the same time, Noerani, a young woman who wore makeup, was beautiful and still unmarried. She arrived at the camp with her father. "The internees were crazy about her,"[118] and much of the novel is about the ways to keep her safe.

There was a court in Boven Digoel, set up by the Dutch authorities with internees' participation, to handle lighter misdemeanors in the camp. *Vrouwenperkara*s, the "women cases," came often before the court. In some of these cases, the court heard about fights breaking out.[119] Some cases are more disturbing than the others to read about. I met a man in Jakarta who was extremely proud of his father, a man of Boven Digoel. Then I read about his father in a camp document:

ON THURSDAY OCTOBER 15, 1936 AT 9:15 at night, internee Soewardi reported that internee [I deleted the name] entered the house of internee Slamet through the back door with an intention to assault Djoeminah, the wife of Slamet. At the time, Slamet was not at home; he was fishing on the river. The said woman Djoeminah cried out, called for help, and the attacker ran away.[120]

"There are so few women in the camp," Dr. Schoonheyt wrote, "that polyandry and homosexuality flourish. All the ladies," and one almost hears the doctor sneering again, "are spoiled and sometimes have to be restrained, lest they ran into each other's hair. *Goena-goena* (witchcraft) is used by male internees to win a female or, if he did, to keep her for himself. Some internees do not leave a house for fear that their wife becomes unfaithful in their absence."[121] This was the image as well as reality: love endangered, sex and promiscuity, pink and purple. "Free love" was a code term in the Indies white press when stories were written about the Communists, and Boven Digoel was the proof. But there were children born in the camp. "The people laugh about it," Dr. Schoonheyt wrote, "indeed, 'fecund Boven Digoel' they call it."[122] "The babies grow here like cabbage."[123]

Mrs. Widayasih was born in Boven Digoel. Mr. Trikoyo was brought to Boven Digoel as a baby, as he liked to say, "as a red baby."[124]

On July 19, 1929, internee Prawirowihardjo wrote to the camp administrator an anxious letter: "My wife is about to give birth. Please, allow me to come and to stay with <u>Mama</u> in the hospital so that I can help her to wash her laundry and the diapers." <u>"Mama"</u> is underlined in ink, evidently by the official. Permission in this case was not given.[125]

Children were brought in, often at a young age, and they were growing up in Boven Digoel. Babies reached puberty and others reached adulthood:

> MONDAY, JUNE 10, 1940 ... NIGHT: 8:10. ... In the house of Maskoen are guests, among them Loekman, Moerwoto with his wife, and Wiranta are recognized. They talk about the boy of Maskoen, who fell from a rose-apple tree.[126]

There is one particularly touching photograph from Boven Digoel, now archived in the National Library in Jakarta. On the picture, there is a family group of internee Aliarcham, former chairman of the Communist Party; his wife, Soekimah; and their two children. The picture must have been taken just before Soekimah and the children were permitted to leave the camp and go back to their relatives in Bandung, West Java. Aliarcham, of course, had to stay and died of tuberculosis in the camp several years later.[127]

The time of Boven Digoel was long enough for those who came to the camp in the prime of their lives, possibly to pass into old age. Natural death was present. In an archival file marked "Invalids in camp section D," for instance, in an undated document, there is under no. 3 an internee, unnamed, "already old, ±sixty years, cannot do any work"; under no. 5, a "very old man"; and, under no. 8, an internee, also unnamed, "old and blind."[128] Internee Raden Mas Samsoe, a former dance instructor at the Sultan Palace in Solo, Central Java, is remembered as living in the camp when "already about eighty years old."[129]

People were dying in the camp in accidents or due to illness or exhaustion. But they were made to live in the camp for so long that many died of "natural" causes:

> THURSDAY, OCTOBER 11, 1934 ... NIGHT: ... 11:25 ... There is a wake in the house of Sroenosari who just died of age. About eight people sit around.[130]

WEDNESDAY, JANUARY 2, 1939 ... MORNING: ... 9:30 ... in the house of Saring whose wife just passed away at childbirth there are guests....
Night: 8:15 ... in the house of Saring ... there are still people ... they *taäziah* [visit a home where someone died].[131]

In Theresienstadt, legal families as well as unmarried lovers were torn apart, as a rule and on principle. But here, too, as in Boven Digoel, the same sense and reality of the modern, namely of a bourgeois family, had been challenged and heightened—to the extreme and as never before.

In some cases one spouse managed to leave before "the cage closed," before the transports to the camps began in earnest. When it was too late to leave, some marriages decided to separate, in the case, that is, when either husband or wife happened to be classified as "Aryan." The non-Jew in the Nazi category was then permitted to stay out of the camp, while the divorced Jewish spouse had to go. There were some "Aryans" in Theresienstadt who were known, in spite of everything, to stay and possibly die with their spouse.

As in Boven Digoel, new marriages and also divorces in Theresienstadt were permitted. In 1944, for instance, ninety-seven weddings, eighty-eight engagements, and twenty (according to other sources, nine) separations were registered.[132] Like in Boven Digoel, marriages in Theresienstadt were radically more "to the point" than those in the outside of the camp. Mr. Uri Spitzer recalled: "Everybody married, for a very simple reason: you could sleep together."[133]

Unlike in Boven Digoel, in Theresienstadt, love happened, but birth could not—except as an exception to the rule, a loophole in the law, or an act of extreme courage or rashness. Policing and medical care were to fashion the camp also that way.

"A human being?" Mephistopheles asks Faust's famulus Wagner, looking at a desk in Wagner's laboratory. "And what amorous pair have you imprisoned in your flue?" "None, God forbid!" Wagner exclaims. "Old-fashioned procreation is something we reject as folly."[134] On the order of the SS administration in Theresienstadt, issued very early in the camp's existence, every pregnancy, if by accident it comes to it, was to be interrupted, whether the woman wished it or not. Dr. Springer, the camp medical officer and internee, wrote after the war, "How large was the number of abortions that were performed I cannot say. But there had to be hundreds of them, perhaps more than a thousand. Not rarely, they had to be done in the second half of pregnancy, in some cases by a caesarean section."[135]

This was definitely to be an un-Klimt image, and un-Klimt bodies were ultimately to be fashioned in the camp. In an un-Klimt way, the bodies of the camp people were to be "buttoned up." Nature cooperated, or, rather, obeyed. "Most of the women," Ruth Bondy later recalled, "stopped menstruating, at least for some time, or their cycle was irregular.... In my experience, they were relieved: there was no cotton, wool, or sanitary pads; improvised pads ... chafed and were not absorbent and it was hard to wash them and the blood-stained underpants."[136] In Theresienstadt, there was not the gaping unnatural gender disparity as in Boven Digoel. Throughout the Theresienstadt camp's existence, the numbers of males and females were roughly equal. Human bodies, sensual bodies, male and female in proportional ratio, were packed in and squeezed even much closer to each other than they were in Boven Digoel—in concentrated intimacy.

So, babies were born in Theresienstadt, in spite of everything. In spite of the awareness that, almost inevitably, the birth would be followed by transport "to the east," for the mother at least.

> JANUARY 22, 1944, Mrs. Fantlová gave birth to the first twins in the Ghetto, they got names Jana and Soňa.[137]

"Several children sat on chamber pots all the time," Mrs. Meyer-Kattenberg said after the war, remembering her room with mothers and children, "and so it went like on an assembly line. Often three or four children sat in a row and, the best of all, if possible, during the mealtime."[138]

Children were growing up in Theresienstadt, too, into puberty and adulthood, only they had much less time for it than in Boven Digoel. Pavel Weiner, just two months after his thirteenth birthday, in his Theresienstadt diary wrote on Monday, November 6, 1944, "Last night I went to steal some potatoes, but instead I found a little kitten. I took it home and played with it. I found out to whom it belonged and early this morning I intend to return it. But first I want to show it to my mother."[139] On Saturday, May 6, 1944, Pavel wrote, "I meet Gustl, who calls me to the washroom, where I see a naked woman! Is it indiscreet?"[140]

Dr. Baume, a Theresienstadt internee and psychologist by profession, did some research among the teenage girls living in the common dormitories of the camp. He analyzed a number of drawings he had asked the girls to make for him. "You can see signs of sadomasochism," he concluded. Dr. Baume also watched when the girls' supervisor decided that one of the girls deserved a punishment for some misbehavior. She consulted with the girls in the common room about what would be the proper disciplinary measure. Some girls suggested "slaps, pinching, striking the legs."[141]

Jehuda Bacon recalled his teenage moment in the camp: "Šmudla's [Dopey, the boys' supervisor] talked to us about sexual questions... about puberty. 'It is OK,' he said, 'to visit each other in bed. But better look for a girlfriend.'"[142] A horrified elderly Philipp Manes wrote, "A seventeen-year-old girl decided to get on transport [to the east] to follow her boyfriend. She did not even let her father know about it."[143] In another place in his diary Manes called this a "moratorium on morals!"[144]

In contrast to the mostly young Boven Digoel, the Theresienstadt camp was at some moments in particular "overflowing with old and overly old people."[145] (Younger people, naturally, were more often able to leave Europe before Hitler got to them.) For instance, on September 9, 1942, according to an official count of the Theresienstadt camp population, "Forty-five percent of inhabitants were over sixty-five years old."[146]

The elder people in Theresienstadt were called *Überaltert* [overage], and one spoke in the camp about *Überaltung* [overaging].[147] "If the elders were able to survive the first and most hazardous weeks," Adler wrote in his history, "they managed to live on in the camp, and in a reasonable state of calm. Especially, when some relative happened to be around." There were two persons known to have arrived at Theresienstadt at the age of one hundred. Both of them, "naturally," died in the camp. But there were many, Adler wrote, who arrived at the camp when they were over eighty, and still some of them saw the liberation. Many of the elderly, wrote Adler, luckily became senile and demented. "They did not understand what was happening to them.... They might call the deportation 'a journey,' or they might take margarine for Swiss butter or the *Einsatz* [the substitute] for Brazilian coffee."[148]

Amid of all the dying, death was medicalized in the camp, and unprecedentedly so. The women in Theresienstadt who made love, happened to get pregnant, and were ordered to get abortions understood it well, and so did the malaria-stricken, pill-fed people in Boven Digoel. Ahead of the times, like in a postmodern utopian hospital, the death in the camps became a simple moment on a ticking clock when one just disappears. "We lost him," or "we lost her," as doctors of our time might increasingly tend to say.

For Martin Heidegger, the great philosopher and ordinary Nazi, "Freeing is taking care of." "One dies lightly in Theresienstadt, no serious illness is needed," wrote Philipp Manes, who survived Theresienstadt but died in Auschwitz.[149] When an internee died in Boven Digoel, the body was brought by friends to a cemetery where the camp bordered the jungle, a wooden plank was planted at the head of the grave with the deceased's name, and the relatives, when their whereabouts could be found, were informed. When a Jew died in Theresienstadt, in the early months, the body was interred in an individual grave, as prescribed by Jewish custom, and it was wrapped in a burial shroud. Later, due to an increasing scarcity of lots, mass graves were opened. Because, as it was explained, of the increasing scarcity of textiles, the bodies were wrapped in paper.[150]

Close to the end of the camp, a "state-of-the-art" crematorium was built for the camp at the edge of the camp, and the ashes of the dead were placed in cardboard boxes, with a name on each one. Still later, the cardboard boxes were opened and the ashes were thrown into the river.

....

"As far as food is concerned," Marcus van Blankenstein reported in the *Nieuwe Rotterdamsche Courant* in September 1928 in his series on Boven Digoel, "in theory, unhulled rice and *mung* beans are on the menu, but in fact, there is only unhulled rice."[151] In fact, even the unhulled rice, which was considered second rate, was not always available.[152] There was always cassava flour, a stuff definitely inferior to any internee coming from a rice-producing region of the Indies, and virtually all of them were.

There was no sheer hunger in the camp; Boven Digoel was neither Auschwitz nor Cayenne. There is not a single report of sheer hunger in all the Boven Digoel documents or testimonies. There was just scarcity, and thus, as in the matters of clothes, jewels, or freedom, a heightened and jarred awareness of food, its nutritional value, its style, taste, and smell.

Meat was being brought to Boven Digoel from outside of New Guinea, mostly as live animals that were slaughtered in the camp. In 1928, for instance, the second year of the camp, 100 cows and 160 goats were brought to and killed in the camp.[153] Most of the fresh meat, of course, was destined for and consumed by the civilian and military officials in the camp. "We get fresh meat once or twice a month at best," an internee wrote in a letter published by an Indonesian paper in July 1929; "if one would not eat kangaroo or cuscus," the internee added.[154]

Or, as we know from other sources, if one had not a stomach for fresh crocodile meat. But in that case, one had to be careful. "Young Mangun," Mr. Trikoyo recalled, "was washing his dishes in the river after a lunch of crocodile, then he took a bath in the river. A crocodile smelled the meat, it attacked Mangun, swam with him in its jaws across the river. There, at the opposite side, as we watched, it ate him."[155]

"The people of the forest, Kaja-Kaja, as they began to visit the camp, brought cassowary eggs, and sometimes a forest pig, in exchange for a piece of cloth or clothing, for [an] iron ax, or for tobacco."[156] In time, the internees managed to raise their own chickens, and some were very good at it. Still, throughout the camp's existence, the staple foods were canned, conserved, and ready-made sardines, corned beef, and salted fish, provided by the authorities or to be bought in an increasing number of camp stores.[157] "Internee Paiso of the camp section C," we read in a Boven Digoel camp registry, "bakes bread and sells it to others."[158]

The camp diet of scarcity made people smell and taste as hardly ever before. "I will never forget," Mrs. Widayasih told me, fifty years later, "*empal*, with white rice, fried tofu, and fried banana, what a smell, and what a taste!"[159] Sago is the edible starch of palm trees. It is known throughout the Indies, and for the Kaja-Kaja people of the forest around Boven Digoel, it is still the staple. In the camp, also, out of necessity, sago was widely eaten, "mixed with edible tuber, taro, and some greens it was cooked in bamboo gear."[160] "Awful," Mr. Trikoyo told me, still making a face, after fifty years. "But, wow, when I was in the camp hospital in bed with malaria," he added, "we could get fried corned beef and legumes!"[161] Internee Kartoatmodjo wrote to his son Soedihiat in Batavia asking for "some spices for the kitchen, you know, clove and nutmeg."[162]

"I disliked *papeda* most of all," Mr. Trikoyo said, recalling porridge made of sago. "I just hoped, at least on holidays, we would not have *papeda*. 'Today,' I thought to myself, 'my mother will make *nagasari*, a rice-flour cake stuffed with bits of banana and steamed in a banana leaf, or perhaps *lemper*, steamed glutinous rice mixed with chunks of chicken meat, or *lemet*, a cake of grated coconut steamed in a banana leaf or corn husk, or even *kakap*, fried fish, that was something really special! That state of wishing on holiday mornings would stay with me for the rest of my life.'"[163] "Doctor was so good," Mr. Trikoyo, said, speaking of his time in the hospital. "When he came to visit us, he always carried a few chili peppers in the pocket of his white coat. As he was leaving he left the peppers with us and sometimes on my bed."[164]

The Boven Digoel camp police made their rounds through the camp, watching, and sniffing:

WEDNESDAY, MAY 29, 1935 . . . MORNING: . . . 9:00 . . . In the house of Internee H. Ishak there is a gathering of several people, the same as usual . . . and they eat.[165]

SUNDAY, NOVEMBER 8, 1936 . . . NIGHT: . . . 9:45 . . . In section C of the camp, in the house of Soekaria, there is a group of five internees. But only boiled cassava is on the table.[166]

SUNDAY, NOVEMBER 7, 1937 MORNING: 9:50 . . . In the house of internee Soemataroena are Wirjosoehardjo and Kartoredjo. They cook a little meal, it is not clear what.[167]

Rarely, if ever before in modern times, was the sense and awareness of nutrition—similarly to the sense and awareness of clothing and fashion—as acute as in the camps. "Vitamins" were valued as never before—mostly, again, because of their absence. "It happened here in this country," Salim recalled, as he and the others in the camp had known very well, "that Professor Christiaan Eijkman earned the Nobel Prize for a discovery that beriberi is caused by deficiency in vitamin B1."[168] "We in Boven Digoel," Salim wrote, "in the beginning used the *mung* beans for prevention of beriberi . . . but later the beans were replaced by B1 tablets." "For cooking and drinking," Salim continued, "we had to use the rainwater, but we knew it was bad for our teeth because it lacked calcium."[169]

Rarely ever before—and rarely ever after until the era of the "organic" "farmers' markets" of our time—so flaming and jarring a significance in the minds of the people have been accorded to greens. The spots where vegetables could be grown in Boven Digoel were extremely few and were located at the edge of the camp. These were precious, *exclusive* plots of land, tiny gardens most of the time, and they were also most intensively cared for by the internees, as well as by the police. They were built in the only area where there was some hope of harvest, which was directly on the banks along the Digoel River. Thus these plots were also the most vulnerable. During the tropical rains, which were regular in Boven Digoel, the river rose and flooded the gardens and often washed them away. The camp police, as much as the internees, watched the plots and watched out for the disaster.

THURSDAY, JUNE 13, 1935. MORNING: . . . 12:10 . . . The camp is calm. . . . *Afternoon:* . . . *3:00.* The vegetable garden at the hospital and the gardens near the river are safe.[170]

Sometimes, a group of Kaja-Kaja people from the jungle came to the camp, Salim wrote, taking a description of this particular episode almost verbatim from Dr. Schoonheyt: "We might give them a large lump of salt, for instance, and they chomped it, and smacked loudly, and spit dripped from their mouths."[171]

This was a catwalk camp, and the table manners of the camp were anxiously kept. Mrs. Zakaria, a child at Boven Digoel, told me how her father, an internee, sent her and her older sister and brother, Chamsinah and Juffri, once a week to the house of *wedana* Singer, the chief of the section of the camp where the family lived. "I was still little," Mrs. Zakaria told me, "and I did not understand much of it. But Chamsinah and Juffri were learning things, how to set a table or how to eat when there were other people around. Our father was progressive, and he wanted us to have manners. Like fork and spoon, you know, and chairs, how to sit, and how to say this or that, well, decorously."[172]

"After a convivial evening," Walter Benjamin wrote in his *Travel Souvenirs*, "someone remaining behind can see at a glance what it was like from the disposition of plates and cups, glasses and food."[173] There is a shopping list saved in the Boven Digoel archive, from the camp government commissary. "Internee Kartaatmadja bought a teapot for *f*1.25, and two liqueur glasses for *f*1; internee H. Sanoesi bought a kitchen knife for *f*1.25 and two zinc plates for *f*0.70."[174] Internee Soewita a.k.a. Soeparma died in Boven Digoel on September 29, 1933, and he left behind "two zinc glasses, one glass (cracked), one spoon, one small pan, one zinc plate, and one small teapot."[175]

SATURDAY, MARCH 30, 1940 ... AFTERNOON ... 4:50 ... Internee Soeroto reports that the Kaja-Kaja who was helping him in his house, ran away and carried with him a small knife and one large teapot, altogether worth *f*3.40.[176]

....

In Europe, on October 30, 1941, in the Nazi Protectorate of Bohemia and Moravia, it was decreed that fish, wine, and garlic must not to be sold to Jews.[177] This meant the Jewish people still living out of the camps. As of June 26, 1942, in Germany, Jewish children were not to receive whole milk but only skimmed milk.[178] After December 1942, the Jews in most of Nazi-occupied Europe were forbidden to purchase "all meats, eggs, white bread, and rolls ... all fruits and vegetables (fresh, dried, or canned), nuts, wines, fruit juices, syrups, marmalades, jams, cheese, candies, fish, and poultry in any state of preparation."[179] Jiří Weil, a Jewish writer waiting for transport in Prague, noted, "I can only buy blood."[180]

After the people were forced into Theresienstadt, the scarcity and awareness of food became new and different. Nutrition, taste, and smell became less crudely a matter of "yes" or "no." The Theresienstadt camp was not Auschwitz, but it was not the Nazi Europe of the camps either. "The supply of food," Professor Utitz testified after the war, "however unsatisfactory, never came to a halt."[181] "There is always some warm food to be got at the central kitchen," wrote Mr. Italie in his camp diary.[182] "The very fact that no one in Theresienstadt remained without food for so much as a single day," wrote Ruth Bondy, "went a long way toward determining the ghetto's character."[183]

The concentration on food supply in Theresienstadt was as intensive as the concentration on clothes or medical care. Documentation of the food in the camp is exhaustively detailed, and so are the food memories—the most uncompromising *spectral analysis* one might say. Adler's history quotes quite a number of "Charts of Food Rations." For instance,

> FEBRUARY 1942: *Daily:* bread 372 g; meat or sausage 31 g; vegetables 8 g; cod with kohlrabi 36 g, sauerkraut 35 g, legume 4 g, substitute coffee or chicory 12 g, potatoes 444 g, substitute butter or fat 18 g, honey 64 g, preserve 16 g, skimmed milk 119 ml, saccharine or sugar 21 g.[184]

"The quality and the preparation of food," wrote Mr. Italie, "is outstanding, but one gets too little."[185] "The food," Mrs. Caransa wrote after the war, "was good and often excellent."[186] There was not hunger of the kind that drives one mad, Ruth Bondy wrote, but "hunger that gnaws like a small mouse."[187]

As in Boven Digoel, in Theresienstadt greens and freshness were a focus of the most anxious concern, articulated again as a lack of vitamins, and minutely measured. "The keeping of [a] minimal level of vitamins was under the control of the camp police."[188] Among the top "typical illnesses" listed, feared, fought against, and talked about all the time was *"avitaminosis."*[189] When the delegation of the International Red Cross had been expected to the camp, Mrs. Meyer-Kattenburg recalled, "The food that day just blew us away. . . . What precisely we got I cannot remember anymore, but one thing I recall distinctly: children had cauliflower for lunch, and it was the first time, it was in 1944 [more than two years into the camp's existence], that they had something so fresh."[190]

Packages from the outside of Theresienstadt, even from the neutral countries abroad, most often Switzerland, were allowed into the camp—with restrictions, of course. As the internees recall, no delicatessen shop window in Berlin, Prague, Amsterdam, or Vienna before the war might have appeared so worth living for. "Packages," Mrs. Meyer-Kattenburg remembered, "they arrived from the Protectorate, from Vienna, but also from Lisbon and Zurich. . . . Honey was perhaps the most valuable article, but there was also powdered milk, oat rolls, pudding in powder, fat, bacon, and sugar."[191] "I got your last package," an internee of Theresienstadt wrote back to a relative still outside the camp, "Sugar..., butter, biscuits, and tomatoes, all was there."[192]

A package to Theresienstadt is a theme of a little book that Otto Weiss wrote in the camp for his wife's birthday. "The almighty God," in the story, took pity on the Jews and sent a package to Theresienstadt. The package was lost, stolen, as often happened, but God did not want to understand. Under an assumed name, as a Jew, he let himself into the camp to search for the lost package: "The loss of the parcel would be a shame, it contained poppy-seed buns, vanilla cakes made with butter, chocolate biscuits, apples, lemons, oranges, onions and garlic, and whole goose liver in fat."[193]

There was a concentrated scarcity and thus a concentrated, spectral, richness of food in the camp. On April 1, 1945, Mr. Italie, one of the practicing Jews in Theresienstadt, wrote, "A kitchen has been designed to serve meals for the Passover. The menu is wonderful, but the kitchen personnel does not appear to be one that would really guarantee strict kosher." On the same day, Mr. Italie wrote again, and with a sense of victory, "I saved some potatoes for the Yom Tov!"[194] Professor Eugen Lieben, another practicing Jew, was respected by many in the camp as a hero. However bad the state of his health (he suffered from tuberculosis, among other things), "he never violated the Jewish dietary laws: no un-kosher food," and to be sure, "no cans."[195]

Not many Jews were willing or able to follow Professor Lieben's example. The majority, in fact, were "modern Jews," "assimilated" long before the camp, from families assimilated for generations. They could not and in most cases did not care much for religious prescriptions; as with clothes, so with food. The camp, through its brutal means, often and radically heightened this modernity in the matter of food. Now, in the camps, the camp people ultimately found, and were forced to find, many forbidden things of life delicious.

There was often horsemeat on the table, and when there was other meat, it was almost exclusively pork and clearly from the slaughter of sick or injured animals. From time to time, there was canned liver paste, and blood sausages from the shop of Karl Schuster, a Czech butcher in the nearby village of Vojkovice.[196]

At the edge of hunger, the Jews of Theresienstadt, as with their clothes, were made sharply aware of food as food, *an sich*, sublime, heightening sight, smell, and taste, suggesting intimacy where there was none. The camp food was as Kantian sublime as anything else in the camp. "Surprisingly," Ruth Bondy wrote after the war, and she could also write "beyond all understanding," "Theresienstadt cooked for twelve special diets, such as for hepatitis, kidney disease, diabetes, and other illnesses."[197]

The staple of the Theresienstadt menu (this was not rice-eating Asia) was potatoes, and, as it was a camp, potatoes *an sich*—potatoes sublime. As in Europe before the camps, but radically more and radically different, there were potatoes as condiments and as a main dish, potatoes in an endless variety—baked potatoes and mashed potatoes, but also "potato cakes, potato dumplings, potato pancakes," "potato goulash," potato salad.[198] Potatoes were the rainbow of the camp smell.

Even more Kantian, there were *buchty*, sugar buns, from potatoes but also from other kinds of flour, traditional in Czech and Czech Jewish households; they became a phenomenon in the camp. The non-Czech-speaking camp people tried their best to translate the word "*buchty*" into their languages and struggled with the word's seven declensions, but then took the Czech name as belonging to them, too. "*Buchty*," wrote Dutch-speaking and Dutch-writing Mr. Italie, are "wonderful *broodjes*, so nicely white."[199] "Once a week," wrote Mr. Bernhard Kold, an internee from Germany, "there were *Buchten*, sometimes with cream!"[200]

Rainer Maria Rilke might have been thinking about the Theresienstadt *buchty*, or *Buchten*, or "wonderful *broodjes*" when he wrote: "Once one entered into the full smell of it, most things were already decided."[201] Women in Theresienstadt would frequently "cook" more sophisticated and choosy dishes than they might ever have done before the camp. "One woman would tell another how she would prepare mushroom sauce with cream and argue about whether it was better to dilute dumpling dough with milk or soda water or with an equal mixture of the two."[202]

The camp people were thrown into a very special and very deep gourmand's den, and table manners, as in Boven Digoel, were expected—or fantasized about—to be exquisite. As Adler wrote, "All the time, there was the greatest shortage of spoons and there were very few plates."[203] Some Jews, Adler adds, especially the elderly, as they arrived to the camp, "sometimes had a couple of cigars or even a bottle of good wine in their trunks," but many "had no spoon."[204]

One could get coffee and tea in Boven Digoel easily; the Indies were the very land of both. There was even quite good Indies and even Dutch beer available in the camp—if one was not too strict a Muslim, that is; but many Boven Digoel internees, being Communists and modern, were not too strict in the matter of beer drinking. Cigarettes were also easily available in Boven Digoel, either the *klobot* type, cornhusk-rolled cigarettes; *kreteks*, with chipped cloves; or the imported Indies, Dutch, and even American brands.

SATURDAY NOVEMBER 17, 1934 ... NIGHT 9:50 ... They smoke "Diëng."[205]

Quite a number of internees in Boven Digoel smoked opium. "Opium eating" was not an offense anywhere in the Indies. Internee Pontjopangrawit was remembered by Mr. Trikoyo as smoking opium. "Uncle Pontjo," Trikoyo recalled, "when he smoked opium, was greatly energized, became quick-witted, and gave fiery speeches."[206]

In Theresienstadt all things alcohol were strictly "contraband." A "good bottle of wine" or "couple of cigars," if one had been foolish or daring enough to carry them to the camp, were almost sure to be confiscated as soon as one arrived.[207] Dedicated attempts were made to produce alcohol in the camp. "To chicory, a little sugar was added and some yeast, and all was closed in a bottle. After several days the liquid became slightly alcoholic, resembling 'beer.'"[208]

Adolf Hitler made his personal and very pink distaste for tobacco well known. Smoking, like alcohol, was "strictly prohibited" in Theresienstadt.[209] The "contraband to be confiscated" included "all tobacco products."[210] When the delegation of the International Red Cross visited Theresienstadt on its inspection, Mr. Eppstein, the head of the Jewish Council of the Elders at the time, welcoming the delegation to the camp, in "elegant tails and a half-top hat, like a true mayor," reprimanded the delegates gently: "Do not smoke gentlemen, please."[211]

Given the smoking prohibition in the camp, Dr. Adolf Metz recalled after the war, "One could easily imagine the price that a Czech gendarme demanded for the tobacco products he was able to smuggle into the camp."[212] The Vlasta, or "Homeland Girl," cigarettes of inferior quality, which outside the camp cost one Czech crown apiece—not cheap—in the camp sold on the black market for "4.80 crowns in the early months and 150 crowns eventually."[213]

"If I only had my pipe here!" Mr. Italie lamented on April 12, 1945, "then I could smoke the tea substitute as the lucky ones here do."[214] "Gold, hard currencies, watches, jewels, and tobacco," Adler wrote, "this all had its price. Occasionally, young women helped themselves to these things by prostitution."[215]

FOUR

Sport

Sport made fashion and was the fashion of the modern and high-modern world, first in the West, but with the Western-colonized world quickly following. In sport clothes, sport manners, sport bodies, and in the sport-fashion truth, modern and high-modern people became themselves.

"It was a sort of sport goods shop, though they sell other merchandise as well," Imre Kertész wrote in the early part of his Holocaust novel-memoir describing the Jewish hero shopping with his son "for the camp." "'Fetch one out of the stockroom for the gentleman, Lovey!' the shop owner commands his wife.... The knapsack met with an immediate approval, but the shopkeeper sent his wife off again for a few other articles that, in his opinion, my father 'can't do without' where he is going." The articles as listed are "a mess tin that could be sealed airtight, a penknife with all sorts of tools that folded into the handle, a belt pouch, and so forth."[1]

Mrs. Demetz, in Prague a woman of fashion but torn out of her middle-class life and on her way to Theresienstadt, wore the sport boots and stockings that she had worn on her hikes in Semmering before the war. Mr. Ginz, also of Prague, not a Jew himself but having a "half-Jewish" son, gave him, as he was leaving for Theresienstadt, "ski boots." As the hero in Josef Taussig's short story, already in Theresienstadt, walked through the camp, he met, we recall, "a little old man in a blue ski cap." "Sport spirit," through the pain of shopping, of packing and departing, through the radically acute sense of clothes, what would be the best for the camp, penetrated the bodies and made the bodies into the bodies for the camp. It made the camp a camp.

Mr. Strassburger, a German Jew, described after the war the young people in the camp: "Especially the ones from Bohemia were fine. It made me melancholic to see them later go on transport to the east. The men were big and strong, women were just *charmant*. In the middle of all the fury and unleashed tempers they stood up brave and unrelenting. They were muscular and attractive.... They had fine bodies and sport spirit."[2]

Georges Perec, whose mother died in Auschwitz, evoked the same thing, just in the extreme of its truth. In his fantasy novel *W, or The Memory of Childhood*, he described a nightmarish camp on a "tiny island off Tierra del Fuego." The camp is "a community concerned exclusively with sport."[3] "Faster, higher, stronger is the proud Olympic motto" of the camp. Sport rules, and all happens in the camp according to the rules of sport. All happens in the camp as in top-performance sport, pushed to the limit. The sport games are the culmination of Perec's camp life. They are called Atlantiada and are held once a month: "The women thought to be fertile are taken to the Central Stadium, their clothing is removed, and they are released onto the track, where they start to run as fast as they can. They are allowed a head start of half a lap before the best athletes."

"The best athletes" then pursue. "One lap is usually all that the runners need to catch up with the women, and as a rule it is right in front of the podium, either on the cinder track or on the grass, that they are raped."[4]

This is how the Perec's camp is made to procreate (how the procreation is controlled), and how some survive. "Very few attempt suicide," Perec says about his fictional camp's internees. "Only sometimes howling is heard on the island, in the outside of the camp, from over the wall."[5]

Sport came into being in the West, spread to the East, and lasted as a dandyish and cruel thing in which every move and the tiniest difference, as in fashion, matter. It became an ideal expression of modern ambition, and thus of pleasure, and thus a healthy thing. Etty Hillesum, expecting to be called to a camp any moment, still in Amsterdam, wrote in her diary in October 1942, "Oh, Lord, give me fewer thoughts first thing in the morning and a little more cold water and exercise."[6]

Sport's significance in Theresienstadt was disproportionate to its significance in the world before the camp and outside the camp. Sport took disproportionately more of the camp people's time, and disproportionately shaped the camp people's bodies and minds.

Soccer was sport number one in Theresienstadt, just as it was the sport number one in Europe of the time. Like doctors (my father might say), the best soccer players ever were the Jews. Many of the best came to Theresienstadt, and their stature and significance became radically greater, suddenly more than it could ever have been if not for the camp.

Pavel Mahrer, born in 1900, played for the Czechoslovak national team before the war and also took part in the Olympic Games of 1924. After the German occupation of the country, initially he was permitted to go on playing in the top Czech soccer league "because of his Aryan looks." After he refused, however, to wear the yellow star, he was transported to Theresienstadt, and there he played for the Butchers. The boys and men of the camp, and girls and women as well, collected autographs from him and other soccer celebrities whenever they met the players in the camp, before or after the matches. "The soccer matches," Max Berger, an ex-internee, recalled, "were visited by scores of fans and also police and even the members of ss in civilian clothes."[7]

There is a now-famous Nazi propaganda film made in and about Theresienstadt, a must-show at all the Holocaust museums, known much better possibly than the camp itself. One long sequence in the film is that of a soccer match, in which the players fight for the ball and there are excited fans in the picture[8]—a fake, like everything in the camps, and increasingly in the world around the camps as well.

But the Theresienstadt boys' magazine *Vedem* reported on soccer often, weeks and months before and after any film was made and irrespective of the film. "The yard of the Dresden barracks is crowded, packed so tight from the attics to the ground that you couldn't stick a pin into it. Fourteen players are running around the field."[9]

Space was limited in the camp; even sports were packed in and squeezed, and the soccer field had to be smaller. Instead of eleven, there were only seven players on each side. The space was limited but the scene was bustling. Špedice (the Movers) played against Kuchaři (the Cooks), Hagibor (the Heroes) against Praha (Prague), S. K. Terezín (Soccer Club Theresienstadt) against Elektrikáři (the Electricians). "The match between the Clothes Distribution Center and the Cooks," a writer for *Vedem* "reported live," "is under way."[10]

There was not only one but several soccer leagues in the camp. They played two series of competitions, in spring and fall, the first season shortly after the camp opened, and the last in the fall of 1944.[11] There was an adult league's divisions A and B, and a youth league. "In the first nine months of the league's existence," Ruth Bondy wrote about the men's league, "144 games were played on the main soccer field in the Dresden barracks."[12] The Dresden barracks was the place where the big matches took place. The Nazi film soccer sequence had been shot there, too.

"Kapr [Carp, a boy's name] and I played a rag ball," wrote Pavel Weiner on Saturday, August 26, 1944.[13] In the scrapbook of a Theresienstadt boy, Erik Baumel, now in the archives of the Jewish Museum in Prague, there is a drawing of just a leg kicking a ball, with a line underneath in a child's hand: "Remember Theresienstadt!"[14]

Besides soccer, they regularly played basketball in Theresienstadt, a sport more elitist in Europe of the time than the mass-played soccer.[15] There was also handball in the camp, not the Ben Shahn kind played in America, but a popular game in Europe of seven players on each side and two goals.[16] "Saturday, May 15, 1944," Adler quoted from one of the programs of the day issued by the Council of the Elders, "at 15:30, a handball match will take place between Holland [meaning Jews from Holland] and the Protectorate [Czech and Moravian Jews]."[17]

There was volleyball and table tennis, a sport particularly suitable for the camp because it required so little space.[18]

There was gymnastics, in actuality as well as in intensive memory. Internee Felix Gustav Flatow was born in 1875 in Berent, West Prussia, and he died in Theresienstadt. In 1896, Flatow was a member of the German national team at the first modern Olympic Games in Athens, and in 1900 he competed in the second games as well. He won gold medals on both occasions.[19] There was group gymnastics, a rage in Europe before and after World War I. Philipp Manes, as only old men can, described a Theresienstadt women's gymnastics team, one of several performing as a group: "They move as one, step forward and step back, they are like a wave, like a sea rising and descending; they form squares and they form circles."[20] There is a flag on display at the Theresienstadt sport exhibition in Beit Theresienstadt, Israel, with letters embroidered: "Hamburg Barracks: women's gymnastics led by Stella Hermann."

Boven Digoel was vastly more a sport place than any village, town, or even city in the colony. Sport was much newer in the Indies than in the West, and more exclusive, definitely dandy. Sporting everywhere in the colony had a distinct catwalk feeling—and imagine sporting in the camp, in the middle of the jungle!

Soccer was number one in Boven Digoel as it was in Theresienstadt. Like a Borsalino hat worn by an Indonesian, soccer was a "novelty" in the Indies. In Boven Digoel, however, soccer was played "practically every day."[21]

> FRIDAY, JUNE 12, 1935 . . . AFTERNOON: 3:00 Agent Soedirman returns to the station and reports that a match between SH and IKOK on the SH soccer field just ended and people are dispersing. The final score was 2:2.[22]

IKOK, I do not understand. And what SH means, even many former internees are not quite sure anymore (or rather, each is sure in his or her way). Some say that SH meant "Seek for Health" or "Sport for Health" (in English);[23] others say Soetji Hati, Malay and Indonesian for "Pure Heart." All agree, however, that SH, whatever it meant, was the strongest soccer team among the many Boven Digoel ever had.[24]

Soccer, as the internees believed at the time, and as many recalled decades later, was the Boven Digoel life, its blood, and certainly its fashion.

> MONDAY, JULY 15, 1935 . . . AFTERNOON . . . 3:50 . . . Scores of people walk to the soccer field of SH to watch a match between IKOK and Zending Juli 1927 [the team of internees who arrived on one ship in July 1927]. . . . There are already about one hundred spectators on the field. The atmosphere is calm.[25]

> SUNDAY, AUGUST 30, 1936 . . . AFTERNOON: 3:20. Soldiers pass the station on the way to watch a match on the soccer field in section C. The match will be between the military and the combination team of internees and civilian officials. The soldiers carry drinks, . . . *4:40*. Agent Maliki leaves the station, to watch. . . . *5:00* Other large group of soldiers, off duty, walks by the station. They go also to watch the match.[26]

One match in particular is recalled by Salim: "I can still see," he wrote, "as if it were now before my eyes, Comrade Hatta locked in a fierce duel for the ball with Father Meuwese [of the Catholic Missionaries of Sacred Heart]. Father Meuwese, his long beard flying in the air, again and again attacks 'the brown monster.'"[27]

Besides "the best," SH and IKOK, there was Kunst en Sport Boven Digoel Vereeniging or KSDV, Dutch for "Arts and Sport Boven Digoel Union," with its own soccer teams, Digoel Voetbal Club or DVC, Dutch for the "Digoel Soccer Club." Some teams had their own youth teams, but also their own B teams and boys' teams. In a letter to the camp authorities dated February 13, 1932, the chairman and the secretary of the DVC asked for permission "to begin a CURSUS for the members." "In the CURSUS," they wrote, "we plan to use several books (on sport). The meetings would take place each Tuesday evening around 7:30, in the house of internee A. Sjaäib."[28] The permission was given.

Pencak, written *pentjak* at the time, and *silat* were the arts of self-defense practiced and revered since ancient times in Java and Sumatra, respectively. They existed in Boven Digoel, too—yet in an uncompromisingly modern mode, as "dances," in the modern-romantic "tradition," or, and this especially, as sports. Those practicing pencak and silat were "trained" by "coaches," and "competitions" were held with fans supporting their men and teams. Like soccer, they were a dandy thing to do. In the camp documents, they were registered as "sport such as soccer."[29] There was one "pentjak team" as a part of the SH club.[30] Two internees, Dt. Saidi Soepoeti and Zakaria, were mentioned as *orang jang treinen* [trainers].[31]

The ROB reported on August 15, 1932, "pentjak training in the houses of Datuk Saidi Soepoeti and Zakaria." Twenty internees, listed by names, signed up for this training course. The word "training" in this, as in many other documents on the camp sport, is in English, that is to say, "Sportish."[32]

There had been boat parades on the Digoel River by the Papua people since before the camp existed. Now, however, as soon as the internees were permitted to put boats on the river, competitions of boating teams were organized.

SATURDAY, JANUARY 9, 1937 . . . AFTERNOON 4:02 . . . Internees sit on the bank of the river and watch the boat races.[33]

There was badminton, as popular in colonial Southeast Asia then as it is in contemporary Southeast Asia today:

SUNDAY, JUNE 14, 1936 . . . MORNING . . . 7:22 . . . In front of Soejitno's house there is a tournament of badminton.[34]

There was even tennis at Boven Digoel, the dandiest and indeed whitest of all the modern sports, while there was no sign of tennis in Theresienstadt. There is a photograph in the archives in Leiden in a file of the daughter of the first camp head, Mrs. Ottow. A small group, all Dutch, all white, Mrs. Ottow among them, poses for a picture behind a tennis net. These were, of course, the Boven Digoel highest-ups.

This was probably the same tennis court Salim described: "In front of the main warehouse," he wrote, "there was a fine tennis court, busy all the time with the civilian officials and military playing ball."³⁵ Internees, however, were playing tennis, too. And police watched.

> TUESDAY, AUGUST 31, 1937, MORNING, 7:00: There are friendly matches to be played today, in badminton and in tennis.³⁶

Bangun Topo, one of the children of the camp, the son of an internee, one of the people I was lucky still to meet, told me, "At a place close to the river there was a tennis court for our parents."³⁷

Mrs. Chamsinah gave me unpublished memoirs of her late husband, the internee Jahja Nasoetion, whom she married in the camp. At one place in the memoirs, an afternoon of one of Jahja's usual days is described: "I came back from the market," he wrote, "rested a little, and then played few games of tennis with my wife and friends, all members of Boven Digoel tennis club."³⁸ "Soetan Sjahrir," Salim recalls, "oh, he did not miss one soccer match . . . and one tennis tournament."³⁹ "Yes, we sure had a tennis court," Mrs. Widayasih, told me, "and wives of internees played, too. Some wore a sarong and a blouse, but many played in a white skirt. We children watched from behind the fence and, sometimes, we could catch a ball that flew over, and kept it."⁴⁰

There was athletics in Boven Digoel. Internee Soewirjo from Pekalongan "organized an athletic club."⁴¹

> SUNDAY, FEBRUARY 21, 1937 . . . AFTERNOON . . . 6:55. In the field of C.V.O. there are heats in track and field.⁴²

There was gymnastics in Boven Digoel, too.

> WEDNESDAY, MAY 27, 1936, on the soccer field of SH, internee Soeroso trains gymnastics with thirty-two children.⁴³

In *Minggat dari Digul*, "Escape from Digoel," the novel written almost certainly by an ex-internee, a young man in the camp is described as a model figure, body and soul of the camp: "He was a guy, well-built and strong, like Jack Dempsey." The novel described the same man once more: "He was like Tom Heeney."⁴⁴ Jack Dempsey and Tom Heeney were boxing champions, in the West and beyond, at the time.

In Rem Koolhaas's *Delirious New York* there is a snapshot of the ultimate modern and the ultimate dandyish in one image. In the most exclusive Manhattan sport club of the 1990s, two men, "naked, have boxing gloves on and eat oysters on ice that a waiter brought to the gym."⁴⁵ There might be something like a companion photograph to the New York scene. Dr. Schoonheyt, in his memoirs of Boven Digoel, published one photograph with a caption: "Boxing is practiced with enthusiasm in the camp." Two internees, unidentified by names, face each other, standing in a perfect boxing pose.[46] They are in the know, and they are naked except for their boxing shorts, boxing boots, and boxing gloves.

....

Roland Barthes was never in a camp, but he was an expert on fashion, and he also wrote about the triviality and triumphalism of sport. Barthes began by thinking of sport as a "human contract": "Ultimately man knows certain forces, certain conflicts, joys, and agonies: sport expresses them, liberates them, consumes them without ever letting anything be destroyed. In sport, man experiences life's fatal combat, but this combat is distanced . . . it loses its noxiousness, not its brilliance or its meaning. What is sport? Sport answers this question by another question: who is best?"[47] Sport translates the serious, even the fatal, into the trivial and back again into the serious. It pleases and envelops, like clothes and fashions, the bodies and souls of the people who aspire, in our case, to be modern and free. Sport fashions the people, properly clothed or properly naked, in endless variants of models, and for all seasons, in the know and on the go, in a shade of pink. "Every moral value," Barthes wrote, "can be invested in the sport: endurance, self-possession, temerity, courage."[48]

More impressively than anywhere in the modern world, sport in the camps fashioned "conflicts, joys and agonies."[49] Fittingly, everything about the conflicts, joys, agonies, and sport in the camps, came together, and had been consummated, in the camp sport uniforms.

In the few sport photographs we have of the Theresienstadt camp, the soccer teams wear uniforms.[50] "Every barrack," Jehuda Bacon recalls, "had its own team and each team had its own flag and dress."[51] The Movers played in blue shirts and white shorts, and Sparta played in dark-red shirts and white shorts; naturally, each of the players had a yellow star on his chest. In an enlarged photograph on the wall in the Beit Theresienstadt sport exhibition, Freddy Hirsch, the "Apollo with a Jewish nose," in a sport posture, wears a gymnast's shorts—and a gymnast's body.[52]

In the collection of the National Library in Jakarta there is a similar picture. A group portrait of a boys' soccer team in Boven Digoel, Vogel, Dutch for "Bird." Boys and young men, with adults (coaches?) standing behind, face the camera, and the boy in front in the middle holds a blackboard with the Vogel emblem. All of the boys, the sons of the internees, wear uniforms for the festive occasion: white trousers, white shirts, and ties.[53]

Soetan Sjahrir wrote on March 25, 1935, from the camp to his brother in Holland: "I have a problem, Tjammie: how to get soccer boots and socks."[54] Progress, fashion, could not be stopped. Already as the internees traveled on the ship up the river to the camp, they could see, "still in the distance, *athletic* figures of the people of the forest, with just plumages of paradise-birds or cockatoos in their hair, shrieking to get our attention."[55]

The Kaja-Kaja, at the edges of the camp and the jungle since the first encounters, were never truly naked to the internees' modern eyes. They either wore "costumes," and when they really wore nothing, to the internees they were "nudists." Thus, the Kaja-Kaja, too, were opened to the change.

> SEPTEMBER 24, 1937. *Theft:* Internee H. A. Chatib reports that following items were stolen from his house: one towel *f*o.90; one sport (tennis) shirt *f*o.50; one soccer dress (shirt) *f*o.50; two pairs of soccer socks *f*o.30, a tin of sardines *f*o.17. The thief probably was a Kaja-Kaja named Joesoep.[56]

> SUNDAY, MAY 23, 1937 ... MORNING ... 10:15, Zainoeddin reports the following clothes stolen: one shirt, one sport shirt, two pairs of soccer socks, two sport shorts, one striped and one black.[57]

> MONDAY, JULY 15, 1935, MORNING, 6:00. Agent Nawawi reports that a pair of soccer socks and one shirt disappeared last night as the laundry was drying on the clothesline.[58]

I would suspect someone like Sjahrir. The police, however, and everybody in the camp appeared to know who it was: it was all the savages' doing.

SOUND

The bell gave a faint tinkle as though it were made of tin and not of copper.... He had forgotten the note of that bell, and now its peculiar tinkle seemed to remind him of something and to bring it clearly before him ...

—DOSTOYEVSKY, *Crime and Punishment*

FIVE

Noise

There were trees around both camps, even inside the camps, and the sound of the trees is often remembered.

The patter of the leaves of the linden, apple, and cherry trees, poplars and chestnuts, had been connected with Theresienstadt. Before it became the camp, Theresienstadt was a Czech town in the middle of the Bohemian countryside. "A river flowed by it and meadows were close and all around. The wind still at the time of the camp, of course, would bring the fragrance of apricots in bloom; birds perched on telephone poles."[1]

"We can hear the warbling of blackbirds," Philipp Manes wrote in his camp diary. "It is March, and it is already beyond doubt that they survived the winter."[2] "Is it true," Elena Makarova asked Arnošt Reiser about his time in the camp, "that because of all the disinfectants there were no birds and no butterflies in Theresienstadt?" "We did not really worry too much about the butterflies," Mr. Reiser said.[3]

There were trees (some were later cut) on what used to be the Theresienstadt town main square, or its Paradeplatz [Exercise Square], as this was a garrison town. Cheeping, twittering, and cooing could be heard from those trees still at the time of the camp, day and night. There were swallows, as everywhere in that part of Europe, marking the seasons.

SUNDAY, APRIL 15, 1945. Spring has now arrived. Spring, the most beautiful thing in the world! . . . The trees are budding and getting new leaves.[4]

All the sounds, of winter, spring, summer, and fall, day and night, were familiar sounds to all the internees.

The sounds of nature in Boven Digoel to the Boven Digoel camp people were radically more of elsewhere. With very few exceptions, the Boven Digoel internees came from the western parts of the tropical archipelago, in fact, from beyond "the Wallace Line" dividing the Austronesian and Asian mainland regions of the world, and their sounds as well. Everything "natural" in Boven Digoel sounded to the camp people as beyond the line, distant and foreign. There were trees *entirely* unfamiliar to them, and birds and their sounds and noises. "Trees in Boven Digoel," ex-internee Salim recalled, "reached to the height of 80, even 100 meters!" Their high canopies of branches, huge and rigid, emitted an uninterrupted dry and harsh rattle of cracking, scratching, and breaking, coming ghastly out of nowhere.[5]

The rains in Boven Digoel had a ferocity that even the tropical downpours the internees knew from their homes in the west of the Indies never approached. The rumble of the rain deafened the camp.

SUNDAY, NOVEMBER 30, 1934 . . . *Night*. . . . There had been only drizzle tonight, but now the wind is rising.[6]

The camp people knew that the rain was coming long before it came, by the sound of it. "Usually it took quite a long time," Salim wrote, "about a quarter of an hour."[7]

In both camps, a river could be heard. Theresienstadt had been founded on the confluence of the smaller Ohře (Eger) and the bigger Labe (Elbe). The Ohře, especially, flowed just under the Theresienstadt walls, and it could be heard in the camp, albeit only gently, from certain spots in the camp, and when it got quiet, mostly at night. The heavy murmur of the mighty Digoel, day or night, could hardly be distinguished from the equally monotonous sound of the trees.

"There were no tigers, elephants, and bears, as the people knew them from their forests at home," Mrs. Widayasih, whose parents came from Java, told me.[8] Dr. Schoonheyt, a big-game hunter, appreciated the exotic: "The muddy banks of the Digoel River," he wrote, "were home to amazing reptiles."[9] To the internees, the reptiles of the place, too, were unfamiliar. "In Boven Digoel," internee Mas Marco wrote in a letter home, "There are not the wild animals as we knew them at home, no elephants, and neither rhinos, nor wild buffalo; just a New Guinea type of wild pigs, snakes, rats, centipedes, and, " he added, "strange kinds of birds. "[10]

"Very few songbirds," Salim wrote, as if he were adding to Mas Marco's account, "almost none." "A Sumatran like me," Salim wrote, "even missed monkeys as they jump from tree to tree back at home" (and how they shout, he might also have said).[11] There were strange-sounding birds. "The birds here," Mas Marco wrote, cannot sing, but "when taught, they can speak." "*Mengoceh*" (talk nonsense) was the word Mas Marco used, and, from the birds, he quickly moved back to the reptiles. "The scariest snakes of them here in Boven Digoel," he wrote, "have four legs, their body is like a Flores dragon—and they have no tongues."[12]

There was an omnipresent absence of familiar sounds. Many internees of Boven Digoel, with clothes, jewels, sewing machines, umbrellas, or, when possible, vitamins, brought songbirds with them, and kept them in cages placed on the long poles in front of their living quarters, as was (and is) the custom in Java, Sumatra, and other western islands. Every morning they put the cages up, and every evening they took them down. Sometimes they brought pigeons.[13] A wife of an internee from Java woke the first morning in the camp: "The dreams of the night were fading away and finally she was completely woken by a cry of a jungle cockatoo, painful and sharp from the trees. That cry of a bird unknown to her made her remember that now, she was in a faraway place."[14] Only slowly, and sometimes never, did the internees learn the birds' and other animals' names: "white and multicolored parrots, hornbills living always in pairs, waders . . . and many *kalongs* (flying foxes)."[15]

Of course, one might give an adventurous spin to what might be heard in the camp, as did a popular Dutch writer, Anthony van Kampen, who some years later wrote about the nature around the camp: "This is the only part of the empire," he wrote, "where the call of the wilderness can still be heard."[16]

Every day in the camp, close to sunset, the noise of mosquitoes and cicadas joined in and then overwhelmed all the other sounds and noises. "Even inside the mosquito net," Mr. Trikoyo recalled, "the buzz of the bugs."[17] "The only sound that might overpower and penetrate the quinine deafness," Krarup Nielsen wrote, referring to the intensive camp medical care, "is the sound of insects, as they, from one moment in late in the afternoon as the day begins to move to its end, begin to call, and swarm, around us, over us, each of us."[18]

At one time, a member of the Theresienstadt Jewish Council of the Elders brought a little cat into the camp. So a tiny meow might be heard at precious moments in the camp. Another time, an Alsatian was spotted in the camp, to all appearances walking by itself. "To see a dog," Hans Günther Adler recalled, "everybody looked in wonder."[19] So perhaps there was some barking. On Sunday, May 21, 1944, Pavel Weiner, a boy at Theresienstadt, wrote in his camp diary, "I stop at the Vrchlabí Barracks to look at the owls who have built their nest."[20]

There were dogs in Boven Digoel. Since long before the time of the camp the dogs had lived with the people of the forest, and the internees began soon to buy or otherwise acquire them as companions for their children and for themselves, too. Yet, as the birds in Boven Digoel "could not sing," these dogs, according to all the testimonies, "could not bark, they just yanked."[21]

Mrs. Zakaria told me about the cat, Berti, she had as a girl in Boven Digoel. "Berti was clever; she liked vegetables but not fish. She could watch a baked fish on the plate on the table, 'You watch!' but she would never take a piece. And, we had a parrot, Jakob, and he could speak. If someone came to our house, Jakob shouted 'Father's not at home!' He was hopping and flying around the house and through the camp, but he always came back. But once, he fell into a pot with boiling water. He died."

From the very early days of the camp, there were chickens. Internees brought some with them (like the sewing machines and umbrellas), and thus there was the noise of chickens in the camp. They often became pets for the children and adults as well, but mainly they were kept for eggs and meat.

> WEDNESDAY, JUNE 9, 1937... NIGHT:... 1:50... In section C of the camp a rooster is heard crying and flapping its wings as it flies over the house of Hadji Maliki. The police run there. It is nothing.[22]

Each attempt to bring back the familiar—the birds that sing, dogs that bark—all the imported, packed-in noise, made the camp stand out as even more foreign and exclusive in the middle of the primeval forest and its primeval sounds. The imported sounds and noises made the camp every bit more edgy, "loudly" announcing the new, the modern, and the future. They were catwalk sounds.

And there were other imported, future-modernity-announcing, and catwalk sounds and noises. Already in a report from June 4, 1927, the first weeks of the camp, one reads, "A trumpet blasted a signal in the military encampment."²³

MONDAY, NOVEMBER 5, 1934 MORNING ... 8:35. The ROB makes rounds through the camp warning internees that tomorrow, Tuesday, November 6, there will be a shooting at the range.²⁴

Salim wrote, "The big drum in the little mosque in section C of the camp beat six o'clock every afternoon for the evening prayer."²⁵

SATURDAY, FEBRUARY 20, 1937 ... NIGHT: 8:00 ... a *bedug* drum is heard again from the courtyard of the mosque.²⁶

The camps were places of concentrated acoustics. Inevitably, typewriters could be heard clicking—the "sound of the key hitting ribbon and paper, the flat forehand swat of the carriage return, after the warning ping ... the tearing of paper."²⁷ Boven Digoel rang out with acoustics that any Indies settlement at the time would rarely emit or hear in such density, except for a very few spots in the supermodern plantation and urban centers. The "government order of December 14, 1926, No. 423," had been issued for Boven Digoel; even before the camp began to function, it ordered "a typewriter for *f*285."²⁸

MONDAY, AUGUST 3, 1936, ... AFTERNOON: ... 3:45. Agent Zainoedin ... leaves the station. He will bring the typewriter to the doctor's office.²⁹

"The telephone wires are being hung," one reads in the Boven Digoel novel *Darah dan Aer-Mata* [Blood and Tears]. Already in March 1927, as the first ships with internees were raising anchors, a Dutch official on a very early inspection tour reported, "There already works a small telephone network."³⁰

THURSDAY, NOVEMBER 8, 1934 ... AFTERNOON: 1:27. A telephone call is received from the military quarters asking for a ROB agent to come and collect an internee who is to be released from prison.³¹

SATURDAY, AUGUST 22, 1936. MORNING. 7:20. A telephone call from the military commander requests that Hadji Sanoesi slaughter a goat and bring it to the headquarters.³²

TUESDAY, JULY 9, 1940. MORNING: ... 10:30. Telephone from the administration asks for the larger typewriter be brought to the main office. The machine is already on the way.³³

"My Corona," Soetan Sjahrir wrote in a letter of March 27, 1935, to his wife in Holland, "I had to leave in Bandung. Fortunately, Hatta has his typewriter here in the camp, and, naturally, I can use it."[34]

The sounds and noises of Boven Digoel, like the sounds and noises of Theresienstadt, the trees, the rivers, the birds, the typewriters, the telephone, each one and all together, to use Ernst Bloch's term, were "cathedralic."[35] They were like the sounds of any space of the world, except that there were the walls all around Theresienstadt, and the jungle all around Boven Digoel. In their listening, the people in both camps were prisoners. In its richness, the acoustic space of the prisoners in both the camps, rather than cathedralic, was cavelike—like Plato's cave. "In Plato's cave," wrote Jean-Luc Nancy, "there is more than just the shadows of the objects being moved about outside: there is also the echo of the voices of those who move them, a detail we usually forget, since it is so quickly set aside by Plato himself in favor of the visual and luminous scheme exclusively."[36] The word "echo," let me add to this, comes from the nymph Echo whose bones turn to stone.

Theresienstadt's high and thick walls were built late in the eighteenth century for the sole purpose of defense. Despite, or perhaps because of, this, they impressed most visitors as beautiful. They stayed as they were built, untouched. All the armies of the nineteenth and twentieth centuries bypassed Theresienstadt's walls on their campaigns between Prague, Vienna, and Berlin. The beautiful gates in the beautiful walls were closed throughout the camp's existence, except when ordered otherwise. When there were sounds and noises of the world behind the walls and gates, they were heard as echoes in the camp.

One large street, "Aryan Street" it was called at the time of the camp, cut through the camp. As Mrs. Kattenburg recalled, "It ran just under the windows of the room of the barracks where many children slept."[37] A truck, tractor, bus, car, cyclist, or even a pedestrian in the world outside could be heard. The sound of motors, tires, and steps heard from the inside had to sound like the strange birds in Boven Digoel that could not sing.

A quite elegant eighteenth-century Church of the Resurrection stood in Theresienstadt town, and now in the camp's main square, locked, too, and with its bells silent. It could not sing. Only, strangely, the clock on the church tower, for a reason unknown, kept working and it could be heard striking hours throughout the camp's history.[38] The bells from a smaller Church of Saint Prokop in a village a few kilometers from the camp could be heard on Sundays, slightly, if the wind blew right. Sometimes, even more distant bells from the town of Litoměřice (during the German occupation, Leitmeritz), could be heard.[39]

A shofar trumpet was allowed in the camp and could be heard at Rosh Hashanah, Yom Kippur, and through the month of Elul.

ORDER CONCERNING SHOFAR PLAYER; DEPARTMENT OF INTERNAL MATTERS, RABBINATE, THERESIENSTADT; SEPTEMBER 14, 1944 26. ELUL 5704

To Mr. Bernhard Kold, here

With this letter, you are installed as a shofar player in Block Q319. Contact Mr. rabbi Dr. Salomonski to inquire about the matter further.

With thanks.

The Director of the Department[40]

In Theresienstadt, as in Boven Digoel, sounds of the world in the middle of the twentieth century were crammed and squeezed, lid closed, into the walled space of the camp. The clicking of typewriters and ringing of telephones could be heard in Theresienstadt, as in Boven Digoel. Even some of the Theresienstadt magazines by the internees, including many issues of *Vedem* and *Šalom na pátek*, were typed. There were no shots heard, as far as I know; no shooting range was close enough, but there were other sounds. A reporter for *Vedem* interviewed Captain Meisl, the commander of a section of the Jewish police charged with keeping "public order" in the camp. The boy journalist clearly had fun with the elder and serious "policeman." "He told us in confidence," the boy-reporter wrote, "that five short blows on his whistle would signal that the police are calling for help."[41]

There were other sounds and noises, more echo-like, Plato-like, cavernous, and cathedralic. "When sirens begin to wail at night," Mr. Manes wrote in his Theresienstadt diary, "we do not have to go to the cellars." It was not expected that the camp might be bombed, if only because the Allies as well as the Germans had more important targets. "Our thoughts," Mr. Manes wrote, listening more than watching, "try to follow the pilot, we imagine the battle in the air . . . the explosions. . . . We could not keep up with them."[42] "On which street in Berlin, on which street in Nuremberg [Mr. Manes's home cities before the war]," at this moment bombs turn buildings in ruins?"[43]

In echoes, also mostly at night, and also impossible to know what was there except the sound, there were the "shrieks" of the forest people around the camp of Boven Digoel, rising up unpredictably and disappearing into the sounds and noises of the jungle. Salim recalled, "A long scream came from unclear direction, rising and falling, announcing that our 'invasion' did not go unnoticed by the savages. They watched our thrust into their world, the shrieks came from several sides, from the forest."[44]

And Krarup Nielsen wrote, "This was a sound as yet unknown, prolonged, plaintive, gruesome.... shriek.... It must have been some beast, that long and piercing howl. But in fact, these were humans, who were giving us a sign of life."[45]

SIX

Voice

In cultures, both Western and Eastern, ancient and modern, it is assumed that neither human nor divine is complete without a voice. "The Lord was not in the wind," says the Book, "the Lord was not in the earthquake . . . the Lord was not in the fire," but "after the fire [there was] still, a small voice, [that] said: 'What doest thou here . . . ?'"[1] It is also assumed, in both the West and the East, past and present, that neither human nor divine really hears unless hearing a voice: "Our ears," says French philosopher Jacques Rolland, "have been educated to hear being in its verbal resonance, an unusual and unforgettable sonority."[2]

There was a voice, a verbal resonance, beneath, above, and through the noise of the camps and of the world surrounding the camps. In its sonority, the camp's voice was palpable and has been remembered. "Marsiki from Blitar [East Java], had a pitch-black face, his profile was sharp, his body strong and squat like that of a peasant, and his voice clapped like a thunderbolt."[3] "Mr. Hermawan, an internee who came to the camp from Bandung [West Java], was young, handsome, and very loud."[4] In Theresienstadt, "The ss men gave orders almost exclusively in voice, by spoken word," Adler recalled, "and there was no way not to hear it."⁵

....

There were rarely visitors to any of the camps, and, even more rarely, a visitor spoke to an internee, except when taking part in order-giving or in interrogation-like asking questions. Rarely a voice could be heard from the outside of the camp.

If a word came from outside a camp, it came mostly as an imagined one. It came silently and had to be helped. It could also be scribbled, or typed, in the outside, and arrive as a letter to the camp, in that kind of an echo. The letter then was helped to a voice in the camp, a voice was beguiled out of it.

As the envelope was being torn open (if the censor did not open it first), and as the pages of paper inside were being touched, unfolded and folded again, as they were turned, the voice was rising from the letter as the paper rustled. At these moments, in the camps, radically and unprecedentedly more than in any modern-time letter reading, by the camp people's to-the-limit eagerness to hear, the paper could sound like a voice. In the camps and through the letters, writing and reading acquired an unprecedentedly strong orphic quality. Already before, in Jean-Luc Nancy's words, writing could have been "thinking addressed."⁶ In the camps, however, letters were voices addressed, received, and listened for.

Censorship of the mail in Theresienstadt "was entrusted to members of the Elders' Council, who would pay for any fault with their heads."⁷ "Censors deleted single words in the text with a black marker."⁸ On January 5, 1943, another of the constantly renewed "General Order of the Jewish Self-Government" had been issued. According to paragraph 8 of the Order, "Illegal exchange of letters will be punished by death. An attempt at it would be punished as the act itself."⁹ Of course, letters were being sent and received, legally or not, and voice in the letters was heard or certainly listened for. Rarely, an inhabitant of a nearby Czech village or a Czech gendarme helping the ss to keep order in the camp, might take a risk, for money, out of compassion or courage. Then a letter might bypass the censor.¹⁰

In Boven Digoel, initially, the internees were strip-searched on arrival, and suspicious letters, "dangerous literature," and sometimes even writing equipment were confiscated. After a few weeks, however, the local commander's eagerness was found excessive by his superiors in Batavia, and most of the books, letters, pens, and paper were returned.¹¹ Still, and throughout the camp's existence, the outgoing and incoming mail was read in the camp office, and the words, and the voice, by this wall around the camp, were "filtered."[12]

> CAMP COMMANDANT BOVEN DIGOEL TO THE RESIDENT IN AMBON, BOVEN DIGOEL JUNE 4, 1927.
>
> I send in attachment: One letter written in pencil and one postcard written in pencil.... The letter is by internee Kariodimedjo and the postcard by internee Soeroto, both contain an unfair description of the state of the camp.[13]

Internee Mas Marco, in a letter that evidently bypassed the Boven Digoel censor and reached a sympathetic newspaper on Java, complained, "In Boven Digoel, an internee even when he or she sends a registered letter or a telegram does not get a receipt in the camp post office. The reason is that all letters pass through the administration and are not handled merely by the post office as they should be. At the administration, even the registered letters are opened and they as well as telegrams are read."[14] One can still hear police running, censor mumbling, and letter writer sighing.

> TUESDAY, OCTOBER 30, 1934 ... AFTERNOON: 1:40. Agent Natoer leaves the station to get a postcard that internee Djamaloeddin Tamin just received from Roestam Effendi in the Netherlands. Natoer comes back with the postcard.[15]

The desire to write, to read, and to speak the written word was radically heightened in the camps by the letters and the voices contained in the letters, sent and received, but most of the time bumped back or filtered through the censors, the wall, the jungle, or the distance. Squeezed in, crammed in, concentrated in the camps, never before in modern time had voice and written word become so tightly one. Voice passed into writing and the written word passed into voices.

In Theresienstadt, the authorities were regularly issuing new, updated, relaxed, or strengthened mail regulations. "This ban on writing letters," Hans Günther Adler wrote about one such order issued in the late spring of 1942, "lasted only to the end of September 1942.[16] "By now," Philipp Manes wrote in 1943, "we are allowed to write one postcard a month."[17] According to Mr. Manes's diary entry a few weeks earlier, the internees were permitted "one postcard in six weeks."[18] In May 24, 1943, Adler wrote, "a new ruling for writing letters was issued: one postcard in three months."[19] And in Manes's diary again, in the entry for April 27, 1943, "After a general ban lasting almost a half of a year, two postcards have reached me from Munich. They were sent in February."[20]

This was called *Schreibturnus* in the camp, a "writing rotation." "We were permitted to write a letter only on a prescribed day, when our turn came up."[21] "Once a month was my writing turn," recalled Mrs. Meyer-Kattenberg.[22] Cards, most easy to get out and to receive, sent from Theresienstadt to Prague, just an hour by a car, often took more than a month to arrive, if they did arrive at all. Cards to and from Germany and other more distant places of Nazi-occupied Europe took much longer.[23] Letters, mostly in the form of cards, sent with SS permission through the International Red Cross to Switzerland and beyond, were expected to take four to six months.[24]

In Boven Digoel, a ship bringing supplies, new groups of internees, and letters, when all went well, arrived at the camp every six weeks. "I am losing my hope," a young woman, her handwriting looks to me, and so her voice sounds to me, like that of a girl, wrote from her home in a small town in Sumatra to her father interned in Boven Digoel. "There is no letter from you," she wrote, "there is no news about you, there is nothing. And here they try to marry me off. Months and months, papa, and no letter!"[25] "News of our families," ex-internee Soemono recalled later in an interview, "might take two months to reach the camp, and then still more weeks to get into our hands."[26]

"One could write," American composer John Cage says in his book *Silence*, "by observing the imperfections in the paper upon which one was writing."[27] Georges Perec said it with greater intensity: "I write, I inhabit my sheet of paper."[28] Franz Kafka, again, said it best. "Writing," he wrote, is a "yearning to write all my anxiety entirely out of me, write it into the depth of the paper."[29] Some pious Jews believed that, of all the holy texts, only the Book of Esther, the book most nakedly of the holy books about the threat of annihilation, the paper or parchment on which it is written, if touched, "makes the hands impure." The Book's, the letter's "eminence and its authenticity" smears the hands because, as Emmanuel Levinas believed, "it can only have meaning in a Jewish body."[30]

The letters sent from and to both Theresienstadt and Boven Digoel, whether for Muslims, the Communists, or the Jews, all more or less approximated the Book of Esther. They approximated the Book of Esther, in fact, as no letters before. Everything written in the camps, more or less, possessed the concentrated identity of pen, pencil, or typewriter, paper, body, and voice. In the Boven Digoel archives in Jakarta, there is a special folder. On each of the loose pages in the folder, next to "number," "name," and "special marks," there is the Esther thing, "left thumb print," "left hand four fingers print," "right thumb print," "right hand four fingers print," in small neatly arranged smears on the paper.[31]

León Ferrari and Mira Schendel were two postwar artists. León was a Latino, and Mira was a Jew. Mira escaped from Germany when she was in her teens. The two worked together, and made prints, drawings, and oil paintings. They called their work "a written materiality," "ingrown language," or, best of all perhaps, a "language as a trembling of the hands, a shudder of the body."[32] They also worked in Braille, "the language of the blind," and at their exhibitions they invited the viewer "to touch" the prints, paintings, or drawings, and even "to wear them out from touching them."[33] They equally appreciated "the physical impression of the typewriter keys striking the paper, inverting the raised dots of Braille."[34] They said "brushstrokes" as they might have said "penstrokes." When they came to summing up their work, they said it was "the endless anticipation of a voice."[35]

With very few exceptions, there were no illiterates in Theresienstadt. The camp was without a doubt more literate that the rest of even so very literate Europe. There were more illiterates in Boven Digoel, but still, again, much fewer, disproportionately fewer than in the Theresienstadt case, compared to the colony that surrounded them. The few who were illiterate dictated their letters to friends or professional scribes. In this case directly, the letter was a voice, or many voices, as people gathered around the one dictating and the one writing, and often voiced their advice and listened.

Because of the walls, the jungle, and the distance, the camp people treasured their letters more, but they shared them more, too, more than they would ever share them before or outside the camps. Internees read letters to other internees, listened, and they whispered them to themselves—letters received, written, and just composed in the head. Many letters were never sent or never received, and the more camp letter they were. They remained in the camps, on their way, or in the distance, as a thought, and as a voice.

"Kartoatmodjo of Boven Digoel wrote a letter to his son Soedihiat in Batavia. Clearly he does not know that his son is in prison."[36] Or:

From police agent A. Mertoadmodjo in Koedoes, [Central Java], *January 26, 1929.* Koesmirah, wife of Boven Digoel internee Sanoesi, asked me to write this letter for her. Koesmirah tells me that her last letter was sent to Boven Digoel on December 4, 1928 and that it was not answered. Koesmirah suffers.... First, please, let her know whether it is true that Sanoesi has died. If he is still alive she wishes to send him cigarettes and clothes. Second, if it is true that Sanoesi died, Koesmirah asks for his photograph and for whatever still might be left in the camp, so she may have something to remember him.[37]

In the same file, next to the letter, there is a page of paper dated April 14, 1929, "a list of items belonging to internee Sanoesi from Koedoes, who has died."

Even after some Jews were sent "to the east," and indeed to the gas chambers, "parcels were still coming to Theresienstadt for the dead men, women, and children."[38] And also the reverse, postcards and letters from now possibly dead persons were arriving at Theresienstadt. Otto Kulka, who went on one of the transports to Auschwitz from Theresienstadt, and who survived, told the story. He was a boy at the time, and as they still were on the train from Theresienstadt, like the others, he was ordered to write a card. "My mother wrote it actually, and I signed the card. A date was written not of the day, March 25, but some day later."[39] Most of the people were dead by the time the mail arrived.

Jehuda Bacon went on a transport from Theresienstadt to Auschwitz on December 15, 1943, and he also was ordered to send a postcard with a false date.[40] People were "believed alive" as the cards arrived. They might be the "truest," meaning most resonating, letters in the camp.

Yehuda Amichai, an Israeli poet, after the war, wrote about letters becoming a voice:

> *And they are brought into the arena to fight with wild beasts*
> *and they see the heads of the spectators in the stadium*
> *and their courage is like the crying of their children, persistent, persistent*
>   *and ineffectual.*
> *And in their back pocket, letters are rustling...*[41]

....

Newspapers in the camps were like letters sent and received, or letters wished for. Like the letters, ultimately in the camps, newspapers rustled and had a voice. Already in the nineteenth century, the philosopher Hegel said that reading newspapers was like a "daily prayer of modern man."[42] It only became fully true in the camps.

It was next to impossible to get hold of a real newspaper in Theresienstadt, and least of all a new real newspaper. In the first few months of the camp, internees were permitted to read the Nazi official *Der neue Tag* [The New Day],[43] but as soon as the situation on the war's fronts got complicated, as the blitzkrieg slowed down and bad news could not be fully blocked, even access to *Der neue Tag* stopped. Afterward, only a sheet properly called *Tagesbefehl* [The Daily Order], had been available. It was distributed by the authorities and then collected again. It was also displayed on the walls or in shop windows as far as there were any.[44]

On a rare, longed-for occasion, a smudged page of a newspaper got through in a package from the outside, disguised as a food- or clothes-wrapping, or a page of a newspaper might be found "as garbage discarded" (it might have been put there by a sympathetic and courageous Czech gendarme or an occasional "Aryan" visitor to the camp). This truly made the news. There were other, also extremely rare, occasions, such as when some Dutch Jews who were transported to Theresienstadt from Westerbork camp in 1944 managed to smuggle some newspapers with them.

Under the heading "WC Paper," Mr. Sven Meyer, a Danish Jew in Theresienstadt, recalled, "From Professor Fernheimer, I managed to exchange a few pages of an old Dutch newspaper for a quarter of a bread loaf.... It was such a wonderful experience to read a newspaper again, even when all of it was old news. How careful I had to be with something so precious. I used no more than a quarter of a page at a time."[45]

In contrast to Theresienstadt, in Boven Digoel, for all practical purposes, there was no censorship of newspapers arriving in the camp.[46] The Boven Digoel internees were even allowed to write to newspapers in the Indies, and some had written and published articles. In this case there was a censor. Still, even without censors, the jungle and the distance worked, as in the case of letters. Like the letters, newspapers in Boven Digoel were a matter of unprecedented rarity, and thus of value, and thus matter to be wished for and read with an unprecedented intensity. Like the letters, the newspapers at Boven Digoel arrived with a ship that returned to the camp, in the best of times, every six weeks. The news traveled long and, like the letters, reached the camp as a delayed echo.

Ex-internee Mohammad Bondan wrote in his memoirs after the war that in Boven Digoel he personally received regularly *Soeara Oemoem* [Common Voice], from time to time, an Indonesian paper from Surabaya; *Pemandangan* [Outlook], from Batavia; and an Indonesian business weekly, *Doenia Dagang* [The Merchant World]. *Poedjangga Baroe* [The New Poet], the Indonesian literary magazine, was also available in the camp. Newspapers arrived even from the Netherlands, including some dailies, with a number of individual issues bundled together, *Nieuwe Rotterdamsche Courant* and *Die Volksblad*, and a weekly *De Groene Amsterdammer*.

Some internees were even remembered reading *New Statesman* and the *Nation*.⁴⁷

Soetan Sjahrir on March 27, 1935, wrote from Boven Digoel to his wife and brother in the Netherlands: "At the moment, I am reading a two-month-old copy of the *Nieuwe Rotterdamsche Courant*.... It is better than all the Indies newspapers together, but these arrive a month faster." "You can only imagine," Sjahrir went on, "how I do gorge myself on the *N. R. Ct.* when it comes."⁴⁸ On July 24, again, Sjahrir wrote to his wife, who evidently had been arranging for the mail, "Yes, *N. R. Ct.* and *De Groene* I still receive regularly."⁴⁹ The next day he added to the letter not yet sent, "I am missing one issue of *De Groene* and one issue of the *N. R. Ct.*"⁵⁰

Coming late, often crumpled and smeared on the long way, like the internees themselves with their umbrellas, as never before, like the holy scrolls, the newspapers in the camps, to recall Emmanuel Levinas, "had a meaning in a body." As they arrived, they went on moving through the camp and soon they were covered, in addition to their travel marks, with their camp readers' fingerprints, stains of tobacco, and perhaps sweat. One should not be misled by the fact that the newspapers were less rare than in Theresienstadt. As Salim recalled, "Sometimes we smoked our cigarettes with tobacco rolled in a newspaper."⁵¹

The newspapers, like letters, had a voice.

> MONDAY, JUNE 24, 1935 ... NIGHT 7:45. Internee Djojodoelkadir reads newspaper *Indonesia Berdjoeang* [Fighting Indonesia] in his house to internee Sawal Rachmat. The article is about the Bolsheviks before the Russian Revolution. Djojodoelkadir reads with a strong voice, full of spirit.⁵²

The police could hear it and they listened for it. The internees were reading aloud to friends as well, it is clear from the police records, as to themselves when alone:

> SUNDAY, MAY 23, 1937 ... NIGHT: ... 8:25. In the house of Soekario in section C of the camp, H. Djaher reads a newspaper about the civil war in Spain.⁵³

> FRIDAY, MAY 24, 1940 ... NIGHT: 9.35 ... Naabas, the old man Leman, and some other people, it is not clear from the outside who, in section B of the camp, read a paper about the war in Europe.⁵⁴

> MONDAY, JUNE 24, 1940 ... NIGHT: ... 9:05 ... Kasman and his wife are alone at home and read a newspaper ... Oesep and Kasiman in the

house of Chamin read newspaper *Adil* [Justice] ... Djojodoelkadir reads a newspaper in Soekariji's house. Potseganda, Poerwawinata, Abdoelrachim, and Moeslid listen ... Maskoen, Kasman and Soeratman are together and read newspaper *Sipatahoean* [The Conscious] in Soeratman's house.⁵⁵

THURSDAY, MAY 30, 1935 ... NIGHT: 8:10. ... In section B of the camp ... Datoek Tan Mohamad reads a newspaper very loudly. He is warned by the police.⁵⁶

As no newspaper, with the despicable exception of the *Tagesbefehl*, was eventually supposed to reach Theresienstadt, the internees produced their own flyers, newspapers, and magazines. "You even put a price on the cover," an ex-writer for the Theresienstadt boys' magazine *Vedem* was asked after the war: "sometimes sixty cents and sometimes seventy cents?" "That was a game," he answered, "the magazine was never published in the true sense of the word; we simply read it aloud every Friday evening."⁵⁷

Vedem was one of the most persistent of the Theresienstadt periodicals. The boys at the Barracks L417 put it together, editorials, reportages, illustrations, every week, for more than two years, between December 1942 and August 1944, until, in August 1944, most of the editors, writers, and illustrators were sent to Auschwitz. *Vedem*, about eight hundred pages of it, is now in the Yad Vashem Archives in Jerusalem and a facsimile of it in the Theresienstadt Memorial in Terezín.⁵⁸ For the boys as for many in the camp around them, the paper was almost completely a voice. "At the general meeting, the new issue of *Vedem* was read to all, then we sang. It was so beautiful, it could not be described in any novel."⁵⁹

In the early weeks of Theresienstadt, before the camp was truly set up, a relative or a friend, still at freedom and courageous enough, might come and get close to the wooden fence that separated the camp from the "Aryan Street" that cut through the camp. Time and place had to be agreed upon beforehand by complicated conspiratorial means. If all went well, they might have a chance to talk for a few minutes, "even when they could not see each other's face."⁶⁰ In one such encounter, described by Adler, a mother of a daughter already interned made several unsuccessful journeys, but it went well this time except that neither could hear much of what the other was saying. "Just close to the end," the daughter is quoted, "I heard distinctly: 'I will try to be back in fourteen days.'"⁶¹

When the worst thing happened, and someone of the Theresienstadt people was put on transport "to the east," as close to death as one can imagine, the voice came forth, closest to a prayer and in its true campness. One of the Theresienstadt women recalled after the war, "In 1944, we 'celebrated' the New Year in Auschwitz. Pepek [Josef Taussig] was there, too. He had washed the blocks and found this book of Rilke in one of them. Through the fence between the male and female camps, he read *The Song of Love and Death* from this book."[62] The same woman recalled, on another occasion in Auschwitz, the same voice: "Once, [Pepek] called us and read fragments from the Bible... from the Book of Judges. In Czech the Bible sounded like an organ. Another time Cicero's speeches against the Catiline Orations. In Latin, by heart, in complete darkness.... Nobody was normal, neither we... let alone the time and place of the happening."[63]

In Kafka's novel *In the Penal Colony*, as a victim, the soldier, is being tortured, and as the words "Honor Your Superiors!" are being inscribed with sharp needles into his skin, as it is getting close to "the sixth hour," and as he is getting close to death—his voice, too, in its exhaustion, silencing, and most camplike, nears to its "completion." "How quiet he grows at just about the sixth hour!," Kafka wrote, "Nothing more happens than that the man begins to understand the inscription, he purses his mouth as if he were listening."[64]

Camps were not a place for a silence and listening about which the seventeenth-century philosopher Gottfried Leibniz wrote so poetically: a calm in which one might hear the world in its fullness, "the state of this world... expressed by the image of murmuring of the ocean or a water mill, or vanishing, or even drunkenness... rumbling... vanishing."[65] Nor were the camps a place for the silence about which Maurice Blanchot wrote already in the time of the camps: "The austere silence, the tacit speech of visible things."[66] Nor was it, most of the time, Roland Barthes's kind of silence, which attempts "to outplay oppression."[67] "On May 1, 1928 at eight o'clock in the morning," Boven Digoel internee Mas Marco wrote in a letter home, "the ship *Segah* arrived at the landing of the camp bringing ninety-eight new internees. It was very hot and many of them were close to fainting. Children cried."[68]

Camps were places between crying and voices, or shrieks rather, of quickly passing moments of pain and joy and calm. There were the "Boven Digoel dinners" in the tropical camp, racy celebrations, Hari Raja, Malay and Indonesian for "Big Days," rather nights, such as were known throughout the colony at the time, on paydays most often, to spend the money, when everybody got drunk and riotous. These were, on the whole, the officials' and guards' events, the *ramai-ramai besar,* Malay and Indonesian for "tumult," and *reuzendrukte,* Dutch for the same. Even some internees were able or willing to participate, namely "when the ship arrived." Salim recalls the moments as fleeting outbursts "of undiluted Wild West in the most of other time lonely and muted corner of the world!"[69]

The camps did not fit Barthes's definition of silence "as a right," the kind of right like that of deafness, "the right 'to turn a deaf ear.'"[70] The camps were neither what Walter Benjamin called places of "moral speechlessness" nor what he described as "the silence of tragic heroes"—even when Benjamin, in the same breath, in this connection, talked about "the silence of the Jews."[71]

"So rise wanderers... raise not your voices, tread firmly in silence," are perhaps the most famous lines from the celebrated Jewish poet Hayim Nahman Bialik's "The Dead of the Desert." Bialik's verses were at least once publicly recited in the Theresienstadt camp, by a Jewish Theresienstadt boys' choir, and the poem was certainly well known and often recited in private.[72] But neither the camp for the Jews nor the camp for the Communists was a place where one could "tread firmly in silence." One could not even dwell or rest in silence for any extent of time in the camps. A Czech Jewish girl, Annetta Makovcová, wrote a poem about her Theresienstadt:

> *Voices jumble, shout and shout more,*
> *Howl and groan, What is going on?*
> *Oh, boy, the neighbors again!*[73]

Pavel Weiner wrote on what he suggested was a typical evening in the camp: "In the barracks, one does hear nothing but kvetching and bleating."[74] There was no escape from the noise of voices like there was no escape from the camps.

Most people in Theresienstadt, with exceptions, throughout their time in the camp lived in barracks. The verb *barrack,* as per the dictionary, means also, and, it seems, properly for the camp, "to jeer loudly." And it was noisy outside the barracks no less. The camp police, the *Ghettowache,* held regularly noisy parades and more often exercises on the Paradeplatz, on the streets, and in the barracks courtyards:

> *Parade March of the Police in the Dresden Barracks:* ... a regiment of ducks is marching.... The entire barracks are laughing.... Shouts and exclamations.... "Do it again!" shout the children.[75]

"Porters sit on the carts next to the post office and offer their services," Gonda Redlich wrote in his Theresienstadt diary on October 14, 1943.[76] No newspapers, really, but noise of colportage. "Colportage," Ernst Bloch wrote as if he heard the camps, "tremolo between illusion and depth."[77]

Children were crying in Theresienstadt as they were crying in Boven Digoel. "The nursery," Gonda Redlich again wrote, "looks out on the Aryan street where the automobiles pass on their way to [Prague]. It may be that the passersby hear the cries of babies."[78] There were moments of silence, it is true, but of a tired and threadbare silence: "A few minutes before the night curfew," Philipp Manes wrote, "the streets become livelier, buzzing and whirring. And then you hear in many languages 'Good night!'"[79]

"Congestion," Rem Koolhaas wrote, is "a system of 2,028 solitudes."[80] Koolhaas wrote about Manhattan, but, using different numbers, he could have written the same about the camps. Camps were the best examples of what Slavoj Žižek called "Phatic communion," "glib chatter, speaking out and listening without telling or hearing anything," "a kind of 'Hello, do you hear me?'" Chitchat, not saying anything, like fashion, but possibly serving as a blanket, a shroud like that in which Etty Hillesum tried to wrap herself, expecting the camp.[81]

One day in September 1933, in Boven Digoel, a suspicion arose among the officials that something might be happening, something dangerous might be said, a voice heard, to put it that way. Specifically, there were reports that a gathering of the internees took place in a house and two speeches sounding as threatening were given. An extensive interrogation was launched. The transcripts of the interrogation make for a sizeable file in the Boven Digoel archives. This was a case when the noise, chitchat, as a shroud, covered everything—even voice.

Interrogation of Moeljodikromo

QUESTION: *What did you hear?* . . .

ANSWER: Nothing. There were many people, talking . . .

QUESTION: *But you stayed until the police arrived and dispersed the people?*

ANSWER: Yes, but I was in the kitchen all the time . . . .

QUESTION: *So what did you hear . . . ?*

ANSWER: I only heard what my friend Wisopo was telling me as I cooked.[82]

Interrogation of Wisopo

QUESTION: *So you heard the people giving speeches?*

ANSWER: I did not hear them. . . . It was *ramai* [bustling]; everybody was talking about this and that.[83]

A jumble of voices might cover the camp and make voice disappear in the process. The cover, to use Benjamin's words about fashion, could be "never anything other than the parody of the motley cadaver, provocation of death . . . bitter colloquy with decay . . ."[84] A jumble of voices could shelter, shroud for a moment. But it was all it was powerful at—cascades of little nothings, of the time, of the season and of a moment.

On Wednesday, October 9, 1934, at 7:20 in the evening an ROB agent in Boven Digoel was sent to the house of internee Boejoeng Moentjak in section C of the camp. "The agent is sent to Boejoeng Moentjak as there are complaints that Boejoeng's house is used by internees to play *troef* [a card game]. The agent reminds Boejoeng that by ten o'clock at night the game has to stop in consideration for the neighbors."[85] On Wednesday, June 9, 1937, at 1:50 in the morning, "In the house of Soekaria in section C of the camp, internees Moeljodikromo, Rahmad and Sastrosoenarto still loudly talk and joke. The ROB orders them to go home. They obey."[86]

By the "General Order of the Jewish Self-Administration" in Theresienstadt, as issued on January 5, 1943, "paragraph twelve," "noise is strictly prohibited."[87] Early in April 1943, five young men attempted to escape from the Theresienstadt camp. They were caught and the SS authorities reacted by prohibiting "all leisure-time activities." The ban lasted from April 7 to May 12. "Dead silence hung over the place," Elena Makarova was told by an ex-internee.[88]

In late 1944, a large group of Dutch Jews arrived at Theresienstadt from the transit camp of Westerbork. People were frantically looking for a friend or a relative who might be lost on the way or might have come before from Westerbork or another place. There was shouting, talking, asking, crying, and laughing when luckily someone found someone. There was noise, buzz, a tumult of voices: "'Sven! Here we are!'—But then," the story of one of the women who were there, the wife of Sven, goes on, or rather ends: "It was shouted: 'Quiet!!'"[89]

SEVEN

Music

An audience in Theresienstadt, 1944. From the Nazi propaganda film, *The Führer Bestows a City upon the Jews*. With permission of the National Film Archive, Prague.

As there were the finest doctors, and the finest sportsmen in the camps, so there were the finest musicians. As with the doctors and the sportsmen, the number of musicians, music performers, and music listeners was disproportionate in the camps, radically higher than among either Europe or the Dutch Indies general public.

Djojo Toegimin of Boven Digoel used to be a bandmaster of a military music corps of the Royal Dutch Indies Army in Magelang, one of the principal military garrisons in Java.[1] Internee Djojo Toegimin is remembered as a "musical expert."[2] Internee Ganda, together with internee Oekar, was active in Boven Digoel, "developing Soendanese [West Javanese] music."[3]

Mohammad Jasin and Sjamsoeddin Katjamata ("The Eye-Glassed Sjamsoeddin") put together a *kroncong* orchestra.[4] *Kroncong*, written *krontjong* at the time, is music often compared to *hawaian* (Hawaiian) music, and at the time of the camp it was popular, especially in the western, most modern and urban parts of the Indies. The kroncong ensembles varied widely, but usually they included guitars, ukuleles, violins, and a singer.

There was gamelan in Boven Digoel, in particular a Javanese and Balinese orchestra of gongs, drums, strings, and voices, classical, ancient, but still widely played in sultans' courts and villages, as well as towns and cities. Internee Pontjopangrawit used to be a distinguished gamelan musician of the Sultan Palace in Solo, Central Java (thus the *pangrawit* title for a scholar musician). In the camp, he became identified with the "Digoel gamelan," a phenomenon perhaps more written about in literature than the camp itself.[5]

With the Theresienstadt internees, the good and often the best of the European musical present and past were brought to a small place. Elsa Porges Bernstein was born in 1886; her father, Heinrich Porges, was a conductor and an illegitimate son of Franz Liszt. He was also known as one of the chief propagators of Richard Wagner. In the camp file of Mrs. Porges, there was a note: "Protected by the Wagner family in Bayreuth."[6] (It did not help.) Paul Ottenheimer, born in 1887, was a conductor of the Vienna court orchestra in his precamp life, and the author of numerous compositions, especially for male choruses. He was especially known in Vienna as the author of an operetta, *Heimliche Liebe* [The Secret Love]. In his precamp life, he was a friend of Richard Strauss, too.[7]

Hans Krása, more of the musical present than the past, had studied with Alexander Zemlinsky in Vienna. In 1926, Serge Koussevitzky conducted in Boston his first symphony.[8] Viktor Ullmann also studied in Vienna, with Arnold Schönberg, and was a member of the circle of composers of the Second Viennese School.[9] Pavel Haas had been one of the last students of

Leoš Janáček.[10] Franz Eugen Klein, before Theresienstadt, was a second conductor of the Vienna State Opera.[11]

On the very first ship of the internees to Boven Digoel, Krarup Nielsen noticed "on the deck, on hooks and spikes, jackets, pans, and backpacks, and also guitars." As the internees were disembarking from the ship, he saw not just the dandy hats, umbrellas, and fancy briefcases but also "mandolins, guitars, and violins, as a part of their baggage."[12]

As the people entered the tropical camp, as they were settling down for years of imprisonment, musical instruments played—indeed played—an oversized role in the internees' lives. "Violins and guitars" are repeatedly remembered and with special intensity.[13] "My late father," Bangun Topo, a boy in Boven Digoel, told me as an old man, "learned to play mandolin in Boven Digoel."[14] Mrs. Chamsinah, a girl in the camp, now an elderly woman, told me several times during one afternoon, "My brother played violin in the camp."[15]

"Internee Djojotoegimin's band," ex-internee Darman recalled, "owned a complete set of instruments."[16] Indeed, there was a jazz band in Boven Digoel. The "memorable Abdoel 'lXarim orchestra," Salim recalled, "included a zinc drum covered with leather and a xylophone made from cans in which butter used to be transported to the camp. Later they managed to buy a real drum, several flutes, and some brass instruments, also cellos, mandolins, and more guitars."[17] Dr. Schoonheyt wrote, "It was the Digoel jazz band. . . . But sometime after the band had been put together, a trouble arose, as the owner of several of the band's instruments was released from the camp and took the instruments with him."[18]

Mr. Trikoyo told me a story about Mr. Pontjopangrawit often told, "Uncle Pontjo has built a gamelan. From scratch!" The "*bonang* (gong-rows) were made of 'milk tins,'" wrote Margaret Kartomi, an Australian scholar who wrote a whole book, an ethnomusicological study, about "the Digoel gamelan."[19] Kartomi wrote, "Internee Pontjopangrawit made a *rebab* [a two-string bowed lute] from sardine tins and animal skin, as he could not obtain the buffalo intestine or bladder parchment. . . . For the most respected instrument of all—the *gong gedhé kemodhong*—Pontjopangrawit and colleagues used a large earthenware water pitcher (normally used in the kitchen)."[20] Salim recalled that Pontjopangrawit also "used iron blades of hoes." "On special occasions," Salim added however, "our musicians could borrow a really fine gamelan from the Boven Digoel military garrison."[21]

In Theresienstadt, in the first weeks, musical instruments were not allowed to the Jews; some exceptions were made to the members of the Jewish Council of the Elders and the Jewish camp police. "But even then," Hans

Günther Adler wrote, "people played music; if only on a mouth harmonica or on a violin that they somehow got in."[22] But as the camp "normalized" and as camp life "developed" into a complete camp life, by the end of 1942, the ban on musical instruments was lifted. Instruments, and also musical scores and notepaper, started to arrive, "legally," with the Jews newly arriving, or they were allowed to be sent to the camp from the plundered and not fully burned Jewish institutions and private homes all over occupied Europe.[23]

With the permission, and, inevitably, help of the ss, a splendid grand piano had been delivered from Germany, on a barge up the Labe River to the camp, and to the living quarters of the head of the Jewish Council of the Elders, Paul Eppstein.[24] (Eppstein, with his family, perished in Auschwitz in 1944.)

Burger-Societeit, "The Club," had been built by the internees with the commandant and camp head's permission, also very early, in Boven Digoel— for music "and other entertainment," and it stood in the very center of the camp. "The Club" was larger than most of the structures in the camp, except perhaps for the hospital. It was built in a tropical style, almost no walls, mainly a roof supported by fine, indeed elegant pillars. It was an imposing site, in a sense a "dominating" site of the camp, a culture center.

There was, also newly built, a "music pavilion" for the camp in Theresienstadt, and it also stood in the very center, at the Paradeplatz [Exercise Square]. It was, Adler wrote, "a nice-looking building, in light form, made of wood, an open structure, and concerts there were to take place daily."[25] "The 'town orchestra,'" wrote Philipp Manes in his Theresienstadt diary, "made itself well-loved." "It performs every day, in the music pavilion, one hour of music, and free."[26] "When Maestro Carlo Taube raises his baton," Mr. Manes wrote about the "town orchestra's" internee-conductor, "the whole space around the music pavilion is packed. People stand and listen— like they used to listen when Prziworski used to play in the Berlin Zoo, in front of the August Café."[27]

In Boven Digoel people, too, played and listened to music, in the Burger-Societeit and also inside their houses, and even "on picnics," during short trips they were allowed inside some limit outside the camp, on the banks of the Digoel smaller and friendlier (and cleaner) Bening River. In Theresienstadt, inside the walls, two former movie houses of the precamp town were eventually opened for concerts by and for the internees. Several other halls in the barracks, some with a podium and some without, began to be used for music. People found places to play music in the barracks' basements and attics, and also in the larger dormitories, among the beds or bunks.[28] Dr. Zucker, a member of the Theresienstadt Jewish Council of the Elders, became well known throughout the camp as a good violinist. "There were regular musical soirées at Zuckers,'" recalled Adler, "the elite met there"; it was a "circle" for the invited.[29]

Each camp had a music of its own, and the difference in genres could not be bigger. But in both camps, music was played and listened to with, one may say, unprecedented, or, one may say, camp, intensity. Greta Kingsberg, a woman in her eighties when I met her in Jerusalem in 2015, was a girl with the most beautiful voice in the Theresienstadt camp, and she was chosen to sing the title role in the Theresienstadt children's opera *Brundibár*. She told me that evening in Jerusalem about the camp, "If you had then stripped me naked, you would find nothing but music."[30]

People intensively composed music in both camps. In Theresienstadt, Viktor Ullmann wrote songs for voice and piano; three sonatas for piano; and an opera, *Der Kaiser von Atlantis* [The Emperor of Atlantis], a requiem on Rainer Maria Rilke's poem "The Song of Love and Death of the Cornet Rilke." He gave lectures in the camp such as "How to Listen to Music" or "Anton Bruckner's Symphonies (with illustrations on the flute)."[31] In a lecture titled "Goethe and the Ghetto," one of the few that survived not just in title but in complete text, Ullmann said, "Theresienstadt has been a school of form for me ... a true *Meisterschule*; a place, to say with Schiller, where one becomes empowered to gaze into the very depth of the secret of artist's work." "I have written a good amount of new music in Theresienstadt," Ullmann also said in the lecture; "Theresienstadt did not restrain my music. It nagged it to go on."[32]

Gideon Klein, Ullmann's colleague and fellow composer, in Theresienstadt, arranged a Hebrew song in the camp, "Bachuri Le'an Tisa?" [Where Are You Going, My Boy?], for a three-voice women's choir; Gideon Klein's song cycle "The Plague," that was also written in the camp, did not survive. Klein was giving lectures in the camp, too, among them one about Mozart, in Elena Makarova's list, on March 3, 1944, and one on J. S. Bach on March 17, 1944.[33] A fellow internee who accompanied Gideon Klein on transport to Auschwitz and on to another camp in Fürstengrube (where Klein died) recalled, "With us, the other prisoners, he was brought for a medical examination and there we all stood and waited, against the wall, naked, under an ss-man guard. In the otherwise empty room stood a piano. To make the waiting easier on himself, the bored ss man asked if someone could play. Klein said he could and, naked like all of us, he sat down and played something of his own repertoire."[34]

Mendelssohn's oratorio *Elias* [Elijah], sung by a chorus of eighty men and women, accompanied by two pianos;[35] Haydn's *Die Schöpfung*; and

Verdi's *Requiem* were performed in the camp.[36] Otto Brod, the younger brother of Max Brod and a close friend of Kafka, too (the third in Kafka's dream of packing at the last moment), was present at the opening night of Verdi's *Requiem* in the camp, in which also his daughter Marianne sang in the choir, and he wrote a review in a camp magazine: "Impressively skillful conducting by Schlächter.... Rhythmic and dynamic clarity. Melodic diversity, energy, and explicit articulation of voices.... Probably, the *Dies Irae* could have been given a greater presto. The piano was out of tune; yet the accompaniment of Frau Pollak was outstanding."[37]

There were operas in Theresienstadt, either in concert or fully staged, in costumes and "with everything,"[38] Verdi's *Aida* and *Rigoletto*, Bizet's *Carmen*, and Rossini's *Guillaume Tell*.[39] Smetana's *Prodaná Nevěsta* [Bartered Bride], a Czech national opera, was performed thirty-five times.[40] Pavel Weiner, a boy in Theresienstadt, wrote on Saturday, August 5, 1944, "Handa gave me a ticket for the opera 'Bastien and Bastienne.' It took place at eight o'clock in the Magdeburg Barracks. Even though I had a ticket for standing, I was able to sit in the first row. It was amazing! Bastien becomes unfaithful to Bastienne and falls in love with the countess. Bastienne cries and Bastien soon forgets about the countess. They make peace with each other and get married. It is by Mozart."[41]

Viktor Ullmann's opera *Der Kaiser von Atlantis* had already been fully rehearsed for the opening night, when most of the singers, musicians, stage hands, and both Ullmann and Peter Kien, the composer and librettist, were sent to Auschwitz.

While everywhere in Nazi Europe it was strictly forbidden to play Jewish composers, in Theresienstadt they performed Mendelssohn as well as Meyerbeer. While jazz music was equally forbidden everywhere in Europe, The Ghetto Swingers performed in the camp: "Martin Roman, the leader; Kohn, Goldberg, Vogel, and Taussig in the brass section; Weiss, Vodňanský, and Danda on reeds; Libeňský, Nettla, Goldstein, and Schumann on percussions."[42]

There were light Viennese operettas in the camp. Original *Das Ghetto Mädel* [The Ghetto Girl], had been performed many times, often to complaints of more serious musical people. There were *schlagers* [hits], while elder people might "sit, lost and fragile, nodding their heads to the tunes from the *Tales from the Vienna Woods* or from *Carmen*."[43] One song banned everywhere else because of its "Yiddish overtones," "Für Mich Bist du Schön" [You Are So Beautiful for Me], was "often heard" in the camp.[44]

On January 9, 1943, nine (according to different memories, sixteen, and according to yet another recollection, ten) young men, who allegedly attempted contact with the outside world, were sentenced to hanging. This was an extremely rare event in the camp. The gallows were erected in a moat running along the walls of the camp and everyone (according to another memory, the Council of the Elders only) had to be present.[45] One after the other, the young men were strangled. With already the rope around his neck, one of them (one memory has it, the last one) began to sing, a hit, a march from a popular 1930s Czech political cabaret: "When we will march by millions, all against the wind."[46] Thinking about the sound of the camps, I try to imagine the song at the moment it ended, the last tone, or shriek of it.

....

Boven Digoel, no less than Theresienstadt, and in spite of the vast genre differences, was touched by music. Like Theresienstadt, Boven Digoel was mapped by music. Through music, it was enlivened and generated, but also contained as a camp.

Marcus van Blankenstein described his arrival with the ship of a group of new internees to the camp in 1928: "From afar, we saw a group of people on the river bank, standing close to each other, all attired in white. They were the internees awaiting the new arrivals. As we came closer, we heard music sound."[47] It had to be the jazz band. "The indomitable Abdul 'lXarim and his jazz band" Salim remembered, "with their 'delightful melodies,' were an inevitable part of the 'Committee-of-Welcome' ceremony prepared for each newly arriving group of internees." "Of course," Salim adds, "we all readily forgave the cacophony of their presentations."[48]

Not merely on special occasions, Boven Digoel sounded with music. It was, as in Theresienstadt, the camp's everyday, day and night, that is, deep into the night, in fact, because in Boven Digoel, unlike in Theresienstadt, there was not much of a curfew.

> SATURDAY, MAY 25, 1935 ... AFTERNOON: 3:30 ... In the house of Oehar[?], section B of the camp, there are many children learning to play mandolin.[49]

> WEDNESDAY, JUNE 23, 1935 ... NIGHT: 9:25 ... In section C of the camp, in the house of internee Soerjosoeprodjo there is a gamelan rehearsal going on. In the house of Soengeb, a group of internees plays muziek.[50]

When an ROB agent wrote *muziek*, to everybody in the camp and in the Indies of the time, it meant "modern" music, mostly "Western" music, that is, perhaps kroncong, but certainly not gamelan. The strong presence of muziek in the camp, again disproportionately strong when compared to the Indies at large, pointed to how exclusive, catwalk, the camp was.

> WEDNESDAY, JULY 3, 1935 . . . NIGHT: . . . 10:00 . . . some people in the camp are rehearsing. Some play guitar with the door closed.[51]
>
> SATURDAY, JULY 22, 1936 . . . NIGHT: . . . 8:05 . . . At Wiriosoedarmo's they play *siter* and *gendang* [a gamelan drum instrument]. . . . Pontjopangrawit can be heard in his house. He plays *gender* [a metallophone, also of gamelan].[52]
>
> TUESDAY, MARCH 28, 1939 . . . NIGHT: 8:00 . . . Karmani, Bondan, and Djojotoegamin play muziek in the house of Padmosoedarmo.[53]
>
> SATURDAY, APRIL 27, 1940 . . . NIGHT: . . . 8:30 . . . The camp feels empty. It is raining, and all is quiet, except the house of Soehoena[?], from which one can hear muziek.[54]

As one walked about the camp when evening approached, Salim recalled, "sometimes one could hear a clear voice of violin from a house a little apart from the others."[55] "From the direction of Auntie Kusen's house," Mr. Trikoyo recalled, "often came a sound of the violin. This was Uncle Suradi."[56] An Indonesian novelist, Misbach Yusa Biran, was born after the time of the camp but remembered his parents, who both were interned in Boven Digoel: "I never heard about the camp from my father, and from mother I heard only a little. In fact all that she had told me was that my father taught himself photography in the camp, that he studied languages in Boven Digoel, Dutch and English, and that, in the camp, he learned to play violin and guitar."[57]

There was singing in Boven Digoel, much less organized than in Theresienstadt, but still, equally diverse in genres and strong in impact. The internees sang individually and in chorus, songs and compositions "modern," "traditional," "folk," "classical," "sophisticated," or "primitive." In 1929, on August 27, during the celebration of the birthday of the Dutch queen and the birth of Princess Irene, for instance, according to the program, "19:35: military music band marches in; 20:00 an internee children's chorus performs songs; 21:00 the celebration officially opens."[58]

On Sunday, December 25, 1936, at 11:10 at night, the camp ROB police reported that in the house of Rahmani there was a rehearsal of "Javanese songs." Men's, women's, and children's choirs had been established by Protestant missionaries, and every Sunday one could hear hymns from a little wooden church at the northern side of the camp.[59] Some men, women, and children of the forest, as time went by, were baptized, and those among them with good voices were admitted to the choir. "The Papuans," Salim, also a new Christian in the end, wrote in his memoirs, "sang the psalms in Latin very well!"[60]

Koranic recitations could be heard from different houses, as prayers, and as songs if one was un-Muslim, secular and/or so much modern.

There was opera in Boven Digoel, too, however, the Theresienstadt people might not recognize an opera in it. The "Malay Opera," or *Stamboel* (the opera was said to come from the West—from Istanbul), was a musical theater, popular in the Indies as much as kroncong, and at the similar social layer of population at the edge of the old and the modern. The stories in the Malay Opera were taken from classics, such as Shakespeare or Calderón, from the old and new Chinese literature, and from Javanese, Malay, or Indian mythology and folklore, all wildly adapted but all keeping a flavor of something coming from the outside.

Mrs. Ottow recalled that she had a piano in the camp. She gave piano lessons to her younger siblings, and, she said, she played herself, "quite a lot,"[61] Schubert or Wagner for piano, perhaps, what else might a young Dutch woman be expected to play at the time? "The petty-bourgeois sterility of the piano etude," Walter Benjamin might say,[62] but in the middle of jungle, I would add.

There were *schlagers*, hits, in Boven Digoel, as they were in Theresienstadt, of a similar kind, much more from elsewhere here than there, of course. Sometimes they were the same songs, from Western films shown in the Indies, or, more specific for Boven Digoel, from the Chinese films, or the handful of films already produced in the Indies: "The melodies like 'Nina Bobo' [Lullaby], 'Ajoen, Ajoen in de Hoge Klapperboom' [Swinging in a High Coconut Palm], or 'Terang Boelan' [Bright Moon] were sung by everybody in the camp," Salim wrote. "To be '*up to date*' [this phrase is in English], our musicians dived into the realm of Western '*schlagers*' [the word is in German], even when their interpretation was of a kind that made the original hardly recognizable."[63] Many internees, naturally, were humming or whistling the hits to themselves. Soetan Sjahrir, Salim recalled, "sang schlagers with enthusiasm" and his favorite appeared to be "Das gibt's nur einmal, das kommt nicht wieder. Das ist zo schön um wahr zu sein!" [It happens once and it does not come back, it is too nice to be true][64]—a song, I should add, "with Yiddish overtones," and, no doubt, hummed and whistled to themselves or sung with enhusiasm by the Jews in Theresienstadt, as well. "My mother was not very musical," Mr. Trikoyo told me, "but we, the children in the camp, liked to sing." "Dutch songs," Mr. Trikoyo explained, "the school songs."

There were marching songs, as in Theresienstadt, so in Boven Digoel. "On Friday, April 29, 1939, at 6:45 in the morning, a ROB agent wrote in the police book, "A company of soldiers marches past the post, in formation and with music."

There were marches composed, sung, and, indeed, marched to in Boven Digoel by the internees. Some were in kroncong style, but often they were written for and played by the internees' own brass band. Mas Marco (who died in the camp) wrote in one of his letters that they sounded "thundering, victorious, never-to-be-defeated mood (do not laugh my reader)."⁶⁵ Internee Mohammad Jassin wrote "March Boven Digoel" in 1927, in the camp:

Boven Digoel in the thicket
In the deep forest
The internment camp
For resisting the Dutch
Boven Digoel in the swamps
The nest of malaria
Boven Digoel in the forest
In the jungle of Papua
*Hurrah-hurrah!*⁶⁶

When the first group of internees arrived at Boven Digoel, which included Salim, as the ship stopped in the Makassar harbor, the internees were locked into the local prison for the night. The next morning they were being taken back to the ship. "On the way to the harbor," Salim recalled, "to the irritation of the guards, we sang the 'Internationale' and other Red songs."⁶⁷

So in the camp:

WEDNESDAY, MAY 29, 1935, MORNING, 9:00. In the house of Wentoek there is Najoan and Barani and they play Red songs on the flute: "Internationale March," "Darah Ra'jat" [Blood of the People], and "La Marseillaise."⁶⁸

"Uncle Pontjo," Mr. Trikoyo told me one day, liked to play songs like "Darah Ra'jat," "Internationale," "1 Mei" [May First], or "Mariana the Proletarian" on one of his gamelan instruments. I have already forgotten much of the lyrics," Trikoyo told me, "but I still remember most of the melodies," and Trikoyo sang to me "almost all," with a fervor. "One day my father had a good day," Trikoyo said as he finished the singing; "he caught good fish and sold it well. He brought me a *wang-wang*, harmonica made in Hong Kong, in C key. I was so happy and I began to play at once, one song after other,

'Enam Djam Kerdja' [Six-Hour Day], 'Doea Belas November' [November the Twelfth, the first day of the 1926 rebellion], 'Tanah Merah di Papoea' [Our Camp in Papua], and, of course, 'Indonesia Raja' [The Great Indonesia]." Though he said his mother was "not so musical," Trikoyo at another moment told me that she was into some songs. "She liked Dutch songs, but sometimes she sang this," and Mr. Trikoyo went back to singing:

The cruel capitalism,
Must be destroyed,
The working class,
Of the World,
Unite, Unite.
Toward victory,
Long live shining days.

....

"Spiritual resistance," Shirli Gilbert wrote in *Music in the Holocaust*, had been "a common concept in secondary writing."[69] "The idea that music comforts and uplifts people, or acts as a vehicle for asserting humanity and dignity," she added, "assumed that music was inviolable by social forces, or that it was immune to the process of politicization and corruption that infiltrated so many aspects of life at that time."[70]

It would be wrong to claim that "the Dutch," through the centuries, into the twentieth century, in Europe, as well as in their colonies, and into the time of the camps, did not love music. It would be even more wrong to deny that "the Germans" loved music and that—however uncomfortable it is to say it—even Nazis loved music. Hitler's and most of his "melody boys'" love of music, of course, might be limited, as one of Hitler's confidants, Albert Speer, said about Hitler, to "Wagner, marches, and operettas."[71]

Certainly, too, the German love of music, and the Nazis' namely, was often "sentimental." Joseph Wechsberg, a Jew who ran to Paris to escape Hitler, later recalled his enquiring about chances of making money by playing violin in a Paris café even after the German army occupied the city and he was stuck in it. "Business wasn't bad," he wrote.[72] There is no escape from it—there was music even in Auschwitz and, as Shirli Gilbert writes, "many considered the existence of music in Auschwitz as a logical extension of the national German passion for music."[73]

SS-Obergruppenführer Reinhard Heydrich, the architect of Hitler's "final solution," the annihilation of European Jewry, was a well-known connoisseur of classical music. In addition to (or together with) planning the camps, Heydrich, as Protector of Bohemia and Moravia, was known as a generous supporter of the Czech Philharmonic.

ss-Obersturmbannführer Adolf Eichmann, a few ranks under Heydrich, and supervising Theresienstadt in particular, was known among his peers for putting together a string quartet from among his subordinated: he played the second violin.[74] In his essay "Listening," Jean-Luc Nancy wrote, "Nazism treats and mistreats in its way the musical arts . . . but Nazism also benefited from an encounter [with music], which was not a chance one."[75] ss men, in uniform or in civilian clothes, it was the general knowledge, regularly visited concerts in Theresienstadt, and listened.

The Dutch, certainly, were not Nazis. Boven Digoel, if only because in Boven Digoel the echoes of Auschwitz were not heard so loudly, was much softer a case. Softer in a sense of music, too, less sharp, less tragic, and less glorious.

"People like to play music," Mas Marco wrote in one of his letters from the camp, "and they also like to be invited to the Dutch controller's house, for the pleasure of it, to play jazz or kroncong or whatever. . . . On the night between the last November 20 and 21, as some people are telling us, the musical ensemble 'Liberty' made of the internees from section B of the camp, was invited to the Dutch controller's house and gave a concert. They played for him and for his wife." "We do not know this with an absolute certainty and it might be just a rumor," Mas Marco continued, "but, if this is true, we are even less certain than we were till now about what kind of people these internees are. Where do they belong? They are Communist, right?"[76]

Mas Marco was one evidently angered by this. In another letter, to be sent with the next ship, he wrote on the subject of music again, "On August 31, 1929, from the house of the camp administrator, J. Block, music was heard. . . . We could only wonder: Do these people as they play, still call themselves the leaders of the people?"[77] Salim, our source for much in the camp, might actually be one of the people playing or listening on these or other occasions, and he made no apology. "After a day of work," Salim, who worked in the camp hospital, wrote in his Boven Digoel memoirs, "we were sometimes invited to the doctor's house. On the front porch of his house 'the Big Uncles' were sitting, the camp administrator, his assistant, our doctor, and one or several of the camp section chiefs. We, the internees, took a place below the porch, on the grass, and in the back of the house."[78] "For an outsider," Salim wrote on another but related subject of music, "and especially for the hard-liners among the Dutch, it was not to be easy to understand this. But we had learned our songs in schools, the Dutch songs, of course. I had been one of the thousands of the Indonesian children," wrote Salim, "who sang Dutch songs since they sat in their grammar-school forms, sang at the top of their voices, and still did in the camp."[79]

All things musical, serious, melancholic, mournful, frivolous, sentimental, revolutionary, or a combination of one or more of the above had been appreciated and practiced everywhere as fashion, a matter of good taste, good manners, and personal dignity. In the camps, music meant radically more. It was all that, and a matter of utmost seriousness, "at the edge of life."[80]

Jiří Weil, waiting in Prague for transport to Theresienstadt, wrote a half story and half diary, as he was expecting the call. At one moment, in the story-diary, he happened to find himself in one of the eateries in the city still opened to the Jews. The people finished eating and four musicians appeared and began to play. "The room grew silent. . . . It was good to sit quietly and listen. I knew that the bloodstains would not appear on the walls of the sanctuary. I knew that people would not writhe when fear caught them by the throat. I knew there was no huddled and trampled city and there never had been. . . . 'Thank you very much,' I said . . . when the musicians finished playing. 'It's a good thing, this music. I never knew that before.'"[81]

The music, in all its triviality, beauty, power, and urgency, helped to establish the camp (or the eatery where the Jews waited for the camp)—the camp order, canon, structure, rhythm, melodies, pitch, harmony, and intonation. John Cage, in his *Silence*, does not mention camps. But his book, like his music, is definitely of and about the time and music of the camps. Cage wrote, and there hardly could be a less-canonical musician than he, "For music, we can substitute a more meaningful term: organization of sound."[82] "For composer," Cage wrote, and he could add for listener as well, we can use even "a more meaningful term," "organizer of sound." "Sound," John Cage wrote, is a "frame."[83]

Music, wrote Ernst Bloch in "The Philosophy of Music," had always a "basilican solidity," always had been "tonal edifice," and it builds "tonal space."[84] More specifically and more to the history of the camps, according to Max Horkheimer and Theodor Adorno in *Dialectic of Enlightenment*, "The utopia which inspired the hopes of the French Revolution had been absorbed potently and impotently into German music and philosophy." Music and philosophy, Horkheimer and Adorno wrote, became "the established bourgeois order [of] entirely functionalized reason."[85]

In 1942 in Theresienstadt, Viktor Kohn composed "Prelude in EDE," a string quartet based on the first three letters of the name of Jacob Edelstein, the first Head of the camp Council of the Elders. The composer instructed the performers on the first page of his prelude: *"poco grave,"* "a little seriously."⁸⁶ By its sublime power of harmony, rhythm, and intonation, even in the wildest cacophony of the Boven Digoel jazz band or in the to-the-limit avant-garde "silence" of John Cage, music demanded order and, indeed, it sounded by an inevitability of repetition, of motifs and phrases, of music.

In Boven Digoel, the police records are full of reports on *repetitie*, Dutch for "repetition" or "rehearsal." One may say "routine." The word "repetitie" appeared as often as "music" and perhaps more. In repetitie, there was the action, the order, and the sense of music.

SATURDAY, APRIL 27, 1940 ... NIGHT: ... 8:30 ... It is still raining. Camp is calm. In the house of Soehoena[?] there is a repetitie ...⁸⁷

King Philip V of Spain, suffering from depression, is said to have given a large pension to the celebrated Italian castrato Farinelli, "so he would sing the same song to him every evening for fourteen years: as if monotony (repetition) by itself were enough to create the retreat."⁸⁸ Sigmund Freud famously argued that repetitive motifs (in dreams) allude to suppressed content. Closer to Boven Digoel, among the Javanese, a mystical practice of *zikir* or *dhikr* was and still is believed to keep or regain spiritual balance. The practice consists of "continuous repetition of a few sacred words or phrases, and rhythmic movements of the head and body."⁸⁹

"I always rehearsed from half past 9 a.m. to 10 a.m.," Alice Herz-Sommer remembered about her playing piano in Theresienstadt, "and after me came Hans Krása."⁹⁰ One can hear the camps as monotony, unbearable unless one hears music. It does not change the deadliness of the monotony, but it makes it musical, and by that virtue, unchallengeable.

People were modern before they came to the camps, and they became even more so in the camps. They used music to bear the monotony. And they succeeded in becoming more musical, and thus more of the camps. Salim, close to losing his mind in the camp (actually, there are reports of him going insane for few months), became "into music." "This was," he recalled, "how I came more to terms with the place, with the jungle around us, and how I made myself at peace with the woods and the beasts, how I was able to learn that the stillness and the loneliness around me had been a consequence of my perceptions not yet fully in control." "I came to terms," Salim wrote, and he might have written, "I made myself to listen." Salim continues: "The sounds ... the voices ... the space ... the solitude that can be made beautiful. ... Promptly at 5:15 p.m., a single cicada begins to hum.

Then, from a distance the soloist is joined by a choir; a high-pitch melody begins and slowly moves, and in an increasing forte. As the clock strikes six, the conductor ticks the music away. Then, there is a pause, just a monotonous croaking of the bullfrogs, and then—the big *bedug* drum can be heard from the mosque."[91]

Only applause was missing—not a rupture and not a chasm: clapping hands. As in Theresienstadt. "A wonderful baritone," Adler wrote about one concert in the Theresienstadt camp. "Encores. . . . The hall was full, and the applause was thundering."[92]

There exists a photograph from one of the Theresienstadt concerts. This is, actually, a still from the Nazi propaganda film about the camp, a fake as fake-ish a fake can be, but music—music sublime—is there. The faces of the internees, listening, in the cave, one feels a chill over how this fake is real. A few rows of people are visible, sitting on chairs; the men all in suits and ties, the women in fine dresses, the concert code. It is written on their faces, as they put them on, they are absorbed by the music. All of them, of course, have a yellow star on their concert best.[93]

The modern world, since the outset of the modern times, first in Europe and then in widening circles beyond, was increasingly into music and ultimately becoming music (like Ulysses trying to hear the Sirens, letting himself be tied to his mast[94]). The camps again were a step to the ultimate. "If it were possible simultaneously to reawaken all the echoes of the memory," Roland Barthes wrote in the late twentieth century, "they would form a concert—perhaps pleasant, perhaps painful, but in any case logical, and without dissonance."[95]

The beauty and the power of music, and camps produced music close to perfection, has been in its being a frame and an order—an order of the limit, the beauty and the power to play, *poco grave* or *stürmisch bewegt*, and to stop, as a conductor or a guard pointed out:

> SATURDAY, AUGUST 25, 1934 . . . NIGHT. . . . 12:10. The ROB goes in the direction from where the music of krontjong is heard. It is the house of internee Padmohoetomo. The agent warns them that the time is already past the hour. They stop. Done.[96]

EIGHT

Radio

The steeple of the Catholic church in the neighboring village could be seen from Theresienstadt's walls and from windows on the higher floors of some barracks. It would be just a short walk to the village if not for the walls and the closed gates. But throughout the camp, in all its corners, the bells from the steeple could be heard.

Everything was done by the authorities, Nazi as well as colonial, to separate the camps from the outside world—including making the camps soundproof. "The Romans," Anton Chekhov reminisced during his visit to the other camps, the Tsarist penal colonies on Sakhalin, "had a form of exile called *deportatio in insulam* (deportation to an island). The main islands utilized for this were Sardinia, Crete, Cyprus, and Rhodes."[1] Boven Digoel and Theresienstadt were to be something close to the islands.

The prison and camp in Pol Pot's Cambodia was Tuol Sleng, Office S-21. It stood in the very middle of the bustle of Phnom Penh, the country metropolis. "In front, the buildings were covered with dense barbed wire, in an attempt to prevent anyone from committing suicide by jumping down the building." In the main building, "each room was closed with glass windows in order to minimize the sound of screaming prisoners during tortures."[2] Some ancient teachers of the Torah spoke "of a world in which prayers cannot pierce the sky, for all the heavenly doors are closed except that through which the tears of the injured pass."[3] Thus, as one can see even from this, there was always some thinking, or fantasy, about getting through.

In Boven Digoel, distance served as the most effective barrier, and not least a sound barrier. This clearly had been a crucial part of the Dutch design when the site for the camp was being decided on, so far from what the authorities considered to be the civilized world—and its sounds. Krarup Nielsen made the measurements as he as a Dane saw it: "The distance from Batavia, the capital of the Indies, to the communist camp on the Digoel River is about the same as the distance from Copenhagen to the North Pole." "Or," he added, "if one prefers the warmer parts, the distance between Batavia and Boven Digoel is like that from Copenhagen to the middle of Sahara."[4]

A Dutch observer, Anthony van Kampen, put it a Dutch way: "Journey from Batavia to Boven Digoel," he wrote, "can take longer than a journey from the Netherlands to the Indies."[5] "To be in Boven Digoel," van Kampen wrote, unnecessarily, "is like to be on the other side of the globe."[6] The Boven Digoel camp was placed about four hundred kilometers from the sea; at the time of the camp, it took a steamer three days and three nights to get up the river from the sea.[7] In the words of Marcus van Blankenstein, the internees traveled on the steamer from the sea to the camp "along the endless disconsolateness of the river, with the banks on both sides covered by [a] dense and uninterrupted wall of jungle."[8]

A Dutch deputy, van Helsdingen of the Volksraad [People's Council], an advisory council of the Indies governor-general, declared in November 1926 as the rebellion was still in progress and Boven Digoel still in the planning stages, "We have always feared Communism, and now it became bloody serious."[9] "Boven Digoel must be on lock and key," was the Indies government response, "it must be tightly closed to all of the outside world."[10]

A former governor of West Java and a member of Raad van Indië, the "Council of the Indies," W. P. Hillen, the highest Dutch official ever to visit Boven Digoel, reported on his inspection tour in 1930, "In the whole of the Dutch Indies there is probably no spot of land where an isolation of a group of people is so complete as in Boven Digoel."[11] Salim described the isolation from the position of an internee, recalling what happened when the government steamer, once every six weeks or so, arrived at the camp. Like everyone in Boven Digoel, he called the steamer "the white ship": "The white ship was the only grasp of the outside world we had. As the ship, by a timetable we knew only vaguely, might be expected to arrive, everyone in the camp wandered impatiently, and toward the downstream, to be most of the time as far down the river as possible. And when we thought we heard the ship's horn from a distance, we all jumped up, with joy, beyond ourselves!"[12]

Theresienstadt was only sixty kilometers from Prague, "set in the Bohemian tranquility of low rolling hills and verdant woods and fields,"[13] in the midst of a familiar, indeed idyllic, setting. There was no impenetrable forest, there seemed to be no impassable distance, and there was no sea. Still, the Nazi ordinances, like the one published on February 26, 1942, stated with confidence and categorically that the Jews would be isolated in the camp. "Isolation," not unlike in Boven Digoel, was a crucial part of the concentrated-camps plan—acoustic isolation not least. The Jews were deported to the camp "in order to prevent whispering propaganda and other subversive activities ... emanating from the Jews."[14] The voices, dimmed already, were to be blocked completely. Isolation, the same thing as concentration, was like the most chilling moment in Dostoyevsky's *Crime and Punishment*, "a door slammed ... a whisper."[15]

"The state of affairs the Nazis wished to create," Zygmunt Bauman wrote in *Modernity and the Holocaust*, "was one of total *Entfernung*—an effective removal of the Jews from the life-world of the German race."[16] If a noise, a sound, or a voice reached the camp from the outside, it arrived modified, and changed often beyond recognition, borne by the walls, by the distance, and by the jungle.

These were not the sounds as emitted in the outside world. They were now sublimely the sounds of the camps. The camp people heard them as the camp, the distance, the jungle, and the walls sound, enriched by the camp people's efforts to grasp the outside world. Mixed with the noises and voices emitted by the camps themselves, the voices, the orders, the whispering, the music, secondhand, they made the camp acoustically complete. "Our camp was so remote, so lonely, so still!" Salim writes, and then he defines the stillness: "The depth of the jungle ... the cry of the animals ... the dragged-out screams from all directions ... the drums of Papuans."[17]

"Like in a fever," Salim recalled, "we have hoped that some awareness of our camp would inspire real protest against our internment, certainly in Holland. There were some speeches given, by some individuals and some groups, but not a single real action. We were bitterly disillusioned!"[18] "A storm of tragic sympathy rages through bourgeois hearts, the kind that always starts buzzing when it's already too late," Kurt Tucholsky wrote about

Europe at the time, but he would be correct about all the other bourgeois-buzz places, and Boven Digoel, too.[19] I once asked an Indonesian friend about the buzz between the camps and the world outside of the camps. He was born after Boven Digoel, but both his father and grandfather were Communists and they talked about it often. He told me, "They in the camp concluded that those in the outside did not speak anymore."[20]

Peter Kien was a young poet, painter, and musician waiting in 1942 to be sent to Theresienstadt. He managed to send a message to a friend who was already in the camp: "There are so few people here," he wrote about Prague still at large.[21] The Jews who were to be sent to Theresienstadt, when their turn came, had to get to the point of departure at the outskirts of Prague on foot or by the tram. "The passengers on the streetcar," Ruth Bondy recalls, "saw the numbered bundles, the eyes red from crying, the farewell glances to the beloved city, and averted their eyes."[22] Not a word, too; luckily the streetcars in Prague were so noisy that a word would not be heard anyway.

There was a new sound to the cities from which the Jews were going—a camp sound, already, in a sense. The people in Prague, for instance, who did not go, or did not go yet, more than before, according to Peter Demetz, consumed "volumes of poetry, eagerly bought theater tickets, and went to movies more often than before (there were three performances daily in every movie house)." Young people, Demetz recalled, more than before, did "listen to, or play jazz music, old and new."[23] When the Philharmonic orchestra in Prague played Smetana's *Má vlast* [My Homeland], Ruth Bondy (who was soon to go) recalled, "the audience burst into enthusiastic applause which lasted fifteen minutes and the conductor kissed the notes."[24]

Some non-Jews, the Czech gendarmes, who helped the ss to police the camp, or some civilians who for some reason got special permission to enter the camp, might risk their lives and talk to the internees, of course, in a whisper.[25] On June 5, 1942, the Jews of Theresienstadt were awakened at five in the morning. "Every one of the residents of the settlement," Gonda Redlich wrote, "was forced to swear by his signature that he did not see the backpack, the bicycle, or gun of the assassin."[26] They might just guess, and it was only whispered among the Jews in the camp, that in that immense distance of sixty kilometers and behind the walls, ss-Obergruppenführer Reinhard Heydrich, the protector of Bohemia and Moravia, was assassinated by a Czech commando sent from London. The Nazi revenge followed in the Czech lands, the real bloodbath, but also it reached the camp in echoes.

The sound of the camps was closed on itself and complete in itself. There were spies in both Boven Digoel and Theresienstadt, the whispers of the spies and about the spies became one with the noises, the voices, and the music.

A group of German women were employed in Theresienstadt by the SS administration. They "cleaned the houses," but, as everybody was aware, "cleaning," they searched for anything forbidden. They were widely believed to steal the internees' property, and they also listened.[27] There was, improbably and whispered about, but in fact real as it became known after the war, "a specially privileged group made of informants of whom some came to the camp already in the service of the SS."[28] "There are Jewish spies in Theresienstadt," wrote Philipp Manes in his camp diary, "who for loathsome reasons betray their own kin."[29] Hans Günther Adler quoted an SS document he saw after the war, a report from just before the end of the war and camp, from late April 1945: "During the recent days, a Jewish informer reports that people in certain circles talk about the surge in the traffic on the roads through and around Theresienstadt. Rumors about it are spreading throughout the camp."[30]

In the letters and memories of Boven Digoel internees, spies were mentioned all the time. Rarely anyone, they wrote and recalled, could be trusted in the camp—the former leaders included.[31] There are a number of documents in the Boven Digoel archives that point the same way.

Report by [name withdrawn by me—R. M.], age twenty-five years, born in Batavia, now of section C of the camp, Boven Digoel, September 26, 1933

QUESTION: *Describe what happened* . . .

ANSWER: On Wednesday, at about 8:30 in the evening the chief of section C called me to his office and instructed me to go to the house of Djaka Dt. Tan Mohamad. A gathering was planned in the house that evening, and I was instructed to report on what would happen there, to remember the names of those who would be there, and to listen to speeches if some are given.[32]

"Internee Moh. Sanoesi," Mas Marco wrote in a letter home, "is suspected to be a spy." In an effort to convince his comrades that he was not a spy, Mas Marco wrote, "Moh. Sanoesi performed some acts as though he was radically against the authorities, like nailing an anti-government leaflet on the fence in front of his house."[33] In the Boven Digoel archives there are also a few letters written by the spies themselves:

BOVEN DIGOEL, JULY 25, 1929

Information For the Highly Esteemed Mr. Assistant Resident in Boven Digoel

Most respectfully! I timidly report that the people arrested yesterday were the right people. But there are still others who are dangerous. They move around the camp every hour of day or night, and they visit homes of other <u>left-wing</u> people. In my humble opinion, their leaders are <u>Bahroedin Said</u> and <u>Soeleman Bastari</u>.... In deepest respect, [the name withdrawn—R. M.] section B of the camp.[34]

The words "left-wing" and the names "Bahroedin Said" and "Soeleman Bastari" are underlined in a pencil different from that of the informant. Clearly, the recipient of the report, the Dutch assistant resident, took notice.

The more the camps were filled with noises, sounds, and voices, whispers and silences, the more complete and self-enclosed they were. The camp acoustics, to use the words of Joseph Roth, not about camps, but about Paris of the time of the camps, was "vibrations created in space and returning to space."[35]

A boy in Theresienstadt, Petr Ginz, exceptionally and extraordinarily sensitive, the chief editor of the boys' magazine *Vedem*, wrote one day about hearing or rather about a dream of hearing:

I dream of hearing the coolie curse in Shanghai and Singapore, the fishermen in Newfoundland, the farmers in Ceylon, the geishas in Japan, the pearl fishers in the Bay of Bengal.

And one day, having learnt about the world and its people through their swearwords, I would return home by steamer across the Pacific. The noise of the ship's screws would lull me and, calmed, I would fall asleep and in my mind the throbbing of the propeller would chant Homer's verses:

Soundly he slept through the night
Sweet dreams his only fetters.[36]

It was suggested that asthma influenced Marcel Proust's "physiology of style" of his *In Search of Lost Time*, and his syntax, which "rhythmically, step by step, enacts his fear of suffocation."[37] For the Jews, for those who prayed, God was reached, or not, by their voice: "Hear, O Israel!" "To be human" for a Muslim, Clifford Geertz wrote, is "to hear in inhalation and exhalation the literal voice of God pronouncing his own name—*hu Allah*."[38]

Such a capacity was certainly acutely present in the camps, too. One of Petr Ginz's friends, also his age, later recalled how they listened at night, in the closed rooms and closed camp: "We listened to the death rattle of the dying and the heavy breathing of couples having sex."[39]

Each camp resounded like Plato's cave. Yet the acoustics of camps was a modern acoustics, state-of-the-art acoustics, with the noises, sounds, voices, and even the echoes to be possibly switched and channeled. The camps were an apparatus as much as a cave.

"Theresienstadt," wrote Philipp Manes about his camp, "is as if it were enwrapped in a sheet of fine and sensitive silver-paper that registers all the energy of the camp." "The news," Mr. Manes wrote, "move fast," "they create an echo that cannot be checked against the original, that is separated from it and mixes with another echo from minute to minute."[40] "The Theresienstadt ghetto," Mr. Manes wrote, "is as delicate and sensitive as a volumeter in an electrical machine. We have no newspaper that would give us news from the outside.... We hear about heavy bombing of German cities...."[41]

The "radio news" became a life-absorbing phenomenon. In the camps the news molded what might become "postmodern bodies." "Biological bodies," wrote Carlo Caduff in *The Pandemic Perhaps* sixty years later, "have increasingly begun to circulate in informational forms, rather than corporeal ones."[42] Already in the camps, as they became the fashion, the bodies became the news.

Hardly ever before, noise, sound, and voice, enwrapped as in tinfoil, sublime in its insubstantiality, overwhelming, moving fast in a closed circuit, so rich in echoes and so ephemeral—was so *instant*. *Instant*, according to a dictionary, means

1. happening or coming immediately; (of food) processed to allow quick preparation; (of a person) becoming a specified thing immediately or very suddenly; prepared quickly and with little effort; producing immediate results; 2. urgent; pressing. 3. *dated* (in business letters) of the current month; 4. *archaic:* of the present moment

The instantness of the camps had been unprecedented. The instantness may be the epitome and even a model for, and a preview of, what Maurice

Blanchot later defined as "actual": "The time when all . . . truths are stories, when all stories are false; no present, nothing but what is actual."[43]

"Rumors are being spread," Gonda Redlich wrote in his Theresienstadt diary on February 27, 1943, touched deeply by the news but not believing it really: "They say that Churchill is dead."[44] In early March, Redlich wrote again, "Parachutists came down upon northern France (note: not true)." And the same day he wrote, "In a conference, the Germans proposed a Jewish state in Alaska, Rhodesia, or Madagascar."[45] Pavel Weiner heard the same things or, rather, listened to the same news:

> JULY 14, 1944, . . . It is rumored that there is a revolution in France, but it doesn't appear to be correct. The rumor probably came about because today is the French national holiday.[46]

> SEPTEMBER 25/26, 1944 . . . All through Theresienstadt, there are rumors about transport . . . that there is a general strike of workers and the railroad people and the railroad tracks are not usable . . . that the railroad cars are not available."[47]

"There was a joke going around in the camp," wrote Emil Utitz in his *Psychology of Life in Theresienstadt Concentration Camp*, "that the war was being moved forward by our gossips." "Judged by what was rumored in the camp," Utitz added, "Africa had been liberated when they were in fact still fighting for Tubruk and Italy capitulated long before the Allies landed in Sicily."[48]

Even the freedom, how could it be otherwise, arrived as a rumor, or instant truth. Eva Ginzová (Chava Pressburger), a younger sister of Petr Ginz, wrote in her own Theresienstadt diary about the last days and hours of the camp:

> APRIL 23, 1945 . . . those who came from Litzmanstadt and Birkenau, what they had to tell! Auschwitz and Birkenau are really the same. Everyone who arrived by transport in Birkenau was immediately stripped and classified. Children under fourteen and people over fifty went immediately into the gas chambers and then were cremated. . . . I wouldn't have believed it if those who had lived through it hadn't told me themselves. I am so worried about what has become of our Petr [who had gone to Auschwitz]. Is he still alive at all?[49]

This was the first time people in Theresienstadt, except some in the Council of the Elders, learned—but still did not believe it. "Rumors aren't always wrong, that's what's so frightening, that shred of truth," wrote Louis-Ferdinand Céline in his *Rigadoon*.[50] The world became "inundated with news," wrote Javanese poet Ranggawarsita in the late nineteenth century, before Céline and before the camps, but already, *actually*, true about the camps:

> With rumors borne on lying lips,
> What merit then in having faith
> In foolish senseless news
> That only breaks the heart.[51]

In gossiping, and in passing the word along, as in "scribbling" and in "idle talk," said Martin Heidegger, a "lack of ground" is signified. The gossiping and passing the word along, the scribbling and the idle talk, however, at the same time, said Heidegger, "guard against the danger of getting stranded." As one "says something groundlessly," nothing seems "closed off any longer."

It is, Heidegger wrote, "uprooted understanding" that makes one feel that one "is still always together with the 'world,' with others, and toward itself."[52] Everything seems to be "in 'the best order,'" and "all doors open." "This tranquillization," as Heidegger called it, makes one "restlessly knowing it all."[53] The Javanese *Recitation of Gatuloco* said, in fact sang, the same: "The gossip you swallow, caring naught for truth. And so you live your lives incapable of death."[54]

Boven Digoel also resounded in its isolation. Like the Theresienstadt camp, in the jungle and at a distance, as if enwrapped in the sensitive silver paper, like a cave and like an apparatus.

This was also a space resounding with rumors. In one especially memorable case, early in 1933, the real news reached Boven Digoel of a mutiny on the Dutch cruiser *De Zeven Provinciën* off the coast of Sumatra. A number of Indonesian sailors were also involved in the mutiny. "The simpler souls among us," Salim recalled, "began to hope. They even came up with 'an information' that the cruiser was about to steam up the Digoel River, to 'knock out' the camp masters, to take us all internees on board and sail to freedom."[55] Doctor Schoonheyt, as always, sneering, or perhaps anxious—he lived in the same camp acoustic space, too—described the moment: "The way in which the reports about the mutiny were received in the camp was amusing. Many internees accepted it as something beyond doubt that the huge cruiser would steam up the tortuous river, that the liberation would take place, and that the internees would cruise around the archipelago in a victory lap." "Only some among the internees seemed to understand," the doctor wrote, "that the mutiny had never had any chance except to fail."[56]

The mutiny on *De Zeven Provinciën* was over in a matter of days. The ship was bombed from the air and the mutineers capitulated. One of the Indonesians among them, in fact, was sent to Boven Digoel.[57] Still the rumor kept reverberating and circulating, and he could do nothing against it. In the wake of another wave of real news, of the Japanese attack on Pearl Harbor in December 1941, and the beginning of the Pacific war, as an echo of *De Zeven Provinciën*, "some internees" listened and whispered again: "The Japanese are about to advance on the camp and they will liberate us all."[58]

The Japanese armies advanced, but they seemed to care about Boven Digoel as little as the outside world in general. Still, a handful of Japanese planes appeared in the skies over Boven Digoel. They even dropped a few bombs on the camp. "The authorities issued an order," ex-internee Joesoef Mawengkang recalled; "We were not to go outside of our houses when a plane appeared. If it happened at night, we were not supposed to make fires in the open. Several times the Japanese planes flew low over the camp and we always ran outside and waved with all we had, sheets, shirts, shorts, everything."[59]

Through the rumors, borne by the walls, the jungle, and the distance, the sheet of silver paper, the camps came into their truth and truly became a part of the world, the world as acoustic space. Rumors became the truth finally, as they had been becoming, gradually through at least two centuries of modern times. In the camps, there was little else than rumor as truth. The camps led the way. They became the sound core of the world.

....

In Theresienstadt the way in which the camp truth of the news traveled was called by the internees themselves JPA, Jüdische Presse-Agentur, the "Jewish Press Agency."[60] *Bonke* was another word widely used, in the plural *Bonken* or *Bonkes*. Philipp Manes explained that it was "a name for every rumor, untrue but needed." "In Theresienstadt," he added, "this word was used every day, and when someone referred to a news item as a *Bonke*, it meant that one should seriously doubt it."[61]

"Even hearsay is a being-in-the-world," wrote Martin Heidegger, as if he knew that he was telling the truth about the world coming, but especially about the camps as they already were.[62] The camp people of Boven Digoel, according to Mas Marco, "were the world's best experts in 'cooking.'" "All the news in Boven Digoel," he explained, "as a 'cook' gets them in his kitchen, became a menu item, or even a dish fantasy." The "cook" spices the news, makes it raw, or medium- or well-cooked. The only rule is that the particular news tastes good and sells well.[63]

In Theresienstadt, Bonkes were also called "latrine news." It meant "news made in latrine, guaranteed."[64] Most properly, also in Theresienstadt, the Bonkes news, echoes traveling around, now stopping, now moving again, in a circle, recharging themselves on the way, were called "tram conductor's stories."[65]

Since the late nineteenth century, the world had increasingly been filled with a new noise, sound, voice, music, and news, actual, instant, circulating, and long-distance, intimate in its vibration, and difficult to "check" back to its source. As it was coming to the moment of the camps, this new sound found its truth and strength in radio. "Young people," Peter Demetz wrote about the Europe of his youth, in the mid- and late 1930s, "excitedly listened to transatlantic musicians." Many of the youth, Demetz wrote, as war broke out in Europe, became "the swing kids, . . . whether in uniform or not."[66] Many went to the camps.

Whether voices or music, or the noise of searching among the stations, radio was always that new thing. By the power of the wonderful new apparatus, the world came close to resembling the camps and the camps to resembling the world. It was a jazzy moment very much. Jazz had been prohibited in Germany since 1933, when the Nazis took over. But the German "*Luftwaffe* pilots listened to jazz on the BBC." "Everywhere" people listened for news, but they got excited by jazz.[67] In the 1930s, at the time of the camps, radio jazz became a rage.

It was not the first time in history when people, to speak with Rousseau, "grasped nothing" and "sensed everything."[68] But never before had the "grasping nothing" and "sensing everything" come so close to the Heideggerian "being-in-the-world" or "closer to the truth." "Do not come near," Peter Kien, a young man, a painter and a poet, wrote in Theresienstadt, "do not come near! . . . Do not come nearer! Love us from afar!"[69] Walls and distance in the camps were all that remained of touching. All the touching had been "condensed" in them, in the walls and the distance—as a long-distance sound.

As a way of grasping, and of gathering all that remained of touching in the camps, a sudden and radical sense of a possibility has arisen. One might listen to a medium, in which the wall and the distance could be negotiated or even pierced. The camp people, ultimately, seemed to grasp what modern people before and outside the camps felt still vaguely: that radio sound, noise, voice, and music, and perhaps they, the listeners, with it, might cut through walls, jungle, and distances. One might even begin to think, in the concentrated, condensed space of the camps, that the piercing and cutting or flying over through the radio might approximate freedom.

The main figure in J. M. G. Le Clézio's novel *The Interrogation* at one moment mumbles to himself, "All the components of the telephone are present in the rhinoceros."⁷⁰ He might be talking about progress in general, as instant and actual.

Long before the camp in the garrison town Theresienstadt came into being, in the rhino time of the camp, all the components of radio, the sounds instant, actual, and long-distance, were already present in the place. In June 1790 was the last test of the new fortress: "The fortress consisted from the outer, middle and inner zones, all connected through an extended network of underground passages of various sizes and functions. The full length of the hallways and galleries for the conduct of water [namely flooding the fortress in the case of enemy attack] *and for listening* reached close to thirty kilometers."⁷¹ A signal given at the commanding post of the fortress had to be clearly heard throughout all barracks and fortifications. In the same way, the camp internees suspected that all sounds, any word spoken at any point of the fortress, could be heard in the commanding—say, listening—post.

"The acoustics in the barracks and in courtyards is splendid," wrote Philipp Manes, who besides being a diarist, and in charge of the Orientation Section of the camp police, was known in the camp as a lover of the arts, and an organizer of the musical events. "When one keeps quiet," Mr. Manes wrote, "every single word, however softly spoken, and every tone, however *piano*, come through crystal clear."⁷² In Theresienstadt, all the components of radio had long been present. But in the camp, crystal clear, actual, instant, and long-distance, they came together.

According to the "General Order of the Jewish Self-Administration" issued on January 5, 1943, and it was only an assertion of standing policy, "It is absolutely forbidden to any ghetto inhabitant to own, or listen to, radio."⁷³ On Thursday, July 20, 1944, one of the rare events, Pavel Weiner was assigned to go outside of the camp's walls, under a Czech gendarme escort, and pick up linden tree blossoms: "We go to the Bohušovice road just outside of the Ghetto.... As we pass the guard [at the gate], we are in the fields, and can see the Aryan highway.... We can see free people, buses, meadows, and houses. Right next to the linden alley, there is a little house belonging to a gravedigger.... The window is open and I can hear the sound of radio coming from the inside of the little house, something I haven't heard for a very long time."[74]

Radio was not physically present in the camp, for the internees certainly, but the more so radio sounded in the camp—and the more than radio it was. The boys' magazine *Vedem* published a regular "Cultural Report" in its issues. "Cultural Report no. 1" reported, "Last week a wonderful lecture series program began [in our dormitory]. The first two lectures had been delivered: Liebstein on television and Ginz on Buddhism."[75]

"On Sunday, November 7, 1943, between 18:00 and 19:30, in the garret under the roof of the barracks on the Langestrasse no. 5, a 'children's revue' by Nora Frýd, *Radiovlnka* [The Little Radio Wave] had been performed for the camp public for the first time."[76] A sketch of the stage set has survived. The Prague Jewish internee-painter Adolf Aussenberg created a "broadcasting studio," with what appears as sound-mixing tables and a set of two amplifiers.[77]

Josef Taussig, the young communist and short-story writer who would soon be reciting Rilke and the Bible to his friends through the fence in Auschwitz, also wrote a short text, "A Radio Reportage from Theresienstadt," to be performed in the camp, "an imaginary radio event," as it is remembered, "with an announcer, chorus and individual voices, full of sparkling humor and acid parodies."[78] The props for this show were a microphone and a red sign that flashed at given moments, "Silence, we are on air!"[79]

Viktor Ullmann's famous Theresienstadt camp opera *Der Kaiser von Atlantis* was as much about death as about radio. Death, as the opera opens, is tired and disgusted by all the new easy, mechanical, and mass ways of killing that take away Death's ancient and decent job. Death refuses to be part of this sham anymore and goes on strike. Without Death, people cannot die, even the terminally ill and those already standing on the gallows. In the end, however, Death is persuaded that things cannot go on this way forever. He will go back to work, but the Emperor, who is guilty of the situation his empire is in, must be the first to die.

The opera is a piece of European musical culture. Among other examples, the Emperor's aria as he departs to die, his "Der Abschied," "The Farewell," is a musical citation of Mahler from his *Das Lied von der Erde* [The Song of the Earth]. The finale of the whole opera is a variation on Martin Luther's sixteenth-century choral *Ein feste Burg ist unser Gott* [A Mighty Fortress Is Our God].[80]

At the same time, even as the curtain raises, before the story begins, "Loudspeaker," a singer playing a loudspeaker, appears on the proscenium, and the first words he sings before the curtain are "Hallo, Hallo." The drama evolves as the Emperor of Atlantis "sits in his study with a telephone and radio that connect him with his ministers." "He sits at his desk before a microphone and a control panel. Next to it, there is a big loudspeaker."

> *Emperor [to his Minister]:* Call Death and get him on the phone right now ... make an announcement, drum it up in every village, at any corner, [broadcast it] on the radio.[81]

As the curtain was to go down at the end of the opera, so it was planned at least before all the cast and both authors went to Auschwitz, four main characters appear in front of the curtain and sing the final quartet: "Girl, Pierrot, Drummer and Loudspeaker."[82]

At the time of Boven Digoel, the Netherlands was a radio empire perhaps second only to Germany. I still remember my parents' precious prewar BluePoint radio in Prague with the names in gold on the dial, "Prague," of course, and "Berlin" and "Hilversum."

Even before the Dutch-Indies camp of Boven Digoel came into its existence, all the components of the radio were already there. On November 24, 1926, weeks before the first internee arrived at the camp, the office of the governor-general of the Indies instructed the government secretary of the colony (in the runic language of the telegraph), "Interning hundreds communists ... stop ... in New Guinea ... stop ... details following ... stop ... personnel and material for hospital ... stop ... radio station and guard ... stop ..."[83]

By the end of January 1927, still before the first ship with the internees arrived, radio connection was installed between Boven Digoel and Ambon, the provincial center of the eastern parts of the archipelago (connected with radio further on with Batavia). A small radio and telegraph station, first just a little hut, under a sergeant major, "was set up," and by the time Salim arrived in 1927, "it was already working."[84] Since then, there was a constant pressure to do more.

> *Report on the trip of the Resident of Ambon to Boven Digoel, September 6 to 24, 1929 ... Journey:* ... The undersigned has to warn in all seriousness the high office of the state that *Retah* [the ship on which the resident was traveling] is not yet equipped with radio![85]

Unlike in Theresienstadt, there was no order in Boven Digoel prohibiting ownership of private radio receivers. Still, I found no record of any private radio in the camp, not only among the internees but also among the

Dutch. There was just the small government radio with a sergeant major, enlarged and upgraded through the years, but nothing more.

But the camp was seen by visitors and, even more, felt by the internees as a radio camp. Krarup Nielsen, already in the camp's beginnings in 1927, wrote, "The latest news is received here, from all over the world." "It is far from being grand," he wrote about the government radio hut, "but in this place, it is as close to being the center of the contact with the whole world as one can think of."[86] "This radio connection," Dr. Schoonheyt wrote a few years after Krarup Nielsen, "is a bridge between us and the civilized world. It is what makes us feel that we do not live in a desert."[87]

SATURDAY, MAY 11, 1935, . . . AFTERNOON 4.36, Agent Soekirman goes to the administrative section of the camp. *Marconist* and radio in order.[88]

"The Red Darling" [Pacar Merah, written "patjar" at the time,] was a hero of adventure series published as cheap slim books and extremely popular in the Indies through the 1930s and into the 1940s. Strangely, they resembled the stories of the Scarlet Pimpernel, an antirevolutionary aristocrat from the time of the French Revolution.

The "real" figure behind the Indies' Pacar Merah was a revolutionary, a former chairman of the Indonesian communist party, Tan Malaka. The only thing common to the French Scarlet Pimpernel and the Indonesian Pacar Merah, but the thing that might explain the how they came together in the fiction and in the minds of the Indonesians, was the way they were always, easily, miraculously, magically escaping the police of the state, the revolutionary in France of the eighteenth century and the antirevolutionary in the Indies of the present, how *instant* and *actual* they were.

Tan Malaka, really, had not been caught, at least not for long, and thus he was never sent to Boven Digoel. Pacar Merah stories, however, were read in the camp, and his travels, escapes, and wonderful appearances all over the world were eagerly followed by the internees. Several close associates of Tan Malaka were caught and were in the camp, including the closest, Djamaluddin Tamin.

Tan Malaka—Pacar Merah—always evaded the police, he was "like an eel," never caught, he was light in touch. Much of his dealing with the world, naturally, was through radio.

In one of the better-known stories of Pacar Merah, "a secret message" is received by a group of Pacar Merah's coconspirators on a ship somewhere off Indonesian islands, escaping, and making ready for the coming revolution: "Comrades! The news from our leader arrived, via secret radio telegraph.... We will now forward the message through radio, to the Headquarters... Djaloemin signed off." Djaloemin was the fictionalized Djamaloeddin Tamin, who in real life sat in the camp. "Djaloemin is still in the cabin of the ship with his three comrades and they still listen to radio. They broadcast in a code they just invented, and which the enemy certainly will not be able to decipher."[89]

Across the jungle and the seas, and through the walls if any might be erected, the news and possibilities via radio were passing and reaching their target. Only radio could do it. "'I am so surprised,' says Djaloemin, the fictional one, not the one in the camp, "The workers' international congress is taking place in Cavite, the Philippines, in the corner of the Luzon island, distant from everywhere, and yet, the speeches, exactly as they are given at the congress, reach the workers hundreds of kilometers away. It is, of course, because the comrades installed loudspeakers and radio."[90]

Viktor Ullmann composing *Der Kaiser von Atlantis* and the internees in Boven Digoel reading Pacar Merah were like Marc Augé's sailors. They traveled, as Augé described them, solitary, hidden from one another by the swelling of the sea, but, connected via the radio, they stayed on course, neck and neck—virtually so.[91]

Radio signal was powerful because it did not get deflected by the swell of the waves, by the jungle or the walls, or the distance, because it did not mix with other sounds or voices on its way, was not hairy or sticky, was not opened to sharing; it passed through, via relays, switches, and other devices, rumors, myths, or fiction, fast and more, instant and actual. It kept clean of all possible knots and hurdles of the human complications along the way. It shot through—"long-distant."

"People spoke of messages," wrote John Cage in *Silence*, "perhaps, because they'd not heard from one another for a long time."[92] Petr Ginz, before going to Theresienstadt, still in Prague, "in a self-invented cryptograph, recorded news from the BBC transmitters, which he secretly listened to even though such activity was severely punished."[93]

> DECEMBER 8, 1941. I was at home in the afternoon. Japan has officially declared war against the United States of America.
>
> DECEMBER 9, 1941. In the morning, I did my homework. The Japanese attacked Singapore.[94]

Philipp Manes, in his sixties, already in the camp, had been experiencing the same thing. Radio seemed able to take in all the world and in an instant;

the instant lasted as long as the radio was on: "There are hills in the distance, far, behind the moats and the walls," Mr. Manes wrote. "From a house of an official, where the windows were left opened, one can hear quiet music on the radio."[95]

This was the best of the radio and of the camps, directly and uncompromisingly through the walls and over the distance—a message, and a signal. The secretary of the underground Communist cell in Theresienstadt—yes, there was such a cell and it had a secretary—was a young man, František Graus (in the 1960s, he became my professor of history at Charles University in Prague). "I retyped Marx's *Das Kapital*, Stalin's *Notes on National Problem*, and foreign radio news," Eva Štichová-Beloda, a member of the cell, recalled after the war. "Where the radio was," she added, "that I do not know; somewhere in the ghetto. I only retyped what Graus gave to me."[96]

According to another testimony, an internee whose name is given only as Drucker, a Jew from Vienna, is said to have organized a "radio underground" in the camp, with members recruited mostly from the Maccabi Zionist Youth. "One of the group," Ruth Bondy told the story, "an electronics engineer, built a radio receiver, which was hidden in the attic of the bakery building, and every evening, one of the members who understood English would listen to the BBC news broadcasts. This was how they first learned that Jews were being gassed in trucks."[97]

There is a radio machine at the Theresienstadt Memorial permanent exhibition on the site of the former camp. It strikes one immediately as too big to hide. Is it a sender, too? Still, it proves the thing that matters, that radio in the camp was a myth unbound, equally profound and modern as radio itself, the yearning for the unlimited, by the camp people then as well as by the visitor to the site now, as they look through the glass of the display case.

The truth of radio in the camps could not be doubted. In Theresienstadt, *Rundfunk* "broadcast" became *Mundfunk* [mouth-cast]. "The *Mundfunk* is amazingly organized," Philipp Manes reported.[98] "From new antennae came ancient folly, wisdom was transmitted from mouth to mouth," wrote Bertolt Brecht, who escaped the camps but lived *completely* in the time of the camps—and of radio.[99] "*Mundfunk* was a word for *Rundfunk* that was absent," wrote Adler, "the news was broadcast by *Mundfunk*."[100] "On the waves of the *Mundfunk* the most fantastic gossip was spread. One could observe how the *Mundfunk* moved from mouth to mouth [*von Mund zu Mund*].... It was a new medium,... a test tube, the news without firm evidence.... Great many *Mundfunk* news were received in rejoicing, and some in triumph. Eyes shone as we whispered to each other, as if we were tuned directly to the heavens: 'Today there is good news!'"[101]

Through the 1930s, there were extremely few radios even in the "free," off-camp Indies. When there was a radio, it was almost exclusively in the western, more modernized parts of the colony. Only in big cities and on the most up-to-date "white" plantations on certain days and certain hours of a day, radio could be listened to. At the moment of Pearl Harbor, as the Japanese began to move south, toward the Indies, as the reality of the Dutch empire crumbled, radio suddenly and radically rose into prominence.

The whole colony at that moment gathered around the radio and listened. Recalling Greta Kingsberg and her being just music in Theresienstadt, one might say about the Indies at this moment, certainly the modern part of it, if you have stripped them naked, you got radio. In Boven Digoel, the internees, the camp guards as well as officials, together, gathered around the radio. In the memories of internee Joesoef Mawengkang, "This was what we began to do. Each day at 10 o'clock in the morning, we all went to the *marconist's* place to get the news about the situation on the battle fronts—the latest broadcast."[102]

This way and through radio, the camp became the Indies and the Indies became the camp. The camp and the Indies gathered around radio—or rather, *in* radio, in the space of radio, a newly emerged fake of freedom, actual and instant, truly modern, as if without walls and barriers, *in* a long-distance nearness.

....

There were gramophones in the camps. Whatever the name or model, these record players had grown in popularity since the nineteenth century, and in the time of the camps they came into their own—like radio, and perhaps more symptomatically than radio. Like radio, in theory, they could be packed in, with the concentrated, condensed, crammed sounds and voices of the world. Unlike radio, without any wire or frequency needed, they could freeze and keep the sound. More than radio, they were the sound of the world at hand, actual, instant, long-distance, and, like NASA food, canned.

There were gramophones physically present both in Boven Digoel and Theresienstadt. They were deemed by the authorities not to be against the security of the camps or against the rules in either camp and they were permitted. They sounded as if there were no walls, no jungle, no sea, and no distance, exactly like the world in the outside, consumer fresh.

It is hard to imagine today how big the presence of the gramophone was in the world of the time. For instance, "Joseph Goebbels," writes Paul Virilio, "had sent fifty thousand fascist propaganda records to gramophone-owning households."[103]

"On Sundays," Ruth Bondy recalled of the last weeks in Prague before she and her friends went to Theresienstadt, "the Havlagah group [Zionist youth] would usually go out with the Rachel group, a sister-group of girls, to hike around Prague." "On rainy days," Bondy wrote, "the group would occasionally meet in the home of one of the members and listen to recordings of classical music."[104] Peter Kien, the librettist-to-be of *Der Kaiser von Atlantis*, described the same weeks of waiting in the same city: "It was a world full of debates and full of culture. There was beautiful music from our gramophone."[105]

After the Jews had been transported to the camps, their apartments were "cleared up," paintings and books were confiscated by the Einsatzstab Rosenberg [The Task Force Rosenberg], "for scientific studies," while "phonographs and records were delivered to the Propaganda Ministry."[106] Still, some Jews managed to pack a gramophone with the bare minimum of the allowed things to the camp.

The members of the Council of the Elders in Theresienstadt met informally, too. Namely Dr. Zucker, who became known in the camp as a music lover, also owned a gramophone. His "splendid collection" of records is often mentioned. "At Zucker's," Adler wrote in his history of the camp, "regularly, there were evenings with the concerts of gramophone music." The Zucker group for the invited had also been known as a "circle of gramophone music."[107]

There were gramophones in Boven Digoel. The world and the camp, also in this case, came together through gramophones.

Already, on the first ship with the internees, Krarup Nielsen noticed gramophones: "Among all the bags and pots and pans, there were gramophones."[108] After the embankment and throughout the camp's existence, gramophones were playing. Each time a ship with supplies, letters, and a new group of internees arrived, the Dutch doctor, the military and civilian officers "came on board of the ship at anchor to drink a glass of gin or two, sit with the crew on the afterdeck, and listen to the soft Hawaiian melodies on the gramophone." The music "floated over the river, into a distance and was coming back in echoes."[109]

The archbishop of Merauke, Adi Seputra, whose diocese included Boven Digoel at the time of the camp, let my son Jan and me in to see the

Missionaries of the Sacred Heart's warehouse in Merauke. It was a large barnlike structure. Inside there were shelves all along, and one could get on the second floor where there still were shelves along the narrow wooden galleries. The shelves were filled with the stuff left behind when a missionary died or was transferred and did not have enough space in his luggage. There were, by categories, "ethnographica" such as to be expected in New Guinea, shields, headdresses, and the plumage of the birds of paradise. There were departed fathers' walking sticks, pans and cups, even Dutch clogs, and hats, a few Borsalinos.

Not one but several shelves were given to gramophones. Some were truly ancient, of the turn of the twentieth century; most were from the 1930s, the Boven Digoel time; and some were certainly from the mission in the camp. There were records, too, stacks of records, some cracked, with labels most often scratched and faded and difficult to read. We deciphered some and it was like we could hear them: *Geschichten aus dem Wiener Wald* [Tales from Vienna Woods]; *Künstlerleben* [Life of an Artist]; Chattanooga Choo Choo—and also, from the 1930s and 1940s, Nazi or semi-Nazi *Flieger sind Sieger* [Pilots Are Victors], and *Wir fahren gegen Engelland* [Then We Sail against Engles Land].

Mrs. Widayasih recalled, "In Boven Digoel, two or three of our neighbors at least, I forgot who they were, owned a gramophone, the one with *Cap Anjing* [Dog Seal]." Mrs. Widayasih refered to RCA, of course, and "His Master's Voice" trademark. "I remember," she added, "that they played waltzes on the gramophone." The Boven Digoel ROB police, who listened, reported gramophones repeatedly:

> MONDAY, DECEMBER 3, ... NIGHT: ... 9:45 ... People appear to be in a happy mood. They walk around the camp, gather in groups, some listen to a siter, and others play a gramophone.[110]

> WEDNESDAY, JULY 1, 1937 ... NIGHT: ... 10:15 In the house of Soewarno it is still loud. They played gramophone and somebody threw a stone at the house. The agent investigates, but no one is found.[111]

> SATURDAY, OCTOBER 9, 1937 ... NIGHT: ... 9:40 ... Internees Najoan and Jahja play gramophone in the house of Kandoer...[112]

> SATURDAY, JANUARY 7, 1939 ... AFTERNOON: ... 2:05. Djalaloedin walks past the station. He says he goes to the house of Aboebakar to set up a gramophone.[113]

SATURDAY, SEPTEMBER 11, 1937 ... NIGHT: 8:50 ... Children of the internees gathered in the front yard of the Asoegari's house and they listen to a gramophone next-door, in the house of Soewarno.[114]

Mr. Trikoyo recalled that in 1935, when he was nine years old, in Boven Digoel, on the gramophone, he heard for the first time the song that later became the Indonesian national anthem, *Indonesia Raya* [Great Indonesia]:

> Uncle Abdul Hamid Loebis had a gramophone, and we have been invited to the house of Uncle Kadiroen, a friend of Uncle Loebis, next to the mosque in section B of the camp. I took my little brother Rokhmah with me, and we were sat down on the bench in the first row with Uncle Kadiroen's children, Soemono and Karno. We watched Uncle Loebis, he took a small needle and fixed it in the gramophone handle. At that time, I did not know yet that the big trumpet on the gramophone was called *loudspeaker*. Uncle Loebis then placed the needle on a black disk—and there came a music and a voice:
>
> *Indonesia my country*
> *Indonesia the beautiful...*
> *Indonesia the pure...*[115]

LIGHT

Facing the auditorium, I see that it is lit by simple petroleum lanterns that are stuck upon on simple chandeliers, like those in the streets, and now, of course, burn only very low. Suddenly, impure petroleum or a damaged wick is probably the cause, the light spurts out of one of these lanterns and sparks pour down in a broad gush on the crowded audience that forms a mass as black as earth. Then a gentleman rises up out of this mass, walks on it toward the lantern, apparently wants to fix the lantern, but first looks up at it, remains standing near it for a short while and when nothing happens, returns quietly to his place in which he is swallowed up. I take him for myself and bow my face into the darkness.

—KAFKA, *Diaries*

NINE

Clearing

The grave of Aliarcham in Boven Digoel, ca. 1934.
From Schoonheyt, *Boven Digoel*.

A space had to be opened inside the existing world in order to put the camps in it, in the middle of Europe as well as in the middle of the New Guinea jungle. There had newly to be a clearing in Martin Heidegger's sense, *Lichtung*: "To say that it is 'illuminated' means that it is cleared in itself *as* being-in-the-world . . . it *is* itself the clearing (Lichtung)."[1] "The *Lichtung* is," says Heidegger, "the clearedness of the there."[2]

"After the rebellion, in early 1927," Mrs. Ottow said in an interview after the war, "my father was asked to set up an internment camp at Boven Digoel. The family stayed after, for a while, in Ambon."[3] Mr. Trikoyo told his granddaughter what he was told by his mother: "On March 20, 1927, at eight o'clock in the morning, the cruiser *Java* anchored near Frederik Hendrik Island. . . . From the sea-faring government steamer *Java* we were transferred to another smaller white ship, which was to take us up the river to Boven Digoel. After another three days . . . on March 23, 1927 at ten o'clock in the morning, we arrived."[4] In other memories, however, in most, it seems, they arrived at night: "Dimly lit, just by two hurricane lamps, the first groups of 'exiles' and their families stepped into the camp."[5]

In Boven Digoel, at first, the people were put in "temporary barracks," which was soon to become section A of the camp. Then a second area was made ready, still close to the river, and it became section B. Still later, sections C and D were "opened," a little further away from the river, and finally sections E, F, and G still deeper into the jungle. Making the camp ready meant cutting the trees, burning the undergrowth, and thus letting in the light. "Opening" the camp meant clearing, clearedness, and, indeed, Lichtung. The stem of the word "*Licht*" means "light." Already the day after the arrival, Salim, who was among the earliest to arrive, writes, "the pioneers entered . . . the jungle. The jungle, it was where our camp . . . will arise! . . . The wild vegetation was to be undone . . . uprooted . . . burned."[6]

"They are working hard," wrote L. H. W. van Sandick, a Dutch high official who visited Boven Digoel soon afterward on inspection. "They are felling the trees and pulling out the stumps, they are digging out the roots . . . they are cutting footpaths through the jungle, into the sections of the camp to be"; and again, "they are opening the camp."[7] The space, the clearing, the Lichtung, the light, spread. "One can still see," Marcus van Blankenstein wrote a year after van Sandick, "the roots of big trees protruding through the surface here and there. Some single trees are still left standing, but they have no chance against the blowing of the wind. At the edge of the jungle, one can see strangely slumped and crooked stems without crowns."[8]

"As I have observed in my previous reports," the administrator of Boven Digoel, J. Blok, wrote to his superiors in September 1928, "a segment of the jungle where section G was to be, had been already in part cut open. But the work had to be abandoned, and it was decided, for the time being, to go on with clearing the jungle to open only six sections of the camp, sections A through F."[9]

Cutting into the forest meant cutting into the darkness. "The crowns of the trees in Boven Digoel," Dr. Schoonheyt wrote, "grow into each other and build up an almost compact canopy of leaves and branches. The sun could rarely get through and, at any time of the day, it is chilly and dark in the jungle."[10] According to Salim, the space to be cleared for the camp to be opened was "dim and primeval."[11]

....

Theresienstadt, built over the past centuries with spires, barracks and houses, moats and walls, was a Heideggerian Lichtung no less, and, at the time of the camps, as new and exemplary as Boven Digoel in the jungle.

The history of Theresienstadt as a camp began by clearing. To concentrate the Jews, the town that had stood for centuries on that site had to be cleared. The evacuation of the mostly Czech population of prewar Theresienstadt—there was one part-Jewish family in the town, some said— began as soon as the idea of the camp took its form, at latest early in 1942.[12] "The town," ss-Obersturmbannführer Adolf Eichmann declared in March 1942, "will be emptied." "*Der Räumung der Stadt*," "the emptying, eviction, of town,"[13] was to happen rapidly. As in Boven Digoel, instantly, like lightning, ahead of itself.

Order by the Reischsprotektor of Bohemia and Moravia regarding the internment of the Jews in the named settlement, February 16, 1942 . . .

Removal of the population from the town of Theresienstadt . . .

Paragraph B 1 E. People who fail to evacuate their homes in eight days beginning today, will be removed and their property will be taken over without compensation.[14]

Even before the evacuation began, almost three months before that, in fact, on November 24, 1941, at 4:30 a.m., the first transport of Jews from Prague arrived in the town. Three hundred forty-two young men were immediately put to work to make the camp ready.[15] This was the *Aufbaukommando* [Construction Commando], the people who made the beginning.

Like Boven Digoel, Theresienstadt was chosen as a site good for clearing. Other places were considered: the medieval Hussite castle Ratiboř or the eastern Bohemian town of Čáslav, for instance.[16] They were rejected, some as too nice, others as too populous, all as too heavy with memory, as it was, too difficult to clear.[17] After much deliberation, Theresienstadt had been declared "suitable."[18]

There was a new light, whether one likes the word in this context or not. It was the light of the time and it beamed on the clearings of both camps. "Deforestation made the camp possible," Dr. Schoonheyt wrote, "it opened one big sunny spot." "From whatever point does one look at the camp," the doctor wrote after almost a decade of the camp's existence, "as a result of the years-long work of trees being felled and bushes burned, the place now makes an impression of almost an unnatural enormousness."[19] "Because of the manner in which the camp was set up," Salim recalled, "too little of shade was left."[20]

"It has been evident from the first moment," a Dutch official visiting the camp noted in the third year of Boven Digoel, in 1929, "that this was not a settlement such as we can see them elsewhere in the Indies. In no ordinary village or town in Java or in other islands, do people have to live without a benefit of a cooling shade, a little of it, at least, where one can find a relief from the sun. Here, this is completely missing."[21]

"What villainy!" Gustave Flaubert wrote about an earlier history of clearing, "First they cut down the trees of liberty."[22] In Boven Digoel, "trees of freedom" were cut down, too, metaphorically, but then a new "tree" was planted to mark the cleared space. "After the first small piece of the jungle was cleared," Salim recalled, "a small official ceremony took place, in the middle of the emerging camp. On a high pole stuck in the ground, a little flag, the Dutch tricolor, was raised."[23]

In Theresienstadt, the bricks-and-stone Austrian-rococo barracks, houses, moats, and walls were not to be cleared out. Rather, much of the chiaroscuro of the past had to go. The radically new light was let in here, too, and it was hard on the eyes here as well. There was no high pole stuck in the ground with a Dutch tricolor in Theresienstadt, but there were Nazi flags, and streamers flying in the camp everywhere. There were other signs of *Geräumung* [making space]—the Catholic Church, for instance, like the pole stuck in the ground, in the very center of the "Jewish settlement," with its doors closed but with its tower clock working.

It is too easy a metaphor to describe the camps as dark places. In fact, and on principle, the camps were spots of concentrated light. The camps' being, like their fashion or their sound, were and marked the culmination of the modern history of light. The people brought to the camps against their will, and often to die, were modern people. They could not help it, and, like their clothes or music, they carried the light with them, packed, crammed, as much of it as they could. Both in fact and on principle, they were the opposites of the ancient prisoners described in the Book of Job, who

> *hate the light,*
> *know nothing of its ways,*
> *avoid its paths...*
> *have no love for the light.*[24]

In both camps, the camp people—Jews as Muslims and as Communists—were the "children of Adam," the first man, "who was given the task of gathering the divine light—the *goodness*—that escaped the vessel broken by creation."[25] Except that now, the light from the broken vessel appeared to shine really hard. As many might think now, as predicted in the eighty-ninth sura of the Koran for Muslims and all the others, a new day broke: "THE DAYBREAK . . . thy Lord standeth on a watchtower."[26]

Whatever the camp people did in the camps, they were enwrapped by the light, like Etty Hillesum's shroud, or like a sensitive silver paper that, in the words of Philipp Manes of Theresienstadt, "registers all the energy of the camp."

Whatever the camp people did, they were the light. Into the clearing, they were the light bearers.

> *Receipt for the valuables of the internees taken for safekeeping*:
> MOHAMED JACOEB. Trunk no. 20: . . . one lamp[27]

> *Content of the luggage belonging to internees*
> . . . *Soetidjah* . . . nine boxes of safety matches.[28]

> *Property of internees*
>
> . . . no. 7. one lamp (without glass) . . . no. 15 . . . two lamps . . . no. 19 one lamp (with broken glass) . . . no. 71 . . . two lamps without glass . . .[29]

Against all odds, the Jews, too, brought light in their overfilled trunks and backpacks into the clearing of Theresienstadt:

> *Warning: The contraband that will be confiscated from the Jews on arrival*:
> . . . candles, matches, cigarette lighters . . .[30]

> *List of items confiscated by the gendarme during the body search*:
>
> . . . a pocket flashlight . . .[31]

"Hanukkah candles," Ruth Bondy wrote about herself and her friends getting ready for the camp (they could be brought into the camp, evidently), "were packed within reach at the top of the knapsack."[32]

....

The camps, in fact and on principle, were toward the light. If the camps were to stay, they had to be constantly recharged.

"Among the internees in Boven Digoel," Krarup Nielsen reported about the first group of the internees, "you find carpenters, electricians, locksmiths, and smiths."[33] "Internee Soegiri was a smith," Koesalah Toer wrote in the list of the Boven Digoel people he compiled after the war.[34] There were not many peasants in Boven Digoel, in sharp contrast to the Indies population at large.[35]

List of internees in Boven Digoel according to their previous profession:

cattle herder ... clerk ... scribe ... assistant scribe ... draftsman ... cashier (in a bank) ... telephone operator ... pawn house official ... post-office employee ... railway man ... tram conductor ... sub-supervisor [*Onderopzichter*] ... nurse ... insurance agent ... Singer [sewing-machine] agent ... teacher in a religious school ... teacher in an elementary school ... assistant teacher ... mosque official ... teacher in a [Christian] mission school ... sergeant ... soldier ... marine ... mechanic ... *fitter* [?] ... chauffeur ... watchmaker, bicycle repairman, and typesetter ... gilder ... tailor ... barber ... laundryman ... village policeman ... small businessman ... batik and hat maker ... fisherman ... tanner ... coolie ... gamelan player ... wajang puppeteer [written *wayang* now] ... journalist and novelist ... circus artist ... paid propagandist ... without profession ... [36]

Internee Markoen Samirata, according to another list, was a "bookbinder," and internee Rosbi a "shipping agent."[37]

There was little, in Boven Digoel, which would fit the romantic, colonial image of "the lazy native." Theresienstadt was just an equally energetic and indeed *brilliant* disproof of an equally romantic European and Nazi stereotype of "the parasitic Jew."[38]

The members of the first transport to Theresienstadt, the Construction Commando, set the tone for the camp. They were all young and strong men between eighteen and forty years old. They volunteered to go first (in the end they would go anyway), and then they were carefully selected by a

Jewish committee, based on their competence—the *sparkle* in them, so to speak. The majority of the Construction Commando and its driving force were "technical experts and engineers and those of other practical professions."[39] Ruth Bondy lists "forty-five specialists in municipal administration, fifteen financial and one postal expert, and fourteen economists, of whom one was a transportation expert . . . six drivers and two switchboard operators."[40]

The men of the commando, the *"fabelhafte Jungs,"* "wonderful youth," as other internees in the camp came to call them, became and remained popular in the camp throughout the camp's existence. A second Construction Commando followed soon after the first, and it, too, enjoyed the high esteem of the whole camp. The "wonderful youth" became role models, and indeed—here comes the history of clearing and of the concentrated light— they became paragons of the camp, meaning the "camp's work ethos."[41]

"When someone from the Construction Commando appeared," as Theresienstadt ex-internee Franz Hahn remembered, "he was like someone above us." There was an "aura" about the members of both of the Construction Commandos.[42] "Their status secured them a good position in the camp [as good as it could be] . . . relatively high-ranking functions on the Jewish 'self-government,'" and "a certain safeguard against deportation."[43]

While in Europe it was still the wife-in-the-household time, 40 percent of the women of Theresienstadt on arrival to the camp declared that they had had a professional life before.[44] If not literally brilliant or sparkling, Theresienstadt—the cage and clearing, by the force of concentrated modernity—was an emergent place. Philipp Manes wrote in his Theresienstadt diary, "No matter what and wherever you look, you can see something is being made, at a lathe, on an anvil, at a smithy. A piece of furniture comes out of the workshop in this place, that it would make proud any big-city cabinetmaker. . . . In another place, men in blue overalls master another job. . . . They all shatter the fairy tales about a Jew who can never work with his own hands."[45] Another man of Theresienstadt, Dr. Jacob Jacobson, who, unlike Manes, survived, used almost the same words as Manes in his report to a Jewish commission after the war: "Wherever you looked in the camp, there was a Jewish worker; with one single exception: no Jew was allowed to work as a chimney sweep."[46]

This was the way the dazzling and hard-on-the-eye light shined on the camps, and indeed out of the camps. There were workshops in Theresienstadt exporting throughout Nazi-occupied Europe: "a cotton-bandage workshop . . . a handbag and satchels assembly line, horn-buttons production . . . a place where board games such as Nine Men's Morris or Catch the Hat were made, and another where mica was split, rabbit fur sheared, or ink dust bottled; there was a silkworm-breeding station."[47]

The Jews, enveloped by the light of the clearing, were working not to be killed. Caught in the light, they were called *"Arbeitswilligen"* by the Nazis, "willing to work."[48] They were imbued with the concentrated will, one may perhaps say.

During the period of planning Boven Digoel, a government forest expert visited the area, checked the soil, and reported that "it is good." Another expert, who made a follow-up visit to Boven Digoel, still an early one, also reported that the soil, "when given a good care," "almost certainly will do well for growing vegetables, fruits, and other products." "Even while," the expert added, "much of Boven Digoel, except the narrow strip of land along the river, is rather barren."[49]

The future of Boven Digoel was painted bright, as a part of the bright idea of clearing. Rubber trees, it was predicted, would grow well in Boven Digoel, and everyone in the Indies had been aware of the rubber miracles, especially in Sumatra, the rubber industry that had helped to build a modern colony. "One can try coffee, too," experts opined.[50] Samples of Boven Digoel lumber were sent to the center of the province in Ambon to evaluate the quality for possible export.[51] "The governor-general wanted to see the internees and their families in the middle of the jungle, together with the government, to found a colony."[52]

Fairly soon, the internees as well as the authorities realized that all was not exactly as the experts predicted. That it was not like that at all. A Dutch official on inspection in Boven Digoel in April 1930 reported, "Initially, vegetables in Boven Digoel came out just fine, but already the second harvest was a disaster. The beans did not push out at all. Rice was even worse, a catastrophe. It is true that the rice looked pretty at first but, as the plants grew, there was no grain."[53] Even so, against all odds, with no way to turn back to, the next fifteen years, the remaining history of the camp, was spent in clearing, expanding, and letting more light in.

Soetan Sjahrir, intellectual, bookish before the camp through and through, wrote in November 1935 in a letter to his wife in Holland from Boven Digoel, "Mieske, I triumphed in cucumbers, but I cannot say the same about the other things. I have now used all the seed I had, and I will see what happens."[54]

The soil of Boven Digoel was poor in calcium, among having other problems, and the few internees who understood something about agriculture knew it as soon as they touched the soil.[55] "Coffee and rubber was supposed to make Boven Digoel rich and the internees have already planted [a] few rubber trees," van Blankenstein reported in 1928, the second year of the camp, but, he added, "most of the expectations are fading fast."[56] In 1928, too, it was reported from Boven Digoel, "Cattle have been tried but results bring only a disappointment."[57] The official who visited the camp in 1930 reported, "I have noticed many attempts undertaken very seriously. But, except the little gardens in front and back of the internees' houses, and contrary to what the experts have predicted, all the attempts till now have failed."[58] Another visitor, and expert, also early in 1930, conveyed "little hope," and he added that "only more disappointments may be expected."[59]

The French author Jean Giraudoux wrote a dreamish novel popular in Europe in the 1930s. Suzanne, a young Parisian woman, was stranded on a Pacific island, but the island, as the author described it, contained everything Suzanne needed, except Paris, of course. The island was a miracle of modern appliances, "a depository of ready-made luxurious objects. The island bears immediately what it has taken civilization centuries to produce, perfect, and ripen . . . the double of every object from the city."[60]

Boven Digoel, and also Theresienstadt, were rather like the other shipwreck experience, that of the eagerly and brilliantly modern Robinson Crusoe. Practically all of what the camp people needed for their new life in the camps, like Robinson, they had "to bring from the ship." The rest they had to build themselves, albeit as "the double," anew "what it had taken civilization centuries to produce, perfect, and ripen." They labored hard for survival, with concentrated will, "from the memory," driven by the image of all that they had been taught in their previous lives, a "glitter of commodity," Walter Benjamin might call it (gloomily).[61] Thus the world *glittered* in the camp.

"Contrary to the promises of the Germans," the transports with the Jews began to arrive at Theresienstadt "before anything had been prepared."[62] Gonda Redlich reported in his camp diary overhearing the first SS commandant of Theresienstadt telling the first head of the Jewish Council of the Elders before the first transport left for the camp: "Don't be afraid. Your situation is good. . . . Everyone will receive a bed and a closet."[63] Others remembered the SS man telling the Jews in the first transport as they arrived and the new clearing was to be opened, "Now you are in the shit. And, now, you show what you can do."[64]

"In the spring of 1942," Kurt Kotouč, one of those who arrived first, remembered, "we were still not allowed to leave the barracks." Only on July 6, 1942, was movement out of the barracks permitted: "The streets of Theresienstadt filled with crowds."[65] "On that day the residents walked about in a daze.... One could now take a walk, indeed walk on pavement (which was not permitted to the Jews when still outside the camps).... Life suddenly took on a fresh flavor; there was something to look forward to, a reason to mop the floor and wear a clean shirt."[66] It was the moment of unprecedented brightness and new energy. "A bakery ... opticians ... watch repair ... shoe repair ... orthopedics ... hairdressers ... housepainters ... roofers, electricians, and plumbers, sewage cleaners, masons, wallpaper hangers (black-out curtain hangers) ... pharmacists ... movers ..."[67] "They worked faithfully," Ruth Bondy wrote after the war about the moment and what followed through the history of the camp. "The work strengthened relationships; it filled the day."[68]

"What the engineers of Theresienstadt accomplished was astounding," recalled Alice Bloemendahl in an interview after the war.[69] "Okay, then listen," Josef Manuel, another Jew of Theresienstadt, told Elena Makarova in 1997. "Our camp was designed for death but well organized for life. You might say that the Jews made everything with their hands."[70]

It was modernity, energy, and light crammed in. One could hear it—and one can still hear a pride, strong, close to despair, but explicit, in many testimonies: "Little would have been accomplished had it not been for the high professional level of the water and electrical engineers, the doctors, technicians, cooks, and all the other professionals working in the ghetto.... Their standards went a long way toward preserving the attitude of pride in one's work.... People worked to the best of their ability without being forced, without the threat of the whip."[71] "All the difficulties notwithstanding," wrote Emil Utitz, "the work ethic was high."[72]

In an iconic album of the late 1920s by the German photographer August Sander, "modern human types" were ordered on a scale of dignity and status. In the portraits in Sander's *Face of Our Time*, "the types" were arranged in an arc, starting at the lower end with a peasant: ascending through a worker, a bourgeois, a student, a politician, a revolutionary, a clergyman, an industrialist, an artist, a writer, and a musician; and then descending again, through a bar waiter and a cleaning woman to the low end of an unemployed worker in a city.[73]

Philipp Manes, charged with leading the "Orientation Section" in Theresienstadt, helping the people who might lost their way in the camp, wrote, "In exercising my duties, I have to deal with people of all classes."[74] "People of all, classes," Hans Günther Adler wrote in his history, could be met in Theresienstadt, "men of big industry, bankers, lawyers, doctors, rabbis, scholars and university professors, teachers, artists, journalists, technicians, small merchants, officials, artisans, peasants, and workers."[75]

"Only after the work is done it is good," wrote Immanuel Kant in the eighteenth century, "only then, and it will never be, comes a rest, and only this rest, is a 'happiness that does not include the least admixture of disgust.'"[76] According to the Marxist Ernst Bloch, two centuries after Kant, "Reason is conditioned by *labor*." "Work is historical," wrote Bloch. It is "the manner in which man adapts himself to his historical development."[77] And then, as Ernst Bloch, a Jew, was writing and running to escape a camp, Rudolf Höss, the SS-Obersturmbannführer and commandant of Auschwitz, put a sign reading *"Arbeit Macht Frei,"* "Work Makes You Free," over the gate of Auschwitz.[78] As with music, if you had them stripped naked, you would find nothing but work.

"In Boven Digoel," van Blankenstein wrote about his visit in 1928, "the internees are putting their lives in order as well as they can, and whoever can see the camp today, cannot but get a favorable impression of their attitude."[79] "There was a period in the camp of forced labor initially," Dr. Schoonheyt wrote. But soon, he wrote, it was abolished as it "dawned" on the authorities "that the internees themselves desired to have their own homes built as quickly as possible, and that they, indeed, would work and help others with their work, eagerly and with diligence, on the construction of the camp."[80]

"Labor," Stefano Harney and Fred Moten wrote in their recent *The Undercommons*, "could easily be mistaken for life."[81] "Everybody wants and can have their own house, own front yard, and own garden," a report on Boven Digoel by a Dutch official stated, and so "they build their own place to stay, as fast as they can, they make designs of their own choice, and they help the others.... It is becoming a movement, to join in the building of the camp. Willingness increases, and everybody except few are at work."[82]

The nineteenth-century Javanese *Serat Wédhatama* [The Supreme Wisdom], teaches, and it sounds like a work chant in Boven Digoel:

Status, property, and skills,
If you come to be lacking
You have lost all trace of humanity.[83]

An ex-internee Marsudi of Boven Digoel told an interviewer long after the camp, "Each new group of arrivals to the camp was welcomed by a reception committee of the internees. The committee informed the new arrivals about the system of *gotong rojong* [mutual help] in the camp. The system was set up especially for building houses. Men worked on the construction and women cooked the meals. Everybody supplied the stuff for the cooking, and we all ate together."[84] "The people as they build the camp together, *are not lazy*," wrote the author and probably an ex-internee in a novel about Boven Digoel. "They made the camp good for themselves and for those who were still to come."[85]

> SUNDAY, DECEMBER 25, 1936 ... MORNING: 11:15 ... Amat Saleh, in section C of the camp, is building a new house and nine men help him.[86]
>
> SUNDAY, JANUARY 24, 1937 ... MORNING: ... 7:55. ... H. A. Chatib builds a house for himself and sixteen men are there and work with him.[87]

"When a new mosque was being built in Boven Digoel," according to another recollection, "internees, Muslims and even the Christians, could be seen busy on the site."[88]

"My father in the camp," Mr. Trikoyo told me, "got skilled in weaving mats of rattan, repairing fishing nets, sharpening saws, and even building boats and constructing houses, all the things one can do with one's own hands."[89] Misbach Yusa Biran heard from his mother about his "grandfather in Boven Digoel carrying stones for paving roads." Biran recalled, "I can still see his shoulders blackened by sun and hard like iron, all this, I believed, from all the heavy loads he carried in the camp."[90] It is clear what Biran was thinking: his grandfather's hands were, as others might call it, work-beautiful: "strong and agile," "burned by the sun," and "know-how full."[91]

In the novel *Darah dan Aer-Mata*, Marija, a woman who was eventually permitted to leave the Boven Digoel camp, returns home to Java. She gets lost on the street and asks a sweeper who happens to be there, working, for directions. It is made clear in the novel that she asks as "the people in Java behave to sweepers," in a "semi-feudal" way. "Has she already forgotten," the author of the novel asks, "what she had learned in the camp, how to talk to working people?"[92]

A few months into the existence of Boven Digoel, fourteen internees, "the most difficult cases to handle," had been punished, pulled out of the main camp, and, so as not to spoil the rest, transported down the river, exiled a second time. A few kilometers downstream from the main camp stood four empty warehouses, abandoned coal storages, and so the new "other camp," where the fourteen were put, was called *Goedang Arang* [the Coal Storage]. Even compared with the main camp, this was really a bad place, muddy all the time and submerged whenever it rained and the river rose. It was a much smaller, more pathetic place, and thus a still more intensive Lichtung.

Journalist van Blankenstein saw Goedang Arang on his visit to Boven Digoel in 1928, and he also met its fourteen inhabitants. He compared the place with the French Cayenne, a Devil's Island of sorts, but at the same time, he found Goedang Arang to be a place of "exemplary" work ethic:

> Imagine this tableau, a daredevil scene, a rough spot at the precipice of a low creek, not a place really to live in. Men, most of them half naked, they walk around. The name of one of them, I am told, is Dahlan. He has long hair and the bearing of a poet. Another man just comes from the jungle. He carries a big axe over his shoulder. The whole place is Crusoe-like. . . . The biggest warehouse has a roof of zinc but no walls, just wooden pillars. Here is the fourteen's sleeping place. A sheet of corrugated iron is nailed upon the warehouse's roof, in the front. There is a drawing on it: a man smoking a pipe and, behind him, in the distance, some kind of Moorish castle. Under the picture, there are verses:
>
> *Al rokende bouwt Kadal zijn luchtkasteel!*
> *Een dwaas blijft droomend bij zijn wenschen staan,*
> *Geeft hem slechts wil, en wijsheid breekt hem baan.*
> *[Of smoke, Kadal built his castle in the air!*
> *In idle wishes fools supinely stay,*
> *Be there a will, and wisdom finds its way.]*

". . . all in Dutch," van Blankenstein adds.⁹³

The space for the camp was being cleared, trees uprooted, barren surface broken, new plants planted. Some plants died, but some grew up, and some blossomed. Through the camp work, as a sign of the camp work, new colors appeared in the clearing, and greater brightness to the light.

> *Boven Digoel, June 11, 1929. To the Assistant-Resident.* In all respect: We undersigned wish to inform you, sir, that we plan to open a new wet (irrigated) rice field. Signed: 1. Boerniat, 2. Hadji Noerdin, 3. Saidiroellah; all three of section C of the camp.⁹⁴

> MONDAY, JUNE 24, 1935 MORNING: . . . 10:50 . . . At the river bank . . . Soewari works on his plot.⁹⁵

> THURSDAY, JULY 11, 1940 MORNING: . . . 7:20 . . . Soetan Arief is seen walking past Kamali's house. He carries a hoe and goes to his plot.⁹⁶

"We used to play with friends," Mr. Trikoyo recalled himself as a child in the camp. "We used to go to the field of Uncle Saleh, which was in the easternmost corner of section B of the camp. The field was newly opened, and it was quite large. The trees of the jungle had already been cut and most of the underbrush was burned and taken away. Part of the field was already hoed and few patches were planted with cucumber." Another time, Mr. Trikoyo recalled, "We went still further on, and there we liked to sit under a big casuarian tree near the bridge between section C and section B. We might watch the father of Warno harvesting beans."[97]

Pemandangan [Outlook] was an Indonesian newspaper sympathetic to the Boven Digoel internees. On July 3, 1935, it published a letter by internee Mohammad Hatta asking a relative in Batavia to send him "a roll of iron wire and some other stuff of the kind, explaining that, next to his house in the camp, he plans to build a chicken coop."[98]

Some months into the camp's existence, like the Theresienstadt people permitted to go out of the barracks and walk on the street, the internees in Boven Digoel were allowed to own *proa*, to paddle a few kilometers up- and downstream on the Digoel River, and to fish.

> MONDAY, JUNE 24, 1935 MORNING: . . . 10:50 . . . Soewarno and Soegiri can be seen building a new boat. Poeradisastra is there, too, and he watches how they are doing. . . . *Afternoon*: *2:25*. . . . the camp is calm. . . . Three boats can be seen on the river and six are pulled out of water.[99]

> FRIDAY, MAY 1, 1936 . . . NIGHT: . . . 3:30 . . . Oesoep of section C returns from fishing. He caught enough.[100]

> THURSDAY, JUNE 11, 1940 MORNING: . . . 7:20 . . . Singdikromo is working on a boat next to his house (he builds a new rudder).[101]

Sawahs, wet or irrigated rice fields, are the treasure and pride of monsoon Asia and the beauty of its landscape. Very fine soil is needed. Sawahs are difficult to build and they are feats of engineering, too. Sawahs were rare in Boven Digoel, but, like the pearls of the Jewesses left at home or perhaps just imagined, sawahs were the camp's memory and ambition.

There appeared in the camp, suddenly, newly, and brightly, coconut palms, and rubber trees, those in spite of the general sense of being a failure, and the more standing out. There even appeared few, rare, but the more glaring and exquisite, orange trees, as well as "fruit trees of all sorts and many sorts of vegetables."[102] Virtually all this, with its colors and beauty, was imported to the camp by the camp people—flowers, plants, and seeds crammed in trunks, or later ordered long-distance and received by mail. Over the years of the camp, the trees and plants "brought from the wreckage" grew, some got sick, and some survived and blossomed, sharp on the eye in the landscape around, and the history around.

"My father planted a coconut tree in Boven Digoel," Mr. Trikoyo recalled.[103] There was coffee growing, in spite of everything, and in spite that coffee had never been grown in the place before, or smelled or tasted.[104] "There is no bamboo in Boven Digoel," van Blankenstein wrote about his visit to the camp in 1928.[105] In the next years, one hears about bamboo in Boven Digoel repeatedly, and also about casuarian trees—the beautiful, dark green trees, again, foreign to New Guinea until the time of the camp, domestic to Java, a tree of love poetry in that now distant island.

Since the very first weeks, when many internees in Boven Digoel still lived in barracks, there emerged little gardens with flowerbeds and, as it had been a long-standing custom in the other parts of the Indies, flower pots that were placed in various arrangements in front of the buildings.

Not exactly Dante's Purgatory, "the flower-bright summit of the hill,"[106] but, on a second look, in fact, yes. "The place," the head of the camp reported already at the end of 1928, "appears quite neat [*net*]."[107] "It is still not fully done," the resident of Ambon reported on his inspection trip to Boven Digoel in May 1929, but, he wrote, "quite a number of the internees' houses already stand and they are neat [net again], and all have front- and backyard gardens planted with vegetables and fruit trees; there is yam, corn, papaya, all for the kitchen, but also flowers. Not much bare space in the garden is left."[108]

"We planted a quite large garden in front of our house," Mrs. Widayasih told me. "Any time of a day, my father was in the garden, busy, taking care of all of this," she counted on her fingers, "jackfruit, soft-fleshed jackfruit, cashew fruit, rose apple, lime, a few canes of sugar, some bananas, and cassava."[109]

"It is a neat camp," Dr. Schoonheyt said when he was in 1934 lecturing in Amsterdam on Boven Digoel, and he used the word "*net*," "neat," again. "The little gardens enliven the whole," Dr. Schoonheyt told his audience in Amsterdam. Dr. Schoonheyt also wrote a series of articles on Boven Digoel in a Dutch paper published in Java, *Javabode*. There is a photograph of already well-grown-up trees, of an alley between the harbor and the camp, in one of the articles, with the caption, again, "A neat [*net*] camp."[110]

The word "*net*" in Dutch, like "neat" in English, according to dictionary, comes from "*nitere*," "to shine." Another meaning of the word, "now obsolete," the dictionary says, is "bright."

In the middle of the Boven Digoel camp was the laid-out and "well-kept 'Orange Park.'"[111] Orange evoked both the Dutch royal color and the fruit brought to the camp by the internees. But flowers seem to return most often in the memories. To Mrs. Zakaria's talking to me, flowers appeared repeatedly. "People liked to plant flowers," she told me, "to bring them from the seeds." "Mother brought many various sorts of seeds with her to the camp, and she planted them in our garden. I remember how proud she was when one seed or another caught on. Guava is truly beautiful when it blossoms, and the jackfruit, we also brought in from Java. And roses."[112] Bangun Topo seemed less interested in flowers. "Yes, there were roses," he told me as I pressed him, and, after some thinking, "and carnations," he added.[113]

The internees brought colors and brightness with them to the camp, as they brought umbrellas, typewriters, or penholders, the colors and brightness of a world that they believed had belonged to them. The camp was made bright and *neat* by cramming and packing. With the lid pushed down, so to speak, not really unpacked, still crammed, in the camps, the camp's overintense sense of bright and neat grew with the passing years, the camp's overintense sense of flowers, trees, seeds, and of it all. If something in the modern world since the nineteenth century ever came near to Charles Baudelaire's *fleurs du mal*, this was it.

The overelegant and natural-artificial word "bouquet," and, indeed, in French, appears more than once in the reports by the Boven Digoel police, all handwritten and most written by an untrained hand. Clearly, bouquetway, this was how the flowers spoke and were important in the camp:

> WEDNESDAY, JUNE 12, 1940 MORNING . . . 9:05: Telephone from the captain; he requests 1 *bouquet* to be delivered; agent L. Ketjil is given the order. He collects the flowers and delivers them to the house of the captain.[114]

The *echt*-colonial flowerpots were already mentioned. They were made of fake marble, snow-white and meticulously arranged on the tiny lawns in front of the internees' houses. They were the superstriking spots of brightness and neatness, beauty spots, to recall the chapter on fashion. The camp was dark, white, red, yellow, pink, the color of banana flower, of a carnation, of a rose. It was much more a garden or park than a field. The houses of the internees, too, the little prisons, were—also something unprecedented in the place—green, red, white, or beige.

It was the culmination of the modern and bright launched long before. The green of Paris, the capital of the nineteenth century, perhaps the beginning of *neat*, as the phenomenon, was also of a packed imported kind. Napoleon saw quite new "public gardens and well-kept parks" in his exile in London. He also quickly understood their importance for keeping law and order. After he became emperor, he installed public gardens and well-kept parks in Paris on a large scale, the Bois de Boulogne being the largest.[115]

According to Walter Benjamin, not just the aim for law and order but "the origin of all present-day architecture ... is the greenhouse." The Crystal Palace, another monument of the new and modern of the time, inside its cast-iron and plate-glass structure, contained "magnificent elm trees."[116] There is a connecting line from Bois de Boulogne and the Crystal Palace to the early twentieth-century New York Central Park's amazing "Tree Moving Machine," and to the neatness of the camps.[117] Gustave Flaubert's image, in his *Sentimental Education*, seems to be ultimate, but he could not see the camps, "the monotonous green expanse like a huge billiard table."[118]

To accent the brightness of the modern of the camps, and to brighten the order, there were sport fields. The better tennis court in Boven Digoel had a surface made of concrete. The lines were white and often repainted. There was a white tennis net, and the shoes of the players were white.[119]

Mrs. Widayasih remembered that tennis shoes were popular in Boven Digoel on and also off the court. "We whitened them with chalk," she told me, "if we had them." The tennis players wore white if they had it, shorts or skirts and shirts. Sometimes women played in sarongs, but they were bright, too. And there were tennis balls, white at the time. Widayasih used to wait for a ball to fly over the fence. "They were like butterflies," she says.[120]

There was the camp, bright, and brighter against the jungle, which was recalled as dark green but most often as just dark. There was the Dutch tricolor brightly flying in the middle of the camp, orange, blue, and white. And when night fell, Salim recalled, "we pulled those orange-blue-and-white mosquito nets over our heads and fold[ed] our feet in."[121]

The internees, held in the camp, built their houses to shine, if only against the jungle, as if shouting (or whispering), "We are here!" The Dutch officials as well as the internees themselves often remarked on the internees' houses being built "in the most unconventional 'styles.'"[122] "There were some truly particular 'beauties' among the camp houses," Salim recalled. "One internee from Japara," Salim gave an example, "covered his whole house, the walls, the doors, and the windows, the pillars, everything, with wood carvings."[123] Did he realize, Salim wondered about the man, that he was in a camp?

"The Wilhelmina Hospital in Boven Digoel was painted white, and its doors and windows were green."[124] In a police book for June 1936 one could read, "The house of clerk Ratumbana is having its windows newly painted."[125] As much as possible, the camp was to be un-drab.

> FRIDAY, JUNE 21, 1935 . . . MORNING . . . 10:20. Agent Soeleman leaves the station to announce an order for general cleaning. . . . *Afternoon:* 12:34. Soeleman . . . give an order to several internees to fix their fences.[126]

The malaria-fighting team in Boven Digoel traced the anopheles-breeding places, collected the larvae, cleaned the camp, and colored the landscape. "They focused on the mosquito-breeding places especially along the river, and especially at times, when the level of water in the river changed. They covered wide stretches of the river banks with Paris green, a larva poison containing arsenic. . . . They covered other breeding places in a radius of about 1½ kilometers around the camp with a thick layer of 'mud,' a dark brown-black petroleum residuum."[127]

This was the time of a new light, and inevitably, of a new darkness, as Ernst Bloch wrote, a darkness that "lightens toward evening."[128] Twilight, certainly, is remembered by the Boven Digoel internees as the most charged moment in the camp. It was the darkness descending that made the camp, actually and instantly, in all its modern, to shine. "At dusk," Salim wrote, "we liked *makan angin* [to eat the wind]. We walked about the camp wherever the mood took us. Some of us sat on the front verandas of their houses, or in their little gardens, and smoked a cigarette under the open sky. This had been 'Boven Digoel at its best!'"[129]

A classical Indies scene of modernity emerging from the darkness, as light, was most famously told by Louis Couperus, a Dutch writer of the turn of the twentieth century, in his novel *The Hidden Force*. A Dutch resident, the top official in a remote Javanese town, walks "to enjoy the breeze," at dusk. The town is "at its best." A native servant follows the resident with a *tali api*, a cord burning at its end, a light no bigger than a burning end of a cigarette. As the resident walks, with the servant behind him, the tiny twinkle of the tali api marks their way—enlightening the town, showing the modern, creating the space. Nothing can be seen of the dark primeval or premodern nature in the light of tali api. There is only, and it stands out sharply—*Burger-Sociëteit* [the club], the church, the clock tower where the town square will soon be, and finally the lighthouse, another light, petroleum or perhaps already electric, a signal of the world.[130]

As dusk fell in Boven Digoel, social gatherings of the internees were held, and they also shined. Often with music, lights beamed into the night. There were *warung*s, the little roadside cafés, serving snacks and drinks, the first one and then two larger ones owned by the Chinese shopkeepers, free people allowed to the camp, and then many more warungs, smaller and some tiny, owned by the internees themselves. At dusk especially, the internees stopped by, they talked, drank tea, coffee, lemonade, or—they were modern people—even beer, in the light of a petroleum lamp or just of a tali api, like Couperus's resident, or just in the light of their cigarettes—their faint glowing miraculously brightening the night.

Some of the warungs grew into noodle places, little eateries, and they too were never empty. Some internees passed through the camp selling *badjigoer goting*, a hot drink made of coconut milk and spices.[131] "There are many *tokotjes* [little shops] and *warungs*," governor Haga of the Moluccas reported on his inspection of the camp in its very early stage. "Some are small, others are larger, almost real cafés, restaurants, and pubs."[132]

FRIDAY, NOVEMBER 9, 1934 . . . NIGHT. . . . 2:15. . . . People still sit at the house of Soewardi, a *warung* in section C.[133]

"Some internees opened little grocery shops," Mrs. Ottow recalled, "and were permitted to order goods from Ambon."[134] They sold sweets, and thus there were always children around.[135] The Tan Toey, a Chinese-owned store, was "a modern restaurant, it had a pool table and served beer with ice."[136] "A dish of rice served on a banana leaf cost thirty cents," Salim recalled, "when it was served by a charming daughter of the restaurant owner, however, the price might be as high as forty cents!"[137]

SATURDAY, SEPTEMBER 12, 1936 . . . NIGHT: . . . 9:50 . . . In many internees' houses lamps still burn.[138]

All these lights in the camp made the surrounding jungle seem even darker.

Lights of hurricane lamps and even of battery-powered pocket flashlights, rather than the old-fashioned petroleum lanterns or even tali api will-o'-the-wisp, moved through the camp. They signaled, among other things, that the ROB police were making their rounds.

SATURDAY, JUNE 29, 1935 . . . NIGHT . . . 1:45. Agent Hadji Sanoesi leaves the station to do his rounds. He takes a hurricane lamp to investigate the landing raft.[139]

There were lights on the river at night. Internees were allowed on the river, and they attached a lamp to each of their boats. There were illuminations on special nights in the camp. Truly artificial light, like above a billiard table, light of the clearing.

Program of the Festivities to Celebrate the Birth of Her Royal Highness Princess Irene Ema Elisabeth and the Anniversary of Her Majesty the Queen, Boven Digoel, August 5, 1939. Fireworks will be performed and there will be a torch march through the camp. Torches are available at the office of the administrator.... At the end of the march there will be a *vreugde-vuur* [Dutch for "fire of joy," fireworks] in Orange Park, opposite the office of the administrator.[140]

In 1855, at the Hôtel du Louvre in Paris, "For the first time, entrepreneurs used electric light on the site, in order to double the day's labor."[141] It was, also, the beginning of the new light. In Boven Digoel, three-quarters of a century later, but still ahead of the time of the colony and much of the world indeed, there was electric light, too. No less dramatic and new in the dark than in Paris in 1855. Electricity, like the Communists, the mosquitoes, and intensive care, became one of the most remarkable attributes of the camp. It accounted for much of the camp's notoriety and historical significance as well—a sign, a blush, and a tag, indicating how far history advanced.

Like the Communists, the mosquitoes, and so on, electricity belonged to Boven Digoel and Boven Digoel belonged to electricity. When Dr. Schoonheyt demonstrated "the well-known internment site in New Guinea" to the audience in Amsterdam, he showed slides, "electric light pictures," of the place. "There is even electric light in the camp," Dr. Schoonheyt told his audience.[142]

Since the first months of the camp, electricity wires were already a part of the camp landscape, of the cleared space. First, the house of the camp administrator got a generator.[143] Almost at the same time, electricity was installed in the Wilhelmina Hospital for the internees.[144] Dr. Schoonheyt recalled that there were "occasions" when the power failed, sometimes for hours at a time. But there was a hospital generator ready to keep the light in times of emergency. "It had its streaks of mood, of course," Dr. Schoonheyt wrote, and sometimes "we could not help it, but had to come back to petroleum lamps."[145] But still, when needed, on the whole, surgeries could be performed even at night.[146]

After a few years, street lighting had been installed in Boven Digoel. The camp became, till the end of the war and the end of the story, the only place with street lighting in the vast Indies area east of Ambon. There were, in the whole of the Indies at the time, only very few electrified places—the largest urban centers and modern plantations. "Here is a jail built in an ultra-modern style," Ho Chi Minh wrote in his *Prison Diary* about his place of imprisonment during World War II in very dark China: "All night the compound is brightly flooded with electricity."[147]

....

In a letter of November 6, 1943, the Auschwitz camp commandant ss-Obersturmbannführer Rudolf Höss, the Kantian,[148] wrote to the office of ss-Sturmbannführer Bishoff, also in Auschwitz. Höss ordered what, so he wrote, was urgently needed for the ultimate camp in his charge: "The following is a list of the plants need to be drawn from our stocks of trees: 200 trees in leaf from three to five meters high; 100 tree shoots in leaf from a meter and a half to four meters high; lastly, 1,000 bushes for use as lining from one to two and a half meters high, all to come from the stock in our nurseries."[149]

This was in accordance with the Nazi *Generalplan Ost* [General Plan East], and the Nazi definition of order implied in the plan, the order in the camps, including "verdant, fecund, and luxuriant." The general plan, of conquest, occupation, and the camps, was in line, in harmony, with the sense of beauty, the rule of the pink. The same rule led to keeping the "Goethe Oak" in the middle of the Buchenwald death camp, keeping it and caring for it intensively.

Theresienstadt was part of the Nazi general plan, and it could not be allowed to be bland and leaden gray. Most of the houses that were part of Theresienstadt, as much as the barracks, "were painted and had small gardens around them, where vegetables were grown for the residents."[150] Some months into the camp's existence, at the edge of the camp, in the moats between the two rows of the fortress's walls, about fourteen meters lower than the top of the walls, soil was brought in, the land was divided in plots and they were assigned as gardens to the internees.

"A piece of land," Philipp Manes wrote, "is now open to us." "The land that was left barren for two hundred years, in a few weeks will become green—the seedlings of tomatoes will shoot into the air . . . there will be lettuce . . . and spinach!"[151] Perhaps not a lot of spinach, lettuce, or tomatoes, and, certainly not much of it on elderly Mr. Manes's plate. But the colors, the green and the red of it!

"What struck the eye immediately in Theresienstadt," an ex-internee recalled, "were the trunks of the trees without branches, always overrun with thousands of starving sparrows."[152] According to many other recollections, however, there were trees left standing in the camp. They might be black and barren in the winter; they were linden trees, most of them,

CLEARING   163

and Theresienstadt was in the northern zone. But when the spring came, cruelly, one should say, the trees got green and then they were in blossom.

"The double row of young linden trees line the Lake Street," Manes wrote in the late spring of 1943 about another part of the camp. "They exude a strong aroma as they gather in blossoms."[153] On Thursday, July 6, 1944, the summertime in the camp, the boy Pavel Weiner wrote, "We have to go pick linden blossoms. . . . We are assigned to linden trees on the square."[154] Internee Ruth Silten, eleven years old at the time, got a letter from the camp administration on November 8, 1944: "You are to present yourself tomorrow, Wednesday the 9th, in the morning at 7:30, at the section of the agriculture at Seestraat no. 3. . . . You will be assigned to a group gathering chestnuts."[155]

A few days before the camp's liberation, on Sunday, April 15, 1945, Pavel Weiner wrote, "Spring has now arrived. Spring, the most beautiful thing in the world! . . . The trees are budding and getting new leaves. How exciting is the rich green color that floods the whole surroundings."[156] Three days earlier, the same spring, Pavel's much older co-internee, Gabriel Italie, wrote in his camp diary, "The trees are now splendid, all of them. In front of the Central Bathhouse there is a walled garden and above the wall one can see a top of a big pear tree. It is dazzling, so full of blossoms!"[157]

There were bouquets in Theresienstadt, as well as in Boven Digoel, and as exclusive. An ex-internee, Mrs. Gerty Spies, remembered years later leaving "a little mug with wildflowers" on Emil Utitz's desk when the old man left his place in the camp library for a moment: "I had picked them for him," Mrs. Spies recalled, "in the moat."[158] Pavel Weiner wrote a long entry in his diary about lilacs. He was assigned, he wrote, to work in the camp garden.

> THURSDAY, MAY 18, 1944 . . . I ask Schwarzbart [internee-supervisor] if he could give me some lilacs. . . . We work until 5:30. . . . It doesn't look like any lilacs will be left for me. I dare to ask again. Schwarzbart says to go around the garden, and somebody there should give me some. I hurry there. . . . Some girls cut a few lilacs for us. I'm very dirty and sweaty. I put the lilacs under my coat and go to the [boys' dormitory]. There, I arrange the lilacs and put a band around them. I go for dinner and take the lilacs to mother.[159]

Announcement by the Jewish Self-Administration, Theresienstadt April 15, 1944. Greenery: From the point of view of health, greenery in Theresienstadt has a special importance in the camp. It can reduce the dust and improve the air. Take care of the greenery and protect it from damage! The fruit trees are raising a particular concern. Any person found damaging a tree or cutting flowers, will be punished.[160]

There were windows without curtains in Theresienstadt, and the fact is often mentioned. But there were windows in the camp, the more striking the less of them there were, shining, brilliant, often with exquisite brought-from-home curtains, and with flowers. There were flowers in some windows in Theresienstadt, and there were flowerpots and flower boxes. "We put a flower box with geraniums in the window, and we put a vase with cut flowers on the table," Catharine van den Berg wrote in her recollection after the war.[161] "From the streets," Manes wrote, "you can see flower boxes."[162] Pansies, fuchsias, geranium, begonias, or pelargoniums were flowers common to Central Europe, but in the camps, like the roses and the carnations in Boven Digoel, they were *imported*.

Laundry on wash lines was allowed in Theresienstadt only at certain hours and certain days, but it appears on many images of the camp, in memorial albums internees wrote for each other's anniversaries, in drawings in letters and diaries, and like the pearls perhaps left at home, they "enlivened the scenery" as they enlivened the memory.

The nighttime curfew in Theresienstadt, unlike in Boven Digoel, was strictly enforced. Throughout, there was *Verdunklung*, a blackout duty, each and every night, only adjusted by an hour for summer- and wintertime. All windows had to be covered by a thick black paper screen, especially made for the purpose.

Announcement by the Jewish Self-Administration, Theresienstadt April 15, 1944 Black-out. Black-out is ordered for every day from 9:00 in the evening till 5:00 in the morning.[163]

The Allied pilots were to see nothing but the dark as they flew over Theresienstadt on their missions.

Electric light had become a necessity for modern Europeans of the 1920s and 1930s; they had already grown fully accustomed to it. There was electric light virtually everywhere in Central and Western Europe, from which the Jews came to Theresienstadt. Public lighting meant for everyone in Europe at the time, naturally, "civilized landscape." It seems even not worth mentioning that there was electricity in Theresienstadt. Still, as never before, as in Boven Digoel, the electric light in Theresienstadt was exclusive, exquisite, and of unprecedented brilliance.

Cafés in Vienna, Prague, Amsterdam, Berlin, Hamburg, and hundreds of other towns and cities before the war from which the people came to Theresienstadt were a significant part of the "civilized landscape," something "one could not do without," a fashion, a style. Each main street, especially, had "plenty of cafés." The Jews came to Theresienstadt from the "civilized places." Even the Jewish women who came to Theresienstadt had been before the war quite accustomed to visiting cafés regularly.[164] Just as the green in Theresienstadt was greener than just green, so the café in the camp would be more than just a café. When late in 1942, memories of cafés, fantasies of cafés, became real, it was more real than just real.

With the SS's permission, a café was opened on what used to be the main square of town before the war. "The café," Adler wrote, "was opened on December 8, 1942, on the site of a prewar restaurant on the main square. The hours were seven days a week from ten o'clock in the morning till seven thirty in the evening." Adler also wrote, "For a visit to the café, special tickets were handed out, valid for a stamped-upon day only and for a two-hour visit as marked on the ticket. . . . At first one hundred, and later five hundred persons could visit the café in one day. . . . There were newspapers [as far as there were any in the camp] available in the café and, in the afternoon after two o'clock, sometimes, an orchestra played."[165] Other times, there were "café-concerts," a piano or a violin, chamber music or a singer. When there was dark over the camp, and it was soon dark much of the year in northern Europe, the lights of the café could not be seen from the outside: there were black-out paper curtains in the windows. But the more it was imagined. There was café light, more than just café light.

Sometimes, on special occasions in Theresienstadt, there were "special illuminations," too. Seder is a ritual meal and service to commemorate the exodus of the Jews from Egypt. "Only the candles," a man recalled of a Seder night in Theresienstadt, "are supposed to give light and it is mysterious to have all the rest of the room unseen. We sit with pillows, and each person's face is in a circle of glowing light."[166] Isaac Bashevis Singer wrote about the memorial candles: "It is said, one can surmise the fate of those in whose memory they were kindled; the flame flickers and sputters when the soul of the departed has not found peace."[167] Ruth Bondy remembered other nights in the camp. When "a soul has departed," she wrote, "we lit memorial candles" and we "recited Caddish for the dead."[168]

The electric light of Theresienstadt, unlike in Boven Digoel, was not a novelty. But like in Boven Digoel, in the Theresienstadt camp, the electricity shined brilliantly, and with unprecedented brightness. Theresienstadt, too, was a victory of the electric light, merciless and unstoppable.

The electric light in the Theresienstadt camp was a light as sharp into the darkness as man had ever made, *Licht an sich*, indeed, like the Nuremberg Nazi Party Congress show captured in Leni Riefenstahl's film, nothing but light, to be switched on and off in an instant, whenever needed, "the triumph of the will."

One of the first actions taken by the Jewish "self-administration" Council of the Elders was "to modernize and to expand for the use by the Jews the existing but small and outdated power net of the place."[169] Alice Bloemendahl got an impression that particularly good care in the camp "was taken of the expansion and modernization of the camp street lighting."[170] On October 7, 1944, Italie wrote in his diary, "Every evening, in spite of all the black-out regulations, neon lights shine on the Bahnhofstrasse."[171]

Albert Speer, Adolf Hitler's architect, is better known for his theory of ruins than for his obsession with light. However, with the Führer's encouragement, Speer designed and "built" a monumental *Lichtdom* [Cathedral of Light], in Nuremberg, and he planned more. These structures, like Leni Riefenstahl's reflectors beaming on the Nazi masses, were made fully of light and of nothing but light. They will be, Speer argued, the ultimate "inspiration" for how empires and men should be built, especially by their unprecedented "linking technique and pathos."[172]

The Nazis did not have enough time to fully build the world around the cathedrals. But much of what they accomplished was Speer-like—houses dimmed but of light, humans in prisons but of light, towers of light, and camps of light. G. L. Durlacher recalled his Theresienstadt days, also like light, nothing but light, its presence and absence:

> I walked through a drafty corridor that cut around all four sides of the huge barracks' inner court. The loose tiles clicked and clacked under each of my steps. Through the arched windows set deep in the thick wall I could see people outside playing ball. On the opposite side, many doors from the corridor were opened to dormitories, and out of them came noise and swells of musty air. People could be seen sitting on their beds. A single bulb from the ceiling in each room gave a sparse light by which reading or writing was all but impossible.[173]

"Night is coming, and now all will become really difficult," Manes wrote about the same time and the same place. "Only above the entrance, one light flickers."[174] And yet another witness wrote, "The attic [where we sleep] is about fourteen by eight meters in size, and there are three electric bulbs for the whole space, each bulb of twenty-five watt."[175]

The camp light was everything, especially by being switchable, light of the will, and it should not be doubted. *Šalom na pátek*, a magazine written mostly by the internee technicians in the camp, published a ditty sent in, as the editor wrote, by a "seven-and-half year old boy Martin Zelenka, living in the camp":

Šetřte světlem
Lidi, lidičky
rozsvěťte svíčičky,
anděl zavřel světlo do garáže,
před ní postavil četné stráže.

[Save the Light:
People, little people,
Light the candles, little candles.
Angels locked the light in a store,
And posted a guard at the door.][176]

"Heavy collective punishment fell on the camp from time to time," wrote Adler in his history of Theresienstadt, "and it made us all, sometimes for weeks, into complete invalids." "The ban on light," he wrote, "was enforced most strictly. Even on the stairs, the washrooms, and the toilets, light was switched off." Sometimes, after some days, Adler wrote, the toilets mercifully were exempted from the "embargo on light." For the rest of the buildings, however, the light remained switched off, sometimes for a whole month. "Not before May 22, 1943," Adler wrote about one very long *Lichtsperre* [ban on light], "the lights had been switched on again, but with a warning that, at the slightest sign of disobedience, the light will be switched off again."[177] On another occasion, "every third day the use of electric light was forbidden, as well as, this time, that of paraffin lamps, too, candles and, of course, of flashlights."[178]

"*Lichtsperre*" was a German and camp term for the ban on light. The premodern was gone, except for the candles at times of rituals. The pre-camp was gone, definitely the custom of Jewish mothers all over Europe, who "would not switch on the electric light until three stars at least had appeared at the window."[179]

TEN

Enlightenment

"We must insist stubbornly," Jean-Luc Nancy wrote, "on the intrinsic membership of fascism in the history of Europe and consequently in its essence or its truth. We must insist on this because the belonging is continually denied or at least made secondary in general, politically conformist consciousness."[1] We must insist stubbornly, too, and in this case, it seems not so difficult to do, on the intrinsic membership of colonialism in the history of the world and consequently in its essence and its truth. Not to do so, also in this case, is to submit to conformist consciousness.

Hannah Arendt famously argued that evil is banal, implying, so it seems, that good has depth.[2] This argument is questionable whether it refers to Nazism or to colonialism. Evil has depth. What Friedrich Nietzsche called "stylized barbarism" appears closer to the truth. Nazism, and colonialism, are *deeply* cultural and *finely* aesthetic; however, this does not reflect nicely on what we might think of culture and aesthetics.[3]

"Nazism," Theodor Adorno and Max Horkheimer wrote, and in my view convincingly, was "the ineluctable outcome of the 'dialectic of Enlightenment.'"[4] So, too, albeit at a greater distance from, yet not in lesser depth, was colonialism. Theresienstadt and Boven Digoel are hugely different but a two-in-one case in the matter. Facing the camps means to think of culture and beauty, and, as a part of it, "to rethink the Enlightenment project itself."[5]

"*Lichtung,*" Martin Heidegger wrote, equals "*clearedness of the there,*"[6] which, he wrote, enables "disclosedness" of being, a "being-in the *clearing.*"[7] Only in clearing, Heidegger wrote, do "we stand in an understanding."[8] The light of the clearing, according to Heidegger, is "defined as care."[9]

Theresienstadt was a camp initially intended "to take care" of "prominent Jews." To be "prominent," in the Nazi usage, but as much in the usage and norm of the whole epoch, was to be modern and enlightened, meaning "civilized," the same as "cultured." The first commandant of the Theresienstadt camp, the ss-Hauptsturmführer Dr. Siegfried Seidl, was "cultured," a doctor of philosophy with a degree from the University of Vienna. Theresienstadt Jews were also "prominent Jews," specifying further, because they were "Jews from Europe."[10] From West and Central Europe, to be more precise, not the *Ostjuden*, as it was accepted, the "less-cultured," "less-enlightened," and "less-civilized," the Jews from Poland or from "further east."

According to one of the early Nazi directives issued in occupied Holland, "Merited Jews, which is artists, physicians, scholars, etc.," were to be sent to Theresienstadt.[11] Whatever happened later, the Nazis kept to this directive to a very large extent: "the Jews of culture," "prominently," were being driven, herded into Theresienstadt rather than to other camps.[12]

There was a disproportionately large number of doctors and musicians among the people of the Theresienstadt camp. And there was a disproportionate number of scientists in the camp, men and women who had enjoyed high respect in prewar Europe and beyond.

To name some at random, Alfred Philippson was a geologist and geographer, and "even in the eyes of the Nazis, he was a scholar of such stature that they permitted him to receive books from the library of the geographical institute at Bonn University and to continue his research in the ghetto."[13]

> To: Professor Dr. Alfred Israel Philippson. Theresienstadt. Protektorat Böhmen und Mähren. Haus Q 408 From: Geographisches Institut der Universität Bonn.
>
> Dear Professor Philippson! For your information: the books that you have requested have already been sent in three packages. I hope they will safely arrive. Of the *Zeitschrift der Gesellschaft für Erdkunde zu Berlin* and of the *Geologische Rundschau* only two issues have been

published so far. I will send to you the next issues as they appear. I hope that, this way, you can get a picture of the current state of the geological and geographical research.

With respect,
[signature illegible]
BONN, DECEMBER 9, 1942[14]

Professor Jacob Jacobson, before the camp, had been the director of the Central Jewish Archive in Germany, and in Theresienstadt, he was not merely permitted but "charged" by the Race Office of the German Empire "to pursue his work on genealogical data from the Jewish family chronicles of the eighteenth century."[15] Samuel Steinherz used to be a major European medieval historian and the rector of the German University in Prague.[16]

There were writers of the highest order driven to Theresienstadt. Not at random, but very personally, Emil Holan was the author of my childhood after the war, when Holan was already dead but I did not know about it. Holan's *Jan Kalista Hockeyista* [Jan Kalista, the Hockey Player], was my absolute favorite when I was eight or ten.[17] Still not at random, Karel Poláček, considered by many to be the greatest Czech humorist writer next to Jaroslav Hašek, of *The Good Soldier Švejk*, but whom I loved more than Hašek, was sent to Theresienstadt, like Holan, then sent "further to the east," where, like Holan, he perished.

Recalling these two is painful enough, but there were many other writers and poets who were sent to this camp; some died, some did not—"the lights" of culture.

There were relatives of the greats, finding themselves in the camp. Baroness Emilia Salvotti was the niece of Heinrich Heine.[18] All three of Kafka's sisters went through Theresienstadt, and all died "in the east." Kafka, again, as if he knew, wrote in his diary in 1919 about a dream he had about the youngest of them, his favorite, Ottla: "Last night, at midnight . . . I woke at about five and heard you at the door of the room calling 'Franz,' softly, but I heard it distinctly. I answered at once but nothing more happened. What did you want?"[19] All four of Sigmund Freud's sisters died in Theresienstadt.[20] On May 6, 1943, Gonda Redlich wrote in his Theresienstadt diary, "The sister of Walther Rathenau asked for a job."[21]

The names of the school degrees that the Boven Digoel people carried to the camp would not mean much to Europe of the time or today; in most cases they would mean nothing. But they shone in the context.

From just one single region of the colony, strongly Muslim Banten, in West Java, there were at one time twenty-five hadjis among the internees in the camp. To be hadji (*haji*) means now, and meant much more at the time, a spiritually inclined person who had devotion, energy, and money to travel over the half the globe, to the holy places in the Middle East, for enlightenment. They were considered learned, seeing the world. At the same time, those sent to Boven Digoel were rebels, which in the Indies, as in Europe, suggested engagement, critical thinking, or both.

There were, in Boven Digoel, still to use the sample of the Boven Digoel internees from Banten, five even more distinguished *Kyai Hadji*s. Nine of the Bantenese were Tubagus, a high aristocratic title which by itself implied prominence and education.[22] Two among the Tubagus, Tubagus Hadji Abdulhamid and Tubagus Kyai Hadji Achmad Chatib, were known to have studied at Al-Azhar in Cairo, the most respected, revered Islamic university in the world.[23]

There were "prominent" internees in Boven Digoel, whose culture-and-learning pedigrees needed less translation for a Westerner. Ali Basjah Siregar, whenever his name was mentioned in the camp, by the other internees or by the authorities, had been described as "a graduate from the English college in Singapore."[24] Three internees in the camp, Clementi Wentoek, Johannes Waworoentoe, and Daniel Kamoe, were known, famous, and prominent as "the students from Moscow." They were of the people of Asia invited to Bolshevik Russia. They appear in the camp documents and they proudly described themselves as the "Group-Moscow in Boven Digoel."[25]

Soetan Sjahrir and Mohammad Hatta came to Boven Digoel later, almost ten years into the camp's history, and they stayed only one year. They were of a later wave of internees who were socialist or nationalist rather than communist. After 1945, Hatta became the vice president of Indonesia, and Sjahrir its prime minister.

At the time of the camp, Sjahrir and Hatta were still a long time away from this. But what already counted in the camp, besides both men's well-articulated political activity, "prominently," was the fact that Hatta graduated from the Rotterdam School of Commerce and fulfilled all the school requirements for a doctoral degree except writing a thesis. He held the degree of *doctorandus*, the single doctorandus in the camp and one of the very few Indonesians with that degree in the Indies. Soetan Sjahrir, Hatta's close ally in politics, matriculated at the University of Leiden.

Nobody knew exactly how much formal study Sjahrir did after his matriculation, in 1929, during the one year he spent in the Netherlands before he chose to go back to the Indies and into politics. But what had been known about Sjahrir as well as Hatta was enough for the rest of the internees, as well as for the authorities, to classify both, Sjahrir and Hatta, as the camp's "academians" and thus, to use the Theresienstadt term, "prominent."

Recent Dutch history of Catholicism in the Indies mentions Boven Digoel in just a few lines, but in them, it has this to say: "The detainees in Boven Digoel belonged to the best-educated inhabitants of the Dutch colony, and there was a vibrant intellectual life in the detention camp."[26]

Internee Gondojoewono was known as a graduate from a four-year course at the School tot Opleiding van Inlandsche Artsen (STOVIA), the first school in Batavia for training "the Indies doctors." The "Indies doctors" were recognized as physicians only in the Indies, but they might go for further education in the Netherlands, to become "real doctors." Gondojoewono practiced on the eastern Indonesian island of Ternate before he was arrested. Soenarjo, another internee, was mentioned rarely otherwise than as "a son of an Indies doctor."[27]

In huge—and dazzling—disproportion to the general population of the Indies, there were a number of former teachers among the Boven Digoel internees, former teachers of religious schools, but even more *onderwijzers*, Dutch for "teachers," teachers in modern, meaning "European," meaning "Western," schools of the Indies.

The camp people in both camps, therefore, the Indies and the European one, brilliantly, were "the people of the book." "Of the Book," in the biblical and Koranic sense, but also in a secular sense, of a book, a book more than just a book.

An Israeli writer, Amos Oz, wrote about his parents, who grew up in Europe before the camps: "They believed that education was an investment for the future, the only thing that no one can ever take away from your children, even if, Heaven forbid, there's another war, another revolution, another migration, more discrimination laws—your diploma you can always fold up quickly, hide in the seams of your clothes, and run away to wherever Jews are allowed to run."[28] One can equally say that they were "the people of the light." For the Jews, as Gershom Scholem, Walter Benjamin's friend, wrote, the Torah, the book, "was the light, the Book of Radiance."[29] Equally so, the Koran for the Muslims was the "Luminous Book!"[30] For the Communists, with Marx and Engels's *Manifesto*, or Lenin's *State and Revolution*, or Stalin or Trotsky, there was radiance in a book as well.

On September 9, 1935, Sjahrir wrote from Boven Digoel to his wife in Holland, "I have just seen in a newspaper an advertisement for Petromax lamp, a new model that burns for *twenty-eight* hours and gives a light of a hundred international candles."³¹ Six weeks later, with the next ship, Sjahrir wrote to his wife again, "It's ten o'clock at night, too early to go to bed. I stay up always until much later and read, of course, under a mosquito net."³²

It got dark at about six o'clock in the evening in Boven Digoel, every day, throughout a year. At six o'clock, the internees struck their lamps to light. They "ate the breeze" and talked and drank coffee or beer, but also read by the light of as new a model of a lamp as they could get. The light then became even more the camp. They heard the light—beneath the noise of mosquitoes and cicadas: "I heard the gas hum in the tubes of the Petromax lamp. It sputtered at first, which caused the wick to glow and temporarily endangered the crown, which was placed more or less loosely on the glass."³³

The Jews were permitted to take fifty kilos "of almost everything" to Theresienstadt. The Boven Digoel people could take more, but they had to pack on very short notice. All took a sample of the world as they knew it, wanted to keep or improve. Books, as lamps, made up a disproportionate share.

"They carried trunks and there were books in each of them," Dr. Schoonheyt wrote about the arrivals to Boven Digoel, in the same tone as he wrote about them carrying umbrellas and bright-colored socks. The new internees were searched on arrival, and initially the literature thought dangerous was confiscated.³⁴ In Boven Digoel, for instance, "a book by the British Premier Ramsay MacDonald entitled *Socialism*, or a book by Firmin Roz, *L'Energie Americaine (Bibliotheque de philosophie scientifique)*." These "unneeded measures," however, were soon corrected and the books were returned to their owners.³⁵

In Theresienstadt, likewise, at first, before the camp settled down as a camp and its concept made clear, some books were deemed contraband and were confiscated on the people's arrival, "as well as writing material including toilet paper."³⁶ As in the Boven Digoel camp, however, after the first weeks, the Jews were left with their books and the camp became what it was till the end. Even many books were left to the Jews in Theresienstadt that in the outside were banned, including those burned on the Opernplatz in Berlin, with Joseph Goebbels orating, the books thought dangerous outside of the camp, Heinrich Heine's, Jakob Wassermann's, Albert Einstein's, and others', by Jews and non-Jews as well.³⁷

"Fifty kilos per person," Ruth Bondy recalled the moment she was getting ready for the camp. "What should one take first? Warm clothing? Food? Bedding? What about toys and textbooks for the children, family photographs, fond souvenirs, Rilke's poetry, or drawing material?"[38]

Very soon after the initial period of uncertainty, libraries were opened in Theresienstadt. The SS office, as it allowed soccer matches in the camp, interfered little with the internees' fashion, it also allowed the libraries. The office even helped with transfers of books to Theresienstadt from the closed Jewish youth training centers, disbanded Jewish academies of learning, not completely burned synagogues, and Jewish apartments from which the Jews were driven to the camps.[39]

"Books, yes, they were," the last head of the Jewish Council of the Elders, rabbi Benjamin Murmelstein, told Claude Lanzmann in an interview after the war. "Jewish books . . . from Warsaw, Breslau, Frankfurt, Amsterdam." "In Theresienstadt," rabbi Murmelstein said, "one could find anything from polar research to [unclear words on the tape]—you could find anything you wanted."[40]

These were, as a rule, public libraries. Every camp person could borrow a book, sometimes for a fee, and sometimes for free. There was a Central Library, and Central Library branches. "In the Central Library," Philipp Manes wrote, "all the books are ordered by categories, and you can instantly get what you need. Hugo Friedmann, our librarian, seems to know each and every book, and he can locate what you asked for in a moment."[41] Professor Emil Utitz, who became the person in charge of the Central Library, and who, as a scholar, also became interested in the individual and collective psychology of the camp, recalled after the war, "My coworkers were in danger of considering themselves a chosen group, so much they loved 'their' library. I had to be on guard lest the librarians might become an exclusive elite, a kind of aristocracy, with its own class consciousness."[42]

Pavel Weiner, age thirteen, wrote frequently in his camp diary about books:

WEDNESDAY, AUGUST 2, 1944 . . . In the morning, I read a book titled *Out of Malayan Jungles*.[43]

WEDNESDAY, AUGUST 9, 1944 . . . Today I was in the library and read *The Merchant of Venice*.[44]

WEDNESDAY, SEPTEMBER 26–28 [*sic*], 1944 . . . We look into the attic of L 218 [barracks]. . . . Books [were] left there. I grabbed several French and English books. One of them is called *How Should a Man Defend Himself?*[45]

Petr Ginz, two years older than Pavel Weiner, made series of "time sheets" in Theresienstadt, where he recorded what books he had read: *"June 1944 . . .* Seneca's *Letters*, . . . London's *The Lost Face*, Alois Musil's *Desert and Oasis*, H. G. Wells's *Christina Alberta's Father*, and parts of Descartes's *Discourse on Method*."[46]

Some of the books borrowed from the Theresienstadt libraries followed the people—or the people followed the books—on the transport "to the east." "They did not mind," Ruth Bondy wrote, "losing a deposit of fifty [camp] crowns for a book."[47] They, the people, and they, the books, traveled to a darker and the darkest place together, as one.

There was the light, and also a smell of books for once—the odor of glue. A workshop was set up in Theresienstadt by the SS administration, where the internees were ordered to bind books for the *Wehrmacht's* soldiers. Some of the books, possibly, might be read, too. For the last weeks of the camp's and the workshop's existence, Norbert Jacques's novel *Dr. Mabuse, der Spieler* is vaguely remembered, on which Fritz Lang based his film trilogy before he left for America.[48]

People carried books to Boven Digoel, too. Mohammad Hatta, one of the two camp academicians, is remembered as the most brilliant example of it, the book light of the camp, making the camp book-enlightened and book-standing-out in the colony at large. There is, in modern Indonesia, no example of a-man-with-books and books-with-a-man like that of Boven Digoel's Hatta.

Hatta was arrested in 1934, soon after he returned from his studies in the Netherlands and took on politics. From his prison cell in Batavia, where he waited for the decision to send him to Boven Digoel, he wrote a letter to the prison director requesting permission to pack his books to make ready for taking them with him to the camp. The permission was given. "Hatta was permitted to leave the prison for three days in a row," Hatta's biographer wrote, "between seven o'clock in the morning and four o'clock in the afternoon, he sorted out the books. . . . Except one trunk with clothes, he did not take any luggage, no baggage, that is, besides sixteen boxes of books. The books went with him from Rotterdam to Batavia, and now to Boven Digoel."[49]

Hatta himself in his own memoirs wrote later in his typical style that he took to the camp "books in boxes, sixteen boxes in all, each a quarter of a cubic meter in size, which came to four cubic meters altogether." "The books took three days to pack," he wrote, "and I got a permission to pack the books into metal boxes."[50]

In the camp itself, "Hatta filled his days with reading." He asked for more books to be sent after him to Boven Digoel, now, as this was a very new place for the academician, for "also books on poultry breeding and on cultivation of vegetables."[51] The books he brought with him and those that he arranged to be sent to him later made a Boven Digoel public library, smaller than the one in Theresienstadt, no doubt, but equally shining in the context.

"Comrade Hatta," wrote Salim, "brought fifteen boxes of books to the camp and we could visit him and borrow his books."[52] Sjahrir, the other academician, who came to the camp with Hatta, wrote to his brother in Holland, on March 9, 1935, "I am reading Goethe's *Faust* and Heine's *Buch der Lieder* now, at Hatta's. . . . Hatta brought with him boxes of books, thirteen or fourteen."[53]

Since books' early times, and certainly since the Enlightenment, prisons, penal colonies, and internment camps were always a space for reading. At least since the liberal and bourgeois nineteenth century, even in the worst prisons and camps, there appeared to be a library. Leo Tolstoy in his *Resurrection* wrote about the feared "Peter and Paul Fortress" in Russia. Prisoners there were also allowed to read and write. "As to books," a prison guard in the *Resurrection* tells a visitor, "we have a library, and the books that are allowed are given to them [prisoners]. Nor are they prohibited from writing. We give them slates and slate pencils so that they can occupy themselves with writing. They can wipe off what they have written and write again and again."[54]

"With the very ship on which I arrived to Boven Digoel, as it was ready to go back," Hatta wrote in his memoirs, "I managed to send a letter to *Pemandangan* [Outlook] magazine with an article about Socrates."[55] He must have written the article on the ship. Next to nothing of what Hatta wrote afterward, in the camp, survived, but he was seen by everyone, and he was remembered, as writing all the time. It was the intensity of writing on a slate with a slate pencil. One small thing, possibly written in the camp (at least Hatta says so), which somehow survived, is a little brochure, a kind of a primer—on Greek philosophy again.[56]

Soetan Sjahrir, the other academician, was too much of a flâneur to carry boxes of books around. But he was equally into writing, equally visible, and almost equally the light of the camp as Hatta was.

Sjahrir wrote almost exclusively letters, but everybody knew it in the camp. Almost all of them were personal, to his wife, his wife's children from a previous marriage, and his younger brother, who lived with them in Haarlem, the Netherlands. These were extraordinarily long letters, lines tightly packed so that they could last, the writing as well as the reading of them, for the six weeks or so between the ships.⁵⁷

In Theresienstadt, Olda Havlová recalled, "Together with Emil Holan, we wrote a children's book. We bound it in cloth and decorated the cover with the Theresienstadt coat of arms."⁵⁸ Quite a number of Theresienstadt diaries, often nicely bound and decorated, can be read in the archives in Jerusalem, Givat Haim (Ihud), in Prague, or at Theresienstadt Memorial. Josef Taussig is remembered as writing a Theresienstadt version of the *Good Soldier Švejk*. The manuscript got lost, but some stories from it survived.

"A cult of magazines emerged in Theresienstadt," wrote historian Vojtěch Blodig.⁵⁹ Satirical (and truly funny) *Šalom na pátek* [Shalom on Friday], was published every Friday in barracks room number 246 BV, "published" meaning that a copy was displayed in the common bedroom for those who wished to come and read. Gerty Spies wrote about "Theresienstadt's rhyming sickness."⁶⁰ Poetry competitions had been organized in the camp, with prizes:

> First prize: two cans of sardines and one loaf of bread; second prize: ten decagrams of honey, ten decagrams of sugar, and ten decagrams of [?]; third prize: ten decagrams of quark, ten decagrams of sugar, and ten decagrams of marmalade.⁶¹

As there were concerts and operas in Theresienstadt, so there were public readings.⁶² The internees began with public readings and lectures as soon as they were allowed to by the SS administration and as soon as the camp settled down, but still in 1942. The last lecture, according to memory, was given in May 1945, in the last days of the camp. According to a list put together by professor Emil Utitz after the war, there were

1. academic lectures
2. language lectures: in English, American [sic], French, Italian, Hebrew, and Yiddish
3. Judaic lectures
4. recitations (arts, literature, poetry)
5. popular lectures (about social problems, for friends of nature, etc.)
6. lectures for people interested in economics and industry.⁶³

One of the "Cultural Reports" occasionally published in the boys' magazine *Vedem* reads, "An important event in our cultural life is the re-establishment of two cultural circles (Latin and Russian)."⁶⁴ For medical workers, "clinical evenings" were organized, with lectures and seminars taking place mostly in the Central Hospital.⁶⁵

Professor Stránský gave a popular lecture on macrobiotics and eugenics among the Jews.⁶⁶ "In this semester [sic] in the English Club, there were heated discussions about whether Shylock really meant to fully consummate his contract with Antonio or whether he did not."⁶⁷ In a "Hebrew Circle" on May 9, 1942, there was "an interesting lecture on [Shmuel Yosef] Agnon."⁶⁸

"Anyone who was there," Adler wrote, "would never forget the evening on the sixtieth anniversary of Kafka's birth. The evening was attended by Kafka's sister Ottilie, by other relatives, and by two schoolmates of the poet."⁶⁹ On Thursday, April 6, 1944, Pavel Weiner wrote, "I talked with my parents and wrote my diary. But then I had to hurry to the *Heim* [youth home] because at eight there was a lecture on graphology."⁷⁰ On June 21, 1944, "in *Bahnhofstrasse*, no. 35 at seven-thirty in the evening, Alfred Engelsmann will give a talk, 'In Free Balloon over the Alps.'"⁷¹

Alice Bloemendahl, a Dutch Jewish woman, had been approached by a Jewish official from the Council of the Elders: "Would you like to go to the *Altersheim* [home for the elderly] to be a woman-reader?" Mrs. Bloemendahl did, and she recalled after the war, "My listeners (they were often seriously ill) lay deep in their pillows.... The listeners in one room varied between seven and twenty, but sometimes there were forty and more.... I began with *Erinnerungen an Frauen*. Two novels, one by Ernst Penzoldt and the other by Theodor Fontane, followed." Then she read Heinrich Heine's "Rabbi of Bacharach" from the *Books of Songs*. "By demand," Mrs. Bloemendahl recalled, "I have also read *Geschichte Napoleons*."⁷²

In one scene of one of the Theresienstadt cabarets, life had been presented as it might be after the war and when the camp would be over. Two clowns meet "after the war" and are trying to remember the name of the camp:

PIDLA HORPATZKY: What was the name of it again? Like some German poet. Was it Schiller? No, it was not that. Some other poet. Who is some other German poet?

FELIX PORGES: Heine? Was that name Heino?...

PIDLA HORPATZKY: No ... oh no. Oh yes! Who wrote *Faust*?

FELIX PORGES: Goethe.

PIDLA HORPATZKY: Yes, correct! Ghetto was the name!⁷³

There were schools in both camps, as there had to be, like in any enlightened place. The camp schools, like books and like clothes, were more, more schools than just schools, and more a site of light than any school before or anywhere else.

The first school in Boven Digoel was founded almost as soon as the military post, the hospital, and the radio station; before the site for the camp had even been fully cleared of trees. Captain L. Th. Becking, the first commandant-administrator of the camp, known as the butcher who brutally suppressed the Communist rebellion in 1926–27, and this was reportedly why he got the job, "founded a school for the children of the internees."[74] The school was a "government school." In 1928, the second school year, for instance, "ƒ1,800 had been appropriated by the government to pay for the school."[75] The school lasted throughout the camp's existence, and throughout that time it was "intensively cared for" by the government:

> JANUARY 15, 1935. The school building is getting a new roof and it is being painted white from the outside.[76]

The Dutch Indies Department of Education and Industry agreed to school for the internees in the camp as a "standard school of a full status" with a link "for its more-gifted students" to advanced, a middle-level education outside the camp. All the students admitted to the government school passed through the first three grades, where the language of instruction was Malay, and, afterward, they were divided in two groups. The "less gifted" were to continue to the fourth and fifth grade, while those found gifted by the teachers were to be admitted to the "connecting" classes in the school, up to the eighth grade.[77]

The administration of the camp, Salim recalled, contributed to the budget of the school generously, including support to a "social and sport club for the students."[78] The language of instruction, as the "gifted" children passed from grade to grade, became increasingly Dutch, until by the fifth grade it became exclusively Dutch.

Mr. Bangun Topo told me that in Boven Digoel he also attended a kindergarten, and he pointed out to me on the map where the building stood; a good site, and close to the river.[79] Mrs. Chamsinah recalled that in the first grade, they learned to write on *papan tulis* with *batu tulis*, on a slate with a slate pen.[80] "In the higher grades," Mr. Trikoyo said, "we all had pens, you know, with pen-holders."[81]

Several lists of students have been preserved and can be found in the camp archive, from the early years of the camp till almost the end, grade by grade:

List of the students of the Government School, Third Quarter, 1941:

seventh grade: one boy, zero girls;
sixth grade: two boys, zero girls;
fifth grade: six boys, zero girls;
fourth grade: two boys, six girls;
third grade: seven boys, five girls;
second grade: five boys, two girls;
first grade: five boys, six girls;
kindergarten: seven boys, six girls;
total: thirty-five boys, twenty-five girls.[82]

In September 12, 1929, the camp administrator J. Blok wrote to the resident in Ambon that, "against the wishes of the internees for a higher school in the camp," he had decided that "this was not desirable." "I think," administrator Blok wrote, "that in a place so small as Boven Digoel, it is useless to have three schools [besides the elementary and the "linking"], and that it would cause an unnecessary burden to the budget."[83]

Yet the internees persisted and then looked for their own ways. "The official school was Dutch," Mrs. Chamsinah told me, "but the internees then got permission to set up a Malay-English school." Malay-*English* school! "The Dutch school," said Mrs. Chamsinah, meaning the government school, "was located in section C of the camp, close to the administration building. The Malay-English school, now, was in section A, where also we lived, and it was the school to which I went."[84] "The government school," says Mr. Trikoyo, "was not the school I went to. My father wished to have to do as little with the government as he could."[85]

"Even before I grew up enough, I often went to school with my older siblings," Mrs. Widayasih told me about the Malay-English school. "There were children from the families who did not want to bow to the government. They did not send their children to the school established by the government where the language was Dutch. The Malay-English school we went to was set up by the internees themselves, and there English was taught from the first grade."

"When I reached the age of six," Mrs. Widayasih told me, "I went to school for the first time as truly a pupil [not just visiting with the older children]. I walked by myself carrying a slate and a slate pencil. The walk from our house to school took only ten or fifteen minutes. It was a nice road, and soon other children joined me on the road. No, no jungle. There were houses of our neighbors along the road, at quite a distance from each other, fifty meters or so, people were smiling at us and we would call out: 'Good morning! Good morning!'"[86]

In 1935, the regime all over the Indies tightened, these were 1930s like everywhere else in the world. By a special "Explanatory Regulation," a "new standard" had been set for schools, as well. Only government schools in the Indies and the private schools that would satisfy a new standard could be accredited. If a private school that did not satisfy the standard and, in spite of the regulation, persisted in teaching, in the term that the Dutch as well as unaccredited schools people used, it became *wilde,* a "wild," school. Such schools were disciplined, and their teachers might be even sent to prison. There was an exception. If there were students from no more than three families at one time in one classroom, they could still be taught legally.[87]

The Malay-English School, set up by the internees in Boven Digoel, was a private school; it did not meet new standards, and thus could not teach as before. But it only made the teaching in Boven Digoel more intensive and more of light. The government school remained open, and the other way of teaching became "wild."

Register of the penalties statement by internee Loekman, eighteen years old.

Internee Loekman . . . It is true that on Saturday, May 16, 1936, at eleven o'clock in the morning, I was giving a singing lesson. I stood in front of the class and wrote notes on the blackboard. This was intended only for my students, the children from only three internee families. However, it is true, that there were other children, too, sitting on the benches in the back of the room, and it is true that they were also writing down the notes. They were from more than three internee families, but they came on their own. . . . It is also true that, in addition to it, there were still some other children. But they were standing outside of the house at the windows, looking in.

Penalty: Eight days prison.

The "wild schools" in the camp, as elsewhere in the Indies, were called more softly "house schools," and thus they are also often listed in the Boven Digoel official documents:

List of students of the house schools in 1940 . . .
Forty students, fifteen teachers.[88]

List of students of the house schools in the first quarter of 1941:
8 teachers, 8 houses (families).[89]

Boven Digoel, the clearing, often felt like one school, a "wild school," that is. Mohammad Hatta is remembered for the sixteen (let us say) boxes of books he brought to the camp, but also for his teaching—philosophy, economics, whatever was asked for and whoever asked. Hatta used to "sign students up" for "twice a week," his biographer says. He taught "after he finished with his own study for the day, and with gardening, and taking care of his chickens."[90]

According to the report by the camp administrator, in 1940, for instance (Hatta was gone by that time), the number of "adult students" in the camp was twenty-three,[91] and there certainly were many more in the really wild, unreported categories. According to the administrator's report for December 31, 1941, in the "evening courses" for adult students, in class number 1, further unspecified, there were five students, in class number 2 there were also five students. In the "afternoon courses taught by internee Sardjono" there were two students, and in "evening courses taught by Achmad Somadi" there was one student.[92]

The Catholic and Protestant missions in the Boven Digoel camp offered classes, too, but exclusively for the children of the military and civilian camp officials. By the second quarter of 1935, there were fifteen boys and six girls attending the Catholic school, and ten boys and nine girls at the Protestant one.[93] There were countless and beyond-registration Islamic courses and Koranic readings in the camp. Internee Achmad Chatib, for instance, was known "teaching for money, giving a course in religion in the mosque as well as coming to the internees' houses."[94]

As in Boven Digoel, there were schools in Theresienstadt, adding substantially to the light of the camp, often being the single light of the camp, making the camp in all its campness a space of enlightenment.

Formally, understood ordinarily, the schools in Theresienstadt were forbidden. On May 16, 1942, as the camp was taking its shape, Gonda Redlich wrote, "Order of the day: . . . teaching will be forbidden."[95] "Any studying was forbidden under the German decree," Nava Shean, a woman of the camp, wrote in her memoirs. "They only allowed 'games' and 'mental tasks.'"[96]

In the town of Theresienstadt, before the camp was established, of course, there used to be schools. The two largest former school buildings became Barracks L 124 and Barracks L 417 in the camp. Throughout the camp's existence, they were still, especially Barracks L 417, called "schools."

Barracks L 417, the more significant of the two, was a big four-story building, just around the corner from the town's and the camp's main square. Its assigned use became that of *Jugendheim* [youth home].[97] Interned children between the ages of four and ten lived in several *Kinderheim*s [children's homes] in the camp; the older boys and girls, between ten and sixteen, lived in *Knaben- und Mädchenheim*s [boys' and girls' homes]; and the youth between the ages of sixteen and twenty were housed in *Lehrling und Jungarbeiterheim*s [students' and young workers' homes].

It was not obligatory for children and young people in the camp to live separately from their families, that is, if they had made it to the camp together. But many families, "at least half of them," after they considered the choice, let their children move into one of the Jugend- or Kinderheims.[98] Jehuda Bacon, who lived in one of the homes for older children, told me, "You should know, many children were not so lucky. Living with their parents in the barracks, they remained poor, uneducated."[99]

There were "supervisors" accredited by the Council of the Elders and assigned to the individual "homes." Almost instantly, the children's homes, in their own Theresienstadt "wild way," became schools, and they grew into schools, as in Boven Digoel, schools more than schools, more schools than ever before and anywhere else.

Textbooks from the prewar schools in Czechoslovakia, Germany, Austria, and the Netherlands were brought into the camp with the other books in trunks and backpacks. All school subjects as in the textbooks and as remembered were taught—languages, history, civics, geography, mathematics, music, and arts.[100] When there were not enough textbooks, which means everywhere, "teachers," called teachers or by other names, "taught from memory and they wrote texts of their own." Instructive examples from classical literature, or exercises of algebra, "from memory, were retyped as textbooks."[101]

"I have also enrolled in a French course," wrote Pavel Weiner on Monday, August 21, 1944, "so I quickly go to Barracks L 216, where the class is being held."[102] The children over fourteen in Theresienstadt were encouraged to enlist in courses in "practical professions," watchmaker, locksmith, agricultural technician, baker, butcher, or electrician.[103] "The favorite in all schools," the boys of Barracks L 417 wrote in their magazine, was "physical education."[104]

There were schools or "schools" in the Theresienstadt camp, informal, even undercover, of many sorts. There was a "school" in the camp for "the children with learning disabilities" and for "disturbed [sic] children." It was run by two internees, husband and wife, who, before the war, were a professional psychologist and an educator.[105]

An exquisite Viennese painter interned in the camp, Friedl Dicker-Brandeis, began to teach painting and drawing in Theresienstadt, first to the girls in Barracks L 410, and later also to boys and to adults all over the camp.[106] Dicker-Brandeis was a graduate of the European most avant-garde Bauhaus arts school, and there studied under luminaries such as Johannes Itten and Paul Klee. The drawings of Theresienstadt children, now in the Jewish Museum in Prague, are her classes' projects. She was transported to Auschwitz in 1944, where she perished.[107]

"We had school every day," a girl in her early teens at the time recalled, "but there was no fixed plan. Teachers changed too often." "When there was a teacher of English, English was taught," the girl recalled, "and when that teacher had to go on transport and there came someone who might not know English but was good in mathematics, so mathematics was taught. . . . The girls, too, came and went."[108] "We were a team. We learned together and, under the direction of 'betreurka' [Czech camp-form of *Betreuerin*, German for a "chaperone," a name the girls in this particular barracks used for a teacher or guardian], we learn geography, history, math. . . . We all are now about thirteen years old and had before this just the elementary school. What will become of us? In the evenings, we usually read."[109]

"I remember to this day," another boy in the camp recalled long after the war, "that we studied the history of the Persian wars and the heroic defense at Thermopylae."[110] The boys in Barrack L 417 came to call their school "the Republic." Like several other homes or schools, they had their own anthem and flag. The anthem "was sung to the tune of a worker's song: 'Like a Tempest Round the World.'"[111] *Vedem* was the "school" magazine.[112]

There were "schools" for adults, too, another component of the camp status, dignity, and light. "Promotions of the Jewish camp policemen," the *Vedem* reported, "are granted according to seniority but also based on good progress in a course in the camp where laws and regulations are taught."[113]

The camps, like schools, more than ever, ultimately, became places of selection. People were tested and placed according to the grades attained—ultimately, at the time of the camps, placed, and discarded. From the very beginning of Boven Digoel, there were lists compiled of the internees who might be considered for special treatment, even for a possible release from the camp. Behavior mattered, but explicitly, ostentatiously, and categorically the person's education figured high on the list.

The list of category A internees who might be considered for release, September 1930

...

3. Markoen Samirata . . . seven years of school in Magelan . . . in the seventh year he dropped out.

...

7. Adam bin Sarpan . . . never attended a school but has acquired some home education. . . . Can read and write.

...

31. Amin, alias Amintapoera . . . native school of the second class.

...

33. Emed, alias Diono, alias Lie Kong Djen . . . school of the second-class.[114]

Schooling made the internees, to echo Robert Musil's term, men (and women) "with qualities." "Sardjono," wrote Koesalah Toer about a prominent Boven Digoel internee, "originally from Priangan, West Java, was a son of a Dutch official in Madura. His father did not legally recognize him, and he was brought up by his mother who was a village woman. But still, Sardjono graduated from the Europese Lagere School (ELS) and Hogere Burgerschool (HBS);[115] ELS was the most elite Dutch elementary, and HBS was an exclusive Dutch high school, in the Netherlands and the more so in the Indies.

The desire to move up in the camp, the desire to be considered for being let out of the camp, and a desire for school became blurred as one burning desire in the camp, a desire for freedom. There is a thick file in the Boven Digoel archives of letters by the internees asking the camp authorities to let their children, with or without their mothers, leave the camp—and to go to school; fathers would stay, of course.

> *To the Assistant Resident, Boven Digoel, June 9, 1929* . . . My daughter Djoemarsih . . . is six years old . . . and we wish to inscribe her in the best school possible. Her grandparents live in Padalarang, Java, and she can stay with them. . . . They can take care of her, and she would like to go. . . . The wife of comrade Sardjono has been permitted to leave Boven Digoel, she goes with the next ship, and she agreed to take our daughter with her and take care of her during the passage. Our daughter would travel at our own expense. In high respect. [Signature illegible][116]

Mohammad Hatta and Soetan Sjahrir, the two "academicians," topped the camp, the camp as school. On June 29, 1935, less than a year after the two men arrived at the camp, there was a debate about their fate in a colonial institution as high as the Volksraad, the "People's Council," in Batavia. The government spokesman told the Volksraad deputies that "a lesser suitability of Boven Digoel as an interning place for intellectuals has been brought to our attention."[117]

On January 4, 1936, several Indies Indonesian papers reported news soon to be confirmed that the two internees indeed were to be released from Boven Digoel. "We might wonder," one of the papers wrote, "why the same treatment could not be extended to more people. But still, at least these two intellectuals are let go," and, the paper wrote, "our thanks go to the government for this."[118]

School in Boven Digoel could become an argument for releasing an internee from the camp. There was no such possibility in Theresienstadt—schools perhaps, but release no. Yet the measure of freedom (in the camp) was based on the level of schooling, too, the level of school achieved before the camp, as well as the results of testing and the grading in the camp. To belong to the camp, people studied. Pavel Weiner wrote:

TUESDAY, APRIL 4, 1944 . . . I was very worried, but I passed the exam. After the exam, I went with Lamm for *gebak* [pastry].[119]

FRIDAY, APRIL 14, 1944. I got my report card today and I have all Excellents and [only] three Satisfactories![120]

WEDNESDAY, JUNE 7, 1944 . . . The *tercie* [third year in Czech gymnasium] ended up well.

FRIDAY, JULY 21, 1944 . . . We have dictation titled "Spring Blossom." It is easy and most likely I will have no mistakes. Then I have to write a composition on the theme "My Friend." Because it seems silly to me, I write about a man who is all alone in the world. I think it will be good. . . . Lichtwitz [a teacher] finally arrives and gives me a test on what I know about Africa. In history I'm tested about Charles IV. I do well in both. Then I go to Room 5 for a test in Judaism.[121]

Pavel was a school-age boy. But also for every position in the camp, the Jewish "self-administration" organized a testing. The camp people tested themselves all the time in the camp, and they had to let themselves be tested. The SS administration of the camp let it be, it, if one may use a pedagogic expression, just "set the standard."

Vily Schönfeld had been a professional graphologist before the war. He was deported to Theresienstadt on July 13, 1943, and was charged by the

Jewish Council of the Elders "to conduct graphological assessment of applicants for any position." He served as the internee handwriting examiner until December 12, 1943, when he was transported to Auschwitz.[122]

The unprecedented yearning for survival in the camps became identified with an equally unprecedented yearning for light. Testing became the motor of the yearning, and thus it was a source of radiance of the camps. As Michel Foucault might say, though he got none of his examples from the camps, this was, and in its most intensive form, "a disciplinary polyphony of exercise," a "pedagogical practice," and a "command pedagogics."[123]

Unattainable freedom, like unattainable truth, as never before, could be understood in a school-like way. "I have 'Excellents' in all subjects," like Pavel Weiner, a Theresienstadt girl (also one of those who did not survive) wrote in her diary in the camp. "Perhaps it is true," she went on, "and I am beginning to believe it, I have changed completely. I am no more who I was in Kyjov [her native town in Moravia]: Cleanliness Excellent, Orderliness Excellent, Manners Excellent, Other Subjects Excellent!"[124]

Camps were injected into the world and expanded, moving the world to what might be the ultimate stage of the Enlightenment. The camps finally brought about what Ernst Bloch wrote at the dawn of camps: "Belief in an already-completed framework of the world and an omen already completely disclosed in the alpha of the absolute idea." The freedom and truth not as "a solitary light" but as "a headmaster." As if he knew all about the camps, Bloch wrote, "The night of the world retreats into the merely ignorant subject," and "here spreads the beautiful warmth of the classroom."[125]

ELEVEN

Limelight

Limelight, more than anything, was the light of the camps. It is wrong to call what happened in the camps tragedy—a scripted narrative, the curtain going up, and down at the end and people going home. Yet the camps were as enlightened as the theater.

Worshipping culture as they surely did, the Germans were often thought, in the modern and civilized world since the eighteenth century, at least, to be the people of the theater. The Germans "were drawn to the theater, as the living incarnation of books, full of pomp and action," wrote Walter Mehring, a Jew who did not go to Theresienstadt because he fled in time.[1] Besides, since the late nineteenth century at least, another view was expressed, and increasingly, that, "the German theatre, stage, and audiences were overrun by Jews—that these had in fact become *Verjudet* [Jewified]." The view, wrote a historian of modern theater, "was often voiced in the early decades of the twentieth century by anti-Semite and Jew alike."[2]

"The Queen of the Night and her allies are killed," William Kentridge described the icon of the modern theater, Mozart's opera *The Magic Flute*. "Love and enlightenment win," Kentridge wrote, "THE STAGE BECOMES

THE SUN."³ Theater convincingly was the culmination of modern human history understood as an increasing light. "The lighting equipment now in use," wrote Antonin Artaud in the 1930s, at the noontime of the camps, is "no longer adequate." Artaud demanded, in the name of the avant-garde, in his *The Theater of Cruelty*, "spreading the light in waves, in sheets, in fusillades of fiery arrows." "Light," he wrote, meaning theater light, "must recover an element of thinness, density, and opaqueness, with a view of producing the sensations of heat, cold, anger, fear, etc."⁴ The spectator in the kind of theater Artaud demanded must be, to use others' words, "dazed and spent."⁵ Theater, through its light, must "physically envelop the spectator."⁶

It is difficult to forget at times that Artaud was in fact not writing about the camps. "The scenes," he theorized about a truly modern and certainly coming theater, "will be played in front of whitewashed wall-backgrounds designated to absorb light."⁷ "Thus," he wrote, "there will be no lost movements, all movements will obey a rhythm; and each character being merely a type, his gesticulation, physiognomy, and costume will appear like so many rays of light."⁸

In Europe and in Germany especially, commentators on culture wrote about "Jewish theatromania."⁹ Friedrich Nietzsche set the tone of the time to come, as in so many things. In *The Gay Science* he stated that the Jews were nothing but actors, "a nation of adaptation, artists par excellence."¹⁰

The camps, and it appeared completely natural and inevitable, were full of theater. The camps were close to bursting with theater, and they were close to being nothing but theater. They were staged, and not just for inspection tours of the higher ups in the camp's bureaucracy or for the eyes and ears of the outside world that might notice. The dazzling light of the camps was concentrated, hard on the eye, the ultimate man-made, switchable, brilliant, multicolored, and scenic light.

"The progressive Westerner," wrote Japanese Junichiro Tanizaki in the 1930s, "is determined always to better his lot. From candle to oil lamp, oil lamp to gaslight, gaslight to electric light—his quest is for a brighter light, to eradicate even the minutest shadow."¹¹ "Light is used," Tanizaki repeated, "for dispelling the shadows."¹²

In Boven Digoel, as far from Europe as it could be, against the jungle, the darkest of the dark, the music pavilion, sometimes called the "Social and Entertainment House" and sometimes the Congresgebouw [Congress Building], was also a place for theater.¹³

On many nights in the camp, Javanese *wayang kulit* [shadow-puppet play] was staged. Each performance, by tradition, began after dark and lasted until the first light in the morning. *Bléncong*, "a specific, usually beautifully ornamented, oil lamp used for traditional *wayang* performances,"[14] was ceremoniously lighted, as a rule with a prayer. A sheet of cloth, *belakang mburi kelir*, a white screen, not unlike the Artaud's "whitewashed wall-backgrounds designated to absorb light," was raised, making for a scene. Flat puppets carved out of buffalo hide, representing gods, heroes, their wives, and servants, were made to move by *dalang*, the puppeteer, sitting behind the screen, between the lamp and the screen. The spectators, in front of the screen, watched the shadows.

"Typically," wrote Benedict Anderson, "the first puppet that the puppeteer brings on stage is described by him as someone who 'yearns for' a loved one or a treasured object."[15] Wayang kulit was repeatedly and with much justification compared to Plato's cave: "Between the fire and prisoners . . . is a low wall built, just as puppeteers have a screen in front of the audience. . . . Tell me, would you think at first that people in this situation have seen anything of themselves or each other except the shadows thrown by the fire onto the wall of the cave in front of them? . . . If they were able to talk to each other, wouldn't you think they would call what they saw real?"[16] In spite of it, no, because of it, as in the cave so in the camps, certainly the wayang play on light could hardly be anything but absorbing.

And when the lamp flame's quenched,
Then everything becomes a void,
Nothing at all exists. . . .
The meaning of the screen is body.
While wayang [the puppet] is the inner soul . . .
The bléncong [the lamp] is the Light of Life.[17]

Ghada Karmi in her recent *Palestinian Memoir* described a wall between Palestinian territories and Israel proper at the Qalandiya checkpoint near Jerusalem. Palestinian activists painted on the wall, on its Palestinian side, something that "looked deceptively realistic," "a 'hole' as if cut out of the wall." One could "see" "blue sky and a patch of green field on the 'other side.'" "So skillfully it was done that one could almost believe it was real."[18]

The most intensive, concentrated care was taken to make the life in the camp look real. In "shops" the Jews "paid" with "money." "The unreal character of the camp life," Hans Günther Adler wrote, "was by this process fundamentally strengthened."[19] The feat of capitalism, commodity, and life-commodity as fetish had been achieved in the camp almost completely and certainly ahead of its time.

A Viennese philosopher, Hans Vaihinger, published a book in 1911 on the culture of the modern. The book became instantly popular in Europe, and its influence lasted well into the time of the camps. It became common knowledge among well-read people, and it was known, of course, in Theresienstadt as well.

The title of the Vaihinger's book and its theme was *The Philosophy of "As If."* Vaihinger overquoted Nietzsche in the book and based much of his argument on what he believed was Nietzsche's. "This is 'the wisdom of the illusion,'" Vaihinger quoted Nietzsche, "the myth must 'be brought back to virility.'"[20] "'We need blindness sometimes,'" was another of Vaihinger's Nietzsche quotes, "'and [we] must allow certain articles of faith and errors to remain untouched within us.'"[21] There is an "abundance of optical errors" in particular, in the contemporary world, and these, too, "we must consciously maintain."[22]

Philipp Manes's Theresienstadt diary was written very much in the spirit and under the influence of Vaihinger, and when it was published after the war, its title, with much justification, was *"Als ob's ein Leben wär,"* "As if it were a life."

Mr. Manes, who did not survive, as we know, lived much of his life in the camp organizing theater, acting in theater, and absorbed by theater. During the fewer than three years given Mr. Manes in the camp, the "Manes Group" put on stage dozens of major works of European dramatic literature as "performance in concert." Goethe's *Faust*, most memorably, was arranged by Manes for two evenings, and between 1943 and 1944 *Faust* was performed "to full house" in the camp six times.[23] The "Manes Group's" theater evenings or afternoons are possibly the most often mentioned events of the camp, cultural or otherwise. *As if* they were the most real thing to happen in the camp.

Philipp Manes's were not the only evocations of Hans Vaihinger in the camp. On a different level and for internees of other tastes, the cabaret of husband and wife Strauss, as famous as Manes's theater in the camp, became especially popular with a song, a *schlager*, a hit, soon almost an anthem of the camp, titled "As If." One of the endless strophes—and more and more were added about all aspects of Theresienstadt life as time went on, but this seemed to be the finale—was sung like this:

There is a café in Theresienstadt
Café de l'Europe as if
And when music there begins to play
One feels as if—[24]

There was a *spectacular* presence of theater in both camps, not the presence in absence, in longing for it, in trying to recall it, as in the case of food or fashion. Theater was real; there was a real theatrical presence in the camp. Each camp, to use Artaud's words not about the camps, was an "absolute action of a spectacle."[25]

Each day and each evening, as long into the night as the curfew at the moment permitted, there was at least one, but often several, stage events in Theresienstadt—books, language, voice, often with music, sometimes in costumes, in the limelight. Nava Shean staged Jean Cocteau's *La voix humaine* in the camp, a story of a woman pleading on a telephone with her lover not to leave her.[26] Her one-woman performance was "kept on the program" throughout the camp's existence until the last weeks of the camp. Nava Shean, originally from Prague, performed *La voix humaine* alternately in Czech and in German.[27]

Shean did not play just Cocteau. She wrote in her memoirs, "I remembered by heart entire books of poetry, sections from plays, scenes of monologues. So I began to travel around the barracks in the evening after work."[28]

"Fashion is a rapid succession of absolute sites," Roland Barthes wrote in his *Fashion System*, "weekend, spring, and the *Riviera* are 'scenes.'"[29] "In fashion photography," Barthes wrote a few pages further on, "the world is usually photographed as a decor, a background, or a scene, in short, as a theater."[30] Joseph Roth, as if complementing Barthes and also as if talking about camp theater in particular, wrote, "Imagination [becomes] livelier than conscience."[31]

A theater stage in the camp, like fashion in Walter Benjamin's sense, was inorganic, "defending the rights of the corpse,"[32] or, in Kafka's sense, it was a wonderful apparatus. The theater sky, as in Samuel Beckett's absurd theater, and as in the camps, is "a sky that is sky only in name, a tree that makes them wonder whether it is one." Perhaps, Beckett was suggesting, his *Waiting for Godot* might be made more convincing "by means of labels, or better still . . . by announcements: 'Well, it seems, this is the sky.'"[33]

Theater stages were being built and played on in the camp in places where someone who was never in a camp would think it impossible—in a theater hall from the precamp times of the town, but also, and more so, in the garrets, attics, and basements of the barracks, in the barracks' courtyards, and in dormitories between the beds.[34] Sometimes the offices of the Jewish Council of the Elders had been cleared in the evening and a play was given, other times stables were used, horses gone long ago.

Nathan the Wise by Gotthold Ephraim Lessing, a play about a Jew saving a Christian girl during the Crusades, by an eighteenth-century German author, had been loved and treasured by cultured people in Germany, Jews as well as non-Jews, no less than Goethe's or Schiller's dramas. *Nathan the Wise* was banned by the Nazis throughout Nazi-occupied Europe. But it was performed in Theresienstadt. The "Manes Group," premiered it on June 19, 1943, and repeated it several times, "in concert," the roles read by actors sitting on the stage.[35]

"And there was a puppet theater," Dr. Adoplph Metz recalled, "as beautiful as one could imagine."[36] Theater in Theresienstadt was cruel in the Antonin Artaud sense, visionary, avant-garde, and beautiful.

František Zelenka was born in 1904 and died in 1944 on a transport from Theresienstadt to Auschwitz. Before the war, he was a stage and costume designer for the Czech National Theater in Prague. Gustav Schorsch was born in 1918 and he also perished. Before the camp he worked as the director of a small experimental theater in Prague. Paradoxically, one might say, but this would not be the right word, only in Theresienstadt did Zelenka and Schorsch get an opportunity to realize their artistic aspirations, fully and ultimately. The Theresienstadt production of Gogol's *The Marriage* in particular, first performed in February 1944, on which they worked together, became not only "the peak of theater production in the camp,"[37] the peak production in the life of the two artists, but possibly the most accomplished piece of theatrical work in that part of the world at the time.

It was, most chillingly, a "work in progress," in the flow of the time, carried by the time. As *The Marriage* was being rehearsed, Nava Shean, who was one of the cast, remembers, "Several actors were 'sent east' and had to be replaced, which meant we had to start over."[38] Gogol's *The Marriage*, Nava Shean recalled, was, and she used Artaud's word, in fact, "cruel satire."[39] The actors, for a performance, received "one hundred grams of sugar and a piece of margarine." For scenery, Zelenka used any available material to be found in the camp, real in the camp, as if real: "logs, sacks, boxes, paper, and huge bed sheets (which were available in abundance due to the many dead)."[40]

Nava Shean remembered Gustav Schorsch, who directed *The Marriage* and many other plays in the camp, as a passionate devotee of Soviet theater director Konstantin Stanislavsky. "Stanislavsky's book, *My Life in Art*, was our beacon. Schorsch quoted it for us from memory."[41]

The poems of François Villon were adapted for stage by Irena Dodalová. Margit Siberfeld, another internee, remembered after the war, "In it I danced."[42] "Theresienstadt," wrote Ruth Bondy, "in some respects, was the most liberal stage in all of occupied Central Europe."[43] Ruth Bondy might also say "the most diverse stage." Zelenka was a Czech Jew, and Schorsch was a German Jew. Nava Shean was from Prague, and she performed her Cocteau both in Czech and in German.

German theater repertory in Theresienstadt brought in and realized by the Jews coming from Germany and Austria was, on the whole, wrote Peter Demetz, "more middle class and conservative." Some theater people in the camp "mocked the Viennese tradition," while others performed it in all seriousness, namely "the sweet operettas of yesterday." They were "often played and greatly enjoyed" in the camp.[44]

> To the Production Workshop, Theresienstadt,
>
> SEPTEMBER 7, 1944
>
> For the next production, I need urgently tails and a large white chrysanthemum
>
> *Signed (Stage Director) Kurt Gerron*

The last-ever theatrical performance in Theresienstadt, Johann Strauss's *Die Fledermaus*, appears to have taken place on April 20, 1945. Of this production, the play's director, Hans Hofer, recalled, "We managed to get dinner jackets and ladies evening dresses from the camp's *Kleiderkammer* [clothes storage]."[45] Josef Taussig, in one of his stories from the camp, described a theater event: "The hall is already packed. Those who got a ticket from a scalper are now finding out that someone else has a ticket for the same seat. But in the end, all are somehow seated, and the show begins as it was supposed to."[46]

On Saturday, January 6, 1945, Pavel Weiner, wrote, "It took some doing on my part to drag [my mother] to the concert, but after, she gave me a kiss out of thankfulness. In the evening, she was so excited that she couldn't fall asleep."[47] There were tickets sold, haggled for, or given away as an award.[48] Honoraria were paid to performers, such as "'bonuses' of sugar, margarine, liver paste, or dumplings."[49] "I was most deeply touched," Manes wrote after one such evening he organized and directed. "Two ladies came to see me afterward, one gave me a whole *buchta* (sugar bun), the other gave me a half."[50]

The theater might have been the ultimate of Theresienstadt, but Theresienstadt was not the end of it. Many, the less lucky, Theresienstadt people were sent "further to the east," and to Auschwitz in particular. Many were not instantly murdered. Namely, the large group that came to Auschwitz from Theresienstadt in January 1944 was put in the "family camp," with barracks for men, women, and children. There, "in the shadow of the crematoria," as Ruth Bondy entitled the final section of her recollections, there was still theater, and, arguably, the most real one.

An adaptation of Walt Disney's *Snow White and the Seven Dwarfs* was "put on in the barracks" in Auschwitz for the Theresienstadt children. It was directed by the youth supervisors from Theresienstadt, and all the roles were played by the children.[51] A staging of *Robinson Crusoe* is also remembered, "with Friday, sailors, and monkeys," as well as a version of Abbé Prévost's *Manon Lescaut* written by the Czech poet Vítězslav Nezval for an avant-garde theater in Prague in 1940. "In concert" a selection from the ballads by Francois Villon was performed. There was also "a puppet theater" played for the Theresienstadt children by Theresienstadt people. All of this, as Ruth Bondy adds, was "drawn from the memories."[52]

For some time the Theresienstadt "family camp" in Auschwitz seemed still to be accorded a "prominent" status—some internees hoped that they would be spared the gas; they could now see the smoke when they looked from their windows. But it finally happened, for most of those in Auschwitz from Theresienstadt, on March 8, 1944.[53]

The files on Boven Digoel theater, like the files on almost all matters of Boven Digoel, are thin. But even from that very little, the overwhelming significance of theater in Boven Digoel is clearly evident. As in Theresienstadt, however without Auschwitz, theater was close to becoming the ultimate of the camp. It enlightened the camp dazzlingly, in limelight.

Program of the Festivities to Celebrate the Anniversary of Her Majesty the Queen and the Birth of Her Royal Highness Princess Irene. 1929

19:45 arrival of the music

20:00 ... theater performance; a costume ball; first cabaret; *pentjak*; *krontjong*; conjuring; second cabaret ... [54]

"Walking through the camp," Mr. Trikoyo recalled, "opposite the house of Uncle Soetan Said Ali, the teacher, you passed the theater building." Boven Digoel, like Theresienstadt, was bursting with theater. There were, in Boven Digoel, too, multiple and often the least probable of stages, of all kinds. Boven Digoel was so much a stage that there was too much of it, for some. "At night," internee Mas Marco wrote from Boven Digoel, "people are cheerful. They gather at the school building to watch theater."⁵⁵ Mas Marco used the Dutch word *"toneel"* for "theater"; it made clear that he was referring to modern types of theater, not to wayang or any kind of "tradition."

In the same letter, Mas Marco wrote about theater, *toneel*, and "decaying morals," of the camp people, especially the most vulnerable among them, the internees' children. The decay, Mas Marco wrote, was "caused by adults speaking and behaving grossly," which comes to a large extent from "watching too much of theater in the camp." "Don't get me wrong," Mas Marco wrote, "I am not one of the prudish people, I do not reject all performing *kunst.*" Here Mas Marco used Dutch again, *"kunst,"* for "art." ⁵⁶

Mas Marco was not prudish. He was an author of some of the funniest, often risqué, novels written by an Indonesian, in his day or ever. What he seemed to be worried about, and what he appeared to be noticing, was an identification of camp with stage. People, he worried, were "forgetting themselves" in theater, becoming spectators, actors, and both. "My feeling just is not in it," he wrote. "I just cannot be expected to fight together, or even share opinions with people who consider themselves leaders, yet still, all they do is to deceive the people, to act as if we were on a podium."⁵⁷

For a particularly high-level visit by the governor of the Moluccas in September 1928, the children of the internees in Boven Digoel rehearsed and then performed "a little theater play" with, as a highlight, a song, "Tussen Keulen en Parijs" [Between Cologne and Paris]. The song is Dutch, and it goes like this:

Between Cologne and Paris
Runs a way to Rome
I will run on it
*We all will run on it.*⁵⁸

For another high-level visit, of the resident of Ambon in May 1929, "the Malay opera was performed by the internees." In the file containing the program of the event there should have been a photograph from the performance. But, evidently, someone unglued it and took it.⁵⁹

It is documented that the Dutch authorities in Boven Digoel, as the German authorities in Theresienstadt, enjoyed the internees' theater and were often seen in the audience. Of course, they had their preferences. The Dutch in Boven Digoel particularly praised and supported the "excellent dancers from Central Java"—"traditional," "ancient," and "harmonious."⁶⁰ "Traditional" puppet shadow play, a wayang theater company, was also established in Boven Digoel by internee Brotosiswojo from Solo, Central Java, and almost certainly there were others, with a warm authorities' approval.[61]

....

There is a mention in the Boven Digoel archives, in a document from May 1929, of an internee who "works as a scribe in the office of the camp administrator." No name is given, but the man is said to be "also a decorator," and, among other things, he is said to have painted a portrait of his supervisor in the office and, also, a "decor, backcloth, wings, and curtains, *trompe l'oeil* for the internees' theater shows."[62]

This file, too, contains neither a photograph nor any other illustration. There is a photograph, however, in Dr. Schoonheyt's archive now in Leiden, of a theater stage from what was clearly one of the "internees' theater shows." The stage represents a street, not much tropical, rather generic European, with two internees shown standing on either side of the scene. The painters of the scene? Two actors in the show?

There certainly were painters in Boven Digoel. One hears about them in memories, and there is a photograph of an internee in the camp, behind an easel.[63] Many of the paintings by the internees in Boven Digoel were done to be sold to sailors who came to the camp with the mail, supplies, and new internees. Some pictures were evidently commissioned by other internees as souvenirs to send home or take with when the time of the camp would be over. An internee, we know, did the cover of Dr. Schoonheyt's Boven Digoel book, a woodcut in kind of expressionist style, a head of Kaja-Kaja.[64]

"Sadikin Donosarono," a Boven Digoel ex-internee called Cus remembered, "was an internee in the camp. His son was a painter, Poeranto Yapoeng, and perhaps the father was a painter, too."[65] "We often went to visit Uncle Noerati," Mr. Trikoyo told me, "he was a skilled painter."[66] Another internee called Soewigno had also been known in the camp as a painter, and after the camp, during the late 1940s, he lived and worked as a painter in Batavia-Jakarta.[67] I asked Mr. Trikoyo about Soewigno, and he was surprised. His older brother's name was Soewigno, Mahmud Siswo Soewigno, and he had been in Boven Digoel with Trikoyo and his family. The name is not very common, but Trikoyo could not recall his brother painting. "Perhaps he did it at home, when he was not with us," Trikoyo suggested.[68]

Like in almost everything, in the matter of paintings Boven Digoel is thin in memories while Theresienstadt is thick. There are numberless examples of the camp paintings, drawings, aquarelles, woodcuts, and even oils and engravings in Theresienstadt, in the widest variety of styles, and, almost as a rule, with the artist's name signed and the history of the particular piece of art known.

Aldo Carpi, a professor of painting at the famous Brera Academy of Fine Arts in Milan, Italy, before he was driven to Theresienstadt, was frequently "commissioned" by the ss officers in the camp to paint their and their families' portraits, some "from life," others from photographs. "There was also demand for Italian landscapes and 'Venetian nudes,' which [naturally] Carpi painted from memory."[69]

"Portraits of the Jewish Elders and members of the Council of the Elders for the Prague ss Headquarters" were also commissioned and painted by the artists-internees in the camp.[70] Mrs. Charlotte Burešová, a professional painter before the war, was now one of those, and, in addition, she "copied works by Rembrandt and Rubens."[71] Other painters interned in Theresienstadt worked on "copies of the old German masters."[72]

Josef (Jo) Spier, a Jewish internee from the Netherlands, already before the war a well-known artist, painted a large number of drawings and watercolors in the camp. His album, *Bilder aus Theresienstadt* [Images from Theresienstadt], was produced in several copies and was being given out as a souvenir to the members of the International Red Cross Committee and some Nazi high-level visitors. All Spier's drawings in the camp were made, as one description has it, in "Spier's characteristic gentle line, colored in bright tones." In addition to the album, Jo Spier did other "occasional art"; most (in)famously, he made a shot-to-shot documentation, in September 1944, of the Nazi propaganda film about Theresienstadt.[73]

On July 20, 1935, ten years before Theresienstadt, Soetan Sjahrir in Boven Digoel wrote to his younger brother in the Netherlands, thanking him for a present: "Tjammie, With the last ship . . . came the calendar with the drawings by Jo Spier. Did you mean to give me a little taste of the times we live in? Indeed, the uttermost nationalistic romanticism rules in Europe at this time."[74]

There were un-Spier and very un-Spier artists in Theresienstadt. Five painters, all of them attached to the Production Workshop, where camp graphs and diagrams for the ss and the Council of the Elders were produced, "in their spare time" produced mostly drawings and water colors depicting "the real life in the camp"—the old, the crippled, and the sick, the coffins, and the empty strollers. The art was pronouncedly expressionist in style, very much like the famous art by Georg Grosz.

The five painters paid dearly for what the Nazis called the "gruesome art." It was discovered that the five had tried, and in part managed, to smuggle their work to an art dealer out of the camp and through him to Switzerland.

All were arrested, and so was their contact, the art dealer. They were beaten and then sent "to the east," where four of them perished.[75] The "gruesome art" was switched off like a voice or radio. The fear of trespassing increased and the camp became more of a camp.

For the winners in the sport and poetry competitions, diplomas were painted, drawn, and engraved—with images of the Theresienstadt rococo ramparts and the gentle Czech hills in the background. A special postage stamp was issued in the camp with an image of the camp, in olive-green, with the same skyline of the walls, bastions, and hills.[76] In the Yad Vashem Archives in Jerusalem there is a calendar, "Theresienstadt 1943," not much different from the one Soetan Sjahrir got from his brother in Boven Digoel eight years earlier. The same artist, Jo Spier, one drawing for every month, "seasonal activity," "in the fields," "at home."[77]

On January 14, 1944, a cable had been received at the *Waffen*-ss office in The Hague, the Nazi-occupied Netherlands, with the subject "Art Restorers for Theresienstadt." Two Dutch Jewish experts, at the time in the camp in Westerbork, were to be sent immediately to Theresienstadt to do some restorations for a planned Linz Museum, a (never realized) darling project of Adolf Hitler.

> The following Jews: 1. Hertog Cohen, ... with his wife Catharine born Velt, 2. Lion Morpurgo, with his wife Rebecca born Natkiel, and their daughter Annie.... The two Jews will be sent to Theresienstadt on the transport leaving January 18, 1944. On the same transport four paintings will be included for restoration.[78]

The camp paintings, drawings, and visual arts generally—avant-garde, kitschy, rococo, or dissenting—were crammed and whipped in the camps into a new awareness of significance within the clearing. Art was both produced and consumed in the closest nearness of the jungle and the walls. Like fashion, sound, and light, camp art was not merely a reflection of, but it merged with the walls, and the jungle surrounding the camps.

In one of the memories of just before the war and the camps, there is an image of an office of a dentist in Prague, one Mr. Klobouk (which is Czech for "hat"). On one of the walls of Mr. Klobouk's waiting room, there is an enlarged photograph showing members of the Athletic Club of Žižkov, the working-class quarter of Prague (I was born there), where the dentist's office was located. Next to it, "tacked up on another wall was a program of the first performance, some years ago, of Karel Čapek's [play] *R.U.R.* at the National Theater, and a framed painting of two birds of paradise with real feathers glued to the picture. This was considered by Klobouk's clientele a major *objet d'art.*"⁷⁹ Marc Augé, after the war, as an anthropologist of Africa and Paris, took walls, what they reflected and "contained," very seriously. He realized the fatality of walls, as well as the chilling facility with which modern man has learned to use and to submit to the walls. Marc Augé would certainly appreciate the bird of paradise glued to the picture on the wall of Mr. Klobouk's waiting room. He watched, on a Paris street after the war, "the broad and precise gesture of people putting up posters." "I have always wondered," he wrote, "how they do it without gluing themselves to the wall."⁸⁰

Aharon Appelfeld, a Jewish writer who spent his childhood in the time of the camps, and whose life was very much touched by the camps, in his novel *Badenheim 1939*, described both the camp time coming and walls being pasted over. As it was becoming evident in the fictional little Eastern European town of Badenheim [spa home] that the Jews would be driven to the camps, the town's Sanitation Department, where the Jews were to be rounded up, changed its appearance. It "now resembled a travel agency festooned with posters ... slogans adorned the walls."⁸¹

Georges Perec, who lost his mother in Auschwitz, knew equally well the feeling, the power, the art, the light emanating from walls: "I put a picture up on a wall," he wrote about himself as a child after the war, "then, I forgot there is a wall.... But I also forgot the picture. I no longer look at it.... There are pictures because there are walls."⁸² Boris Lurie, who passed through Auschwitz, again and again, throughout his postcamp life, obsessively came back, also in his art, to a problem, a mystery, a ghost of a poster, of a picture on the wall. He collected posters, signboards, and frivolous advertisements often, as well as these most horrific photographs of the Nazi mass murders, and he pinned—and glued—the images, photographs, posters, and "torn papers" onto his own paintings on the walls of his atelier in New York that thus became his home.⁸³

Theresienstadt's walls were being covered, and, as the camp time went on increasingly so, by posters, murals, paintings, drawings, and announcements. There was no time for or interest in erasing the commercial signs on the facades of Theresienstadt town from the time before the camp. They gave the camp even more of a feeling of being in a (cruel) theater:

> Tailor's Jan Hochman Theresienstadt Street no. 3. We custom make affordable men's suits.
>
> Magister J. BAVLNKA Pharmacy at the House at the Crown.
>
> *Pro trappera: dýmka od Zieglera!* [For each trapper: pipe from Ziegler!]⁸⁴
>
> *František Horvát,* Delicatessen.⁸⁵

"The blue distance which never gives way to foreground or dissolves at our approach, but only looms more compact and threatening, is the painted distance of a backdrop," wrote Walter Benjamin. "It is what gives stage sets their incomparable atmosphere."[86] Baudelaire, before Benjamin, was fascinated with painting as stage backdrops. "The renunciation of the magic of distance is a decisive moment in Baudelaire's lyric poetry," wrote Benjamin.[87] Jacques-Louis David, at the turn of the eighteenth century, "counseled his pupils to draw from nature"—"as it is shown in panorama," he specified, "the panoramas' plastically arranged foreground," "painted background."[88]

Even the inner walls in Theresienstadt became facades-as-backdrops. The orders and warnings issued by the Nazi administration, as well as the repetitions of the warnings and orders by the Jewish Council of the Elders, covered the inner walls. The Theresienstadt children's drawings and paintings are exhibited today in Holocaust museums all over the world. In the camp, as they were made, most often, they were pinned or glued to the walls, in the rooms where the children slept. "Above every bed," Jehuda Bacon recalled, "there was some decoration, some picture, some image, like that of Prague."[89]

"Inside," Klara Caransa remembered of the nursery and kindergarten in the Theresienstadt camp, "the walls were covered with fantasy images by painter Aussenberg."[90] "In the central room," Adler wrote about the same place, "as one walked around, the walls were just a continuous sequence of murals."[91] Jo Spier, in his memoirs, recalled these walls, too, "Little Red Riding Hood, Tom Thumb, Cinderella, Snow White."[92]

Early in 1945, with the ss permitting or looking the other way, the prayer room in the Magdeburg Barracks, according to a "Jewish survivor's report," "was renovated and redecorated by Jo Spier, a gifted and versatile artist, who had also painted pictures for the ss Club House."[93] "The cheerful facade," wrote Ernst Bloch in his *Traces*, "is even stranger than the usual happy ending."[94] When the many people were transported from Theresienstadt to Auschwitz, close to the end of the war, and of their lives, there, in the children's barracks, they still, newly, again, covered the walls with paintings: "Drawings of Indians, Eskimos, black children, a palm tree and monkeys, an illustration from Snow White [were] drawn on the walls of the block by Dina Gottlieb."[95]

There were not many walls in Boven Digoel. The tropical climate demanded building light, often without walls at all, just a roof on pillars. The internees' houses were small, the walls were mostly of woven reeds, rattan, bamboo, and the like, and there was not much of an interior anyway, or space to hang, pin, or glue pictures, inside or outside. There were fences rather than walls. The camp was not good for murals.

But there was a kind of painted wall in Boven Digoel, even more suggesting pictures-as-backdrops, theatrical and even more absorbing than the painted walls in Theresienstadt. There was a silver screen in Boven Digoel, separating the camp from the outside, enclosing the camp as in a shroud, emanating light.

In contrast to Theresienstadt, movies were permitted in Boven Digoel. Film reels were imported, and screenings were supported and often visited by the authorities. "Now, films here are shown regularly," the resident of Ambon reported on his inspection visit to Boven Digoel in November 1929.[96]

MONDAY, SEPTEMBER 17, 1934 . . . MORNING . . . 6:30: A telephone call from the main office. They ask that all the people working on the repair of the movie house, except four, to report to the main office for another job.[97]

Regularly, there were reports in the Indies newspapers about the Boven Digoel movie theater and movie time. One day it was reported as a thing of the past, or a myth, and another day as opened again.[98]

"The launching of the sound film," Benjamin wrote in his exchange with Theodor Adorno in 1938, "must be seen as the industry's effort to end the revolutionary hegemony of silent film, which tended to evoke reactions that were difficult to control and therefore politically dangerous."[99] In Boven Digoel, however, and until the end, it appears, only silent films were shown. It is true that internees repeatedly complained about the thing not being modern enough.

In the Indies, at the time when the future Boven Digoel internees were children or very young, at the turn of the century, movies were the greatest novelty. Eddy du Perron, a Dutch writer of the same age as many of the internees, who spent his childhood and youth in the Indies, remembered his first full-length and, of course, silent, films at the time, *Zigomar: The King of the Bandits*, *The Story of a Poor Girl*, and, later, *Quo Vadis*, *Spartacus*, and *Cleopatra*. "A Javanese brass band accompanied the movies with the same cheerful, sentimental circus tunes and in all seriousness played "Ach, du lieber Augustin" when the Roman warrior and the Egyptian queen took their leave of each other."[100]

In Boven Digoel, the Papua people from the jungle came sometimes to watch. These might still be the films that du Perron saw few years earlier. The most popular among the Kaja-Kaja, several internees wrote that they recalled, were "Tarzan, Tom Mix, and Douglas Fairbanks."[101]

There was a sense of *poco grave* in the frivolity of "Ach, du lieber Augustin" played at a wrong time. There was, to use Jean Baudrillard's words—in the film at that time everywhere, but truly true in the camp—"entrenchment as technological and psychedelic fantasy," a "machinery of special effects," "common hemorrhage into technology," and "a holocaust of means."[102] There was no light, except this light, in the middle of the Boven Digoel jungle, when Tarzan met Jane.

The people in Boven Digoel, like anywhere, not just the Kaja-Kaja when they came to the movies, were not allowed to touch the screen—just as the people of Theresienstadt weren't supposed to touch the walls. Here worked the technological truth, too, and not to be doubted: everybody in the know and on the go, knew it; also in the jungle camp. You touch the screen and, even more certainly than if you touched the wall, you would lose everything.

More unquestionably than the wall, too, the screen was full of light. The screen was the wall of light, and it gave light only, as long as one kept away. The screen, its light, then, generated the community of people, in the camp as well as on the outside. Because of the screen there was, in Paul Virilio's words, a "coupling of bodies with objects of unusual brilliance"[103]—a brilliance, to use Jean-Luc Nancy's words, that is "pushing your outstretched hand away."[104]

The silver screen permitted, and demanded, a "gaze . . . without touching, if touching then as 'afterglow.'"[105] "We greet the hills there behind the walls," Philipp Manes wrote in his Theresienstadt diary as if he were writing from a cave or, better yet, as if he were seeing a movie. "A distant hill with a black cone at its top, the town of Czech Litoměřice in the mist, with a spire that, sometimes, can also be seen."[106] Hugo Friedmann, the Theresienstadt librarian, organized tours for his friends, cointernees, through the camp. "In the New Alley (Q 4), the most noteworthy is house no. 4, in the most charming rococo style. . . . From an old Theresienstadt resident, who had first been evacuated from the town and then returned to the camp as a Jew, I was told that in this house used to be a pharmacy with a Jewish owner."

Then Friedmann "took" his tour groups to "Ramparts III," theatrically, without really touching, because no internee in fact was allowed to enter the place. "Ramparts III is the only place from which the free horizon and open landscape can be seen," Friedmann told the groups. "It is an exotic panorama, with the volcanic caps of the Bohemian Central Hills as a backdrop. The old church spires of Czech Litoměřice can be seen. . . . Sunsets here offer a bewitching show in many colors. The romantic charm of this view, of course, had long been known by Adrian Ludwig Richter, Caspar David Friedrich, Philipp Otto Runge, and Georg Friedrich Kersing, who all painted here. For us, the contemporary inhabitants, naturally, this has a theoretical attraction."[107] The camp people saw the world, "which sometimes can be seen," from behind the walls, or rather on the walls like on the screens. The walls covered the view, even much of the skies and the hills. They offered the complete view; the complete view was on the walls. The walls were the screen, the light, and the afterglow, the whole picture as the camp people got it. The German word for the walls surrounding the Theresienstadt camp—a word that everybody in the camp knew and used—was *die Schanzen*. The word "*Schanzen*," according to dictionary, means, "ramparts, walls, especially military," but also "hope, outlook, and possibility of success," like the English "chance."

The time was over in modern history, and completely so in the time of the camps, for a moment of surprise like that of the Lumière brothers' first films, the locomotive rushing at the audience, bursting out of the screen. Now it was only, and for the camp people behind the walls and in the middle of the jungle ultimately, to stand back and watch.

The world behind the walls and the jungle was "the 'other side of transparency.'"[108] "We ride on wooden horses," they sang in a Theresienstadt cabaret.[109] Limelights did not burn. Their power was virtual.

A transparently brilliant, dazzling, colorful, enlightening, silver, supermodern limelight burned in the camps that "only reveals everything in which you cannot partake."[110] Samuel Weber, in his study of the theatrical, wrote of "opacity." The opacity of theater, he wrote, is "irreducible," and it "defines the quality of theater as *medium*."[111] It suggests touching, but in fact theater is "transforming 'mere images ... into real beings,'" producing "a high degree of acquiescence." "It may gild poverty," Weber writes, for instance, "but it cannot transcend it." [112]

In Theresienstadt there was no real silver screen. In the matter of cinematographic progress, Boven Digoel was ahead of Theresienstadt. Yet, the Theresienstadt people, nonetheless, thought about film, and lived the film, like they thought about and lived fashion or radio. Jacob Edelstein was the first Jewish head of the Council of the Elders in the camp. Some people who knew him from Prague before the camp, when they spoke fondly about him and the life before, recalled that he used to have "only one weakness: from time to time he would slip away from his office and disappear into the darkness of the Arcades or one of the many other cinemas in the neighborhood, to see a thriller or Western."[113]

There were ultimately intensive film memories and film feelings in Theresienstadt. Even before the camp, as the people were packing, there were film expectations, images untouchable, yet bruising. Dr. Jacobson, one of the camp people, recalled after the war, "We had been told in Berlin that Theresienstadt had a cinema; in actual fact, there was no cinema in which films were shown. There was a cinema building in Theresienstadt, but when I arrived, it was crammed with people who slept there. Later it was refurbished and used for concerts and, sometimes, for religious services."[114] "There were no movies, and no movie house," wrote Adler in his Theresienstadt camp history.[115] But there were film rumors! On November 27, 1943, Gonda Redlich wrote, "They want to fix the cinema."[116] There were film jokes, dark jokes, as the best jokes are: "Do you know that the last two films shown in Theresienstadt before the Jews were brought in were *The Final Lap of a Big Race* and *At the Last Stop of a Cable Car?*"[117]

On second thought, actually, Boven Digoel was not ahead of Theresienstadt as far as film was concerned; not in all aspects, at least. There was no film, and no movie house in Theresienstadt, but Theresienstadt itself, completely, became a film.[118]

Gonda Redlich describes in his Theresienstadt diary the very driving of the Jews into the camp as the building of a film city. In Prague, the Jews were ordered to gather for transport at a site where the annual Prague fairs used to take place, "a great barnlike building."[119] "Something like a *yarid hamizrach*," Redlich described the place and the Jews waiting to be taken to trains. He later crossed out the term, but still it is there, crossed out, in his published diary, yarid hamizrach, Hebrew for "oriental fair."[120] Pavel Weiner's mother, in her own memoirs, wrote, "The Fairgrounds resembled a gypsy camp."[121]

Elena Makarova, who spent many of the recent years studying Theresienstadt, once told a story of her Jewish childhood in Russia,

> As a child, I used to sit next to old men on a park bench and ask them what they thought about life. The answers generally did not console me. Perhaps, the only old man whose experience did not seem to me wasted was my grandfather, an illiterate provincial Jew. He perceived life as a sacrament. He did not have enough intellect or education for logical reasoning: the most attractive thing to him was the circus which, to my knowledge, he had never seen. "In the circus there is everything," he used to say. "There a person is cut in half in front of an audience, and he remains alive."[122]

On January 20, 1943, the arrival of the first Dutch Jewish transport to Theresienstadt was filmed. "The people from the Nazi Protectorate of Czech and Moravia film weekly *Aktuality*, 'Current Events,' arrived. For the first time, films were being shot in the camp."[123] But the main event was to come a few months later with the making of a "documentary," *Der Führer schenkt den Juden eine Stadt* [The Leader Bestows a City upon the Jews].[124]

The music to the film was pieced together "exclusively from the compositions of Jewish authors, Mendelssohn, Bruch, Dauber, Offenbach, Krása, Haase, and others."[125] "It has to be admitted," wrote a recent author of a study of the film, trying to make some sense of what kind of "fake" this was, "that the visual authenticity of the film is considerably greater in many aspects than most people think. Much of what is shown in the film, in Theresienstadt really existed and was a part of the everyday life of the prisoners—not just in 1944 [when the film was made], but before. Many scenes were shot in spots that were not 'beautified.'"[126]

Some Jews reportedly declined to participate in making the film. František Zelenka, for instance, who had produced Gogol's *Marriage* in the camp, is said to have refused and was sent to Auschwitz as a punishment. But others agreed—Kurt Gerron, famously, and most propitiously for the film. Kurt Gerron was a prewar German film and theater superstar, known by everyone in the film world, among other things, as a partner of Marlene Dietrich and Emil Jannings in Josef von Sternberg and Heinrich Mann's *The Blue Angel*. Gerron accepted and, according to most witnesses, worked energetically, to the best of his artistic capacities, as the director of the film.[127]

The Jews of Theresienstadt, many much less willing than Kurt Gerron but having no way to do otherwise, became stars and extras in the film. They walked in front of the cameras, showed themselves working, sporting, playing music, "doing the everyday." Several performances of the camp theater, concerts, and lectures were filmed. The Jewish Elder Rabbi Murmelstein later recalled how the SS arranged for the children who were to sing in the opera *Brundibár*, which was also filmed, that they "should get some hours of quartz lamps 'mountain-sunlight,' so that they would tan and look healthy."[128] On Friday, September 1, 1944, Pavel Weiner wrote in his diary, "I go to the Dresden Barracks [to see] the soccer match, Sparta vs. Jugendfürsorge [youth care]. It will be filmed. . . . The match ends as expected, eight to one in favor of Sparta. I am also filmed. During the intermission, a German screams that we must cheer louder for the players."[129]

"Film is truth twenty-four times a second!" said Jean-Luc Godard.[130] Marc Augé, in his *Paris, années 30*, shows some photographs taken in Paris days before the war started and weeks before the Jewish transport to the camps began. He describes the faces on the photographs, namely an "expression of individuals attending the departure of kin." In these particular snapshots, he notices a "strange value," a flash: "*un baluchon* [a backpack] carried by a man hurrying to get out of frame."[131]

But there is no way out of the frame when either a photograph or a film are well taken, and in the frame resides much of their power. Subjects, either in or out of focus, are framed, and this is the work of light as well.

The power of the light, photography, film, or theater, like walls and jungle-as-a-wall, besides the framing, is also in their flatness. They are conceived so as that it would make no real sense to look behind a screen, or to turn a photograph around. Karl Rossmann, the hero of Kafka's *Amerika*, driven far from home, picks up a photograph out of his travel trunk and attempts to make out his parents: "He gazed all the more attentively now at the [photograph] lying before him and tried to catch his father's eye from various angles. But his father refused to come to life, no matter how much his expression was modified by shifting the candle into different positions; nor did his thick, horizontal moustache look in the least real. . . . His mother, however, had come out better; her mouth was twisted as if she had been hurt and were forcing herself to smile."[132] But, and Kafka made no secret about it, the mother's part of the story was dubious. In fact, there was not much hope, except for the Kafka's hero to enter the photograph himself.

The camp people lived in the frame and by the light. Were they not the light and the film, Rabbi Murmelstein reasoned to Claude Lanzmann after the war, "the Red Cross would not have come to see us."[133] In fact, he added, some Nazis (and this is well documented in other sources) thought about killing everybody in the end. The "liquidation of Theresienstadt," Rabbi Murmelstein said, "might have been postponed because they wanted to finish the film."[134]

Some people lived in film and in the light to the end. Taken from Theresienstadt in the later part of the war, and after the film was finished, they were transported to Auschwitz. After the days of journey, as the train stopped, "they had experienced the rushed exit from the cars into the bright light of projectors."[135] They still were not getting out of frame. The light they were dazzled with beamed. The scene, and the world, completely, were enlightened.

IV

CITY

The city, the station, not a crack, as far as I can see, no damage... looks funny, almost suspicious, a small town like this, absolutely peaceful, you can't help wondering: what are they waiting for?

—CÉLINE, *Rigadoon*

TWELVE

Blocks

Theresienstadt from inside the walls, ca. 1943. With permission of the Theresienstadt Memorial, Terezín.

Since the Enlightenment at least, there were geometers as models, brains, and as morals, as the truth. Geometers bore the truth. Captain Ahab knew of this as he addressed Pip in *Moby-Dick*: "True art thou, lad, as the circumference to its center."[1] Whatever space was true, in the world, it was true as a truth of geometers. In the truth, all may be geometrically defined, "contour, melody, dance or phrase, story or recital, montage or palette, volume, grain, frame, or cadence."[2]

"What 'exists' really in geometric space is univocally decided in all its determinations, in advance," Edmund Husserl wrote in *The Crisis of European Sciences and Transcendental Phenomenology*. "Our apodictic thinking," he argued, "proceeding stepwise to infinity through concepts, propositions, inferences, proofs, only 'discovers' what is already there, what in itself already exists in truth."[3] The "praxis of perfecting," us being "interested in these ideal shapes," "constructing," means that "we are 'geometers'" and live in a "self-enclosed world of ideal objects."[4]

As the family of Trikoyo arrived at Boven Digoel with the first group of internees, his mother told Trikoyo later, he was just a baby at the time, the place was still nothing but fallen trees and burned remains of the jungle, some plain spots, and, she said, "several barracks." "Imagine," Mr. Trikoyo, as an old man, told the story to his granddaughter, "we slept on the logs from fallen trees, just unvarnished logs. People who were able to bring mats, unrolled the mats. But my family had to go on very short notice, and they did not bring anything."[5]

Internee Mas Marco arrived at Boven Digoel on June 21, 1927, and he wrote in a letter home, "There already stand fourteen barracks, each thirty meters long and four meters wide, with roofs of sago-palm leaves and walls of logs.... Inside of each barrack, a person is given a space to sleep, two-by-two meters, and an additional space to eat and to store their personal belongings, two-by-two meters. The internee families with more than one child may be allotted four-by-four meters times two."[6] This was ideally so, Mas Marco wrote. In fact, but still geometrically, as more and more people were arriving, "even the families with four children may not get more than two-by-two meters." Individual houses, Mas Marco wrote in the same letter, began to be built, with the permission of the authorities, as fast as possible. "In section A of the camp," Mas Marco wrote, "after a few months, there already stand twelve houses... each four-by-four."[7]

These were all rudimentary and crude dwellings, but built, in their basic and elementary way, according to the truth of the geometer-architects. Boven Digoel was crude and rudimentary, but, into the wilderness, to use the words of Ernst Bloch again, a "rectangular flashing world of functional forms."[8] "Maybe," Jean-Luc Nancy wrote, "maybe this world could be saved by beautiful geometric designs in *n* dimensions, with elegant axonometries; but then everything would have to float, hanging in midair and," he added, "bodies *must* touch the ground."[9] Such a world, Nancy wrote, would essentially be "diagrams, networks, topological graftings, mass geographies."[10] One has to think about the beauty of Kafka's apparition of a body again: "The two distinct pairs of lines that outlined his legs crossed and softly merged with the lines outlining his body."

In another Kafka text, *In the Penal Colony*, the same beauty is described, that of a "wonderful apparatus," in fact a torture and killing machine around which the penal colony is built and through which it is being explained. The commanding officer of the camp shows the explorer the scheme of the apparatus, proudly, a technical drawing on a large sheet of paper: "All explorer could see was a labyrinth of lines crossing and recrossing each other, which covered the paper so thickly that it was difficult to discern the blank space between them. 'Read it,' said the officer. 'I can't,' said the explorer. . . . 'Yes,' said the officer, 'it's no calligraphy for school children.'"[11]

It was geometry, not for everyone but in truth. Much could be explained in Theresienstadt by the scarcity of paper, but it does not explain everything. Often, we find letters by the internees, diaries, notes, and, very much so, poetry, written on *Makulatur*, spoilt sheets or pages written only on one side, recto full, verso ready. Equally often, we find many letters, poetry and so on, written on clear technical paper and unfilled forms from the various departments of the camps: there was an industry in the camp of producing technical drawings, diagrams, networks, "not calligraphy for school children."

The lines and shapes and schemes of planes are visible under the text and between the lines of Theresienstadt camp people writing. They stand up. Erna Popper-Furman, one of the camp girls at the time, and a student in the arts classes of Friedl Dicker-Brandeis, made her own pretty monthly calendar in the camp. At the top of the page (I think it is "March") one can read *Lieferschein* [delivery note] *Nr.— von—194—* [No—from—194—]. At the bottom of the page is a dotted line for the *Unterschrift d. Empfaengers* [signature of the recipient].[12] The handwritten ink on the calendar got pale over the years and almost disappeared. The preprinted lines of the form remain as new.

The original score of Viktor Ullmann's Theresienstadt opera *Der Kaiser von Atlantis* was also written on unfilled internees' information forms.[13] Le Corbusier, possibly the most important ideologue of the new space in the twentieth century, an architect and certainly a geometer, did not write about the camps but at the time of the camps. He declared that the new world might be "fixed on a piece of paper." "It is a plan of battle,"[14] he wrote in his *Towards a New Architecture*, "sensorial rhythm (light and volume) can . . . thus be achieved."[15]

Geometry, as Edmund Husserl understood it, was the pinnacle of the modern, and nowhere more completely than in the camps. "In front of and behind," Imre Kertész recalled of his arrival at the pinnacle of the camps, Auschwitz, "as far as the eye could see, was a long row of similar barns, and over to the left as well there were absolutely identical rows, at regular distances and intervals in front, behind, and to the side. Beyond that was that broad, dazzling, metaled road."[16] "On that vast, completely flat terrain," Kertész also wrote, "it was no longer really possible, at least in my eyes, to keep track of the paths, squares, and identical buildings."[17]

On May 18, 1942, still in Prague, waiting for his transport to Theresienstadt, still going to school (now a school for Jewish children only), Petr Ginz, not yet of the camp people, not yet fully, wrote, "In the morning at school, in the afternoon at home. I am redoing the map of *Gross-Deutsche Reich* because I was told that in the one that I had in my exercise book, Moravia looked like a sausage."[18]

The supermodern ideal of the camps was correct, exact, and utopian. Étienne Cabet's hero narrates his journey to Icaria, the perfect island of the nineteenth century: "'It is perfectly symmetrical,' I exclaimed."[19] His Icaria guide agrees: "You may see two circles, one made up of twenty squares and the other of forty. The squares are almost equidistant one from the other and are spread out throughout the city. Look at the streets, all straight and wide. There are fifty large ones that cross the city parallel to the river and fifty perpendicular to it. . . . Icaria is, in fact, a model of the terrestrial universe."[20]

"Remember," wrote Ludwig Wittgenstein, "that one is sometimes convinced of the *correctness* of a view by its *simplicity* or *symmetry*."[21] In the so-called Production Workshop in Theresienstadt, the selected, and indeed the best artists of the prewar times, were engaged to fulfill multiple tasks of technical drawing, projecting the facts of the camp's production and growth. They were charged to produce diagrams and charts that were then regularly submitted to the Jewish Council of the Elders and some sent further on to the SS authorities of the camp.

The construction activities in the camp and the organization of living conditions in the first two years are recorded in a historical survey titled "Geschichte des Ghetto Theresienstadt, 1941–1943" [History of Theresienstadt

Camp, 1941–1943], a folder produced by the Production Workshop, dated December 31, 1943, fifty-two pages of text, mostly illustrations, charts, and graphs.[22]

Some of the charts also made at the Production Workshop are now on display in one of the camp's former barracks. They disturbed me when I saw them for the first time, as perhaps Robert Jan van Pelt, a Dutch historian of architecture, might have been disturbed when, in the Moscow archives, he discovered the architectural plans of Auschwitz. The charts, diagrams, and schematic drawings of Theresienstadt, like the plans of Auschwitz, are upsetting by their soulless beauty, sublime in their awesomeness. This might be what the commanding officer in Kafka's *Penal Colony* might have meant.

The large sheets of the Theresienstadt graphs and diagrams are not crowded but neatly structured. The numbers and letter symbols are written in the most readable technical fonts and arranged in perfect rows and columns. They made sense spatially as well as literally. They might be statistics, but, in their impact, they are geometry, too.

The technical-statistical-geometric drawings of Theresienstadt, crime scenes, are sublime in how hard-core they are depicted, en face, in profile, from the top, from beneath. Bedřich Fritta, later to perish as one of the five producing "gruesome art," directed the program.

There is a large chart-diagram-plan-picture by Peter Kien, also a poet and the librettist of Ullmann's opera, *Der Kaiser von Atlantis*. Kien's chart is called "*Raumnot* [Lack of Space]," and is among the Production Workshop's most beautiful. A camp's barrack is *clinically* cut through, to show all the section from the roof to the basement, exposed. The figures of the Jews are drawn as sitting, standing, and lying in beds, on each floor—the attic, the fourth, third, second, and first floors, and the basement. The people, or icons rather, are tagged with numbers. *Einwohner* [inhabitant] and *Fläche* [surface] are what this is essentially (and only) about.[23] They incarnate what Edmund Husserl wrote about when he argued that the metamorphosis or new truth of humans is one of "abridgments" or "silhouettes."[24]

The "geometric" drawings by Bedřich Fritta, Peter Kien, and others of the Production Workshop appear scarier than the "gruesome" Georg Grosz–like paintings some of the artists paid for by their deaths. It may have been, of course, also a case of anxiety uncompletely suppressed: "Only the diagram," wrote Rem Koolhaas, "gives a bearable vision."[25]

"Above every bed," as Jehuda Bacon, a boy of Theresienstadt, told me, "there was some decoration or picture." But Mr. Bacon continued, "On the main wall, there was a bulletin board where the achievements and the failings of each of us were marked by dots of different colors, and there was also a graph of our progress." "There were points penciled in, as the time went on," Jehuda Bacon said, "with an explanation of why each point was given."[26]

In Boven Digoel, the landscape and the river, and certainly the jungle, were much harder to be made in "two-by-two" or "four-by-four." Still, the camp was no less true, in Captain Ahab's wisdom, "true as the circumference to its center." The Dutch flag on the pole stuck in the middle of the clearing in the beginning, at the conception, was the center, and it gave the same sense of geometry to the camp. The barracks and soon the houses, and soon the people, were to fill and realize the space.

There are in the Boven Digoel archives also loose sheets of paper, far from the beautiful technical sheets of Theresienstadt, often just a part of a page from a notebook, with a few lines in pencil, in which an internee asks the authorities for permission to leave the barracks and to build his own house, to open, to clear, a plot of land at the edge of the jungle, to plant a fruit tree or a bed of vegetables in his garden. Sometimes a doctor's signature and sometimes a short note is there, too, certifying that the place asked for is a healthy place and that there is no concern about the tree or the plot. But always, as clearly required, a sketch is drawn on the piece of paper, most often without a ruler or compass, "like a sausage," Petr Ginz might say, but the lengths, the widths, and the depths are clearly marked, in meters and sometimes centimeters, and allowing for a good eye and steady hand, the angles, mostly right.

Boven Digoel, true to itself like the circumference to its center, to the flag, proved and grew as a surface space, *Fläche*; the surface was charted first as an idea and then, step by step, the camp emerged in the real. "As our ship was getting close to the camp," wrote Krarup Nielsen about the first trip to Boven Digoel, "we saw that the banks of the river at the point of the camp rose *circa* twenty meters above the level of the river." The camp itself, Krarup Nielsen wrote, "was a third of a kilometer in length and *circa* a half kilometer in width. The cleared terrain was planned to expand up to one square kilometer."[27]

The police in Boven Digoel made up of the internees, as everywhere in the Indies, was called the *ronda* (from French *la ronde*, "watch") as the agents, indeed, were making rounds. One of the ronda tasks in the camp, besides watching, listening, and fulfilling little tasks now and then for the authorities, was *mengukur tanah*, in Malay or Indonesian "to measure land"—to circle the camp and to survey the land, policing the geometry and the truth of the camp.

> SATURDAY, SEPTEMBER 18, 1937 ... AFTERNOON, 1:00: Agent Moenandar surveys the land beyond camp section A, which is planned to be cleared. Internees H. Moekmin and Soeleman Bt. want to make it into an un-irrigated rice field.[28]

In March 1939, a group of six internees applied for permission to clear a patch at the edge of the jungle for a vegetable garden. They produced a letter with their names in a neat column, and a sketch of the area, on which their respective future garden, divided in six, was marked. The letter was written in an unlearned hand, but the sketch, however uneven, was purely geometric, there was all that was needed, names—with the internees' numbers—and measures:

> To the camp administrator
>
> 1. Kaling *gelar* Malim Batoeah no. 1251: ... see sketch; 46 × 55 m.
> 2. Hartadjani no. 1018 ... see sketch; 33 × 47 m.
> 3. Jasin no. 1003; ... see sketch; 24 × 36 m.
> 4. Soedirodo no. 1380; ... see sketch; 94 × 150 m.
> 5. Abdoelsalam no. 1445; ... see sketch; 60 × 60 m.
> 6. Amalredjo no. 1402, ... see sketch; 60 × 80 m.
>
> BOVEN DITEL, MARCH 6, 1939
>
> *[Signatures]*[29]

Geometry, measurements, sequences and progressions of names, was the way how one was to find one's place, the way in which the camp as a whole was defined, and the way in which it breathed. On September 5, 1935, internee Soewandi sent his request:

> To the camp administrator
>
> Soewandi no. 458; ... see sketch; length +40 m width +35 m = +1400 m2.
> BOVEN DIGOEL, SEPTEMBER 5, 1935
>
> *[Signature]*

On July 31, 1936, internees Prijokoesoemo and Maskoen sent theirs:

> To the camp administrator
>
> Prijokoesoemo no. 157; . . . see sketch; length 30 m width 20 m;
> Maskoen no. 186; . . . see sketch length 30 m width 20 m. . . .
> BOVEN DIGOEL, JULY 31, 1936
>
> *[Signatures]*[30]

The sketches, and the lines of the sketches, the angles and the measurements, more accurately, intimately, and categorically than the jungle and the walls, articulated the camps and *delineated* the camps' people. Each and every house, yard, and garden, indeed, every room in an internee's house, was sketched, ordered, and came into being as ordered and sketched.

Every house with its yard and garden in Boven Digoel, by a special order, "had to be separated with a fence from the neighbor's."[31] The fences were in most cases made of shrubs and sometimes of cotton trees. The fences as lines declared the plan, "a plan of battle," as Le Corbusier might say. "Only the internee who obeyed the order about the fences," wrote Joesoef Mawengkang, who spent almost ten years in Boven Digoel, "might at least live under an illusion that one day, at some point, he might be considered for release from the camp."[32]

> FRIDAY, JUNE 21, 1935 . . . AFTERNOON: *12:34:* Agent Soeleman and the camp administrator . . . make rounds in section B of the camp. . . . They are reissuing the fence order to the internees who still linger. . . .
> *1:21:* Agent Soedirman leaves the station. . . . He goes to repeat the fence order to internees Saparman and Djaidin. . . .[33]

Mrs. Zakaria, recalling the camp, recalled the flowers and recalled the fences. She told me that the fences were made of flower bushes, and some of bamboo. "Quite nice," she said, "not very high, you could see over."[34]

Register of the criminal cases before the magistrate

> 1. Midjamdja, +40 years old. . . . He is reported as still not having a fence around his house, yard, and garden. . . . Found guilty of misdemeanor, by article *1* sub *b* of the *Netheidsverordening* [the Neatness Ordinance]. Fined *f*5.— and ten days of prison.[35]

The moment the jungle was cleared and the first barracks were built, before houses, and before fences, the telephone lines appeared in Boven Digoel. First one line, and then a net over the camp, on the poles, marked and cut the camp in its own straight way and in the spirit of the clearing. The lines did not follow the sketches along which the barracks, houses, yards, gardens, and fields were built, but they comported with them, and accented the camp design as unquestionably geometrical. They proved geometry to be the soul and the completion of the camp. The telephone lines, flagrantly visible, signified the modern against the jungle, the river, and everything not yet in the line way, indeed, *in the line*. They signified lasting, too, the camp time that had no end and no beginning. They were, straight or curved, the length without breadth.

In Theresienstadt, the geometric spirit had been in place more than a century before the Nazis made a camp of it, however a spirit still protomodern, Habsburg-enlightened, rococo style. On October 10, 1780, "the first stone" (an equivalent of the pole with the Dutch tricolor in Boven Digoel) "was ceremonially laid by the emperor himself, in the presence of the commander-in-chief of his army, Count Moritz Lacy and the head of the army construction, Karl Pellegrini."[36] Theresienstadt was based on a sketch, an idea of Marquis de Vauban, the seventeenth-century French genius in fortress building and, equally so, in ballistics, in other words a true architect-and-geometer.[37]

"The construction of fortifications," says the hero of W. G. Sebald's *Austerlitz*, a novel very much also about Theresienstadt, "clearly showed how we feel obliged to keep surrounding ourselves with defenses, built in successive phases as a precaution against any incursion by enemy powers, until the idea of concentric rings making their way steadily outward comes up against its natural limits."[38] Theresienstadt was built on the idea of concentric rings, its "fortification and siegecraft, *escape* and *courtine, faussebraie, réduit*, and *glacis*," got their meaning, their truth, in "the star-shaped dodecagon behind trenches."[39]

Two years after the first stone for the fortress Theresienstadt was laid, Theresienstadt was declared a town. "The space inside the walls not used for military purposes was divided into 288 building parcels." Next to military garrisons, houses for civilians were built. "The character of the civilian buildings was still determined by military purposes and so their stern functionality was made to fit into the military character of the town."[40]

Hugo Friedmann, the Theresienstadt camp librarian who would perish in Auschwitz, who took other internees on architectural tours through the camp, believed that Theresienstadt was worth the interest.[41] Theresienstadt, he lectured his groups, exemplified an extraordinarily fine layout of a fortress, the correct shape of a star with five bastions each, with fort points between each of bastions.[42] As an actor in one of the Theresienstadt cabaret shows quipped, meaning both the yellow tag and the geometry, "They found a city in the shape of a star."[43]

Erika Taube, a girl of fifteen at the time, wrote a poem in Theresienstadt called "The World Is Round." "The world is round, / and still has many corners."[44] A report on the camp by a survivor says, "*Theresienstadt ist baulich symmetrisch* [Theresienstadt is architecturally symmetrical]."[45]

"The town was built with military precision," Ruth Bondy wrote, "five long streets lengthwise, eight short streets across, all at right angles to one another. A square in the middle." "A ten-minute walk from one end of each of the long streets to another—and the barracks were also uniform, with an identical number of gates and inner yards."[46] "Each long street measured seven hundred meters."[47] More than a star. A boy of Theresienstadt, age ten at the time, wrote,

Thus at least I see it
Theresienstadt
a square kilometer
alone in the world.[48]

Dr. Adolf Metz, an ex-internee of Theresienstadt, recalled after the war, "The town had eight great military barracks with a large number of casements and underground corridors, and eight hundred small houses in dully-straight five long and eight crosswise streets." "There were no sights, no monuments, nothing," Dr. Metz added, but he was right only in part.[49] There was the square, a square square indeed, in the middle of the camp. And there was "the first stone," not visible but certainly in the exact center of the square.

....

ss-Obergruppenführer Reinhard Heydrich, the Reichsprotektor of Bohemia and Moravia, at a meeting of the Nazi high-level officials, at the end of October 1941, declared not for the first time that "after the Jews are deported to the East," which meant after Europe would be cleared of the Jews, "Theresienstadt will become a German settlement, a model bridgehead to strengthen German-ness in the accordance with the Führer's plan."[50] *Musterlager* [model camp] (also "template camp") was the code term often used by the Nazis, and very much so for Theresienstadt.[51] From a model camp for the Jews to a *Mustersiedlung* [a model settlement], it was the idea.[52]

Architects and urban planners thinking in lines and planes, geometer-architects, have always come close to an idea and the possibility of a model, but never as close as in a model camp.

When Hélène Gaudy, a French writer, visited recently Theresienstadt, as she wrote in her *Une île, une forteresse* [An Island, a Fortress], she found one thing still there from the time of the camp, unchanged: "At the corners of certain streets, still decipherable inscriptions, 'Block' followed by a number."[53] "Block," indeed, often interchangeable with "barracks," became a name for geometric idea par excellence, in stone, in brick, in concrete, or in iron, in the modern and supramodern cities as well as in the camps.[54]

Toward the moment of the camps, Le Corbusier and other "geometers who practice architecture" enthused over and designed "exclusive employment of straight lines and square-sets."[55] "We must clear our minds of romantic cobwebs," Le Corbusier wrote.[56] Mr. Trikoyo, as we talked one day in his little three-room house in Tangerang, in east Jakarta, began to speak about one of his father's friends, Mr. Soendoro. Soendoro used to be a builder, a site manager, in Semarang, Central Java, before he was interned in Boven Digoel at the same time as Trikoyo's father. "In Boven Digoel," Trikoyo told me, "Soendoro got active again, and he was known to help the Dutch authorities in planning the overall layout of the camp."[57]

When it was over, Mr. Trikoyo went on, he, like the others, got out of the camp. He arrived in Jakarta, after the war, what used to be Batavia, the capital of the colony, and now was the metropolis of the independent Indonesia. He was truly surprised, he told me. One day he happened to find himself in *Kebayoran Baru* [The New Kebayoran], a southern suburb of Jakarta, or a satellite town, rather, in fact the last urban project the Dutch architects began to develop just before the Indonesian Republic took over in 1949, and which the Indonesian- and Dutch-trained architect Soesilo was just finishing. The straight and wide avenues, uniform layout, and large squares. Mr. Trikoyo told me, it suddenly reminded him of Soendoro and the camp.[58]

In one of the lectures and shows before the war, while Boven Digoel was still very much existing, Dr. Schoonheyt, when he talked about Boven Digoel in Amsterdam, described no blocks but "the little houses of the internees." However, "The camp can easily be imagined somewhere in Java," he said, "as a model settlement."[59]

Hendrik Freerk Tillema was a contemporary of Dr. Schoonheyt and of Boven Digoel, and of Le Corbusier, in fact. He was a pharmacist, adventurer, and entrepreneur, and perhaps most of all, an amateur architect-as-geometer. Tillema was not involved in designing Boven Digoel, at least not directly, but his ideas, his plans, his sketches were highly relevant. Boven Digoel might be considered a not-far-from-the-tree-fallen fruit of his thoughts, or fantasies.

Like Le Corbusier, Soendoro, and Schoonheyt, Hendrik Tillema was led to believe that one had to begin from a clear clearing, a complete one. No truly modern Indies settlement, he argued, "could be improved unless it is built anew," the creation of a new town from a tabula rasa, "naturally" oriented, as the winds blew, opened to the winds, with wide streets lined with trees, and houses adapted to tropical heat and humidity.⁶⁰

Hendrik Tillema did not call his idea *"la cité radieuse"* like Le Corbusier, but easily could have. Nor did he call it *Icaria* like Étienne Cabet. The name he chose for it was *Kromoblanda*, a composite of *kromo* [native], and *blanda* [Dutch], meaning the natives and the Dutch inspired by the architecture in Kromoblanda will live together. He also called his invention a *modelkampong* [model village/quarter]. He did not care to design "a guardhouse" for his "model village," and neither "there is a watchtower around the compound," because he trusted that "the provision of facilities and well-ordered space would guarantee the self-regulation of human behavior." Kusno Abidin, who studied Tillema closely, commented, "The new visual order, was to serve as a symbol and instrument of urban modernity."⁶¹

In Dostoyevsky's *Crime and Punishment*, which takes place in Saint Petersburg, the mid-nineteenth-century Russian metropolis, it is not so much winds and wide avenues as "blocks," or barracks, that convey the city: "door slammed . . . a whisper. There must have been numbers of them—almost all the inmates of the block."⁶²

Blocks belong to the modern and the supermodern city inevitably, logically, conveniently, cheaply, architecturally, ideally, and geometrically. Thought deeply, they were cubes: a square in layout and in all the other measurements, in three dimensions—width, length, and depth. Cubes and squares were concepts, Platonic forms, through which the power of geometry could be most profoundly conveyed. In blocks, the cubes, incarnations in barracks, cubes, tenement blocs, "hive-dense tenements,"⁶³ the power of cubes and geometry was ultimately affirmed.

As Jacob Riis wrote in 1889 about another modern metropolis, tenement blocks in New York at the time "harbored" three-fourths of the city's population.⁶⁴ It, rather than Dostoyevsky's Saint Petersburg, was the true beginning. Still a century later, with the time of camps in between, Paul Virilio wrote about "the fourth world's" "contemporary urban ghettos"—in blocks.⁶⁵ At roughly the same time as Virilio, Ulrike Meinhof, of the Red

Army Faction, declared, "That is where we came from: from ... the desolate concrete public housing, the cell-prisons, asylums, and special prison sections."[66] She meant blocks.

"We must create," Le Corbusier declared as this was getting truly in motion, "the mass-production spirit ... of living in mass-production houses ... great blocks of houses with successive setbacks, stretching along arterial avenues."[67] Rem Koolhaas wrote not about Auschwitz or Theresienstadt or Boven Digoel but about Manhattan above Fourteenth Street:

> Fabricated motherland ... a system of rectangular plots ... a neat symmetrical pattern ... grid ... rectilinear streets ... supposed improvements by circles, ovals, and stars ... straight-sided, and right angled-houses.[68]
>
> Each block ... turn[ed] into a self-contained enclave of the Irresistible Synthetic ... a dry archipelago of blocks.[69]

"Through volume," according to Rem Koolhaas, the city of blocks "cannot avoid being a symbol."[70]

Mr. Trikoyo, in recalling the camp, again and again quoted to me measurements, planes, and angles. Some of the most emotional parts of his memory were shaped that way. Recalling his mother telling him about the first weeks in Boven Digoel, he spoke of "blocks," and in blocks, "block no. 5, sixty by four meters"[71]; or, to put it another way, he spoke of and in rectangles.

Sometimes, and ultimately, in Europe as in Asia, the blocks and cubes were called "boxes," and *Koffers* [coffers, suitcases, or trunks]. "I live in a zinc trunk now," Soetan Sjahrir wrote to his wife about himself in Boven Digoel.[72] The internees in the camp walked through the streets of blocks. The main street in the Boven Digoel camp was called *Blokweg* [Block Street]. "It runs," as the official registry of the camp described it, "past the Tantoy's Chinese store, past a dry rice field, through the administration section, past the house of internee Soenarto, and as far as the center of section C."[73]

To use Joseph Roth's expression about some groups of European populations not yet in the camps, they were "boxed up."[74]

In 2002, in the Jewish Museum in New York, I saw the Holocaust exhibition *Mirroring Evil*. One exhibit, "Concentration Camp Set" by Zbigniew Libera, presented a Nazi camp, clearly a death camp, as a model "ready to sell."[75] A build-a-city toy, a little camp had completely been constructed—and could be dismantled and rebuilt again, and again—of black and white Lego blocks. It was explained in the displayed "advertisement" that the plastic cubes fit together so well because they were so simple, pure in the idea of them, in other words, so perfect to build a town, a city, a camp, and camp people.

Theresienstadt, an internee wrote in his diary, consisted of "blocks each of twenty-five to thirty houses. The courtyards of all the blocks are connected with each other by bridges or floor passages."[76] "This fortified town," wrote W. G. Sebald, who saw the place after the war, was "laid out like Campanella's ideal sun state, to a strict geometrical grid."[77]

"Barrack," explains Ruth Bondy, was "a 'block' in the camp language."[78] All the barracks, or blocks, of Theresienstadt were built with the same design: "the quadrangular courtyards with archways and wide encircling loggias." Hugo Friedmann, on the architectural tours he led in Theresienstadt, pointed out the blocks and the cubes of the camp to his cointernees. "They are," he said, "pleasantly reminiscent of the architecture of Southern monasteries."[79]

Blocksperre [the block-embargo], Jehuda Bacon explained, was a heavy punishment: "The people were forbidden to come out of their block to the streets."[80] The Theresienstadt camp central hospital's official name, and so it was usually called, was "Block E VI." All blocks in the camp had their *Blockarzten* [block doctors], and every block doctor was supervised by a *Blockchefarzt* [a block chief doctor]. There were "block pharmacies."[81]

Along with "block," another word commonly used to describe and articulate Theresienstadt space was "*quartier*," "quarter." It was a leftover from the time it was a military garrison, but it fit and was as soundly geometric as "block."[82] "Each one of us as we were checked into the camp," Hans Günther Adler recalled in his history, "had been assigned to his [or her] *quartier* of the camp."[83]

Blocks and quartiers, fit together, articulated the place better than the Lego cubes, more "organically" because they still could be divided and subdivided while not losing their building potential, their architectural and geometric truth, but, quite the opposite, confirming the wholeness, and making the truth even more convincing.

Already about the New York City of the late 1880s Jacob Riis wrote that subdivision was the rule and the work in progress: "The conversion of houses and blocks into barracks, and dividing their space into smaller proportions [is] capable of containing human life within four walls."[84] Imbued with historical optimism and by the power of reason, reason of land surveyors and geometric-architectural reason, innovation proceeded not as overcrowding, it was not in the reason's vocabulary, but through "miniaturization." The "large rooms were partitioned into several smaller ones, without regard to light or ventilation," and thus the blocks "became filled from cellar to garret."[85]

Michel Foucault wrote about "partitioning" as a potential and dynamic of "disciplinary space." "Disciplinary space," he wrote, "tends to be divided into as many sections as there are bodies or elements to be distributed." This is "a procedure," he wrote, "aimed at knowing, mastering, and using." "Discipline," Foucault wrote, though he might have written "geometry" or "architecture as geometry" as well, "organizes an analytical space."[86]

In his manifesto *Towards a New Architecture*, Le Corbusier wrote with emphasis, "*Take a flat which is one size smaller than what your parents accustomed you to.*"[87] He went on in the same text, imagining and suggesting a "university quarter" (quartier indeed). "What the student wants," Le Corbusier wrote in the 1920s about the coming generation, "is a monk's cell, well-lit and heated, with a corner from which he can look at the stars." "Every student," Le Corbusier added, "has a right to the same type of cell." Moreover, this plan, he concluded, "allows for indefinite expansion."[88]

In Boven Digoel, Mr. Trikoyo recalled, "Our family was given four mosquito nets and mother sewed them together into a large one so that the whole family might sleep under a single cover." In the barrack in which they were first put, sixty meters long and four meters wide, the internees hung whatever clothes and sheets they had to divide the space, to create some sense of privacy for each family. "But these were not real walls, mainly cloth," Mr. Trikoyo said almost happily, "so that we children could run, or crawl through and throughout, from one family to another."[89]

On Tuesday, June 26, 1932, at 12:30 p.m., internee Moeljowidjojo reported to the Boven Digoel camp ROB police that his trunk with clothes and other items had been stolen and that he suspected internee Soeprapto. A detailed report on the interrogation that followed, of both Moeljowidjojo and Soeprapto, was filed. In the same folder, this time expertly drawn, is a sketch of the accuser's house, each room measured and numbered: the porch; room number one, two, three, and four; the kitchen, the backyard, and an outhouse. The gate through which the thief possibly got in is highlighted in red. There is a diagram of the thief's suspected movement through the house. Next, there is another sketch, equally clear and detailed, of possible approaches to Moeljowidjojo's house, to point out, namely, how vulnerable the house was to a thief approaching from the road.[90]

We can still walk in, or break into, the house, and check the camp for safety. We can still follow the people as they dwelled and felt or did not feel safe; we can still analyze them. We can still see how through these sketches the camp people could be silhouetted and disciplined.

On November 1, 1941, so late in the camp's history, internee Moestapha sent a letter to the camp administration requesting permission to build an extension, a new back porch to his house. The extension, he wrote, would be three by three and a half meters, and he pointed to "an attached sketch." On November 3 (one month before Pearl Harbor), the back-porch addition was approved.[91]

The house of Mohammad Hatta, though it belonged to one of the two "academicians" and to a "privileged" internee in Boven Digoel, was not much different from the houses of the others. Like the others, it was modern, not really eagerly, but self-confidently so.

The house had a front porch, a "gallery," we do not know how deep, but about four meters long. Through the porch that faced the main road, one entered a "hall," hardly a corridor, in fact, "wide about seventy-five centimeters," leading through to the other end of the house. In the "hall," one on the right and one on the left, there were two doors to the only rooms of the house. Both rooms were of equal size, two meters wide and "a little more" in depth. One of the rooms was used by Hatta as his "bedroom," and the other as his "study" (sometimes called "library"). In the backyard, in a roofed part of it, was a kitchen. Beyond, there was an outhouse, "bathroom and WC," as it was called.[92]

In my very rough calculation, the whole "roofed" house, excluding the porch and the backyard, could not be much larger than five meters by five. Imagine the energy and the spirit of the modern in the camp allowing for, and certainly growing out of, such a "deeply meaningful" and "inevitable," concentrated division and subdivision!

Soetan Sjahrir, the other "academician" in Boven Digoel, described his house in a letter to his family in Holland in July 1934:

> The tiny house is a camp model, that is, you can see many houses of the same model in the camp. It is not really ugly. It has a layout five by three, it is three meters high and it is divided in two. The larger room is three by three meters, the other is smaller, and I use them as a sitting room and a study, respectively. Both rooms have large windows which can be almost fully opened, so the house has quite good ventilation. A little structure separated from the house serves me as a kitchen, it is three meters long and two meters wide.[93]

The time of Boven Digoel was still the time of the ships as virtually the only transport for long-distance travel, and Mrs. Ottow recalled that her family, traveling to the camp, brought their own furniture.[94] This was, of course, the family of the camp administrator. But internees as well could take much more to the camp than clothes and bare necessities. Most of the Boven Digoel internees were able to fill the blocks and cubes of their living space in the camp with things, small and large, shipped from home. Sjahrir, in one of the first letters he sent to his wife in Holland, described how his ship to Boven Digoel stopped in a port on the way: "I spent my last pennies on a little table, four folding chairs, and one deck chair," he wrote, "it all cost ƒ2½, and is made of ironwood!"[95]

Another internee, Jahja Nasoetion, in memoirs his widow let me read, described an experience of going the opposite way, from Boven Digoel, as the camp was being evacuated in 1943 and the internees were being moved to Australia. Jahja lamented the loss of things he had brought in and now had to leave behind, "Most of the room furnishing," he wrote, "beds, chairs, sofa, buffet, a large mirror."[96]

"Strive for four things," an ancient Javanese code instructs a believer, "a capacious vehicle, a roomy house, an excellent garment, and a bright lamp. A roomy house means abundance of talk conducive to good; an excellent garment means courtesy; a bright lamp means true and real wisdom."[97] Which might be answered by Gershom Scholem's "It is a profound truth that a well-ordered house is a dangerous thing."[98]

The Austrian Hermann Broch wrote in his novel *The Realist* that "all young girls in the better-class bourgeois families were in the most intimate manner bound up with problems of architectonics, [namely] awareness of the secret harmony and counterpoint exemplified in the arrangement of the furniture and pictures."[99] Broch's "young girls of 1910," about whom he wrote here, became adult women at the time of the camps. One of them, in fact, Hermann Broch's mother, died in Theresienstadt.

ss-Obergruppenführer Reinhard Heydrich, the Reichsprotektor of Bohemia and Moravia, and the man who thought of Theresienstadt as a model camp, no less than "the young girls of 1910," exhibited high sensitivity to the problem of "architectonics" and "arrangement of the furniture and pictures." On December 15, 1941, at least, he issued a "strictly confidential" order for "Jewish property" in the protectorate to be registered, in good-household categories:

1. kitchen furniture
2. bedroom furniture
3. carpets
4. books

5. paintings
6. other art
7. musical instruments
8. glass and porcelain
9. small pieces
10. perishables.[100]

"From the emptied Jewish homes in Prague," wrote Adler, "furniture was sent to Theresienstadt." Much of it appears in testimonies. Furniture of lost homes was stored in Theresienstadt barracks' "basements, attics, or left in the open."[101] Some of the tables, chairs, mirrors, and paintings brought to Theresienstadt had been redistributed to the internees to make up their own camp *as if* bedrooms, *as if* sitting rooms, and *as if* studies.

Especially the older Jews and particularly those coming from Germany arrived at the camp with "some expectation." They believed, or forced themselves to believe, that indeed Theresienstadt was a "camp for the prominents," much better than other camps, as little as they knew about this and them, and that they might be able to survive in Theresienstadt somehow decently until the war would be over. "They brought curtains," wrote Adler, "vases, family memorabilia, and much of the other stuff of not much use in the camp. . . . Then they were loaded like cattle on the trucks or tractor-trailers."[102]

"The houses stood grim, windows without curtains," Philipp Manes wrote about some houses and barracks in Theresienstadt.[103] There were other barracks and houses and parts in the camp, however. The "prominents'" quarters of the camp, namely. The Jews decorated for their military service in World War I on the German or the Austrian side, "Jewish-but-well-known" artists, scholars, and some other "categories," were "entitled to three and a half square meters of living space per person."[104] Most of the "prominents" in Theresienstadt were assigned the living space in *Seestraße* [Lake Street], at the edge of the camp. "There one can find," wrote Mr. Manes, "little houses with halls with windows and rooms with high ceilings and iron beds."[105]

In the windows of the prominents, but not only in them, there were curtains. Certainly in the gossip circulating through the camp, in the Bonkes, in some houses of the "prominents," there were paintings on the walls, and even carpets. The fact that Paul Eppstein, the head of the Jewish Council, even got a grand piano (not gossip), was widely known in the camp.[106] Paul Eppstein's successor, the last head of the Jewish Council of the Elders,

Rabbi Murmelstein, told Claude Lanzmann in an interview after the war that his living quarters were especially equipped for making the Nazi film about the camp:

> MURMELSTEIN: My apartment was filmed.
>
> LANZMANN: Your apartment in Theresienstadt?
>
> MURMELSTEIN: ... During the city beautification, the order arrived that an architect from the Prague Opera House would furnish my apartment.[107]

It might be without relevance that the last Theresienstadt camp commander, SS-Obersturmführer Karl Rahm, who was put in charge of the "beautification" of the camp in 1944, was a toolmaker in his precamp life.[108] "Beautification," as Rabbi Murmelstein noted, was a program of staging the camp, staged anyway, so making it even more staged, specifically for an expected visit of the International Red Cross delegation and for the shooting of the film. Sometimes "beautification," *Verschönerung*, has been translated as "embellishment."

Baron Georges-Eugène Haussmann, remaking Paris, in the metropolis of the nineteenth century, in the city of the wide and straight boulevards radiating from the Arc de Triomphe, like a fan from a pole with a tricolor, a new city center, in a perfect image, especially in the sketch, all modern, also talked about "embellishment." More to the point, some talked about "strategic embellishments," or "*aérer, unifier, et embellir*," "air, unity, and embellish."[109]

In one of the plays written and performed in Theresienstadt, in November 1943, an interior is described in detail, it stars in the play. It is the apartment of the chief warden in a prison. The warden, in fact, is a prisoner, too. Yet, for the moment, he is allowed to live, he was assigned "a two-room beauty with paintings and carpets, a fine collection of gramophone recordings, and a delightful lap dog."[110]

Before they were driven to the camp, as they were preparing for Theresienstadt, the Jewish women were "knitting from unraveled wool, and sewing new clothes from old."[111] In the European cities, as the Jews expected to be put on transport any moment, Jewish workshops had been organized, "duvets were sewn," "more comfortable for the trip than quilts."[112] The better-off Jewish families "exchanged the white bed linen of the bourgeoisie for the coarser striped sheets of the lower classes."[113] They gathered whatnots and toys. Petr Ginz, still in Prague, wrote in his diary, on Friday, October 31, 1941, "In the morning I was supposed to go to school, but instead I went to say goodbye to the Miluškas and the Jiřinas, [who are going to the camp]. I brought little Pavlíček something to play with while traveling: a tank and a monkey that jumped and turned somersaults, but which scared him terribly."[114] (As I write this, I have a little mug from Carlsbad on my desk, with "Rudi" written on it in gold letters. Mr. and Mrs. Löwi from the floor above us brought the little mug for me from Carlsbad when I was a child. They were saying I was "theirs." I played also with a wooden tank in their apartment and got a wonderful scooter from them. Only much later did I find out that I was a substitute for their two sons, who had been taken to Theresienstadt and then disappeared into the camps "further in the east.")

These were the whatnots, always and in the camps, too, to fill the architectonics, to fix the sense of home, and, now, in the supermodern world and in the camps, to give a sense to geometry, to install a sense of the world, in the camps ultimately, as blocks and cubes.

"The Hamburg Jews," Dr. Jacob Jacobson remembered of Theresienstadt after the war, "had brought their own scrolls of the law, their own ark curtains, their own prayer shawls from Hamburg."[115] People were filling the blocks with heightened energy, to live and survive. They divided and subdivided the blocks into smaller and still smaller units with the same motivation. In this way, they articulated the cubes and the blocks, made them intense, and categorical more than ever before.

"Interiors-as-cockpits" were said to be growing in numbers in the cities of Europe after the war. In Theresienstadt already, the interiors-as-cockpits reached a stage of "self-contained universes."[116] On October 9, 1943, Mr. Schliesser of the camp administration commissioned the internee workshop to make a file cabinet for his apartment in the camp. On September 9, Mr. Streshnak, also of the camp administration, ordered a toy horse to be made for his son.[117] Another Theresienstadt document, from May 14, 1943, mentions the "repair of a sport car for ss Officer Heinrich Claussen."[118]

In Boven Digoel no less, the new privacy was being fabricated by subdividing blocks and filling the cubes. The more minimal the flat was, the more subdivided the communal space was, the more intimate the internees felt to be to the whole and to the camp, the more private was the camp. Partitioned, square or quadratic, abstract, the more it felt one's own.

The Boven Digoel camp ROB police in its criminal report on December 11, 1936, described a "case no. 51":

Break-In: This morning, internee Priokoesoema reported that last night one rice-cooking pot, price +*f*2, was stolen from his kitchen. He suspects that the pot was stolen by a person who grabbed the pot by pushing a hand through a hole in the roof. The hole and the roof are such that anyone could easily reach the pot with a hand. The pot stood on the stove.[119]

Jehuda Bacon described his youth home in Theresienstadt. "*Madrich* [Hebrew for 'leader' or 'youth educator']," Mr. Bacon recalled, "was very strict about the order in our room. Nothing might be just stuffed or thrown around to disturb the good impression of the place. The important thing for each one of us, was to behave in the home as to make it like at home."[120] Gonda Redlich wrote in his diary about a visit he made to a children's arts-and-crafts exhibition opened in the camp. "The children express their ideals," he wrote, and he was especially moved by "one beautiful model of an apartment."[121]

By the summer and fall of 1942, the early months of the camp, the average area of the living space for a person in Theresienstadt, according to Adler, fell under two-by-two meters. In the attics of the barracks, where a large number of the internees lived, at that time, the average living space fell to 1.6 meters per person.[122] Moreover, "being in an attic like this," Gonda Redlich wrote on August 29, 1942, "is a true Hell. On a summer afternoon, the suffocating air and stench hover like a cloud above the people, trapping their souls."[123]

Still, and even more, the process of partitioning kept on running and it accelerated. The logic of the miniaturization was being strengthened as the people wished against the odds to live as they had lived before. The blocks, from the basement to the attic, as in Peter Kien's drawing, were cut through, divided and subdivided. "Light isolation," mostly lathe-thin boarding or sheets of plywood that sometimes, somehow, became available, was used as the ever-new separation of ever-tinier units.

Dormers in the roof in the attics of the barracks were somehow enlarged so that they became "almost windows," electric wires were pulled from the walls, and connected so that even little ovens could be installed in newly created spaces. "Upgrading," Adler wrote, "was more or less legal."[124]

The thinner the separation, the more a dwelling took on a meaning of being a home. The thinner the wall, the purer and more categorical was the line, the length without breadth, the geometric paradigm.

Mansard was originally a Parisian architectural style, mostly known for its treatment of rooms directly under the apartment houses' roofs, designed for servants. In the Theresienstadt camp, "mansard" became a name in the camp language for a single-occupant or family living space, built under the roof of a barrack, by dividing, and subdividing, and subsubdividing the attic. "Mansards" became increasingly common and increasingly smaller as the camp time went on, as the camp lives went on, or rather, as they developed. There were "luxurious" mansards, one described by Adler, with a surface of sixteen square meters, with (for some reason) "three sofas," "an armchair, a wardrobe, and a nice large mirror."[125]

"Hacienda," according to *Šalom na pátek* magazine, was another camp name in Theresienstadt for "a kind of living space, built on top of a three-story bunk by pushing two bunks together, and barring the view into the inside by sheets, with the aim of facilitating friendly communication between the occupant of the hacienda and a friend of the other sex."[126] As the camp continued to live, and mature, some "haciendas" built on top of the storied bunks began to be called "villas."[127]

Karel Poláček, a Czech Jewish writer who later died "further in the east," lived in a "*kumbálek*" in Theresienstadt. A kumbálek, a little *kumbál*, Czech for "cubbyhole," was a space or room in the camp built in a block most often on the ground floor or in the basement, where the place of storage and the like used to be in the precamp times. People recalled that it was quite a blessing for Mr. Poláček, because he could still write while in the camp. "One could visit him," one former internee recalled of Poláček's kumbálek, "one only had to bow deeply."[128]

There was a prelude to almost everything in the camps. "They all sleep in wooden drawers, two stories one above the other," Joseph Roth wrote about the recent immigrant Jews in Berlin from Poland in the late 1930s.[129]

There were large dormitories in Theresienstadt where more than four hundred people slept. Most of the rooms in the camp were smaller, for eight or ten people. In most of the rooms, "there were two-level and in some places three-level bunks."[130] The height of such a "bed" for one person on average was at some points in time regulated as eighty centimeters, with a length of one meter seventy centimeters, and width of sixty-five centimeters.[131]

In a Theresienstadt girl's *Album von Vera Nath* [Album of Vera Nath], today in the Jewish Museum in Prague, there is a watercolor picture of a girls' dormitory: two-storied bunks, each with a comforter and pillow of the same shape, all neatly arranged, at right angles, nothing beyond the line outlined by the bunks. It would be most easy to make a technical drawing of it and still keep the full sense of it. In a sense, it is a technical drawing.[132]

In Auschwitz, they called the two- and three-story beds, still *progressively* smaller and much smaller than in Theresienstadt, again, "boxes."[133]

Better still, perhaps, Rem Koolhaas's terms should be called for. Writing in 1990 about Singapore, about its futuristic architecture, Koolhaas wrote about "'flatted' multilevel factories."[134]

The smaller the space, the more intensive the care. The camp women in Theresienstadt "put covers on the mattress, hang pictures of their dear ones over the bunk, place a doily on the board at its foot and put their belonging on it." Those who had eventually to go "further east," as they were leaving Theresienstadt, Ruth Bondy wrote, "lost yet another home."[135]

This has usually been called overcrowding. But in the truth of the camp, in the sense of increasingly concentrated modernity, it was miniaturization. The art of living was designed and driven toward the minimal. Under each bed in Theresienstadt, or, if there was no space, next to it, there were the people's "closed trunks full of necessities."[136] "Our keepsakes are under our beds," wrote Philipp Manes. "Our whole world is under the bed."[137]

"I got a bed D," Mrs. Mayer-Kattenburg recalled, "which meant that it was at the end of the row. On the side of the bed there was a space just for me, like for a king, to use it, all available only to me!"[138] There was trouble at one point in the older boys' home. "Dr. Jáchim meant well," wrote the boys in their *Vedem*. "He has a valid argument, it is not indeed very hygienic, that we kept all our things between the wall and bed, behind our heads. But this is our last spot of privacy, and we are desperate because they try to take it away from us." "You must let us," the boys begged the boys' home's block physician, Dr. Jáchim, "to keep the last half a meter behind our heads."[139]

"In what sense is logic something sublime?" Ludwig Wittgenstein wondered, and so do I throughout the book.[140] Theresienstadt, once more, was not Auschwitz. It was just toward Auschwitz, and along the line. In Auschwitz, Primo Levi recalled a "ritual of 'making the beds.'" In Auschwitz, like everything, it was deadly. Immediately after reveille, Levi wrote, came *Bettenbauen* [bed building]. The bunks in the rows had to look "like a rectangular parallelepiped." Each tiny imperfection was "punished publicly and savagely." Specially selected groups of prisoners, *Bettmachzieher* [bed after-puller] groups, "checked transversal alignment [with] a string the length of the hut."[141]

Boven Digoel was not Auschwitz either. Trikoyo, with other children in Boven Digoel, could still run or crawl under the cloth partitions between the family private space through the barracks.

Boven Digoel was also not the Indonesian postindependence and postcolonial camps and prisons of the mid- and late 1960s, where thousands of "suspected communists" (and there were quite a number of the Boven Digoel ex-internees still alive among them) had been concentrated by the new military regime, as in the case of Boven Digoel, without a trial, and also for an unspecified time. One of the "Salemba prison people," from a jail in Jakarta, recalled the space given to him and the others, post–Boven Digoel and post-Theresienstadt, but equally geometric, at least in his memory. Indeed, a geometry lesson:

> In Salemba prison, nine of us lived together in a cell of about 160 cm by 240 cm. The sleeping positions had to be planned. For instance, if the legs of person A were to the left of person B, then the legs of person B also had to be to the left of person A, parallel to it, so that the legs of A and B did not get entangled. If five of us were to place their heads toward the west or north, the remaining four had to have their heads toward the east or south. Good planning and *caranya berukuran* [taking measurements] allowed us to interlock and go to sleep.[142]

Friedrich Nietzsche, never in a camp but with an acute sense for the modern and the high modern, and for geometry, described his superman, the man of the future, as "rectangular in body and soul."[143]

....

The new of the twentieth century had been announced by the European avant-garde, cubism especially, with its "interlocking planes; flattened, dissected, and recomposed forms"; sculptures such as those of Alexander Archipenko or Umberto Boccioni, with their "planar logic"; the "new being-thought-of in terms of cubes and curves." The twentieth century brought about a new, "strange charm offered by the divided plane," and, indeed, "the appeal of the active, mysterious portioning," an unprecedented wave of "constructional pleasure ... totally geometrically hypertrophied."[144]

The new era was marked, driven, and determined by "a mass ... enveloped in its surface."[145] Surface, increasingly. "*Portes-fenêtres*," "French doors," and "balconies, kept very narrow,"[146] became the logic of this new. Pedro Gadanho quoted Siegfried Kracauer's *The Mass Ornament*: "The most significant revelation about the nature of the modern metropolis is in the surfaces."[147]

The geometry of the surface, Le Corbusier believed, was the crucial principle of the new. "Doors and windows," he wrote, these "holes are often the destruction of form."[148] In the case of iconic buildings of the twentieth century such as the Empire State Building, "the skin is all or almost all ... setting the windows, in the metal frames, flush with the outer wall [so that] not even shadows are allowed to break the upward sweep of the tower."[149]

In Theresienstadt, the Jewish camp police took intensive care that windows were flush with the outer wall, as well. The *Ordnerwache* [Order Watch], another specialized Jewish police section, had been on duty day and night. Petr Ginz wrote in the boys' magazine about how the police "go after the people who spit, litter, spill water, or have their eiderdowns hanging out of the window after 8 a.m."[150] *Šalom na pátek* was trying to make a joke of the matter: "Hiršík aired his comforter in the window. This is just him, he forgot all about the comforter and was unmasked as a *säumiger Lufter* [sluggish airer]. The block elder punished him with one day without food—poor Hiršík!"[151]

The windows, in the metal frames, flush with the outer wall, not disturbing the wall in the least, no holes making the surface unsmooth, were twentieth-century modern. "Do you want flowers on the windowsill, Gleb," Dasha, a true Bolshevik, in Soviet Fyodor Vasilievich Gladkov's 1925 novel *Cement*, asks her lover who disappointed her by not being Bolshevik enough. And what about "a bed overloaded with feather pillows?" Dasha asks in a crescendo of sarcasm.[152] In Theresienstadt, if bad came to worse, one could easily be sent to Auschwitz for "breaking the facade."

The forest surrounded Boven Digoel, with myriad niches and shadows between the trees and bushes, and holes, and the river flowing and overflowing the land, making bizarre-shaped lakes and spots of dry land, unpredictably. One needed truly a camp to make this into a wall, a plane, or a facade.

Boven Digoel was made truly, modern flat by the very originary act of clearing. "Deforestation of the camp," Dr. Schoonheyt wrote, "created a sunny spot." "Against the background of the huge trees of the primeval forest where the clearing ends," the doctor wrote, "the spot gives a sense of enormous expanse."[153] The sense of flatness of the Boven Digoel clearing and camp was further accentuated by the stubs of trees left protruding from the surface here and there, catching moss and rotting. Boven Digoel was avant-garde and en route to the future, a flat surface, a plane, like a drawing desk still with the work going on, a blank slate, keeping people captive, and flattened, too, a *"tabula rasa* created by a restless technization."[154]

Like Koolhaas's super-modern Singapore fifty years later, Boven Digoel was a "'virgin' land," built over with "slabs" on a "razed plane"[155]—and like Theresienstadt. Gabriel Italie wrote on October 22, 1944, hyperbolically, or rather, in the logic of a flattened place, "Just a couple of years ago, when [the camp of] Theresienstadt did not yet exist, there was a desert here."[156]

In fact, to call Mr. Manes's statement hyperbolic is questionable. In Theresienstadt, indeed, "contrary, to the promises by the Germans that the ghetto would be ready before the transports to the camp began, there was nothing there."[157] What the Jews faced when they arrived, Adler wrote, suggesting a desert, not unlike Mr. Manes, "was 333,056 m^2 area. Forty-two percent of the area had been built over, 12 percent of it was still not being used. The 42 built-over percent was parceled into streets, squares, courtyards, and gardens."[158]

"Area," Ernst Bloch thought, "this salvation of man and of being is thought in terms of an ontology in two dimensions, because it excludes all reference to height, as if there was some fear that one might confuse height and sky."[159] Everything, including depth, increasingly in modern times, was thought of in terms of flatness. Height became a modality of flatness. Skyscrapers, the tower blocks, the watchtowers of the modern, increased this significance of flatness. "Skyscrapers" according to Koolhaas, are a "sheer territorial multiplication," flatness multiplied.[160] "Shallow basements," Benjamin noticed already in the 1930s, "have taken the place of deep cellars." This could have happened, Benjamin added, speaking of progress, because of "the use of concrete and cement."[161]

Increasing hardness was an inevitable quality and condition of flatness. "Houses of reinforced concrete," wrote Francis Picabia in the same time, at the same moment, as Benjamin, this is "our era for you!"[162] "Hardness," Martin Heidegger wrote at the same moment, "is experienced by touching."[163]

The agricultural consultant of the Indies government, E. H. Tietjens, in the planning phases for the camp, reported that the soil in Boven Digoel was "fertile."[164] This suggested that the soil in Boven Digoel could be ploughed, hoed, turned over, and that roots would take in the soil's depth, some depth certainly. Very soon, however, almost as soon as the soil was touched, it was learned that the soil of Boven Digoel "is not good for agriculture." Besides, it became evident and a factor that "the community of internees in large portion consists of office people," not peasants, certainly. "The first real rains and following storms washed away the top layer of the soil. In almost no part of the new clearing anything could be planted more than once, at most twice, before the soil either washed away or becomes too thin for planting."[165]

"All the attempts to do agriculture in Boven Digoel totally failed," wrote Salim.[166] "As a possible agricultural colony," Marcus van Blankenstein reported already in 1928, "Boven Digoel is a disconsolate enterprise." "Beneath a shallow layer of soil," van Blankenstein specified, "lays an impenetrable ground."[167]

The camps brought about an unprecedentedly profound, calculated, functional, hard, and unswerving, all-absorbing sense of the surface and of the superficial. It stayed with us. A British artist, Richard Long, in the 1980s, set out to walk through the English countryside. He walked by compass, through fields, woods, and towns. What he demonstrated with his walk about the world was, to say it simply, that he left no traces. A friend of Long expanded on the experiment. He filmed his own effort to break the surface and "to bury himself in." The two men resembled the camp people as well as us. They also resembled biblical Job, in the sense that antiquity is still with us. Job complained to God, and God gave him instruction, or he possibly joked. "'Stamp,' said we, 'with thy foot.'"[168]

The soil was either not there or it was gone, the area was flattened beyond what the clearing had already done, and this was the camp of the future. Masun Samadjirdja, a Boven Digoel ex-internee, recalled in an interview after the war, "The delegates of all the sport teams in Boven Digoel selected a former irrigated rice field that had failed to produce, to become the new soccer field."[169] The soil became crusty and stale. The shallow became flat and hard. Measured, categorically rectangular, with the white lines sharp on the eye, straight and carefully renewed, the failed field became almost purely an idea, almost abstractly a sign of the camp, the camp dynamics, a paragon of the camp. It could still go further, and better. In the new edition of his book published in 1940, Dr. Schoonheyt included a picture of a tennis court with the caption, *"De cementen tennisbaan voor de geïnterneerden* [The concrete tennis court for the internees]."[170]

"Shallow instability," Gilles Lipovetsky argued in his *The Empire of Fashion*, possesses a potential to become "a permanent system."[171] Martin Heidegger, again, quoting a German fable with clear biblical overtones, suggested, "Let [the human] be called 'homo,' for it is made out of humus (earth)."[172] "I'm auscultating the ground," Louis-Ferdinand Céline described the most precarious moment of his clinging to life, as Paris was being "flattened" by the Allied bombing early in 1945.[173]

"Argument and logic," William Kentridge said in one of his Harvard lectures, "became something on top of the world, hovering over its surface, rather than embedded in it."[174] Lined, rectangular, categorical, geometric, and flat, there had been increasingly nothing to articulate the modern of the camp better than the soccer field on the failed rice field. The line was the rule. The camp people, on the sport field especially, between the lines, moved on command, by the rules and by their own flattened will. The line was everything. You trespassed and you were out.

Sublime, hard-core, straight-lined, the sport fields empty or in action, were truly the camp:

> *camp:* Origin: from French *camp, champ*, from Italian *campo*, from Latin *campus* "level ground," specifically applied to the *Campus Martius* in Rome, used for games, athletic practice, and military drill.

And also:

> camp: a facility at which athletes train during the off-season.

Theresienstadt, too, as clearing, progressed from uncharted landscape to blocks, bunks, haciendas, and sport fields.

"The bastions at the walls of the Theresienstadt fortress," Adler wrote, "were initially forbidden to the people of the camp. But after few months, one bastion, called *Südberg* [South Hill], behind the barrack A II, was opened to the camp public, and we built there playgrounds and sport fields."[175] "On the South Hill," Adler continues, "people played soccer, and spectators loudly cheered their teams."[176] On June 23, 1943, Bernhard Kold wrote in his camp diary, "We went to see two good soccer matches on the well-kept sport field on the Bastion III (the South Hill)."[177]

"There is a fine soccer field on the walls," Hanuš Kominík, a boy in Theresienstadt, wrote in *Vedem*; "with two new goals," he added.[178] "On the South Hill," Gonda Redlich wrote, "the guards on the watchtower keep an eye on the game, lest the people running after the ball attempt to escape."[179]

In Boven Digoel, as if to challenge the huge space still uncharted and not yet built over, there were sport fields even more of importance. "The soccer field in section C was largest," Mrs. Widayasih told me, "and it had also a tribune for the spectators."[180] During the matches, internees in stalls sold *sirop* [sugar water], and, as Mrs. Widayasih told me, "there was never sirop as good as that at home." "Sour-sweet," she recalled, "it had a light-red color, and there was a special fragrance to it."[181]

> SATURDAY, JUNE 29, 1935 ... AFTERNOON ... 3:55 ... In the soccer field of *Sutji Hati* [Pure Heart], there are about ten children, all pupils of the wild schools. They stick a new goal pole in the ground; among them can be recognized Soemarko and some of his friends.[182]

> SATURDAY, MAY 30, 1936 ... NIGHT: 11:10 ... In the house of Natar Zainoedin there is a meeting of the Committee to Build a New Sport Field.[183]

THIRTEEN

Streets

The Jews in Europe as well as the Communist rebels in the Indies, as it all began, were driven on the road, like Stepan Trofimovich in Dostoyevsky's *Demons*, who lost everything and believed he had to leave everything he had, and get "dressed 'for the road.'"[1] "Transportation means perambulators on the move," wrote Philipp Manes in Theresienstadt. He recalled, as he was dragged away from his Berlin middle-class home, grateful for the moment that he had no children. "Depending just on your muscular power," he wrote, "you put a bigger one of your two rucksacks on your back, strap a smaller one on your chest, take a bedroll in the left hand and a smaller trunk in the right hand."[2] In fact, in reality and according to the rules, he was not allowed even that much.

On September 9, 1943, Philip Mechanicus, a Dutch-Jewish journalist interned in the transit camp in Westerbork, wrote in his camp diary, "Men and women stop one another on the ... road and ask: 'Where are you going? Theresienstadt? Germany? Auschwitz?'"[3] Etty Hillesum, who became Philip Mechanicus's friend in Westerbork, wrote in her diary on July 27, 1942, still waiting in Amsterdam, just before she had to go, "And there are always the canals beside which I walk and which I engrave more deeply on my memory, so that I need never again be without them."[4]

Petr Ginz, also still in Prague and waiting, like Etty Hillesum in Amsterdam, wrote in his diary the same thing:

Preparations

While walking, I tried to absorb, for the last time, the street noise I would not hear again for a long time (in my opinion; Father and Mother are counting on just a few months).[5]

Salim, of Boven Digoel, recalled his own journey to Boven Digoel that took place on the ship. They sailed for weeks until they reached the point where the Digoel River flowed into the sea. At that point, Salim recalled thirty years later, one of the crew on the ship pointed to the water that changed its color from the blue of the sea to the muddy brown of the river: "He told us," Salim wrote, "as the lighter color of the water was disappearing and we entered the darker waters, 'This is what the river does, soon you are at home.'"[6]

There were stops on the road. There were, throughout Europe in the 1930s, as there are today, sites for recycling scrap metal, glass, old textiles, paper, or bones. *"Sammelstellen,"* "collecting sites," they were called in German. By 1941, as the moment of the camps arrived in Europe, sites with the same names, Sammelstellen, and often at the same locations, became gathering places where the Jews (and the Communists, and the homosexuals, and anyone who deserved it in the Nazis' minds) were being "collected" for transport.[7]

"After formalities were satisfied," wrote Max Berger, recalling his own being collected for Theresienstadt, "our identity card was stamped *'ghettoisiert* [ghettoized]'"[8] The recycling sites themselves changed only slightly as the people-for-the-camps began to be collected instead of scrap metal, old paper, and bones. They remained, sort of, recycling sites, too. People, logically, in the spirit of the time and perhaps ahead of its time, became stuff, useful, more or less.

As the transports to the camps began to move in earnest, Heinrich Himmler, the camp and now also transport architect, logically, began using a language of the road, and "of the stuff." "'Let nobody tell me,'" Himmler said in the fall of 1941 (the war with the Soviet Union was already on at the time but it was still going well), "'that we can't park them in the marshy parts of Russia!'"[9] After a while, as the war with the Soviet Union stopped going well, in the same way, the Nazis began to speak about "parking them" in the camps.[10]

Siegried Kracauer, in the 1930s, in a study of Paris of the nineteenth century, wrote about the emergence in the modern world of the "jargon of the boulevards."[11] The Nazi use of words such as "collection sites" or "parking" was not merely an extension or even a remnant of the jargon of the boulevards. It was the jargon's upgrading, building a functional and instrumental language in its ultimate. Etty Hillesum, in one of her letters from Westerbork, wrote about the camps as new settlements on the road, "these great human warehouses."[12]

"We're all sitting inside, and we don't have a clue. Train's leaving!," Kurt Tucholsky wrote in 1920, a German Jewish writer who fifteen years later died in exile, possibly by suicide. Tucholsky's mother, and it seems almost like a cliché, died in Theresienstadt.[13]

Michel Chevalier, quoted in Walter Benjamin's *Arcades Project*, wrote in 1852, long before all this, "For the transport of war materials in railroad cars, [was] set up the equation: forty men equal six horses."[14] At the time of World War I, the Austrian army manual prescribed forty-six men, or six horses and four men, for one freight carriage.[15] In the French army in the same war, "big freight cars took 'eight horses or forty men.'"[16] Hans Günther Adler, referring to the transport of the Jews to Theresienstadt, reported "seventy to eighty persons in one cattle car." "Before the fall of 1944," he added, "passenger cars were still sometimes used, but one was squeezed in them no less."[17]

There was a famous exchange caught on film at the trial in Jerusalem in 1960 of Adolf Eichmann, who was responsible for Theresienstadt in the Nazis' overall system of the camps. It was one of the rare moments when Eichmann, otherwise aloof in his glass box, got truly agitated. The exchange had been about how many Jews, according to the Nazi rules, were to be fitted into one cattle car.

From documents and testimonies, it is clear how seriously the Nazis thought about roads, parking, and warehouses. In the minutes of a discussion at the Reichssicherheitshauptamt, the main Nazi office for security, on March 6, 1942, SS-Obersturmbannführer Adolf Eichmann expressed "worries" about the "technical carrying out" of transports, to Theresienstadt specifically: "The trains are meant for only seven hundred persons," he insisted, and seemed to become angry, "but they are used to transport one thousand Jews."[18] Let us calculate, seemed to be the dictum:

Instruction by Reichssicherheitshauptamt office IV B 4a, August 1, 1942
Transport to Theresienstadt

1. 550 Jews from Nurenberg,
2. 180 Jews from Fürth,
3. 128 Jews from Bamberg,
4. 142 Jews from Würzburg (8 Jews as reserve)

1,000 Jews

Leo Baeck, an influential rabbi in Berlin before the war, recalled his being loaded "for the road," to Theresienstadt: "It was as if I were a horse."[19]

"The train cars for transport," Philipp Manes wrote in his Theresienstadt diary, and he used a vocabulary very much of the time, "are loaded with human-mass."[20] Jehuda Bacon, in an interview in Jerusalem in 2013, talked of his road-to-Theresienstadt experience as of "fear of *Einladung*." In an interview otherwise conducted in Hebrew, Mr. Bacon used a German word for "loading." In the same interview, instead of "*Einladung*," he once used "*Einwagonieren*," German for "loading in a railway car."[21]

In a telephone conference between ss-Sturmbannführer Hans Günther of the main security office in Berlin and the ss office in The Hague, on January 25, 1943, the officers talked about "*die Verschiebung nach Theresienstadt*," "dispatching to Theresienstadt."[22] "*Abschiebung*," "moving on," was another word of the language. ss-Obersturmbannführer Adolf Eichmann, in a report to the Nazi higher office on March 6, 1943, had Jews "*nach Theresienstadt abgeschoben*."[23]

The trains to the camps were to move through the European landscape, as Richard Long would move forty years later, leaving no traces. In a secret telegram from the ss headquarters in The Hague, the occupied Netherlands, an order was sent, on April 15, 1943, to the office in Utrecht, the main railway junction on the border between the Netherlands and Germany. Under the heading "Trains from the Netherlands to Theresienstadt," one reads, "The Transport Command in Utrecht is herewith reminded that closed cars must be made available for a train from Amsterdam to Theresienstadt that will leave on April 21, 1943. . . . The train must be enabled to travel at a normal and steady speed. It has been reported in recent days that trains are sometimes left on tracks for days."[24] Jiří Weil, a Czech Jewish writer, looking still from the outside, wrote about a train from Prague to Theresienstadt: "When the train departed [from the Prague station], nobody noticed, because it looked like an entirely ordinary freight train moving slowly as it should, along the tracks, with covered cars that might be carrying cement or gun mounts."[25]

Oldřich Böhm, a boy of Theresienstadt, and a young poet, wrote,

Strange train
Closed hermetically
Up to the roof
Full of sighs
In cattle cars
The human freight.[26]

"The cars were closed and sealed," Adler wrote.[27] "Sheets of metal were nailed over the windows," wrote Manes.[28] It cannot be helped, Kafka was traveling with the Jews on one of these trains. Or, certainly, their memories of the prewar train travels did: "A short Frenchwoman got into the next compartment, with outstretched arm announced that our full compartment was not '*complet*,' and pushed in her father and her older, shorter sister, who looked at once innocent and lewd and who tickled my hips with her elbow."[29]

It was the stage of history for the architects as geometers to come into their own. The people were put on the road and driven in blocks and to blocks. They were, in other words (of that language) "packed in boxes." Indeed, the train cars, long before but now most fittingly, were called "boxcars."[30] When in Theresienstadt, Gonda Redlich noted in his diary that one day, expecting a new transport, somebody asked the chief of the Czech gendarmes, who was organizing the arrival, how many people were coming. "Janeczek answered: 'three boxcars of Jews.'"[31]

Being on the road, never before was one on the road so fully, so complete, and so absorbingly. Never before could the journey toward the modern, the light, give so complete a feeling of "being on the road." In another premonition, Hermann Broch wrote in a novel published long, but not long enough, before the camps and the transports to the camps: "The train goes roaring on at full speed, apparently darting towards a goal ... in the painful liberty of the open that makes an attempt to turn and walk in the opposite direction.... the traveler ... presses his nose flat against the windowpane as he used to do when he was a child."[32]

Being on the road makes the modern unstable, and this is the constant of the modern. The modern makes "foreign" every place one leaves, passes through, and moves toward. "For lack of changing one's life," Marc Augé wrote, we built up "a symbolic system" that allows us "to change the train"[33]—sometimes, we cannot do even that.

Erna Furman, who spent her teen years in Theresienstadt, recalled later, in an interview with Elena Makarova, how her mother, who traveled with her to Theresienstadt and beyond on these trains, was slowly losing her mind. She became suspicious of everybody, especially of the Jews, Mrs. Furman said. She repeatedly tried to get out from the train ("change the trains," Marc Augé may perhaps say). In October 1942, Mrs. Furman recalled, "Mother escaped from the train, again thinking that Jews were after her. It took place when the train was still in the station and not running. And again, it was Jews against her, not the Germans. It was tough."[34]

What seemed really to matter was the loading—and thus, the calculation of the mass and the measurement of the space. An ex-internee of Westerbork recalled that nothing was likely to give the SS commandant of the camp a "greater offense than a disorderly transport. Instances were known in which, upset by the improper disposition of the train's human ballast, he would condescend to assist and with his own gloved hand push the wretched victim, some man, woman, or child, inside the packed door, like so!"[35] At the loading of transports from Theresienstadt further on, Adler recalled, "unemotional cold bureaucratism had been observed."[36]

The people on the way to Boven Digoel were packed and loaded, too, and, in the context of history and modernity, with the same zeal, measurement, calculation, and efficiency.

In most cases, after being arrested and their papers stamped, the camp-people-to-be were locked in the cells of local prisons for a time, to wait, so to speak, until they were put on the road. Then, in general, they were loaded into police cars and driven to a train station, to be transferred further to the nearest seaport.

Mohammad Hatta wrote in his memoirs, "Bondan and I, with our trunks, were ordered to step in a police car. Inside it was dark and constrained. The back of the car was partitioned into three sections, each section just big enough for a single person to stand up. It turned out, as we began to move, that the section in front was occupied by Soetan Sjahrir, who had been picked up before from the Tjipinang prison. I stood in the middle section, and Bondan in the last one, behind me."[37]

Mohammad Bondan wrote about his memories of the same moment: "In the police car, there was no space to sit down, we were just standing in little boxes [*kotak-kotak*] and, through the journey, we had to focus on keeping balance. From a tiny opening for ventilation in my little box, I could see Kramat Street, Gunungsari Street, and other places in downtown Jakarta as we passed by."[38] The partitions between Hatta's, Sjahrir's, and Bondan's sections were thin, and soon they discovered that they were able to talk to each other. "We could talk," Bondan recalled, "and what Sjahrir said, had been conveyed to me by Hatta, who stood between us. What I answered went through Hatta the same way in the opposite direction." It was as if there were telephones in the police car. "We chatted happily, delighted that we were together, however we could not see each other's faces."[39]

Jahja Nasoetion, another man transported to Boven Digoel, wrote in his memoirs, "I left the cell of the prison in Batavia, where I had spent, 'a retiree from the world,' two years, four months, and forty days. In front of the prison gate stood waiting a closed prison car."[40] The car drove Jahja through Batavia to the port. "From the inside of the car I could not see outside, and from the outside nobody could see who was in the car, and even whether the content of the car was human."[41]

Then there was a ship waiting. The *Melchior Treub* government steamer for Hatta and his friends. "The ship," Hatta recalled, "sailed first to Surabaya [East Java] and it stopped there. But it dropped its anchor at a great distance from the docks and it stayed in the harbor for the shortest time necessary. There were, as we later heard, people who somehow learned that we were on the ship and who would have liked to say goodbye to us. But this was not to be."[42]

....

A compact, clean, well-charted, and hard surface was required for the roads to be dependable. No depth, and no softness; one might get stuck on a soft road. Softness was as bad as a crumbling wall. Roads should be metallic, ideally, like the channels of long-distance communication.

Hardness, long before the camps, had been an essential part of the truth of the modern—its efficiency, its being up the wall and on the road—a man-made hardness, of jewelry and of Heidegger. "In stone we feel the natural spirit of the mass," A. G. Meyer wrote in 1907 and was quoted in Benjamin's *Arcades Project*, but, he added, "iron is, for us, compressed durability and tenacity."[43] The man-made hardness, essential, became, inevitably or progressively, the same thing, a matter of culture, and it became beautiful: "Cast iron, wrought iron, ingot iron, winding iron staircases, cast-iron girders, iron lattice ... polished iron, dazzling copper, fashion of the time, delicate like embroidery, yet hard."[44] Jules Michelet, the great French historian of the

Revolution, at the outset of the high modern, in the mid-nineteenth century in Paris, stood "pale and feeble" in front of a new, high-modern iron construction. "Man," he said, "is only the humble servant of those steel giants."[45]

There was a new "beauty of brightly painted concrete," Ernst Bloch wrote closer to the camps' time. "Concrete cannot be set on fire; it is healthy," Bloch also wrote. "Without concrete we would have no usable modern house ... [or] airtight windows.... The weak flesh cannot survive alone, and reaches for a husk."[46] Harder is "denser," wrote Le Corbusier again, with much greater self-assurance than Bloch.[47] "The war has shaken us all," Le Corbusier wrote, meaning World War I.[48] "*Architecture or revolution* ... steel and concrete ... the Stone Age, the Bronze Age, the Iron Age ... reinforced concrete ... [new] aesthetics of construction ... *surface* ... tubes replacing the encumbrance of tramways..."[49]

The hardness did not mean eternity. Like radio, the hardness could and, indeed, should be, actual and instant. There was significantly, besides the concrete and iron, a papier-mâché hardness. Papier-mâché was a stuff, too, used by architects and urban planners for building models, to sketch their concepts quickly. There was a cardboard hardness, too; plastic hardness would come later. The iron, concrete, papier-mâché, or cardboard buildings and cities, and ultimately camps, were not supposed to have roots, to "grow," as though possessing, to use words of Joseph Roth, "an organic secret." They were not supposed, still Roth, to "rustle like trees."[50] Whatever the new stuff they were made of, they were supposed to be impressive, and habitable, as pop-up shows: "*Pop-up* (of a book or greeting card) containing folded cut-out pictures that rise up to form a three-dimensional scene or figure when the page is turned."[51]

In Boven Digoel, the camp people built up their houses, delineated, conceived, mapped their living space with whatever material they could find. In Theresienstadt they often used lathe-thin boarding or plywood, "sheets of artificial wood,"[52] other "light isolation desks,"[53] or even cardboard. They would have used plastic, no doubt, if the era of plastic had already begun. They would have used concrete if they had had access to it. The camps signaled what was coming, "the beauty of airports," as Rem Koolhaas might point out. In the airports, Koolhaas wrote about our present, "There are no walls, only partitions."

When Maxim Gorky, the preeminent Soviet writer, visited the true and only Luna Park at Coney Island in the 1920s, he described it as "hell very badly done."[54] Benjamin, more down to earth, considered Luna Park "a prefiguration of sanatoria," and he might include it among the embodiments of what he called the "cult of the ephemeral."⁵⁵ "It is of just such ridiculous thin material that the new parts of cities are built," wrote Joseph Roth, and he knew it was serious and a sign of the future: "There are walls you can pinch between finger and thumb," and, he added, "airy filmy walls."⁵⁶

This was a filmy hardness of theater wings and backdrops, or, still closer, a film studio. It allowed for making quick and radical changes, meaning conquering the world.

In the mid-nineteenth century, as the first Dutch ships of adventurers and conquistadors arrived at the shores of New Guinea, "on widely scattered beaches the Dutch commanders erected escutcheons—iron plates embossed with a coat of arms and the label *Nederlandsch Indië*—then shot off cannons and tossed out trinkets to impress the Papua onlookers. They punished the coastal troublemakers, ambushing villages, burning houses, and seizing anyone who failed to escape."⁵⁷ The escutcheons, I guess, were made of iron. There is another report, this time from the camp already established and from almost a century later. On a lined page torn from a notebook, a letter by an internee, dated June 15, 1929, sent evidently from *Tanah Tinggi* [Higher Ground], a section of the camp built off the A-to-F sections of the main settlement, the toughest section of the camp, a "second camp" of Boven Digoel, for the least obedient internees, still an hour or so by motor boat further up the river, still deeper into the wilderness:

> *The Highly Esteemed Assistant Resident Sir*
> *Boven Digoel*
> With respect.
>
> You must remember, when you visited Tanah Tinggi, I approached you and made a request. I had to leave all my stuff in the main camp when, in haste, I was moved from the main camp. I was told then, that all my things would be shipped after me as I need them very much.
>
> When you visited Tanah Tinggi, you told me that I should make a list. I delivered the list to you, and waited. . . . Several boats have already come from the main camp, but my things were not on any of them. . . .
>
> Might it be that you have forgotten? . . . As the weeks pass on, I worry that my things may be spoiled or stolen. . . . I have put them all together with great difficulty and some of them I have made myself. . . . So, here again, is the list: one foot-pedal sewing machine, two tables, one chair, one bench, one kitchen made of concrete, two bedboards plated with zinc.⁵⁸

There is a little note in pen next to each item on the list, clearly by the hand of an official in the main camp: "found" or "not found." Next to the "kitchen made of concrete," "found," there is in addition a question mark by the same hand. As though the officer had not heard about the modern on the march. But he may be excused; even Mrs. Kandinsky, the wife of the most avant-garde European painter of the time, Wassily Kandinsky, had been puzzled when they visited one of Le Corbusier's houses in Saarbrücken, and she was shown, among other furniture in the house, a "desk and a bookshelf made of concrete."[59] The Boven Digoel internee's letter concluded,

> Even when I do not have too high an expectation anymore that you would help me, the Most Respected Sir, I send you my greeting.
> *Signed Soendoro.*[60]

We have already heard about internee Soendoro. He was the friend of Trikoyo's father, a builder first in Semarang before the camp and then, according to Trikoyo, helping the Dutch authorities to build Boven Digoel. He was the man who made Trikoyo think of Boven Digoel when he saw, after the war, the high-modern avenues and blocks of the "New Kebayoran" in Jakarta.[61]

Papier-mâché, cardboard, iron, and concrete hardness was imported and established in the camps, like roses or like the best doctors there ever were. Etty Hillesum, in one of her letters from Westerbork, wrote, "We sleep on the bunks brought here from the disbanded Maginot Line."[62] The Maginot Line was a defense wall built in 1930 to defend France against Germany and after 1940, as the Nazis invaded France, put out of service. In Westerbork, they also got iron stoves from the Maginot Line, and Philip Mechanicus described them in his camp diary as "a low affair with a top surface about a meter square on which a great number of mess-tins and pots and kettles and jugs can stand at the same time."[63]

The other camp's people, like those of Theresienstadt, had to wait a little longer for a kind of Maginot hardness to appear and mold (indeed) their lives. Only after the less lucky of the Theresienstadt people got to Auschwitz, as Ruth Bondy recalled, were their blocks furnished (indeed) with all kind of things, "whatnots," "from the surplus equipment of German Rommel's campaign in Africa."[64]

Qualities such as "fitting" or "usable" came to fully dominate the thinking of the time and more so the camps—to "hardwire" the time and more so the camps. "A primary orientation to thingness," wrote Heidegger, "initially merely material, gets stamped as something good." "Good" Heidegger wrote, becomes the same as "the useful thing at hand."⁶⁵

Hardness was essential for the camps as the epitomes of the world. The Soviet classic by Fyodor Vasilievich Gladkov was aptly titled *Cement*, and it was read since the 1920s everywhere, including the camps, as long as they could get the book, a story of progressive hardness, the hardness of the future. The book describes a utopia, articulating the twentieth century as much as Le Corbusier did. This was the scene, or a stage rather: "Coal and cement. Slag and soot. Filigree-towers of the electric conveyor. Smokestack higher than the mountains. Net-work of cables."⁶⁶

In Boven Digoel, the barracks and houses initially had bamboo, rattan, or grass thatched walls and palm-leaf roofs because, initially, it was so distant from everywhere. But soon, as soon as possible, the walls "had been plastered over to give the appearance of normal walls."⁶⁷ The walls initially might have been lighter and permitted better ventilation than plastered walls. But the more real the camp was to be, the harder the stuff it should be built of. This was an escutcheon and iron and the concrete of the real. Internee Salim wrote, "Our hospital was put on a base made of stone."⁶⁸ "The hospital's walls," Trikoyo recalled, "were all of stone and still covered with a layer of cement painted white. The floors in the hospital were of ceramic tiles, and the roof of the hospital was of zinc."⁶⁹

Siegfried Kracauer, writing about Berlin of 1930 and the city's "pleasure barracks," meaning movie theaters and dancing halls for the aspiring lower-middle and lower classes, described the barracks as "the true symbolic centers of the world," "the white-collar worker's pipe dreams in stone, or rather in stucco."⁷⁰

The houses of the internees in Boven Digoel, wrote historian Takashi Shiraishi, "were relatively well-built, made with wood and zinc roofs, some with plastered walls."⁷¹ Shiraishi also mentions "well-kept stone houses for the low-ranking civilian and police staff."⁷² But the true, iconic hardness of Boven Digoel was zinc.

"In Boven Digoel," it was repeatedly complained by the officials, "one can still find parts of military barracks built of rough untreated timber and even with roofs of sago palm fronds."⁷³ Yet there was zinc, and more zinc was coming. It was more, a rage, a culture, zinc in all its incarnations and uses. The "shopping list for Mr. Sanoesi" included "two zinc plates, *f*0.70; zinc finger bowls, *f*0.70."⁷⁴ "The water flows in the camp as it wishes, and it flows away wherever it finds a slope and an open way," Marcus van Blankenstein wrote from Boven Digoel in 1928. "The best solution," he suggested, and he saw it already happening, "is to collect the water on a zinc roof."[75] "As I walked along the main street of camp section C," an official wrote in a report on his inspection a year after van Blankenstein, "on the right, already stood a warehouse with a roof of zinc."[76]

For the time being, not concrete but zinc was the new and the true of the camp. "In the soccer field in camp section C," Mrs. Widayasih recalled, "there was a tribune for the spectators that had seats of wooden planks but a roof of zinc."[77] Internee-musician Pontjopangrawit was remembered building in the camp "some of his gamelan instruments from zinc containers."[78] Zinc was the thing.

> TUESDAY, JULY 28, 1936 . . . NIGHT: 9:10. Internee Ibing reports to the ROB agent that behind his house a group of Kaja-Kaja makes a racket every night, shouting and beating on zinc plates.[79]

"They can earn a premium of thirty cents a day," the Boven Digoel administrator Blok reported in December 1928 on the ways in which he tried to inspire the internees to work more and better. "More of them, however, I find motivated by a possibility that they might be allocated zinc, especially for the roofs of their houses. Often, they just ask for zinc without it even entering their minds that they might just go to the forest and get lumber for their roof."[80] "Even Papuans," there was another report on times changing, "do not want to live anymore under the thatched-palm-leaves roof, when they can get hold of a zinc sheet."[81]

On June 18, 1929, internee Soemobasir from camp section B wrote a letter "in all respect" to the assistant resident in Boven Digoel:

> I live in a house that is as yet not covered with zinc. I have already asked for zinc once but was told that I would have to buy it. But I have no money. . . . If I buy zinc I would have nothing to buy food with. I need 130 (hundred thirty) small sheets of zinc to cover my roof. . . .
>
> In all respect, again.
> *Signed Soemobasir.*[82]

Mr. Trikoyo describes the grave site, the most revered grave in the camp, of Aliarcham, the former Communist Party chairman, who, as we have seen, died in the camp. "Above the grave," Mr. Trikoyo told me, "stood a light wooden structure but with a zinc roof."[83]

WEDNESDAY, JUNE 12, 1935, MORNING: . . . 11:30. Internee Soeparman can be seen walking past the police station, carrying small plates of zinc to cover, he says, bags of his rice and other supplies that lay in the open.[84]

Soetan Sjahrir wrote to his brother in the Netherlands on March 27, 1935, "There are houses here that are built completely of zinc plates. . . . Now, the roofs of almost all the houses here are of zinc."[85] And to his wife Sjahrir wrote in the next letter, on April 21, 1935, "The roofs are usually of zinc, the walls of thatched bamboo, wood or again of zinc sheets."[86]

The skyline of Boven Digoel, "songline" as Rem Koolhaas called it, writing about Singapore, indeed "sang" of zinc. "In the distance," Salim wrote about his return after some months from a stay in a hospital in Ambon, "as you were coming up the river to the camp, the first signs of the settlement you saw, were the zinc roofs!"[87]

The camps were not supposed, to use the words of Joseph Roth again, to contain "an organic secret" like the cities of the old; their walls were not supposed to "rustle like trees." There was a new sense of the natural, the natural process of concentration, condensation—and crystallization—"crystal," according to the dictionary, "a piece of a homogeneous solid substance having a natural geometrically regular form with symmetrically arranged plane faces." The camps, radically more and more rapidly than the rest of the high-modern world, became crystal-clear and crystal-hard. As in crystals, again, it was the geometry and the purity of planes, lines, angles, barracks, cubes, and people that cause the camp's strength, integrity, and hardness.

According to Max Horkheimer and Theodor Adorno's *Dialectic of Enlightenment*, it was a long process that now—they wrote this in the closing months of World War II—reached its highest point. "Enlightenment thinking," they wrote, "already contains the germ of the regression." It gives an opening to "the technologically educated masses" into a world not fully manageable, and this builds up "the fear of truth, which *petrifies* enlightenment itself."[88]

Hard, truly hard things were packed for the camps, and with as much care, and anxiety, as books, for instance. These hard things, like the books, equally, were part of the camp dialectic of enlightenment.

**List of the items left by the internees with the captain
of the HMS Java for safekeeping**

Internee Hartadi, alias Koesmo: A nickel watch with a chain, and a little pack of nails.[89]

"I have packed a hammer for the camp," ex-internee Bernhard Kold of Theresienstadt recalled, "and hooks and nails. The work tools were so very important and nobody in the camp would even for a minute let his eyes off his toolbox."[90] "The tools were in great demand," Alice Bloemendahl remembered, "and each wooden plank, and every little piece of timber, of a pipe, or of a wire."[91]

Like food, fashion clothes, or books, real or fantasy, the ironmongery, hammers, cogs, pliers, and screws were acute in the camps, and *essential*. The horror of the camps might reach to heaven, but they were, *in essence*, useful and efficient "'flatted' multilevel factories."[92] The hardness, and the impenetrable flatness, only thought about by Le Corbusier and others, was the architectural and moral reality of the camps.

On July 20, 1942, Nava Shean, on her way to Theresienstadt, in the collection site in Prague, waiting, scribbled in her diary, "*The Fairground Palace*. We have been here for two days already. We sit or lie on the concrete floor over our backpacks."[93] On November 12, 1943, Philip Mechanicus wrote about the Westerbork camp, "Life is becoming more trying, wetter, and muddier."[94]

In Boven Digoel, the roads and streets of the camp were paved, in sharp and indeed shocking contrast to the roads and streets of the still largely dusty, and when it rained, wet and muddy colony. Even the most modern Indies towns and cities were largely unpaved. Surface in Boven Digoel was, to use the word again, hard. The camp police, the *ronda*, as they made their rounds, could even be described, if the word was already there, as "surfing." "Cruising," indeed, was used:

> MONDAY, JUNE 14, 1937 ... NIGHT: ... 7:58 ... The police [*ronda*] is cruising [*ber-kruising*] the camp.[95]

Shoes and bare feet, still, in Boven Digoel, very much stamped on the hard surface as the people walked, making a sound that, if it was still needed, revealed the camp's hardness. Ultimately, in Auschwitz, the sound was—on hard surface and asphalt, too—that of "the crude clogs with their wooden soles."[96]

Hard and, ever more, paved roads and streets, as well as, inside the home, floors of stone, concrete, or tiles, since long before the camp, were the modern of the Indies. In the Indies, since the turn of the twentieth century, on entering a house, one knew in an instant whether the house was of the new time, that is, Westerner's, in most cases. "You entered the wide and long hall of the house, and its floor were [*sic*] completely marble.

Behind the dining room was the pantry, where blue-and-yellow tiles replaced the marble floors."[97]

The hardness of the surface, "stamp with thy foot," became a fundamental matter of culture, new, energetic, and arriving. In the cleared spots in the jungle around Boven Digoel, inspired, enlightened by the camp, the Catholic Mission of the Sacred Heart did much of letting the light in, and of paving the surface.

Visit to the Church

The inhabitants of Okaba [Papua] are curious. There is so much to see at the *tuans* [masters] ... colorful windows that you cannot just take eyes off, and, when you lay down, the pleasant and cool concrete floor.[98]

Soetan Sjahrir wrote in a letter, "We have not real floors in our houses. The only place where you can enjoy the luxury of a concrete floor is the house of the camp administrator. We, on the whole, have just the ground for flooring, the clay hard stamped."[99]

The roads and streets in Boven Digoel, indeed, on the whole, had been made hard. "As you passed a little bridge," Salim at one place in his memoirs leads his reader through the camp, "there was a graveled path."[100] Dr. Schoonheyt, in his Amsterdam lecture about the camp, pointed out these two aspect of the camp with emphasis: "zinc roofs" and "gravel of the streets."[101]

Boven Digoel was set up on the muddy and flood-prone low bank of the river. But the hardness welcomed visitors, inspecting officials, as well as the new arriving internees. Already at the first steps, as one went from the ship and the river to the camp, there was an imposingly large and solid landing place. Next to the zinc roofs and paved roads, this was a signature of the camp. The words of Kafka in his *In the Penal Colony*, describing the first and lasting impression of the penal colony by Kafka's explorer, in Boven Digoel again rung true: "Mostly harbor works, nothing but harbor works."[102]

"The raft," Mr. Trikoyo recalled of the Boven Digoel landing place in his memoirs, "was not like the rafts usually were and still are on the rivers in Java. This raft was large, made of huge boards and beams held together not by the usual spikes, but by iron bolts. The whole was secured to the hooks deep in the bank of the river with a cable that was as thick as my arm."[103] The raft was watched no less than the people were.

MONDAY, JUNE 24, 1935 . . . AFTERNOON . . . 4.35. Agent Hadji Sanoesi goes to check the raft. The water is rising, the cables have already pulled the whole ladder above the level of the water. There is still no reason to worry.[104]

SATURDAY, MAY 16, 1936. MORNING . . . 8:50 . . . Water is still high. The ladder is already far from the bank. The main cable to the raft is checked. It holds fast.[105]

FRIDAY, MAY 24, 1935. MORNING . . . 11:00 . . . The concrete foundation of the raft is fine, and the raft sits back again. The camp is calm.[106]

The survival of Boven Digoel's continuing existence, significantly, was based on not taking in water. Camps were not supposed to leak. Nobody thought about dry foundations and leaking as much as the people of the camps—except Le Corbusier, perhaps. "Instead of forming foundations by excavating and constructing thick foundation walls," Le Corbusier suggested "concrete piles."[107] Reinforced concrete would be best but where not available, piles of hard wood, bricks, or stone should work. The builders of Theresienstadt held that view long before Le Corbusier. "Do you know," the magazine *Šalom na pátek* asked, "that a large part of Theresienstadt is built on oak gratings, similar to Venice?"[108]

On piles, with thick and solid landing places, leak-proof, mold-proof, and flood-proof, on hard surface, what George Perec wrote in horror was true also about Theresienstadt and Boven Digoel: "The camps were working smoothly."[109]

On the charts and diagrams, with the little silhouettes of people, the smoothness can be seen. Rails, and rail connections, ran smoothly, from a station to the camp, from one camp to the next, as well as the waterworks under and above the ground, canalization, the chlorine-treating station, the excavation of a sink for drainage, a pump station, all of it was about controlling the flow, of water, of trains, of people. The leaks were controlled, ideally, settled, as on the graphs and the diagrams.

The "Little Fortress" of Theresienstadt, also called "Fort B," was designed to guard the Ohře/Eger River and the Labe/Elbe River.[110] One of the most important offices in Theresienstadt, run by the Jewish Council of the Elders under SS supervision, was Der Wasserdienst [the Water Service].[111] Before the war, the inhabitants of the town were still getting much of their water from local wells. After the Jews arrived, the Water Service took it upon itself to modernize the water supply radically. "The Jewish engineers and workers," Max Berger, a former internee, wrote after the war, worked without rest and in a short time they connected almost every house to an all-camp water system. In barracks, closets with flushing water, and also washrooms with showers, were installed.[112]

Like the plumbed trains, the plumbed police cars, and the plumbed ships, the plumbed water system was there to prevent leaking. Water, like people, flowed smoothly and did not overflow. "In two years, between the summer of 1942 and the summer of 1944, Jewish workers have built up an integrated canalization and water-distribution net complete."[113]

This drive for smoothness referred not just to modern or even high-modern. It referred to revolutionary. In his own time Alexander Ulyanov tried to assassinate the Russian tsar, was captured, and executed. His brother, Vladimir, the future Lenin, inherited a favorite book of his brother, Nikolai Chernyshevsky's *What Is to Be Done?* There were long passages in the book on "drainage," canalization, and water distribution systems, strange only at first glance. "To avoid Tsarist censorship, Russian radicals referred to mechanical processes such as 'draining' to indicate revolutionary means."[114] In Étienne Cabet's *Travels in Icaria*, three-quarters of a century before Lenin, "the streets are paved or constructed in such a way that water never collects on them, for there are frequent openings through which the water goes into underground canals."[115]

It was not perfect in the camps, not yet. The rivers, at least, were not fully under control, nor were the rains, and floods were a threat both to Boven Digoel and to Theresienstadt. But they were ready as best as they could be. When a boy-editor of *Vedem* in Theresienstadt interviewed a Jewish camp policeman, the officer talked about all the things the police were doing. "He said that the camp police were also owners of a pontoon bridge that could be used in the case of flooding."[116]

This was a peak of what Ernst Bloch called the era of the "lavatorial" universe, as close, at least, as the world ever got to it. Canalization, irrigation, and drainage were to allow for water and waste to flow safely in pipes, as the people were to flow safely in special pipelines for people. Hygiene, health, and plumbing were to keep the camp running smoothly. "Technological cold," it might be said about the camps, which is also what Ernst Bloch said about the advanced modern.[117]

In Boven Digoel, the houses, front yards, backyards, and gardens of the internees were separated by fences of bamboo and flower bushes. But the truth of the camp, the truth of a line were ditches. They were dug according to a plan, with precision; they were watched by the police; and orders were issued for them to be regularly cleaned. They were part of the camp's integral *gotenstelsel* [gutter network]. "The gutter network," Salim recalled, "was given a special importance. Many of these water and waste channels were not just a ditch in the earth. They were built of bricks strengthened by mortar, and, often, they were covered with zinc sheets."[118]

There was a brickyard in Boven Digoel with most of its production specifically being the bricks for the gutters.[119] And, then, indeed, there was the concrete:

Day Report June 1936

Work plan for today . . . building concrete gutters.[120]

WEDNESDAY, JULY 1, 1937 MORNING . . . 7:28. A captain arrives. With the camp supervisor, he will inspect the reinforcing of a gutter behind the administrative office.[121]

"Tubes replace the encumbrance of tramways," wrote Le Corbusier in his *Towards a New Architecture*.[122] Tubes and ditches, canals, armatures, strengthened with bricks and concrete, covered with zinc sheets, or just earth stamped with one's feet, like the closed police cars, trains with windows nailed over, and ships anchoring far from the harbor, were remaking the world, and they most categorically articulated the camps. They were Benjamin's "Arcades," *Passagen*, the Parisian passages, novelty of the nineteenth century, but mightily upgraded.

The camp people of Boven Digoel and Theresienstadt, but much more smoothly than Benjamin's flâneur, passed through, in much more an efficient way were driven through, programmed, and secured through.

"The arcade," Benjamin wrote, "is a city, a world in miniature."[123] Each time I was in Berlin, before the Wall came down, one or other friend, an inhabitant of the eastern part of the city, which was the only place where, as a citizen of Czechoslovakia, I could then go, told me sooner or later a piquant observation but still as in wonder. Throughout all the time of Germany's separation, they said, the only thing still connecting Berlin's, and, in fact, Germany's and in fact the world's two parts was the city's sewage system. The shit flowed through.

....

"The necessity for order," Le Corbusier also knew, was contained in the line. "The regulating line," he wrote in his manifesto in 1923, "brings satisfaction to the understanding."[124] Through lines, he wrote, "man rings in unison with universal order."[125] "Geometry is the language of man," and it is "made possible only by lines"; "Harmony" is a "moment of accord with the axis," and it is "the axis" that gives "intensity to the volume."[126] A "chord inside us is struck when we see it; the axis is touched," when we "touch the axis of harmony."[127]

Michel Foucault might be talking about the same line. By walking up and down the central aisle of the workshop, Foucault famously wrote, one builds up "discipline." Walking the line, giving adequate significance to the line, Foucault wrote, "is an art of rank."[128]

Lines, the foundations of pure geometric order, attained their highest material significance in the camps. The camp people, as hardly any group of humans before the camps, were ordered by line, lived in line, were filed, filed away, and left hanging, by a thread, *file*, being from the Latin *filum*, "thread."

"Even babies in perambulators," Adler wrote in his history of the camp in Theresienstadt, "had to join the march."[129] The people were waiting in the barracks' corridors, moved slowly along the long walls, or just "stood in line."[130] According to the Theresienstadt Daily Order No. 12 Concerning Children's Visits to Parents, Dated December 27, 1942, "The children living in children's homes are allowed to see their parents once a week."[131] "This was devastating," Adler wrote, "to watch the children led by the gendarmes or Jewish police. They were gathered in groups, ordered into a closed formation, and thus led through the camp."[132] Karel Fleischmann, a physician before the war who also practiced as a doctor in the camp, left notes about life in the camp (he did not survive). In one of them, he talks about "the endless line of waiting patients."[133]

A line, a queue, in Czech is *fronta*, which was also the language spoken by Dr. Fleischmann and, in fact, by a majority of the Jews in Theresienstadt. The word *fronta* originated probably at the time of World War I when Czech men fought on the *fronts*, "the battle front," and the women stood in long lines, "the other front," and so they called it, to buy bread and what might still remain in the shop. In Theresienstadt, there were *fronty*, plural for *fronta* [fronts], queues, all the time, and people were waiting in them, lining up in them, for everything. The camp was always in a queue, in line, moving only one way, forward. At the camp latrines, connected with the Theresienstadt water system, people are remembered pleading, "Gentlemen, the line is as far as to the courtyard. Please, put your trousers on later."[134]

There was geometric wisdom to the lines. The French writer Louis-Ferdinand Céline described the quasicamplike experience of applying to be hired as a shop floor worker in Detroit at the end of the 1920s: "You can't go wrong," a man in the line told him, "just follow your nose."[135] Then Céline and the other men were all stripped naked and passed through a medical check. "When we had our clothes back on, we were sent off," Céline wrote (he should have rather written "sent on"), "in slow-moving files, hesitating groups."[136]

According to paragraph seven of the "General Rules of the Jewish Self-Administration" in Theresienstadt, "The food must be collected under the supervision of the elder of each room on the block, in orderly lines."[137] In Auschwitz, just a moment before humanity imploded, at the peak of it, the line became still more of a line. Imre Kertész wrote: "Bandi Citrom [a more experienced fellow prisoner] instilled in me that the only secure place . . . in a marching column was always in the middle of a row; that even when soup was being dished out one would do better to aim, not for the front, but for the back of the queue, where you could predict they would be serving from the bottom of the vat, and therefore from the thicker sediment."[138] One way to read about it, think about it, and write about it, calmly, is also to hold on to the line, "the linearity of language, one thought following another."[139]

Ruth Bondy remembered my beloved writer, Karel Poláček, in Theresienstadt. "Like everyone else, Poláček used to wait in line near the kitchen window with his dish in hand, his ration slips in his pocket, his soup spoon stuck in the lapel of his coat." Among the few things, too, Karel Poláček managed still to write in the camp was "Reflections on the Art of Walking with a Bowl of Soup": "History tells of heroes who could carry iron chains with heads erect. But only a slave, who has since childhood been taught to bend his back, can carry a full bowl of soup. If he walks straight, with his head raised toward the sky, half the soup will spill, and he will return home more hungry than when he left."[140]

....

The architecture and geometry of the camps was "cold, lucid, dispassionate."[141] There was to be no touching if the camps were to work smoothly; the lines were to be tangential. "Tangential," in geometry, is not, like some etymologies might suggest, related to the Latin *tangere or tangent*, meaning "to touch" or "a touch." Rather the opposite, *noli me tangere*, "do not touch me," seemed what "tangential" meant, and what truly mattered in the camps; tangential, as in the story of Christ's resurrection, in Jean-Luc

Nancy's interpretation, "where touching does not touch and where it must not touch." This seemed to be indeed the camp people's ultimate "art," "tact," and "grace," their being of the place and not to perish, their way to live on.[142]

Neither Theresienstadt nor Boven Digoel was Auschwitz. The bodies of Theresienstadt and Boven Digoel internees were not crushed. They were not even to come close to crushing, like swerving cars should not, not even to screeching. In the camps, there was to be what Zygmunt Bauman called "neigbourlessness."[143] The body of being in Theresienstadt and in Boven Digoel was not in blows, in beating and bloodying. The body of being in the camps was in touching, in Jean-Luc Nancy's sense, lightly and, most of the time, *almost* touching.

The matter of the two camps, unlike of Auschwitz, was very much still a "matter of tact," and an individual body in the camps was very much still "a body of sense."[144] Touching was exercised as "*excription* of [a] body," a body "abandoned at its limits." Even the "grafting" in Kafka's *In the Penal Colony*, which in the end killed the victim, touched a body at "tangential points."[145] The man in Kafka's novel is done to death by having letters calligraphically written onto his body: "Obey your superiors!" Which read like a schooling.

This was what was to be happening in the camps, "the human body [being] raised to the dignity of signs"—to use Antonin Artaud's words from his mad and true *The Theater of Cruelty*.[146] One has to think again about the tattoos in Auschwitz, and about the absence of them in both Boven Digoel and Theresienstadt. One has to think again about the yellow star, sewed on clothes, by a thread, or hung around the neck by a string or a chain. One has to think again, the same thing, how rare are contemporary photographs of the Kaja-Kaja, the native people of the place, greeting a "white" person, or even a "brown" internee, rubbing a nose against a nose, even so lightly touching.[147]

Philipp Manes wrote in his diary about Theresienstadt, "The camp is a way of turning away from morals. It is a moratorium on morals."[148] "Turning away" and "moratorium" suggest a move to a distance.[149]

When the French talk about the subway network in Paris, two lines coming together, "crossing" each other, Marc Augé noticed, they say "*correspondances*." When the Italians talk about the same thing in Rome, coming together and crossing the rail lines, they speak of "*coincidences*."[150] This suggests well a move in which the camps were "turning away," and into a "moratorium." Like the subway networks, and like the calligraphy on the tortured body in *In the Penal Colony*, the thinking, designing, and being in the camps was to be cautiously and for the sake of survival, a "moratorium," "meticulous interlacing of lines,"[151] "intersecting without crisscrossing."[152] When there might be "*approaches*," matters of life or longing for them in the camps, as between two subway trains getting close together, there was to be "*avoidances*."[153]

It is "the principle of least resistance," wrote Paul Virilio, that is "so dear to engineers." "Equilibrium," in the minds of engineers, engineers-as-architects and engineers-as-geometers, can be achieved only when one "avoids accidents." The engineers' true world is "a world utterly suspended on the threshold of a final operation."[154] Only there the substance rests, only on it can the smooth move (or "moratorium") be planned, and can a perspective be envisioned—"the dreary perspective of the train station," wrote Walter Benjamin as if he were completing Paul Virilio's thought, the perspective of a train station "with the small altar of happiness at the intersection of the tracks."[155]

Zygmunt Bauman wrote in his *Modernity and the Holocaust*, "The road to Auschwitz was built by hate, but paved with indifference."[156] "Internees often came to our house, to talk to my father," said Mrs. Ottow, a daughter of the Boven Digoel administrator, with a touch of blasé. "Several of them were coming to visit."[157]

> FRIDAY, AUGUST 31, 1934, MORNING, 8:20. Internees are walking past the station. They go across the bridge to the administrative section, to take part in the reception to celebrate the Queen's birthday . . . 8:35 . . . extra police are sent to the place.[158]

Their road—this was why they could go, and perhaps sing—was "paved with indifference."

A few months into Boven Digoel's existence, the central government in Batavia reprimanded Captain Becking for being "overeager." The "general police rule" in the camp, they reminded him, is that of "calm and orderliness," and nothing beyond "a generally understood interpretation of police surveillance." "Any lack of willingness on the side of the internees to cooperate should not be met with intensifying the force on the side of the camp administration, as you suggest," Captain Becking was told, "but in each specific case through a careful approach and persuasion."[159] It was to become the principle that the people of the administration, including the military guarding the camp, in their contact with the internees had to "behave with 'tact.'"[160]

"I admit willingly," internee Salim wrote, "that we in Boven Digoel were not mishandled. The Dutch distanced themselves meticulously from all the blameworthy methods of physical disciplining and punishment which, alas," Salim added with hindsight, "were happening at the time in other parts of the world. The means by which the Dutch managed to keep us 'on our knees' for so long, were more efficient." Salim then listed "the means": "1. climate, 2. malaria, 3. jungle, 4. solitude, 5. nostalgia." "I am still impressed," Salim wrote, decades later, "by the people who came up with such a brilliant and elegant game, and who were able to play it with human lives for such a long time!"[161]

"No one understood it better than he," Jean-Paul Sartre wrote about Martin Heidegger, perhaps the greatest philosopher of the twentieth century but who also played a Nazi game, that man is "a being of distance."[162] "The place of *Dasein*," the being-there, Heidegger wrote, "can be apprehended only by 'distancing' [*Entfernung*]."[163]

Heidegger suggested thinking about "*time* as the possible horizon."[164] Which meant that the point that one moves toward is never reached. "One seeks the original model," Maurice Blanchot wrote about the other side of the trajectory, "wanting to be referred to a point of departure, an initial revelation, but there is none."[165] Modern humans lived, and the camp people exemplarily so, in "the continuity of expectation." "Eternal deferral makes eternal expectation possible [as] the thrall of a specter [as] a perception of the present as a vanishing moment."[166] Dasein meant lives at the present as a vanishing moment, and, in the camps, such lives came to their completion. Life, according to Heidegger, "does not traverse.... [It is] always a heedful being toward what is approached and de-distanced.... Dasein essentially dwells in de-distancing.... De-distancing... is something that Dasein can *never cross over*."[167]

Rabbi Joachim Prinz, in a speech given in April 1935 in Berlin, suggested something like Heidegger, and, like Heidegger, not just about the lives of the Jews—about dedistancing and the impossibility or futility of an effort to cross over. "The ghetto is the 'world,'" Rabbi Prinz said, and "ghetto" would soon be translated as "camp." "Outside is the ghetto. On the marketplace, in the street, in the public tavern, everywhere is ghetto."[168]

Whenever a new transport with Jews arrived at Theresienstadt, and whenever a transport was leaving the camp for "further to the east," after the rails were extended into the camp, all the streets through which the train moved were *absperrt* [closed off]. The doors and windows of all the barracks and houses along the street had to be shut. "The closing off [*Absperrung*] was organized and checked up on by the camp's Jewish police."[169] The people in the houses and barracks, who were not going, tried to get as close to a window as possible. On March 31, 1942, Gonda Redlich wrote in his diary about a new transport arriving: "Women quarreled with each other by the window as there was not enough place for everyone."[170]

"The streets," Philipp Manes wrote," through which the miserable human train [*Menschenzug*] is moving, are sealed."[171] Like the police cars, the trains, and the ships, like the plumbing, the principle and the game was to avoid crashing and crossing, tarrying, blocking, or clotting, any stoppage except when planned and ordered. Pierre Bourdieu might call it "*deuce* violence."[172] In the Malay world they would call it *perintah halus* [a gentle order from above].

Heinrich Himmler, the principal architect-as-geometer of the camps, ordered the ss elite troops he commanded to be strong by, in effect, being blasé. He knew enough about human contact to worry that by applying "more direct" methods, the ss men themselves might suffer by the tension and become, in Himmler's words, *Nervenkranke oder Rohlinge* [neurotic or brutish].[173] The "Stormtroopers" were notorious for a "direct approach." It was known that most of the rank-and-file Stormtroopers "were recruited from the lower classes."[174]

Physical violence, "direct approach," occurred in Theresienstadt at times, when a rule of the camp was overstepped—from either side.[175] But, as in the Boven Digoel camp, the people of Theresienstadt generally spoke about touching as tangential, scary in its possibility and in the absence of the direct. They spoke and knew about a permanent presence of violence, but, as with fashion or radio, to say with Avital Ronell, as a *"présence-à-distance."*[176]

At the very beginning of the Theresienstadt camp, as it was still taking shape, as already mentioned, several young men were hanged.[177] Adolf Eichmann, learning about it, as the last head of the Jewish Council of the Elders in Theresienstadt told Claude Lanzmann, "considered it a mistake." "It did not fit into his plans." "I did not want this," Eichmann is supposed to have said, "this could have been avoided."[178]

Cases of "storm methods" existed in Theresienstadt, but they were seen and remembered as "cases," not as the norm. One of the ss men, ss-Scharführer Rudolf Heindl, was such a case. He "became violent with women when he got drunk."[179]

After the first weeks and as the camp "stabilized," Ruth Bondy recalled, "the ss were no longer a regular sight, though, like evil spirits, they still appeared from time to time for surprise inspection." "Once," she recalled, "an ss driver intentionally ran down and killed an old woman. Another time an old man failed to raise his hat and then tried to block the blows by the ss man, and was shot. Another man was shot by one of the leaders of the ss 'kindergarten' [this is how the internees called the junior ss-men] because he happened to pass an ss man having trouble with his tractor, and refused to help the German."[180] "However," Bondy wrote, "most of the camp residents had only rare contact with the Germans, and this built in them a sense of living in a walled-in and sheltered haven."[181]

"We would see the Germans rarely," wrote also Adler, "and rarely did we have anything to do with them, except when one of us violated the issued instructions"—*verstößt gröblich*, wrote Adler, "grossly violated," and, he might add, when an ss officer grossly violated the instructions. "This," Adler repeated, once more "happened exceptionally." "The communication between the internees and the Germans," he added as if in explanation, "was almost always done in writing."[182] The camp, Adler specified in another place in his history, worked (and touched) "as an administrative machine that worked through notes and transcripts [*Aktenvermerke*]."[183]

Many internees in Theresienstadt, of course, knew Franz Kafka's writing, and also his *The Castle*, the story of K., a land surveyor who comes to a foreign place and tries to find his way through it. There are village people, who are aloof or scared, and there are the people at the castle, who are unapproachable. The land surveyor K. tries to get to Klamm, an official at the castle, to get his orders. But K. only suspects that Klamm is the one who might give him orders. He cannot even be sure whether the man they point to him as Klamm is Klamm indeed. At one moment, K. is advised by a Klamm's secretary, perhaps Klamm's secretary, to send Klamm a "protocol."

"Will Klamm, then, Mr. Secretary," asked K., "read the protocol?"

"No," replied [the secretary], "why should he? Klamm can't read any protocol, in fact he reads none. 'Keep away from me with your protocols,' he usually says." For who can hide anything from Klamm?[184]

It may be added as a footnote that the people of Theresienstadt, indeed, called the camp offices of the Council of the Elders or the ss headquarters either *Der Stab* [the Staff] or *Das Schloss* [the Castle].[185]

"*Aktenvermerke*," Adler wrote, and "protocols," he might say, "in the way they were written as well as in their content, were abstract and impersonal. All the communication in the camp, between the Jewish Council of the Elders and the ss, and between the Jewish Council, the ss, and the camp population was carried, by *Aktenvermerke*." As if Adler felt that still more explanation was needed, he added, "Or, in abbreviation. '*Vermerken*.'"[186]

Despite the people in the camps being crammed into an unprecedentedly "intimate" space, with the lid put on, in both camps there had been coldly, impersonally, cruelly, blasé, little violence—not just between the guards and the internees but also among the internees themselves. Throughout the existence of Theresienstadt, there is not a single record of a Jew being murdered by a fellow Jew (with the exception of one "official" liquidation of a Jewish informer). Nor was there one incident in the camp of robbery, rape, or serious physical assault.[187]

There were cases of theft in Theresienstadt, numerous cases, in fact, and they were harshly, some say too harshly, punished by the camp courts, run by the Jewish internees themselves.[188] The unrelieved tensions found an outlet in a raised voice, a word of reproach, and, but only rarely, in a fist-fight, a slap across the face, or a shove, which almost always were regarded as misdemeanors and were reported as such to the Jewish court. The sentences were regularly published in the *Tegesbefehl* [The Daily Order].[189]

Decision of the Camp Court

Case X/1–583: sentenced to 14 days for stealing 2 kg of bread from the Central Bakery of the Jewish Self-Administration

Case 1387: sentenced to 5 days for an attempt to use another's food card to collect a lunch.

FOURTEEN

Suburbs

Both camps, Boven Digoel and Theresienstadt, as a matter of course, often without a second thought given to it, were called "towns." Theresienstadt, of course, *was* a town before the camp. But Boven Digoel, even more "incongruously," was called a town from the first moment, as the trees and bushes in that nothing-before place were still being cut and burned. Not rarely, both of the camps, in fact, were called cities.

Westerbork, from which many of the people went to Theresienstadt, a camp set up "by a stroke of the pen" in the middle of the north Netherlands' swamps and dunes, was called a town as well, and by the internees themselves. Indeed, it was called a "city in the making."[1] Etty Hillesum in her diary wrote about Westerbork as about a city complete—one particular part of the camp, she wrote, "makes you feel you are in a squalid slum, another will give the impression of a solid middle-class district."[2]

Dr. Maurice Rossel, the International Red Cross delegate who visited Theresienstadt in 1944, saw the camp, and so reported to the Red Cross headquarters, as "a normal provincial town." "Our astonishment was huge,"

Dr. Rossel recalled in an interview long after the war, "to find in the ghetto a lively city with an almost normal life."³

It was later often and almost generally argued (with a feeling of relief and even comfort) that the camp Dr. Rossel saw was "staged" just for Dr. Rossel's visit. It was a stage, as we have seen, but not just for the few days of Mr. Rossel's visit; it was a stage fully lived throughout the camp's history. It was a stage, besides, no more and no less than the world at the time and since the time of the camps began.

Throughout the camp's existence, the internees, whomever one listens to, expressed a strong city, even metropolitan, feeling. Ruth Bondy wrote about the will of the internees, in spite of everything, to build a "Jewish city."⁴ Erika Taube, a teenage girl of Theresienstadt, wrote in her notebook of verses about *der Aufbau dieser Stadt* [building this town].⁵ "There was no movie house in the camp," Hans Günther Adler wrote, "but sometimes it all felt as a big city."⁶

Often, and as a matter of course, too, as if no further explanation were needed, the same descriptions, "urban," "town," and even "city," were attached to Boven Digoel by the authorities as well as the internees. Nothing urban, certainly, existed in the place before. In all the senses of the modern, it wasn't even a "place" before. Yet, already in August 1, 1928, in the second year of the camp, a letter by a Boven Digoel internee published in a Semarang newspaper in Java bore the headline "Boven Digoel in the Future," and it contained "details about the camp expansion." According to the author of this particular letter, "Boven Digoel is slowly on its way to becom[ing] a city of the future, a big city with its own agricultural and even plantation environs."⁷

Agricultural projects soon became a fiasco in Boven Digoel, and the more the notion of the camp as a city flourished—just urban, purely urban. In the final months of the camp, a top-level Dutch official visited the camp and wrote in his report back that Boven Digoel "is in fact a complex of a center and 'suburbs.'"⁸ The "Block Street" in Boven Digoel, like "Station Street" in Theresienstadt, or "Boulevard des Misères" in Westerbork, were, as Le Corbusier or Baron Haussmann might say, "the strategic axes" of the town.⁹

The streets and boulevards in all towns and cities of modern times lead, in both ways, to the suburbs. Samuel Beckett wrote in a letter to friends about his return from London to Paris that all "went without hitch till I lost my way in the *boulevards extérieurs!*"¹⁰ Friedrich Nietzsche believed that a street became the most dangerous space, or line, of the modern.¹¹

Louis-Ferdinand Céline believed that "the last judgment will take place in the street."[12] Kafka wrote about a dream he had about a street—and, one may say, a *passage*: "I walked through a long row of houses at the level of the first or second floor, just as one walks through a tunnel from one carriage to another. I walked very quickly, perhaps also because houses were so rickety that for that reason alone one hurried. The doors between the houses I did not notice at all, it was just a gigantic row of rooms."

At that moment in Kafka's dream the street gets even more strangely familiar—and we know it is a camp: "They were perhaps all rooms with beds through which I went.... I felt abashed to walk through people's rooms at a time when many of them were still lying in their beds.... I stepped back among a number of men, who seemed to be waiting against the wall near the opening of the stairway, on which there was a small amount of traffic."[13] The diary written in the Theresienstadt camp by Mr. Durlacher was, as we like to say today, Kafkaesque.

The Hamburg barracks

I walked through a drafty corridor that cut around all four sides of the huge barracks' inner court. The loose tiles clicked and clacked under each of my steps.... On the opposite side, many doors from the corridor were opened to dormitories, and out of them came noise and swells of musty air. People could be seen sitting on their beds.[14]

In 1929, in his essay "The Return of the Flâneur," Walter Benjamin wrote that "the cult of 'dwelling' in the old sense, with the idea of security at its core, has now received its death knell." "Giedion, Mendelsohn, and Le Corbusier," Benjamin wrote, "are converting human habitations into the transitional space of every imaginable force and wave of light and air."[15]

It was a century-long development or more. "They spoke of Paris as *la ville qui remué*," the city that never stops moving, that stirs, Benjamin wrote about Paris in the nineteenth century.[16] Kurt Schwitters, a German painter and poet, wrote the same early in the twentieth century: "In the war, I discovered my love for the wheel."[17] In Kafka's nightmarish *The Metamorphosis*, a little before Schwitters, a man turned into a bug is shown as on his back trying to move, no wheels: "He would have needed arms and hands to raise himself; instead he had only these numerous little legs which were in constant varied motion and over which he had no control."[18]

Gershom Scholem, the best friend of Benjamin, grew up in Berlin and was deeply affected by the city, the high-modern and the just-precamp city of wheels. "I would spend long periods of time," Scholem recalled, "staring across the Spree at the long-distance trains that went by the station at relatively low speeds." Reading the signs on the train cars held a particular fascination to the boy Scholem. "I was fascinated," he wrote, "by the strange place names, which I later looked up in Andreä's big family atlas at home." "Frequently," Scholem continued, "the destinations were emphasized with larger letters than the interim stops, and thus names like Hoek van Holland, Eydtkuhnen, and Oświeçim (a name that sometimes appeared on express trains) became familiar to me."[19] Oświeçim, of course, is the Polish name for Auschwitz.

"Speed," Paul Virilio wrote half a century later, *"confirms* everything that was initially contained in territorial reorganization."[20] Speed confirms cities, and even more so it confirms camps. Already Paris in the nineteenth century, wrote Benjamin, was "an artificial city, in which the [inhabitants] (and this is the crucial point) no longer feel at home."[21] To be of a city was becoming ever more equivalent to Blaise Pascal's "We're all aboard."[22]

The modern was becoming modern ever more by being built or, as filmmaker Andrei Tarkovsky may put it, "sculpted" by speed.[23] "The rush, the haste, the speed is essential," Le Corbusier enthused. He got so hyperbolic about "steel and concrete" in large part because, using them, a building may be "completed in three days."[24]

"In the course of two months," Krarup Nielsen reported about Boven Digoel's first days as he heard about them, "one hundred native soldiers and six hundred prisoners were brought from various garrisons and prisons in the colony and descended upon the spot." "It required a great energy," he added, "to made a whole city [sic] arise in such a short time. Naturally, at the moment," Krarup Nielsen wrote when the first internees arrived, "it is still far from being completed. The ship on which we arrived brought also a large amount of material and equipment. Now, hundreds of men are busy with digging, sawing, and hammering. The new buildings are raising up with a stunning speed."[25]

Just as when building a Western metropolis after a devastating fire, there was an "urgent need" to build Boven Digoel "swiftly and expediently."[26] The pace of construction in Boven Digoel was fast, and fully in the rhythm of the time—as in Manhattan, where at the same historical moment, in fact, the Empire State Building was shooting up. "At some point," wrote Koolhaas about the Empire State Building, "the 'velocity' of this automatic architecture reach[es] 14½ stories in ten days."[27] As in the most modern cities and metropolises, but really from scratch, the spirit of the times produced the camp as a part of the general culture of the world, a "composite, provisional, and ephemeral reality."[28]

....

Unlike in Manhattan, there were no vehicles in Boven Digoel to speak of—in fact, none whatsoever. But thoughts about vehicles, their presence in absence, ideas and plans for vehicles, missing vehicles, made the camp into a to-the-limit traffic place, a place sculpted by speed, indeed, a velocity site. More than any high-modern city and metropolis in the real, more than in Kurt Schwitters's war-induced love for wheels, and more than in Benjamin's or Pascal's ideas of Paris, the camp's foundations rested (moved) on wheels.

The waters of the Digoel River rolled on in the immediate vicinity of the camp. Standing on the bank, being of the camp, watching the river, one had to feel after a while that the camp moved at the river's speed and that the river stood still. The deadlier still it was in the camp, the faster the camp moved. "One was overtaken by a feeling," Salim recalled, "that one traveled at full speed, deeper and deeper toward the middle of the jungle."[29]

During the early years of Boven Digoel, "there were two or three automobiles in the whole immense island of New Guinea."[30] As the years went on, a few motor vehicles appeared in the biggest towns of the island, in Merauke or Hollandia, but this was hundreds of kilometers away from Boven Digoel, and there were no motor roads in between—in fact, no roads at all. But one should not ignore details. "The ship," Krarup Nielsen reported on the disembarking of the soldiers at the camp, "as it came to the landing place of the camp, let the soldiers out, their wives, shrieking children, toddlers, and babies, bags, a few birdcages, and sewing machines. Someone was so naive as to bring a bicycle to this place."[31]

So, there was a bicycle with the first ship, but still more than eight years later, in 1935, as Dr. Schoonheyt wrote, "there is neither a train, nor a single car in Boven Digoel.... The only traffic there is, is an oxcart that about once a week could be heard rattling through the camp." And, yes, once there was a "speeding bike" mentioned by the doctor.[32] A Dutch official on his inspection of the camp, in 1930, complained that the Boven Digoel police corps was too large. It was "superfluous," the official wrote. "One commanding officer and fifteen agents, and there is no traffic to be directed!"[33] Internees agreed:

> SATURDAY, JULY 31, 1937 ... NIGHT: 7:00 ... Anda, Sangari, Soewandi, and Zainal Abidin in the house of Kasangali talk about the police in Java. They say, at least, their job over there is to direct traffic.[34]

Still, and the more so, there had to be a desire for the urban-as-traffic, and among both the authorities and the internees. A disproportionately large number of the internees came to the camp from either cities and towns of the Indies, or from Batavia, the Indies metropolis. Many more came from the suburbs and environs of towns, cities, and the metropolis. The urban was very much a part of their beliefs and a great part of why they rebelled.

In Kwee Tek Hoay's "Drama in Boven Digoel," published at the time of the camp, a "modern girl," who would later in the novel follow her father to Boven Digoel, goes to another "modern girl's" wedding in Batavia: "Noerani took a *délman* [two-wheeled buggy] to the house.... As she paid the cab, she looked at the two cars already parked at the curb. Both nice. Hudsons. Both with all the gadgets. One of them a sedan."[35]

Mrs. Widayasih, in her memoirs, wrote that when she was a child in Boven Digoel, she knew perfectly well how cars looked, how they sounded, and even how they smelled. She knew this, she wrote, from her camp school textbooks: "Through all the time in Boven Digoel," she wrote, "I never saw a motorcycle, and, of course, not a single car. There was not even a horse, maybe one. Not until the evacuation of the camp, until we left the camp and reached the sea, I saw my first truck. It carried stone or sand, I think, for the road repair."[36]

There was a short moment, which Widayasih was either too little to remember or did not think important. A group of prospectors appeared in the vicinity of Boven Digoel, in 1937, and soon a search for possible reserves of gold a few kilometers from the camp started, another clearing in the jungle. For a few months the place became busy, and the rumbling of trucks might occasionally be heard from the camp. Even a small airstrip was built for the gold mine, and so some planes might be seen flying over.

> FRIDAY, APRIL 20, 1937. MORNING ... 6:45. A detachment of the military in closed formation and with music march through the camp in the direction of the airfield.[37]

In less than two years it was discovered that there was no gold, or not enough to be worth the trouble. The trucks left, and there were no more planes or the sound of trucks.[38] There are surprisingly few memories of it. But certainly, it had to add to the Platonic velocity of the camp.

Mr. Bangun Topo was about Mrs. Widayasih's age, and thus also probably too small to remember the details of the gold-mine planes. Still, he recalled planes, in Boven Digoel style. He sang to me about them. "With the other children in Boven Digoel, in kindergarten," he told me, "we sang many songs. My favorite was *'In de Vliegmachine'* [Dutch for In the Airplane]." "When I grow up," Mr. Bangun Topo sang as if he were back in the camp, "I will fly in an airplane."[39]

According to Rudolf Höss, the commandant of Auschwitz and Himmler's subordinate, "Himmler has chosen for Auschwitz the site he did, because it was easily accessible by rail."[40] Auschwitz was chosen, to use again an expression from Benjamin, as "yet another settlement along a highway."[41]

Auschwitz, and also Theresienstadt and Boven Digoel, were designed as road sites, the cities on the road. Or more, something like Singapore later, "a Maki-an city," of Fumihiko Maki, a Japanese architect with "an ultramodern version of a passage." He "sculpted" Singapore by "linkages" and "traffic focal points," lines and points on a diagram, "city corridors, rooms, and transportation exchanges," connectors to "district shopping centers."[42] In the case of the camps, certainly Maki-an, but in horror and supra-hypermodern, the connectors were "open-ended."

Camps, as long as they function well, function smoothly, are instant and actual, but also very much premonitions and blueprints. "This all gives an impression of a midway," wrote the Dutch writer Beb Vuyk in another camp diary about a Japanese internment camp in the Indies, historically next to Boven Digoel, this time for the Dutch during World War II. "Trucks are constantly arriving overloaded with furniture," wrote Vuyk.[43]

"Camp," according to the dictionary, is "a place with temporary accommodations of huts, tents, or other structures, typically used by soldiers, refugees, prisoners, or travelers." "Camping," the dictionary adds to the definition, "attracts people of all ages." "The camp," Giorgio Agamben wrote in his *Remnants of Auschwitz*, "is the place in which no one can truly die or survive in his own place."[44] He could write *"la ville qui remue."*

Mr. Trikoyo recalled what he was told about his family packing for Boven Digoel: "My older brother hesitated to board the ship but they told him that his things would be sent after him."[45] "People tend to forget," Krarup Nielsen wrote, "that the true impact of the Communists being sent to the camp was the whole of the Indies brought in motion."[46] Georges Perec sensed the same moment and feeling in Europe, a wish for "there to exist places that are stable, unmoving, intangible, untouched."[47]

In official reports, Boven Digoel was regularly called *doorgangskamp* [a transit camp], or, grammatically wrong but true to the meaning, a "through-go camp."[48] Other times the Dutch reports called Boven Digoel a *doorgangshuis* [a transit house].[49] Mr. Durlacher, a Dutch Jew, in his Theresienstadt diary written in Dutch, used to call the European camp *doorgangsbarakken* [transit barracks], or "through go barracks."⁵⁰ (He could say "*Passagen*.")

In an internal note of the Dutch Indies government about Boven Digoel in 1934, into the seventh year of the camp, an official concluded, "The state of the camp can now be considered consolidated."⁵¹ A deputy in the Volksraad, the governor-general's advisory council, the next year, declared that "slowly, the public is beginning to get accustomed to the fact that Boven Digoel is in fact a permanent place."⁵² Salim recalled, writing about the same time, "Our circumstances, changed from staying in temporary barracks to a sort of living in town."⁵³ It was a stationary life, sort of like waiting for the next ship, or at a railway station, "with its anxieties about train connections."⁵⁴

Mrs. Ottow, of the elite of the camp elite, perhaps best articulated the permanency of the camp and the extraterritorial, off-the-ground feel of it: "Life in the camp was very lonesome," Mrs. Ottow said, "but we kept ourselves busy, I personally by studying piano, reading, and translations. I knew it was *tijdelijk*."⁵⁵ "*Tijdelijk*" is Dutch for "temporary," "provisional," or "interim."

In Theresienstadt, as in Boven Digoel, and as in Paris, Berlin, Amsterdam, or Prague, only radically more, "even after the extremely difficult first months of the initial period, when Theresienstadt was especially unstable, still nobody in the camp felt really 'at home.'"⁵⁶ It was like being amid "the whirr of a thousand sewing machines," Jacob Riis might say, knowing New York fifty years earlier.⁵⁷ Only there was radically more of it in the camp—being locked in one place, in constant inquietude, in fear of being moved on, in the case of Theresienstadt still "further to the east," transported to, what had been whispered about, in trembling, "the destination open-ended," or, with an even greater trembling, "the final destination"⁵⁸—toward an improbable point where the two rails of a track come together.

Helen Fein, a historian of the Holocaust, believed that she knew how the camp people saw it. "The threat of collective death was not anticipated because the social organization of the political economy of the ghetto created differential death chances every day."⁵⁹ Lenka Lindtová, a teenage girl of Theresienstadt and, in the camp, in love for the first time in her life, wrote a short poem, "For Moly." Moly was her boyfriend, who had just been put on a transport to Auschwitz. It was not known in the camp, just in trembling, what kind of destination it really was. It was in fact known only as Birkenau in Theresienstadt, which somehow still sounded like having something to do with "birchwoods." Anyway, Lenka wished *to stay* with Moly, which meant *to go*:

Thu ne pamu
Já chci domů
Chci aspoň do Birkenau...
[Thu ne pamu
I want to go home
Or at least to Birkenau...][60]

"Any genuine stabilization of the society of Theresienstadt," wrote Zdeněk Lederer, a boy a little younger than Lenka Lindtová back then, "was prevented by deportation... all privileges were of a temporary nature."[61]

Like Boven Digoel, Theresienstadt was thought of and lived as a "*provisorium*." The internees as well as the camp authorities thought of the camp as a temporary arrangement.[62] At the "final-solution" Wannsee Conference in January 1942, Theresienstadt, still only a blueprint, was categorized as a "transit ghetto," *Durchgangsghetto*.[63] "To be sure," Raul Hilberg wrote in his *The Destruction of the European Jews*, using a railwayman's language, too, "Theresienstadt had never been intended to serve as more than a stopover."[64]

Theresienstadt was suspended between transit and stopover, and it was the camp's dynamic permanency, its life energy. In a Theresienstadt cabaret song long as a train trip, after each of the countless strophes, there was a refrain:

This is why we want forever,
we want forever,
in Theresienstadt to live

In Theresienstadt to live.

Just you try to get us out,
Sorry, sorry.
We do not want to go![65]

A high-modern house should be like a car, Le Corbusier thought, and he indeed named one of the single-family houses he designed Maison Citrohan, with a clear nod to the French automaker Citroën.[66] Even more, "Liners... airplanes...," Le Corbusier wrote, should be "standards for the dwelling house.... The 'house-machine'" should be "practical as an 'innovation trunk.'"[67]

Paul Virilio, who had already lived through the next stage, when many of Le Corbusier's fantasies became true, wrote, "Architecture is in constant movement, while dwellings have become no more than anamorphoses of thresholds." "Architecture," wrote Virilio, is "no longer in architecture, but in geometry; the space-time of vectors, the aesthetic of construction is dissimulated in the special effects of the communication machines, engines of transfer and transmission; the arts." And here Virilio almost becomes Kafka, and one of the camps. "Dwelling," he writes, is on the way "to disappear in the intense illumination of projection and diffusion."[68] "You're as well-off here as anywhere else," wrote Bertolt Brecht, "So you may as well stay."[69]

Albert Speer, Hitler's architect, remembered that Hitler "spoke of the *Autobahnen* [the expressways] as his 'Parthenon.'"[70]

"The pace, I sensed, was also quickening," wrote Imre Kertész about his being on his way from one of the worst camps to another of the worst.[71] *Laufschritt* [run-walk, a run or quick march], wrote Kertész, was the Nazi and camp word for it.[72] That day, on the way from Auschwitz to Buchenwald, Kertész recalled, they got down from the train, and in their run-walk, they "passed by a statue that stood on the green sward of a clearing wedged between the two forks that the road took here. . . . From the stripes carved into its clothing and its bald cranium, but above all from the whole demeanor, it was immediately apparent that this was seeking to portray a prisoner. The head was thrust forward and one leg kicked out high behind in imitation of running, while the two hands, in a cramped grip, were clasping an incredibly massive cube of stone to the abdomen."[73] Leonard Baker, a Jew who passed through several camps and then to Theresienstadt, remembered his moving on: "To the East," he wrote, "we dragged our feet."[74]

They could often hardly move, but still they were "in a hurry." And here comes the premonition of modern people again, Marc Augé's people as if of the camps, "occupied by the urgency of their everyday life," in "more or less rapid flow," always "behind schedule."[75] Or better still, the man of Martin Heidegger, "on the track," "being 'in on it,'" "at a quicker pace," "*verfallen* [falling prey]," "completely taken in by the world," in "a mode of groundless floating," "in 'busyness.'"[76]

Rudolf Vrba, an Auschwitz survivor famous for his many other testimonies, put it in the extreme. There were, in the ultimate camp, he said in a biblical and American-Western idiom, "only two kinds of workers at the Buna site: the quick and the dead."[77]

In Theresienstadt, Ruth Bondy wrote, "On July 2, [1942,] the city" (she meant the camp) "was officially handed over to the Jews, and four days later, on a stifling summer day, the ghetto rejoiced." "It was a thrilling day, filled with excitement and expectation. The Czech gendarmes, who had guarded the barrack gates since the ghetto opened, left in the afternoon, and at 6 p.m. the gates were opened. The inmates were free, free in the small enclave inside the walls."[78]

"When the block embargo ended," Jehuda Bacon recalled of the same moment, "everyone ran outside into the streets."[79] "Today," Gonda Redlich wrote on July 7, 1942, five days later, "we went outside." Redlich went outside with his wife and their baby—yes, they managed somehow to have a baby and keep it, too. Redlich's diary entry continues, "For the first time without a police escort."[80] "Every ghetto inhabitant," wrote Adler, "inside the limits of the camp, was free to move."[81] Ruth Bondy again recalled, "The residents walked about in a daze. . . . One could now take a walk, indeed walk on pavement."[82]

"These were streets," recalled Mrs. Meyer-Kattenburg, of Theresienstadt, "where one could meet a neighbor taking a walk."[83] Peter Kien, a poet and a painter, wrote a poem about the streets in Theresienstadt, a poem, in my view, more completely-street than could ever be written anywhere but within the walls.

Oh, streets, precious streets
With bustle and trot
Worried and anxious
Please
Come, oh, come, take us in![84]

"Of course, we are aware that we are behind the walls," Philipp Manes wrote. "But, inside the walls, we feel like human beings, still in our minds, who just have to withstand a certain limitation of personal freedom."[85]

"One day after another," the same Philipp Manes complained in (or to) his diary, "we do not have a quiet hour."[86] Mr. Manes meant here mainly his duty as a leader of the camp Orientation Section, helping the people who got lost to find their place in the camp. "The bed," Kafka wrote in his *In the Penal Colony*, about the torture tool on which the victims were killed, is a "wonderful apparatus." It "quivers in minute, very rapid vibrations." "You will have seen similar apparatus in hospitals," the penal colony commander explained to Kafka's explorer, "but in our bed the movements are all precisely calculated."[87]

The camps were quivering. In the camps, tumult, that sense and notion of time, also reached a kind of apex of long historical development. In the camps, more than ever before and more than in the outside in the era of the camps, one felt "temporality as a 'time calculation.'" "'Time,'" more than ever, was being "experienced in such calculation."[88] *"Reckoning* with time," wrote Martin Heidegger, as if he decided to speak about the camps at last, is "seen in the quantification of time."[89] "The use of the clock," Heidegger added, "becomes more refined."[90]

In Theresienstadt, as in the other Nazi camps, "wristwatches were confiscated from Jews upon arrival and were sent to the soldiers at the front. Only physicians and some other professionals who needed watches for their work were given special dispensation to have one."[91] Time, ultimately in the camps, became calculated, and so its geometry was assured, fitting into the geometry of the camp space: "A pure succession of nows, without beginning and without end, in which the ecstatic character of primordial temporality is leveled down," "measured as such so that nothing is to be found except distance and number."[92] The final imperative of now was fixed by the calculation of time: "The succession of nows is uninterrupted and has no gap."[93]

Philipp Manes had not a single quiet minute to spare, first of all, because of his duties as the chief of the camp Orientation Section. The camp people whom Philipp Manes's Orientation Section was helping home were equally restless. "They were restless," wrote Adler, "they moved between places, sometimes forty to fifty of them in one day, and only after long hours of searching, were they brought home."[94]

It was all increasingly the matter of calculation, and numbers and tagging. On August 23, 1942, Gonda Redlich wrote, "A woman new to the ghetto was unable to find her way home. She cannot say or understand anything. Luckily for her, she was carrying linen stamped with the number IV 786."[95] The Roman numeral was the number of the block, and the Arabic numeral the number of the room in the block.

The camp was a town, a city, and a metropolis in large part due to the aimless wandering of its inhabitants. Increasingly, to put it right, there was channeling. Petr Ginz described in the boys' magazine *Vedem* a Jewish camp policeman who stood on duty at a block's gate. "He provides information, and he sees to it that people as they walk on the sidewalk, keep on the right side (laugher)."[96]

"The ghetto continues to grow apace," Gonda Redlich wrote on June 10, 1942. "People walk in the streets. Traffic is especially heavy between six and eight in the evening."[97] Josef Taussig wrote on Friday, June 21, 1944, in one of the letters to his wife, who was also in the camp but in another block, "My father [who was also in the camp, quite unruly and getting into fights with other elderly men] got a 'ticket' from one of the police."[98] There was a special section of the Jewish police ultimately put together, the OD, *Ord-*

nungsdienst, or Order Section. Its primary duty was "to maintain order in food lines and at other assembly points."[99]

"There is no time for real 'visiting,'" Etty Hillesum wrote about Westerbork as Philipp Manes wrote about Theresienstadt, "nor is there any quiet place anywhere to sit down and be together. People talk to each other in passing and outdoors. Really, one keeps walking around all day long."[100] Etty Hillesum's friend Philip Mechanicus wrote about the same "city" and about the same "traffic." "In the camp," he wrote, "wheelbarrows substitute for a place to sit down. You find left-around wheelbarrows everywhere, in front of the large barracks and small barracks, under a clump of trees, or just in the middle of nowhere, on the flat expanse of field." As Mechanicus wrote, there were virtually no places to sit besides wheelbarrows.[101]

The "ordinary" traffic was rare, but the camp traffic was sublime and roaring by its absence. On Wednesday, April 19, 1944, Pavel Weiner wrote, "When I arrive at the bakery, Rahm [the camp ss commandant] is just leaving on his motorcycle."[102] "We did not see any ss man," Max E. Mannheimer of Theresienstadt recalled after the war, "apart from the commandant who occasionally rode on horseback through the ghetto streets."[103]

"One day," Jo Spier, the Dutch-Jewish painter in Theresienstadt, remembered, "the ss-Scharführer Heindl, came to the room where we, the artists-internees worked. He picked out one of us, [a] quite well-known Dutch [Jewish] painter and ordered a portrait, of himself on a motorcycle as he is riding through a deserted camp."[104] ("Horses are made of chromium steel / And little fat men shall ride them," George Orwell wrote in his *Why I Write*.[105]) The same ss-Scharführer Heindl was also remembered as "touring the streets in his car inspecting buildings and people at work."[106]

"On the streets," wrote Theresienstadt internee Gabriel Italie, "there is almost no traffic. Only pedestrians and, now and then, a truck or a tractor with a trailer carrying a load of bread, potatoes, or coal passes by, always escorted by Czech gendarmes. Other than that, one can only see handcarts and very rarely a bicycle, motorcycle, or a passenger car with the Germans." Mr. Italie, a man from Holland, and probably thinking of Holland and not of Auschwitz, added "nobody walks in clogs."[107]

Some of the "traffic" facts of Theresienstadt stir a special Indies echo in me as I write. "Nearly all transport in the ghetto," another witness of Theresienstadt recalled, "was via rickshaw pulled by the ghetto inmates."[108]

"The junior ss men, 'the ss kindergarten,' served as drivers of most of the cars, trucks, and tractors. Jews were forbidden to drive a vehicle of any sort."[109] "Two Jews decorated with stars push a trolley," Mrs.

Meyer-Kattenburg described later what, she wrote, was what the street was really about.[110]

"There aren't enough horses to pull the wagons," Gonda Redlich wrote on August 13, 1942, meaning carts, or trolleys.[111] Bread, potatoes, coal, and the dead were transported on the carts or trolleys pushed by men. *Šalom na pátek* called a hearse, a pushcart on which the dead were carried, a "funeral tram."[112] Jiří Vogel, one of the Theresienstadt technical people, it is remembered, "designed a new type of hearse for the camp and also a perambulator, but neither design could be fully realized."[113]

Several funeral hearses to be pulled by horses, used by the Jewish communities in Europe before the war, were brought by the SS to Theresienstadt. "The hearses' decorative poles were cut off to make the carriages lighter," so that they could be pulled by people. "It is possible," one observer wrote, "that some of the [gilded and otherwise richly decorated] pales [cut from the hearses] were eventually used in theater performances, almost certainly in a fairy tale about *Prinz Bettliegend* [Prince Call-It-Sick]."[114]

"Ambulances," also pulled by men, were seen and heard moving through the streets of Theresienstadt, and speeding (trotting?) when there was an emergency. "Initially four people and two trolleys made the hospital transport," wrote Dr. Erich Springer in the report he wrote after the war on the camp health system. Later, Dr. Springer wrote, the "fleet" was "built up to have eight pairs of people on standby." Still later "we constructed a special lightweight two-wheel cart with attached pull bars. . . . It worked. Just a few minutes after a message had been received, the patient could be brought to the hospital."[115]

A fire engine could also be seen and heard on the camp streets when there was a fire, or when the firemen trained. During the Red Cross's second and last visit to Theresienstadt, on April 13, 1945, standing in front of the camp fire station, the third and last head of the Jewish Council of the Elders, Rabbi Murmelstein, gave a demonstration to the guests by activating a fire alarm. "The Jewish firefighters were ready in forty-five seconds."[116]

....

Neither Theresienstadt nor Boven Digoel were Auschwitz. "On the whole," Adler wrote, "most of the time, the tempo [in Theresienstadt] was fast but not murderous."[117] "Tempo" rather than rushing a victim into exhaustion and death was typical of Theresienstadt as well as of Boven Digoel. There was a cultural space around the time, which overwhelmed people. Tempo was a buzzword for the time.

This is what made the sport so serious a matter, filling the camps and expressing the camps so thoroughly. "Between six and eight o'clock in the evening, the big courtyard of our barracks is used as a soccer field," wrote elderly Mr. Manes. "People stand in rows, and all the windows and arches of the arcades in the upper floors are full. . . . Rhythmically, the crowd is shouting: 'Tempo! Tempo!'"[118]

"Thousands of nervous people," Gonda Redlich wrote at the same time and sort of about the same thing, "live with fear in their hearts. They are afraid and struggle to remain here. They race, race back and forth, during the day and at night, without a rest."[119] "Run out, run in, speed up everything," clowns sang in the Theresienstadt cabaret.[120] In a speech to the camp people on June 23, 1944 (shortly before he would be taken from the camp and shot), the second head of the Jewish Council of the Elders, Dr. Paul Eppstein, classified the camp population as consisting of two groups. "The first, or vegetative, type clings to the past and lives from day to day. The second type takes an active part in the town's life."[121]

In fact, Theresienstadt, without cars, *was* traffic. Ruth Bondy wrote that the camp was "constant traffic." "People arrived at the ghetto," she wrote, "and they were deported to the east."[122] The camp was traffic, it was the streets, and stations, inside the houses and inside the people. On Friday, May 19, 1944, Pavel Weiner wrote about his youth home: "Franta" the supervisor was "angry that the *Kofferlager* was not put in order yet."[123] *Kofferlager*, German *Koffer*, for "trunk," and *Lager* for "camp," was how the boys called a room in the barracks where the people's luggage was stored, and ready.

Everything of the world had to be squeezed and crammed into the trunks as the people were leaving for the camps. And it was there, just waiting for the next section of the journey. The whole camp became a Kofferlager and could be so called. "Trunk and Me" was another cabaret song in Theresienstadt:

Just a thing, a leather type,
Carried in time, carried in place
The trunk is me, I am the trunk.[124]

"More people than one cares to count," Avital Ronell wrote in *The Test Drive*, not just about the camps, "live in such a world of improvable distress . . . stranded with an unprovable reality."[125] The camps were a culmination moment of modern-humanity's rational and enlightened distress caused by an unprovable reality. The camps were a culmination of what Hegel called the "fear of erring." Hegel also wrote, and here he sounded as if he could have known the camps, "The fear of error reveals itself as a fear of the truth."[126]

"It's the mark of a narrow world," Joseph Roth wrote at the outset of the camps, and in contrast to Hegel, he wrote it for the Jews, "that it mistrusts the undefined."[127] It was so scary, increasingly, for increasing numbers of people, and for the Jews in Europe in particular, with unknown future, that "no one [was] supposed to ignore Reason, as none was excused from knowing the law."[128] Even before the camps came into full swing, and never before so badly, did the world come to suffer from "the acute ailment called precision."[129]

"From the very first day of my life in prison," Fyodor Dostoyevsky wrote in his *Memoirs from the House of the Dead*, "I had begun to dream of freedom. Calculating when my term would come to an end became my favorite occupation, in a thousand different forms and applications."[130] Max Horkheimer and Theodor Adorno, after decades of progress since Dostoyevsky and his camp, and with (vague) knowledge of the camps, in their *Dialectic of Enlightenment* wrote, "For enlightenment, anything which does not conform to the standard of calculability and utility must be viewed with suspicion." "Numbers," they wrote, "became enlightenment's canon.... Bourgeois society is ruled by equivalence. It makes dissimilar things comparable by reducing them to abstract quantities."[131]

"People live to add, subtract, and divide time on the abacus of waiting," wrote Vladislav Vančura, a Czech writer, a non-Jew (but he was shot by the Nazis, as an example, in Prague, in June 1942).[132] Now, it was happening, what had been long in coming, wrote Adorno and Horkheimer, "losing one's own name."[133] "The standardization of the intellectual function," they wrote, became "the law of large numbers."[134] "If someone learns to calculate," wrote Ludwig Wittgenstein, "doubt gradually loses its sense."[135] What remains, he added, is "the general rule of multiplying."[136]

In Theresienstadt, calculated by an ex-internee, published in England after the war and adjusted to the English currency, the daily upkeep was "a threepence per head" in 1942, "a fourpence per head" in 1943, and "a fivepence per head" in 1944.[137] "Food," Gonda Redlich wrote on April 27, 1943, "is distributed according to a ration card. It is a card divided in rows and columns of little squares, each square for a day. You lose a square, and you do not eat."[138] "*Punktkarte*" was the German word in the camp for a ration card, a "point card."[139]

On Tuesday, June 13, 1944, Pavel Weiner wrote, "At home, I notice that I have again lost my *Menaška* [Czech camp slang for "*Menagekarte*," German/camp for "food card"], so I am forced to go to the *Menagekartenstelle* [the food cards office]."[140] In Kafka's *The Trial*, the hero, the victim, Josef K., still at home, is visited by two "warders" (the trial will end in his execution), and he is asked to identify himself. Like Pavel Weiner, Josef K. panicked: "At last he found his bicycle license and was about to start off with it to the warders, but then it seemed too trivial a thing, and he searched again until he found his birth certificate."[141]

The yet undistributed "food cards" and other cards for control of the camp life were kept in a *Kartothek*, or *Kartei*, a "catalogue," "registry," or "card file." "In the catalogue," wrote Mr. Manes, "each person is grasped [*erfaßt*] and schematized [*schematisierd*]."[142] On November 9, 1943, terrifying news spread through Theresienstadt that Jacob Edelstein, the head of the Jewish Council of the Elders, had been arrested; nobody knew what might come next. The camp SS commandant, it became gradually known, "paid a surprise visit, seizing some of the registry records. Charges were raised against the [Edelstein's] staff involving manipulation: errors and 'discrepancies' in the lists."[143] Jacob Edelstein, his wife, and their teenage son were taken to Auschwitz and later killed. This was the distress, the uncertainty, and the fear of erring at its highest.

"We helplessly register," wrote Rem Koolhaas.[144] He called the space thus created and kept "Junkspace." But what could he, or we, really know? How far and deep it might go! The Jews before being herded to the camps were handed forms to register "The Contents of Emptied Apartment":

1. Furniture and other (number and price)
    a. bedroom
    b. living room
    c. pantry
    d. bathroom
    e. kitchen
    f. balcony, winter garden, attic, cellar, various
2. paintings, art, antiquities, jewelry, gold (as far as found in the apartment)
3. table silver, cutlery, crystal
4. table cloth, etc.[145]

There are two photographs of an unidentified warehouse, possibly in the camp. The "furniture and other" from the pillaged Jewish homes is stocked along the walls up to a vaulted ceiling. In "photo no. 2" there are chairs and desks, in "photo no. 3," labels in German are visible: "comforters and bedding," "pillows small: group II," "pillows large: group III," and "pillows large: group II."[146]

In Boven Digoel, fear of erring and belief in calculation was no less careful or life-defining.

Large parts of the Boven Digoel archive are taken up by the most detailed records of the food distribution center of the camp. There are numbers and names, silhouettes, in columns. In the first six months of 1930, for example, in January, internee Atmosoemarto, one child under three years old, and one child over three years old, received food and other daily needs at the value of ƒ29.33; in February, ƒ24.40; and so on, for each month, which came to a total, in six months, of ƒ179.79. Internee Soedono, single, in the same period received food at the value, total, of ƒ46.84. Internee Teroenosari, two adults, two children above three years, and two children under three years, received stuff for the whole year, a total of ƒ256.73. Under internee Teroenosari, down in the columns, was a note: "One son died." A grand total of the supplies distributed among the internees in this particular period, judging from this particular document, was ƒ20,952.13.[147]

According to another document, for June 1935, with the internees classified in groups, group I got full rations, group II only rice, group III did not get fish, and group IV got half rations, except for rice, of which the internees in the group got a full ration. In that month, the daily full rations were rice, 0.60 kilogram; salted fish, 0.072 kilogram; salt, 0.016 kilogram; tea, 0.006 kilogram; mung beans, 0.02 kilogram; Javanese (brown) sugar, 0.02 kilogram; palm oil, 0.012 liter; and white sugar, 0.01 kilogram. Those with a full ration also got 2.5 liters of petroleum per month.[148]

There were multiple card systems, vitally important in their calculated uncertainty and in the internees' as well as the authorities' fear of error.

> FRIDAY, SEPTEMBER 14, 1934 ... AFTERNOON: ... 3:40 Telephone call from Mr. Rifai, switchboard operator. Sergeant Sangoen requests that ROB agent Moh. Ali be sent to him and bring the address cards.[149]

"The card index," wrote Benjamin in his *One-Way Street*, "marks the conquest of the three-dimensionality of script.... Everything that matters is to be found in the card box."[150] "That wisest of books: the phone book," Joseph Roth wrote with an equally strong suggestion that still more was coming.[151]

Walter Benjamin, as we saw, also noticed in the mid-1930s the fashion of metal plaquettes worn on jumpers or overcoats, displaying "the initial letters of the bearer's first name."[152] Georges Perec, ten years after Benjamin, already wondered "why so very many people take pride in showing off handbags bearing the monograms of the manufacturer." "I can understand," Perec wrote, "people attaching some importance to having their initials on the things they are fond of (shirts, suitcases, napkin rings, etc.), but the initials of a supplier?"[153]

Everything that mattered in the camps could be found, one is tempted to say, originated, in the card index. In order to function, the cards had to be filled out correctly and filed alphabetically.

In December 1932, exact day is missing, the third birthday of the daughter of internee Moeksin was celebrated in Boven Digoel. Her name was Energi, Malay or Indonesian for "energy."[154] A daughter of another internee, Soebroto Pasoeroehan, born in Boven Digoel, on March 21, 1931, is recorded in the camp's card index as "Crisis Money," spelled like that, in English. Soebroto also had a son, born in Boven Digoel on June 26, 1932, and the son's name was Digoelaniem. The meaning of "Digoel" in the baby's name is clear. The meaning of "aniem," to me, is not. But ANIEM was a generally known abbreviation under which the *Algemeene Nederlandsch-Indische Electriciteits-Maatschappij* [The General Dutch-Indies Electric Company], was known. So, perhaps, "energy" again?

And so on. Internee Soemotaroeno, alias Sadimin, had a daughter, born in Boven Digoel on July 14, 1929, whom he named Natura, which was not to mean "nature," in all probability, but "*natura*," as in government rations distributed not in money but *in natura* [in kind] to the internees who did not volunteer to work on the government projects in the camp. Natura had a brother, born in Boven Digoel on June 29, 1933, who was given the name Digoelawas, which meant "Digoel Watch Out." The daughter of internee Soedarmo, born in Boven Digoel on November 14, 1937, got the name Doenia, meaning "the world."[155]

"My younger brother," Mrs. Widayasih wrote in her memoirs, "was also born in Boven Digoel, and he was given a name *Pitunov*. His birthday was on November 7."[156] November 7, of course, was the date of the Bolshevik Revolution in Russia in 1917. "Pitu" in the little Pitunov's name comes from Javanese for "seven," and "nov" from "November." In the Boven Digoel card register, indeed, there was everything that mattered, sort of. I also found an internee Darmosoejoedno, "a tinsmith," and his wife Soemijati, who had a baby son and his name was Lenin.[157]

This was *la lutte finale*, but equally so, acts born of "improvable distress." Anton Chekhov described another camp, before Boven Digoel and Theresienstadt. The names the internees of the Sakhalin penal colony gave to themselves, he suggested, were as much a battle for identity as a way of forgetting. "The most commonly used given name," he noted, "was Ivan, and surname 'Don't-Remember.'" Some other names Chekhov listed (and he indeed compiled a card index as he traveled through the place) were "Mustapha Don't-Remember and Vasily Countryless." Chekhov also met "a penal convict called Good-Looking Can't-Remember-My-Relations."[158]

In Theresienstadt, Ruth Bondy (she just died in Tel Aviv as I am writing this) recalled, "In the late afternoons, women walked on the *Bastei* [bastion], jackets hung loosely over their shoulders, as it was always the custom, or fashion, in Central Europe. One would overhear conversations. '*Küss die Hand, gnädige Frau.*' '*Habe die Ehre, Herr Doktor*'" (German for "I kiss your hand, Madam." and "Your servant, Doctor.")[159] "In Theresienstadt," Philipp Manes wrote, "everyone has to have a title."[160]

In June 1936, Heinrich Himmler informed all the relevant offices of the Reich that Hitler did not wish Jews "to carry the name[s] Siegfried and Thusnelda," to give some examples. They were Wagnerian names, Germanic names, the codes that, attached to a Jew, might "enchain" the Germanic the wrong way. Two years after Himmler's directive, in August 1938, the Nazi decree "stipulated that Jewish men had to add to their regular first name the middle name Israel, and Jewish women, the name Sara, unless they already had a first name included in the Interior Ministry's approved list."[161] In Theresienstadt, too, of course, Israel and Sara, like a Jewish star, had to be used.[162]

Many Jews in Europe in the nineteenth and twentieth centuries, and many of those who eventually arrived at Theresienstadt, actually, "were very fond of the name Siegfried," the Nibelungen hero, the dragon slayer.[163] For many of them, Siegfried indeed meant Wagner, and Wagner indeed meant Germany. Like Goethe the German, or Mendelssohn the Jew, it was the Germany they loved and many of them fought for in the World War I.

The people were given their names at birth, and they carried them to the camps like the clothes, jewels, or books they managed to pack for the journey. The transport to Theresienstadt, wrote Ruth Bondy, "included eight Werfels, fifty-five Freuds, and 106 Mahlers (one named Gustav)."[164] But there were also Jews in Theresienstadt named Himmler, Hess, and Rosenberg, as well as Wagner. There was even a Hittler interned in Theresienstadt, although his given name was Sheindel and he spelled his name, surely happy for the difference, with a double *t*.[165]

On Thursday, November 30, 1944, Pavel Weiner wrote, "A man who used to be named Adolf, now calls himself Abraham."[166] There was in Theresienstadt, compared to Boven Digoel, a subtler but no less concentrated coding.

The first baby born in the camp was given the name Tomáš, like the first president of the Czechoslovak Republic, Tomáš Masaryk, who was credited with building up a democratic state in the middle of Europe and with keeping good conditions for the Jews in the state before the Nazis came.[167]

"Haven't you got that yet?" Joseph Roth wrote to a friend, writer Stefen Zweig, as the Nazis went on conquering one nation of Europe after another. "The word has died," Roth wrote, "men bark like dogs."[168] But Roth, in this case, might be missing the point a little. What might rather be happening was what Gottfried Wilhelm Leibniz three centuries earlier noticed as "the *lingua universalis* of logic."[169] Barking it might be to many, but it was the coding again, rational and indeed enlightening, exact, correct, functional, and enforced for the sake of order, "a thing as magnificent as music or algebra."[170]

Robert Service, three centuries after Leibniz, in his history of the Bolshevik Revolution wrote about "*Sovnarkom*" (abbreviation of Soviet National Committee). "The title was a joint idea of Lenin and Trotsky. Lenin was delighted: 'That's wonderful: it has the terrible smell of revolution!'"[171] Maybe it was not exactly what Leibniz had in mind. Or Ludwig Wittgenstein, when he wrote about the "symbolism of chemistry, and the notation of infinitesimal calculus." Wittgenstein also wrote about the "suburbs of our language," and it might be that. "It is easy," he wrote, and we hear Joseph Roth again, "to imagine a language consisting only of orders and reports in battle."[172]

A community of humans, named, titled, initialed, numbered, arranged alphabetically and numerically, in columns, this was the idea, the plan, and, as long as time allowed, the emergent reality of the camps:

Register of Mutations for 1932 and 1933: ...

MARCH 4, 1932: Soegijarto, son of internee Mardjohan, was born and got written in under no. 507 ... [173]

MARCH 19, 1932: Internee Mas Marco ... passed away. He had no. 235 ...

In Theresienstadt, when a person went to the latrine, he or she was locked in the cubicle from the outside by the internee on duty (who was also to check after each visit if the place was left clean).[174] After the person relieved himself or herself, he or she called out his or her number. It was a code. It worked, except when, let's say, an only-Czech-speaking Jew went in, and a non-Czech-speaking person, or a person not wishing to understand, was on latrine duty. But, according to most testimonies, it did not happen often; there was German one could communicate with in the end.[175]

"All the doors are identical," Joseph Roth wrote about the world he was living in, "only the numbers on them are different."[176] There was always a linkage between fate, number, and the book. In the seventeenth sura of the Koran, called "The Journey," Allah tells Mohammad, "And every man's fate have we fastened about his neck: and on the day of resurrection will we bring forth to him a book which shall be proffered to him wide open."[177] Now, profoundly as never before, it was happening. "The number is everything," Philipp Manes wrote in Theresienstadt.[178]

This again was happening for some time. "The man-instrument," wrote Honoré de Balzac, "is a sort of social zero, and no matter how many of them there are, they will never form a sum unless preceded by some numerals."[179] Rabbi Leo Baeck remembered after the war: "I was in Theresienstadt the number 187894."[180] Imre Kertész wrote about numbers in a death camp: "64921 in my own case, for example. It was advisable, I was informed, to learn as soon as possible, how this was to be pronounced in German clearly, intelligibly, and in a distinctly articulated fashion, thus: '*Vier-und-sechzig, neun, ein-und-zwanzig.*'"[181]

Adler, like Rabbi Leo Baeck, recalled entering the camp: "Now I was B1 214."[182] Numbers and abstraction go together, and they became one in the camps. "Abstraction," Zygmunt Bauman wrote, "is one of the modern mind's principal powers. Nazi legislation, propaganda, and management of social settings took care to separate the one and only 'abstract Jew' from the many 'concrete Jews' known to the Germans as neighbors or workmates." It was the established proposition, a Platonic form, "the exceedingly popular stereotype of the 'Jew as such.'"[183]

"We carried a piece of cloth with a transport number hung over our neck," Jehuda Bacon recalled of his journey from Theresienstadt to Auschwitz.[184] Even the newborns, we saw already, "were given their transport number, instantly at birth."[185] "Numbers dangle from their necks," wrote a Czech writer waiting in Prague to go and watching the others as they were departing, "numbers go with them every step of the way."[186] Francis Picabia never went to a camp, but, like Kafka and Benjamin, he was a poet, and so he sensed them going: "The sound of your sentences hangs from you like those bells cattle wear around their necks and which ring when they come down from the mountains of suggestions."[187]

Those who went all the way had their numbers, as their ultimate and final identity, tattooed on their arms. Some of them, those who survived, if asked by their grandchildren, for instance, would call their number, with the full privilege of truth, their *"Himmlische Telefonnummer,"* German for "celestial telephone number."[188] These were whole numbers, and arithmetic sequences. As Yevgeny Pavlovich in *The Idiot* tells the prince, "If you like, I will analyze you to yourself on my fingers."[189]

....

"The prisoners in Theresienstadt," a historian wrote, "were easy to line up with the help of their numbers." "Each set of numbers," she explained further, "began with a letter, and then the next in alphabetical order.... Places of origin were in Roman numerals."[190] "The transport numbers," Ruth Bondy recalled, "were now called identity numbers."[191] Correctly, a poem by a Theresienstadt internee called "Hope" ran like this:

> *Wife, granny, the little ones, and I*
> *Each with a transport number*
> *From ninety-two*
> *To ninety-five.*[192]

On Monday, April 13, 1942, Petr Ginz, still in Prague, still waiting, wrote in what is now called his Theresienstadt diary: "In the morning [on the way] to school, they announced a new transport, and it's all names with L: Lev—, Löv—, Löw—, and so on. So, we are worried about the Levituses."[193] "Do you know," the camp magazine *Šalom na pátek* asked its readers in the "Entertainment" column, "that the name of the first man in Theresienstadt, in alphabetical order, is *Aach* [Czech for 'Ah']?"[194]

It was a serious intention of Josef Taussig, a young Theresienstadt internee, a Jew and a Communist, to write a new *Good Soldier Švejk* in the camp, along the line of famous Jaroslav Hašek's Czech satire. (Bertolt Brecht later wrote his own "sequel" to *Švejk*; his "good soldier" meets Hitler on the snowy plains at Stalingrad.) Taussig, as many later recalled, worked hard on his *Švejk* manuscript. Neither he nor the manuscript survived, but so much of it is known: at the time when the transport of Jews to the camps were already in progress, in Prague, Švejk went into the municipal office to get a tag for his dog (he had a business of selling stray and stolen dogs, as Hašek's original did). Švejk gets into the wrong line, is mistakenly stamped "J," for "Jew," on his identity card, and is sent to Theresienstadt.[195] In spite of the fact that Švejk is an "Aryan." This is the joke.

The power of the list, of categories, and more purely of letters of the alphabet and of numbers, made people into parts of a form and thus into other people, and things into other things, people into things and into commodities, usable and disposable, into a "reserve," Heidegger's word, to shelve the people.

A "Talmud Commando," under the SS order and supervised by the Jewish Council of the Elders, had been established in Theresienstadt. The Talmud Commando's duty was to catalogue religious books brought into the camp from the pillaged Jewish places. The head of the Council of the Elders, Rabbi Murmelstein, who was in charge of "the project" ex officio, "used the system of the Prussian State Library." The internees for the Talmud Commando were selected from among prominent scholars and religious figures interned in the camp, some possibly brought to Theresienstadt for the purpose. The project was well started, but it was left "half done," Adler wrote, for, in the fall of 1944, somebody might change his mind, and virtually all the Commando members were sent to Auschwitz.[196]

The books in Theresienstadt's main library, much more diverse than just books about religion, were also shelved and catalogued, well ordered, "commanded," and, sure, alphabetically by their author, and by their subject, their genre, or their language. As if a fire were to break out and firefighters were ready, "One can get in a moment a book one needs," Philipp Manes wrote. "Mr. Hugo Friedmann [the associate librarian and also the architecture-tours guide in the camp] knows each and every book by sight and where to find it. Before you know, he is back from the stacks and brings it."[197]

The power of the list rested upon letters, codes, and numbers, in rows and columns, not just designation and accumulation but sorting and ordering as well. Once put on paper (and they could be "barked out" also), being on a list became one's identity and, indeed, oneself. *Kaoem Moeda* [The Youth] was an Indonesian nationalist paper in Bandung, West Java. In August 1928, it published an article under the headline "The Innocent People in Boven Digoel." "When a list of the people to be sent to Boven Digoel in this particular group was being put together," the paper wrote, "some names got onto the list by mistake."[198] These names got on the list and a number was attached to each of them, and, at least as far as we know, no correction has been made. Other people are worried and afraid, the paper wrote, "that they will also in the future be put on some of these transport lists."[199]

In fact, some corrections were made. Internee Jahja Nasoetion recalled of his journey to Boven Digoel:

> After we have sat three days in Surabaya prison, they led us to the ship, *Fomalhaut*, in the harbor. With us, there was a man who was also going

to Boven Digoel, Comrade Sjuib, from West Sumatra. He already had spent several years in the camp and now he was going back because it was discovered that he was released in error. His name had been put on the list instead of that of Comrade Ahmad Maliki from Bandung. After Comrade Sjuib, on a ship from Boven Digoel, had arrived in Surabaya, there already was a telegram from the camp reporting the mix-up, and so, of course, he had to go back. It was truly sad to watch the man, who now had to send a letter to his family that he was going back to the camp because of an administrative error by the colonial government.[200]

Georges Perec wrote, in this particular case not about the camps but about the catalogue of exhibited items at the "Universal Exposition 1900" in Paris. "There is something at once uplifting and terrifying," he wrote, "about the idea that nothing in the world is so unique that it can't be entered on a list."[201]

"Behind each name on the list," Adler recalled, "an SS officer added either 'T' or 'O,' so that there could be no mistake."[202] "T" meant Theresienstadt, and "O" meant *Ost*, "the east." One could analyze the camps, ultimately, on one's fingers. The "Little Fortress," in Theresienstadt, was also, or better, known as "Fort B."[203] The main camp therefore was "Fort A."

All the blocks in Theresienstadt, and all streets for some time, for the experimental moment that lasted through much of the camp's existence, were renamed, coded, or tagged, each with a number and a letter only. It made for clear and useful geometry, too. So, for a time, at the height of the camp, there were only *Langsstrassen*, German for "long streets," and *Querstrassen*, German for "crosswise streets," or rather, as they became known and generally called, *L-Strassen* and *Q-Strassen*. Numbered blocks stood in line, in arithmetic and alphabetical sequence, from one wall of the camp to the opposite end. Even the word *"Strasse"* disappeared from the code. So, for instance, one lived in L 1 or Q 2.[204] Again, the Theresienstadt cabaret sang it best:

This is our world
We all are "in"
In the South, and in the North
In nine Q's, and in six L's.[205]

In the Yad Vashem archives in Jerusalem I came upon a thin file of lose pages all dated "Theresienstadt, September 7, 1943." There is a list: addresses in the camp, with a note that these are where letters from the outside arrived,

"L 211, L 120, L 114, Q 309."[206] On Friday, April 28, 1944, Pavel Weiner described how he looked for the mother of his friend, Franta Springer. He needed to talk to her very much and ask about Franta, if he was still in the camp. Pavel went from block to block: "I get there, but I am told that Mrs. Springer has moved away." Finally, "I go to the registry office [*Evidenz*] and I am told that she is at Q 501, so I finally go there."[207]

The coding, as it was, contained in the principle of alphabetical and arithmetical sequence, could be extended beyond the walls, like the signal of the radio, it could not be stopped, in fact. Mr. Jiří Franěk, who had traveled from Theresienstadt "further on" and survived, told Elena Makarova, "Birkenau was divided in two camps: A-Auschwitz and B-Birkenau. Inside Birkenau there was camp A-1, women's camp, A-2, that's where we [the Theresienstadt people] were, and A-3 was under construction. A-2 was divided into A-2a, A-2b and, I think, A-2g. Next to us, there was a Gypsy camp, A-2c. A-2d was a mixed camp, where my brother was and where he perished. He had gone there earlier. The main camp was A-2b, a rectangle, with a long side of 300 m, located in the center of the big camp."[208]

Boven Digoel, colonial-wise, jungle-wise, "the last place where wilderness calls could still be heard," was, no less than Theresienstadt, lettered, numbered, coded, and listable. In the middle of the "primitive," the sections of the camp were named, and no other names were ever used by either the authorities or the internees, by the first six letters, "A," "B," "C," "D," "E," and "F." "Five of the six planned camp sections, A, B, C, D, and E," reported Marcus van Blankenstein in 1928, "are already built and internees live there."[209] Section F, in fact, in spite of efforts, was never really finished. The jungle won, in this case.

The rest of the place, however, progressively was being refined, tuned, cleared, if not in everything, certainly in coding, expansion of coding, codes, subcodes, and sub-subcodes. In July 1940, the next to the last year of the camp, the "Registry of the houses currently inhabited by the internees" listed section "C" of the camp and showed it on an attached map, as made of "Store Street," "Block Street," "Alleys I–III," "Alleys A–E," "Digoel Street," "Alleys IV–VII," "Alley AA," "Alley BB," "Alley CC," and "Alley DD."[210]

When we talked about the coding in Boven Digoel with the late Willem Wertheim, a sociologist of Indonesia, who was born in Saint Petersburg in 1907, he reacted by telling me that it was "like with us." Streets in the new and fashionable part of Saint Petersburg, where young Wertheim spent his childhood during World War I and the Bolshevik Revolution, were also "grouped in a numbered series," First Rozhdestvensky Street, Second Rozhdestvensky Street, and so on, and so on.[211]

The coding, as Rem Koolhaas argues about Manhattan, might also be called an "exterminating principle" of "cyclic restatement," a "creation and destruction irrevocably interlocked" in the "suspense" of "escalating intensity."[212] It is the memorializing of one's number and pronouncing it correctly. The space given to the camp people, like the space of Manhattan or Saint Petersburg, was designed, coded, and numbered so that it "can now be multiplied *ad infinitum*."[213]

The camp people were not the first, but they lived the culmination. Like nobody before them, they were tabulated into lines and columns that had no end. The line was temporal as much as alphabetical, numerical, and geometrical. Each camp, like a modern metropolis which was not there yet, became "a city of the perpetual *flight forward*."[214] As Benjamin wrote to Adorno in 1935, and in the camps his observation was most true: "Things are hollowed out, and as ciphers, draw in meanings."[215]

Even the internees talked about "*Project* Theresienstadt."[216] There is a small octavo *Kontobuch* [book of accounts], in the Yad Vashem archives, catalogued under a number and letters by which it can be filed and found again. The Kontobuch has about twenty pages all covered by handwriting. These are poetry verses by a married woman in the late forties, a mother, who, I guess, had never written poetry or anything "literary" before. I learned from the poems (not meant for me) that she was separated from her husband and her two children by the circumstances of the time. It was for them that she wrote the poetry, awkward, and full of the most personal memories, and sensual desires inspired by the loss. She hoped to see them all again, and she was afraid, at the same time, that she would be put on the list.

On September 7, 1944, it happened. She would go to "Birkenau," and she had two days to pack. The scribbling in the Kontobuch becomes less readable, page by page quickly filled, now, close to the last page are often illegible. It is still poetry—in fact it is now more poetry. Her last entry, September 9, 1944, is almost unintelligible.

The most beautiful summer day in the last three years,
the hills . . .
call to the registrar [kartei] . . .
first to the Stadium to get a ticket . . .
through puddles of water . . .[217]

"We have achieved what was foretold," wrote Gilles Deleuze in his *Desert Islands*, "the absence of any goal. Errancy has ceased being a return to the origin; it is no longer even aberration, which would still presuppose a fixed point."[218] "The new arrivals," wrote Adler about Theresienstadt, "carried their bags, and marched in four rows, led by the Czech gendarmes and the camp police." The journey from the railway station nearest to Theresienstadt, before an extension to the camp was built, was three kilometers long and took the new arrivals two to three hours. They walked. "The final destination," Adler wrote, and he could say, "a fixed point," the final destination "was the Sluice Gate."[219]

The *Schleuse*, German for "Sluice Gate," Dutch "*sluis*," was known to the Theresienstadt internees coming from all places and speaking all languages. Originally a purely engineering term, used also by the eighteenth-century builders of Theresienstadt, it described the fortress's (or whatever engineering) system of water control. The Schleuse was a part, or gadget, of the system that regulated the path through which water flowed. Now, in the camp, *Schleuse* came to mean a gate, a special gate building, in fact, most of the time in block E VII, where the new arrivals were stopped and they and their bags were searched. Each person and bag, before being let through, was stopped, controlled, and, with more or less "contraband" seized, let pass through. Thus, they had become camp people, anew or more. The process was called *"Durchschleusung,"* German for "sluicing."[220]

Thus, "the final destination" of Adler, and "a fixed point" of Deleuze, in fact, was no closure. It was just a moving further on, into the camp, and, if death did not take one first, of course, to another camp, and more to camp, like in numerical or alphabetical sequence, as the water flows.

To facilitate the system, after some months of the camp buildup, a train line was extended into the camp.[221] Still the new arrivals had to pass through "the sluice." Still there was nothing but the stopovers on the line. This is a poem by a fifteen-year-old boy of Theresienstadt about the first train arriving on the new line reaching into the streets of the camp:

The First Train

. . .

I close my eyes. So, this is what an unbeating heart
Of steel, driven by steam, looks like.
It gives the world no choice at all.
Under your wheels, my dear, I go a little further.[222]

The Sluice Gate was not the final point but the essence of the camps. In fact, through the Sluice Gate nothing of the disturbing or rebellious past was supposed to pass, not even the present, to use Maurice Blanchot's words, "no present, nothing but what is actual." To pass through the Sluice Gate was "the step not beyond."[223]

The ways of the camps were "Lordly"—as Marc Augé wrote, meaning the Paris Metro in this case—"like those of the Lord . . . impenetrable: they are traveled endlessly."[224] Close to it, the ways of the camps were "suburban." Into suburbs, the "network grows ceaselessly."[225]

Walter Benjamin called a space that was growing around him in 1938 "into ever-wider circles," the "*taedium vitae*," "weariness of life" or "world-weariness."[226] This might be why he was so serious about his *Arcades Project* as a passage of modernity. In *The Arcades Project*, he quoted Louis Veuillot's *Les odeurs de Paris*, from 1866, "complaining that the architecture of the new Paris, despite its eclecticism, is uniformly tedious in its recourse to 'the emphatic and the aligned.'"[227]

Reading Benjamin into the camps, a place where "destiny finally ebbed,"[228] one may be tempted to call the camps the capitals of the twentieth century, as he called Paris the capital of the nineteenth. Suburbs, even more than in Benjamin's Paris, would become downtowns. As the people approached the camps, entered them, and died in them, as the camps were planned and mapped, either from the outside in or from the inside out, there were to be no edges. Toward the edge, the wall, the jungle, the screen, the feeling of the camp intensified, the camps got purer, more sublime, and all-embracing. Through the taedium vitae, the suburban became the fullness of life thus given.

"Do you think," Karl Rossmann asked Fanny in Kafka's *Amerika*, "that I'll get a job here too?" They speak about the Nature Theatre of Oklahoma, the company that offered jobs and new lives. "Most certainly," said Fanny, "why, it's the greatest theatre in the world. . . . I've not seen it yet, I admit, but some of the other girls here, who have been in Oklahoma already, say there are almost no limits to it."[229] "Why has the theatre not opened yet?" asked Karl. "Oh yes," said Fanny, "it's an old theatre, but it is always being enlarged."[230]

Kafka, in 1912, initially called his novel *Der Verschollene* [The Man Who Disappeared].[231] Everybody is aiming for, moving to "the greatest theatre in the world" in the novel. Pointing to a man who evidently is going the same way, Karl asks a supervisor (or is he a guard, or perhaps a train conductor?), "He has a wife with him too and a small child in a perambulator. Are they coming too?" "Of course," said the man, and he seemed to smile at Karl's doubts. "We can use all of them."[232]

V

SCATTERING

And suddenly there was a great earthquake, so that the foundations of the prison were shaken: and immediately all the doors were opened, and everyone's bands were loosed. And the keeper of the prison awaking out of his sleep, and seeing the prison doors open, he drew his sword, and would have killed himself, supposing that the prisoners had been fled. But Paul cried out with a loud voice, saying, "Do thyself no harm: for we are all here."

—Acts 16:26–28

FIFTEEN

Nausea

There are some reports about the authorities of both Theresienstadt and Boven Digoel fearing internees' resistance. In one Theresienstadt memoir "Marxist-oriented Zionists" are mentioned and their "illegal" magazine, NICOC, which means "Spark." One of the group, Pavel Löwinger, reportedly "translated selected pages of Marx's *Capital* from Yiddish into Czech."[1] The same testimony mentioned Communist "party-oriented discussions" in the camp. The author of the testimony added, "I believe that the same was done by the Zionists, that they probably also held meetings; in our, Communists' case, we usually called it 'study sessions.' Here I got to learn something about Marx's *Capital* for the first time. The thin booklet was a selection, and they put 'Latin grammar' on the cover." However, "Up to the very end," this witness concluded, "as I look at it now, all these activities make the impress of rather pointless efforts."[2]

There is a suggestion in Hans Günther Adler's history of Theresienstadt that the last SS commandant of the camp worried whether a number of the internees, former officers of the Austrian, German, Dutch, or Czechoslovak army, might be capable of some action, as the fronts of World War II were coming closer to Central Europe and to the camp.³ Yet nothing of the kind, as far as it is known, really happened in Theresienstadt.

"Yes, I am impressed by this," Claude Lanzmann said during an interview after the war with the last Theresienstadt head of the Jewish Council of the Elders, Rabbi Benjamin Murmelstein, the only one who survived the war. "I am impressed," Lanzmann said, but we hear "depressed," rather, "by this general passivity to the end."⁴

Dr. Maurice Rossel, the delegate from the International Red Cross, visited the Theresienstadt camp in 1944, and he, also in an interview with Lanzmann, similarly recalled his surprise and indeed disbelief. "I got the impression at the time," Dr. Rossel said, "that the behavior of the people was also such that ... it was ... very antipathetic. The attitude of the Jews in this city," meaning Theresienstadt; "and I ask myself still today, I still believe it—in spite of all that I have been told—this subservience and this passivity, it is something I have never digested."⁵ A few minutes later in the interview, Dr. Rossel said, "One would expect a wink ... a ... a ... a nothing. ... And ... still now, I don't understand that these people knew, as I know, as one says now, that they were lost, damned..."⁶

An internee who survived Theresienstadt later told a story about the camp's last days, in fact a story of the camp's liberation. He recalled an "incident that happened in Theresienstadt in those closing days." All the German guards had already fled, and the Russians had not yet arrived. ss-Obersturmführer Karl Rahm, the last camp commandant, suddenly appeared on the street: "On a bicycle and without a weapon, he pedaled from gate to gate, closing the doors of the offices, collecting the keys. ... The Jews watched him from the sidewalks and from the windows of the crowded barracks. ... There was no one else present at this time except the Jews and this German soldier. ... Not one person lifted a stone to throw at him. They could have strangled him if they wanted."⁷

In another text, this time from Theresienstadt long before the liberation, an unknown author wrote an essay on Czech folk tales. The original typescript survived and is now filed in the Jewish Museum in Prague. It has marginalia written in pen, and typos and grammar are carefully corrected in the same pen. It shows a high level of author conscience but also learning. There is a clear influence of the avant-garde structuralist Prague Linguistic Circle of the 1930s on the text's argument.

One Czech fable, similar to German story "The Long, The Fat, and The Keen-Sighted," is analyzed in the essay in particular detail. Three friends,

The Long, The Fat, and The Keen-Sighted, decide to take a stand and to defend a city threatened by an evil king. The evil king's army marches toward the city gate, and the moment comes.

> The Fat squats as wide as he is, in the middle of the gate, facing the evil king's army. He makes himself even fatter than he usually is, and he clogs the gate with his barrel of a body completely. The evil king's army attacks, and, now, The Fat opens his big mouth. Mistaking the kisser for the gate, the army marches in. The Fat, to the ultimate mirth of all the city people, who came to watch, spits out the soldiers, officers, and generals of the enemy one by one. The last soldier, who somehow got stuck in, causes The Fat to sneeze and the soldier is catapulted "beyond the nine hills."

The last words of the essay, which was probably read at one of the camp public performances, are "We all can learn from the wisdom of the people."[8]

The "wisdom of the people," like everything else in the camp, was spectacular. The "wisdom of the people" as a possibility of resistance, like radio or traffic, was spectacularly present in the camp by its absence.

There were many variations of "The Long, The Fat, and The Keen-Sighted" story. The one most strongly affecting the people was probably a play about Esther. The Old Testament story of the Jewish heroine Esther is recalled by the Jews every spring in the celebration of Purim. It used to gain a special popularity and significance at historical moments of Jewish oppression, and, thus, ultimately again, in the camps. The Esther of the Book of Esther was a Jewish concubine of a Babylonian king, and she, at the last moment, together with the wise Jew Mordechai, miraculously saved her Jewish nation in exile from Haman, the king's evil advisor, who with his sons planned the Jews' annihilation.

Theodor Lessing, a Jewish philosopher (assassinated by the Nazis in 1933 in Mariánské Lázně, Marienbad, Czechoslovakia), referred to Purim as "the suspension of all borders."[9] The feast has a sound dimension, too. Every time Haman's name is mentioned, for instance, during the Purim service in a synagogue, "the children twirl noisemakers."[10] The evil voice is silenced with the noise.

The avant-garde and arguably best theater in prewar Prague, led by a Communist, E. F. Burian, prepared the Esther story to be performed on its stage in 1939. Then the Nazis occupied Prague and the play was banned, but the text survived and was somehow smuggled into Theresienstadt.

Some of the Burian collaborators interned there took the text and repeatedly, not just at Purim, performed it in the camp before truly excited audiences. Always shining in all testimonies, it ended in triumph and a song:

> King to the servants:
> *Still today you hang Haman.*
> *Let Haman hang.*
> *I name Mordechai his successor.*
> . . .
>
> The crowd around the throne:
> *Down with Haman.*
> *Long live Mordechai.*
>
> Narrator:
> *The same day Esther asked the king to abolish Haman's laws. . . .*
> *Haman and his ten sons were hanged, and there were no more enemies. A clear day rose beyond the mountains—from each Jewish face shone a smile, from each lip flew a song.*
> *(All sing).*[11]

The spectacular was there, in all its heaviness and edginess. On June 7, 1943, Gonda Redlich wrote, "Yesterday, two German officers slapped each other. Both were drunk. A wonderful spectacle."[12]

Mrs. Widayasih might refer to the very same thing in Boven Digoel: "My mother told me: 'What chance does a *katé* [a Javanese midget horse] have against an Australian stallion.'"[13] (A *Dutch* stallion, she might say, but this was how the saying went on Java and in Boven Digoel.)

There are files with petitions in the Boven Digoel archive, submitted by the camp people to the officials at various levels of the camp authority. Some of the letters are written with flair. Others are just scribbled, and it is clear, even from the handwriting, that some were composed in despair. One kind of petition is very polite, the second less so, and the third shows a dramatic lack of what even the sender might call good manners. As a rule, they all seem to be dispatched with little expectation of real effect. Some, those more daring or more resigned, were being sent again and again. They were like other letters sent from the camp home, into the open, in a monotonous rhythm of a repetition—as re-petitions.

Some, again, were spectacular.

BOVEN DIGOEL, AUGUST 18, 1929

To:

The Most Esteemed Sir, the Assistant Resident of Boven Digoel

With all respect and most humbly ... I request an audience with His Excellency the Governor of the Moluccas when he comes on his announced visit to the camp.... The points I wish to talk to him are:

1. The situation of the internees in Boven Digoel at the present as compared with the years 1927 and 1928.
2. The reasons for Boven Digoel internees' dissatisfaction with the government.
3. The question of rice in the camp ...

With greetings and respect.
Signed, S. Achmadsjah, camp section B[14]

"Some our friends in the camp," Mas Marco wrote in one of his letters from the camp, "intentionally drop rubbish in the camp, and some others behave in manners that are not polite to talk about."[15]

There were other ways opened to the internees, as if through a screen. Reading in the "List of the Offenses Handled by the Magistrate in Boven Digoel," internee Midjamdja stood accused, for instance, of doing nothing. As of November 30, 1935, he still had not built a fence to mark the boundaries of his house and front yard. Internee Midjamdja admitted that there were still no fences around his house and declared, "I do not know whether I would ever want to build them." He was convicted, ordered to pay a fine of ƒ5, and he was sent to prison for four days by the force of Article 1, Sub B of the Neatness Ordinance.[16] Internee Djaja was called before the magistrate on July 15, 1937, for the same offense, and he said at his sentencing, "I can do what I wish to do, because I am here just as an exile."[17]

There were dramatic speeches in Boven Digoel and as echoes or rumors they circulated in the camp. On August 27, 1929, an internee-spy reported a gathering of the fellow internees a day before in the mosque of section C, where about a hundred persons attended "to honor Hadji Achmat, who died." After the prayers for the dead, the spy wrote, there were "*voordrachten*," which is Dutch for "speeches," but rather "lectures," "about the deceased, how full of energy he used to be in the movement and in teaching Communism, how significant his role was in the Sumatra uprising [of 1927], and that we all should follow the example he has given."[18]

On Friday, May 24, 1935, the Boven Digoel ROB police reported that at 9:38 the night before, in the house of internee Soemasaroeno, in section B of the camp, a number of internees and their family members, all "known as radicals," "sat around the room and talked." The police agent overheard them saying that, "in their opinion, the government *fears* the Communists."[19] It had to be the official reading the report who underlined the words "known as radicals" and the word "fears." When the governor of the Moluccas visited the camp on one of his inspection tours, "Someone spat at his feet."

On Tuesday, November 6, 1934, at 8:40 at night, a piece of paper appeared affixed, it is not said how, to the fence in front of internee Natar Zainudin's house. An hour or so later another leaflet was discovered by a police agent on the wall of internee Said Ali's house. The same day, still a third piece of paper was discovered on the bridge to the camp section B, near the house of internee Abdoel Madjid, a.k.a. Rangkajo Boengsoe.[20] These were leaflets, judging from the fact that "DHM" was written on all of them, but the meaning of the three letters of the alphabet was mysterious. We do not know the internees' interpretation, but the police read the "DHM" as *De Helden Moed*," Dutch for "The Hero's Courage." In the police report a line below one of the "DHMs" is quoted as well, which ran, "The government is responsible for feeding the internees." The police probably ordered the leaflets or posters (no size of them is given) to be destroyed. At least, I did not find any in the file.[21]

There were demonstrations in Boven Digoel, something that was unimaginable in Theresienstadt. On Friday, May 1, 1936, at 7:30 in the morning, the children of the internees, as an ROB police agent reported, "boys and girls in their best," gathered in front of the houses of internees Kadiroen and Moeljani. Teachers of the "wild schools" were also present. At 8:45, internee Soeroso, one of the teachers, was overheard by the police explaining to the children the difference between rich and poor. "We are the people without money, the poor ones," Soeroso said. "The people who have money are the rich class. We are the proletarians and they are the capitalists."[22]

It was May Day. The ROB police still reported that in section C of the camp "many internees appear to be visiting each other's houses." From the house of internee Soekaria music was heard, people played kroncong, and they sang "songs with lyrics of bad morals." From the singing voices, the ROB agent, however, could not recognize who namely was signing.

At 9:15, still the same morning, three children of internees were brought to the police station because they did not obey the police order to stop singing "the Internationale." At 10:30 other children, all students of the wild schools, were reported marching "to and fro" in front of the *wedana*'s, district chief's, office. Internees Djaétoen and Moekandar led the march, and, the agent reported, the children have passed the wedana's office three times already. At 10:50 the agent counted thirty-one children marching. At 2:20 in the afternoon, several internees in the house of Matsari were overheard talking about the three children taken to the police station in the morning.[23]

On Friday, September 11, 1936, it was the turn of the camp authorities to celebrate—the Dutch royal princess was getting engaged in The Hague. On the night of the occasion, at 9:10 in the evening, the police reported that the internees' houses were "almost all dark, except for those with small children." "It gives an impression," the police agent submitted, "of antipathy."[24]

There had been just one single case in the fifteen-year history of Boven Digoel when the Arnaudian cruel theater became indeed bloody, spilling offstage, so to speak. On September 17, 1929, the Boven Digoel administrator sent an urgent telegram to Batavia in which he reported a "protest-march by the internees," "some of them armed with hatchets, knives, and sticks." The marchers had been "warned," the telegram reported, and a few arrests were made. However, internee Kartodanoedjoe "resisted arrest," and internee Madasin "came to his help," "displaying tailor scissors." "A soldier cut Madasin's throat with a sword." Madasin "was dead instantly."[25]

Still six years after this happened, in 1935, Dr. Schoonheyt wrote, and as far as all the documents show, he was right, "To this day, this was the only physical encounter between the authorities and the internees in Boven Digoel with lethal consequence." In fact, he could have written the same on the closing day of the camp.[26]

Special *selamatans* [ceremonial meals] were held in the camp by the internees every year on anniversary of Madasin's death. Speeches and lectures were given. The authorities, every year, too, sent spies to the selamatans, to watch and listen. When "disorderly behavior" was noticed, the culprit was punished by a fine and a few days in prison.

Trial Proceedings:

... On September 13, 1933, the accused Hadji Adenan, invalid, living in section C of the camp ... visited section B ...

QUESTION BY THE MAGISTRATE: *"Was this an evening to celebrate Madasin ... ?"*

ANSWER: "There was food, and two speeches, one by Reksosiswojo and the other by Poeradisastra."[27]

These were events irritating to the administration. When Aliarcham, the former chairman of the Communist Party and possibly the most respected internee in the camp, died of tuberculosis in the Tanah Tinggi section of the camp, Aliarcham's corpse was carried by government motorboat downstream to the main camp to be buried at the internees' cemetery. Dr. Schoonheyt was the camp medical officer at the time; he accompanied the body, and later wrote about the moment in his memoirs. As the boat was coming to the main camp, the doctor wrote, he saw the internees standing shoulder to shoulder along the bank of the river, in silence, paying respect to the dead.

The doctor recalled the moment with irritation, and he was more irritated, he wrote, a few days later when some of the internees came to his door and offered to sell him a photograph they had taken of Aliarcham's grave.[28]

As in the case of the killed Madasin, there were, in the years to come, memorials on the anniversary of Aliarcham's death, and they too were watched. Some years they happened, other years, evidently, they did not.

WEDNESDAY, JULY 1, 1937 MORNING: . . . 11:00 . . . Camp is calm. There is no sign of anything connected with the anniversary of Aliarcham's death.

The sense of resistance thickened in the camps by the absence of a possibility to resist. The desire to resist, possibly thicker in the camps than anywhere else and any time before, because there was no outlet to it, thickened even more thickly into a desire to escape. Emmanuel Levinas might describe something close to the desire, close to an ultimate desire, in his essay *De l'évasion* [On Escape], written in 1935, Levinas being a Jew, and writing at the dawn of the time of the camps for Jews. The desire, Levinas wrote, is "without the return to its point of departure," it is "neither caress, nor liturgy," it does not "fade into complacency or exhaustion."[29]

The camps were designed not by a butcher—no matter how they may have turned out—but rather, to use the language fitting the age of reason, by a "totalitarian scribe."[30] In the twentieth century, whatever violence it might eventually come to, as Carl Schmitt wrote, "the political concept of battle becomes discussion." The "will to repel the enemy," wrote Schmitt, "turns into a rationally constructed social ideal or program, a tendency or, a calculation."[31] This was the cold violence that the world was coming to embrace, and the camps, again, were spearheading the trend.

Neither Boven Digoel nor Theresienstadt were Auschwitz. Whatever the harshness in these two camps, the real horror was that they were still, and more than ever, the clearings. Their horizon was still there, and more than ever, with more light than ever, as a screen. Mohammad Hatta could still give a lecture in Boven Digoel, as he probably never would be inspired to give anywhere in the Indies, titled *Pengantar ke Djalan Ilmu dan Pengetahuan* [Introduction to the Way to Learning]. Purely light. The lecture, which was published after the war as a small book, dealt with "knowledge and science" and "different ways to achieve knowledge."[32]

The "objective violence" to which the cold, blasé brutality led, with its heights again in the camps, did not imply crashes but "introductions," "ways to achieve," and "contributions." The "objective violence" before it culminated in the camps and since before the camps, in Slavoj Žižek's words, was a reflection of a "self-enhancing circulation of capital,"[33] and, with it, of enlightened people, "capital" meaning value in the bourgeois world, "enlightened people" meaning those in the camps as well as outside of the camps.

"Every partial system," wrote Hermann Broch about the twentieth century, "considered a value system must imitate the structure of the total system, whether it be a simple reflection of that or its distorted perversion."[34] The total system of the twentieth century determined the dynamics and desires of the partial systems of the camps. The camp people of Boven Digoel, like the camp people of Theresienstadt, and like the modern people of Europe and Asia, lived, some more and some less in a cage, and all in one "ideosphere."[35] This was how their horizon was given to them, and how each one's story "never stop[ped] speaking inside his head."[36]

The culture of the twentieth century and subculture of the camps "oscillate between an amelioration of historical importance and a catastrophe."[37] "The problem is one of adaptation."[38]

"Nothing less than a compass is required, if you are to find your way," Walter Benjamin quoted Jacques Fabien of the mid-eighteenth century.[39] This compass, according to Edmund Husserl, becomes "a method of idealization and construction, an infinite and yet self-enclosed world."[40] Geometry, again, created ritual settings, and nothing ideally exists anymore *"outside of ritual settings."*[41]

"Clearing" comes to mean "the extermination of space as the field of freedom of political action." It is in its own way a dynamic and energetic space: in clearing, "the more speed increases, the faster freedom decreases."[42] "Anyway, we only break down open doors," wrote Louis-Ferdinand Céline.[43] Jacob Riis, who, like Céline, was never in the camp but lived in that age, tells us that recidivists in New York in 1889 were called "Revolvers," meaning revolving doors rather than pistols.[44] "One cannot flee it, not even in flight," Ernst Bloch wrote, "even the most resistant are taken on capitalism's wings."[45] "You seek imaginary landings in the continual movement of resting places," Dadaist Francis Picabia wrote, "what madness!"[46]

....

"The internees," Krarup Nielsen wrote, expressing a feeling about Boven Digoel similar to what Dr. Rossel believed he saw in Theresienstadt, "appear to accept their lives with Eastern fatalism."[47] The "Eastern fatalism," however, appears to be a term misplaced in this case.

In the wake of the Communist uprisings in 1926 and 1927, the authorities in the Indies panicked and interned many "suspected Communists," people having nothing to do either with the Communists or with the uprisings. Several men and women known as Saminists were also among the deported "suspects."[48] They all came from Java, called themselves "children of Adam," and rejected all of what they saw as the trappings of the modern life, such as taxes by modern governments as well as modern schools. Collectively, clearly an example of "Eastern fatalism," they became a dark spot on the Boven Digoel camp clearing.

"These followers of Samin are not completely normal," wrote a camp official in a report in 1935, and "they belong to the worst-disposed element in the camp. They are against any kind of cooperation with the government; entirely."[49] The Saminists were a close-knit group, even though, in one case, it appears that a Communist internee, not a Saminist, joined the group.

> SATURDAY, JUNE 1, 1935 . . . NIGHT . . . 8:40 . . . Sjamsoedin joined the "Oeripist" group.[50]

"Oeripists" was another name for the followers of Samin.

The Saminists, or Oeripists, *did not belong*, and so their actions, or non-actions rather, were so disturbing to the authorities of the camp, and perhaps also to the internees themselves.

> SATURDAY, NOVEMBER 28, 1936, MORNING: 10:15. Two Oeripists, Karioredjo and Partosentono, refuse to tell the police on duty their camp numbers.[51]

One day in 1938, one of the sheep brought to the camp for slaughter escaped to the forest. Two of the Saminists-Oeripists "who knew well how to handle sheep," on their own of course, ventured after the animal into the jungle. They caught the sheep, slaughtered it themselves, and divided the meat between their folk. According to some reports, they might give some meat to the other internees, too. When they were interrogated by the camp magistrate, they "calmly admitted what they did and said that God sent the sheep to them."[52]

Another time, two of the Saminists disappeared. The others of the group, when they were interrogated, told the police that the two went "to visit their brother." There was no brother. "The two Saminists disappeared, and the people did not know where to look for them," Mrs. Widayasih recalled. "After several days," she said, "nobody knew how the man died, a corpse of one of the Saminists was found at the edge of the jungle, not far from the camp, near the place where internees used to pound their rice."[53]

The Saminists were free of the camp because they did not belong, and they were free as long as they did not belong.

There were some other camp people in Boven Digoel, not Saminists-Oeripists, modern, Communist, but not unlike the Saminists, absolutely so. Both the authorities and internees often found themselves describing them in the same way, as "firm characters," "principled," "upright," or, the same thing in the camp, "recalcitrant," "implacable."[54] In a heated debate about Boven Digoel in the Volksraad in Batavia, in December 1928, a deputy described the Boven Digoel internees as divided into three distinct groups; *de goedgezinden* [the well-disposed]; *de halfslachtigen* [the half-hearted]; and *de onverzoenlijken* [the recalcitrant].[55] In a confidential circular letter, in August 1935, the Indies procurer general described the recalcitrant in Boven Digoel as "unmanageable."[56]

The "unmanageable" were also called "consequential" or "radical."[57] The "recalcitrant," "unmanageable," "radical," or "consequential," as time passed and camp was getting settled down, one by one, with family if they had one, were sent to Tanah Tinggi, up the river, still deeper into the jungle. But unlike whereto the Saminists ran, it was a clearing again and more so, where the light was still harder on the eyes, and which became still more purely of the camp. It was not Auschwitz either, but it was Boven Digoel in its ultimate.

According to Salim, who spent months there, Tanah Tinggi was a "depressing and debilitating place." "Only a truly strong in body and soul," Salim added, "the *jago's*, could withstand the conditions there for a prolonged period of time."[58] *Jago* (written "*djago*" at the time), in Java, Sumatra, and other islands, means a "cock," a "champion," or a "charismatic leader," "die-hard," as Salim explained, switching into English. The people of "the second camp," Salim wrote, meaning Tanah Tinggi, did not take any orders, were seen as a "potential threat," and, Salim concluded, were "nihilists."[59]

"There was yet another division in the prison," Fyodor Dostoyevsky wrote of his Siberian camp in Tsarist Russia, "that of those who were completely desperate."[60] In his *Memoirs from the House of the Dead*, Dostoyevsky devoted a special chapter to the "Desperate People." In his description, they also seemed to be the core of the camp and, at the same time, only-almost belonging to it. "It is difficult," Dostoyevsky wrote, "to say much about desperate characters in prison, as elsewhere, there are rather few of them."[61]

Comfortingly, in the long tradition of the enlightenment and the age of reason, insanity was an explanation. In the end of ends, the recalcitrants, the nihilists, were mad because they did not move the camp way and, ergo, the modern way. They did not move as the camp moved and the world moved. They halted and, in the most extreme cases, stood still.

"The threat today is not passivity but pseudo-activity," Slavoj Žižek concluded his essay *Violence*. "The truly difficult thing," he wrote, "is to step back, to withdraw. . . . Sometimes, doing nothing is the most violent thing to do."[62]

"Indecision," Kafka wrote in his *The Castle*, "seemed a mad idea in connection with such an organization."[63] By "mad idea" Kafka might mean mad courage, maybe even something close to Benjamin's utopian, romantic, suspicious-to-all-Hegelians, "dialectics at a standstill."[64] Or, perhaps, even closer to "holding oneself in the truth," as proposed by Heidegger (who proved himself neither mad nor courageous enough in the "holding").[65] Perhaps the "madness" was close to "liberty." "In this negation," Maurice Blanchot wrote, "men stand forth erect in the liberty of the 'I am,'" "not dispersed, but entirely gathered together . . . because of the firmness." "At a certain moment," Blanchot added, "in order to act it is necessary to cease acting . . . lest I lose my way in aimless roving."[66]

Jean-Paul Sartre describes one of his rational heroes: "Sick people always annoyed him a little—especially madmen because they were wrong."[67] Very few rational people have the courage, or madness, to admit that: "Philosophy . . . is born out of a withdrawal from the conditions found in a world of gods, sacrifices, hierarchies, hieroglyphs, and hierophanies." "It is born out of a withdrawal of the reasons of the world."[68] There are very few courageous enough, as Ernst Bloch wrote, or mad enough to believe in a "sense of equilibrium that lets the bourgeois shake his head at excess."[69]

There were quite a number of "Boven Digoel psychopaths."[70] The "mad" were concentrated in the camp, there was proportionally, radically more of them in the camp than in the world outside the camp.

In 1933, Dr. Muhamad Amir, an Indies expert in psychiatry about whom we know nothing else, arrived at Boven Digoel to conduct research on the mental health of the Boven Digoel internees. He found, among about four hundred inhabitants of the camp at the moment, "thirty cases indicating insanity or chronic mental disorder."[71] Other cases of documented, registered madness could be found through the camp archive. In one file, on a piece of paper, with the letterhead "Shell" on top, possibly torn from the doctor's notebook, there is a scribbled date, February 28, 1932, and a short list also in longhand of "the abnormals." "Roesman, no. 350," originally from Rembang, has a note behind his name: "truly psychopathic." Other "cases" are listed only as their camp numbers: "139, 350, 630, 795, 994, 1198, 1241, 1264, 1260, 421."[72]

The mentally disturbed people, meaning disturbed enough to be listed, were used by the doctor, clearly, and by the authorities in general to signify the fundamental "normalcy" and "sanity" of the camp as a whole.

> FRIDAY, JULY 12, 1935 . . . AFTERNOON: Agent Soedirman returns to the station. He watched the match on the SH soccer field. . . . Soedirman reports that Atmadja, the madman, was also there to watch. He wore clean clothes and seemed to be washed. Only his hair is still long, and he gets easily excited.[73]

"Our doctor often told us," Salim recalled, "that the mentally ill in the camp were 'nails in his coffin.'" "The medication against psychosis that we have today," Salim explained, writing in the 1950s, "was unknown in the time of the camp." "There were cases of total dementia," according to Salim." "These people," says Salim, "gradually sunk into themselves, into their own thought world," into "their neuroses and psychoses."[74]

"There might erupt a sudden moment of fear, or an attack, by *gendroewo*, for instance, a [Javanese!] malevolent spirit of the forest, might be imagined." "Those who became aggressive," wrote Salim, "were restrained and, in rare cases, temporarily [*sic*] evacuated."[75]

There is yet another list in the Boven Digoel archives, from 1932, of another nine internees who were diagnosed as mentally ill. The names are not easy to decipher, but one of them looks like Salim's.[76] According to a letter exchange between the resident of Ambon and the Boven Digoel authorities on May 31, 1929, internee Salim, indeed, is reported as having returned from Tanah Tinggi back to the main camp "because it is feared that he might be driven to complete insanity."[77] In 1935, Salim is mentioned again, this time in the ROB police book. He lived in the main camp now, yet his "mental health" was still clearly questionable:

TUESDAY, JUNE 4, 1935 . . . AFTERNOON . . . 3:35 . . . Police are sent to A. C. Salim to ask whether he would like to become a teacher [of the government school] as a substitute for internee Najoan . . . 4:50 . . . Salim does not feel like taking Najoan's job, because he worries that his nerves might give way again.[78]

One might say that the camp was a madhouse. But rather, normalcy was made acute. The madness was most carefully kept to itself.

On Friday, May 29, 1936, at 2:55 in the morning, internee Dt. Koening was heard "to cry in his house." The police were called, and Dt. Koening was found sitting inside his house in a chair with his head down on the table. "When asked, Dt. Koening said that it was nothing. Then he took a deep breath and said: 'Ah, how far my thoughts have flown!'" He was ordered to close the door of his house, which he had left open all night, and to go back to sleep. "He obeyed."[79]

"Internee Liantoe, in a moment of despair, killed himself. He cut his artery, and with his blood he wrote a testament on the wall of his house."[80] (The internee Liantoe's testament has not come to us.) "Internee Kusno Goenoko, a teacher of the government elementary school in Boven Digoel, who was sent to Tanah Tinggi, tied a stone with a towel to his body and threw himself into the river." Several days later his corpse was found in the mud of the river bank, several kilometers below Tanah Tinggi. "He was buried there on the spot."[81]

Tanah Tinggi was expected "to isolate the bad elements among the internees from attempting to disturb the spirit of the rest of the camp."[82] "The camp at Tanah Tinggi," the camp administrator reported repeatedly, "is designed for the core, the least cooperative among the internees."[83] "Tanah Tinggi section of Boven Digoel is a place where everything is simple (primitive)," wrote *Soeloeh Ra'jat Indonesia* [The Torch of Indonesian People], in an article titled *Soeara dari Boven Digoel* [Voice from Boven Digoel]. "When the doctor from the main camp comes on visit to Tanah Tinggi, the people there just shake their heads and reject the pill."[84]

"The men in Tanah Tinggi," recalled one of the Tanah Tinggi people after the war, "wore only pajama trousers, sleeveless undershirts, and sometimes their chests were bare. Women wore sarongs."[85]

In April 1930, Governor W. P. Hillen inspected the main camp and also traveled to Tanah Tinggi. In a section of his report "Situation in Tanah Tinggi," Hillen described "a sharp contrast" between Tanah Tinggi and the main camp. "In Tanah Tinggi," he wrote, "the people live totally by themselves and among themselves. There is not a single one among them who would be well-disposed to the Indies government or the Boven Digoel authorities."

"There are in Tanah Tinggi forty-three houses in total," Hillen reported in 1930, "with 115 inhabitants, seventy internees, and forty-five family members. The houses are set up strictly on the spots chosen by the internees themselves. Each house stands separate from the other, surrounded by trees and small, not very well kept yards and gardens. The authorities built a road from the riverbank landing place up to the camp which lies on a steep slope. But, other than that, there are no roads. Internees refuse to build them, which makes even their mutual visits, most of all in the evening, all but impossible." "Still," Governor Hillen reported, "the houses are of the same quality as the houses of the internees in the main camp, and could be described as sufficient." The government rations of salt fish, oil, and the like, like basic medications, were stored in a small warehouse on the river bank and distributed to the internees twice a week.

"When I visited the camp," Governor Hillen wrote, "the inhabitants of this unusual community did not appear to take any notice of me . . . in spite of the fact that my visit was announced long before and everybody had to know that I was coming." "I took a long leisurely walk through the place for almost two hours, and I often stopped to give the internees a chance to address to me with complaints or questions. But the people behaved as if they had not seen me. Either they stayed in their houses, or, when somebody happened to be outside, they just went on with whatever they were doing, working in the garden or just sitting on the porch and reading. Only one internee turned his back on me."[86]

Five years after Hillen's visit, in a document dated January 15, 1935, the Boven Digoel authorities reported that the internees of Tanah Tinggi were "again" reminded that they had to build fences around their houses, as it was the long-standing and largely observed rule in the main camp. "To this moment," the report complained, "not a single one in Tanah Tinggi did so. They will be asked again. The fence must be one meter high. If in one month the fences are still not standing, punishment will follow according to law."[87] I did not find any other report in the archives of either compliance or punishment.

One might think of a revolution, as the Paris revolution of 1830, for instance. The hero of Flaubert's *Sentimental Education* walks through the Paris streets during a short pause in the fighting—leisurely, he is a bourgeois—as if on an inspection. "Further on, he noticed three paving stones in the middle of the roadway, presumably the beginnings of a barricade, and then some broken bottles and coils of wire intended to obstruct the cavalry."[88]

On August 27, 1929, the police reported, not a little surprised, that the internee Agoes Soeleman, now in section A of the main camp, "demands that he be sent to Tanah Tinggi."[89] On June 1, in the same year, a group of six recalcitrants already interned in the tough second camp wrote to the administrators informing them that their families, still in the main camp, could be sent up the river to them in Tanah Tinggi because, as the recalcitrants wrote, "The place has already been made ready for them."[90]

"Even a few years ago," Dr. Schoonheyt wrote in 1935, "it was strictly forbidden to us to enter the camp of the recalcitrants without an armed escort. But it has become apparent that the measure is superfluous."[91] The Dutch policy to Tanah Tinggi, perhaps even more than to Boven Digoel, was blasé, which is liberal, holding internees without violence, without blood being spilled, even without a touch. The policy worked both ways. Dr. Schoonheyt described one of his regular visits to the upper camp to bring some medication and eventually to bring a seriously sick or dead internee back to the main camp.

> Just before landing, by some mechanical defect, the motor of our boat suddenly stopped. The boat stopped in its progress and then slowly, by the force of the current, began to move back. The pilot still managed to throw a rope so that its other end fell in the middle of the group of internees, who sat on the landing raft and watched. I shouted at them to grab their end of the rope and pull us to shore. But they appeared in no mood to do so. They did not move a finger, just looked at the rope, moving slowly back as well, and some of them could even be heard laughing as our boat was carried away!

As in Flaubert's *Sentimental Education*, like the three paving stones in the middle of the Paris roadway, it might signal the beginnings of a barricade. But the motor of the boat was repaired, and the doctor reached the camp only slightly delayed. No punishment is mentioned, as there was no law against what the internees did. Except that, as Dr. Schoonheyt concluded his story, "While some supplies were being carried on shore, we set up a big banquet-table on the deck of the boat and, in full view of the internees, had a good *ijsttafel* feast, rice, fish, and meat, desert and coffee."[92]

What was happening in Tanah Tinggi certainly made a bourgeois "shake his head at excess."[93] The people of Tanah Tinggi were like the people in the main camp, only more so. In the Boven Digoel official report for the second quarter of 1935, another visitor described his inspection of Tanah Tinggi. During a walk through the camp he saw "a fine bunch of bananas hanging from a tree." "How much does it cost?" the official asked an internee who happened to work nearby in a garden. The internee answered the official and the official reported it: "Here we own and sell nothing. If you wish the bananas, just pick them from the tree."[94]

There was no revolution, however some might see it coming. Early in 1943, Charles O. van der Plas, the high official of the Dutch Indies government, in Australia in exile by this time already, visited Boven Digoel, preparing the camp evacuation ahead of the advancing Japanese. The Tanah Tinggi inhabitants, van der Plas wrote as he found them, are "extremely dangerous psychopaths," "professional criminals," "antisocial people," and "their knowledge of communism is muddled." "The people of Tanah Tinggi," van der Plas went on, "are lunatics, and they all live in barricaded houses, armed with wooden spears."[95] He also noted that, while the people of the main camp were ready to be evacuated to Australia, several of the Tanah Tinggi people did not want to go.

....

The "Little Fortress" in Theresienstadt, or "Fortress B," to some extent was like Tanah Tinggi in Boven Digoel. It was built at the same time as the main garrison, only a little apart from the main fortress and town, as a part of it. But almost instantly it came to be used as a prison. Most famously, Gavrilo Princip, the assassin of Archduke Ferdinand, "whose seven bullets started the Great War," was incarcerated and he died there.

The Gestapo, the Nazi secret state police, began to put political prisoners in the Little Fortress after March 1939, when German armies occupied Czechoslovakia. The prisoners in the Little Fortress were not necessarily Jews. The Little Fortress was a prison for the enemies of Hitler, people of all nationalities and political convictions, the Communists, the officers of the prewar Czechoslovak army, the priests, and the sport and trade union leaders. The Little Fortress was a place of regular beatings, torture, and executions.

Mr. Austerlitz, the hero of W. G. Sebald's novel of the same name, spends most of his visit to Theresienstadt searching for his past life, in Theresienstadt's main camp. It is only after he returns from the visit that he comes upon some stunning photographs of a prison that makes him think about Theresienstadt again: "At the time of my first visit to the Bohemian ghetto, I could not bring myself to enter, [but] my true place of work should have been there, in the little fortress of Theresienstadt."[96]

The Little Fortress, or "little fortress" as Sebald wrote it, was "theoretically" a ten-minute walk from the main camp, across the bridge over the

Ohře River, on the highway from Theresienstadt to Prague. But "in fact" it was isolated even more than Tanah Tinggi. No internee from the main camp, or anybody else except the prisoners and the guards, by any secret path, could ever reach the place, except when taken there. It was then as bad thing as to be taken to Auschwitz, and worse, because it loomed "so close." Only imagined, it was felt in the main camp, more than Tanah Tinggi, as a place of madness, a place on the brink of belonging to life, or behind the cliff.

Though the Little Fortress could not be seen or heard from the main camp, the prisoners of the Little Fortress almost daily and at certain hours were led along the main camp walls. Their columns passed through the "Aryan Street," in fact, through the main camp, and directly under the windows of some barracks. The people in the main camp saw and heard the columns, and they knew what it meant, and even more what it was supposed to mean: "The Little Fortress was the feared Theresienstadt camp prison from which few came out alive."[97] What could the people do but close their windows?

Karel Poláček, at the time when he already knew that he was going to the camp but was still waiting for transport, wrote to his lover, Dora, who was also waiting, "I beg you," he wrote her in a letter on April 19, 1942, "talk to nobody and if you have to, talk low—make yourself into nothing."[98]

On March 6, 1943, he sent her another letter: "Don't let the fear come to you . . . don't go for a walk, nature is not worth it."[99] On March 15, 1942, Poláček, in a letter to Dora, quoted an entry from a dictionary: "*Lycantropy*: metamorphosis of a human into a wolf, when the wolf keeps both human reason and its savagery." And he added, "Don't be sad, this planet is not worth it (and currently it is covered with mucus)."[100] On April 12, 1943, Poláček wrote, "I'm training myself not to be curious and I've made some progress with it."[101]

In a Jewish legend of a pogrom in Prague, in the medieval times, the Messiah is moved at last to help the Jews and He enters the city. "Only the madman Tanchum recognized the Messiah."[102] "Milena is right," Kafka wrote in his diary on January 18, 1922, about Milena Jesenská, his Czech lover, "fear means unhappiness but it does not follow from this that courage means happiness. . . . Not courage then," Kafka concluded, "but fearlessness with its calm, open eye and stoical resolution."[103]

As in Boven Digoel, there was a disproportionately large number of "insane" or "mad" people in the Theresienstadt camp, at least other internees as well as the guards called them thus. As in Boven Digoel, reading the documents and listening to the testimonies, there is often a strong sense that these people were the burden, meaning the core and the meaning of the camp.

Professor Emil Utitz, soon after the war, wrote a book-length study on Theresienstadt camp psychology. He listed several "typical cases." In the camp's "house for the mentally sick," for instance, "there was a patient," Utitz wrote, "suffering from a delusion of grandeur. He imagined himself to be a member of the camp's Jewish Council of the Elders, and as such he demanded unconditional obedience from all the doctors, staff, and other patients. He behaved like a prince, or like he thought a prince might behave."[104]

Adler appended to his Theresienstadt history a glossary of the words widely used in the camp, mostly German, whether the internee or the guard was a native German, Czech, Dutch, or Danish speaker. One word stands out particularly in the glossary. "*Siech*," German for "ailing," "infirm," in the camp meant, wrote Adler, "what in other camps was called 'Musulman' or a 'weary Sheikh.'"[105] It was a word in a male form always, but a Siech could be a woman, a camp person, who slowed down as a reaction to the camp, and then, Adler wrote, "stopped moving," as it was interpreted by Adler and almost everybody in the camp, waiting for death.

Gathering all the forces of optimism in us, we might find some affinity between the Siech, plural *Siecher*, the mad, the "Musulmans," "weary Sheikhs," and the people in Tanah Tinggi who "stopped moving" "entirely gathering together," who, against the camp moving, stood still, became supernumerary, numerical sequence broken.

According to the Nazi laws enforced everywhere in occupied Europe and, of course, in Theresienstadt, "willful self-mutilation was punishable by death." One was seen as resisting by just slowing down or even stopping completely, by detaching oneself, and even by choosing one's own death. The choice, the Nazi reasoned, and correctly it had often seemed, might allow one to get off. In a novel by Hans Fallada about Nazi Germany, written an uncomfortably short time after the war, a German man, a worker, in the greatest distress, on the brink of crashing, or perhaps resisting, and certainly yearning to get himself out of everything, is about to harm himself, to place his hand under an electric saw in a factory where he is working. At the last moment, he recalled the Nazi law and "his hand recoiled."[106]

One was strictly forbidden to touch one's body, but, for sure, one was supposed, recalling Kafka's wonderful apparatus, to let oneself be engraved.

"How could there even be suicides when everyone is happy?" a visitor exclaims, shown around Étienne Cabet's nineteenth-century Icaria. A citizen of Icaria agrees about the happiness and explains: "Violent passions hardly exist anymore, nor, consequently, do madmen."[107] In Thomas More's "first" *Utopia*, "anyone who takes his life without the approval of the priests and the senate is considered unworthy of either burial or cremation, and his body is cast into a swamp, unmarked, and dishonored."[108]

"As there were regulations of births," Adler wrote about Theresienstadt, "so there were regulations about deaths and suicides."[109] According to Ruth Bondy, "Compared with the rate among the general population . . . the number of suicides and suicide attempts were high, but, considering the level of personal distress, the figures were very low: out of 120,000 people who arrived at the ghetto in the first two years, only 768 tried to commit suicide, and only 246 succeeded."[110]

....

Some internees in both camps believed there was a God, and God's will, and, therefore, that some gates, to heaven, in the last instance, still could be opened.

The internees, generally with the authorities' consent and sometimes help, built several mosques in Boven Digoel. There also, as well, a Catholic and a Protestant church were built. Contrary to the postwar myths and loose memories to the contrary, there was never a total ban on either private or public prayer in Theresienstadt. Ruth Bondy described how "one after another synagogue opened up in the various barracks, the attics, the office rooms, and the performance halls."[111]

Theresienstadt was made by the Nazis as a camp for the Jews, and the camp was one of the Nazi policies to make Jews into "Jews by race." There were Jews in the camp, Jews by Nazi definition of "blood." People, in fact, of many religions as well as secular people were concentrated in the camp. There were numerous Roman Catholics in the camp, and "Catholic services were regularly held in the ghetto (not in the church on the main square, which was closed). There were Protestants among the Jews in Theresienstadt, and they held services of their own."[112]

Rabbi Unger preached to the Jews in the Lecture Hall of the Theresienstadt Magdeburg Barracks. "The Jews from Hamburg had brought their own scrolls of the law, ark curtains, and prayer shawls from Hamburg," Jacob Jacobson recalled. "Public Seder celebrations," he wrote, too, "were held, and they were well attended."[113] The Zionist feminist rabbi Regina preached in Theresienstadt, and with fewer restrictions by conservative Jews, it seemed, than she could ever have had in the place she came from, in prewar Berlin.[114]

Many Jewish families in Theresienstadt celebrated Christmas, whether or not only to please the Jewish children who were accustomed to the festivities in prewar Germany, Czechoslovakia, the Netherlands, and Denmark.[115]

On Sunday, December 24, 1944, Pavel Weiner wrote in his diary, "*Christmas Eve:* I think this will be the saddest Christmas Eve in my life."[116]

Still, Adler wrote, "one did not get an impression in Theresienstadt, that religious life was in the foreground."[117] "Religious life," he wrote, "played a relatively small role. The majority of the younger internees had only a loose connection to religion."[118] The camp did not become a holy place, not really. On Friday, May 5, 1944, Pavel Weiner wrote in his Theresienstadt diary, "I am scolded because I didn't have my hair cut. My mother says I look like a rabbi."[119]

"Don't think that all the boys born here are circumcised," Gonda Redlich lamented on May 4, 1944. "There is a child here who is several years old. The doctor recommended circumcision, but the parents wouldn't hear of it." "In general," Redlich added, "there are uncircumcised Jews, children of mixed marriages and 'modern Jews.' Their parents view ritual, especially circumcision, as barbaric."[120]

Of course, there were many who kept to or even "discovered" religion in the camp, but the gate was not opened. In Boven Digoel, internee Salim was one of the internees who left Islam and became Christian. Some Jews in Theresienstadt, assimilated to cultures in which their families had lived often for several generations, became Jews of faith in the camp. Rabbi Leo Baeck, in the Theresienstadt camp, finished his *Dieses Volk: Jüdische Existenz* [This People: Jewish Existence], a book of theology that became the most profound Jewish testament of the time.[121] Religion was allowed in the camps, and it became a part of the camps, not crashing through the wall and across the distance, however, but written on the wall, so to speak, projected on the screen, like desire for freedom, and in some cases like madness.

....

Emmanuel Levinas, at the very moment of the camps' emerging, in 1935, published his essay "On Escape." As he wrote later, "On Escape" was meant "to bear witness" "on the eve of great massacres." The world, this was the essay's core and burden, had reached the point when "consciousness of having no way out was tied to a determined anticipation of impossible new thoughts."[122]

"Nausea" is to Levinas in the essay the crucial word to describe "being and time" in that moment. "Nausea," Levinas wrote, "manifests the nothing."[123] It is "the manifestation of nothingness *as a return*," of "the nothing as the pure *fact of being*," of "the return of nothing into an unalterable binding presence."[124]

In the vertigo of return, facing the revolving gates, screens, mirrors, and receding horizons, in the Heideggerian "clearing," wrote Levinas, we are "revolted from the inside." This is a "revolting presence of ourselves to ourselves." This is "the nausea," the "impossibility of being what one is," and being "at the same time riveted to ourselves, enclosed in a tight circle that smothers."[125] "Only the nakedness of being in its plenitude and its utterly binding presence."[126] Of course, humans are still defined and moved by a "need." "But this need," Levinas concluded, "is not oriented toward the complete fulfillment of a limited being, toward satisfaction, but toward release and escape."[127]

When Levinas wrote his essay in 1935, Martin Heidegger was already a rector of the University of Freiburg and already speaking for Hitler. The first Nazi camps were already a fact and they were "working smoothly." Heidegger already accepted, and certainly taught, that the one gesture of freedom still left was to become a being "closed in on himself,"[128] Dasein, but only up to the wall. Levinas realized, in contrast, that he lived in a time of "hysterical bodies"—the individuals, the societies, the camps, and the worlds—that "cannot be unfolded or opened up."[129]

Reading Levinas, and Heidegger, and the camp testimonies, one is reminded again of the "tragicomic" (Dr. Schoonheyt's word) and yet epochal event on that ship to the Boven Digoel camp, when a couple of internees held a seasick soldier and helped him to vomit over the railing into the sea.[130]

SIXTEEN

Escape

Lilly Joss Reich, "Locals and Emigrants," Morocco, 1940.
With permission of the Wien Museum, Vienna.

Gonda Redlich reported a "funny occurrence." "A man died of sepsis in the camp, and a clerk of the Jewish burial society registered the cause of the death mistakenly [as a dark joke?], instead of *Sepsis* as *Skepsis* [skepticism]."[1]

Karl Marx, quoted by Walter Benjamin, said that every modern human being, really, lives in "a hostile dwelling."[2] "The picture of dissatisfaction," wrote Kafka about his world closer to the camps than Marx's, is "presented" as "everyone is perpetually lifting his feet to escape from the place on which he stands."[3]

The people caught in that modern kind of space, and the camps were the most exemplary and perhaps ultimate case of it, try to build "abstract barricades,"[4] try to arm themselves with "imperturbable patience," or they "submit."[5] In each case, to say with Jean-Jacques Rousseau, they might "play a tune by turning a handle."[6]

The people caught in that kind of space, till they resign, may try "to abandon those parts of self we can no longer sustain."[7] Of course, there is that "persistent sense of horizon" or of "the banal."[8] In a New York tenement-bloc quarter, in the late 1880s, after a "mother had thrown herself out of the window, and was carried up from the street dead," one of so many similar cases, Jacob Riis overheard a neighbor saying, "She was 'discouraged.'"[9]

As their ship moved slowly up the Digoel River to the camp, Salim recalled, the internees were "utterly depressed." "With the greatest difficulty, we even had to stop one of us so that he did not jump over the ship railing!"[10] Several Boven Digoel suicides were explained by the authorities and also "by the neighbors" as that the internee "could not bear anymore to see the degradation of the camp."[11] We live, Ernst Bloch wrote in *The Spirit of Utopia* at the same time, in "the interior, the exterior, and the superior"; "despair remains."[12]

The camp people were people of the book, and their despair, inevitably, was a "despair of language."[13] "I am reading *Na dnŭ*, 'On the Bottom,' now, by Gorky," wrote Karel Poláček to Dora just days before they took them both to Theresienstadt. "From this I quote, and write this into my diary, too." They decided, a letter or two earlier, to write a diary together, in case, probably, something happened to one of them only. This is what Poláček instructed Dora to write down from Gorky:

ZATIN: Words—There is yet one word: transcendental.

BUBNOV: What does it mean?

ZATIN: I do not know—I forgot—

BUBNOV: So why do you say it?

ZATIN: Oh—I am fed up with our common words, my dear! With each of them. I have heard each one at least thousand times.[14]

Louis-Ferdinand Céline, in his *Journey to the End of the Night*, recalled, "My father talked to himself in corners. He was afraid of being carried away."[15] "It haunts us," Bloch wrote, "this halfness," "the anguish of finitude," the "nothingness from out of lived anguish, a modality of the psyche leading further than did negation."[16]

The world of the 1930s and the camps perhaps ultimately became not a place for anyone to allow oneself to be vulnerable, and, wrote Bloch, "only a vulnerable person can love his neighbor."[17] The world, and camps perhaps ultimately and perhaps as a premonition, became a space where one could not risk one's essence, or body, being raptured. Rapture being, Bloch wrote, a "signification, as the one-for-the-other."[18]

Bloch called these moments of rapture, moments of "astonishment" and "glimmering."[19] Levinas called them moments of "being's coming to itself."[20] For Philippe Nemo, these were moments of "the mad manifestation of the Law's absence."[21] Heinrich Heine, as poets can, said it perhaps best: "If we go through history, Madame, we find that all great men have been obliged to run away once in their lives."[22]

"I could never grow reconciled to that life," Dostoyevsky wrote about himself and his Siberian camp.[23] He was there, one of his co-internees remembered, "like a captured wolf."[24] Kafka, a Jew caught in Prague, is said to have compared himself to a *kavka*, a "jackdaw" (the name of one of his ancestors had evidently been transcribed by mistake as *"Kafka"*). *Kavka*, the jackdaw, Kafka is said to point to a little gray bird that artisans in Prague liked to keep at the curb in front of their shops. They clipped the bird's wings and *kavka* hopped on the sidewalk in front of the shop to entertain the passersby.[25] (One cannot but think about Klee's and Benjamin's *Angelus Novus*. The angel's wings do not look good for flying either.)

"It is hard to leave the harbor and to venture into the limitless," wrote Hermann Broch.[26] In order to escape, Broch added, "We must lose ourselves in the darkness of the invisible."[27] To attempt an escape, wrote Dostoyevsky, meant to play with fate. "The gamblers," he wrote, "usually played very simple games. They were all games of chance."[28]

Schanzen [walls], in German and in Theresienstadt, also meant "chances." Hans Günther Adler wrote about one such game of chance designed and played in the camp. He quotes the instructions:

1. *Schleuse* (Sluice Gate)—throw dice twice . . .
2. Uncle in bakery—jump forward to 19 . . .
3. Uncle in the Council of the Elders—jump forward to 15 . . .
12. God's help—jump forward to 26 . . .
35. Latrine occupied—pass twice . . .
50. *Sow* (Hebrew for "the end").[29]

....

In Boven Digoel "Register of the Internees," filed under no. 101, internee Achmat bin Hoesin of Camp Section A, is listed: "Ran two times already. The first time, in 1932, he turned and came back. The second time, he perished?"[30] (Note the question mark.)

The military barracks in Boven Digoel, *tangsi* [garrison] "were encircled with barbed wire and there was a watch post at each of the four corners."[31] Not so the camp itself. On this, Dr. Schoonheyt wrote, "We can rest assured that Boven Digoel as it is at present fully satisfies conditions for an internment camp, based on the following: 1. excellent layout, 2. bearable climate, 3. satisfactory state of health in the camp, 4. difficulty of an escape, 5. scarce and backward Papua population which is still immune to communist and nationalist propaganda."[32]

Still, all measures were taken to make escapes truly impossible. To the people in Tanah Tinggi, no fishing boats were allowed. In the main camp, boats had been allowed, but under conditions and strict daily control. Government rations, in the main camp, were distributed twice a week, and each internee and all family members had to present themselves at each of the "roll calls," appels, a good way to check that everyone was still in the camp. Malaria pills were distributed in the same way, during additional appels. But, above this, there was the jungle. No efforts were made by the busy camp authorities to cut paths into the forest or, the same thing, along the river.[33]

There was no wall, not even a fence around the camp. One could just step into the jungle, and walk deeper into the jungle. "Tracking the escapees in this immense landscape," a camp administrator reported in 1930, "is like looking for a needle in a haystack. . . . Nonetheless, *pour acquit de curiosité* [to satisfy one's curiosity]," the official added for some reason in French, "search patrols are being sent out."[34]

There are statistics and diagrams, of course. In January 1929, for instance, which was less than two years into the camp's existence, the total number of escape *attempts* in the quite small camp was reported as sixty-one. Some of those who had attempted an escape had been returned by one of Papua tribes around Boven Digoel in exchange for rewards, usually in the form of money, tobacco, and iron tools. Others, who got so far as across the Dutch Indies border, had been returned by the British authorities from the British Thursday Islands between New Guinea and Australia, or from the British, eastern half of New Guinea.

There existed an international-law treaty between the two imperial powers, and the escapees, of course, did not have visas. All the rest of the escapees from Boven Digoel in this period, according to the documents, after wandering in the jungle for days and sometimes weeks, either perished by exhaustion, illness, Papuans, or wild animals, or they turned back and returned to the camp by their own remaining strength.[35]

Boven Digoel, the camp and the clearing, was an act of colonialism, expansion of the empire, and invasion of the modern. "The settler," in the general colonial narrative, "is portrayed as surrounded by 'natives,' inverting... the role of aggressor so that colonialism is made to look like self-defense."[36]

In Boven Digoel, the guards and the internees were the settlers, too. "On the whole," ex-internee Joesoef Mawengkang wrote after the war, "the Kaja-Kaja people feared the internees because they saw them walking around the camp with machetes and axes. Besides, the Kaja-Kaja believed that the military in Boven Digoel were there in the camp to ensure the safety of the internees, and this was why the Kaja-Kaja did not dare to touch us when we were in the camp."[37] The camp authorities, on their side, did not make a secret of the fact that the people of the forest are dangerous folk. On the contrary, one or another official or soldier might quip where the internees could hear them, "The meat of the internees is thought tastier than the meat of most other animals." Some of the internees, and all more or less subconsciously, accepted this as "the truth."[38] To escape through the jungle would mean to cross the marshes where one can easily drown, and find a way across at least one, but more likely several, rivers, Digoel, Fly, Mandobo, Kaoh, and Mayu, all treacherous and full of crocodiles.[39]

The idea of escape surrounded Boven Digoel like the jungle, the horizon, the truth, and the banal. The people, as long as they lived in the camp, some more and some less, all were being toward-the-escape. But, as in Heidegger's morale that nauseated Levinas, only the mad really attempted to crush into, or cross, the line.

WEDNESDAY, MAY 21, 1936 ... NIGHT ... 2:10 ... Internee Hardjo is not at home. According to the explanation given to the police agent by internees Hadji Adenan and Soegiri, Hardjo's neighbors, he has been on the river already for two days, fishing. He has not yet returned.[40]

Internee Hardjo did return, and he brought fish.

The real attempts at escape did not match the suspicion of guards watching for breakouts, as well as the temptation of the internees watching for a chance, both the fantasies of escape. There is a novel, a thriller, a fable, a fantasy, a utopia written by a Boven Digoel internee most probably, after he was released, and while the camp was still in existence:

> There were five men who decided to run. Each of them carried provisions for the journey. Some carried 50 kg and others only 25 kg. Pandoe, who was still weak after a recent illness, carried 15 kg.... At his belt, each of them had a machete or an ax. Each carried a blanket, and wore a shirt, a pair of trousers, and a pair of shoes. In their bags there was rice, salt fish, chili pepper, matches, and tobacco. Each of them also carried a pocket flashlight *Eveready*, a plate, and a coffee cup. Quinine pills, of course, could not be left behind, five bottles of them.... Pandoe carried no rice or fish, only a cardboard of *Cabin* biscuits.[41]

"Some comrades," wrote internee Mas Marco in a letter from the camp, "ran twice, Goesti Djohan Idroes, for instance, originally from Borneo."[42] "Thomas Najoan, our Jungle Pimpernel," Salim wrote, invoking again the French legend about disguise and escape, "tried to escape three times.[43] The report by governor Hillen on his visit to Boven Digoel in the summer of 1930 contains a mention of this Thomas Najoan. Hillen described an interrogation of the "well-known Najoan," then in Tanah Tinggi, the tougher camp, after his first capture. "When I asked him," Hillen wrote, "whether he might run again, he answered me with complete calm, 'Perhaps, if I would feel like it.'" "This person," Hillen commented (we should say "shaking his head at excess"), "used to have several good professional jobs, saw a great number of places in the Indies, and had even visited the Netherlands. Now this! It suggests an abnormal psyche."[44]

Najoan "felt like that" and ran again, twice, in fact, after he met governor Hillen. The second time he was brought back from the Thursday Islands. The third time he attempted to escape during the last months of the camps, in 1941. "As far as I know," Salim wrote, "this time he went alone!... We heard nothing more about him." "Perhaps" Salim guessed, "his dried skull hangs in one of the Papua tribe houses."[45]

On March 13, 1930, a Sumatra paper, *Pewarta Deli* [The Deli Reporter], published an editorial about Boven Digoel escapees, or rather, about those who had tried. The paper wondered what despair might be pushing the camp people. "These people," the editorial opined, "rather than remain in the camp, are willing to die."[46]

Or, to say it again, they were mad. In a Boven Digoel "Register of Internees Not Sound in their Mind (Mentally Abnormal)," dated March 1, 1932, "Raden Amat, invalid, originally from Semarang [Central Java], interned since March 28, 1927, was seen, disappearing into the jungle, and loudly crying. A party of people, police and internees, was sent to search for him, and he was found, still at the edge, but already in the jungle, south of camp section A." It is not clear from the record whether Raden Amat was found alive or dead. In the same file, internee Soekarman, also originally from Semarang, "in the camp since November 15, 1928, became insane sometime around the middle of 1931. Twice he disappeared into the jungle, and he was also heard crying."[47]

The author of the novel about Pandoe and his friends trying to escape included his own comment on the story: "Whoever decides to run must have the courage to die. Whoever thinks it is enough merely to live, should not attempt to run." Indeed, the Pandoe story ends in what might be madness, but what also might be a sharp edge of reason: "Pandoe appeared to want to die, but he did not want it to happen by his own hand."[48]

The ideas of resistance, and of escape, suicide, madness, and utopia, came closer to each other in the camps than any time before and anywhere else. These ideas, so inherently diverse throughout modern history, merged into one idea in the camps. But "ideas" is perhaps not the best word. Perhaps "moments" is better, or even "bursts," of despair, or even laughter "as a wink, impertinent, outrageous, insane."[49] When Thomas Najoan answered governor Hillen, it was, to say with Gilles Deleuze, "untimely," and "never reducible to the political-historical element."[50]

Barthes wrote about the same moment of escape or perhaps resistance, as about a "possibility that language does not exist, does not take place." There was, according to Barthes, something exhilarating, even freedom perhaps, in "'becoming mute' like a vowel."[51] However, Barthes himself did not attempt to get there. He knew, or he believed to know, that "terrorism doesn't talk" and achieves nothing in this way except giving an "impression of madness, of horror."[52] To attempt an escape, or even to think about an escape, ultimately in the camps, implied that one was willing to be "exempt from meaning."[53] "And where, I ask you," Céline wrote, "can a man escape to, when he hasn't enough madness left inside him?"[54]

This might be what both Heidegger and Levinas in this case called *"Absturz* [the plunge]."[55] A moment that might achieve "freeing the horizon," but that is, at the same time, "toward death," yes, admittedly, perhaps, "freedom toward death."[56] Dostoyevsky was of the same opinion, recalling his camp. Thinking of escape, he wrote, was "a mournful desire for an abrupt display of personality."[57] Immanuel Kant called this moment, of "radical Evil," according to Georges Bataille, "that *evil* committed against our own interest, demanded by an imperious desire for freedom."[58] One thinks of the Saminists, or Oeripists, of Boven Digoel again. Their desire for freedom did not exclude a freedom in death.

In the "General Regulations for Jewish Self-Government," issued in Theresienstadt on January 5, 1943, by the camp commandant SS-Hauptsturmführer Dr. Seidl, paragraph 10 states, "Leaving the ghetto without an authorization is considered an attempt at escape. The gendarmerie has an order immediately to fire."[59]

Adler attempted to compile a list of escape attempts throughout the duration of the camp. He found thirty-one cases of people who were released for various and often unclear reasons, "with the SS authorization."[60] As for the escapes, "in all, only thirty-three persons, out of the more than 140,000 internees who have passed through Theresienstadt, succeeded in running away."[61]

One term for the escapees from Theresienstadt, not unlike in the Boven Digoel camp, was "deserters."[62] Virtually all of the extremely few attempts at escape and of the even fewer successful escapes, Adler noted, "were undertaken by [strong and] young Czech Jews."[63]

The only "detailed" and "factual" description of an escape, from the moment of setting out, through crossing the line, to being elsewhere, off the camp, as far as I know, comes from two testimonies, both years after the war. Both of these stories are spectacular, and both have no ending. We are told how the escapee got "up the wall," "down the wall and away," and away, into an empty countryside, into empty mountains, at a greater and increasing distance from the camp. The distancing is crucial, and it is the substance of these escapes.

"I decided to climb the fortress walls at night," Evžen Hilar told a conference about the history of the camp in 1965, how he climbed the wall and how he ran: "How high are the ramparts? How far will the rope reach? . . .

If only [the ss man] Heindl would not take his dog for his usual walk on the ramparts.... In the distance, the clock of the Czech Litoměřice church strikes midnight." "I looked for a shelter in Czech farms abandoned by evacuated farmers," Hilar said. He ran to "neutral Slovakia," the eastern part of former Czechoslovakia, which means he ran a distance of four hundred kilometers or so. He ran "to the Orava region," to the north of Slovakia, and then still more to the east, to the Slovak Low Tatras mountains. Finally, "to its highest peak, Rozsutec." There, Evžen Hilar's story ends (the story was told in 1965 in Socialist Czechoslovakia): "Captain Ivan, the first Russian fraternal kiss on both cheeks."[64]

Otto Kuhn was the second former Theresienstadt internee who, to the same conference, gave a description of his successful escape. "We made our escape," Otto Kuhn said, "from the Podmokly Barracks on the first summer day, on June 21, 1943, at about midnight." "We climbed over the wooden fence and got into the moat under the walls. None of the guards... noticed anything.... We took hearty leave of each other, wished ourselves all the best and good luck, and said, 'Till we meet again, after the war U Fleků.'" U Fleků was the good soldier Švejk's famous watering hole in Jaroslav Hašek's novel and in Prague. It was a common saying among the Prague inhabitants especially, when people were making *as if* they surely would meet again, "After the war at six U Fleků."

"Alas," Otto Kuhn ended his story: "we never met again," "I was the only one of the four to get out in one piece.... I was hiding in dens and in the ditches in the woods... looking for fruits and berries in the forest.... During the night I walked toward the south then east.... I reached the Hostýnské Mountains [in Moravia, between Bohemia and Slovakia]."[65]

Escapes, or rather attempts at escapes, led to the only two public executions in the history of the Theresienstadt camp. "For the rest of the war no more executions took place within the ghetto."[66] "On April 9, 1943," Adler wrote, "we all were forbidden to leave the barracks and the electric lights in the barracks were switched off as a punishment for another attempt to escape the camp."[67] On Friday, April 21, 1944, Pavel Weiner wrote, "As I wake up, the first thing in the morning I hear is the news of the disappearance of two boys from the ghetto. They are from our school."[68] On Tuesday, July 18, 1944, Pavel came back to the event: "Presumably, Sklárek, one of the escapees, had his hair dyed by the barber Lavecký. The barber was arrested and beaten."[69]

When one was able to glance over the Theresienstadt camp walls, one could see Czech landscape toward the blue low hills, orchards, little groves, villages, and single farms, the town of Litoměřice with its spires. Escape did not look impossible. However, what might appear to be orchards, forests, villages, hills, and the town was a Heideggerian horizon that "could be apprehended only by distancing."

"Why did so few prisoners take this risk?" Zdeněk Lederer, a former internee, asked. One reason why, Lederer answered himself, was a blurred line dividing the camp and the world. The camp was located in the world of the camps, and one is reminded again of Céline's "And where, I ask you, can a man escape to?"[70] The situation of Jews after they were deported to Theresienstadt, Lederer wrote, "was different only in degree from their position before their deportation. Their life had been insecure, they had been outcasts from the beginning of the German occupation, and" for the Czech Jews namely, who were the majority in the camp, "their destination, Theresienstadt, was after all in Bohemia and not very far from Prague."[71]

Besides, the sweet Czech landscape, the orchards, fields, towns, and villages surrounding Theresienstadt, was not so different from the jungle around Boven Digoel, when one thought of real touching.

Anti-Semitism, according to general agreement, was much less rampant in Masaryk's Czechoslovakia than in most of the rest of the central Europe. The Czechs living around Theresienstadt would not, with few exceptions, report a Jewish escapee, exchange him, so to speak, "for money or an iron ax." But neither would they easily offer to help. The Czechs living around Theresienstadt, throughout the landscape, and up to Prague, my uncles and aunts, my parents, were not, with few exceptions, like the wild Papua tribes. But they, too, now lived in a large, European camp suburb. And the punishment for helping a Jew, if found out, was death.

"Do you understand, sir, do you understand what it means when you have absolutely nowhere to turn?" the desperate Marmeladov, at the end of his ways, in Dostoyevsky's *Crime and Punishment*, asks people barely listening in the Saint Petersburg tavern.[72] Elena Makarova mentioned a girl in Friedl Dicker-Brandeis's art class in the Theresienstadt camp. She "drew a house in the middle of the picture. The path stopped short before the house and didn't reach it."[73]

....

Camps became the energy of the world, the "electric" of the world, as Jules Michelet might say using his new nineteenth-century vocabulary.[74] Not any more Benjamin's and Baudelaire's Paris as a pointer to the future. Through the camps, the world in its fullness, to use Heidegger's exalted twentieth-century phrase, "came forth into being"—through the camps, the camp fashion, sound, light, and geometry, and through the camp people's madness, resignation, and insistence on, thinking at least of, an escape.

Even those who, in the world of the camps, now, were not locked in the camps but lived in the camps' suburbs, who touched upon the camps only lightly, tangentially, became the people of the camps and, from the moment of touching, they thought of an escape. If they insisted, they were punished in the manner of the camps. If they kept on insisting, they were scattered. Being scattered, they marked, stigmatized, tagged, and mapped the world, made it meaningful or madly without a meaning, for themselves and, indeed, for us.

Dr. Schoonheyt, even when after 1935 not any more physically in camp, being touched by the camp once, was one of the persons to be of the camp forever.

When Dr. Schoonheyt retired from Boven Digoel after his term of duty ended, he became the chief medical officer of Tanjung Priok, the harbor in Batavia. He wrote a memoir of Boven Digoel, and the book became a bestseller in the Indies and in the Netherlands as well. The doctor became a celebrity and soon was on a lecture circuit, talking about the camp both in the Indies and in the Netherlands. Almost as soon as that, he became involved with the National-Socialist Bond, the NSB, a proto-fascist and eventually Nazi, Indies, and Dutch party and movement.[75]

As World War II broke out in Europe in the fall of 1939 and, on May 10, 1940, Germany invaded the Netherlands, the Dutch-Indies authorities, expecting an imminent Japanese invasion, arrested the NSB leaders and sympathizers as a potential fifth column, and concentrated them in newly opened camps. Dr. Schoonheyt was prominently among them.

Boven Digoel, evidently never absent from the doctor's mind, now came back in full. "Initially," Dr. Schoonheyt wrote in his autobiography after the war, coauthored with Anthony van Kampen, "the NSB people were designated 'traitors' by the government. After a short time, as no crime was proved to them, they began to call us 'dangerous to the state.'"[76]

This was the same label and the same (lack of) judicial process that the Communist rebels of 1926 and 1927 got, and it was not lost on Dr. Schoonheyt. "Next step, we were classified as 'potentially dangerous,'" and the next step still, "we became 'the embittered.'"[77] A few, a burden and a core among the NSB-ers in the camp, those truly resentful, "persisting," were indeed called *"onverzoenlijke"* [recalcitrant], the same term that had been used for the Tanah Tinggi people. Dr. Schoonheyt, now, was one of the recalcitrants.[78]

The NSB-ers, Dr. Schoonheyt, too, were sent to the camp on the basis of Articles 20 and 37 of the Indies Staat van Oorlog en Beleg, SOB [State of War and Siege].[79] These articles were the same on the basis of which the rebels without trial, back in 1926 and in all the years thereafter, were being sent to Boven Digoel.[80] "Now, I could clearly see," Dr. Schoonheyt recalled after the war, "as I too became a victim of the government psychosis. I thought back to Boven Digoel, and I understood how the internees might have felt back then."[81]

Dr. Schoonheyt was taken to the Tjipinang prison in Batavia first (Soetan Sjahrir, for instance, had waited there for his transport to Boven Digoel a few years ago).[82] From Tjipinang, with the others, Dr. Schoonheyt was shipped to Onrust Island, just off Batavia. In the words of Dr. Schoonheyt's autobiography, it was "an improvised Netherlands concentration camp."[83] On Onrust Island, Dr. Schoonheyt even noted, however only in passing, "there were also Jews in the camp."[84] These were the Jews defined as German nationals caught by the war in the Indies and, "as Germans," considered the enemies of the Dutch.

As a man of the camp now, and not merely tangentially, Dr. Schoonheyt, as recalcitrant, thought of "nothing but escape." "Run!" he summarized his thoughts at the moment. And like a true camp man, he asked immediately, "But where?" as if he were quoting Céline or Lederer or Marmeladov. "One moment," he recalled after the war, "an idea came to me, to make use of the Japanese ship [it was still before the Pacific war started] that was just anchored in the harbor only a few hundred meters from our camp."[85]

Then Dr. Schoonheyt and the others of the NSB were transported to another camp, in Ngawi, East Java. In September 1942, a liberal and antifascist Dutch weekly in Bandung, West Java, *Kritiek en Opbouw* [Criticism and Structure], wondered "whether the misbehaved NSB-ers, who are now in the Ngawi camp, should not be sent to Boven Digoel."[86]

Dr. Schoonheyt in fact thought about the same. "I wrote a letter asking the governor-general to send me with my wife and daughter to Boven Digoel. There, at least, we could stay together as a family, and not behind a barbed wire. The answer came quickly, and it was negative. Even Boven Digoel was too good for me! Government would not favor me with Boven Digoel!"[87]

Then came still another "concentration camp," Schoonheyt uses the term again, in Ambarawa, Central Java. "We slept on straw matrasses on the ground and were merely given mosquito nets." It was like Salim in Boven

Digoel speaking: "The nets were in orange, white, and blue colors," wrote the doctor. "A remarkable experience," he added, "to be sheltered from the mosquitoes by the imperial colors."[88]

After other few months, Dr. Schoonheyt and most of the others of the NSB were put on a ship that sailed—to where they were not told. It was in the opposite direction from Boven Digoel, this they knew instantly. The ship sailed westward, but also to the very end of the world and the (still surviving) Dutch empire. On the ship, Dr. Schoonheyt recalled, "Suddenly it has dawned upon me, what a barbaric system."[89]

After weeks on the ocean, they arrived at Suriname, the Dutch West Indies, South America—again, as if the world of the camps had to present itself in its fullness and, indeed, global unity. Dr. Schoonheyt and the other NSB-ers were taken to where another "concentration camp" was made ready for them, fifty kilometers south of Paramaribo, at a spot on the Suriname River called "Joodse Savannah," "the Jewish Savannah."

There were no Jews there anymore. But, as Dr. Schoonheyt and the others arrived, they found a large number of Jewish gravestones, some overturned, most of the place covered by the wild vegetation that, in order to build the camp, "had to be cut and cleared."[90] This was a spot where, "running away from the fifteenth-century persecution in Spain and Portugal, some Jews escaped and found a refuge."[91] They built a Jewish community there, and lived in Joodse Savannah for more than the next three centuries. (A beautiful, small, wood-carved seventeenth-century synagogue of the Joodse Savannah was recently taken apart, shipped to Jerusalem, and restored in the Israel Museum.)

On November 4, 1942, Dr. Schoonheyt attempted to escape. His attempt was madness, and the story of it, as he told it himself, reads like a Boven Digoel novel written by an ex-internee. "Our provisions consisted of some crusts of hard and stale bread. Because of our unfamiliarity with the terrain and lack of experience with bushwhacking, as we found later, we walked in circles through the jungle that surrounded the camp, and never got further than a few kilometers from the camp."

"At one moment," Dr. Schoonheyt writes—now a reader expects a Papuan to appear but he gets an Indian—"we arrived at the edge of a small field of an Indian, where he grew some cassava and a few pineapples. The roosters cried."[92]

Anxious about the Indian, they slept that night at the edge of the field but in the jungle. In the morning one of the group cut himself on a sharp leaf and was bleeding badly. "In no time, we learned later, the Indian, his name was Paulus, discovered the tracks of blood." "He came upon us." "The prize on our heads," Dr. Schoonheyt noted, "was ƒ100, plus a hunting rifle."[93]

Like most attempts at escapes from Boven Digoel or from Theresienstadt, the attempt at escape by Dr. Schoonheyt from the Jewish Savannah failed. Like the other camp people, running, they moved in circles and never, except in dreams or as a myth, got far from the camp. Through their running, their horizon only became more enlightened and more distant. The camps became more camps.

Dr. Schoonheyt and the other escapee were brought back to the camp, and they were kept there beyond the end of the war, until 1946 in fact. Many of the remaining months and years in the camp, Dr. Schoonheyt recalled, the best moments of it, he spent in wandering as far as they were allowed to go, to the banks of the Suriname River. "For me," he recalled, "the late afternoons especially, just before a signal was given that we had to go back to the barracks, were the most beautiful hours of the day." "These were the loveliest moments. I had found a quiet spot on the river. I sat there and followed the stream with my eyes. There were so many amazing sunsets that I often got in a state of ecstasy and wondered: 'Is this river Suriname or is this river Digoel?'"[94]

The Boven Digoel first commander, Captain L. Th. Becking, like Dr. Schoonheyt, became active in the NSB after he retired from the camp.[95] Like Dr. Schoonheyt, he was arrested, passed through several camps in the Indies, and was also interned in the Jewish Savannah. There, he got sick and, in spite of Dr. Schoonheyt's best attempts (he was allowed to care for his cointernee as a physician), Captain Becking died in the Paramaribo hospital still as a prisoner of the camp.[96]

Dr. Marcus van Blankenstein, the distinguished Dutch journalist who reported on the Bolshevik Revolution and peace conferences after World War I, and who visited Boven Digoel in 1928 and wrote a series of articles about Boven Digoel that made the camp well known throughout the Indies and the Netherlands, also touched the camp and the camp touched him, forever. Besides, van Blankestein was a Jew.

After his Boven Digoel "episode," van Blankenstein focused on Germany. He remained a prominent journalist. In August 1933, eight months after Hitler's coming to power, the German Embassy in the Netherlands announced that it was taking legal steps against van Blankenstein, namely because of his comments about the German president, General Hindenburg. This referred to van Blankestein's several articles published in the previous March and April accusing Hindenburg of the "mishandling of the German Jews." The German consul general in The Hague was quoted as referring to van Blankenstein as a "dirty Jew."[97]

A decade after witnessing Boven Digoel and writing also about the impossibility of escape, van Blankenstein was himself on the run. Three days after Germany invaded the Netherlands, on the morning of May 13, van Blankenstein ran, better to say biked, this was Holland, from his villa in Wassenaar to the British Embassy in The Hague, about fifteen kilometers away. With the British consul's help, he got to the Rotterdam harbor, where the British torpedo boat *Windsor* waited for refugees to take them to England.[98]

Safely in England, van Blankenstein became the chief editor of the Dutch exile magazine *Vrij Nederland* [The Free Netherlands].[99] In this paper, on August 15, 1942, he published one of the earliest reports about "the Jewish transports from Amsterdam to the East accelerating." He warned that if the rate was kept at the present speed, "by June 1, 1943, not a single Jew will remain in the Netherlands."[100]

Germany did not invade England, and van Blankenstein never went to a Nazi camp. It might be said that he escaped. Or that he survived on the periphery of the camps.

The older brother of van Blankenstein, Philip, worked until the outbreak of the war as a radiologist in a Jewish hospital in Rotterdam. He did not escape. In 1940, he was arrested and taken first to Westerbork and then to Theresienstadt. "Shortly afterward, he was sent on a transport to Auschwitz and as far as it is known, on October 15, 1944, he died in a gas chamber." On August 3, 1943, van Blankenstein's sister, Hanna, with her husband, Juda Souget, and their daughter Judith made the same journey, and they also perished. Hanna and Juda's other daughter, Jet, also died in Auschwitz on September 17, 1943. The youngest brother of Marcus van Blankenstein, Louis, managed to run before the Nazis invaded the Netherlands, and he got to the Dutch Indies.

One might say "the periphery of the camps," but in fact the camps were expanding. Louis van Blankenstein escaped to the Indies, but, as the Japanese occupied the Indies in the spring of 1942, he was interned in one of the camps the Japanese established for the citizens of their enemy-nations.[101]

Parlindoengan Loebis was an Indonesian youth activist at the time of Boven Digoel, but either not radical or lucky enough not to be sent to the camp. On the contrary, in 1932, he was chosen and sent on a government scholarship to study medicine in the Netherlands.

"I left for the Netherlands, August 6, 1932," Loebis wrote in his memoirs after the war, "on a German ship of the Norddeutscher Lloyd."[102] "The ship moved forward at low speed, because according to the Versailles Peace Treaty, no German vessel was allowed to sail faster than ten knots per hour."[103] Speaking of touching, "Two days after we left Aden on the way to Europe," Loebis recalled, "in the middle of the Red Sea, our ship met and passed *Saarbücken*, a ship on which Dr. Mohammad Hatta traveled, from his studies in Holland on his way back to Indonesia."[104] Hatta, without knowing it yet, traveled back to Indonesia as a stopover, before being taken "further on to the east," to Boven Digoel.

After Loebis reached the Netherlands, he joined the Indonesian student organization in the Netherlands, Perhimpoenan Indonesia [the Indonesian Association]. "Not all Indonesian students in the Netherlands," Loebis wrote, "had the courage. They looked at us as *berkarakter mantap*." "*Berkarakter mantap*" is Malay or Indonesian for "unwavering" or "of steady character,"[105] but, were Loebis to end in Boven Digoel and not in the Netherlands, the word might be "recalcitrant." "The Indonesian Association," Loebis continued, during the late 1930s "came to be considered a Communist fellow traveler."[106]

On January 31, 1938, "celebrating the birth of a princess of the Royal House," Loebis signed a letter to the governor-general of the Indies in the name of the Indonesian Association. The letter congratulated the governor-general on the happy occasion that "warms the hearts of all Her Majesty's subjects," but used the opportunity to "remind His Excellency that many of Her Majesty's subjects still live under Article 37 of the penal code."[107] This was the code, of course, under which the Boven Digoel people (and also Dr. Schoonheyt a little later) were being sent to camps.

In October 1940, the Netherlands being already occupied by Germany for four months, Loebis passed his final examination and began a medical practice in Amsterdam. This step was made easy, he recalled, because the Jewish doctor who had held the practice before had left Loebis his office as he was transported to the camp.[108] Before Loebis himself had enough time to organize his new place, for suspected anti-German activity, he was arrested, too.

From prison, Loebis was sent to his first camp, in North Holland near Alkmaar. In this camp, he recalled later, especially members of the Dutch Communist Party and of other left-wing parties were interned.[109] But there was, as an internee, also, Mr. Charles Welter, a former Dutch minister of the colonies and before that a member of the Dutch Indies Volksraad [the People's Council], as well as of the Raad van Indië [the Council of the Indies].[110] By remote control, at least, Welter was also one of the Dutch top officials responsible for Boven Digoel.[111] "All we needed most at the moment," Loebis wrote about this first camp of his, "was *cabé* chilli pepper, and *sambal*."[112] Loebis says he somehow managed to get some, and Welter shared in it.

In October 1942, Loebis was transported to "Camp Heinkel," one section of the Buchenwald concentration camp complex—"near the town of Weimar," Loebis explained to his Indonesian readers.[113] "After delousing," Loebis wrote, "they gave us kind of striped pajamas and a beret with the same stripes, like the uniform the convicts wear in Sing-Sing." Their shoes were made of wood, and "soles were also from wood."[114]

"On the whole," Loebis wrote, "the German guards behaved correctly to me as a doctor."[115] "There was a tree in the middle of the camp," Loebis also notes, "they called it Goethe's Oak. Goethe was a German writer." Loebis met Soviet prisoners in the camp.[116] "They often said," he wrote, "'*Siskoyeno, toch crematorium*,'" which in Loebis's hearing and transcription of Russian should mean, "Nothing much matters, but crematorium."[117]

Loebis also met "*the Musulmans*," a kind of Theresienstadt "Siecher" or "weary Sheikhs," not cobelievers in Islam, as he assured his readers, but those who had resigned. "If there was an empty bed in the infirmary, some I managed to check in . . . these poor people. Once a German doctor came on inspection and told me: 'Loebis, this is not a mosque, this is an infirmary,' meaning, 'We do not accept Musulmans.'"[118]

Loebis saw the Jews in the camp, too. He had heard about "the killings," if even vaguely, as rumors. "As the doctors, we feared," he wrote, "that were the Germans [to] decide to kill the Jews in the camp, we would be ordered to do it."[119] "Jews wore yellow stars," Loebis wrote, and "their barracks were separated from ours. We could see them only when they passed by collecting the trash. As a rule, they were being sent away soon after they arrived, perhaps, people said, to other camps in Poland."[120]

"The top Communist functionaries," Loebis wrote he heard, "were interned in the camp, like Thälmann [the chairman of the German Communist Party, shot in Buchenwald, indeed, in 1944], and other important people like Masaryk [the former president of Czechoslovakia, who died in 1937], Dollfuss [the former chancellor of Austria, who died in 1934], and others."[121] "We often passed by the barracks where they were kept," Loebis wrote, "but we never saw them."[122]

"When I was in Buchenwald," wrote Loebis, "a German friend told me one day that a group of Dutch 'honor prisoners' was brought to the camp."[123] This rumor was true. Indeed, the Germans took a group of high-level

Dutch officials into custody after their army occupied the Netherlands in May 1940, and the group was brought to Buchenwald. These were "Buchenwald hostages," as they became to be known afterward, held as ransom for a possible exchange for the German officials interned by the Dutch government, especially in the colonies.

This was to remain a "secret agreement," as is clear, for instance, from an exchange between the German offices in The Hague and in Berlin in August 1942.[124] In addition to three former Dutch cabinet ministers, there were seventeen former members of the Dutch parliament in the group, nine former mayors, ten aldermen of city councils, the secretary of a provincial government, and a number of members of regional councils.[125] An important, if not crucial, segment of the group had been in the past connected with the Indies and therefore directly or indirectly, *tangentially*, with Boven Digoel.

For the Dutch "Buchenwald hostages," as Boven Digoel and Theresienstadt for the others, the camp was not Auschwitz. As far as I know, all Buchenwald hostages survived the camp except one, Dr. ter Haar, a professor at the Batavia Law School in the Indies. He died in Buchenwald.[126]

Soccer was not played in Buchenwald, and neither was music. After a short while, however, the group was moved to De Ruwenberg, in the Netherlands, still a camp, but a better place. Here, indeed, soccer appears in the documents, including scores: "Press against Parliament, 1–3," "Lawyers against Mayors . . . Professors against *Dominees* [ministers of the Dutch Reformed Church]."

This might appear as a little Indies in Nazi-occupied Europe. The names, without which neither the Indies nor Boven Digoel could be imagined, were on the list of the De Ruwenberg internees: "Savornin Lohman in the goal, Logemann as a back, the fast-footed Geyl with Boeke as a forward."[127] They played music in the camp and, in fact, they played virtually the same songs as the internees in Boven Digoel played. In between the numbers, food and drinks were prepared at a table they called *Waroeng Java*, Malay for "Java stall."[128] They wrote, together and individually, several diaries.

> *De Ruwenberg, April 16, 1943* . . . Thanks to our friends in the outside, of the Association of the Indies Retirees, a number of musical instruments were brought to the camp, and a small orchestra was put together. We play mainly *krontjong*, of course. The *krontjong* melodies are especially and exquisitely suited to the evenings here in the camp, at the time when the days are almost over. And how lovely do the *krontjong* songs then cling through the silent nights![129]

There is no mention of other music, in fact, except kroncong. "*Our Indies orchestra!*" is a title of another entry in a group's collective diary. "On the New Year's Eve [of 1943]," it says, "we played *krontjong* songs like 'Senang hati' [Malay for "Happy Heart"], 'Lief Indië' [Dutch for "Beloved Indies"], and Deleman's 'Gestelmars' [Dutch for "Constitution March"]."[130]

There were lectures, and series of lectures, and a sort of university even. "We are hearing," a diary entry has it for October 29, 1942, "regular lectures in Latin and Greek. Drewes teaches Arabic and Malay. In the last couple of weeks, eighteen lectures were given, of which fourteen had some relation to the Indies."[131]

There were Jews among the hostages, mostly former high-level officials, and a majority of them, again, connected with the Indies. The "Aryan" hostages worried what the future might bring for their Jewish colleagues and friends. The Jews among the hostages, naturally, feared more. The "Aryans," in their own fear, tried not to appear to turn their faces the other way. While still in Buchenwald, the hostages, "Aryans" as well as Jews, could see the Holocaust from almost an immediate proximity: "Every morning, a small group of emaciated Jews with food buckets from the kitchen passes our block."[132] "Last night, a group of newly arrived Dutch Jews stood on an appel since half past twelve at noon to half past seven in the evening, seven hours, at attention, to exhaustion."[133]

The world of the camps expanded expeditiously. They sprawled like suburbs. Salomon Zwarenstein Strijen was born to a Jewish family in Holland on October 10, 1886. Between 1920 and 1941 he lived and worked in Poerwokerto and Semarang, East and Central Java. He died in Auschwitz on August 27, 1943. David Coenraad Gomperts, who used to work as a director of the Cultuurmaatschappij [Plantation Company] in the Indies, must have been caught while in retirement from the colony, in the Netherlands. He died in the death camp of Sobibor, Poland, on May 7, 1943.

Catharine van den Berg was born in 1917 in Rotterdam. "My father originally came from Bukovina [East Carpathians]," she told an interviewer in the Yad Vashem Holocaust Memorial in Jerusalem after the war. "When Germany invaded the Netherlands in the spring of 1940, father thought of moving with us to Spain." It did not happen. "First," van den Berg said, "my parents-in-law were taken away."

QUESTION: There was no other way of escape? Perhaps to Indonesia?

ANSWER: There were no more ships going out.[134]

Ziegfried de Lima was born in The Hague, in the Netherlands, in October 1916. In 1940, unlike family van den Berg, without family, he managed to get on a ship to the Indies. "I arrived in March 1940," he said, also in an interview at Yad Vashem, "I had four hundred guilders in my pocket and a postcard, on which I had written an address of somebody in Bandung who was supposed to give me a job." There was no job, so de Lima signed up for the Dutch-Indies army. "I was assigned to the Harley-Davidson riders in Java," he said. In early March 1942, the Dutch in the colony had capitulated, Japan occupied the Indies, and de Lima was caught and interned in a camp. He was moved from camp to camp. The end of the war found him in the prisoners-of-war camp on the "Railway of Death" on the Thai-Burmese border.[135]

Yvonne Bouwer, like Mr. Strijen, Mrs. van den Berg, and Mr. de Lima, was Jewish. She was a little girl and lived in Holland when the German army occupied the Netherlands in May 1940. "My parents," she recalled after the war, "got us on the last ship leaving for the Indies. They planned to go further on to Australia," but they "missed the boat" in Java. "It was our luck," Bouwer said, "because the ship sunk."

Bouwer's story is even more spectacular than the others, or it might be just more purely a camp story. Because Yvonne's family missed the ship, they had to stay in the Indies and the war caught up with them. All they did in the following months was try to evade the Japanese camp. Gradually all "whites," Jews as well as non-Jews, and soon many of the "mix-bloods," had to go.

After few weeks both of Yvonne's parents were taken away. Mrs. Bouwer said that even though she was a Jewess, her skin was fair at the time, and she had light, almost-blond hair and very light eyes. It gets complicated; colors had the opposite politics in the Indies of the time and in Europe of the time: "So, I kept dyeing my hair black, and washed my face and body in pomegranate juice to make my skin dark. I wore dark glasses so that I might be mistaken for a native. In this way, hidden in a garden cabin of a good Javanese family, I did not have to go."[136]

The world seemed to be opening through the modern centuries; or one might call it shrinking. The camps suddenly brought the moment close, and into the present. Longing to move, to escape, became the essence of the opening of the world, or its shrinking, and for an increasing number of people it became the only thing that still remained of life. In a letter of September 6–7, 1943, Jopie Vleeschouwer, a young Dutch Jewish woman, wrote to a friend about Etty Hillesum, who was just taken from the Westerbork camp on a transport, not to Theresienstadt, as she might have hoped, but to Auschwitz. "You feel quite drained at first," Jopie wrote to a friend about Etty, "but life goes on. As I write this she moves close and closer to the East, where she once wanted to travel so much."[137]

Professor Willem Wertheim more than anyone else has inspired me to embark on the study of modern Indonesia. I met Wim Wertheim for the first time when I still lived in Prague, in 1969, in his office in Amsterdam with a big picture of Che Guevara on the wall. He seemed already quite old to me. In the late 1920s, in search of a job as young Dutch lawyer, he had gone with his wife to the Indies. They stayed there through World War II and Indonesian independence. In the late colonial Indies, Wertheim became an important liberal figure, and he taught at the law college in Batavia, where he was a colleague of several people who became the "Buchenwald hostages" in 1940.

Wertheim was a Jew, and he told me about "another Czech," a Czech Jew that is, Harry (at the time Heinz) Benda. Harry Benda was born in Liberec, German Reichenberg, at the Czech-German border, north of Prague, in 1919. He was just out of the gymnasium when his parents sent him in a hurry away from Czechoslovakia, in fact from Europe, to escape the Nazis. "We met Harry Benda," Wertheim recalled, "in Batavia, on March 11, 1939." It was four days exactly, before the German army entered Prague. "He was very worried," Wertheim wrote, "about the situation in his land."[138]

Harry Benda, then a professor of history at Yale, wrote me several letters in 1968 and 1969 suggesting that I move to Cornell and study Indonesia like him.

"Despite his age," Wertheim wrote in Benda's obituary in 1972, "he attained such good credentials with a Dutch trading company, by which he was employed, that they entrusted him [in 1941] with the management of their branch in Semarang." Then the war caught up with him anyway, and Benda was interned, in fact, in the same camp as Wertheim, who, inevitably, was put in a Japanese camp, too. "In our common camp," wrote Wertheim, "he expressed to me his wish to drop his commercial career after the war, despite his excellent prospects, and to pursue an academic ambition."[139]

....

The story is not leaving me. As I write this, individuals, groups, crowds, and masses with no fixed address wander through Europe and through the world, full of longing, and aimless. When they dream, especially on the brink of waking up, they must be dreaming of the camps. On September 7,

1920, in Prague, four years before he died and twenty-two years before Theresienstadt became a camp, Kafka wrote to Milena:

> LAST NIGHT, AROUND 8:00 in the evening, I looked in from the street on the banquet hall of the Jewish Torhaus, where well over one hundred Russian-Jewish emigrants are being housed—The hall is packed... while they wait here for the American visas; later at about 12:30 at night, I saw them there all asleep one next to the other.... In a few weeks one will be in America. Of course, it's not that simple; there have been cases of dysentery, there are people standing outside shouting threats through the window, there's even fighting among the Jews themselves.[140]

A large number of the Austrian socialists, Jewish and non-Jewish, in 1934, fourteen years after Kafka wrote this, were running from Vienna and Austria after the crushing defeat in the civil war and following rise of the extreme right wing.[141] Bruno Kreisky, one of the party leaders, and a Jew, like many if not most, ran to the neighboring still democratic Czechoslovakia. He stopped for a while and ran further, to Sweden.[142] Otto Bauer, another Socialist leader, escaped to Bratislava, the Slovak capital of Czechoslovakia, and then to Paris, where he died in 1938.[143]

There were the crowds and masses about to move soon, but at first they were the people with names. Bertolt Brecht, Erich Maria Remarque, Lion Feuchtwanger, Oskar Kokoschka, Heinrich Mann and his brother Thomas, Peter Weiss—these ran to and through Prague and further to Paris, Stockholm, or Moscow and beyond. But many more ran wherever they believed a gate was open, into another camplike space. They were Jews, half-Jews, and non-Jews, left-wing, in-the-middle, or right-wing, or just the "freedom-loving," carrying in their running the (fear of the) camps with them.

Milena Jesenská, a Czech woman to whom Kafka wrote, in my view, his most beautiful letters (she eventually died in the Ravensbrück camp), an ardent Communist, at the time of impending war worked as a journalist in a prominent liberal Prague weekly, *Přítomnost* [The Present]. In sheer despair, Jesenská wrote about the refugees flowing into Prague and Bohemia. "People without documents," she wrote, "on foot, with empty hands. Wandering among us."[144]

It was a cruel theater, as yet not exclusively behind the walls, and so for everyone to see, not just for the people already in the camps. These were Jews and non-Jews running, thus humans of the same blood, you and me. These were the famous and often the most famous people of the whole era of culture preceding the camps, and now the greats were moving, stopping for a while, and running again.

These people ran the only way they knew, through places equally great in culture and as spectacular as themselves, through ports and stations with exotic names and with connections, so they hoped, over the sea, through metropolises and fashionable seaside resorts, as the camps, perhaps, certainly, could not reach here. Through their running, the ports, stations, metropolises, and seaside resorts began, and more and more, to resemble the camps.

Sanary-sur-Mer was a spectacular place, well known to the "best of European society" since the nineteenth century. It was a summer resort on the French Riviera about fifteen kilometers west of Toulon.[145] By the mid- to late 1930s, as the world of camps was expanding and efforts to escape intensified, Sanary-sur-Mer grew into what poet W. H. Auden, one of the people going there, would call "the malicious village of exile."[146]

Thomas Mann, Lion Feuchtwanger, Arnold Zweig Ludwig Marcuse, Ernst Bloch, Bertolt Brecht, Franz Werfel, Alma Mahler,[147] Aldous Huxley (who wrote his *Brave New World* there), and the list goes on, spent time at Sanary-sur-Mer, some, not all, as refugees, but increasingly many, as they ran, looking for a temporary shelter and planning to run further on. Not really a camp, and not really a village, but certainly a space—or a stage, or a catwalk—of concentrated modernity.[148]

Some ran, to use Milena Jesenská's word, "aimlessly." Others, as Kurt Tucholsky said, tried "to stop a catastrophe with their typewriters" but soon realized there was no chance in it. As Tucholsky also wrote, "You can't whistle against the ocean."[149]

Joseph Roth, if caught, would certainly have been put in the camp, and ranked as a "recalcitrant." In his effort to keep his dignity, he could not do anything but keep on running. In running, he exemplified in the highest the ethos of running at the time, which was to keep alive a glimmer of freedom.

On the morning of January 30, 1933, the day Adolf Hitler was appointed chancellor of Germany, Joseph Roth, who happened to be in Berlin at the time, "boarded the Paris train, and never set foot in Germany again."[150] After five years of wandering, settling down, and running away, mostly in what he called "sweet France"—"remember, there was a certain Dreyfus," he wrote to Stefan Zweig about it[151]—in increasing despair, waiting for the US visa promised to him again and again, superficially judged, he appeared in the end to be a defeated man, a "holy drinker" as he called it himself. But he died on the run, free in that (only) possibility of running on, alone, on May 27, 1939, in a third-rate hotel in Paris, of an alcohol overdose, as one report, or rumor, has it.

Roth was an Austrian Jew and Benjamin was a German Jew in the end, as the camp categorization went. Already before Hitler came to power, Benjamin thought of leaving his native Germany, of leaving Europe, in fact, to go somewhere, and he often thought of Palestine. He planned on learning Hebrew in the late 1920s, and by a historical accident, or was it the network already at work, chose as his teacher (because he was of the circle of the well-to-do Jewish intellectuals of the city) a distinguished Berlin rabbi, Leo Baeck, who fifteen years later would be taken to Theresienstadt.[152]

Like Joseph Roth, Walter Benjamin left Germany when Hitler came to power, and never returned. Like Roth, Benjamin wrote, in my view, his best texts as he ran—through the *spectacular* Riviera, Mallorca, and then Sweden, staying mostly in shabby hotel rooms, supported by, and increasingly dependent upon, his friends, whose numbers grew progressively smaller and finally close to zero. As the war broke out, Benjamin, in Paris at the time, was arrested by the French authorities as an "enemy German" and held for several months in a camp indeed. Luckily, he was released before Germany overran France. Like Roth, in an increasing state of despair, Benjamin waited for the US visa repeatedly promised to him. He learned English, with Hannah Stern, later Arendt, and he is remembered as displaying a large map of Manhattan on the wall above his writing desk, as long as he had a desk.[153]

As Hitler moved toward Paris in the spring of 1940, Benjamin moved south, toward Spain, to wait there for the visa, and possibly to board a ship. In Marseille, he met another man running. "I ran into an old friend," Arthur Koestler recalled, a little too theatrically, but perhaps it was true. "The German writer, Walter Benjamin, was making preparations for his own escape . . . by a different route. . . . He had thirty tablets of a morphia compound, which he intended to swallow if caught; he said they were enough to kill a horse, and gave me half of the tablets, just in case."[154] After walking over the Pyrenees, already in Spain, on September 25, 1940, an exhausted Benjamin got some news that the Spanish would turn him back, false news, as it became clear the next morning. But Benjamin had already swallowed the poison. When Bertolt Brecht, one of his remaining friends, a non-Jew but equally on the run, heard about Benjamin's suicide, he declared this, with, as usual, a correct sense of history, a successful escape.

On the Death of the Refugee W. B.

*I'm told you raised your hand against yourself
Anticipating the butcher*

. . .

. . . you destroyed a torturable body.[155]

....

The world was never circumvented so fully and with so much energy as now at the time of the camps and through attempts to escape the camps—for the first time perhaps, since the Age of Great Discoveries when the modern had been announced. The people touched by the camps and running to escape the camps rounded the world. Their running completed the world, as it had been known. As if its round shape had finally been proved.

Djamaloeddin Tamin and some other members of Tan Malaka's group of Communist rebels were caught, sent to Boven Digoel, spent there years, and, probably, much of the time thought of escape. Djamaloeddin Tamin for some time taught children in the Boven Digoel government school for internees, and was also known as earning some money, chickens, eggs, and fish by working in the camp as a tailor.

Tan Malaka, and some other members of his group, were not caught. Tan Malaka evaded Boven Digoel and kept on running. He kept out of the camp by being "elusive as an eel," and he appeared at the most unexpected places all around the world. Many of the people in the camp, and other people possibly threatened by the camps and running, thought of Tan Malaka as their hero. Fictionalized Tan Malaka, Pacar Merah [The Red Darling] of the thriller series, as we have seen, was wildly popular in the Indies, and undoubtedly it was read in the camp, too.

One day, Pacar Merah, or Tan Malaka, or if not him personally, one of his lieutenants, might be in Tokyo, the next day in Moscow, in Berlin, or in Manhattan, in some sea resort, too, in the cities and sites evidently known to the author and his readers from tourist guides, other novels, or magazines. Tan Malaka or Pacar Merah or the lieutenants moved as rumors, as Bonkes, as *berita masak*, virtually, actually, instantly, through the world as a radio network rather than a real world.

In one of the stories, the Tan Malaka/Pacar Merah people escaped the "imperialist police" by a hair's breadth, hiding in a mosque in the Boi de Boulogne, and the next moment they are described listening to Josephine Baker in a theater in the city singing "*J'ai deux amours, mon pays et Paris.*"

Could not they, one wonders, should not they, in that Paris mosque or in the Folies Bergère, in that world of the camps, in the camps' suburbs, as they ran, meet Benjamin or perhaps Joseph Roth, just a little drunk?

In 1931, Erika and Klaus Mann, the children of Thomas Mann, together wrote *Das Buch von der Riviera* [A Book about the Riviera], which at the time appeared still more a tourist fantasy than a guidebook on how to run away. Among the places described in the book is Saint-Tropez, but also Sanary-sur-Mer.[156]

The next year, in 1932, still early in the time of the camps in Europe, Erika Mann helped to produce what appeared to be a tourist project again, *Ein Reisefilm unter der Führung von Erika Mann* [A Travel Film directed by Erika Mann].[157] At this time, Erika Mann was already described in the Nazi press as a "flat-footed half Jew." She performed in the film as a tourist guide, in a tourist guide's uniform. She talks to a group of well-dressed European tourists, explaining their "forthcoming trip together." The trip, she says, will lead them to Marseille and then across the Mediterranean Sea, through Morocco to Timbuktu. Erika speaks, "Ladies and gentlemen! The people over there, beyond the sea, just now celebrate Ramadan, the major feast of their year. . . . We will spend some time with them. . . . We will arrive exactly at the right moment."[158]

Erika Mann's "tourist short film" appears ghastly when one watches it even eighty years later. The trip would soon be done, and repeated, and sometimes by the same routes and by the same people, but without much hope of a return. Later, after it all seemed over, after the war, in the 1950s and 1960s, the same route would be surfed in a truly tourist way. Still later, in our day, migrants from Africa would take over the routes, be schlepping somewhere or away from somewhere.

Lilly Joss Reich was born to a Czech "Aryan" father and an Austrian Jewish mother. Before the war, Lilly Joss was a professional art photographer in Vienna. Her portrait of Albert Einstein from 1937 is possibly the most frequently reproduced portrait of the man. In 1940, Lilly Joss, as a half-Jew, was running from Vienna and from under the shadow of the camps, of Theresienstadt, indeed, because this was where many Viennese Jews were being sent. She got as far as Bordeaux, on the French coast, and took a ship to England. But "the first night on the ship" they were told that "the ship had to change its course and sail not to England but to Casablanca in Morocco."[159]

Lilly Joss had a Rolleiflex camera with her, and waiting for a ship to America, she did what she knew how, and took photographs in Casablanca.

Her portraits of the everyday life in the city, at first glance, like Erika Mann's film, look like images of European bourgeois on vacation. On a second glance, however, one can see European exiles, women especially, awkward in their European clothes; they look like winter clothes packed in a hurry.

In one of the pictures, Jewish women sit in a park, next to Arab women in flowing Arab clothes, sitting on the same benches, with children, hard to say whose are whose, playing together. The pictures had to be taken not far from Rick's Café, the *Casablanca* one, which never really was. A caption Lilly Joss probably attached herself to one of the photographs later, when a ship took her to America, states the obvious: "The scene makes an impression of tourists rather than emigrants."[160] "Again and again," Benjamin wrote in his fragments-essay *Einbahnstrasse* [One-Way Street], "in Shakespeare, in Calderón, battles fill the last act, and kings, princes, attendants, and followers 'enter, fleeing.'"[161]

In 1940, the year Lilly Joss's photographs were taken, *Jüdisches Nachrichtenblatt*, the "Jewish News," a Prague paper for the Jews still there, in Nazi-occupied Central Europe, and, of course, thinking of running, wrote "Bolivia is the land of the future. . . . Don't be afraid of snakes and mosquitoes."[162] As Europe was becoming gradually Hitler's, and as Britain and the United States were gradually closing their borders to Jewish immigration, new and increasingly "exotic" countries were suggested as a place to run to—Brazil, or Alaska, which, as *Jüdisches Nachrichtenblatt* wrote, was "unjustly suffering from a negative image."[163] A settlement in the Virgin Islands was suggested.[164]

With the blasé attitude of the Nazis for a time still permitting exit to the Jews, Hanna Steiner, a representative of the Jewish Council in Prague, "undertook a trip to Berlin and Hamburg [in 1940] to negotiate with shipping companies and consulates of neutral countries. While in Germany she also conferred with the consuls of Santo Domingo, Venezuela, and Ecuador."[165]

"Many return from places like Argentina, Brazil, and Australia after only a short time," Joseph Roth wrote from his Paris exile, at the same time, on his run. Humanitarian committees made promises, but "countries proved unable to keep the promise the committees made on their behalf."[166] "The world hasn't helped much, not even out of expediency," wrote Roth. "But then," he added, "how could one have looked to a world like this for help?"[167]

At the end of 1940, *Jüdisches Nachrichtenblatt* mentioned Shanghai, China, as "a goal and a bridge."[168] Then Manchukuo, in East Asia, under Japanese control, was to be "a gate."[169] Manfred, a cousin of Emil Utitz, "wanted to leave 'civilization' behind." "So, he accepted a minor position in the Philippines, which, he explained, was definitely out of Hitler's reach."[170] He avoided the war in Europe, and he avoided Theresienstadt or some other Nazi camp, "only to fall into the hands of the Japanese in Manila." "Together with his wife and son, he was rescued by American troops from the Japanese camp in the early spring of 1945."[171]

On September 4, 1940, a group of about 3,500 Jewish refugees from Vienna, Prague, Brno, Berlin, Munich, and Danzig (Gdańsk) gathered in Vienna.[172] They still got permission and set out on their way. After the most difficult trip on the Danube River all the way to the Black Sea, into the Mediterranean, they came so close that they could see Haifa on the horizon—only to be pushed away by the order of the British authorities in Palestine. They went on. After weeks of further journey, with the ship breaking apart as it sailed, and with the crew assaulting the women, they finally reached the tropical island of British Mauritius.[173] Like the people in Lilly Joss's Casablanca photographs, like Etty Hillesum always dreamed to do, they reached the Orient.

In Mauritius, they were put into a camp, naturally, a hastily adapted prison. Many of the Jews spoke German among themselves, and they all came from Nazi Europe, so to the British colonial rulers of the island they could easily be spies, or enemies. "In spite of their utter physical and mental exhaustion," wrote Elena Makarova, who came upon the Mauritius story while researching Theresienstadt, "it remains etched in their memories—the incredible beauty of the scenery . . . the red flame trees that dotted the green countryside at that time of the year—a lovely contrast to the backdrop of the mountains."[174]

It is argued that when the Mauritius Jews got their permit to leave Central Europe in September 1940, the Nazis might still have preferred to get rid of the Jews rather than kill them. But the war enveloped Europe, and it eventually blocked even the last remaining routes of the Jews' possible escape. In summer 1940, SS-Obersturmbannführer Adolf Eichmann informed a representative of the Jewish community in Prague that only the way through Lisbon and the one to the east, and then to the Far East, still remained open.[175] On June 22, 1941, Hitler attacked the Soviet Union, and the Nazi-Soviet front cut the eastern route. On August 23, 1941, Heinrich Himmler officially ended all Nazi policies still allowing for Jewish emigration.[176]

It was the newly proven roundness of the world, and its fullness. The US president, Franklin D. Roosevelt, asked Benito Mussolini to allow Jews to move to Ethiopia, which was under Italian rule. Italy was friendly to Hitler but at the time still ambiguous in her attitude toward the Jews. In his response, reportedly, "Il Duce wondered why the refugees could not be settled in the United States."[177]

....

Dr. Hans de Vries of the Netherlands Institute for War Documentation in Amsterdam, now the Institute for the Holocaust and Genocide Studies, talked to me at Café Luxembourg near the institute about what he believed was a very important feature of Theresienstadt—about the Indies.

We talked about "Barnevelders," a group of "Nazi-privileged" Dutch Jews, higher-level and mostly high-level officials, well-known writers, artists, musicians, and the like, as well as the Jews who had converted to Protestantism, a group of about 650 persons in total. These people were arrested by the Nazis after the German occupation of the Netherlands, like all the other Jews, but then their ways separated, and they ended up in Theresienstadt. De Vries's parents were also "of the Indies," they spent a large part of their life there, and they also went to the Nazi camps. "Were they not of the Barnevelders?" I asked. "Oh, no!" he said, "they were just simple people."

In January 1943, the Barnevelders were gathered and transported together to a special camp, the nineteenth-century castle De Schaffelaar, in the central Netherlands, near the little town of Barneveld, thus the name of the group. It was not too bad a place. Given the time and the prisoners, it was an exclusive place. There was music, and theater, and sport, and free movement on the grounds of the castle and its gardens. In a matter of months, however, beginning in late September 1943, the exclusive camp experience abruptly ended, and some, and soon all, of the "Barneveld Group" were moved to Westerbork.

Still in Westerbork, the Barnevelders were housed in a special barracks, and as another internee of Westerbork, not in the group, recalled, they "constituted the 'camp intelligentsia.'" On September 4, 1944, as the group, now 560 persons in all, they went to Theresienstadt.[178]

On September 23, 1944, the SS authorities in Theresienstadt informed the Jewish Council of the Elders in the camp—the Elders were charged with making up the list, SS men provided "merely" numbers and categories— that the "Dutch nationals whose names figure as 'Barnevelders'" "must not be included" in any transport.[179] Indeed, it appears that the highest survival rate of any Theresienstadt group was in the "Barneveld group."[180] It also appears that not a single one of the group was sent to Auschwitz.[181]

Among the "Barnevelders" of Theresienstadt, a "privileged" among the "privileged," for instance, was Emanuel Moresco, born in 1869 in Amsterdam but spending his whole long and brilliant career in or with the Indies. Between 1927 and 1929, Moresco was the vice president of the Council of the Indies. At the time of his arrest, in 1940, he was the general secretary of the Netherlands' ministry of the colonies.[182]

We do not know how exactly the Indies were present in Theresienstadt, and whether Boven Digoel was ever mentioned. There are no reports of Salim-like or Dr. Schoonheyt–like Indies flashes back, no mention of kroncong music or rijsttafel cuisine in the camp, as far as I know. Neither Emanuel Moresco nor any of the other "Indies people" of Theresienstadt, as far as I know, left memoirs, and I did not find anybody still alive. There is just an entry, which Elena Makarova, again, has found, going through the lists of the lectures by the Theresienstadt internees, a two-line announcement with a short bio:

> *Schor (née Spiro) Barbara.* Born on March 18, 1868 in Częstochowa [Poland]. Deported to Theresienstadt from Berlin on December 17, 1942. Deported to Auschwitz on December 18, 1943. Perished.
>
> *Lecture July 27, 1943*: "Memories of My Life in the Netherlands East Indies."[183]

And this: On April 7, 1943, Mr. Italie wrote in his diary, "Yesterday evening for about two hours I listened to 'gamelan' . . . pans and pots from the kitchen somebody was drabbling, clashing and crashing with a verve."[184]

SEVENTEEN

Dust, or Memory

"Abraham Moshe, it's worse than you think."
"What could be worse?" asked Abraham Moshe, ironically.
"Abraham Moshe, the atheists are right. There is no justice, no judge..."
"Then who rules the world, rabbi...?"
"A total lie.... A heap of dung—"
"Where did the dung come from?"
"In the beginning was the dung."

—ISAAC BASHEVIS SINGER, *Gimpel the Fool*

The camp people trying to escape or just thinking about escape, and those precious few who actually ran and got beyond a line, toward the next line, when they persisted, were scattered. When recalcitrant still, they were scattered off and beyond the clearing, and off and beyond the memory.

Something similar to that, a premonition or precedent, had been happening, also en masse and in despair, and for a long time. During the Crusades, "totally fed up with their lives," "whole villages of men set out. It is only afterward that a frightened papacy tried to give this movement direction by leading off to the Holy Land."¹ The worst, already then, were the mad and the children. The children's crusades got in the way and then completely out of hand, and most of the kids had to be killed or were sold into slavery.

The "Street Arabs," in the New York of Jacob Riis's time, late in the nineteenth century, at the outset of the early high-modern, were children and "runaways," "a set of hardened little scoundrels," Jacob Riis wrote, "quite beyond the reach of missionary effort," vagabonds, and each a vagabond "acknowledging no authority," "with his grimy fist raised against society whenever it tries to coerce him." Theirs was "sturdy independence, love of freedom, and absolute self-reliance." "To steal a march on them is the only way." They live "wild lives," nothing "holds them fast."²

In the Soviet Ukraine of the 1920s, already at the time of the camps and the revolutions, on March 8, 1927, Sergei Prokofiev wrote in his diary about his visit after years back to his homeland and the city of Kharkov. That night, "On the way we remembered that there were many *bezprizorniye* [homeless children] in the south. They run around in large gangs, one of them jumps under your feet to knock you down, while the others steal your bags and purses, often using knives or infecting you with syphilitic bites. Fortunately, the streets were quiet."³ "This pupil has not learned how to ask questions," wrote Ludwig Wittgenstein in his essay *On Certainty*. "He has not learned *the* game that we are trying to teach him."⁴ But still, Wittgenstein insisted, "Something must be taught us as a foundation."⁵

Anton Chekhov wrote on his visit to the Tsarist Sakhalin penal colony, "To come across escaped convicts in the Siberian forests is a misfortune. The escapees," this is what he heard, "are 'more terrifying than any bear.'"⁶ There was a fear of "sometimes being mauled by a bear, sometimes attacked by escapees."⁷ "Fear of escapees is enormous," Chekhov wrote, "rumors [of them] induce dread."⁸

In Vietnam, in a supposedly postcamp time, after thirty years of war, the people still tried to escape from their recent modern. There were hundreds of thousands of "invisible neighbors" in Vietnam, the dead of the past "improperly buried," "displaced spirits," "street-wandering ghosts."⁹ And "nothing is more frightening," the Vietnamese were saying, "than an encounter with the ghost of a prisoner."¹⁰ If it happens, "the goods offered to the spirits may include a traveler's bag."¹¹

"Man," wrote Ernst Bloch (he meant woman, too), "rises up, a bird of the soul, to disappear . . . where the body has no more walls."¹² Yet, David Napier, as if he were answering Bloch, the too-utopian, pointed out that on the way up, man (or woman) is "still with walls," still cannot do much more than "confound what is socially prescribed"[13]—in other words, be a vagrant, "vagrant," in a dictionary definition,

> . . street person, homeless person, tramp, hobo, drifter, down-and-out, derelict, beggar; itinerant, wanderer, nomad, traveler, vagabond, transient; *informal* bag lady, bum; *literary* wayfarer; *in ornithology* . . . a bird that has strayed or been blown from its usual range or migratory route. Also called *accidental*.

Dr. Albert Schweitzer, a great organist, a famous missionary, and not without his own kind of complicity in the camp-making logic of modern times and colonialism in particular, wrote in his autobiography, "For a time, I thought I would someday devote myself to tramps and discharged convicts."[14] In the end Dr. Schweitzer decided to go as a doctor to Africa.

Vagrant and tramp move by loitering. A vagrant (and tramp) still, according to a dictionary, is "someone who hangs around downtown after the stores are closed and appears to be deliberately wasting time traveling indolently and with frequent pauses." Workers, at the moment they began to form themselves into a crowd and then a class, on their own way to escape to freedom, became to the bourgeois "genuine outsiders," "veritable nomads," an "external population."[15] Even in the so-called workers' states of the twentieth century, when men (or women) persisted, they became "disorderly' people . . . without any discipline," and, according to even Georg Lukács, driven by "anarchism of vagabondage."[16]

There is a long history of this, too, going back, at least, to the era of the Plague, slavery, Ireland, Virginia. Contemporary German historian Alf Lüdtke wrote about modern Europe in the first half of the twentieth century before the time of the camps, "Vagrants were chased and arrested, 'mad' people were increasingly detained in special institutions; compulsory education was enforced by the police, at least in the towns and cities."[17] "Unwanted animals are not killed," wrote Joseph Roth in the 1930s, already on the run, "but there are a lot of stray dogs and cats."[18]

Rudolf Höss, the future commandant of Auschwitz and the *Arbeit Macht Frei* man, since early on in his career had worried about the "problem of the vagrants and asocials."[19] Heinrich Himmler, Rudolf Höss's future supervisor, already when still just a chief of police in Bavaria, "ordered the first dragnet operations to clean the province of the undesirables." Himmler sent the vagrants mostly to Dachau, a place near Munich and under his supervision, a camp that when opened on March 21, 1933, became the first of the Nazi concentration universe. "The upright citizens of Bavaria were relieved," wrote historians Debórah Dwork and Robert Jan van Pelt, "The sole dissenting voice came from the Chamber of Commerce. It feared that, as concentration camp workers were not paid, camp products would undercut the competition."[20]

"The bourgeoisie had no qualms about using the camps to clean up its streets," wrote Dwork and van Pelt.[21] Cleaning and clearing were the catchwords, the codes now coming into their true use. Instantly, and repeatedly, there were issued "police instructions and measures against immorality and hostility toward the state." The Dachau concentration camp's "basic law" seemed to be first putting a Nazi stamp on the "pink face." There was a whole section in the law referring to "Grousers and Grumblers."[22]

There had been vagrants in the Indies, no less than in Europe, and, at least suspected, grousers and grumblers, that kind of external population. Like in Europe, there was a close connection of vagrants or suspected vagrants with the camp, with Boven Digoel. Like in Europe, the camp, the center of outsidedness, exemplified the working of the system, the web, and modernity as a whole.

A Malay paper, *Sinar Sumatra* [The Ray of Sumatra], on February 6, 1930, published its comment on "a desertion" by several internees from Boven Digoel. This time, they got as far as the Thursday Islands. "We were told," the paper reported, "that in fact these were recalcitrant Communists who would rather die than ask the government for mercy.... They evidently could not keep still, and all they had done was to think about how to run away. The military in Boven Digoel, however, usually could sniff it out and know how to keep these people in, or, like in this case, to bring them back." "Were not these people kept in the camp," the author of the article concluded, "they might end stirring up even the Papuans to rise against the government."[23]

On February 28, 1930, an author who signed himself Si Paoel [Paul] in another Sumatra paper, *Oetoesan Sumatra* [The Sumatra Messenger], reacting probably to the same attempt at an escape from Boven Digoel, painted an even more frightening picture for his readers, certainly the government and its well-meaning subjects. The people who have tried to escape from Boven Digoel, Si Paoel wrote, imagine—they might escape and wander! And they might even become the new *Geuzen*! This was a historical reference every child with just a little colonial Dutch education understood. *Geuzen* [beggars] were the sixteenth-century guerrillas who started the rebellion against Spain out of which the independent Dutch Republic emerged.

Thomas Najoan, the "Jungle Pimpernel," tried to escape from Boven Digoel three times, and he perished in the forest on the third attempt. Salim recalled how he met Najoan when, after his second attempt, he was being taken back to the camp. Salim was at the same time coming back too, on a ship from a long stay in the hospital in Ambon. "As we arrived to the rode in Dobo," Salim wrote, Dobo being the last sea port before ships entered the Digoel River mouth, "and as we idled on the deck, we saw a small motorboat, and in it a person waving to us. To our pleasant surprise he turned out to be Thomas Najoan." It emerged that this time he got as far as the Thursday Islands, almost Australia. "Not before long," Salim went on with his story, "Najoan was climbing on board to go on our ship with us to Boven Digoel. Still on the ladder, he shouted up to us: 'Australia is so boring, I am going back to Uncle Bintang!'"[24]

It should be explained why they all, Salim and his friends, and Najoan, laughed. Uncle Bintang was a Boven Digoel guard. "*Bintang*" in Malay and Indonesian means "star." He might have acquired the nickname, one story went, because he earned a medal while serving in the Dutch anti-Aceh war at the turn of the century.[25] But a further explanation is needed, and Najoan actually gave it to his friends himself. He tried, he said, to escape the camp, in order to reach the "stars," indeed, Lenin and Stalin first of all. But it has always turned out in the end to be Uncle Bintang and the camp.

"And at night stars rise like the bubbles of the drowned," poet Yehuda Amichai wrote decades later.[26] Walter Benjamin wrote about stars at the same time as Najoan was running. "It is not," he wrote, "that what is past casts its light on what is present, or what is present its light on what is past; rather, image is that wherein what has been comes together in a flash with the now to form a constellation."[27] Najoan probably thought the same way. Of course, he knew that Lenin, for one, was dead for years already, but, clearly, he did not care.

"The 'subject of free choice' in the Western, 'tolerant,' multicultural sense," wrote Slavoj Žižek, "can emerge only as the result of an extremely violent process of being torn out of a particular lifeworld, of being cut off from one's roots." This is, in Žižek's argument, "the hugely liberating aspect of this violence."[28] "Truth," wrote Benjamin, arguing the same, "wants to be startled abruptly at one stroke, from her self-immersion, whether by uproar, music, or cries for help."[29]

Kafka, in 1922, wrote about "steadfastness": "I don't want to pursue any particular course of development; I want to change my place in the world entirely, which actually means that I want to go to another planet."[30] "Throw you hearts over all borders," Walter Mehring, a Dada poet and a Jew, sang in 1933 in Paris, in his *Emigrantenchoral* [Emigrants Choir], as he was on the run from Germany to Austria, from Austria to France, and from France to America.

Build yourself a nest!
Forget. Forget.[31]

There is a little of a Najoan story in Theresienstadt. "An astronomer," Gonda Redlich wrote in his camp diary on January 8, 1943, an elderly Jewish man, laid in the hospital, awaiting his transport "to the east." He was telling the friends who came to visit him that he had "new ideas about the structure of the moon that are completely different from contemporary science." "I heard him speak," Redlich wrote, "though I did not understand the subject."[32] While in the camps, those who kept talking about an escape, or the stars, or the moon—the same thing—spoke in what León Ferrari and Mira Schendel, two artists at the turn of the twenty-first century, will describe as a moment when "language becomes 'cosmic word dust.'"[33]

A transcript survived of one of the lectures professor Emil Utitz gave in Theresienstadt, and it can be found in archives of the Jewish Museum in Prague. Professor Utitz reminded his audience of an often-told story of the Greek philosopher Thales, who was often also recognized as the father of geometry. Thales observed deeply the stars to predict the weather, paying no attention to anything below, including the Thracian servant who tried to alert him to a well in his way. Thales stumbled and fell on his nose. How funny![34]

Running, or looking toward the stars, or running and looking toward the stars, the camp people, perhaps, were expressing an "unstoppable need to find an absolute position."[35] Friedl Dicker-Brandeis, who in Theresienstadt taught arts to children and later to adults as well, is remembered by one of her teenage students: "Sometimes [Friedl] suggested themes—a woman in a hat walking through a deserted street on [a] windy evening or a story of an African animal." Other times she told the class to draw "with a complete freedom—where would they like to be, what they wished, what they could see from their windows, and what was most important."[36]

Georges Perec recalled, "Between my eleventh and fifteenth year," these were the first few years after the war, when he already knew that his mother perished, probably in Auschwitz, "I filled whole exercise books: human figures unrelated to the ground, which was supposed to support them, ships with sails that did not touch the masts and masts which did not fit into the hulls, the machines of war, engines of death, flying machines and implausible mechanical vehicles with disconnected nozzles, discontinuous cordage, disengaged wheels, rotating in the void; the wings of the planes were detached from their trunks, their arms were out of their torsos, their hands gave them no grasp."[37]

I did not find any children's art from Boven Digoel, and Mrs. Widayasih, Mr. Trikoyo, and every one of their friends, children at the time, told me that they did not remember any. From Theresienstadt, there are hundreds of pieces of children's artwork. The children painted and drew what clearly appear as sexual, spatial, or funeral fears and horror of the space. But they all painted or drew paradise, too, a tropical paradise, in fact, with palms, wildflowers, and strange animals, even camels. This was Palestine, they were told, where they might go if they survived. But "to all appearances," in the full meaning of the art, dreams, nightmares, and the camp, and I have no doubt about it, the warm regions they painted and drew to escape to, in a dream, too, were the Indies, and New Guinea, and Boven Digoel.[38]

Looking at it soberly, if some sobriety were possible, it was Palestine, Eretz Israel. Heinz Prossnitz was a young man in 1944 and still waiting in Prague to be taken to Theresienstadt—where he went eventually, and then to Auschwitz, where he died. For him, wrote Ruth Bondy, who was his friend, "crumbs of news about Palestine were like the pieces of bread Hansel and Gretel scattered in the dark forest."[39] "God knows," Heinz Prossnitz wrote, still in Prague, on his eighteenth birthday, "what will become of me. After all, I want to immigrate to Eretz Israel and to take part, body and soul, in establishing our state. But the climate?"[40]

....

One of the last books Joseph Roth was able to finish was *The Leviathan*. He described it, too, as "of my best."[41] As in Benjamin's case, the best books were written on the run. *The Leviathan* was published in 1940 by the Amsterdam publishing house Querido. However, before the book could be fully distributed, Germany occupied the Netherlands. Emanuel Querido, Querido Publishers' co-owner, a Jew like Roth, went into hiding, was betrayed and deported, and in 1943 "gassed by the Germans."[42] The whole stock of Joseph Roth's *The Leviathan*, not yet sold, fell into the hands of the occupiers and was "pulped by the Germans."[43]

During the last months of Roth's life, Dorothy Thompson, a prominent American writer at the time, journalist, and radio broadcaster (in 1939 *Time Magazine* named Thompson the second-most-influential woman after Eleanor Roosevelt),[44] translated one of Roth's novels, *Job*. On January 21,

1939, when Roth had only four more months to live, Dorothy Thompson wrote to him:

> Dear Mr. Roth:
>
> On behalf of the American PEN Club, I have the honor to invite you to be a special guest at the World Congress of Writers to be held on invitation of the New York World's Fair on May 8, 9, and 10, 1939.... Living expenses will be paid and entertainment provided for the three days of the Congress....
>
> This Congress will provide an opportunity for the writers of the world to publicly and freely state their belief in the personal freedoms without which the creation of literature is impossible, in a setting commanding international attention....
>
> Sincerely,
> *Dorothy Thompson, President*[45]

The three days all-inclusive at the congress and the opportunity to freely state his belief in personal freedom did not happen. Joseph Roth died, and the rest was a remainder. Blanche Gidon, who translated Roth's works into French, managed to get hold of the papers Roth left after his death. It was a sparkle, an accident, a *coincidence*, a chance meeting. The papers Mrs. Gidon was able to gather after Roth's disorderly death found their way into a newly established Leo Baeck Institute of Jewish Studies in New York. The name giver and the first director of the institute was Theresienstadt's rabbi Leo Baeck.[46] Roth got a grave that may easily be overlooked, at the Thiais Cemetery south of Paris.

Benjamin's grave, or a "grave" rather, is as if the man was still on the run. Hannah Stern-Arendt, with whom Benjamin was taking English lessons in Paris in a waning hope of escaping to America, visited "Benjamin's grave" in Spain after the war and described what she found: "A grave with Benjamin's name scrawled on a special wooden enclosure was being shown to visitors. The photographs in my possession clearly indicate that this grave, which is completely isolated and utterly separate from the actual burial place, is an invention of the cemetery attendants who, in consideration of the number of inquiries, wanted to assure themselves of a tip."[47]

Surrealist André Breton encouraged his fellow poets in the 1930s: *"Lâchez tout* [Drop everything].... Drop your wife, drop your girlfriend....

Park your children in the woods.... Take to the road!"[48] The Dadaist precursors of Breton, it was said with some hyperbole, in the cities "arrived by train and disappeared into Oceania by steamer."[49] Paul Éluard, close to both Dada and surrealism, and to Communism, too, escaped to Batavia in a dream: "In the heavy heat, and beneath a vertical sun, white Dutch women with milky skin go by, their heads bare."[50]

Max Ernst, a friend of Éluard and all the rest, wrote, dreamed, about the "Dutch Indies," too, without going into the particulars, as poets could: "The human eye is decorated with tears from Batavia."[51] But it took the moment of the camps, being touched by the camps at least, for "the escapism" to become real.

Robert Desnos was of the circle of exciting and visionary "irresponsibles." Louis Aragon, of the same group, wrote about Desnos as a "unique modern sage" with "strange ships in every fold of his brain."[52] Desnos had been one of the leading figures of the surrealist movement. In his poetry, he traveled "through all the seas." Then the moment of the camps came. Desnos, not a Jew, was arrested in France, transported to Auschwitz, survived this camp and was transported to other camps, and, finally, close to the end of the war, to the Theresienstadt Small Fortress, Fortress B. There, in June 1945, a month after Theresienstadt, the prison and the camp, were liberated, exhausted, not killed, Desnos died.[53]

....

As the camps were liberated in Europe, in 1945, the gates of the camps opened and the internees who survived came out. But the world that awaited them, now, was the world of the camps. The new histories of the liberated people opened, in the words of Kwon Heonik, writing about another camp people after another war and years of suffering, in another part of the world, "multiple histories of displacement."[54] Or, like the delicate prince in Dostoyevsky's *The Idiot*, the camp people were, now, "more or less allowed to run free and expose [their] wounds."[55]

There were no straight or honest questions to ask the people who had just left the camps: how did they feel while running? Also, there were no straight and honest answers they could give. Perhaps a timetable. In one of the taped interviews professionally and routinely conducted in the Yad Vashem Holocaust Memorial in Jerusalem as an effort to deal systematically with the memory of the Holocaust, a Memorial's interviewer questioned a Theresienstadt survivor, Mrs. Jacqueline Philips.

Today is July 9, 1993. . . .

QUESTION: *You were born as Jacqueline Shpetter?*

ANSWER: Yes

QUESTION: *Were you born in Borneo, Indonesia, in 1924?*

ANSWER: Yes. But in 1933, my father retired and so the family decided to go back and live in Holland again . . .

Fast forward.

QUESTION: *After the war you began in Holland again?*

ANSWER: Yes. . . . But all was finished. I went to America, back to Holland, to Indonesia, and to Australia—first to New Zealand, that is, and then to Australia. There I became religious. Last year, I decided to move to Israel.[56]

In mid-May 1945, as the evacuation of the Theresienstadt camp began, buses and trucks from the outside began to arrive. Jo Spier, a painter and now a liberated Jew, recalled "two very pretty German buses." More buses like that came, Spier recalled. Some of them belonged to the *Stadtbahn Köln* [City Transport Cologne], and some to the *Stadtbahn Essen* [City Transport Essen]. "In all these years in the camp," Spier wrote, "we never saw anything so pretty." "On the sides of the buses there was written in chalk: 'Germany welcomes back her Jews.'"[57]

Mrs. Leontine Fels–de Jong was born in Batavia in 1931. When she was eighteen months old, the family moved back to the Netherlands. When Germany invaded the Netherlands, they were arrested. They were ranked as "prominent Jews" and interned in Barneveld, and then they were transported to Theresienstadt. Mrs. Fels–de Jong told her story in 1995 as part of a video project funded by the Spielberg Foundation. She can be seen on camera describing, near the end of the interview, what she found when she came back to the Netherlands from the camp.

Friends and neighbors, she says, had been asked, as they went to the camp, to keep some valuables and furniture for them, which they somehow saved from confiscation but had to leave behind. Mrs. Fels–de Jong shows on the camera a photograph of a baby, herself, with her parents in the Indies—a typical colonial photo, the father in a rattan lazy chair, the baby on his lap, and the mother smiling above them, all three, the parents and the baby, in all-white. We hear the voice of the interviewer, "What else remained?" Leontine Fels–de Jong shows a list she evidently typed after she came from the camp and had since carried throughout her travels, the things that remained: "a standing lamp, a Chinese kimono, a little round table of oak wood, a parlor palm plant."[58]

Parlindoengan Loebis, like the other camp people in Europe, walked out the gate in the spring of 1945. "The first night," Loebis wrote in his memoirs, "we had to sleep under a *cemara* tree behind a ditch at the edge of a highway."[59] It might be a slip of the tongue, or rather the way memory played with him. Loebis, the Sumatran, released from the European camp, spent that first night under what had to be some kind of the northern European spruce, fir, or pine. But he wrote "*cemara*," a casuarian tree of the tropics, the most fragrant, and most often sung about, in Sumatran and Javanese poetry.

"The road," Loebis continued, "was full of people coming out of the camps." "Some people carried musical instruments, and in the evening they played as the others were preparing food, if there was any." The music they played "was mostly jazz." The musicians Loebis met were "Hungarians who used to play in the European hotels before the war." It is not said if they kept together through the camps or got together while interned. Loebis asked them to play "I Can't Give You Anything but Love, Baby."

"The last days of April [1945]," wrote Loebis, "were increasingly busy on the roads. There were large crowds of liberated people, and they all moved to the west. Also tanks and all kinds of other vehicles passed by. [Was it seized German army stuff, or is it just Loebis's memory?] On the tanks one could see men, women, and children. Everybody was driving, riding, or walking to the west, because they all were afraid of the Russian Army, which, as everybody said, had already reached Berlin."[60]

"The ecological dream-notion of total recycling (in which every remainder is used again)" is "the ultimate capitalist dream," wrote Robert Smithson in 1962 explaining his *Asphalt Run*. It is also, he added, "proof of how capitalism can appropriate ideologies which seem to oppose it."[61] Like Loebis and others from the camps in 1945, but fifteen years later, Smithson walked, or better said, tried to walk "across the continent." "It was hard," he said, "to find suitable sites in Europe for making works [leaving traces?] because 'everything is so cultivated.'"[62] He might say, "recycled."

Photographs from the "real" Nazi camps are well known, and they make one wonder: how can people look at them, put them behind museum glass, and try to explain them? The heaps of dead bodies were not to be found in

Theresienstadt, but some corpses of the Theresienstadt people, those who had been taken to Auschwitz and other camps "further east," surely were in the heaps. There is no better "description" of this than that of Boris Lurie, a survivor, an artist, and Robert Smithson's partner in trying to remember beyond the limit: "The skull-like grimaces that confront viewers and fix them with dead eyes, coagulate into ciphers of bodies that no longer seem to promise anything. They have been sucked dry, and the sensuality shown seems to be a contortion, a deformation of desire that has become unreal."[63]

Lisa Gidron, a young woman liberated from Theresienstadt, remembered her first months out of the camp: "We got married in the autumn 1945, the day after Yom Kippur, in the main synagogue in Prague. Everybody was crying—the first marriage after the *Shoah* [Holocaust]. We made it, we are still alive . . . ! We will give birth to children."[64]

Tom Segev, an Israeli historian, wrote about envoys sent by the Zionist leaders from Palestine, even before the state of Israel was declared, to Europe, to look among the Jewish people just out of the camps for potential immigrants to Palestine. The Zionist envoys knew where to go, to the "displaced-persons camps"—yes, camps again! The camps were set up, and their numbers grew, throughout the liberated continent, to accommodate the Jews, many of them, if not majority of them, who did not know where to go. "At first, I thought they were animals," one of the envoys from Palestine later recalled. "There were families that lived five, six couples in one room, their entire sex life and everything together." Segev commented, "Since they were always in camps, and had suffered greatly, he [the envoy] concluded that 'for them it was natural.'"[65]

"Again and again," Segev added, "the envoys expressed their amazement that so many of the survivors quickly married and had children."[66] "It is hard to describe their longing for a normal life," another man on the same mission is quoted by Segev.[67] "I don't like the term survivor. After all, aren't we all survivors?" wrote Valy Weiner, the mother of Paul Weiner, the boy of Theresienstadt, in her own short autobiography,[68] meaning all those who were in the camp as well as those who were not.

Some of the Jews who walked out of the gates of the camps returned "home," now forever in quotation marks, to the countries where they had lived before the war. Often, too often, after they had experienced the reception they did, many decided to move again. Many ran directly or with stopovers to America, as the quotas, still in force, permitted, that is to say. Many, often the most bitter, courageous, or lost, the *recalcitrant*, some directly and some after running and stopovers lasting for months and years, moved to Palestine, Eretz Israel, the Jewish Homeland, the Jewish State.

The Jewish War of Independence against the British, rising Arab nationalism, and tensions between the Jews and Arabs all escalated at that precise moment. Palestine was a world with an expanding, "war-cultivated," hard surface, as much as the rest of the world. This was also what some called "the Arab miracle," walking on the land, and leaving the land without so much as leaving a trace. "Tens of thousands of homes were suddenly available."[69] "Hundreds of thousands of Arabs fled, and were expelled from their homes. Entire cities and whole villages were repopulated in short order with new immigrants, most of them Holocaust survivors."[70]

"Some of the fresh Zionists," Ruth Bondy wrote about the Theresienstadt camp people who moved to Israel, she one of them, "chose new Hebrew names: Jindra became Avri, Willy, Zev; Paul, Dov, Edith, Naomi. Others stuck to their old names or their names stuck to them."[71] They were often called *"yekeh"* by the Jews living in Palestine since before the war, as the German Jews used to call "Eastern" Jews from Poland, especially Galicia, before the war.[72] Now *"yekehs"* came generally to mean all the Jews coming from Europe. Sometimes the word was "simply translated," and the Holocaust survivors were referred to as "German."[73]

Amos Oz, an Israeli writer who came from a family of pre-war settlers and who lived through the mid- and late 1940s as a child, remembered how dire the situation in Palestine was, especially as the State of Israel was (about to be) declared: "We ate black bread with slices of onion and olives cut in half, and sometimes also with anchovy paste; we ate smoked fish and salt fish that came from the depth of the fragrant barrels in the corner of Mr. Auster's grocery; on special occasions we ate sardines, that we considered a delicacy."[74] It had to look for those who experienced it now very much like Theresienstadt's menu. What they were learning as they passed from day to day in Palestine, the news, was very much camplike, too. "It was slowly dawning on those whose families had not arrived," Amos Oz recalled, "that the Germans had killed them all."[75]

Israel became the suburb of the camps, and sprawling. There was not eerie but real closeness between the camps they came from and the place they came in. The language, certainly, remained that of clearing.

"Nobody used the word 'Palestinians' in those days," wrote Amos Oz, recalling how the Jews referred to the Arabs. "They were called 'terrorists,' *'fedayeen,'* 'the enemy,' or 'Arab refugees hungry for revenge.'" "We," wrote Oz, "have craftily grabbed more and more of their land."[76] It was an old-new, *altneu*, clearing. The people of the new Israel, including the new arrivals, and those from Theresienstadt among them, lived most purely and symptomatically in *kibbutzim*, which translated as "ingathering" but actually meant a fortress.[77] Like the internees of Boven Digoel in their camp watching for the Papuans in the dark forest, or like the recalcitrant in Tanah Tinggi, the Jews in the old-new land, carrying guns, were dressed "in shorts and singlet."[78]

"The ficus and pine trees, the myrtle bushes, the bougainvillea and ligustrum shrubs" in hot and desert Palestine welcomed the people accustomed to apple and linden trees in Theresienstadt and before "mosquitoes buzzed around them."[79] And the earth, for years and sometimes till they died in Israel, remained to them thin and just a surface. As the Israeli poet Yehuda Amichai wrote,

Forced
Always to emigrate once more from the smell
My life is stretched out this way, it grows very thin.[80]

When the gates of the camps opened, the camp people carried the light of the camps into the world, expanding the clearing. "Think what would naturally happen to them if they were released from their bonds," asks Plato talking about the cave. "Suppose one of them were let loose and suddenly compelled to stand up and turn his head, and look and walk towards the fire; all these actions would be painful, and he would be too dazzled to see properly.... Don't you think he would be at a loss, and think that what he used to see was far truer than the objects now being pointed out to him?"[81]

The people from Theresienstadt who emigrated to Palestine, "to some extent," as Ruth Bondy put it, began to see the camp of the just-ended past "as a place to look back at with longing." In the camp, she wrote, meaning Theresienstadt, "they were still near their parents, siblings, and friends; many of them experienced their first love there." They "went to school" there. In the camp, they still "knew nothing about the existence of the mechanized extermination of gas chambers."[82]

The ex-Theresienstadt people now in Palestine began to meet again, if they ever stopped. At Givat Haim (Ihud), a Jewish settlement one hour by car north of Tel Aviv, a sizeable group of the Theresienstadt people had settled. They began to do "conferences." At the meetings that became regular during the 1950s, they organized soccer tournaments and played "a singalong around a campfire, as in the days of the Zionist youth movement."[83]

"Upon arrival," historian Tom Segev wrote, "the new immigrants were often looked down on as an uprooted mass of refugees with no pride and no dignity. Some called the new arrivals "the people of the *She'erith Hapletah,* 'the Surviving Remnant.'"[84] With Jan, my son, we met one of them in 2014, an elderly man from prewar Czechoslovakia who lived in "Kibbutz Masaryk" near Haifa. He told us that he had come to Israel in 1945 and that then, so he said (should I keep it here?), at least once he was called *sabon*. "Soap," he explained.[85]

Boris Lurie, a Jew who survived the camps, left for the United States, and spent the rest of his life as an artist in New York, wrote, "Most survivors of the National Socialists' mass extermination, no longer felt comfortable in the world of those who had been spared."[86] A "survivor" of the Theresienstadt camp who came back to Prague, where he lived before the war, and one of those who stayed, told his interviewer that the tragedy of his generation was "that we actually have beautiful memories of Theresienstadt."[87]

Palestine, and Israel, again, was the most of this. In the world of camps after the camps, it was a concentration of what was happening to the Jews from the camps and to those never in the camps but watching the Jews from the camps. "Jerusalem," wrote Yehuda Amichai, "is full of used Jews."

> *Jerusalem is full of used Jews, worn out by history,*
> *Jews second-hand, slightly damaged, at bargain prices . . .*
> *. . .*
> *Jerusalem's a place where everyone remembers he's forgotten something*
> *but doesn't remember what it is. . . .*
> *This is the end of the landscape.*[88]

Except, that this was not the end of the landscape. The used Jews of Israel became the exemplary people of the "new worldliness of the world." About Kibbutz Gevaram at the time of Israel's victorious Six-Day War, in 1967, on the front line, Yehuda Amichai wrote,

> *In a wooden shack, I once saw*
> *books by Buber and Rilke on the shelf*
> *and prints of Van Gogh and Modigliani.*
> *It was on the eve of deadly battle.*
> *And there's a grove of eucalyptus trees,*
> *pale, as if sick with longing.*
> *They don't know what they're longing for*
> *and I tell them now in a quiet voice:*
> *Australia, Australia.*[89]

It was not the end of the landscape. One thing still left was to look to the stars. Half a century after the war, with many camp people still alive, an Israel astronaut was selected for the next flight of the space shuttle *Columbia*. His name was Ilan Ramon, his mother was a Holocaust survivor, and he looked for a memento to take with him up there. He consulted the Yad Vashem Memorial and with their help chose a drawing by Petr Ginz, a boy of Theresienstadt, the editor of the Theresienstadt boys' magazine *Vedem*, who perished in Auschwitz in 1944. The picture, appropriately enough, represented the boy's image, the camp's image of the moon landscape. The *Columbia*, on which Ilan Ramon was flying, as it is known, burned on its way back, upon reentering the Earth's atmosphere, on February 1, 2003. "It would have been Petr's seventy-fifth birthday," Petr's sister told me in her house in Omer, Israel.[90]

....

On July 11, 1928, still very early into the camp's existence, a Chinese-Malay newspaper in Batavia published an interview with the widow of a Boven Digoel internee who had died in the camp. The woman had returned from New Guinea to Java, and now, she told the paper, her husband came back with her as a ghost.[91]

Of the few internees in Boven Digoel who "got mercy" and for whatever reason were allowed to leave the camp before its final evacuation in 1943, as well as of those who "perhaps" escaped, who disappeared into the jungle or down the river, little was known "for real." Those who came home after the camp was liquidated in 1943, and after the long detour, being still interned in Australia and arriving in Indonesia, of some of them, as late as in 1947, only fragmentary information exists, most of it ghastly, too.

Achmad Basuki Siradi, a Boven Digoel internee, originally from Surakarta, Central Java, was released from the camp for reasons unstated a short while before the Japanese invaded the Indies in 1942 and before the whole camp was evacuated. On his return, immediately it seems, he joined the Communist Party again, an underground group at the time. After the Dutch capitulated soon afterward, the Japanese, the new rulers in the Indies, arrested Siradi, clearly on new or old charges of being a Communist. The Kenpeitai, the Japanese military police, tortured Siradi, so much still is known, and this is the last time Siradi is mentioned anywhere.[92] Hadji Achmad was let go from Boven Digoel at the same time. He, too, it appears, resumed underground activities; he, too, was arrested by the Japanese; and he, too, "disappeared."[93] Soekindar, equally so, was released from Boven

Digoel and arrested by the Japanese, and the last thing we know about him was that he sat in a prison in Semarang, a town on the north coast of Java.[94]

Osa Maliki Wangsadinata was also released from Boven Digoel before the time. He also fell into the Kenpeitai's hands, but he survived. He lived to join the Indonesian Revolution in 1945, as a member of the Barisan Pelopor Istimewa [Special Student Unit Corps].[95]

Soetan Sjahrir, the "academician" in Boven Digoel and as such released after just one year in the camp, spent the Japanese occupation in hiding. After 1945, with a clean record of not collaborating with the occupiers, he quickly rose in the political space of the independent state and became the first prime minister of the republic in November 1945.[96] Mohammad Hatta, the other "academician," was released from Boven Digoel at the same time as Sjahrir. He did collaborate with the Japanese, second only in importance to "the leader," Soekarno. When Soekarno proclaimed Indonesian independence on August 17, 1945, he became the first president, and Hatta the first vice president.

Hatta's larger-than-life statue now stands in the center of where the Boven Digoel camp used to be. In a storage area of what local people (wrongly) point out as "the colonial prison of Boven Digoel" (it was a prison, but long after the camp was gone, in the 1950s), my son and I, on our visit in 2013, found "the Hatta bench." Or so a label said on what remained of a wooden bench. The "original" and "no doubt" "Hatta bench" is in one of the old photographs in Salim's memoirs. It is said by Salim in the memoirs that it was a bench where Hatta "took his rest there and read."[97]

Like the Hatta statue, the figures of the two "academicians" and prominent politicians after the war overshadow whatever memories there might be of "the other" Boven Digoel. The fates of the mass of the people of Boven Digoel, and they seemed similar to one another, appeared sporadically, flashes at the crossroads, to use Kwon Heonik's words about the Vietnamese dead, as "traveling ghosts." Like in Heonik's history, "traveling bags as if" were often offered to the people of Boven Digoel when they appeared—to get them away, back on their road. Some in Indonesia were "simply killed," or, those who were ghosts, "killed again."

During the bloody war of independence, the exhausted and increasingly anxious Soekarno government tried to do what it could to convince the "Free World," the United Kingdom and the United States, that it was not really revolutionary, and certainly not inclining toward Communism. Diverging forces in Indonesia were fighting for the future character of the republic, whether nationalism would mature into a movement for a social change and how fast. In September 1948 in the town of Madiun, East Java, the struggle grew into an open military confrontation of Indonesians with Indonesians. The Communist Party of Indonesia, legal in the new state, had been accused of plotting to overthrow the Soekarno government and was crushed. Many of the Boven Digoel ex-internees, "survivors," whether involved in the affair or not, as "well-known Communists," appeared among those hunted down and killed. As a rule, the whereabouts of their graves, or corpses, are unknown.

Those who survived, the former Boven Digoel people, tried to become invisible. A few still went into politics or into government service, but cautiously. They were helped, I was told by some of them, by the fact that the government did not put "the Boven Digoel question" on a form they were asked to fill when applying for a job. This was Indonesia, nothing was clearly defined; at the same time the people from the camp were getting a small government pension. But, again I was told, it was not worth the trouble, or the risk, and many did not care to apply. Moreover, the steady inflation soon made the pension laughable. As I met them, in the 1980s, 1990s, 2000s, and 2010s, they were still looking over their shoulders.

Another "Communist *putsch*" was crushed in Indonesia in the fall of 1965. Between 500,000 and a million people, suspected of being Communists or having left-wing sympathies, were murdered in one of the largest holocausts in modern time. Boven Digoel people, quite old by the time if still living, wherever found, were either killed or put in prison, or camp again. In the words of Salim, who watched the events from his new home in the Netherlands, "All former Boven Digoel internees were . . . now eliminated"; "all"; "*áálle*," Salim added, of course hyperbolically, and clearly in horror, "really all."[98]

Mr. Trikoyo was one of the Boven Digoel people who "were sent back." He spent eight years in a camp on Buru, the island in the middle between Java and New Guinea. He was let go after eight years. "We all became *manusia usia lanjut MANULA*," he liked to say, "people of advanced age." I told him about Jerusalem being full of "used Jews." He laughed.[99]

Mr. Trikoyo once showed me on his computer a list of seventeen "children of Digoel," as he called them, his friends who were children in the camp. All of the seventeen at the time lived not far from Mr. Trikoyo, and he had planned some kind of a reunion. But he was not sure "if anyone would come."[100] They did not come.

Mr. Trikoyo was still very much alive when we were seeing each other between the 1990s and the 2010s. He was at his computer every day, and he still received visitors. He had a stroke a few months after he was released from the Buru camp, in the mid-1970s, and he was still partially paralyzed. He typed with one finger of his left hand, "the better hand," he told me. What Heidegger said, quoting Nietzsche, fit Mr. Trikoyo perfectly: "In anticipation, *Dasein* [being there] ... guards against 'becoming too old for its victories.'"[101] More than ever before, and it might be the world around him, Mr. Trikoyo looked recalcitrant.

In front of Mr. Trikoyo's house in Tangerang, East Jakarta, was a large vacant square with a highly improvised basketball court, and a mosque in the back. Even without the prerecorded muezzin calls to prayer five times a day and without the basketball court, it would have been a very noisy place. Still, much of the time Mr. Trikoyo spoke in a low voice. "Have you ever told your neighbors about the camps?" I asked him, after we knew each other better. "No," he said and pointed to the next door on the left side and to the next door on the right side across the narrow driveways (with no cars).

"Do not they know?" I asked.
"No!" he said.
"You've lived in this house for how long?"
"Eight years?"
"And at the place where you lived before. The people knew?"
"No!"[102]

Mrs. Widayasih, another "child of Digoel," spoke with me around the same time I talked to Mr. Trikoyo, and told me a story about the spring of 1966, at the height of the massacres. Vigilante groups, clearly with the Indonesian army as a backup, roamed through the streets of Jakarta day and night looking for Communists. Mrs. Widayasih lived with her husband and her father, a Boven Digoel ex-internee who was still alive, and she was not sure whether they had them already on some of their lists. She was sure, however, that even if they did not, were they to find the stacks of the old copies of *Bintang Timur* [The Eastern Star], a Communist magazine her father read and kept, "they would know." It would mean another camp. "Father was always stubborn like a horse," Mrs. Widayasih told me, "but he was old and weak, too." He could merely watch, she said, how his daughter and her husband were making fire of the *Bintang Timur* in the backyard of their house. "Who was the worst?" I asked. "The neighbors," Mrs. Widayasih said without a moment of hesitation.

Mr. Bangun Topo, another "Digoel child," told me on one of my visits to his house in Eastern Jakarta that even the members of his family on his wife's side never knew about his being in the camp. "I got in the army, you understand," he said in explanation.[103]

Yudo Widiyastono was born in Boven Digoel to an internee named Soekarno, not the national leader and later president. But his father might have gotten the name to pay homage to the leader. Yudo's grandfather was a Boven Digoel internee, Kadiroen, a recalcitrant, who spent most of the time with his large family, including Yudo and Soekarno, in the toughest-of-the-tough Tanah Tinggi section of the camp.

I met Mr. Yudo in his house in a middle-class neighborhood of Depok, a town that was a one-hour drive south of Jakarta. His name, Yudo, means "Battle" or "Struggle." Mr. Yudo told me that he was too small in the camp to remember very much, and that even as a teenager and young adult, from his parents, or from anybody, he heard very little about the camp. "Boven Digoel was *off*," he said, using the English word even when he otherwise spoke Indonesian. Only after his father died, in the 1970s, did the family find out that, all those years, the old man was writing about the camp, "a memoir," "and there," said Mr. Yudo, "is everything."

"Copyedited pages," Yudo said, "it is just waiting to go to the printer." "When?" I asked, and who can imagine my excitement. "Can I see it now?" "Oh no, we are still waiting for the situation to be more *aman*," he said, "*aman*," in Indonesian, means "calm" or "safe." Mr. Yudo explained that that would be "when we retire," meaning, when there will be no danger of people "discovering Communists" in them and of such hard-won careers made "unsafe."

Many of the "Boven Digoel children" and "Boven Digoel grandchildren" have reached quite high positions in the independent Indonesia, as government officials, and many of them, in fact, in the military—as they saw it and told me—in large part because they did not talk about "being of Digoel." I probably will not see Yudo's father's memoir, ever. Dust is settling on it somewhere. It may be, in fact, this single stack of paper, never seen, covered by dust and turning into dust, that I am writing this chapter about.[104]

Mrs. Chamsinah, another "child of Digoel," her fifty-or-so son Kiki told me, is not afraid. Chamsinah never wrote about the camp, he said, but "she is an organizer." In the last year, in fact, she had put together a list of the Boven Digoel people still alive, the "Digoel children," that is, and planned "a reunion." All was already done, the envelopes with addresses, and the letters of invitations. "But some people were anxious. It did not happen."[105]

Tatiana Lukman [Loekman in the old transcription] is the oldest of the five children of M. H. Loekman, a man whom we recall listed in the Boven

Digoel police records as the youth teaching music to the internees' children, against the rules, to children from more than three families. Loekman survived, came back to Indonesia, and became active in the Communist movement again. During the 1965 and 1966 massacres, he disappeared and almost certainly was killed.[106]

Tatiana Lukman lived near Utrecht in the Netherlands when I visited her in June 2011. She still believed Khrushchev was "a dirty revisionist," which, she said, her father taught her.[107] In 2008 Tatiana published a book about Boven Digoel. The little book, rather a manifesto, has the title *Panta Rhei: Tidak Ada Pengorbanan yang Sia-Sia* [Everything Flows: No Sacrifice Is in Vain].

Tatiana Lukman was born long after Boven Digoel. Half a century after Boven Digoel, and more than twenty years after her father disappeared, in 1988, she traveled to Australia to look for the graves of the Boven Digoel people who had been evacuated there in 1943. Some died there "in transit," Tatiana's grandfather and grandmother on her father's side among them.

She might be more successful than Hannah Arendt searching for the grave of Walter Benjamin, or she might be more persistent. First, in the catalogues of the National Library in Sydney, Tatiana found the names of eight former Boven Digoel internees who died and were buried in Australia. Second, she then took a trip three hundred kilometers west of Sydney, to the town of Cowra, where most of the Boven Digoel people were put after they arrived in Australia. In Cowra, she found the graves, eight concrete slabs, that is, with name posts no longer there. But she copied the plan of the cemetery from the Sydney library and she believed she found the graves she had come for.[108]

This might be the end of the landscape. What might come next? Some "Digoel children" told me that Tatiana visited them in Jakarta on her way. Mostly, she irritated them, they said, with her dogmatic and unbending stories she was telling them about what had "really" happened in the camp.

J. M. G. Le Clézio, in his novel *Desert*, describes Aamma, a Tuareg woman: "Sometimes Aamma tells the story differently, as if she doesn't really remember very well."[109] This may be a way.

I met Mr. Moedakir on my next-to-last trip to Indonesia, on the outskirts of Serang, a provincial town ninety kilometers west of Jakarta.[110] I was given the telephone number of his granddaughter by another child of Boven Digoel, and I called her to make sure Mr. Moedakir would be at home. "Sure, he will," she said and laughed. "Go west of the town," she told me, "till you come to the big bamboo tree. Then turn left."

Mr. Moedakir was six years younger than Mr. Trikoyo, and they were friends in Boven Digoel. Moedakir was the son of internee Mohamad Isa.[111] Like Mr. Trikoyo, two decades and three years after he got out of Boven Digoel, after "the 1965 affair," he was sent to a camp again, on Buru.

According to Zarathustra, "The individual can experience himself only at the end of his wandering." Mr. Moedakir, as I arrived, took my hands into his, squeezed them, and said they felt like the hands of Mr. Campbell. Clarrie Campbell was an Australian labor-union organizer who worked with the Indonesians after they were evacuated from the camp to Australia, and who saw most of them leave for Java in 1947.[112]

Trikoyo had warned me about Mr. Moedakir's "fluent talking." Indeed, as the talk went on, I did not understand much of what the old man was saying. He was speaking fast and without interruption, except for a short breath and a sip of coffee now and then. The Javanese taxi driver who took me there, and who sat there with us throughout the visit, an Indonesian native speaker, told me on our way back that he did not understand much either.

I felt like Louis-Ferdinand Céline, who described trying to talk to a friend amid the deafening noise of Paris burning, the city attacked by the Allied planes in 1945. "What if," wondered Céline, forgetting about the planes, "he was answering me after all? Maybe I just couldn't hear him? What if my own noise was drowning it out?"[113]

There was not much furniture in Mr. Moedakir's house. His daughter told me, with him listening and nodding as she talked, how her mother, Mr. Moedakir's wife, after they put Moedakir in the camp again, sent him to Buru in 1966, she "married temporarily." Mr. Trikoyo's wife, in fact, had told me the same thing about herself. In order to survive, they had to have some man. Mrs. Trikoyo, actually, had a child from the "temporary marriage"; Mrs. Moedakir had two. After the internees returned, Moedakir after thirteen years in Buru, Trikoyo after eight, the women often, and in both Moedakir's and Trikoyo's cases, rejoined the men. "They had their time in the camps," Mrs. Moedakir laughs, "but we, what could we do?"

Mr. Moedakir's father, Mohamad Isa, an ex-internee of Boven Digoel, got back to Java from Boven Digoel and Australia in 1947, and died "here," Mr. Moedakir pointed toward the open door of the house, meaning in this town. At the time of "the *Madiun*," in 1948, "he was not killed," Mr. Moedakir said, "he died."

After he came from Boven Digoel via Australia, Mr. Moedakir himself worked as a *becak*, a rickshaw driver. Why was he arrested and sent to the second camp in 1966? The *dukun*, shaman, local witch healer, predicted it. That is why.

Mr. Moedakir is bald, the skin is paper-like, thick yellow with big dark-brown and black spots, stretched tightly over his skull, and equally so over his bony face. I am not sure if he could see me at all. They say he is "legally blind," but so am I. His eyes are light gray, almost white, and empty, sky-empty. He has had several strokes and has to be washed and helped to the bathroom. The rest of the time, he sits in a wheelchair the whole day, facing the open door.

As Mr. Trikoyo said, he was fluent indeed, no stopping. He appeared particularly proud and his voice rose at those moments, of his memory for numbers, both from Boven Digoel and from Buru: "77," "143," "586," "5." I recognized some of them, and checked others back in the hotel. All correct.

....

"From this point on, there are memories," Georges Perec wrote in *The Memory of Childhood*, "fleeting, persistent, trivial, burdensome—but there is nothing that binds them together."[114] "In Eastern Europe," Ruth Bondy wrote, "thousands disappeared without anyone knowing their names anymore." Well, not really, she corrected herself, and with a clear hint of bitterness, or melancholy, or burdensome memory: "There are some names extant and in fact many, on the wall of the Pinkas Synagogue [in Prague], and in fact the list is supposedly complete," she wrote, when compared, that is, to the names "in the memorial book and in the two computerized card files."[115]

Some upgrades to the Pinkas Synagogue in Prague, related to memory, were embarked upon already by the Nazis in 1942. The upgrades were a part of Hitler's project of a monumental all-Europe or all-Reich Jewish Museum, perhaps to be established in Prague. Imposing, and dead, Jewish culture was to be put on display, to complement the German museums of equally imposing and dead Greek and Roman cultures, for the next thousand years of the German Reich. A team of Jewish scholars was ordered to collect and catalogue the ritual and other "objects of the Jews" from the synagogues and Jewish homes of Europe, as long as these had not yet been plundered or burned completely to ash.

The team picked up, set to work, some of the team lovingly so, no doubt—these were treasures close to extinction and still possible to save. One after the other and in the end, all except one, it seems, the members of the team were transported to, and perished in, the camps. One of the two survivors of the original team, Dr. Hana Frankensteinová-Volavková, had been deported to Theresienstadt close to the end of the war, survived, and became the first director of the newly opened Jewish Museum in liberated Prague.[116]

Georg Wilhelm Friedrich Hegel, and many others of his time and since his time, was well aware that the very symbolization of a thing always "equals its mortification."[117] A German artist, Wolf Vostell, of the camp generation, created a large painting to be exhibited at one of the Auschwitz trials in Frankfurt, titled *Wir Waren so eine Art Museumsstück* [We Were a Kind of Museum Piece].[118]

"When we put up a sign or a label—this event happened in this space, this monument is erected to the memory of—we admit defeat," said William Kentridge in a recent Harvard lecture.[119] "The wrenching of things from their familiar contexts," wrote Walter Benjamin, equals "the normal state for goods on display."[120]

At the site of the Pinkas Synagogue in Prague, after the war, the Jewish Museum installed a memorial wall: "Eighty thousand names are recorded," Ruth Bondy wrote in one of her books on Theresienstadt, in a chapter titled "Roll Call."[121] "The names project," she wrote, is built, first, upon "an alphabetical index of all the deportees according to the lists of transport," and, second, upon "a record of the deceased." "The names of all the women," she added, are "written with the suffix -ová or -á, as is customary in Czech, even if they came from German-speaking families." It means they were never called these names when alive. All the first names of the people on the wall are written in their Czech version. Whatever these people might be called when still alive, Ernst, Franz, Georg, Ignaz, Rosalia, Elizabeth, Johanna, they are memorialized, silhouetted on the wall, as Arnošt, František, Jiří, Hynek, Růžena, Eliška, Jana.

I have to check the next time I am in Prague whether the memorial wall is built of bricks, of marble, or perhaps of concrete. In any case, it appears, to quote Ruth Bondy for the last time in this book, "What is written on the wall cannot be changed."[122] This is still a screen that cannot be touched. The "documentary" *Der Führer Schenkt den Juden eine Stadt*, Theresienstadt on the silver screen, became better known after the war, in fact, more real in our world of camps, than Theresienstadt itself.[123]

The people, whose names are on the wall and cannot be changed, even typos, have be made immortal by the force of the wall—or screen. The Javanese survivors of Boven Digoel, who got no wall after the fact, might recognize the Pinkas Synagogue memorial wall as *Martaya*, "a deathless void."[124]

There are crowds of tourists from all over the world now in Prague, queuing to see the Pinkas Synagogue, the adjacent Old Jewish Cemetery, and the memorial wall. There must be children and grandchildren of Theresienstadt among them. It is too late for many survivors to be there. To some of the visitors the wall might be a "hidden death," "an excess of negativity, a loss or a remainder in surplus," "something supernumerary in relation to all calculation," a "repeated possibilization of the unprecedented."[125] To others it might be one of the wailing walls, like the major one in Jerusalem, Yehuda Amichai wrote about:

> *Tourists . . .*
> They squat at the Holocaust Memorial.
> They put on grave faces at the Wailing Wall.[126]

"The visitors to Auschwitz," wrote Dwork and van Pelt on the history of the camp and town after 1945, "are not told that the crematorium they see is largely a postwar reconstruction."[127] "Museums?" wrote Rem Koolhaas, "no cemetery would dare to reshuffle corpses as casually in the name of current expediency."[128]

Whenever I go to Theresienstadt, I try to walk the route they walked, three kilometers from the nearest railway station in Bohušovice. Later they built a railhead directly to the camp, and, as I walk, I look for the remnants of the tracks. Google helps: "This railhead does not exist today anymore. It was shortened after the war, it was electrified, and until the 1990s, it served the local company, *Zelenina Terezín* [Vegetables Theresienstadt]. As such it was used when several films were made related to Theresienstadt during World War II."[129] The "Boven Digoel Heroes Cemetery" was built in the 1970s, during the Buru camp time. It is behind the statue of Hatta, on the site where the camp cemetery used to be. The dead lie there, or one should assume so, and they are rearranged, now all under identical and rectangular concrete slabs, ½ by 1½ meters, in straight rows, the long and the shorter ones, Ls and Qs, one may say, having a flashback to the streets of Theresienstadt. The layout of the cemetery is Icaria-like, symmetrical; all the graves are numbered, and many names are misspelled.

Boven Digoel now is a provincial town, a sprawling settlement of houses very much like those one finds anywhere in modern Indonesia. The "new people" are coming from the western part of the archipelago, mostly Muslims. They own also the only two eateries in Boven Digoel, and two small bed-and-breakfasts. The Catholic priest is also an Indonesian. Mass is held every day, and the church is visited almost exclusively by the

Papua people. Some live in the settlement and others still visit from the jungle.

Mr. Benedictus is a Papua chief of the local voluntary defense in Boven Digoel. We met by chance when Jan and I took a walk, and he told us that he knew everything about Boven Digoel, and especially its past. He heard it from his parents, he said, who were born around 1966. He took us around, first to the former house of the administrator of the camp, he said, then to the former camp hospital. We did not take our map with us that afternoon so we could enjoy undisturbed our walk and Mr. Benedictus's pointing to sites and telling us what we saw. Both the administrator's buildings and the hospital stood on a small overhang over Digoel, and there truly was a beautiful view of the river, as both Salim and Dr. Schoonheyt indeed wrote that there was.

Of the few buildings that Mr. Benedictus said were still from the time of the camp, only foundations made of concrete, where there had been such foundation, survived. On some of these foundations, platforms, in fact, Papua families built huts of palm leaves and metal sheets (was it zinc?).

"Our graves," Salim wrote in his memoirs—he never visited Boven Digoel after 1943—"were well cared for by us until our last days in the camp." "On simple little wooden planks above the graves stood names," he wrote. "Only with the time, in an exposure to the winds, the rains, and the sun, some of the names became hard to read."[130] "If I were ever go back to visit," Salim wrote, "and if I still might find some traces, it would surely be the graves."[131]

The Boven Digoel Heroes Cemetery can be called a "cementery."[132] The amount of concrete used there, holding the graves together and keeping the names readable, makes the present in the cemetery, in the words of Ernst Bloch, "become unpresent." The present turned unpresent, Bloch wrote, "drifts like debris down some nameless river [through a] wholly unfeeling universe."[133] It makes it possible, or so one may at least try, at the Heroes Cemetery more than anywhere, to make the dead become unpresent and "go on living," as in Kafka's *Metamorphosis*—to honor the dead's memory: "'He has to go,' cried his sister, 'that's the only solution, father. You just have to try to get rid of the idea that it's Gregor. That we believed it for so long, that is our real tragedy.... If it were Gregor, he would have realized long since that it isn't possible.... He would have gone away of his own accord. Then we wouldn't have a brother, but we would be able to go on living and honor his memory.'"[134]

When Kafka sent *Metamorphosis* to the publisher, the story of the young man Gregor who is changed into an insect, Kafka was very particular about possible illustrations for the story: "The insect itself is not to be drawn. It is not even to be seen from a distance.... If I may make a suggestion of my own about the illustrations, I would choose scenes such as: the parents and the chief clerk by the closed door, or, better still, the parents and the sister in a lighted room, in which the door to a completely dark room stands open."[135]

The Prince in Dostoyevsky's *The Idiot* tells the ladies, once at a tea, how on his travels in Europe he witnessed an execution. The ladies are curious. "I did not like it at all," he says at last, "and I was rather ill afterward, but I admit that I was riveted to the spot, I could not take my eyes off it."[136] "At the sight of ruins," the prophet Jeremiah said, "the pious man must 'whistle,' remain 'appalled,' and 'shake his head.'"[137]

Before the world falls apart, however, the camps might become a tourist space, holding the world together.

BOVEN DIGOEL TOURS

A six-day trip will discover the cultural and historic sites of Merauke and Boven Digoel.
Do experience the hidden world on an adventure that you will never forget. Price from €1,199 per person.
...

Day 4 from Bupul to Boven Digoel:
After breakfast, you will travel to the high point of the trip, Boven Digoel, a journey lasting about ten hours, during which you will see the splendid Digoel River. After arrival to Boven Digoel, free time.

Day 5 Boven Digoel:
Find out about Boven Digoel. You will visit a traditional market, a waterfall of the Bening River, bening meaning "clear," and a prison from the colonial period where the first president of Indonesia, Soekarno, was jailed.

Day 6 Boven Digoel:
The end of this trip. After breakfast, you will be transferred to the next site of your choice, an Agats village, the Oksibil Mountains, or back to Merauke, either by plane or by car.

DEVA GROUP UTRECHT[138]

Rem Koolhaas wrote, and this is also the last quote from him in this book, "The upward curve of tourism" is "about to intersect the downward graph of historical presence."[139]

In Theresienstadt, I used to have coffee at the Hotel Imperial, before it went bankrupt, I think in 2014. With "the best snacks in town," the only snacks in town, in fact, it was located on the main square of town and former camp, next to where the Gestapo offices used to be. There used to be a glossy folder on each table on the hotel terrace. I have stolen the folder. It invited me to spend a weekend "In Imperial Theresienstadt." There were nineteenth-century frescoes of romantic landscapes in the hotel's dancing hall, and this was perhaps what the folder meant: "Stay with us," it read, "You will be mollycoddled by history."

In the building of the former youth home, where also the boy's magazine *Vedem* was edited, after the war a permanent exposition was installed titled "The Public Security Corps and Revolutionary Traditions of the North Bohemia Region." After 1989, with the "revolutionary" regime in Czechoslovakia gone, "the marble panels were removed from the inner walls of the museum of the police and revolution, and the crystal chandeliers of the museum were taken down." The place, in the words of a Czech historian, "returned to its original look."[140]

On October 17, 1991, the Theresienstadt Memorial was ceremoniously opened, a whole town in fact, turned into a museum.[141] Mrs. Greta Kingsberg, the young singer in the camp who if you stripped her naked you'd find only music, told me a story when I saw her in 2015 in her house in Jerusalem. She decided to visit Theresienstadt, still hesitantly, for the first time after fifty years of life in Israel. At the main building, where the museum route now began, she was asked to buy a ticket. "I was here already," Greta told the woman at the box office, with a poker face. So, she tells me, and slaps her knee, "They let me in again!"[142]

Elena Makarova, when we once took a walk in Theresienstadt, told me what her deepest impression of the place was: "Theresienstadt after six," she said, "all tourists are gone."

Very few people stay in town after six; the buses leave and one sees only a person or a group of two or three, now and then, on the street. These are most often the patients from the home for the mentally ill, where restrictions seem to be loose. Drug and alcohol addicts have been added to the patients recently.

This seems to be quite a standard situation. It happened to me after 1989, not just once, almost exactly as it happened to Mr. Austerlitz in W. G. Sebald's novel, and before 1989. Mr. Austerlitz wanders on a deserted Theresienstadt street, "except for a mentally disturbed man who crossed my path among the lime trees of the park with the fountain, telling I have no idea what tale in a kind of broken German [sic], frantically waving his arms, before he too, still clutching the hundred-crown note I had given him, seemed to be swallowed up by the earth, as they say, even as he was running off."[143]

....

In an interview in 1975, Claud Lanzmann asked Rabbi Benjamin Murmelstein, the last head of the Jewish Council of the Elders in Theresienstadt:

QUESTION: *Since when do you live in Rome?*

ANSWER: Since 1947.

QUESTION: *Do you have some pictures from Theresienstadt?*

ANSWER No, no.

QUESTION: *You have nothing?*

ANSWER: No, no, no.[144]

I asked the same question of Mr. Moedakir, and, in the same words, he, and in fact all the Boven Digoel people I still had a chance to meet, answered the same way and in the same words. "Look there!" they could easily quote the Old Javanese *Ramayana*, "the city is all covered and hidden under an ashy gray dome."[145] The books, letters, and photographs turned to ash most easily. "Holocaust" comes from Greek *"holokauston,"* from *"holos,"* whole, and *"kaustos,"* burned.

I talked to Mr. Tobi Siregar, one of the "Digoel children," shortly before his death (as I talked to all of them shortly before their deaths). He told me about a "nostalgia trip" he and five of the other "Digoel children" recently made to the site of the former camp. Did he still find something? "No, no, nothing," he said, like Rabbi Murmelstein. "Well, oh yes," he corrected himself, "a mortar, half-buried in the ground." Tobi's father used to earn some additional money by husking and grinding rice for the camp people, and it might have been his. "Have you taken it with you home?" He slapped his knee like Greta Kingsberg telling me about her return to Theresienstadt. "You're so funny! It was too heavy to take on the plane." "It must be still there," he added after a short pause, "in the grass."[146]

Nothing new, only now it seems even more the everyday. This is William Kentridge's modern telling of an old story: "The bank at the edge of the River Styx, where Charon deposits those headed for the black darkness of Hades. He keeps in his boat the attributes they have shed. A suitcase of teeth, a pile of shoes, a sheaf of words, an old stone discus. Held in trust on account, waiting to be decoded, for the shards to be rearranged, to be made new."[147] There is a future, some believe, in suitcases of teeth that may be returned, in ashes and dust, in the remainder. The Book of Job speaks of a man "whose foundation is in the dust."[148] Heidegger wrote (after Nietzsche), "Authentic historicity, understands history as the 'return' (*Wiederkehr*)."[149]

Mr. Trikoyo, with his wife sitting next to him, told me that he was lucky. His wife, I already knew, married another man after they took him to his second camp, the Buru camp, in 1966. "I am lucky. I have a son from my wife here, who married another man while I was in the camp. If it had not happened, and if the other one did not make her pregnant, I would not have a son, because I cannot anymore. After the interrogation by the police in Jakarta, I became impotent. Still today I have not recovered."[150] "In certain conditions, which attach them to the very movements of things," Gilles Deleuze wrote in his *Desert Islands*, "humans do not put an end to desertness, they make it sacred," they are "ready to begin the world anew."[151] "Miracles" happen, wrote Emmanuel Levinas in *Beyond Memory*, "those that take place upon the return from exile and dispersion."[152]

Gilles Deleuze, however, also warned, and his warning is especially pertinent to a historian: "If you're trapped in the dream of the other," he wrote, "you're fucked."[153] The last time I saw Mr. Trikoyo in his house in Tangerang, he embraced me as I was leaving, and, for a moment, I felt his sweat on my face. Somebody said wisely that the best way to write is to write in panic. This is, at least, how one can get a little closer to his "human subjects," while running, too, or trying to, or at least thinking about it.

NOTES

Introduction

1 Lyotard, *Heidegger and "the Jews,"* 22.
2 Lyotard, *Heidegger and "the Jews,"* 81.
3 Lyotard, *Heidegger and "the Jews,"* 27.
4 Lyotard, *Heidegger and "the Jews,"* 80.
5 "For finer purposes of life, little was available. Terror of the sublime maddened all minds." Bellow, *Mr. Sammler's Planet*, 89.
6 Wittgenstein, *On Certainty*, 9, 58.
7 Adorno, *Aesthetic Theory*, 339.
8 "Joy," in Singer, *Gimpel the Fool*, 125–26.
9 Beckett, *Letters*, 4:546.
10 Brecht, *Poems*, 320.
11 Beckett, *Letters*, 1:553.
12 Barthes, *Fashion System*, 292.
13 Canetti, *Crowds and Power*, 227.
14 "On the Image of Proust," in Benjamin, *Selected Writings*, 2:265.

Chapter 1. Clothes

Kafka, *Diaries, 1910–1913*, December 16, 1911, 180.

1. Thea Höchster, "Konto-buch," YVA 033 7136.
2. Presser, *Destruction of Dutch Jewry*, 534.
3. Hillesum, *Interrupted Life*, 43.
4. Juhasz, "Tztzit–Ritual Fringes," in Juhasz, *Jewish Wardrobe*, 51.
5. Balzac, *Treatise on Elegant Living*, 26.
6. Chekhov, *Sakhalin Island*, 91.
7. Adler, *Theresienstadt*, 1:122.
8. Stepan Trofimovich, on his final journey, was "dressed 'for the road.'" Dostoyevsky, *Demons*, 595.
9. Riedmann, *Ich bin Jude*, 77.
10. Adler, *Theresienstadt*, 2:277.
11. Weil, *Life with a Star*, 111.
12. On June 1, 1943, the railhead into the camp was ceremoniously opened. Adler, *Theresienstadt*, 3:696.
13. Bondy, *Elder of the Jews*, 250.
14. Balzac, *Treatise on Elegant Living*, 1.
15. Shean, *To Be an Actress*, 35.
16. Kafka, *Diaries, 1910–1913*, October 28, 1911, 120.
17. BDA 91.
18. BDA 91.
19. Nielsen, *In het Land van Kannibalen*, 102–3.
20. Schoonheyt, *Boven-Digoel*, 263. Unless noted otherwise, the 1936 edition is used.
21. Mechanicus, *Waiting for Death*, September 19, 1943, 161.
22. "Lijst dari nama2 barang2 jang ditinggalkan oleh Djaidin al. Mardjoen," Boven Digoel, December 20, 1932, in BDA 308.
23. "Lijst dari nama2 barang2 jang ditinggalkan oleh Soewita al. Soeparman," Boven Digoel, October 7, 1933, BDA 47.
24. "Politie Dagboek," BDA 212.
25. YVAF 1550.
26. Italie, *Het Oorlogsdagboek*, 491.
27. Italie, *Het Oorlogsdagboek*, 520–21.
28. Pavel Weiner, *Boy in Terezín*, 216–17.
29. Manes, *Als ob's ein Leben*, 73.
30. "Testimony of Frieda (Kuttner) Cohn," YVA 01-291, 7.
31. Adler, *Theresienstadt*, 1:126.
32. "Nieuws v.d. Dag," IPO 1931.
33. "Voor Inhouding op Loonen," Boven Digoel, October 18, 1937, BDA 122.
34. "Keng Po," October 4, 1927, IPO 1927.
35. Soetan Sjahrir, letter to Duchâteu, Boven Digoel, November 9, 1935, n.p., KITLV.
36. "Register brieven," 1929, BDA 33.
37. "Register brieven," 1928, BDA 32.

38. "Register van Verstrekte Toelatingsbewijsen," 1932–35, BDA 275.
39. Italie, *Het Oorlogsdagboek*, 64.
40. Italie, *Het Oorlogsdagboek*, 94.
41. Interview with Trikoyo, Tangerang, Indonesia, July 7, 2008.
42. "Politie Dagbook," BDA 212.
43. Barthes, *Fashion System*, 24,
44. Testimoy by W. A. Ottow-Blok, Heemstede, third part, February 23, 1999, MGI 1316.2.
45. Internee Toepin registered on the ship as he went to Boven Digoel: "a box no. 11: sewing machine." "Directeur der Strafgevangenis," Medan, March 3, 1927, BDA 91.
46. Interview with Trikoyo, Tangerang, May 17, 2011.
47. Interview with Widayasih, Jakarta, January 23, 2009.
48. M. van Blankenstein, "Het verbanningsoord," *Nieuwe Rotterdamsche Courant*, September 13, 1928.
49. M. van Blankenstein, "Het verbanningsoord," *Nieuwe Rotterdamsche Courant*, September 11, 1928.
50. "Politie Dagboek," November 17, 1934, BDA 210.
51. "Politie Dagboek," June 19, 1936, BDA 212.
52. "Politie Dagboek," May 1, 1936, BDA 212.
53. Widayasih, *Masa kanak-kanak*, 1:26.
54. Mas Marco, *Pergaulan Orang Buangan*, 58.
55. Schoonheyt, *Boven-Digoel*, 35.
56. Schoonheyt, *Boven-Digoel*, 129.
57. Schoonheyt, *Boven-Digoel*, 39.
58. Schoonheyt, *Boven-Digoel*, 110. Edmund Husserl wrote in *The Crisis of European Sciences*, "Reason is a broad title. According to the old familiar definition man is the rational animal, and in this broad sense even the Papuan is a man and not a beast" (290).
59. Widayasih, *Masa kanak-kanak*, 1:30.
60. Interview with Zakaria, Jakarta, May 10, 2011.
61. "Women in the Theresienstadt Ghetto," in Bondy, *Trapped*, 52.
62. Bondy, *Elder of the Jews*, 47.
63. Pressburger, *Diary of Petr Ginz*, 21.
64. Demetz, *Prague in Danger*, 75.
65. Redlich, *Terezín Diary*, 126n9.
66. "Dr. M. Rossel. Delegierten de C.I.C.R. April 23, 1944," in Kárný et al., *Theresienstädter Studien*, 1996, 289.
67. "Aus einen Brief an Frau Irma Doll und Herr Friedmann," November 21, 1946, YVA O.2/985, 4.
68. Ab Caransa, "Theresienstadt. Schizofrenie in steen," NIOD 809/17, 27.
69. "Letter by Dr. F. Saron," February 9, 1946, 3, YVA 07/6-4-8. See also Dr. Jacob Jacobson, "Jewish Survivors Report. The Daily Life, 1943–1945," March 1946, YVA 164/105, 12.
70. Josef Taussig, "Terezínské korso po roce," JMP 326.
71. Manes, *Als ob's ein Leben*, 304.

72. Alfred Meril, Kurt J. Hermann, and Cpt. Charlie Ross, "A Trip to Ghetto Theresienstadt," YVA 07/6-4-3, 3.
73. Lipovetsky, *Empire of Fashion*, 23.
74. "Fashion," in Benjamin, *Arcades Project*, 66.
75. "Fashion," in Benjamin, *Arcades Project*, 62–63.
76. Barthes, *Fashion System*, 300.
77. "Fashion," in Benjamin, *Arcades Project*, 79.
78. Balzac, *Treatise on Elegant Living*, 76.
79. Translator's introduction to Balzac, *Treatise on Elegant Living*, xiii. On "cruelty" in dandyism, see also Sartre, *Baudelaire*, 133.
80. Perec, *Species of Spaces*, 60.
81. Winston Churchill's speech in the House of Commons on June 22, 1941.
82. Dostoyevsky, *Demons*, 427.
83. Lederer, *Ghetto Theresienstadt*, 74.
84. Adler, *Theresienstadt*, 1:174.
85. "Rapport van het lid van de Raad van Nederlandsch-Indië, W. P. Hillen, over de interneeringskampen aan de Bovel-Digoel," July 22, 1930, ARA Vb. 1 Nov. 1930 lr. K24.
86. Testimony by a former internee Darman on January 9, 2001, quoted in Toer, *Tanah Merah*, 85; Toer, *Tanah Merah*, 48.
87. "Verslag van de reis van den Resident van Amboina naar Boven Digoel," May 14–31, 1929, ARA, Vb 12 Jan 1939 E1: Mr 1964x/1930, 24.
88. Weiss, *And God Saw*, 13n2.
89. Adler, *Theresienstadt*, 2:277.
90. Lanzmann, *Benjamin Murmelstein*, 151.
91. Pavel Weiner, *Boy in Terezín*, 108.
92. Manes, *Als ob's ein Leben*, 234.
93. YVAF 59609.
94. Heidegger, *Being and Time*, 56.
95. *Šalom na pátek*, in "Humor as Weapon," in Bondy, *Trapped*, 85.

Chapter 2. Beauty Spots

1. Leviticus 19:27–28.
2. "Contempt for the Torah as Idolatry," in Levinas, *Time of the Nations*, 43.
3. Pérez-Oramas, *Tangled Alphabets*, 27.
4. Nancy, *Corpus*, 45.
5. Dostoyevsky, *House of the Dead*, 134.
6. Broch, *Sleepwalkers*, 23.
7. Levi, *Drowned*, 113.
8. Levi, *Drowned*, 39.
9. Adler, *Theresienstadt*, 1:127.
10. Josef Taussig, "Terezínské korso po roce," JMP 326.

11 "Proces-verbaal: Directeur der Strafgevangenis voor Doortrekkende en Huis van Bewaring te Batavia," January 29, 1927, BDA 166.
12 "Proces-verbaal," January 26, 1927, BDA 166.
13 "Politie Dagboek," BDA 251.
14 "Politie Dagboek," BDA 251.
15 Dostoyevsky, *House of the Dead*, 12.
16 Nielsen, *In het Land van Kannibalen*, 91–92, 103.
17 Adler, *Theresienstadt*, 1:84–85.
18 Dr. Adolph Metz, stellv. Leiter des Gesundeitsamtes von Theresienstadt Ghetto, "Theresienstadt," YVA 033/3257, 27.
19 "Fashion," in Benjamin, *Arcades Project*, 80.
20 Jiří Bruml, "The Cap (A Feuilleton)," "Vedem," in Křížková, *We Are Children*, 121.
21 Bondy, *Elder of the Jews*, 244.
22 Manes, *Als ob's ein Leben*, 364.
23 Manes, *Als ob's ein Leben*, 495.
24 Manes, *Als ob's ein Leben*, 518–19.
25 Balzac, *My Journey*, 49.
26 Flaubert, *Sentimental Education*, 327.
27 Ruth Bondy, "The History of the Closing Gates" in Bondy, *Trapped*, 30. Two months earlier, "Jews in the Nazi Protectorate of Bohemia and Moravia were forbidden to buy caps." Demetz, *Prague in Danger*, 98.
28 Djati, *Menjadi Tjamboek Berdoeri*, 28.
29 "Afschrift: Bevelschrift," Tjipanas, April 15, 1927, BDA 1.
30 BDA 214.
31 Agamben, *Remnants of Auschwitz*, 68.
32 Adler, *Theresienstadt*, 1:85. "Eyes left, caps off" will be the manner in Auschwitz. Levi, *Drowned*, 135.
33 Kafka, *Trial*, 223.
34 "Addendum to the Brecht Commentary: The Threepenny Opera" (1937), in Benjamin, *Selected Writings*, 3:258.
35 "Hitler's Diminished Masculinity" (1934), in Benjamin, *Selected Writings*, 2:792–93.
36 "Bernhard Kold: Tagebuchfragment aus dem Jahre 1943," YVA 02/387, 5.
37 Nielsen, *In het Land van Kannibalen*, 93–94.
38 Schoonheyt, *Boven-Digoel*, 63.
39 Schoonheyt, *Boven-Digoel*, 165.
40 Interview with Trikoyo, Tangerang, July 28, 2008. See also Tri Ramidjo, *Kisah-Kisah*, 87.
41 The "Jewish face" was a sort of "Oriental face," too, "yellow, Oriental skin is also part of the standard image of the diseased Jew." "A Dream of Jewishness on the Frontier," in Gilman, *Jewish Frontiers*, 141. According to "the view in the scientific thought-collective in Europe of the nineteenth-century and certainly with strong residues to the twentieth . . . the Jews were black." Gilman, *Jew's Body*, 165.

42. Adler, *Theresienstadt*, 1:109, 1:124.
43. Karel Fleischmann, "Terezínské panoptikum," March 1944, JMP 326. "A descriptive analysis of banknotes is needed," wrote Benjamin. "For nowhere more naively than in these documents does capitalism display itself in solemn earnest." "One-Way Street," in Benjamin, *Selected Writings*, 1:481.
44. Adler, *Die verheimlichte Wahrheit*, 179.
45. "The Miracle of the Loaves," in Bondy, *Trapped*, 19.
46. Dr. Jacob Jacobson, "Jewish Survivors Report: The Daily Life, 1943–1945," March 1946, YVA 164/105, 12.
47. "Aussage von Otto Bernstein," in Hájková, *Die fabelhaften Jungs aus Theresienstadt*, 131.
48. Manes, *Als ob's ein Leben*, 159. See also Franz Kafka writing to Milena Jesenska about her *echt* Czech father, Prague, August 4, 1920: "Naturally for your father there's no difference between your husband and myself; there's no doubt about it, to the European we both have the same Negro face." Kafka, *Letters to Milena*, 136.
49. Mrázek, *Sjahrir*, 9.
50. Kracauer, *Salaried Masses*, 38–39.
51. Dwork and van Pelt, *Auschwitz*, 77.
52. Demetz, *Prague in Danger*, 43.
53. Demetz, *Prague in Danger*, 120. Another contemporary, and a Jew, noted the same. The German women in Prague, he wrote, held a "dim view of cosmetics and permanent." "These '*Walküren*' wore white woolen stockings, dirndl-dresses." Wechsberg, *Sweet and Sour*, 68.
54. Ruth Bondy, "Women in the Theresienstadt Ghetto," in Bondy, *Trapped*, 52.
55. Redlich, *Terezín Diary*, 125.
56. Adler, *Theresienstadt*, 2:449.
57. Alfred Meril, Kurt J. Hermann, and Cpt. Charlie Ross, "Trip to Ghetto," YVA 07/6-4, 3.
58. Lipovetsky, *Empire of Fashion*, 69.
59. Koolhaas and Foster, *Junkspace*, 26.
60. BDA 125.
61. Kwee, *Drama di Boven Digul*, 523–24.
62. Adler, *Theresienstadt*, 1:126. See also "Bernhard Kold: Tagebuchfragment aus dem Jahre 1943," YVA 02/387, 6.
63. Bondy, *Elder of the Jews*, 47.
64. Adler, *Die verheimlichte Wahrheit*, 119.
65. Manes, *Als ob's ein Leben*, 304.
66. Ruth Bondy, "Privileged until Further Notice," in Bondy, *Trapped*, 102.
67. "Opgave van in bewaring genomen goederen voor door Hms. 'Java' overgevoorde gein," n.d., BDA 122. See also "Porces-verbaal," Tanjoeng Priok, January 31, 1927: "nickel watch (Weltham Massachussetts) . . . nickel watch ("Robinson" with chain) . . . 14 karat gold ring (seal ring) . . . copper wristwatch . . . wristwatch"; "Patent London," BDA 166.

68 Lipovetsky, *Empire of Fashion*, 136.
69 Testimony of Jehuda Bacon, Jerusalem, February 13, 1952, NIOD 270c/118, 9.
70 Manes, *Als ob's ein Leben*, 59, 126.
71 Adler, *Theresienstadt*, 1:143.
72 Kafka, *Amerika*, 286.
73 "Fashion," in Benjamin, *Arcades Project*, 72. "In Paris, the fashion that summer, [1933], the summer in which uniforms had become so horribly fashionable in Germany, was for women to dress à l'uniforme.... The women wore that kind of thing for fun, and nobody thought anything of it." Haffner, *Defying Hitler*, 249.
74 "Fashion," in Benjamin, *Arcades Project*, 72.
75 The story goes on: "'You are picking a wrong race,' I said, furious. The SS man roared with laughter and said, 'you might as well get used to it.'" Edgcomb, *From Swastika to Jim Crow*, xviii.
76 H. M., "Ghetto Cops," in "Vedem," September 23, 1943, in Křížková et al., *We Are Children*, 120.
77 Josef Taussig, "Terezínské korso po roce," JMP 326.
78 Spier, *Dat alles*, 56.
79 Utitz, *Psychologie života*, 57.
80 An ex-internee quoted in Toer, *Tanah Merah*, 150.
81 Redlich, *Terezín Diary*, 122.
82 "Adornment," in Wolff, *Sociology of Georg Simmel*, 340–41.
83 Schoonheyt, *Boven-Digoel*, 263.
84 Barthes, *Fashion System*, 20, 263.
85 Makarova, *University*, 384.
86 Dostoyevsky, *House of the Dead*, 143–44.
87 Testimony by a Boven Digoel ex-internee, Marsudi, June 16, 1976, in *Citra dan Perjuangan*, 78.
88 "De Commissaris van Politie," Tandjoeng Priok, January 31, 1927, BDA 238. See also "Komandan Militer," Tandjoeng Priok, January 31, 1927, on "reception of 25 American shackles," BDA 243. "American shackles," I learned, were a well-known prop in the 1930s, used by film studios, particularly in gangster films. See Poláček, *Povidky*, 1089.
89 Kafka, *Diaries, 1914–1923*, March 15, 1914, 29.
90 Benda, "From Prague to Theresienstadt," 257.
91 Balzac, *Treatise on Elegant Living*, 66.
92 Juhasz, "Externally Fashioned Aspects of Jewish Dress," in Juhasz, *Jewish Wardrobe*, 15.
93 Juhasz, "Externally Fashioned Aspects of Jewish Dress," 20.
94 Hilberg, *Destruction*, 1, 177.
95 Hilberg, *Destruction*, 1, 178.
96 P. Roth, *Operation Shylock*, 217.
97 Hilberg, *Destruction*, 1, 178.
98 Weil, *Life with a Star*, 64.
99 Kertész, *Fatelessness*, 10.

100 Bondy, *Elder of the Jews*, 224.
101 Whiteley, *Appel Is Forever*, 28.
102 Hájková, *Die fabelhaften Jungs aus Theresienstadt*, 132.
103 Bondy, *Elder of the Jews*, 224.
104 Demetz, *Prague in Danger*, 142.
105 Demetz, *Prague in Danger*, 142–43.
106 Hillesum, *Interrupted Life*, Thursday, April 30, 1942, 128.
107 C. Mayer-Kattenburg, "Onze belevenissen tydens de Jodenvervolgingen in de tweede Wereldoorlog," 1945, NIOD 244/920b, 40.
108 "Tagesbefehl," June 16, 1942, in Adler, *Theresienstadt*, 1:85.
109 Pressburger, *Diary of Petr Ginz*, April 16, 1942, 99.
110 Weil, *Life with a Star*, 181–82.
111 Adler, *Theresienstadt*, 1:liv.

Chapter 3. Pink Bodies

1 Henri Focillon, "Vie des forms" (1934), in "Fashion," in Benjamin, *Arcades Project*, 80.
2 The "Medizin," of Gustav Klimt (1897–98) survived and was kept in the estate of Dr. Hermann Wittgenstein, a cousin of Ludwig Wittgenstein, until 2014, when it was bought by the Israel Museum in Jerusalem.
3 Heidegger, *Being and Time*, 83.
4 Erich Springer, gew. Leiter der Krankenhauses in Theresienstadt, "Das Gesundheitswesen im Theresienstadt Ghetto," 16, YVA M-1/E37 02/525, 5, 17.
5 Springer, "Das Gesundheitswesen im Theresienstadt Ghetto," 26.
6 Adler, *Theresienstadt*, 2:493.
7 Heidegger, *Being and Time*, 307.
8 Heidegger, *Being and Time*, 337.
9 Heidegger, *Being and Time*, 338.
10 Adler, *Theresienstadt*, 2:523.
11 Ruth Bondy, "Women in the Theresienstadt Ghetto," in Bondy, *Trapped*, 52. For a similar postwar report by an internee working as a nurse in the camp surgery, see "Protokoll Frau M.L.," YVA 140–02/1024.
12 Adler, *Theresienstadt*, 2:504.
13 Italie, *Het Oorlogsdagboek*, 155.
14 Redlich, *Terezín Diary*, 80.
15 Elon, *Pity of It All*, 274.
16 Springer, "Das Gesundheitswesen im Theresienstadt Ghetto," 3.
17 Mirawati, *Inventaris Arsip Boven Digoel*, 1.
18 "De telegram from 1ste Gov. Secr. 138x no.1060 verbond begrooting," ARA Mr. 1247x/26, 1250x/26, 1153x/26.
19 Salim, *Vijftien jaar*, 138. Unless noted otherwise, the second expanded edition from 1980 is used.

20 Salim, *Vijftien jaar*, 138. In Schoonheyt, *Boven-Digoel*, 158, there is a photograph of the Boven Digoel hospital pharmacy with full shelves indeed.
21 Shiraishi, "Phantom World of Digoel," 94.
22 Nielsen, *In het Land van Kannibalen*, 108.
23 L. H. W. van Sandick, Gouverneur van Ambon, "2e rapport Boven Digoel," November 5, 1927, ARA, Mr. 1107x/27.
24 Schoonheyt, *Boven-Digoel*, 58.
25 Schoonheyt, *Boven-Digoel*, 156.
26 M. van Blankenstein, "Het verbanningsoord," September 11, 1928.
27 "Tractmente en formatie Wilhelmina Ziekenhuis ingaande Februari 1932," Boven Digoel, January 29, 1932, in BDA 46. See also "Rapport van het lid van de Raad van Nederlandsch-Indië, W. P. Hillen, over de interneeringskampen aan de Bovel-Digoel," July 22, 1930, ARA Vb. 1 Nov. 1930 lr. K24, 12.
28 In this file there are several documents concerning Boven Digoel patients sent for treatment in the military hospital in Amboin; e.g., Ishak, BDA 201. A group of five internees was sent to the military hospital in Amboina on July 8, 1929; see BDA 201. On July 11, 1929, internees Supardi and Tajib were sent to the military hospital "for a surgery." BDA 201.
29 "Memorie van Overgave van Aftredende Gouverneur den Molukken J. T. Tideman," ARA Mr. 699x/30.
30 Salim, *Vijftien jaar*, 167.
31 "Politie Dagboek," BDA 212.
32 "Politie Dagboek," BDA 212.
33 "Politie Dagboek," BDA 212.
34 "Politie Dagboek," BDA 251.
35 "Politie Dagboek," BDA 251.
36 Mawengkang, *Boven Digoel*, 58.
37 Mas Marco, *Pergaulan Orang Buangan*, 3.
38 Hatta, *Berjuang dan Dibuang*, 158.
39 Widayasih, *Masa kanak-kanak*, 1:14–15.
40 Interview with Bangun Topo, Jakarta, August 11, 2008.
41 Bondan, *Memoar*, 47.
42 *Citra dan Perjuangan*, 89. On the "*kinine-doofheid*," see Nielsen, *In het Land van Kannibalen*, 122.
43 "Politie Dagboek," BDA 210.
44 "Politie Dagboek," BDA 210.
45 "Politie Dagboek," BDA 212.
46 "Politie Dagboek," BDA 251.
47 Dr. Jacob Jacobson, "Jewish Survivors Report: The Daily Life, 1943–1945," March 1946, YVA 164/105, 3.
48 Ruth Bondy, "Women in the Theresienstadt Ghetto," in Bondy, *Trapped*, 58.
49 Else Dormitzer, "Leben in Theresienstadt," September 1945, YVA 02/392, 2.
50 Shean, *To Be an Actress*, 35.
51 Adler, *Theresienstadt*, 2:513. "On April 24, [1945,] was among the young children for the first time diagnosed *Fleck*-typhoid." Adler, *Theresienstadt*, 1:212.

52 Pavel Weiner, *Boy in Terezín*, 97.
53 Dr. Adolph Metz, stellv. Leiter des Gesundheitsamtes von Theresienstadt Ghetto, "Theresienstadt," February 9, 1946, YVA 07/6-4-8, 20.
54 Bondy, *Elder of the Jews*, 362.
55 Metz, "Theresienstadt," February 9, 27, 1946, 27.
56 Makarova, *University*, 498. For an order of "300 kg Zyklon" for Theresienstadt, see Adler, *Die verheimlichte Wahrheit*, 141.
57 Weiss, *God Saw*, 57.
58 Pavel Weiner, *Boy in Terezín*, 67.
59 Josef Taussig, "Die Theresienstädter Kabarette," in Kárný et al., *Theresienstädter Studien*, 1994, 226.
60 Ruth Bondy, "The Miracle of the Loaves," in Bondy, *Trapped*, 148.
61 "The Changing Image of the Theresienstadt Ghetto," in Bondy, *Trapped*, 12.
62 Others were assigned to *Klodienst*, "latrine duty." Weiss, *God Saw*, 38n27.
63 "Oldřich Böhm's diary, February 1943," JMP 326 L 502, 4.
64 Lenka Lindtová wrote, "I was thinking of you, as I went to havaj." Lenka Lindtová, "Mamince," JMP 325.
65 Pavel Weiner, *Boy in Terezín*, 207. "When there was no toilet paper, people used wet rags that they rinsed after use." Weiss, *God Saw*, 42n32.
66 "Op de verklaring van Villanus [van Blankenstein] in het Soer. Hdbld.," in "Bintang Timoer," August 15–20, 1928, in *IPO* 1928.
67 "Overleden, Boven Digoel, 1927–34," BDA 269.
68 "Doodsoorzaken der in Boven Digoel geïnterneerden en hunne gezinsleden over het jaar 1940," BDA 129.
69 Interview with Trikoyo, Tangerang, July 5, 2010.
70 Salim, *Vijftien jaar*, 206.
71 Oen, *Darah dan Aer-Mata*, 6.
72 Salim, *Vijftien jaar*, 15.
73 "Memorie van Overgave van Aftredende Gouverneur den Molukken J. T. Tideman," ARA Mr. 699x/30.
74 BDA 210.
75 BDA 211.
76 BDA 211.
77 BDA 211.
78 Tanpa Nama, "Minggat dari Digul," 249.
79 Bloch, *Spirit of Utopia*, 10–11.
80 Adorno, *Jargon of Authenticity*, 69–70.
81 Interview with Trikoyo, Tangerang, July 5, 2010.
82 Adler, *Theresienstadt*, 2:411.
83 Metz, "Theresienstadt," February 9, 1946, 2–3.
84 Bondy, *Elder of the Jews*, 362. See also "Nach dem Clo und vor dem Essen Haendewaschen nicht vergessen!" in Felix Eptein, "Imaginierte Erinnerung an Theresienstadt," 1, YVA 02/229.
85 Adler, *Theresienstadt*, 2:333.

86 *Šalom na pátek*, December 31, 1943, 118, YVA 064.64, 117. See also "Vorschriften für die Instandhaltung der Aborte und Kanäle," in Adler, *Theresienstadt*, 2:334.
87 *Šalom na pátek*, December 31, 1943, 125, YVA 064.64, 117.
88 Manes, *Als ob's ein Leben*, 176.
89 Ginz, "Rambles," in "Vedem," in Křížková et al., *We Are Children*, 118.
90 Manes, *Als ob's ein Leben*, 157.
91 Testimony of Jehuda Bacon, Jerusalem, February 13, 1952, NIOD 270c/118, 9.
92 Pavel Weiner, *Boy in Terezín*, 73.
93 Paul Weiner, *Terezín Remembered*, 5.
94 "Das Recht des jüdischen Siedlungsgebietes Theresienstadt: Erste Fassung: Ghettorecht in Theresienstadt Zusammengestellt nach dem Stande vom 15 Juli 1944," YVA 064/399, 10.
95 Redlich, *Terezín Diary*, 103n9.
96 Max Berger, "Zpráva o pobytu v Terezíně," YVA 07/6-4, 12.
97 Jiří Grünbaum, "Rambles Through Terezín," in "Vedem," Křížková et al., *We Are Children*, 104–5.
98 Max E. Mannheimer, "Theresienstadt and from Theresienstadt to Auschwitz," YVA 07/6-4, 8. Hannah Arendt mentions the defense lawyer of Adolf Eichmann at the trial in Jerusalem, in particular, Dr. Servatius's amazing conviction that killing by gas must be regarded as "a medical matter." Arendt, *Eichmann*, 95.
99 Mirawati, *Inventaris Arsip Boven Digoel*, 2; Salim, *Vijftien jaar*, 84.
100 The Reichsvereiningen der Juden in Deutschland, established in July 1939 on the order of the SS, issued a "Heimeinkaufverträge," an "agreement to sell home." "On the basis of these Agreements, some believed that they were taken to an old persons home of the Theresienstadt spa [Kurort Theresienstadt]." Adler, *Theresienstadt*, 1:xlix. When Mr. Austerlitz of W. G. Sebald's novel visited Theresienstadt after the war and looked into the shop window of the Antikos Bazar, the antique shop (which is still there), he saw, among other things, "the tin advertising sign bearing the words *Theresienstädter Wasser*." Sebald, *Austerlitz*, 196. A girl who survived Theresienstadt, Helga Weissová, is quoted after the war: "C'est ridicule, mais on dirait que Terezín doit se transformer en station thermal." Gaudy, *Une île, une forteresse*, 96.
101 Adler, *Theresienstadt*, 1:108.
102 See "as a wife of an internee and not his lover." "Gobée, De Adv voor Inlandsche zaken," January 14, 1937, ARA Vb. 2 Oct. 1937 M27 Mr. 149x/37.
103 "Gouv Oostkust van Sumatra. Aan den Gouverneur van West Java te Batavia," June 1, 1927, BDA 200.
104 "Gouv Oostkust van Sumatra. Aan den Gouverneur van West Java te Batavia," June 1, 1927, BDA 200.
105 "Fashion," in Benjamin, *Arcades Project*, 79.
106 *Citra dan Perjuangan*, 83.
107 "Politie Dagboek," BDA 251.
108 Interview with Widayasih, Jakarta, January 23, 2009.
109 Resident den Molukken B. J. Haga "Boven Digoel Verslag," April 5–21, 1936, ARA Vb. 2 Oct. 1937 M27.

110 Salim, *Vijftien jaar*, 241–42.
111 Schoonheyt, *Boven-Digoel*, 186.
112 Salim, *Vijftien jaar*, 241.
113 Oen, *Darah dan Aer-Mata*, 86.
114 Toer, *Tanah Merah*, 78.
115 For 1931 there are thirty-nine letters asking for being sent away; in 1932, twenty letters; in 1933, twelve letters; in 1934, four letters; in 1935, eight letters; in 1936, six letters; in 1937, four letters; in 1938, six letters; and in 1939, twelve letters; here the files end. BDA 144.
116 "Politie Dagboek," BDA 251.
117 Salim, *Vijftien jaar*, 248.
118 Kwee, *Drama di Boven Digul*, 512.
119 Salim, *Vijftien jaar*, 124.
120 "Wedana-rapport," August 27, 1932, BDA 238.
121 Schoonheyt, *Boven-Digoel*, 186.
122 Salim, *Vijftien jaar*, 179. "In 1929–1930, there was born 120 babies per year ... in 1934–35 ... about 160 babies." Salim, *Vijftien jaar*, 242.
123 Schoonheyt, *Boven-Digoel*, 91.
124 Interview with Trikoyo, Tangerang, July 28, 2008.
125 BDA 300. Sunday, October 28, 1934. On the request the official wrote in big letters and underlined "Kon niet!" [Cannot!].
126 "Politie Boek," BDA 251.
127 Uncatalogued photography collection of the National Library in Jakarta: *"Gambar bersama Bp. Aliarcham,"* "Family portrait of Mr. Aliarcham."
128 "Staat Invaliden Kamp D," n.d., BDA 293.
129 Testimony by ex-internee Darman, September 23, 2001, in Toer, *Tanah Merah*, 98.
130 "Politie Dagboek," BDA 210.
131 "Politie Dagboek," BDA 251.
132 Adler, *Theresienstadt*, 2:478.
133 Testimony by Uri Spitzer in Makarova, *Boarding Pass to Paradise*, 86.
134 Mephistopheles and Wagner in Goethe, *Faust*, 2:6836–39.
135 Springer, "Das Gesundheitswesen im Theresienstadt Ghetto," 23.
136 Ruth Bondy, "Women in the Theresienstadt Ghetto," in Bondy, *Trapped*, 53.
137 *Šalom na pátek*, March 17, 1944, 117, 149, YVA 064.64. Births and "unverified additions" to the Theresienstadt camp population were 247, according to Hilberg, *Destruction*, 2:455.
138 C. Mayer-Kattenburg, "Onze belevenissen tydens de Jodenvervolgingen in de tweede Wereldoorlog," 1945, NIOD 244/920b, 61–62.
139 Pavel Weiner, *Boy in Terezín*, 191.
140 Pavel Weiner, *Boy in Terezín*, 39. "The women in the bakery talk about things which I would rather not mention here." Pavel Weiner, November 2, 1944, 90.
141 Redlich, *Terezín Diary*, 111.
142 Jehuda Bacon, in Adler, *Theresienstadt*, 2:556.
143 Manes, *Als ob's ein Leben*, 435.

144 Manes, *Als ob's ein Leben*, 61.
145 Adler, *Theresienstadt*, 1:110.
146 Adler, *Theresienstadt*, 2:694.
147 Adler, *Theresienstadt*, 1:lvi.
148 Adler, *Theresienstadt*, 2:545–46.
149 Manes, *Als ob's ein Leben*, 103.
150 Rothkirchen, *Jews of Bohemia and Moravia*, 266.
151 M. van Blankenstein, "Het verbanningsoord," *Nieuwe Rotterdamsche Courant*, September 16, 1928.
152 "Memorie van Overgave van Aftredende Gouverneur den Molukken J. T. Tideman," ARA Mr. 699x/30, 27.
153 "Rapport van het lid van de Raad van Nederlandsch-Indië, W. P. Hillen, over de interneeringskampen aan de Bovel-Digoel," July 22, 1930, ARA Vb. 1 Nov. 1930 lr. K24, 16.
154 "Soeloeh Ra'jat Indonesia," July 10, 1929, *IPO* 1929.
155 Ramidjo, *Kisah-Kisah*, 79.
156 Tanpa Nama, "Minggat dari Digul," 265n34.
157 Interview with Trikoyo, Tangerang, July 5, 2010.
158 "Bevolking-Register der Geinterneerden," n.d., BDA 103.
159 Widayasih, *Masa kanak-kanak*, 1:4.
160 Becking, "Reisverslag," KITLV 53/1992/4, 9.
161 Interview with Trikoyo, Tangerang, January 30, 2012.
162 "Keng Po," October 4, 1927, *IPO* 1927.
163 Interview with Trikoyo, Tangerang, July 28, 2008.
164 Interview with Trikoyo, Tangerang, July 28, 2008.
165 "Politie Dagboek," BDA 211.
166 "Politie Dagboek," BDA 212.
167 "Politie Dagboek," BDA 251.
168 Salim, *Vijftien jaar*, 414–15.
169 Salim, *Vijftien jaar*, 308–9.
170 "Politie Dagboek," BDA 211.
171 Salim, *Vijftien jaar*, 183.
172 Interview with Zakaria, Jakarta, May 10, 2011.
173 "Travel Souvenirs," in Benjamin, *Selected Writings*, 1:472.
174 BDA 125.
175 "Staat van de goedern," Boven Digoel, October 7, 1933, BDA 47.
176 "Politie Dagboek," BDA 251.
177 Ruth Bondy, "The History of the Closing Gates," in Bondy, *Trapped*, 30.
178 Hilberg, *Destruction*, 1:152.
179 Hilberg, *Destruction*, 1:153n11.
180 Weil, *Life with a Star*, 17.
181 Utitz, *Psychologie života*, 9.
182 Italie, *Het Oorlogsdagboek*, 412.
183 Bondy, "Theresienstadt Ghetto," 304.
184 Adler, *Theresienstadt*, 2:344.

185 Italie, *Het Oorlogsdagboek*, 491.
186 Ab Caransa, "Theresienstadt: Schizofrenie in steen," NIOD 809/17, 13.
187 Ruth Bondy, "The Changing Image of the Theresienstadt Ghetto" in Bondy, *Trapped*, 12.
188 Über die *Möglichkeit der Ghettoisierung im Protektorat*, in "Dokumentation zur Errichtung des Theresienstädter Ghettos 1941," in Kárný et al., *Theresienstädter Studien*, 1996, 270.
189 Adler, *Theresienstadt*, 2:519–20.
190 C. Mayer-Kattenburg, "Onze belevenissen tydens de Jodenvervolgingen in de tweede Wereldoorlog," 1945, NIOD 244/920b, 82.
191 Mayer-Kattenburg, "Onze belevenissen tydens de Jodenvervolgingen," NIOD 244/920b, 82.
192 "Ein Bericht von Frau Käthe Goldschmidt über Hugo Friedmann: Aus einem Brief an Frau Irma Doll," November 21, 1945, YVA 02/985, 1.
193 Weiss, *God Saw*, 12.
194 Italie, *Het Oorlogsdagboek*, 542.
195 Makarova, *University*, 356.
196 Adler, *Theresienstadt*, 2:351.
197 Ruth Bondy's note to Otto Weiss. A request form for the dietary kitchen is reproduced in Adler, *Die verheimlichte Wahrheit*, 214.
198 Manes, *Als ob's ein Leben*, 77. Adler, *Theresienstadt*, 2:357. For "potatoe cakes," see Italie, *Het Oorlogsdagboek*, February 7, 1945, 530.
199 Italie, *Het Oorlogsdagboek*, February 7, 1945, 493.
200 Bernhard Kold, "Tagebuchfragment aus dem Jahre 1943," YVA 02/387, 7–8.
201 Rilke, *Notebooks*, 211.
202 Ruth Bondy, "Women in the Theresienstadt Ghetto," in Bondy, *Trapped*, 55.
203 Adler, *Theresienstadt*, 2:448.
204 Adler, *Theresienstadt*, 1:107–8.
205 "Politie Dagboek," BDA 210.
206 Ramidjo, *Kisah-Kisah*, 77–79.
207 Adler, *Theresienstadt*, 2:270–71.
208 Adler, *Theresienstadt*, 2:375.
209 Dr. Jacob Jacobson, "Jewish Survivors Report: The Daily Life, 1943–1945," March, 1946, 10, YVA 164/105. "In 1941, at the opening of the Institute for Tobacco Hazards Research in Jena, the editor Johann von Leers argued that the Jews were responsible for introducing tobacco into Europe and that they continued to use the tobacco trade as a means of destroying Aryan culture." "Smoking Jews on the Frontier," in Gilman, *Jewish Frontiers*, 105–6.
210 Adler, *Theresienstadt*, 2:270–71.
211 Redlich, *Terezín Diary*, 149.
212 Dr. Adolph Mettz, stellv. Leiter des Gesundheitsamtes von Theresienstadt Ghetto, "Theresienstadt," YVA 033/3257, 7.
213 Adler, *Theresienstadt*, 2:375.
214 Italie, *Het Oorlogsdagboek*, 554.
215 Adler, *Theresienstadt*, 2:286.

Chapter 4. Sport

1. Kertész, *Fatelessness*, 11.
2. Hájková, *Die fabelhaften Jungs*, 131.
3. Perec, *W, or The Memory of Childhood*, 7.
4. Perec, *W, or The Memory of Childhood*, 125.
5. Perec, *W, or The Memory of Childhood*, 133.
6. Hillesum, *Interrupted Life*, October 22, 1941, 5–6.
7. Max Berger, "Zpráva o pobytu v Terezíně," YVA 07/64, 12.
8. Originally without a title, as far as it is known, the fragments of the film that survived were edited together after the war as *Der Führer schenkt den Juden eine Stadt*, "The Führer Bestows a City upon the Jews."
9. Unknown author, "Sport in Terezín," in "Vedem," in Křížková et al., *We Are Children*, 52.
10. Unknown author, "Sport in Terezín," 52.
11. Adler, *Theresienstadt*, 1:180. The "Fussball-Liga" table with the names of the teams is reproduced in Adler, *Die verheimlichte Wahrheit*, 249.
12. Bondy, *Elder of the Jews*, 382–83.
13. Pavel Weiner, *Boy in Terezín*, 136.
14. "Můj památník: Erik Baumel," September 5, 1943, JMP 324a.
15. Adler, *Theresienstadt*, 2:240. Manes, *Als ob's ein Leben*, 358.
16. Adler, *Theresienstadt*, 1:180.
17. Adler, *Theresienstadt*, 1:180.
18. Adler, *Theresienstadt*, 1:240, 2:553. On volleyball, see "Dr. M. Rossel. Delegierten de C.I.C.R. " April 23, 1944, in Kárný et al., *Theresienstädter Studien*, 1996, 295.
19. Adler, *Theresienstadt*, 2:136.
20. Manes, *Als ob's ein Leben*, 316.
21. Schoonheyt, *Boven-Digoel*, 185.
22. "Politie Dagboek," BDA 211.
23. "Hulppolitierapport: Vergadering Voetbalclub S/H.," BDA 324.
24. Testimony by ex-internee Maskun Sumadirdja, August 25, 1976, in *Citra dan Perjuangan*, 86.
25. "Politie Dagboek," BDA 211.
26. "Politie Dagboek," BDA 212.
27. Salim, *Vijftien jaar*, 246.
28. "Bestuur E.V.C.[?]," February 13, 1932, BDA 313.
29. *Citra dan Perjuangan*, 80.
30. Salim, *Vijftien jaar*, 240.
31. "Boven Digoel, August 14, 1932, Daftar nama2 orang jang a kan mengadakan trainen 'Pentjak' boeat keramaian 'Peringataan 31 Agustus 1932,'" BDA 80.
32. "Bestuur Comite," Boven Digoel, August 15, 1932, BDA 80.
33. "Polietie Dagboek," BDA 212.
34. "Polietie Dagboek," BDA 212.

35 Salim, *Vijftien jaar*, 121. "The tennis court," meaning evidently the one for the officials, "could be rented and the charge will be reimbursed from the local treasury." "Verslag van de reis van der Resident Ouweling van Amboina naar Boven Digoel," September 6–24, 1929, in ARA, Vb. 12 Jan. 1939 E1: Mr. 1964x/1930, 18.
36 "Politie Dagboek," BDA 251.
37 Interview with Bangun Topo, Jakarta, August 11, 2008.
38 Nasoetion, *Perdjuanganku*, 75.
39 Salim, *Vijftien jaar*, 248.
40 Widayasih, *Masa kanak-kanak*, 1:12.
41 Toer, *Tanah Merah*, 116; see also *Citra dan Perjuangan*, 86.
42 "Politie Dagboek," BDA 212.
43 "Polietie Dagboek," BDA 212. "Register van de strafzaken, behandelt en afgedaan door den Magistraat, 1935–1936," BDA 164.
44 Tanpa Nama, "Minggat dari Digul," 227–28.
45 Koolhaas, *Delirious New York*, 182.
46 Schoonheyt, *Boven-Digoel*, 184.
47 "Soccer," in Barthes, *What Is Sport?*, 61–63.
48 "Soccer," in Barthes, *What Is Sport?*, 45–55.
49 "Soccer," in Barthes, *What Is Sport?*, 65.
50 Many photographs and even some film fragments are kept in a special sport room of the Givat Heim Ihud Theresienstadt Memorial in Israel. In the images, the soccer teams are all in uniforms.
51 "Testimony of Jehuda Bacon," Jerusalem, February 13, 1952, in NIOD 270c/118, 9.
52 Enlarged photographs of Freddy Hirsch and a woman gymnast in a gymnastic dress, demonstrating certain positions, are also on the wall of the sport room in Givat Heim Ihud.
53 Schoonheyt, *Boven-Digoel* (1940 edition), 198.
54 Soetan Sjahrir, letter to Sjahsam Boven Digoel, March 27, 1935.
55 Salim, *Vijftien jaar*, 84; emphasis mine.
56 "Politie Dagboek," BDA 251.
57 "Politie Dagboek," BDA 212.
58 "Politie Dagboek," BDA 211.

Chapter 5. Noise

Dostoyevsky, *Crime and Punishment*, 7.

1 Weil, *Life with a Star*, 115.
2 Manes, *Als ob's ein Leben*, 144.
3 Testimony by Arnošt Reiser, 1998, New York, in Makarova, *University*, 417.
4 Pavel Weiner, *Boy in Terezín*, 20.
5 Salim, *Vijftien jaar*, 315.
6 "Politie Dagboek," BDA 210.

7. Salim, *Vijftien jaar*, 165.
8. Widayasih, *Masa kanak-kanak*, 1:2.
9. Clippings from Haarlem's Dagblad, June 17, 1933, 3, "Waar het Boven-Digoel gebied, van en oud Haarlemmer," in *Collectie Schoonheyt*, 1.
10. Mas Marco, *Pergaulan Orang Buangan*, 147.
11. Salim, *Vijftien jaar*, 316.
12. Mas Marco, *Pergaulan Orang Buangan*, 147. There was a Wallace line dividing the Asian and Pacific flora and fauna universe. It cut between where the internees came from and where the camp was.
13. Oen, *Darah dan Aer-Mata*, 86–90.
14. Oen, *Darah dan Aer-Mata*, 68.
15. Salim, *Vijftien jaar*, 101.
16. van Kampen, *Jungle Pimpernel*, 341.
17. Interview with Trikoyo, Tangerang, July 28, 2008.
18. Nielsen, *In het Land van Kannibalen*, 122.
19. Adler, *Theresienstadt*, 3:678. "In the spring or summer of 1942 the Jews had to get rid of their house animals, such as dogs, cats and canaries." Adler, *Die verheimlichte Wahrheit*, 46.
20. Pavel Weiner, *Boy in Terezín*, 58.
21. Salim, *Vijftien jaar*, 318.
22. "Politie Dagboek," BDA 212.
23. "Gezaghebber Boven Digoel aan den Resident van Amboina," Boven Digoel, June 4, 1927, BDA 5.
24. "Politie Dagboek," BDA 210.
25. Salim, *Vijftien jaar*, 140.
26. "Politie Dagboek," BDA 212.
27. Kentridge, *Six Drawing Lessons*, 30.
28. In "Memorie van Overgave van Aftredende Gouverneur den Molukken J. T. Tideman," 17, in ARA Mr. 699x/30.
29. "Politie Dagboek," BDA 212.
30. "Bevolking-Register der Geinterneerden," March 26, 1927, BDA 103.
31. "Politie Dagboek," BDA 210.
32. "Politie Dagboek," BDA 212.
33. "Politie Dagboek," BDA 251.
34. Soetan Sjahrir, letter to Maria Duchâteau, Boven Digoel, March 27, 1935.
35. "The Philosophy of Music" in Bloch, *Spirit of Utopia*, 58.
36. Nancy, *Listening*, 75n42.
37. C. Mayer-Kattenburg, "Onze belevenissen tydens de Jodenvervolgingen in de tweede Wereldoorlog," 1945, in NIOD 244/920b, 64.
38. Weiss, *God Saw*, 39.
39. Evžen Hilar, "Escape from the Ghetto," in Council of Jewish Communities, *Terezín*, 285.
40. Adler, *Die verheimlichte Wahrheit*, 240.
41. "Rambles through T M" (probably Herbert Maier), "Vedem," in Křížková et al., *We Are Children*, 121.

42　Manes, *Als ob's ein Leben,* 219. Mr. Manes here recalls Schiller's *Mary Stuart,* of course, looking at the clouds from her prison: "Fast fleeting clouds! ye meteors that fly; / Could I but with you sail through the sky! /. . . ."
43　Manes, *Als ob's ein Leben,* 163.
44　Salim, *Vijftien jaar,* 81.
45　Nielsen, *In het Land van Kannibalen,* 98–100.

Chapter 6. Voice

1　I Kings 19.
2　Jacques Rolland, "Getting Out of Being by a New Path," in Levinas, *On Escape,* 9.
3　Testimony by ex-internee Harsutejo, November 10, 2003, in Toer, *Tanah Merah,* 74.
4　Testimony by ex-internee Darman, June 29, 2002, in Toer, *Tanah Merah,* 149.
5　Adler, *Theresienstadt,* 2:256.
6　Nancy, *Corpus,* 19.
7　Makarova, *University,* 50.
8　Ruth Bondy, "The Miracle of the Loaves," in Bondy, *Trapped,* 141.
9　Adler, *Theresienstadt,* 2:464.
10　"Many of the Czech gendermes behaved in an outstanding way to the prisoners. They often risked their lives to help us." "Jo Singer: Erlebnisse in Wien und Theresienstadt," in Miroslav Kárný, "Die Gendarmerie-Sonderabteilung und die Theresienstädter Häftlinge," in Kárný et al., *Theresienstädter Studien,* 1996, 137.
11　"Memorie van Overgave van Aftredende Gouverneur den Molukken J. T. Tideman," ARA Mr. 699x/30, 17.
12　Deputy Van Helsdingen in the "Volksraad," in Kwantes, *De Ontwikkeling,* 2:651.
13　"Gezaghebber Boven Digoel aan den Resident van Amboina," Boven Digoel, June 4, 1927, BDA 5.
14　Mas Marco, *Pergaulan Orang Buangan,* 113.
15　"Politie Dagboek," BDA 210.
16　Adler, *Theresienstadt,* 1:li.
17　Manes, *Als ob's ein Leben,* 301.
18　Manes, *Als ob's ein Leben,* 248.
19　Adler, *Theresienstadt,* 3:696.
20　Manes, *Als ob's ein Leben,* 248.
21　Adler, *Theresienstadt,* 1:li.
22　C. Mayer-Kattenburg, "Onze belevenissen tydens de Jodenvervolgingen in de tweede Wereldoorlog," 1945, NIOD 244/920b, 66.
23　Adler, *Theresienstadt,* 2:575–76.
24　Makarova, *Boarding Pass to Paradise,* 68.
25　Oen, *Darah dan Aer-Mata,* 71.
26　Testimony by an ex-internee Soemono Moestapha about Tanah Tinggi section of the camp, in Toer, *Tanah Merah,* 223, 225.
27　Cage, *Silence,* 70.

28 Perec, *Species of Spaces*, 11.
29 Kafka, *Diaries, 1910–1913*, December 8, 1911, 173.
30 "The Translation of the Scripture," in Levinas, *Time of the Nations*, 34–35.
31 BDA 116.
32 Pérez-Oramas, *Tangled Alphabets*, 15.
33 Pérez-Oramas, *Tangled Alphabets*, 38.
34 Pérez-Oramas, *Tangled Alphabets*, 39.
35 Pérez-Oramas, *Tangled Alphabets*, 34.
36 "Keng Po," October 4, 1927, *IPO* 1927.
37 BDA 297.
38 Dr. Jacob Jacobson, "Jewish Survivors Report: The Daily Life, 1943–1945," March 1946, YVA 164/105, 18.
39 Otto Dov Kulka, "Bericht über das 'Theresienstadt Familienlager' in Auschwitz-Birkenau," 3, YVA 03/2896. *Naamlijste van afzenden brieven uit Theresienstadt en jodse "arbeids-kampen" 1943–1944*, NIOD 187/166H.
40 "Testimony of Jehuda Bacon," Jerusalem, February 13, 1952, 11, NIOD 270C/118.
41 "Elegy," in Amichai, *Selected Poetry*, 58.
42 Nancy, *Philosophical Chronicles*, 39.
43 Demetz, *Prague in Danger*, 39.
44 Weiss, *God Saw*, 44.
45 Mayer-Kattenburg, "Onze belevenissen tydens," 60.
46 "The internees in Boven Digoel ... have access not only to books on religion and educational fairy tales, but also Malay and Dutch newspapers." "Djawa Tengah," February 9, 1931, *IPO* 1931.
47 Toer, *Tanah Merah*, 32–33. Bondan, *Memoar*, 50. "We are happy to report that while we have printed 1000 copies of our paper initially, we have now to double the number. In Boven Digoel our newspaper has 35 readers." Dewan, February 18, 1930, *IPO* 1930.
48 Soetan Sjahrir, letter to Maria Duchâteau, March 27, 1935.
49 Soetan Sjahrir, letter to Maria Duchâteau, July 24, 1935.
50 Soetan Sjahrir, letter to Maria Duchâteau, Sjahsam, and children, July 25, 1935.
51 Salim, *Vijftien jaar*, 141–42.
52 "Politie Dagboek," BDA 211.
53 "Politie Dagboek," BDA 212.
54 "Politie Dagboek," BDA 215.
55 "Politie Dagboek," BDA.
56 "Politie Dagboek," BDA 211.
57 Křížková et al., *We Are Children*, 36.
58 See also Erik Polák, "Úloha časopisů v životě terezínských dětí a mládeže," in Kárný and Blodig, *Terezín v konečném řešeni*, 138.
59 "Testimony of Jehuda Bacon."
60 Bondy, *Elder of the Jews*, 330–31.
61 Adler, *Theresienstadt*, 2:583.
62 Makarova, *University*, 367.
63 Makarova, *University*, 414.

64 Kafka, *In the Penal Colony*, 204.
65 "The Method of Dramatization," in Deleuze, *Desert Islands*, 101.
66 Maurice Blanchot, in Barthes, *Neutral*, 93.
67 Barthes, *Neutral*, 23.
68 Mas Marco, *Pergaulan Orang Buangan*, 75.
69 Salim, *Vijftien jaar*, 155.
70 Barthes, *Neutral*, 109.
71 Walter Benjamin, in Fenves, *Arresting Language*, 238.
72 Bondy, *Elder of the Jews*, 329.
73 Annetta Makovcová, "Básně," October 20, 1943, JMP 326.
74 Pavel Weiner, *Boy in Terezín*, 206.
75 Anonymous, "Parademarsch Ghettowache in the Dresden Barracks," in "Vedem," in Křížková et al., *We Are Children*, 122.
76 Redlich, *Terezín Diary*, 133.
77 Bloch, *Traces*, 51.
78 Redlich, *Terezín Diary*, 107.
79 Manes, *Als ob's ein Leben*, 317.
80 Koolhaas, *Delirious New York*, 125.
81 Žižek, *Violence*, 66–67.
82 "Proces-Verbaal Moeljodikromo," September 13, 1933, BDA 171.
83 "Proces-Verbaal Soekandar al. Wisopo," September 26, 1933, BDA 171.
84 "Fashion," in Benjamin, *Arcades Project*, 62–63.
85 "Politie Dagboek," BDA 210.
86 "Politie Dagboek," BDA 251.
87 Adler, *Theresienstadt*, 2:464.
88 Makarova, *University*, 62.
89 Mayer-Kattenburg, "Onze belevenissen tydens," 72.

Chapter 7. Music

1 Testimony by ex-internee Darman, September 23, 2003, in Toer, *Tanah Merah*, 57.
2 Tri Ramidjo, *Kisah-Kisah*, 52.
3 Testimony by ex-internee Darman, 59.
4 Testimony by ex-internee Darman, 84.
5 Kartomi, *Gamelan Digul*, 16–17.
6 Hyndráková et al., *Prominenti v ghettu*, 127, 207.
7 Hyndráková et al., *Prominenti v ghettu*, 173.
8 Makarova, *University*, 230.
9 Blodig et al., *Kultura proti smrti*, 25.
10 Blodig et al., *Kultura proti smrti*, 25. The Jewish Museum in Prague has Pavel Haas's manuscript of his song on the words of Chinese poetry, "I overhear the wild goose's voice"; JMP 319a.
11 Makarova, *University*, 478.

12 Nielsen, *In het Land van Kannibalen*, 92.
13 Toer, *Tanah Merah*, 84.
14 Interview with Bangun Topo, Jakarta, May 15, 2011.
15 Interview with Chamsinah Nasoetion, Jakarta, May 9, 2011.
16 Testimony by ex-internee Darman, 57.
17 Salim, *Vijftien jaar*, 239–40.
18 Schoonheyt, *Boven-Digoel*, 181–82.
19 Kartomi, *Gamelan Digul*, 28.
20 Kartomi, *Gamelan Digul*, 32.
21 Salim, *Vijftien jaar*, 240.
22 Adler, *Theresienstadt*, 2:587.
23 Adler, *Theresienstadt*, 2:588.
24 Trude Simonsohn, "Erinnerung an Paul Eppstein," in Kárný et al., *Theresienstädter Studien*, 1996, 128.
25 Adler, *Theresienstadt*, 1:166.
26 Manes, *Als ob's ein Leben*, 356.
27 Manes, *Als ob's ein Leben*, 312. There is a Theresienstadt photo of the camp orchestra in the open in YVAF 32650, and a photo of a "concert in the park" in YVAF 15650.
28 Adler, *Theresienstadt*, 2:588.
29 Adler, *Theresienstadt*, 2:603.
30 Interview with Greta Kingsberg, Jerusalem, May 14, 2015.
31 Makarova, *University*, 525. The Jewish Museum in Prague has Ullmann's manuscript of his song on Rilke's "The Lay of the Love and Death of Cornet Christopher Rilke," JMP 318d.
32 Victor Ullmann, "Goethe und Ghetto," YVA 064/65.
33 Makarova, *University*, 479.
34 Slavický, *Gideon Klein*, 21, 24.
35 Manes, *Als ob's ein Leben*, 366.
36 For testimony by an eye- (ear) witness, see Margit Silberfeld, "The Requiem by Verdi without Music Score," YVA 03/889; also YVA 492/11–5; and Furman, *Ways of Growing Up*, 197.
37 Makarova, *University*, 216.
38 For an incomplete list of the operas, see Adler, *Theresienstadt*, 2:592–94.
39 Kuna, *Hudba na hranici života*, 193–208.
40 Kuna, *Hudba na hranici života*, 183–92.
41 Pavel Weiner, *Boy in Terezín*, 111.
42 The picture and playbill are in the Theresienstadt Memorial Hall of Music. See also Adler, *Die verheimlichte Wahrheit*, 251.
43 Bondy, *Elder of the Jews*, 345. "When a sentimental song sounded '*Im Prater blühen wieder die Bäume*,' cried all the Viennese." Utitz, *Psychologie života*, 23.
44 Adler, *Theresienstadt*, 2:530.
45 Rothkirchen, *Jews of Bohemia and Moravia*, 237.
46 Bondy, *Elder of the Jews*, 262.
47 M. van Blankenstein, "Het verbanningsoord," September 11, 1928.

48 Salim, *Vijftien jaar*, 113.
49 BDA 211.
50 BDA 211.
51 BDA 211.
52 BDA 212.
53 BDA 251.
54 BDA 251.
55 Salim, *Vijftien jaar*, 142.
56 Interview with Trikoyo, Tangerang, January 27, 2008.
57 Misbach, *Kenang-Kenangan Orang Bandel*, 15, 20.
58 "PROGRAMMA der feestavond, BDA 83.
59 Salim, *Vijftien jaar*, 124.
60 Salim, *Vijftien jaar*, 253.
61 Testimony by W. A. Ottow-Blok, Heemstede, first part, January 3, 1999, MGI 1316.2.
62 "An Outsider Makes His Mark" (1930), in Benjamin, *Selected Writings*, 2:309.
63 Salim, *Vijftien jaar*, 119.
64 Salim, *Vijftien jaar*, 248.
65 Abdoel 'lXarim M.s. "Pandu Anak Buangan," 107–8.
66 Testimony by ex-internee Darman, June 29, 2002, in Toer, *Tanah Merah*, 25.
67 Salim, *Vijftien jaar*, 110.
68 "Politie Dagboek," BDA 211.
69 Gilbert, *Music in the Holocaust*, 2, 11.
70 Gilbert, *Music in the Holocaust*, 3.
71 Fest, *Die unbeantwortbaren Fragen*, 61.
72 Wechsberg, *Sweet and Sour*, 265.
73 Gilbert, *Music in the Holocaust*, 195.
74 Hilberg, *Destruction*, 2:246.
75 "March in Spirit in Our Ranks," in Nancy, *Listening*, 50.
76 Mas Marco, *Pergaulan Orang Buangan*, 108–9.
77 Mas Marco, *Pergaulan Orang Buangan*, 125–26.
78 Salim, *Vijftien jaar*, 125.
79 Salim, *Vijftien jaar*, 233.
80 This is in the title of Milan Kuna's book *Hudba na hranici života*, "Music in Terezín at the Edge of Life."
81 Weil, *Life with a Star*, 156–57.
82 Cage, *Silence*, 3.
83 Cage, *Silence*, 5.
84 "Philosophy of Music," in Bloch, *Spirit of Utopia*, 35, 37.
85 Horkheimer and Adorno, *Dialectic of Enlightenment*, 66.
86 See a page of chamber music signed "Viktor Kohn, Terezín 1942," in JMP 319a.
87 "Politie Dagboek," BDA 251.
88 Barthes, *Neutral*, 144.
89 Benedict Anderson, "The Suluk Gatoloco I," *Indonesia* (CMIP), 32:123n22.
90 Alice Herz-Sommer, "Aufzeichnungen den pianistin," YVA 033.2356.

91 Salim, *Vijftien jaar*, 151–52.
92 Adler, *Theresienstadt*, 1:205.
93 See, for example, a photo of the audience, including Maxmillian Adler, father of the historian, and Leo Baeck, in a still from the Nazi propaganda film *Der Führer schenkt den Juden eine Stadt*, YVAF 4433249.
94 Horkheimer and Adorno, *Dialectic of Enlightenment*, 26–28.
95 Barthes, *Neutral*, 167.
96 "Politie Dagboek," BDA 210.

Chapter 8. Radio

1 Chekhov, *Sakhalin Island*, 435.
2 *Toul Sleng Genocide Museum*, n.p.
3 "Ideology and Idealism," in Levinas, *Of God*, 13.
4 Nielsen, *In het Land van Kannibalen*, 106.
5 van Kampen, *Een kwestie van macht*, 76.
6 van Kampen, *Wijkende Wildernis*, 208. "On the old primitive map of the world from the time of the early discoveries, there used to be marked 'finis terrae'— the end of the world. Just of that spot is Merauke." Nielsen, *In het Land van Kannibalen*, 140.
7 Schoonheyt, *Boven-Digoel*, 29.
8 M. van Blankenstein, "Het verbanningsoord," September 8, 1928.
9 Deputy Van Heldingen, in *Handelingen Volksraad*, November 18, 1926, 343.
10 "Memorie van Overgave van Aftredende Gouverneur den Molukken J. T. Tideman," ARA Mr. 699x/30, 189.
11 "Rapport van het lid van de Raad van Nederlandsch-Indië, W. P. Hillen, over de interneeringskampen aan de Bovel-Digoel," July 22, 1930, ARA Vb. 1 Nov. 1930 lr. K24.
12 Salim, *Vijftien jaar*, 153.
13 Bondy, *Elder of the Jews*, 249.
14 See the ordinance of February 26, 1942, in YVA 07/6-4.
15 Dostoyevsky, *Crime and Punishment*, 139.
16 Bauman, *Modernity and the Holocaust*, 120.
17 Salim, *Vijftien jaar*, 112.
18 Salim, *Vijftien jaar*, 157.
19 "The Homeless," October 2, 1920, in Tucholsky, *Berlin!*, 86.
20 Interview with Tejo, Jakarta, May 11, 2011. Mr. Tejo speaks both about his father and grandfather in relation to Boven Digoel, and about his own experience as an internee at the camp at Buru in the 1960s and 1970s; on Buru, see chapter 17.
21 Heukäufer, *So wenig Menschen*, 36.
22 Bondy, *Elder of the Jews*, 234.
23 Demetz, *Prague in Danger*, 107.
24 Bondy, *Elder of the Jews*, 126.

25. Miroslav Kárný, "Die Gendarmerie-Sonderabteilung und die Theresienstädter Häftlinge," in Kárný et al., *Theresienstädter Studien*, 1996, 137.
26. Redlich, *Terezín Diary*, 51.
27. *Beruška* (plural *berušky*), from Czech *beru*, "I take away." *Beruška* in Czech actually means "firefly." See Adler, *Theresienstadt*, 1:xxxiii–iv.
28. Hyndráková et al., *Prominenti v ghettu*, 49.
29. Manes, *Als ob's ein Leben*, 193.
30. Adler, *Theresienstadt*, 1:209.
31. "Fadjar Asia," June 5/10, 1930, *IPO* 1930.
32. "Proces-Verbaal Soekandar al. Wisopo," BDA 171.
33. Mas Marco, *Pergaulan Orang Buangan*, 21.
34. BDA 201.
35. "Honor to the Roofs of Paris!" (1930), in Roth, *Report from a Parisian Paradise*, 203.
36. Petr Ginz, "The Life of an Inanimate Object," in "Vedem," in Křížková et al., *We Are Children*, 66.
37. Jacques Rivière, "On the Image of Proust" (1929), in Benjamin, *Selected Writings*, 2:246.
38. Geertz, "Impact of the Concept of Culture," 53.
39. "Recollections of Kurt Kotouč," in Křížková et al., *We Are Children*, 101.
40. Manes, *Als ob's ein Leben*, 224.
41. Manes, *Als ob's ein Leben*, 111.
42. Caduff, *Pandemic Perhaps*, 115.
43. Blanchot, *Step Not Beyond*, 55.
44. Redlich, *Terezín Diary*, 105.
45. Redlich, *Terezín Diary*, 23.
46. Pavel Weiner, *Boy in Terezín*, 92.
47. Pavel Weiner, *Boy in Terezín*, 163.
48. Utitz, *Psychologie života*, 18.
49. Křížková et al., *We Are Children*, 73.
50. Céline, *Rigadoon*, 147.
51. Florida, *Living in a Time of Madness*, 8, 10.
52. Heidegger, *Being and Time*, 164.
53. Heidegger, *Being and Time*, 171.
54. Benedict Anderson, "The Suluk Gatoloco I," in *Indonesia* (CMIP), 32:148n99.
55. Salim, *Vijftien jaar*, 237.
56. Schoonheyt, *Boven-Digoel*, 176.
57. Salim, *Vijftien jaar*, 237.
58. Salim, *Vijftien jaar*, 343.
59. Mawengkang, *Boven Digoel*, 148.
60. Ab Caransa, "Theresienstadt. Schizofrenie in steen," NIOD 809/17, 60.
61. Manes, *Als ob's ein Leben*, 476n2.
62. Heidegger, *Being and Time*, 150.
63. Mas Marco, *Pergaulan Orang Buangan*, 153–54.
64. Adler, "Wörterverzeichnis," in *Theresienstadt*, 1:xliv.

65 Bloch, *Traces*, 59.
66 Demetz, *Prague in Danger*, 107.
67 Demetz, *Prague in Danger*, 110.
68 Rousseau, *Confessions*, 20.
69 Heukäufer, *So wenig Menschen*, 164.
70 Le Clézio, *Interrogation*, 142.
71 Blodig, *Terezín v konečném řešeni*, 11; emphasis mine.
72 Manes, *Als ob's ein Leben*, 154.
73 Adler, *Theresienstadt*, 2:464.
74 Pavel Weiner, *Boy in Terezín*, 97. There is a letter of appreciation sent after the war by an ex-internee Greta Kubátová to a Czech former gendarme in the camp, captain Karel Salaba. She thanks him for leaving the radio on when she was cleaning floors in the SS Headquarters. July 27, 1945, JMP 357/07.
75 Ginz, "Culture report," in "Vedem," in Křížková et al., *We Are Children*, 150.
76 Adler, *Theresienstadt*, 2:597.
77 The watercolor, now in the Yad Vashem Art Museum, is reproduced in Plaček, *Double Signature*, 67.
78 Makarova, *University*, 366–67.
79 Peschel, *Divadelní texty z terezínského ghetta*, 133.
80 David Broch, "Skryté významy: symboly v terezínske hudbě," in Kárný and Blodig, *Terezín v konečném řešeni*, 114.
81 Peter Kien, "Poetry," YVA 72/70, 38.
82 Peter Kien, "Poetry," YVA 72/70, 42.
83 "Cablegram no. 1283x," September 24, 1926, in ARA Mr. 1247x/26, 1250x.
84 Salim, *Vijftien jaar*, 83.
85 "Verslag van de reis van der Resident Ouweling van Amboina naar Boven Digoel," September 6–24, 1929, Amboina, November 18, 1929, ARA, Vb. 12 Jan. 1939 E1: Mr. 1964x/1930, 18.
86 Nielsen, *In het Land van Kannibalen*, 108.
87 Schoonheyt, *Boven-Digoel*, 59.
88 "Politie Dagboek," BDA 211.
89 Matu Mona, *Pacar Merah Indonesia*, 1:95, 1:97, 1:102.
90 Matu Mona, *Pacar Merah Indonesia*, 1:163.
91 Augé, *In the Metro*, 16.
92 Cage, *Silence*, 98. "In my opinion, sound is more suggestive than the image," Adolf Hitler said in 1933. Fascism appropriated "Christian-liturgical elements" in its sonic ritual. In its radio programs about the war, "some of the additional sound effects included the sighs of wounded soldiers." Birdsall, *Nazi Soundscapes*, 35, 41, 43, 114.
93 Pressburger, *Diary of Petr Ginz*, 41n.
94 Pressburger, *Diary of Petr Ginz*, 48.
95 Manes, *Als ob's ein Leben*, 69.
96 Makarova, *University*, 134.
97 Bondy, *Elder of the Jews*, 303.
98 Manes, *Als ob's ein Leben*, 338.

99 Brecht, *Poems*, 386.
100 Adler, *Theresienstadt*, 1:xlvi.
101 Adler, *Theresienstadt*, 2:581–82.
102 Mawengkang, *Boven Digoel*, 150.
103 Virilio, *War and Cinema*, 31.
104 Ruth Bondy, "The Miracle of the Loaves," in Bondy, *Trapped*, 121.
105 Heukäufer, *So wenig Menschen*, 12.
106 Hilberg, *Destruction*, 2:498.
107 Adler, *Theresienstadt*, 2:603.
108 Nielsen, *In het Land van Kannibalen*, 91.
109 Nielsen, *In het Land van Kannibalen*, 119–22.
110 "Politie Dagboek," BDA 251.
111 "Politie Dagboek," BDA 212.
112 "Politie Dagboek," BDA 251.
113 "Politie Dagboek," BDA 212.
114 "Politie Dagboek," BDA 212.
115 Ramidjo, *Kisah-Kisah*, 184–86.

Chapter 9. Clearing

Kafka, *Diaries, 1910–1913*, November 19, 1911, 156.

1 Heidegger, *Being and Time*, 129.
2 Heidegger, *Being and Time*, 388.
3 Testimony by W. A. Ottow-Blok, Heemstede, second part, January 3, 1999, MGI 1316.2.
4 Ramidjo, *Kisah-Kisah*, 68.
5 Salim, *Vijftien jaar*, 85.
6 Salim, *Vijftien jaar*, 81.
7 L. H. W. van Sandick, Gouverneur van Ambon, "1e rapport Boven Digoel," May 24, 1927, 19, ARA, Mr. 739x/27.
8 M. van Blankenstein, "Het verbanningsoord," September 8, 1928.
9 J. Blok, "Rapport A van den Assiko," Boven Digoel, September 1928, 1, ARA Vb. 10 Dec. 1928 V21: Mr. 992x/28.
10 Schoonheyt, *Boven-Digoel*, 226.
11 Salim, *Vijftien jaar*, 81.
12 Bondy, "Theresinstadt Ghetto," 311.
13 "Bericht über die im Reichssicherheitshauptamt Amt IV B 4 Statgefun. der Besprekung," March 6, 1942, NIOD 270c/119, 2.
14 "Der Reichsprotektor in Böhmen und Mähren Heydrich, Prague, February 16, 1942," JMP 52.
15 Lederer, *Ghetto Theresienstadt*, 14.
16 Meeting, October 10, 1941, Heydrich, Eichmann, and others present; Hyndráková et al., *Prominenti v ghettu*, 21.

17 Adler, *Theresienstadt*, 1:26–27.
18 Cablegram no. 1283x, September 24, 1926, ARA Mr. 1247x/26, 1250x.
19 Schoonheyt, *Boven-Digoel*, 66.
20 Salim, *Vijftien jaar*, 133.
21 Verslag van de reis van den Resident van Amboina naar BD van den 14den t/m 31sten Mei 1929, ARA Vb. 12 Jan. 1939 E1: Mr. x/1930, 38.
22 Flaubert, *Sentimental Education*, 429.
23 Salim, *Vijftien jaar*, 82.
24 Job 24:13–17.
25 Jonathan Safran Foer, "Introduction," in Pressburger, *Diary of Petr Ginz*.
26 Sura 89, "The Daybreak," Koran, 54.
27 "Directeur der Strafgevangenis," Medan, March 3, 1927, BDA 91.
28 "Proces-verbaal: Algemeene Politie Batavia," January 31, 1927, BDA 166.
29 "Bezittingen van Tanah Tinggi," 1939, BDA 214.
30 Adler, *Theresienstadt*, 2:270–71.
31 Bernhard Kold, "Tagebuchfragment aus dem Jahre 1943," YVA 02/387, 3.
32 Bondy, *Elder of the Jews*, 400.
33 Nielsen, *In het Land van Kannibalen*, 111.
34 Toer, *Tanah Merah*, 105.
35 Toer, *Tanah Merah*, 225.
36 "Indeeling der in Boen Digoel geinterneerd naar genoten schoolopleiding en vroeger beroep," 1940, BDA 318.
37 "Staat A vermeldende de namen van en verdere byzonderheden omtrent de ballingen, wie interneering toestand kan werden opheven," ARA Vb. 1 Nov. 1930 Ir K24: Mr. 896x/30.
38 "The assumption, even among those physicians who saw this as a positive quality, was that the Jews were innately unable to undertake physical labor." Gilman, *Jew's Body*, 52.
39 Hájková, *Die fabelhaften Jungs aus Theresienstadt*, 120.
40 Bondy, *Elder of the Jews*, 242.
41 Hájková, *Die fabelhaften Jungs aus Theresienstadt*, 120–21.
42 Franz Hahn, in Hájková, *Die fabelhaften Jungs aus Theresienstadt*, 122.
43 Hájková, *Die fabelhaften Jungs aus Theresienstadt*, 121.
44 "Women in the Theresienstadt Ghetto," in Bondy, *Trapped*, 44.
45 Manes, *Als ob's ein Leben*, 276–78.
46 Dr. Jacob Jacobson, "Jewish Survivors Report: The Daily Life, 1943–1945," March 1946, YVA 164/105, 7.
47 Sebald, *Austerlitz*, 237. "Rabbit shearing and splitting mica with a sharp knife by women sitting on stools. The mica was divided into the leaves for the Luftwaffe." Weiss, *God Saw*, 55nn49–50.
48 Sebald, *Austerlitz*, 250.
49 J. Blok, "Rapport A van den Assiko," Boven Digoel September 1928, ARA Vb. 10 Dec. 1928 V21: Mr. 992x/28, 13–14.
50 M. van Blankenstein, "Het verbanningsoord," September 16, 1928.
51 Schoonheyt, *Boven-Digoel*, 200.

52 Shiraishi, "Phantom World of Digoel," 97.
53 "Drie Jaar Boven Digoel-Schandaap: Het Rapport van W.P. Hillen," in De Socialist, 2e jrg. No. 102, Vrijdag 12 September 1930," in Hatta, *Verspreide Geschriften*, 524.
54 Soetan Sjahrir, letter to Maria Duchâteau, Boven Digoel, November 25, 1935.
55 MvO Gouv. der Molukken R. J. Koppend, April 1934, Deel II, Geheim, ARA 59ff.
56 M. van Blankestein, "Het verbanningsoord," September 8, 1928.
57 "Ticheman aan Gouverneur General, Interneeringskamp Boven Digoel," March 2, 1929, ARA Vb. 17 Juni 1930 A14.
58 Resident de Molukken B. J. Haga, "Digoelverslag" I, November 8, 1930, ARA Nov. 1930 Ir K24: Mr. 853x/35
59 "Tideman to Dir. van Landbouw Buitenzorg," March 22, 1930, ARA Vb. 12 Jan. 1939 E1: Mr. 1964x/1930.
60 "Desert Islands," in Deleuze, *Desert Islands*, 12–13. The novel is Jean Giraudoux's *Suzanne et le Pacifique* (1921).
61 "Paris Capital of the Nineteenth Century, Exposé (of 1939)," in Benjamin, *Arcades Project*, 18.
62 Ruth Bondy, "Women in the Theresienstadt Ghetto," in Bondy, *Trapped*, 47.
63 Redlich, *Terezín Diary*, 49.
64 Bondy, *Elder of the Jews*, 3–4.
65 "Recollections of Kurt Kotouč," Theresienstadt, 1944, "Vedem," in Křížková et al., *We Are Children*, 101.
66 Bondy, *Elder of the Jews*, 287.
67 Adler, *Theresienstadt*, 2:399–400.
68 "The Changing Image of the Theresienstadt Ghetto," in Bondy, *Trapped*, 13.
69 Alice Bloemendahl, "Theresienstadt with a Difference," YVA 02/452, 2.
70 Testimony by Josef Manuel (Manzi), Nahariya, Israel, 1997, in Makarova, *University*, 382.
71 Bondy, "Theresienstadt Ghetto," 311.
72 Utitz, *Psychologie života*, 33, 50–51.
73 Sander, *Photographs*, 11.
74 Manes, *Als ob's ein Leben*, 48.
75 Adler, *Theresienstadt*, 2:309.
76 Ernst Bloch quoting Kant, in Bloch, *Traces*, 74, 76.
77 "On Death in the Thought of Ernst Bloch," in Levinas, *Of God*, 36–38; emphasis in source.
78 Dwork and van Pelt, *Auschwitz*, 102.
79 M. van Blankenstein, "Het verbanningsoord," September 8, 1928.
80 Schoonheyt, *Boven-Digoel*, 268. "At that time the people did not understand anything. They felt like inhabitants of a fortress, were full of confusion and loneliness, and they accepted the guidance of Captain Becking, listened to his story, and with enthusiasm opened fields and built the camp as a place to stay." Oen, *Darah dan Aer-Mata*, 3–4.
81 Harney and Moten, *Undercommons*, 54.
82 "Memorie van Overgave van Aftredende Gouverneur den Molukken J. T. Tideman," ARA Mr. 699x/30, 27.

83 Robson, *Wédhatama*, 33.
84 Testimony by Marsudi, June 16, 1976, in *Citra dan Perjuangan*, 78.
85 Oen, *Darah dan Aer-Mata*, 8; the emphasis on "are not lazy" (*tida males*) is mine.
86 "Politie Dagboek," BDA 212.
87 "Politie Dagboek," BDA 212.
88 *Citra dan Perjuangan*, 80.
89 Interview with Trikoyo, Tangerang, May 17, 2011.
90 Misbach, *Kenang-Kenangan Orang Bandel*, 6.
91 Le Clézio, *Desert*, 258.
92 Oen, *Darah dan Aer-Mata*, 75.
93 M. van Blankenstein, "Het verbanningsoord," September 15, 1928. The verses van Blankenstein quoted are a Dutch rendition of the poem "The Birth of Flattery" by George Crabbe, 1754–1832, an English poet known, among other things, for inspiring Benjamin Britten's "Peter Grimes."
94 "Menghadap Padoeka toean Assistent-Resident," June 11, 1929, BDA 204.
95 "Politie Dagboek," BDA 211.
96 "Politie Dagboek," BDA 251.
97 Ramidjo, *Kisah-Kisah*, 71.
98 Letter from Mohammad Hatta to "Pemandangan," July 3, 1935, IPO 1935. I asked Mrs. Zakaria, "Did the internees have many chickens in Boven Digoel? How many?" She thought and said, "Hundreds." Interview with Zakaria, Jakarta, May 10, 2011.
99 "Politie Dagboek," BDA 211.
100 "Politie Dagboek," BDA 212.
101 "Politie Dagboek," BDA 251.
102 Schoonheyt, *Boven-Digoel*, 65.
103 Ramidjo, *Kisah-Kisah*, 139.
104 M. van Blankenstein, "Het verbanningsoord," September 8, 1928.
105 M. van Blankenstein, "Het verbanningsoord," September 8, 1928.
106 Canto VIII in Dante, *Purgatory*, 129.
107 J. Blok, "Rapport van den Assiko," Boven Digoel, September 1928, ARA Vb. 10 Dec. 1928 V21: Mr. 992x/2–3, 28.
108 "Verslag van de reis van der Resident Ouweling van Amboina naar Boven Digoel, May 14–31, 1929," ARA Vb. 12 Jan. 1939 E1: Mr. 1964x/1930, 38.
109 Widayasih, *Masa kanak-kanak*, 1:8–9.
110 Schoonheyt, "Bij de ballingen van BD," Javabode, April 19, 1934, a clipping in *Archief Schoonheyt* 1.
111 Shiraishi, "Phantom World of Digoel," 104.
112 Interview with Zakaria, Jakarta, May, 10, 2011.
113 Interview with Bangun Topo, Jakarta, May 15, 2011.
114 "Politie Dagboek," BDA 251.
115 Benjamin, *Arcades Project*, 123.
116 Benjamin, *Arcades Project*, 158.
117 Koolhaas, *Delirious New York*, 22.
118 Flaubert, *Sentimental Education*, 208.

119 Photo of the *"cementen tennisbaan,"* "tennis court with surface of concrete," in Schoonheyt, *Boven-Digoel* (1940 edition), 170.
120 Widayasih, *Masa kanak-kanak*, 1:12.
121 Salim, *Vijftien jaar*, 115.
122 "Verslag van de reis van der Resident Ouweling van Amboina naar Boven Digoel," van den May 14–31, 1929, ARA Vb. 12 Jan. 1939 E1: Mr. 1964x/1930, 38.
123 Salim, *Vijftien jaar*, 140.
124 Interview with Trikoyo, Tangerang, July 5, 2010.
125 "Dagrapport," June 1936, BDA 18.
126 "Politie Dagboek," BDA 211.
127 Schoonheyt, *Boven-Digoel*, 85–86.
128 "The Shape of the Inconstruable Question," in Bloch, *Spirit of Utopia*, 194.
129 Salim, *Vijftien jaar*, 152.
130 Couperus, *Hidden Force*, 44–48.
131 Oen, *Darah dan Aer-Mata*, 8.
132 B. J. Haga, "Verslag Boven Digoel medio Augustus 1934," ARA Vb. 7 Mei 1935, W8, 2.
133 "Politie Dagboek," BDA 212.
134 Testimony by W. A. Ottow-Blok, second part, January 3, 1999.
135 d'Amour, *Taufan Gila*, 84.
136 Shiraishi, "Phantom World of Digoel," 105.
137 Salim, *Vijftien jaar*, 217.
138 "Politie Dagboek," BDA 212.
139 "Politie Dagboek," BDA 212.
140 "PROGRAMMA der feestavond ter gelegenheid van de verjaardag van H.M. de Koningin en de geboorte van H.K.H. Prinses Irene," August 5, 1939, BDA 83.
141 G. d'Avenel (1894), in Benjamin, *Arcades Project*, 167.
142 "Interneeringsoord BD. Voordracht met lichtbeelden door dr. L.J.A. Schoonheyt," in *Archief Schoonheyt* 1.
143 "Rapport van het lid van de Raad van Nederlandsch-Indië, W. P. Hillen, over de interneeringskampen aan de Bovel-Digoel," July 22, 1930, ARA Vb. 1 Nov. 1930 lr. K24, 14.
144 Salim, *Vijftien jaar*, 138.
145 Schoonheyt, *Boven-Digoel*, 45–46.
146 van Kampen, *Een kwestie van macht*, 84–85.
147 "Nanning Prison," in Ho Chi Minh, *Prison Diary*, 60. Rosalind Morris recalled the statement by Ho Chi Minh, whose name means Light Bearer, in her debate with William Kentridge: "I am reminded of the apocryphal remark attributed to Ho Chi Minh when he was asked 'What is your assessment of the Enlightenment?' He said, or is said to have said, 'It's too soon to tell.'" Kentridge and Morris, *That Which Is Not Drawn*, 17.
148 See the paragraph on *Arbeit Macht Frei* above. Hannah Arendt was disturbed and has a disturbing comment about Eichmann declaring himself a Kantian. See Arendt, *Eichmann in Jerusalem*, 120–22.
149 Perec, *Species of Spaces*, 90.

150 Bondy, *Elder of the Jews*, 440.
151 Manes, *Als ob's ein Leben*, 288.
152 Baker, *Days of Sorrow*, 3.
153 Manes, *Als ob's ein Leben*, 263.
154 Pavel Weiner, *Boy in Terezín*, 84.
155 Adler, *Die verheimlichte Wahrheit*, 193.
156 Pavel Weiner, *Boy in Terezín*, 220.
157 Italie, *Het Oorlogsdagboek*, April 12, 1945, 546.
158 Spies, *My Years in Theresienstadt*, 83.
159 Pavel Weiner, *Boy in Terezín*, 55.
160 Adler, *Die verheimlichte Wahrheit*, 237.
161 Testimony by Catharine van der Berg, December 2, 1998, YVA 03/11.
162 Manes, *Als ob's ein Leben*, 290.
163 Adler, *Die verheimlichte Wahrheit*, 237.
164 Hájková, *Die fabelhaften Jungs aus Theresienstadt*, 134.
165 Adler, *Theresienstadt*, 1:128. "Substitute coffee with sugar, substitute tea, in summer lemonade and in exceptional cases, ice-cream." Dr. Jacob Jacobson, "Jewish Survivors Report: The Daily Life, 1943–1945," March 1946, YVA 164/105, 11.
166 Whiteley, *Appel Is Forever*, 28.
167 "By the Light of Memorial Candle," in Singer, *Gimpel the Fool*, 65–66.
168 Bondy, *Elder of the Jews*, 262.
169 Dr. Adolph Metz, stellv. Leiter des Gesundeitsamtes von Theresienstadt Ghetto, "Theresienstadt," February 9, 1946, YVA 033/3257, 2.
170 Alice Bloemendahl, "Theresienstadt with a Difference," YVA 02/452, 2.
171 Italie, *Het Oorlogsdagboek*, 494.
172 Fest, *Die unbeantwortbaren Fragen*, 65.
173 Durlacher, *Quarantaine*, 63.
174 Manes, *Als ob's ein Leben*, 423.
175 "Bernhard Kold: Tagebuchfragment aus dem Jahre 1943," YVA 02/387, 4.
176 Martin Zelenka, in *Šalom na pátek*, April 3, 1943, YVA 064.64, 17.
177 Adler, *Theresienstadt*, 1:146.
178 Weiss, *God Saw*, 28.
179 Oz, *Tale of Love and Darkness*, 65.

Chapter 10. Enlightenment

1 "March in Spirit in Our Ranks," in Nancy, *Listening*, 5.
2 Arendt, *Eichmann*, 231. See also van Pelt and Westfall, *Architectural Principles*, 127–28.
3 On Nietzsche's idea of "stylized barbarism," see Horkheimer and Adorno, *Dialectic of Enlightenment*, 101.
4 Quoted in Žižek, "Afterword: Lenin's Choice," in Žižek, *Revolution at the Gates*, 299.

5. Žižek, "Afterword: Lenin's Choice," 299.
6. Heidegger, *Being and Time*, 388; emphasis in source.
7. Heidegger, *Being and Time*, 164; emphasis in source.
8. Heidegger, *Being and Time*, 8.
9. Heidegger, *Being and Time*, 334.
10. "Notitie van Werther, ISdS Den Haag IV B 5 over besprekingen in Berlijn RSHA" (Reichssicherheitshauptamt), March 3, 1943, NIOD 270c/591.
11. "B.d. S. IV B 4. Vermerk für SS-Stubas. Zoepf. Betreft: Theresienstadt," The Hague, January 25, 1943, NIOD 270c/623.
12. Bergen-Belsen was the other camp similarly designated, but its "prominent" status did not last long, and it developed into a predominantly annihilation camp.
13. Ruth Bondy, "Privileged until Further Notice," in Bondy, *Trapped*, 99–100.
14. The postcard is in Adler, *Die verheimlichte Wahrheit*, 290.
15. Hyndráková et al., *Prominenti v ghettu*, 102.
16. Ruth Bondy, "Roll Call," in Bondy, *Trapped*, 199.
17. Blodig et al., *Kultura proti smrti*, 227. Emil Holan survived the camps but died soon after the return to Prague. He gave lectures in Theresienstadt titled "Film-Shooting at Barrandov Film City," "On Jirka's Great Invention," and "On the Czech Railways." See Makarova, *University*, 47.
18. Ruth Bondy, "Privileged until Further Notice," in Bondy, *Trapped*, 102.
19. Kafka, *Letters to Friends*, February 1, 1919, 212–13.
20. On Sigmund Freud's sisters in Theresienstadt, see Gilman, *Jew's Body*, 236.
21. Redlich, *Terezín Diary*, 116.
22. Toer, *Tanah Merah*, 154.
23. Toer, *Tanah Merah*, 37, 40.
24. Toer, *Tanah Merah*, 43.
25. Matanasi, *Thomas Najoan*, 19.
26. Steenbrink, *Catholics in Indonesia*, 2:251.
27. Schoonheyt, *Boven-Digoel*, 163–64.
28. Oz, *Tale of Love and Darkness*, 173.
29. "Introduction," in Scholem, *Zohar*, vii.
30. Sura 43, "Ornaments of Gold," Koran, 135.
31. Soetan Sjahrir, letter to Maria Duchâteau, Boven Digoel, September 9, 1935.
32. Soetan Sjahrir, letter to Maria Duchâteau, Boven Digoel, November 25, 1935; emphasis in source.
33. Du Perron, *Country of Origin*, 79.
34. Schoonheyt, *Boven-Digoel*, 263.
35. Resident de Molukken B. J. Haga, "Verslag Boven Digoel" I, 3, ARA Vb. 1 Nov. 1930 Ir K24: Mr. 853x/35, 3.
36. Adler, *Theresienstadt*, 2:271.
37. Dr. Adolph Metz, stellv. Leiter des Gesundeitsamtes von Theresienstadt Ghetto, "Theresienstadt," February 9, 1946, YVA 033/3257, 5.
38. Bondy, *Elder of the Jews*, 233.
39. Bondy, *Elder of the Jews*, 347.
40. Lanzmann, *Murmelstein*, Rome, 67–68.

41 Manes, *Als ob's ein Leben*, 398.
42 Utitz, *Psychologie života*, 31.
43 Pavel Weiner, *Boy in Terezín*, 106.
44 Pavel Weiner, *Boy in Terezín*, 115.
45 Pavel Weiner, *Boy in Terezín*, 165.
46 From Petr Ginz's "Time Sheets," in Křížková et al., *We Are Children*, 67.
47 Bondy, *Elder of the Jews*, 347.
48 Dr. Jacob Jacobson, "Jewish Survivors Report: The Daily Life, 1943–1945," March 1946, YVA 164/105, 8.
49 Riyadi, *Hatta*, 238.
50 Hatta, *Berjuang dan Dibuang*, 138–39.
51 Riyadi, *Hatta*, 246–47.
52 Salim, *Vijftien jaar*, 141.
53 Soetan Sjahrir, letter to Sjahsam, Boven Digoel, March 9, 1935.
54 Tolstoy, *Resurrection*, 348–49.
55 Hatta, *Berjuang dan Dibuang*, 151.
56 Hatta, *Alam Pikiran Junani*.
57 A selection of the letters was published as Sjahrazad, *Indonesische Overpeinzingen*, by De Bezige Bij in Amsterdam in 1945. The original letters were recently acquired by KITLV in Leiden.
58 Olda Havlová's recollectons in Makarova, *University*, 152–53.
59 Blodig et al., *Kultura proti smrti*, 178.
60 Spies, *My Years in Theresienstadt*, 21.
61 Manes, *Als ob's ein Leben*, 220.
62 Max Berger, "Zpráva o pobytu v Terezíně," YVA 07/6-4, 3.
63 Original typewritten page compiled by professor Utitz in July 31, 1945, JMP 320a.
64 "Cultural Correspondent (Kurt Kotouč)," in "Vedem," in Křížková et al., *We Are Children*, 148.
65 Erich Springer, gew. Leiter des Krankenhauses in Theresienstadt, "Das Gesundheitswesen im Theresienstadt Ghetto," YVA M-1/E37 02/525, 8.
66 JMP 320b-8.
67 Alice Bloemendahl, "Theresienstadt with a Difference," YVA 02/452, 2.
68 Redlich, *Terezín Diary*, 41.
69 Adler, *Theresienstadt*, 2:599.
70 Pavel Weiner, *Boy in Terezín*, 13.
71 "Program of Lectures," JMP 320b-4.
72 Alice Bloemendahl, "Theresienstadt with a Difference," YVA 02/452, 1. Krapp, in Samuel Beckett's *Krapp's Last Tape*, recalls reading Theodor Fontane's novel *Effi Briest*. Beckett himself wrote to a friend, "Scalded the eyes out of me reading *Effi* again, a page a day with tears again." Beckett, *Letters*, 3:586n3.
73 Peschel, *Divadelní texty z terezínského ghetta*, 251.
74 Mirawati, *Inventaris Arsip Boven Digoel*, 1.
75 "Rapport van het lid van de Raad van Nederlandsch-Indië, W. P. Hillen, over de interneeringskampen aan de Bovel-Digoel," July 22, 1930, ARA Vb. 1 Nov. 1930 lr. K24, 16.

76 HPB van Langen, "Opgave van gebouwen en woningen in het internoeringskamp Boven Digoel 4de kwartaal 1934," December 8, 1932, in ARA Vb. 7 Mei 1935 W8, 2.
77 "Onderwyzvoorziening te Boven Digoel. Wd Dir van Ond. en Eerrend." ARA Vb. 12 Jan. 1939 E1: Mr. 2614x/1930.
78 Salim, *Vijftien jaar*, 242.
79 Interview with Bangun Topo, Jakarta, August 11, 2008.
80 Interview with Chamsinah Nasoetion, Jakarta, May 9, 2011.
81 Interview with Trikoyo, Tngerang, July 28, 2008.
82 "Opgave leerlingen v/d wilde scholen," BDA 319.
83 J. Blok, "Boven Digoel Rapport," September 12, 1929," ARA Vb. 12 Jan. 1939 E1: Mr. 1964x/1930.
84 Interview with Chamsinah Nasoetion, Jakarta, May 18, 2011.
85 Interview with Trikoyo, Tengerang, January 30, 2012.
86 Interview with Widayasih, Jakarta, January 23, 2009; see also Widayasih, *Masa kanak-kanak*, 1:7–8.
87 B. J. Haga, "Verslag Boven Digoel medio Augustus 1934," 25, ARA Vb. 7 Mei 1935 W8.
88 "Aantal leerlingen," 1940, BDA 129; "Opgave leerlingen v/d wilde scholen," 1940, BDA 319.
89 "Opgave leerlingen en onderwijzers van de naturalisten op ultimo 1e kwartaal 1940," BDA 318.
90 Riyadi, *Hatta*, 246–47.
91 "Opgave leerlingen."
92 "Avondcursussen," BDA 319.
93 "Woningen in het interneeringskamp, 2 kwartaal 1935," ARA Vb. 1 Nov. 1930 Ir K24, 9.
94 Toer, *Tanah Merah*, 40.
95 Redlich, *Terezín Diary*, 43.
96 Shean, *To Be an Actress*, 32.
97 Adler, *Theresienstadt*, 1:xli.
98 "Mothers were not obliged to transfer their children to the homes, but most of them did so." Ruth Bondy, "Women in the Theresienstadt Ghetto," in Bondy, *Trapped*, 60.
99 Interview with Jehuda Bacon, Jerusalem, May 15, 2013.
100 Kasperová, *Výchova*, 158–59.
101 Šormová, *Divadlo v Terezíně*, 75.
102 Pavel Weiner, *Boy in Terezín*, 129.
103 Max Berger, "Zpráva o pobytu v Terezíně," YVA 07/6–4, 3.
104 Křížková et al., *We Are Children*, 39.
105 Redlich, *Terezín Diary*, 109n14.
106 Furman, *Ways of Growing Up*, 19.
107 The best on Dicker-Brandeis is Makarova, *Friedl Dicker-Brandeis*.
108 Diary of Helga Weissová, 171.
109 Diary of Helga Weissová, 159.

110 Otto Dov Kulka: Bericht über das "Theresienstadt Familienlager" in Auschwitz-Birkenau, YVA 03/2896.
111 Testimony by Zdeněk Ornest in Adler, *Die verheimlichte Wahrheit*, 36.
112 Kasperová, *Výchova*, 156.
113 "Vedem," in Křížková et al., *We Are Children*, 121.
114 "Opgaaf van personen wier interneering zou kunnen opgehoven: Behoort by den geheimen brief van het Radslid Hillen van September 19, 1930," ARA Vb. 1 Nov. 1930 Ir K24.
115 Toer, *Tanah Merah*, 99.
116 "Aan den Assistent-Resident van Boven Digoel," Tanah Tinggi, June 9, 1929, BDA 205.
117 Regeringsmachtigde voor algemeene zaken bij de Volksraad aan Gouverneur General, June 29, 1935, in Kwantes, *De Ontwikkeling*, 4:318.
118 "Pemandangan," January 4, 1936, IPO 1936.
119 Pavel Weiner, *Boy in Terezín*, 9.
120 Pavel Weiner, *Boy in Terezín*, 16.
121 Pavel Weiner, *Boy in Terezín*, 99.
122 Makarova, *University*, 510.
123 Foucault, *Discipline and Punish*, 159. The term "command pedagogics" was coined by a foremost Bolshevik pedagogue, Anton Makarenko, who worked with the *bezprizorniye*, "uncared for," children of the revolution. Makarenko organized colonies for the children on the principle of "command pedagogics." Later these colonies, or camps, were transferred to a commune established by Cheka (GPU). Murto, *Makarenko*, 178. See also Lukács, "Makarenko," 191–236.
124 Kasperová, *Výchova*, 171.
125 "The Shape of the Inconstruable Question," in Bloch, *Spirit of Utopia*, 184–85.

Chapter 11. Limelight

1 Mehring, *Lost Library*, 75.
2 Anat Feinberg, "Stagestruck: Jewish Attitudes to the Theatre in Wilhelmine Germany," in Malkin and Rokem, *Jews*, 59.
3 Kentridge, *Six Drawing Lessons*, 42.
4 "The Theater of Cruelty (First Manifesto)," in Artaud, *The Theater and Its Double*, 95.
5 Faulkner, *Fable*, 17.
6 "The Theater of Cruelty (Second Manifesto)," in Artaud, *Theater*, 125.
7 "Theater of Cruelty (First Manifesto)," in Artaud, *Theater*, 96.
8 "Theater of Cruelty (First Manifesto)," in Artaud, *Theater*, 98.
9 Bernhard Greiner, "German and Jewish 'Theatromania': Theoder Lessing's Theater-Seele between Goethe and Kafka," in Malkin and Rokem, *Jews*, 106–7.
10 Jeanette R. Malkin, "Transforming in Public: Jewish Actors on the German Expressionist Stage," in Malkin and Rokem, *Jews*, 167.

11 Tanizaki, *In Praise of Shadows*, 48.
12 Tanizaki, *In Praise of Shadows*, 58.
13 Shiraishi, "Phantom World of Digoel," 107.
14 Anderson, "The Suluk Gatoloco I," *Indonesia* 32, 133, 133n50.
15 Anderson, "The Suluk Gatoloco I," *Indonesia* 32, 135.
16 Plato, *Republic*, 2:109.
17 Anderson, "The Suluk Gatoloco I," *Indonesia* 32, 136.
18 Karmi, *Return*, 46–47.
19 Adler, *Die verheimlichte Wahrheit*, 184.
20 Vaihinger, *Philosophy*, 343. See also recently Kwame Anthony Appiah,' *As If: Idealization and Ideals* (Cambridge, MA: Harvard University Press, 2017).
21 Vaihinger, *Philosophy*, 346n1.
22 Vaihinger, *Philosophy*, 352n3.
23 Furman, *Ways of Growing Up*, 197.
24 "From a Cabarette of the Ehepaar Strauss," in Peschel, *Divadelní texty z terezínského ghetta*, 297.
25 "The Theater and the Plague," in Artaud, *Theater*, 23.
26 Demetz, *Prague in Danger*, 162.
27 Šormová, *Divadlo v Terezíně*, 66.
28 Shean, *To Be an Actress*, 26.
29 Barthes, *Fashion System*, 252.
30 Barthes, *Fashion System*, 301.
31 Roth, *Hotel Years*, 73–74.
32 "Fashion," in Benjamin, *Arcades Project*, 79.
33 January 3, 1951, in Beckett, *Letters*, 2:218–19.
34 Dr. Adolph Metz, stellv. Leiter des Gesundheitsamtes von Theresienstadt Ghetto, "Theresienstadt," February 9, 1946, YVA 033/3257, 3, 5.
35 Furman, *Ways of Growing Up*, 136.
36 Metz, "Theresienstadt," 3.
37 Gogol seemed to fit the camps. Anton Chekhov noted on his visit to the Sakhalin penal colony, "for example at Alexandrovsk in 1888, an amateur production of *The Marriage*." Chekhov, *Sakhalin Island*, 279.
38 Shean, *To Be an Actress*, 42.
39 Shean, *To Be an Actress*, 42.
40 Shean, *To Be an Actress*, 100, 43.
41 Shean, *To Be an Actress*, 42.
42 "Testimony by Margit Silberfeld, né Kampert," in Plaček, *Double Signature*, 90.
43 Bondy, *Elder of the Jews*, 327.
44 Demetz, *Prague in Danger*, 163.
45 Hans Hoffer's testimony, in Šormová, *Divadlo v Terezíně*, 94.
46 Josef Taussing, "Totéž ale v šatně," JMP 326.
47 Pavel Weiner, *Boy in Terezín*, 215.
48 Bondy, *Elder of the Jews*, 365.
49 Adler, *Theresienstadt*, 2:612.
50 Manes, *Als ob's ein Leben*, 207.

51 Ruth Bondy, "Games in the Shadow of the Crematoria," in Bondy, *Trapped*, 166.
52 Ruth Bondy, "Games in the Shadow of the Crematoria," in Bondy, *Trapped*, 167.
53 Rothkirchen, *Jews of Bohemia and Moravia*, 258.
54 "PROGRAMA DER FEESTE ter gelegenheid van de geboorte van H.K.H. Prinses Irene Ema Elisabeth," Boven Digoel, August 5, 1939, BDA 83.
55 Mas Marco, *Pergaulan Orang Buangan*, 76.
56 Mas Marco, *Pergaulan Orang Buangan*, 157. Another theater form is mentioned, "the Javanese *tembang* (reciting Javanese poems)." Shiraishi, "Phantom World of Digoel."
57 Mas Marco, *Pergaulan Orang Buangan*, 159.
58 M. van Blankenstein, "Het verbanningsoord," September 13, 1928.
59 "Verslag van de reis van der Resident Ouweling van Amboina naar Boven Digoel," May 14–31, 1929, ARA Vb. 12 Jan. 1939 E1: Mr. 1964x/1930, 36.
60 Schoonheyt, *Boven-Digoel*, 183.
61 Toer, *Tanah Merah*, 27.
62 "Verslag van de reis van der Resident Ouweling van Amboina naar Boven Digoel," May 14–31, 1929, ARA Vb. 12 Jan. 1939 E1: Mr. 1964x/1930, 35.
63 Schoonheyt, *Boven-Digoel* (1940 edition), 195.
64 The woodcut, signed by Soewigno, is in *Archief Schoonheyt 2*.
65 Testimony by ex-internee Cus, March 22, 2003, in Toer, *Tanah Merah*, 96.
66 Interview with Trikoyo, Tangerang, January 30, 2012.
67 Toer, *Tanah Merah*, 116.
68 Interview with Trikoyo, Jakarta, May 11, 2011. On Soewigno, see also Salim, *Vijftien jaar* (1976), 238–39.
69 Aldo Carpi's memoir, "Diario di Gusen," Torino, Einaudi, 1993, in Agamben, *Remnants of Auschwitz*, 50.
70 Dr. Jacob Jacobson, "Jewish Survivors Report: The Daily Life, 1943–1945," March 1946, YVA 164/105, 8.
71 Plaček, *Double Signature*, 41.
72 Blodig et al., *Kultura proti smrti*, 57.
73 Blodig et al., *Kultura proti smrti*, 53.
74 Soetan Sjahrir, letter to Sjahsam, Boven Digoel, July 20, 1935.
75 Green, *Artists of Terezín*, is focused almost entirely on those artists in the camp. See also Leo Haas, "The Affair of the Painter of Terezín," in Council of Jewish Communities, *Terezín*, 158.
76 YVAF 5220. "The SS and perhaps also Czech gendarmes made a brisk business with those curiosities." Adler, *Die verheimlichte Wahrheit*, 234.
77 YVA 064.64.
78 "Bilderrestauratoren für Theresienstadt," The Hague, January 14, 1944, NIOD 77/1322.
79 Wechsberg, *Sweet and Sour*, 62.
80 Augé, *In the Metro*, 61.
81 Appelfeld, *Badenheim 1939*, 33.
82 Perec, *Species of Spaces*, 36.
83 Kugelmann, *No Compromises!*, 64, 78.

84 *Šalom na pátek*, April, 30, 1943, YVA 064.64, 117.
85 Ruth Bondy, "Humor as Weapon," in Bondy, *Trapped*, 87.
86 "One-Way Street," in Benjamin, *Selected Writings*, 1:468.
87 "Central Park" (1938/1939), in Benjamin, *Selected Writings*, 4:72.
88 "Paris, the Capital of the Nineteenth Century" (1935), in Benjamin, *Selected Writings*, 3:34–35.
89 Jehuda Bacon, in Adler, *Theresienstadt*, 2:554–55.
90 Ab Caransa, "Theresienstadt: Schizofrenie in steen," NIOD 809/17, 18. According to other memories, the painter was Jo Spier.
91 Jehuda Bacon, in Adler, *Theresienstadt*, 2:557.
92 Spier, *Dat alles*, 72.
93 Jacobson, "Jewish Survivors Report," 15.
94 Bloch, *Traces*, 138.
95 Ruth Bondy, "Games in the Shadow of the Crematoria," in Bondy, *Trapped*, 167.
96 "Verslag van de reis van der Resident Ouweling van Amboina naar Boven Digoel," September 6–September 24, 1929, ARA Vb. 12 Jan. 1939 E1: Mr. 1964x/1930.
97 "Politie Dagboek," BDA 210.
98 "Djawa Tengah," February 9, 1931, IPO 1931: "In a follow up to a previous article, author signed '101' reported that the internees in Boven Digoel have movies at the present."
99 "Exchange with Theodor W. Adorno on 'The Paris of the Second Empire in Baudelaire'" (1938), in Benjamin, *Selected Writings*, 4:111.
100 Du Perron, *Country of Origin*, 187.
101 Shiraishi, "Phantom World of Digoel," 104.
102 Baudrillard, *Simulacra*, 59.
103 Virilio, *Aesthetics*, 82.
104 Nancy, *Noli me tangere*, 15–16.
105 Bloch, *Traces*, 61.
106 Manes, *Als ob's ein Leben*, 144.
107 The manuscript of Hugo Israel Friedmann, "Kunstführung durch Theresienstadt (illustriert von Professor Alfred Bergel), November 1943," is in YVA 05/41. Here it is quoted from Adler, *Die verheimlichte Wahrheit*, 244–46.
108 Pérez-Oramas, *Tangled Alphabets*, 35.
109 David Broch, "Skryté významy: Symboly v terezínské hudbě," in Kárný and Blodig, *Terezín v konečném řešeni*, 113.
110 Koolhaas and Foster, *Junkspace*, 9.
111 Weber, *Theatricality*, 7; emphasis in source.
112 Weber, *Theatricality*, 11.
113 Bondy, *Elder of the Jews*, 54.
114 Jacobson, "Jewish Survivors Report," 12.
115 Adler, *Theresienstadt*, 2:585.
116 Redlich, *Terezín Diary*, 136.
117 *Šalom na pátek*, December 31, 1943, YVA 064, 147. These were the real films played at the time.

118 Similarly, Philip Mechanicus walked through the Westerbork camp and wrote in his diary, "Past hut and look-out towers that looked as if they were made of cardboard. The atmosphere at Westerbork is like that in a film city." August 2, 1943, Mechanicus, *Waiting for Death*, 110.
119 Sebald, *Austerlitz*, 178–79.
120 Redlich, *Terezín Diary*, 15n6.
121 V. Weiner, *Recollections*, 1.
122 Makarova, *Boarding Pass to Paradise*, 16.
123 Hyndráková et al., *Prominenti v ghettu*, 53. Hans de Vries, "Židé z Holandska do Terezína," in Kárný and Blodig, *Terezín v konečném řešeni*, 55.
124 For documents on the film shooting, see Adler, *Die verheimlichte Wahrheit*, 229–33.
125 Karel Margry, "Nacistický propagandistický film o Terezíně," in Kárný and Blodig, *Terezín v konečném řešení*, 222.
126 Margry, "Nacistický propagandistický film o Terezíně," 223.
127 Spier, *Dat alles*, 119.
128 Lanzmann, *Benjamin Murmelstein*, 267.
129 Pavel Weiner, *Boy in Terezín*, 144.
130 Virilio, *Aesthetics*, 60.
131 Tom Conley, "Introduction," in Augé, *In the Metro*, xix–xx.
132 Kafka, *Amerika*, 104.
133 Lanzmann, *Benjamin Murmelstein*, 268.
134 Lanzmann, *Benjamin Murmelstein*, 172.
135 Ruth Bondy, "Games in the Shadow of the Crematoria," in Bondy, *Trapped*, 160.

Chapter 12. Blocks

Céline, *Rigadoon*, 235.

1 Melville, *Moby Dick*, 581.
2 Nancy, *Pleasure in Drawing*, 103.
3 Husserl, *Crisis of European Sciences*, 22.
4 Husserl, *Crisis of European Sciences*, 227.
5 Ramidjo, *Kisah-Kisah*, 4, 169.
6 Mas Marco, *Pergaulan Orang Buangan*, 3.
7 Mas Marco, *Pergaulan Orang Buangan*, 4–5.
8 Bloch, *Spirit of Utopia*, 13–14.
9 Nancy, *Corpus*, 9.
10 Nancy, *Corpus*, 11.
11 Kafka, *Penal Colony*, 202–3.
12 Furman, *Ways of Growing Up*, 117, 121.
13 Plaček, *Double Signature*, 44–45.
14 Le Corbusier, *Towards a New Architecture*, 180.
15 Le Corbusier, *Towards a New Architecture*, 183.

16   Kertész, *Fatelessness*, 102.
17   Kertész, *Fatelessness*, 102.
18   Pressburger, *Diary of Petr Ginz*, 107.
19   Cabet, *Travels in Icaria*, 19–20.
20   Cabet, *Travels in Icaria*, 20.
21   Wittgenstein, *On Certainty*, 14; emphasis in source.
22   A major part of it was republished under the title "Otto Zucker: Theresienstadt 1941–1943," in *Theresienstädter Studien und Dokumente* (1995), 264–71.
23   See Adler, *Die verheimlichte Wahrheit*, 147.
24   "From Consciousness to Wakefulness: Starting from Husserl," in Levinas, *Of God*, 18.
25   Koolhaas and Foster, *Junkspace*, 19.
26   "Testimony of Jehuda Bacon," Jerusalem, February, 13, 1952, NIOD 270c/118, 11.
27   Nielsen, *In het Land van Kannibalen*, 107–8.
28   "Politie Dagboek," BDA 251.
29   "Register permohonan memboeka tanah," Boven Digoel, March 1, 1939, BDA 89.
30   "Register permohonan memboeka tanah," Boven Digoel, July 31, 1936, BDA 271.
31   "Verslag van de reis van den Resident van Amboina naar BD van den 14den t/m 31sten Mei 1929, ARA Vb. 12 Jan. 1939 E1: Mr. 1964x/1930, 38. Also see M. van Blankenstein, "Het verbanningsoord," September 11, 1928.
32   Mawengkang, *Boven Digoel*, 66.
33   "Politie Dagboek," BDA 211.
34   Interview with Zakaria, Jakarta, May 10, 2011.
35   "Register van de strafzaken, behandelt en afgedaan door den Magistraat," BDA 164.
36   Makarova, *University*, 20.
37   "Guibert systematically implemented the chronometric measurement of shooting that had been suggested earlier by Vauban." Foucault, *Discipline and Punish*, 150.
38   Sebald, *Austerlitz*, 14.
39   Sebald, *Austerlitz*, 15.
40   Blodig, *Terezín*, 11.
41   Makarova, *University*, 43.
42   Blodig, *Terezín*, 129.
43   "Tři doby země Levoty," in Peschel, *Divadelní texty z terezínského ghetta*, 167.
44   Erika Taube, "Die Welt Is Round," JMP 326.
45   Erich Springer, gew. Leiter des Krankenhauses in Theresienstadt, "Das Gesundheitswesen im Theresienstadt Ghetto," YVA M-1/E37 02/525, 19.
46   Bondy, *Elder of the Jews*, 250.
47   Ruth Bondy, "The Theresienstadt Ghetto: Its Characteristics and Perspective," in Bondy, *Nazi Concentration Camps*, 305.
48   This is a little poem exhibited in the former "School" building in Theresienstadt Memorial, signed by "Hanuš, Löwy and Bachner."
49   Dr. Adolph Metz, stellv. Leiter des Gesundheitsamtes von Theresienstadt Ghetto, "Theresienstadt," in YVA 033/3257, 1.

50 Hyndráková et al., *Prominenti v ghettu*, 23.
51 Jacob Presser, "Introduction," in Mechanicus, *Waiting for Death*, 6.
52 Adler, *Theresienstadt*, 1:143. Nazis often called Theresienstadt "Musterghetto." See, for example, "the minutes of Heydrich's Prague Conference (October 10, 1941).... Evacuation to Eastern territories would follow and then the whole area might be used for a model Government settlement." Rothkirchen, *Jews of Bohemia and Moravia*, 234.
53 Gaudy, *Une Île, Une Forteresse*, 44.
54 Koolhaas, "Singapore," 1015.
55 Charles-François Viel (1805), in Benjamin, *Arcades Project*, 166–67.
56 Le Corbusier, *Towards a New Architecture*, 238.
57 Interview with Trikoyo, Tangerang, May 17, 2011.
58 Interview with Trikoyo, Tangerang, May 17, 2011.
59 "Interneeringsoord BD: Voordracht met lichtbeelden door dr. L.J.A. Schoonheyt Amsterdam, November 11, 1937," newpapper clippings, in *Archief Schoonheyt* 1.
60 Abidin, *Appearance of Memory*, 193.
61 Abidin, *Appearance of Memory*, 194.
62 Dostoyevsky, *Crime and Punishment*, 139.
63 Faulkner, *Fable*, 3.
64 Riis, *How the Other Half Lives*, 20.
65 Virilio, *Speed and Politics*, 77.
66 Ulrike Meinhof, "Armed Anti-Imperialist Struggle," in Kraus and Lotringer, *Hatred of Capitalism*, 276.
67 Le Corbusier, *Towards a New Architecture*, 61.
68 Koolhaas, *Delirious New York*, 18–19.
69 Koolhaas, *Delirious New York*, 97.
70 Koolhaas, *Delirious New York*, 101.
71 Interview with Trikoyo, Tangerang, July 5, 2010.
72 Soetan Sjahrir, letter to Maria Duchâteau, on board the *Albatros*, February 21, 1935.
73 "Recapitulatie: Huizen bewond door geint," Boven Digoel, July 2, 1940, BDA 129.
74 Roth, *Hotel Years*, 13.
75 Kleeblatt, *Mirroring Evil*, 17–19. On the scandal and especially on Elie Wiesel's reaction, see Eiko Grimberg, "A Failed Portrait," in Kugelmann, *No Compromises!*, 165.
76 "Bernhard Kold: Tagebuchfragment aus dem Jahre 1943," YVA 02/387, 10.
77 Sebald, *Austerlitz*, 189.
78 Ruth Bondy, "Games in the Shadow of the Crematoria," in Bondy, *Trapped*, 158.
79 Makarova, *University*, 24.
80 "Testimony of Jehuda Bacon," 9. See also Weiss, *God Saw*, 55n49.
81 Springer, "Das Gesundheitswesen im Theresienstadt Ghetto," 20, 26.
82 Adler, *Theresienstadt*, 1:lvi.
83 Adler, *Theresienstadt*, 2:273.
84 Riis, *How the Other Half Lives*, 10.
85 Riis, *How the Other Half Lives*, 9.

86 Foucault, *Discipline and Punish*, 145.
87 Le Corbusier, *Towards a New Architecture*, 123.
88 Le Corbusier, *Towards a New Architecture*, 260.
89 Interview with Trikoyo, Tangerang, May 17, 2011.
90 "Proces-Verbaal: Opgave van gestolen en teruggevonden goederen van Moeljowidjojo," July 26, 1932, BDA 170.
91 "Aan de Rovimeester," Boven Digoel, November 3, 1941, BDA 11.
92 Riyadi, *Hatta*, 241–42.
93 Sjahrir, letter to Maria Duchâteau, Boven Digoel, July 24, 1935.
94 Testimony by W. A. Ottow-Blok, Heemstede, third part, February 23, 1999, MGI 1316.2.
95 Soetan Sjahrir, letter to Maria Duchâteau, on board the *Albatros*, February 21, 1935.
96 Nasoetion, *Perdjuanganku*, 78.
97 Drewes, *Early Javanese Code*, 23.
98 Scholem, *Kabbalah and Counter-History*, 76.
99 Broch, *Sleepwalkers*, 398–99.
100 JMP 60.
101 Adler, *Theresienstadt*, 1:152.
102 Adler, *Theresienstadt*, 1:108.
103 Manes, *Als ob's ein Leben*, 169.
104 Hyndráková et al., *Prominenti v ghettu*, 61.
105 Manes, *Als ob's ein Leben*, 263.
106 Hyndráková et al., *Prominenti v ghettu*, 62.
107 Lanzmann, *Benjamin Murmelstein*, 67–68.
108 Blodig et al., *Perpetrators of Crimes*, 6.
109 "Paris, the Capital of the Nineteenth Century" (1935), in Benjamin, *Selected Writings*, 3:42.
110 "Ghetto-Zeit / Der Böse Traum," November 2, 1943, in Heukäufer, *So wenig Menschen*, 197.
111 "Women in the Theresienstadt Ghetto," in Bondy, *Trapped*, 44–45.
112 "The Miracle of the Loaves," in Bondy, *Trapped*, 125.
113 Bondy, *Elder of the Jews*, 247.
114 Pressburger, *Diary of Petr Ginz*, 40.
115 Dr. Jacob Jacobson, "Jewish Survivors Report: The Daily Life, 1943–1945," March 1946, YVA 164/105, 15. "Many of the most religious communities, mainly Moravian, had brought with them their Torah, Magillah, Shofar, Kiddush goblets, and candelabra." Rothkirchen, *Jews of Bohemia and Moravia*, 266.
116 Koolhaas, *Delirious New York*, 157.
117 Adler, *Theresienstadt*, 2:428–29.
118 Blodig et al., *Perpetrators of Crimes*, 16.
119 "Police report / Internment camp / 1936–1937," December 11, 1936, BDA 212.
120 "Testimony of Jehuda Bacon," 9.
121 Redlich, *Terezín Diary*, 126.

122　Adler, *Theresienstadt*, 2:325.
123　Redlich, *Terezín Diary*, 67.
124　Adler, *Theresienstadt*, 1:153.
125　Adler, *Theresienstadt*, 2:339.
126　*Šalom na pátek*, April 30, 1943, 62, YVA 064.64.
127　Adler, *Theresienstadt*, 1:lvii.
128　Tydlitát, *Karel Poláček a divadlo*, 288.
129　Roth, *Hotel Years*, 109.
130　Adler, *Theresienstadt*, 1:liv.
131　Adler, *Theresienstadt*, 2:328–29.
132　Brenner-Wonschick, *Die Mädchen von Zimmer 28*, 87. Also, a drawing by Helga Weissová, another girl from the same dormitory, "Betten in Zimmer 28," 209.
133　Kertész, *Fatelessness*, 147.
134　Koolhaas, "Singapore," 1019.
135　"Women in the Theresienstadt Ghetto," in Bondy, *Trapped*, 46.
136　Adler, *Theresienstadt*, 2:367.
137　Manes, *Als ob's ein Leben*, 194.
138　C. Mayer-Kattenburg, "Onze belevenissen tydens de Jodenvervolgingen in de tweede Wereldoorlog," 1945, NIOD 244/920b, 59.
139　"Z" in "Vedem," in Křížková et al., *We Are Children*, 51.
140　Wittgenstein, *Philosophical Investigations*, 36.
141　Levi, *Drowned*, 116–18.
142　Djati and Anderson, *Menjadi Tjamboek*, 54. This happened "*diatas pembaringan beton*," "on the floor of concrete."
143　Nietzsche, *Thus Spoke Zarathustra*, 20.
144　Bloch, *Spirit of Utopia*, 28, 30.
145　Le Corbusier, *Towards a New Architecture*, 2.
146　Benjamin, *Arcades Project*, 212.
147　Pedro Gadanho, "Generative Atmopshere," in Eisenschmidt and Mekinda, *Chicagoisms*, 170.
148　Le Corbusier, *Towards a New Architecture*, 39.
149　Koolhaas, *Delirious New York*, 141.
150　Petr Ginz, "Rambles," in "Vedem," reprinted in Křížková et al., *We Are Children*, 118.
151　*Šalom na pátek*, December 31, 1943, YVA 064.64, 125.
152　Gladkov, *Cement*, 28.
153　Schoonheyt, *Boven-Digoel*, 66.
154　"The Age of Neutralizations and Depolitizations (1929)," in Schmitt, *Concept of the Political*, 93.
155　Koolhaas, "Singapore," 1044, 1059.
156　Italie, *Het Oorlogsdagboek*, October 22, 1944, 499.
157　"Women in the Theresienstadt Ghetto," in Bondy, *Trapped*, 47.
158　Adler, *Theresienstadt*, 2:320.
159　"On Death in the Thought of Ernst Bloch," in Levinas, *Of God*, 42.

160 Koolhaas, *Delirious New York*, 88.
161 Benjamin, *Arcades Project*, 122.
162 "Picabia Versus Dada" (1927), in Picabia, *Beautiful Monster*, 325–26.
163 Heidegger, *Being and Time*, 89.
164 Salim, *Vijftien jaar*, 125, 130.
165 *Citra dan Perjuangan*, 88–89.
166 Salim, *Vijftien jaar*, 125.
167 Quoted in *Het Digoelschandaal*, 11.
168 Sura XXXVIII—Sad, *Koran*, 127.
169 Testimony by Maskun Sumadirdja, Jakarta, August 25, 1976, in *Citra dan Perjuangan*, 86.
170 Schoonheyt, *Boven-Digoel* (1940 edition), 170.
171 Lipovetsky, *Empire of Fashion*, 4.
172 Heidegger, *Being and Time*, 191.
173 Céline, *Normance*, 238.
174 Kentridge, *Six Drawing Lessons*, 14.
175 Adler, *Theresienstadt*, 1:xxxiii.
176 Adler, *Theresienstadt*, 1:176.
177 "Bernhard Kold: Tagebuchfragment aus dem Jahre 1943," 10.
178 Hanuš Kominík, "The Ramparts," in "Vedem," in Křížková et al., *We Are Children*, 143.
179 Redlich, *Terezín Diary*, 117n4.
180 Widayasih, *Masa kanak-kanak*, 1:19.
181 Interview with Widayasih, Jakarta, January 23, 2009.
182 "Politie Dagboek," BDA 211.
183 "Politie Dagboek, BDA 211." In the spring of 2009, in the New York MOMA, I saw an installation by the German artist Martin Kippenberger that filled a whole huge mezzanine of the museum. It was called *Happy End of Franz Kafka's Amerika* (1994), and it was to represent a place where the hero of Kafka's unfinished novel was supposed to end his journey. The place was rectangular and marked by straight white lines, like a perfect soccer field. Lounge chairs and sofas were all over the place in the most bizarre positions, beach umbrellas shading huge orange eggs. It was clearly a space of interrogation at the same time. A few mannequins were installed, either facing each other or looking blank, possibly waiting. One could sit and watch from the wooden benches of low tribunes built on all four sides. It was not a camp, exactly. Kafka called it the greatest theater. See also a review of the installation by Natalie Haddad in *frieze magazine* 120 (January–February 2009): n.p.

Chapter 13. Streets

1 Dostoyevsky, *Demons*, 595.
2 Manes, *Als ob's ein Leben*, 422.
3 Mechanicus, *Waiting for Death*, September 9, 1943, 151–52.

4   Hillesum, *Interrupted Life*, 193.
5   Pressburger, *Diary of Petr Ginz*, 19.
6   Salim, *Vijftien jaar*, 111.
7   Vlasta Schönová and Walter Traub, "Loutkové Divadlo Domova B2 Q609," in Peschel, *Divadelní texty z terezínského ghetta*, 147n15.
8   Max Berger, "Zpráva o pobytu v Terezíně," YVA 07/6–4, 1.
9   Dwork and van Pelt, *Auschwitz*, 295.
10 Lanzmann, *Maurice Rossel*, January–March 2009, 46.
11 Kracauer, *Jacques Offenbach*, 204.
12 Hillesum, *Interrupted Life*, letter of December 18, 1942, 254.
13 "The City's Face," November 16, 1920, in Tucholsky, *Berlin!*, 36.
14 Michel Chevalier (1852), in Benjamin, *Arcades Project*, 598.
15 *Pěšky světovou válkou*, catalogue of exhibition, Prague, 2009, 47.
16 Céline, *Rigadoon*, 115.
17 Adler, *Theresienstadt*, 2:291.
18 "Bericht über die im Reichssicherheitshauptamt Amt IV B 4 Statgefun. der Bespreking," March 6, 1942, NIOD 270c/119, 2–3.
19 Baker, *Days of Sorrow*, 3.
20 Manes, *Als ob's ein Leben*, 317–18.
21 Interview with Jehuda Bacon, Jerusalem, May 15, 2013.
22 "Die Verschickung to Theresienstadt," The Hague, January 25, 1943, NIOD 270c/623.
23 "Bericht über die im Reichssicherheitshauptamt Amt IV B 4 Statgefun. der Bespreking," 2.
24 "Zug aus den Niederlanden nach Theresienstadt," The Hague, April 15, 1943, NIOD 270c/624.
25 Weil, *Life with a Star*, 162.
26 Oldřich Böhm, "Vídeňský vlak," August 20, 1942, JMP 326.
27 Adler, *Theresienstadt*, 2:292.
28 Manes, *Als ob's ein Leben*, 466.
29 "Travel Diaries," in Kafka, *Diaries, 1914–1923*, 251.
30 Levi, *Drowned*, 17.
31 Redlich, *Terezín Diary*, April 30, 1943, 115.
32 Broch, *Sleepwalkers*, 293–94.
33 Augé, *In the Metro*, 58.
34 Furman, *Ways of Growing Up*, 61.
35 Boas, *Boulevard des Misères*, 30.
36 Adler, *Die verheimlichte Wahrheit*, 20.
37 Hatta, *Berjuang dan Dibuang*, 142.
38 Bondan, *Memoar*, 33.
39 Bondan, *Memoar*, 33.
40 Nasoetion, *Perdjuanganku*, 71.
41 Nasoetion, *Perdjuanganku*, 71.
42 Hatta, *Berjuang dan Dibuang*, 142.
43 A. G. Meyer (1907), in Benjamin, *Arcades Project*, 156.
44 A. G. Meyer (1907), in Benjamin, *Arcades Project*, 156, 163, 167.

45 Jules Michelet (1846), in Benjamin, *Arcades Project*, 168.
46 Bloch, *Spirit of Utopia*, 13, 18.
47 Le Corbusier, *Towards a New Architecture*, 191.
48 Le Corbusier, *Towards a New Architecture*, 233.
49 Le Corbusier, *Towards a New Architecture*, 8, 13, 92, 37, 60.
50 "Avignon," in Roth, *Report from a Parisian Paradise*, 98.
51 Marchetti and Quinz, *Dysfashional*, n.p.
52 Redlich, *Terezín Diary*, 87.
53 Adler, *Theresienstadt*, 1:153.
54 Maxim Gorky quoted in chapter on "Boredom" in Koolhaas, *Delirious New York*, 29.
55 "One-Way Street," in Benjamin, *Selected Writings*, 1:487. "Exchange with Theodor W. Adorno on the Essay 'Paris, the Capital of the Nineteenth Century'" (1935), in Benjamin, *Selected Writings*, 3:64n5.
56 Roth, *Hotel Years*, 28, 37.
57 Rutherford, *Raiding the Land*, 182.
58 "Naar Assistent-Resident," June 15, 1929, BDA 204.
59 Kandinsky, *Kandinsky und Ich*, 143.
60 "Naar Assistent-Resident," June 15, 1929, BDA 204.
61 "Internee Soendoro from Semarang" is listed under no. 75, as arriving to the camp on March 23, 1927. "Bevolkingsregister Boven Digoel," 1934, BDA 110. In another list, "Bevolkingsregister," there is a cross made with pencil at Soendoro's name, and a date written in, September 25, 1936. A note says, "*Aan zwartwaterkoorts overleden* [died of malaria]." BDA 120. I did not find Soendoro's grave in the Boven Digoel cemetery.
62 Hillesum, *Twee brieven*, 28.
63 Mechanicus, *Waiting for Death*, November 8, 1943, 184.
64 "Games in the Shadow of the Crematoria," in Bondy, *Trapped*, 161.
65 Heidegger, *Being and Time*, 96–97.
66 Gladkov, *Cement*, 2. For "Review of Gladkov's Cement" (1927), see Benjamin, *Selected Writings*, 2:47: "Gladkov inaugurated a new epoch in Russia. His masterpiece, *Cement* . . . imported the argot of the Bolsheviks into literature."
67 Du Perron, *Country of Origin*, 155.
68 Salim, *Vijftien jaar*, 138.
69 Ramidjo, *Kisah-Kisah*, 82.
70 "An Outsider Makes His Mark" (1930), in Benjamin, *Selected Writings*, 2:309.
71 Shiraishi, "Phantom World of Digoel," 107.
72 Shiraishi, "Phantom World of Digoel," 104.
73 L. H. W. van Sandick, Gouverneur van Ambon, "2e rapport Boven Digoel," November 5, 1927, ARA, Mr. 1107x/27, 33.
74 BDA 125.
75 M. van Blankestein, "Het verbanningsoord," September 11, 1928.
76 "Verslag van de reis van der Resident Ouweling van Amboina naar Boven Digoel," May 14–31, 1929, ARA Vb. 12 Jan. 1939 E1: Mr. 1964x/1930, 38.
77 Widayasih, *Masa kanak-kanak*, 1:19.

78 Mas Marco, *Pergaulan Orang Buangan*, 75.
79 "Politie Dagboek," BDA 212.
80 J. Blok, "Rapport A van den Assiko," Boven Digoel September 1928, 1, ARA Vb. December 10, 1928, V21: Mr. 992x/28.
81 van Eechoud, *Vergeten Aarde*, 228.
82 "Naar Assistent-Resident," June 18, 1929, BDA 204.
83 Interview with Trikoyo, Tangerang, January 27, 2008.
84 "Politie Dagboek," BDA 212.
85 Soetan Sjahrir, letter to Sjahsam, Boven Digoel, March 27, 1935.
86 Soetan Sjahrir, letter to Maria Duchâteau, Boven Digoel, April 21, 1935.
87 Salim, *Vijftien jaar*, 112.
88 "Preface to the New Edition (1969)," in Horkheimer and Adorno, *Dialectic of Enlightenment*, xvi; emphasis mine.
89 "Opgave van in bewaring genomen goederen voor door Hms. 'Java' overgevoorde geint," n.d., BDA 122.
90 "Bernhard Kold: Tagebuchfragment aus dem Jahre 1943," YVA 02/387, 4.
91 Alice Bloemendahl, "Theresienstadt with a Difference," YVA 02/452, 3.
92 Koolhaas, "Singapore," 1019.
93 Shean, *To Be an Actress*, 24.
94 Mechanicus, *Waiting for Death*, November 12, 1943, 187.
95 "Politie Dagboek," BDA 212.
96 Levi, *Drowned*, 113.
97 Du Perron, *Country of Origin*, 76, 79.
98 De Witte, *Kaja-Kaja*, 14.
99 Soetan Sjahrir, letter to Maria Duchâteau, Boven Digoel, April 21, 1935.
100 Salim, *Vijftien jaar*, 134.
101 Interneeringsoord BOVEN-DIGOEL, Voordracht met lichtbeelden door dr. L.J.A. Schoonheyt Amsterdam, November 11, 1937, in *Archief Schoonheyt* 1.
102 Kafka, *Penal Colony*, 214.
103 Ramidjo, *Kisah-Kisah*, 55.
104 "Politie Dagboek," BDA 211.
105 "Politie Dagboek," BDA 212.
106 "Politie Dagboek," BDA 211.
107 Le Corbusier, *Towards a New Architecture*, 60.
108 *Šalom na pátek*, December 31, 1943, YVA 064.6, 147.
109 Perec, *W, or The Memory of Childhood*, 19.
110 Blodig, *Terezín*, 11–12.
111 Weiss, *God Saw*, 25.
112 Max Berger, "Zpráva o pobytu v Terezíně," YVA 07/6-4, 11.
113 Bloemendahl, "Theresienstadt with a Difference," YVA 02-452, 2–3.
114 Chernyshevsky, *What Is to Be Done?*, 182n89.
115 Cabet, *Travels in Icaria*, 36–37.
116 H. M., "Ghetto Cops," in "Vedem," in Křížková et al., *We Are Children*, 120.
117 Bloch, *Spirit of Utopia*, 10–11.
118 Salim, *Vijftien jaar*, 140.

119 Resident den Molukken B. J. Haga "Boven Digoel Verslag," April 5–21, 1936, ARA Vb. 2 Oct. 1937 M27, 4.
120 "Dagrapport," June 1936, BDA 18.
121 "Politie Dagboek," BDA 212.
122 Le Corbusier, *Towards a New Architecture*, 8, 13, 92, 37, 60.
123 "Paris, the Capital of the Nineteenth Century" (1935), in Benjamin, *Selected Writings*, 3:32.
124 Le Corbusier, *Towards a New Architecture*, 3.
125 Le Corbusier, *Towards a New Architecture*, 31.
126 Le Corbusier, *Towards a New Architecture*, 72, 189–90.
127 Le Corbusier, *Towards a New Architecture*, 212, 220.
128 Foucault, *Discipline and Punish*, 144–46.
129 Adler, *Theresienstadt*, 2:268.
130 YVAF 1017751014.
131 Lederer, *Ghetto Theresienstadt*, 17n4.
132 Adler, *Theresienstadt*, 1:98.
133 Adler, *Theresienstadt*, 2:535.
134 "Oldřich Böhm's diary, February 1943," JMP 326 L 502.
135 Céline, *Journey*, 192.
136 Céline, *Journey*, 193–94.
137 "Allgemeine Ordnung der Jüdischen Selbstverwaltung [declared by] des Herrn Lagerkommanant SS-Hauptsturmführer Dr. Seidl," January 5, 1943, YVA 064/399.
138 Kertész, *Fatelessness*, 136–37.
139 Kentridge, *Six Drawing Lessons*, 52.
140 Bondy, *Elder of the Jews*, 307.
141 "The Shape of the Inconstruable Question," in Bloch, *Spirit of Utopia*, 179.
142 Nancy, *Noli me tangere*, 13.
143 Bauman, *Modernity and the Holocaust*, 123.
144 Nancy, *Corpus*, 87.
145 Nancy, *Corpus*, 11. There is a tension in the word: "a tangent continually touching the peripheral complexities of the state." Kierkegaard, *Concept of Irony*, 183.
146 "The Theater of Cruelty (First Manifesto)," in Artaud, *Theater and Its Double*, 94.
147 Boelaars, *Papoea's aan de Mappi*, 144.
148 Manes, *Als ob's ein Leben*, 61.
149 "Foreword," in Levinas, *Of God*, xiv.
150 Augé, *In the Metro*, 7.
151 Augé, *In the Metro*, 53.
152 Augé, *In the Metro*, 6.
153 Napier, *Age of Immunology*, 31.
154 Virilio, *Aesthetics*, 103.
155 Benjamin, *Arcades Project*, 155.

156 Bauman, *Modernity and the Holocaust*, 125.
157 Testimony by W. A. Ottow-Blok, Heemstede, first part, January 3, 1999, MGI 1316.2.
158 "Politie Dagboek," BDA 210.
159 "Memorie van Overgave van Aftredende Gouverneur den Molukken J. T. Tideman," ARA Mr. 699x/30, 184.
160 Schoonheyt, *Boven-Digoel*, 270.
161 Salim, *Vijftien jaar*, 146.
162 Sartre, *Baudelaire*, 38.
163 Heidegger, in Garrido, *On Time*, 51.
164 Heidegger, *Being and Time*, 1.
165 "Sleep, Night," in Blanchot, *Space of Literature*, 268.
166 Caduff, *Pandemic Perhaps*, 23–24.
167 Heidegger, *Being and Time*, 102–6.
168 Bauman, *Modernity and the Holocaust*, 123.
169 Adler, *Theresienstadt*, 1:xxx.
170 Redlich, *Terezín Diary*, 31.
171 Manes, *Als ob's ein Leben*, 230.
172 Lüdtke, "Organizational Order of *Eigensinn*," 314.
173 Hilberg, *Destruction*, 3:1080–81.
174 Hilberg, *Destruction*, 3:5.
175 Bondy, *Elder of the Jews*, 254.
176 Ronell, *Telephone Book*, 9.
177 Dr. Jacob Jacobson, "Jewish Survivors Report: The Daily Life, 1943–1945," March 1946, YVA 164/105, 5.
178 Lanzmann, *Murmelstein*, 148. One more case of execution in the camp is mentioned. One Pavel Masárek was hanged behind the Aussig blocks because he allegedly attempted to attack an SS-man, Bergel. Blodig et al., *Perpetrators of Crimes*, 14.
179 Lanzmann, *Murmelstein*, 163.
180 Bondy, *Elder of the Jews*, 285–86.
181 Bondy, *Elder of the Jews*, 286–87.
182 Manes, *Als ob's ein Leben*, 338.
183 Adler, *Theresienstadt*, 2:256.
184 Kafka, *Castle*, 150. "Klamm" is "ravine" in German. In Czech, however, the language of Kafka's mother, "*klam*," the same pronunciation, means "illusion" or "deception."
185 Weiss, *God Saw*, 25.
186 Adler, *Theresienstadt*, 1:xxx.
187 Ruth Bondy, "The Theresienstadt Ghetto: Its Characteristics and Perspective," in Bondy, *Nazi Concentration Camps*, 305.
188 Bondy, "Theresienstadt Ghetto," 306.
189 Bondy, "Theresienstadt Ghetto," 306. On the Jewish Court, see also Max E. Mannheimer, "From Theresienstadt to Auschwitz," YVA 07/6–4, 6.

Chapter 14. Suburbs

1. Boas, *Boulevard des Misères*, 4.
2. Hillesum, *Interrupted Life*, letter of December 18, 1942, 254.
3. Lanzmann, *Maurice Rossel*, January–March 2009, 4.
4. Bondy, *Elder of the Jews*, 3–4.
5. JMP 326.
6. Adler, *Theresienstadt*, 2:585.
7. "Bahagia," July 26, 1928, and August 4, 1928, IPO 1928.
8. Van der Plas, "Memorandum," March 13, 1943, in Noonan, *Merdeka in Mackay*, 274.
9. Benjamin, *Arcades Project*, 124.
10. Beckett to Donald Page, June 8, 1961, in Beckett, *Letters*, 3:418.
11. "Hitting the Streets: Ecce Fama," in Ronell, *Finitude's Score*, 63–82.
12. Céline, *Journey to the End of the Night*, 308.
13. Kafka, *Diaries, 1910–1913*, October 9, 1911, 88–90.
14. Durlacher, *Quarantaine*, 63.
15. "The Return of the Flâneur" (1929), in Benjamin, *Selected Writings*, 2:264. "On the Boulevards the dandies lived, so to speak, extraterritorially." Kracauer, *Jacques Offenbach*, 96.
16. Benjamin, *Arcades Project*, 516.
17. Huelsenbeck, *Dada Almanac*, 158.
18. Kafka, *Metamorphosis*, 13.
19. Scholem, *From Berlin to Jerusalem*, 13–14.
20. Virilio, *Bunker Archeology*, 18.
21. Benjamin, *Arcades Project*, 129.
22. Augé, *In the Metro*, 70.
23. Tarkovsky, *Sculpting in Time*.
24. Le Corbusier, *Towards a New Architecture*, 8, 231.
25. Nielsen, *In het Land van Kannibalen*, 107–8.
26. Stanley Tigerman, "Preface," in Eisenschmidt and Mekinda, *Chicagoisms*, 6.
27. Koolhaas, *Delirious New York*, 141.
28. Augé, *In the Metro*, 12.
29. Salim, *Vijftien jaar*, 98.
30. van Eechoud, *Vergeten Aarde*, 136.
31. Nielsen, *In het Land van Kannibalen*, 102.
32. Schoonheyt, *Boven-Digoel*, 93.
33. "Rapport van het lid van de Raad van Nederlandsch-Indië, W. P. Hillen, over de interneeringskampen aan de Bovel-Digoel," July 22, 1930, in ARA Vb. 1 Nov. 1930 lr. K24, 24.
34. "Politie Dagboek," BDA 212.
35. Kwee, *Drama di Boven Digul*, 186.
36. Widayasih, *Masa kanak-kanak*, 1:14.
37. "Politie Dagboek," BDA 212.

38 Shiraishi, "Phantom World of Digoel," 106.
39 Interview with Bangun Topo, Jakarta, May 15, 2011.
40 Dwork and van Pelt, *Auschwitz*, 279.
41 Benjamin, *Arcades Project*, 407.
42 Koolhaas, "Singapore," 1051, 1068.
43 Vuyk, *Kampdagboeken*, 13.
44 Agamben, *Remnants of Auschwitz*, 104.
45 Ramidjo, *Kisah-Kisah*, 4.
46 Nielsen, *In het Land van Kannibalen*, 91.
47 Perec, *Species of Spaces*, 91.
48 L. H. W. van Sandick, Gouverneur van Ambon, "1e rapport Boven Digoel," May 24, 1927, ARA, Mr. 739x/27, 19.
49 "Memorie van Overgave van Aftredende Gouverneur den Molukken J. T. Tideman," ARA, Mr. 699x/30, 189.
50 Durlacher, *Quarantaine*, 27.
51 B. J. Haga, "Verslag Boven Digoel medio Augustus 1934," ARA Vb. Mei 7, 1935 W8, 10. The same words, "geconsolideert ... maar toch," can be seen in B. J. Haga's report on the camp two years later. B. J. Haga, "Aantal geinterneerde werkwilligen," December 2, 1936, ARA Vb. 2 Oct. 1937 M27 Mr. 149x/37, 1.
52 *Handelingen Volksraad*, 1935–36, 720.
53 Salim, *Vijftien jaar*, 112.
54 Kafka, *Metamorphosis*, 8.
55 Testimony by W. A. Ottow-Blok, Heemstede, first part, January 3, 1999, MGI 1316.2; emphasis mine.
56 Adler, *Theresienstadt*, 2:283.
57 Riis, *How the Other Half Lives*, 85.
58 Hillesum, *Twee brieven*, 16. Křížková et al., *We Are Children*, 16.
59 Jacques Fein quoted in Bauman, *Modernity and the Holocaust*, 134.
60 Lenka Lindtovaá, "Molymu," JMP 325.
61 Lederer, *Ghetto Theresienstadt*, 85.
62 Adler, *Theresienstadt*, 2:393.
63 "Notulen van de zg Wannsee conferentie te Berlijn. Besprechungspunten Koll," January 20, 1942, NIOD 270c/74, 8.
64 Hilberg, *Destruction*, 2:456. "Heydrich's ... statements ... in Prague in October 1941 reveal ... that from the outset the T ghetto was never meant to be anything more than a way station." Ruth Bondy, "The Theresienstadt Ghetto: Its Characteristics and Perspective," in Bondy, *Nazi Concentration Camps*, 304.
65 Makarova, *University*, 268.
66 Le Corbusier, *Towards a New Architecture*, 240.
67 Le Corbusier, *Towards a New Architecture*, 4, 8, 116.
68 Virilio, *Aesthetics*, 74.
69 Bertolt Brecht's "Ninth Poem," in "Commentary on Poems by Brecht," in Benjamin, *Selected Writings*, 4:235–36.

70 Fest, *Die unbeantwortbaren Fragen*, 40. "The Autobahns were not simply new forms of *tabula-rasa* rationality. . . . According to Fritz Todt, writing in 1934, 'The German road must be an expression of its landscape, and an expression of the German essence.' . . . Autobahns literally may be said to have set the course for the more subjective forms of national conformity." Kwinter, "Mies and Movement," in Mertins, *Presence of Mies*, 87–88. Nazism, according to Yehuda Bauer, was very much "the racial soul expressed in esthetically conceived trains and highways." Bauer, *Rethinking Holocaust*, 85.
71 Kertész, *Fatelessness*, 85.
72 Kertész, *Fatelessness*, 226.
73 Kertész, *Fatelessness*, 123.
74 Baker, *Days of Sorrow*, 7.
75 Augé, *In the Metro*, 18.
76 Heidegger, *Being and Time*, 167–71.
77 Rudolf Vrba, in Dwork and van Pelt, *Auschwitz*, 231. "A ghastly note of incongruity to the bedlam were groups of quiet men in impeccable civilian clothes, picking their way through corpses they did not want to see, measuring timbers with bright yellow folding rules, making neat little notes in black leather books, oblivious to the blood bath." Dwork and van Pelt, *Auschwitz*, 231–32.
78 Bondy, *Elder of the Jews*, 287.
79 "Testimony of Jehuda Bacon," Jerusalem, February 13, 1952, NIOD 270c/118, 9.
80 Redlich, *Terezín Diary*, 55.
81 Adler, *Theresienstadt*, 1:35.
82 Bondy, *Elder of the Jews*, 287.
83 C. Mayer-Kattenburg, "Onze belevenissen tydens de Jodenvervolgingen in de tweede Wereldoorlog," 1945, NIOD 244/920b, 40.
84 Heukäufer, *So wenig Menschen*, 155.
85 Manes, *Als ob's ein Leben*, 339.
86 Manes, *Als ob's ein Leben*, 57.
87 Kafka, *Penal Colony*, 196.
88 Heidegger, *Being and Time*, 223.
89 Heidegger, *Being and Time*, 392.
90 Heidegger, *Being and Time*, 395.
91 Weiss, *God Saw*, 45n37.
92 Heidegger, *Being and Time*, 314, 398.
93 Heidegger, *Being and Time*, 401–2.
94 Adler, *Theresienstadt*, 1:111.
95 Redlich, *Terezín Diary*, 66.
96 Petr Ginz, "Rumbles," in "Vedem," in Křížková et al., *We Are Children*, 118. "The Ordnerwache . . . stands in the gates to the barracks shouting 'Rechts gehen!' (walk on the right) all day and all night." H. M., "Ghetto Cops," in "Vedem," in Křížková et al., *We Are Children*, 120.
97 Redlich, *Terezín Diary*, 56.
98 "Josef Taussig: Dopisy Věře," JMP 326.
99 Weiss, *God Saw*, 29n24.

100 Hillesum, *Interrupted Life*, around June 26, 1943, 280.
101 Mechanicus, *Waiting for Death*, September 9, 1943, 151.
102 Pavel Weiner, *Boy in Terezín*, 21.
103 Max E. Mannheimer, "Theresienstadt and from Theresienstadt to Auschwitz," YVA 07/6–4, 6.
104 Spier, *Dat alles*, 40.
105 Orwell, *Why I Write*, 7.
106 Lederer, *Ghetto Theresienstadt*, 77.
107 Italie, *Het Oorlogsdagboek*, 490–91.
108 Weiss, *God Saw*, 48n41.
109 Weiss, *God Saw*, 42n48.
110 C. Mayer-Kattenburg, "Onze belevenissen tydens de Jodenvervolgingen," 56.
111 Redlich, *Terezín Diary*, 64.
112 *Šalom na pátek*, April 30, 1943, YVA 064.64, 23.
113 Blodig et al., *Kultura proti smrti*, 53.
114 Peschel, *Divadelní texty z terezínského ghetta*, 179n15.
115 Erich Springer, gew. Leiter des Krankenhauses in Theresienstadt, "Das Gesundheitswesen im Theresienstadt Ghetto," YVA M-1/E37 02/525, 18–19.
116 Adler, *Theresienstadt*, 1:205.
117 Adler, *Theresienstadt*, 2:407.
118 Manes, *Als ob's ein Leben*, 63.
119 Redlich, *Terezín Diary*, 79.
120 Peschel, *Divadelní texty z terezínskeho ghetta*, 169.
121 Makarova, *University*, 375.
122 Bondy, *Elder of the Jews*, 274.
123 Pavel Weiner, *Boy in Terezín*, 54.
124 Peschel, *Divadelní texty z terezínského ghetta*, 165.
125 Ronell, *Test Drive*, 103, 106.
126 Hegel, in Heidegger, *Hegel's Concept of Experience*, 10.
127 "The White Cities," in Roth, *Report from a Parisian Paradise*, 73.
128 Virilio, *Aesthetics*, 40.
129 Barthes, *Neutral*, 96.
130 Dostoyevsky, *House of the Dead*, 114–15.
131 Horkheimer and Adorno, *Dialectic of Enlightenment*, 3–4.
132 Vančura, *Rodina Horvátova*, 315.
133 Horkheimer and Adorno, *Dialectic of Enlightenment*, 24.
134 Horkheimer and Adorno, *Dialectic of Enlightenment*, 28, 66.
135 Wittgenstein, *On Certainty*, 9.
136 Wittgenstein, *On Certainty*, 17.
137 Lederer, *Ghetto Theresienstadt*, 73.
138 Redlich, *Terezín Diary*, 115.
139 For the "point card," see illustration in Blaufuks, *Terezín*, n.p.
140 Pavel Weiner, *Boy in Terezín*, 67.
141 Kafka, *Trial*, 511.
142 Manes, *Als ob's ein Leben*, 237–38.

143 Rothkirchen, *Jews of Bohemia and Moravia*, 244.
144 Koolhaas and Foster, *Junkspace*, 35.
145 Adler, *Die verheimlichte Wahrheit*, 65–67.
146 Council of Jewish Communities, *Terezín*, 7.
147 "Specificatie-staat de vivres-prijzen die aan de naturalisten averstrekt woorden over eerste halfjaar 1930," Bestuur Toko, Boven Digoel, June 30, 1930, BDA 92.
148 "Aantooning aankomende hoevelheden natura voeding over de maand Juni 1935," BDA 35.
149 "Politie Dagboek," BDA 210.
150 "One-Way Street," in Benjamin, *Selected Writings*, 1:456.
151 Roth, *Hotel Years*, 156.
152 "Fashion," in Benjamin, *Arcades Project*, 72.
153 Perec, *Species of Spaces*, 157.
154 "Opgave de terugkeerenden en gezinsleden van de geint. per G. M. S. Reiger," Boven Digoel, December 4, 1932, BDA 141.
155 "Bevolkingsregister Boven Digoel," 1939, BDA 102.
156 Widayasih, *Masa kanak-kanak*, 1:11.
157 "Bevolkingsregister Boven Digoel," 1939, BDA 144.
158 Chekhov, *Sakhalin Island*, 66, 78.
159 Caransa, "Theresienstadt. Schizofrenie in steen," NIOD 809/17, 18.
160 Manes, *Als ob's ein Leben*, 253.
161 Hilberg, *Destruction*, 2:611–12.
162 Adler, *Theresienstadt*, 1:xli.
163 Bondy, *Trapped*, 185. Gershom Scholem wrote, "When my grandfather became an enthusiastic Wagnerian in the 1850s, he henceforth called himself Siegfried Scholem, and it was under this name that his printshop was entered into the trade register. On his gravestone, which may still be seen at the Jewish cemetery at Weissensee in East Berlin, the Hebrew inscription still refers to him as Scholem Scholem, but the German inscription on the front reads Siegfried. The gravestone of my father (1925) bore no Hebrew inscription." Scholem, *From Berlin to Jerusalem*, 5.
164 "Roll Call," in Bondy, *Trapped*, 188.
165 "Roll Call," in Bondy, *Trapped*, 181.
166 Pavel Weiner, *Boy in Terezín*, 203.
167 Hájková, *Die fabelhaften Jungs aus Theresienstadt*, 132.
168 Michael Hofmann, "Joseph Roth: Going over the Edge," in *New York Review of Books*, December 22, 2011, 80.
169 "In formula *calculemus* ('let's calculate') Leibniz imagines that one day we could forge some sort of conceptual algebra that would make a sign correspond to each concept. One would then write questions as one pose[s] an equation, and they could be resolved by calculation." "The Spanish Path" (2005), in Atlan, *Selected Writings*, 212.
170 Von Hofmannsthal, *Lord Chandos*, 119.
171 Service, *Stalin*, 147.

172 Wittgenstein, *Philosophical Investigations*, 7.
173 "Register der Mutatie-Rapporten 1932 en 1933," BDA 93.
174 Weiss, *God Saw*, 41.
175 Redlich, *Terezín Diary*, 90.
176 Roth, *Hotel Years*, 28.
177 Sura 17, "The Journey," Koran, 166.
178 Manes, *Als ob's ein Leben*, 423.
179 Balzac, *Treatise on Elegant Living*, 4.
180 Baker, *Days of Sorrow*, 3.
181 Kertész, *Fatelessness*, 124.
182 Adler, *Theresienstadt*, 2:277.
183 Bauman, *Modernity and the Holocaust*, 227.
184 "Testimony of Jehuda Bacon," 9. "Women stood in line with their numbers over their necks like a cattle for slaughter." "Tagebuch von Vally Fink," April 11, 1942, YVA 02/444, 2.
185 Adler, *Theresienstadt*, 2:526.
186 Weil, *Colors*, 53.
187 "Jesus Christ Rastaquouère," in Picabia, *Beautiful Monster*, 227.
188 Kertész, *Fatelessness*, 107.
189 Dostoyevsky, *Idiot*, 628.
190 Hájková, *Die fabelhaften Jungs aus Theresienstadt*, 121.
191 Bondy, *Elder of the Jews*, 437.
192 JMP 326.
193 Pressburger, *Diary of Petr Ginz*, 98.
194 *Šalom na pátek*, December 31, 1943, YVA 064.64, 147.
195 Nora Frýd's recollections, in Makarova, *University*, 285.
196 Adler, *Theresienstadt*, 2:609. "Germans appointed approximately twenty rabbis to sort out the books, put them in catalogs, and index them with the intention of saving future museums this work." Makarova, *University*, 123.
197 Manes, *Als ob's ein Leben*, 398.
198 "Kaoem Moeda," August 13 and 30, 1928, and September 8, 1928, *IPO* 1928.
199 Abdoel 'lXarim M.s. "Pandu Anak Buangan," 100.
200 Nasoetion, *Perdjuanganku*, 72–73.
201 Perec, *Species of Spaces*, 192.
202 Adler, *Theresienstadt*, 1:122.
203 Blodig, *Terezín*, 12.
204 Springer, "Das Gesundheitswesen im Theresienstadt Ghetto," 19. "From 1943, the streets in the ghetto, which previously were marked by letters and numbers, were given poetic sounding names." "Privileged until Further Notice," in Bondy, *Trapped*, 93.
205 Peschel, *Divadelní texty z terezínského ghetta*, 299.
206 YVA 16/51.
207 Pavel Weiner, *Boy in Terezín*, 30.
208 Testimony of Jiří Franěk, in Makarova, *University*, 176.
209 M. van Blankenstein, "Het verbanningsoord," September 11, 1928.

210 "Recapitulatie: Huizen bewond door geinterneerden," Boven Digoel, July 2, 1940, BDA 129.
211 See also Collectie Wertheim IISH, 165.
212 Koolhaas, *Delirious New York*, 13, 15.
213 Koolhaas, *Delirious New York*, 82.
214 Koolhaas, *Delirious New York*, 123.
215 "Exchange with Theodor W. Adorno on the Essay 'Paris, the Capital of the Nineteenth Century'" (1935), in Benjamin, *Selected Writings*, 3:63.
216 Manes, *Als ob's ein Leben*, 53.
217 Thea Höchster, "Konto-Buch," YVA 033. 7136.
218 "The Fissure of Anaxagoras and the Local Fires of Heraclitus," in Deleuze, *Desert Islands*, 156–57.
219 Adler, *Theresienstadt*, 2:268.
220 Bernhard Kold, "Tagebuchfragment aus dem Jahre 1943," June 18, 1943, YVA 02/387, 3.
221 "The railroad track has been completed. The Jews have built (it). The camp commander has ordered an especially nice steam engine and, with several Nazi officers, opened traffic on the railroad. At night, the officers celebrated so much they didn't know where they were." 29v-6vi43, in Redlich, *Terezín Diary*, 119–20.
222 Hanuš Hachenburg, "Vedem," in Křížková et al., *We Are Children*, 89.
223 Blanchot, *Step Not Beyond*, 55.
224 Augé, *In the Metro*, 9.
225 Augé, *In the Metro*, 20.
226 "Exchange with Theodor W. Adorno on 'The Paris of the Second Empire in Baudelaire'" (1938), in Benjamin, *Selected Writings*, 4:163.
227 Benjamin, *Selected Writings*, 4:195n32.
228 Faulkner, *Fable*, 22.
229 Kafka, *Amerika*, 279. "'Oh,' said Fanny, 'we always make great preparations in case there should be a great crowd'" (280).
230 Kafka, *Amerika*, 280.
231 Kafka, *Letters to Felice*, 35.
232 Kafka, *Amerika*, 281.

Chapter 15. Nausea

1 Hanuš Schimmerling, "Židovská mládež v hnutí odporu," in Kárný and Blodig, *Terezín v konečném řeššení*, 120.
2 Schimmerling, "Židovská mládež v hnutí odporu," 120.
3 Adler, *Theresienstadt*, 1:187.
4 Lanzmann, *Benjamin Murmelstein*, 275.
5 Lanzmann, *Maurice Rossel*, 40.
6 Lanzmann, *Maurice Rossel*, 48.

7 Baker, *Days of Sorrow*, 318.
8 JMP 320c-6:20.
9 Bernhard Greiner, "German and Jewish 'Theatromania': Theoder Lessing's *Theater-Seele* between Goethe and Kafka," in Malkin and Rokem, *Jews*, 112.
10 Baker, *Days of Sorrow*, 193.
11 "Fragments of the text of Esther," an original carbon copy of the play as performed in Theresienstadt, can be found in JMP 318c.
12 Redlich, *Terezín Diary*, 120. "A resistance organization had finally been set up in Auschwitz [among the people who arrived from Theresienstadt].... The occasion was the imminent gassing of a large number of Czech Jews from T., who had been kept for six months in the so-called family camp inside Birkenau. The Jewish Sonderkommando wanted the Jews in the family camp to set fire to their barracks, while a revolt would take place in the crematoria, but the families could not be convinced that their lives were about to be extinguished until they were in the changing room, confronted by armed ss men and dogs." Hilberg, *Destruction*, 3:1047. "The proposal was apparently made to [Freddy Hirsch] by roof repairman David Schmuelevsky, a member of the communist underground in Auschwitz." Bondy, *Elder of the Jews*, 421. "The communist underground which planned the revolt with the councelors of the dormitory, estimated that out of twelve thousand camp inmates, perhaps thirty of forty would get away" (443–44).
13 Widayasih, *Masa kanak-kanak*, 1:5.
14 The letter is in BDA 257.
15 Mas Marco, *Pergaulan Orang Buangan*, 7–8. "39. Soekarman secton C... Brutal toward the officials... 131. Kartodanoedjo section C.... Altercation with an agent of ROB, sentenced to 3 months in prison." "Bevolking-Register der Geinterneerden," Boven Digoel, n.d., BDA 103.
16 "Register van de strafzaken, behandelt en afgedaan door den Magistraat" in "Resident den Molukken B. J. Haga "Boven Digoel Verslag," April 5–21, 1936, ARA Vb. 2 Oct. 1937 M27.
17 "Bevolking-Register der Geinterneerden," Boven Digoel, n.d., BDA 226.
18 "Politie Dagboek," BDA 252.
19 "Politie Dagboek," BDA 211.
20 "Politie Dagboek," BDA 210.
21 "Politie Dagboek," BDA 243.
22 "Politie Dagboek," BDA 212.
23 "Politie Dagboek," BDA 212.
24 "Politie Dagboek," BDA 212.
25 "Tideman naar Gouverneur General," September 17, 1929, ARA Vb. 12 Jan. 1939 Mr. 1964x/1930. See also Assistant Resident J. Blok naar Resident van Amboina, "Relletjes te Boven Digoel," September 22, 1929, ARA Vb. 12 Jan. 1939 Mr. 1964x/1930.
26 Schoonheyt, *Boven-Digoel*, 207.
27 "Proces-Verbaal," Boven Digoel, September 26, 1933, BDA 171.

28 Schoonheyt, *Boven-Digoel*, 178. There is a photo of the grave and of the dead Aliarcham; so, perhaps, the doctor bought the photographs in the end.
29 Rolland, "Annotations," in Levinas, *On Escape*, 81.
30 Virilio, *Speed and Politics*, 18.
31 Schmitt, *Concept of the Political*, 71, 72.
32 Hatta, *Pengantar ke Djalan Ilmu*, 1.
33 Žižek, *Violence*, 10.
34 Broch, *Sleepwalkers*, 635.
35 Barthes, *Neutral*, 91–92.
36 Barthes, *Neutral*, 92.
37 Le Corbusier, *Towards a New Architecture*, 269.
38 Le Corbusier, *Towards a New Architecture*, 288.
39 Jacques Fabien (1863), in Benjamin, *Arcades Project*, 136.
40 Husserl, *Crisis of European Sciences*, 26.
41 Napier, *Age of Immunology*, 34.
42 Virilio, *Speed and Politics*, 142.
43 Céline, *Mea Culpa*, 3.
44 Riis, *How the Other Half Lives*, 60.
45 Bloch, *Traces*, 14.
46 "Jesus Christ Rastaquouère," in Picabia, *Beautiful Monster*, 227.
47 Nielsen, *In het Land van Kannibalen*, 92.
48 *Citra dan Perjuangan*, 99.
49 "Verslag 3e kwartaal 1933," ARA Vb. 7 mei 1935 W8, 2.
50 "Politie Dagboek," BDA 211.
51 "Politie Dagboek," BDA 212.
52 Toer, *Tanah Merah*, 155.
53 Widayasih, *Masa kanak-kanak*, 1:20–21.
54 "Rapport van het lid van de Raad van Nederlandsch-Indië, W. P. Hillen, over de interneeringskampen aan de Bovel-Digoel," July 22, 1930, ARA Vb. 1 Nov. 1930 lr. K24.
55 *Handelingen Volksraad*, November 8, 1929, 1649.
56 Resident den Molukken B. J. Haga, "Boven Digoel Verslag," April 521, 1936, ARA Vb. 2 Oct. 1937 M27, 2–3.
57 Mas Marco, *Pergaulan Orang Buangan*, 171.
58 Salim, *Vijftien jaar*, 274.
59 Salim, *Vijftien jaar*, 169.
60 Dostoyevsky, *House of the Dead*, 305.
61 Dostoyevsky, *House of the Dead*, 128.
62 Žižek, *Violence*, 183. "Socrates came to himself by standing still." Kierkegaard, *Concept of Irony*, 442. In Hegel's view, "Socrates was deservedly condemned to death" (193).
63 Kafka, *Castle*, 31.
64 "Paris, the Capital of the Nineteenth Century" (1935), in Benjamin, *Selected Writings*, 3:40.
65 Heidegger, *Being and Time*, 253.

66 "The Essential Solitude and Solitude in the World," in Blanchot, *Space of Literature*, 251. "Sleep, Night," in Blanchot, *Space of Literature*, 266.
67 "The Room," in Sartre, *Wall*, 25.
68 Nancy, *Philosophical Chronicles*, 4.
69 Bloch, *Traces*, 41.
70 Salim, *Vijftien jaar*, 364–65.
71 Bijkerk, "Selamat Berpisah," in Suwardi, *Koloni pengucilan*, 70.
72 "Bevolking-Register der Geinterneerden," Boven Digoel, February 28, 1932, BDA 264.
73 "Politie Dagboek," BDA 211.
74 Salim, *Vijftien jaar*, 222.
75 Salim, *Vijftien jaar*, 151.
76 "Bevolking-Register der Geinterneerden," Boven Digoel, February 28, 1932, BDA 264.
77 "Verslag van de reis van den Resident van Amboina naar Boven Digoel," May 14–31, 1929, ARA, Vb. 12 Jan. 1939 E1: Mr. 1964x/1930, 61.
78 "Politie Dagboek," BDA 212.
79 "Politie Dagboek," BDA 212.
80 Toer, *Tanah Merah*, 70.
81 Toer, *Tanah Merah*, 69.
82 "Resident van Amboina naar Controleur van Boven Digoel," July 5, 1928, ARA Vb. 10 Dec. 1928 V21: Mr. 992x/28.
83 HPB van Langen, "Het interneeringkamp Boven Digoel 3e kwartaal 1934," October 1, 1934, ARA Vb. 7 Mei 1935 W8, 2.
84 "Soeloeh Ra'jat Indonesia," July 10, 1929, *IPO* 1929.
85 Toer, *Tanah Merah*, 224.
86 "Rapport van het lid van de Raad van Nederlandsch-Indië, W. P. Hillen, over de interneeringskampen aan de Bovel-Digoel," July 22, 1930, ARA Vb. 1 Nov. 1930 lr. K24, 14.
87 HPB van Langen, "Interneeringskamp Boven Digoel, 4de kwartaal 1934," December 8, 1934, ARA Vb. 7 Mei 1935 W8, 2, 4.
88 Flaubert, *Sentimental Education*, 309.
89 "Politie Dagboek," BDA 252.
90 BDA 204. The letter is written in pencil, with some nonchalance and certainly not much respect. Mas Marco is among eight signatories.
91 Schoonheyt, *Boven-Digoel*, 212–13.
92 Schoonheyt, *Boven-Digoel*, 214.
93 Bloch, *Traces*, 41.
94 "Woningen in het interneeringskamp," ARA Vb. 1 Nov. 1930 Ir K24, 3.
95 Letter from van der Plas to H. J. van Mook, April 18, 1943. ARA Collection no. 176 H. J. van Mook, translation by Harry A. Poeze, in Poeze, "From Foe to Partner," 62.
96 Sebald, *Austerlitz*, 283.
97 Weiss, *God Saw*, 41n30.
98 Poláček, *Poslední dopisy Doře*, 22.

99 Poláček, *Poslední dopisy Doře*.
100 Poláček, *Poslední dopisy Doře*.
101 Poláček, *Poslední dopisy Doře*.
102 Goodman, *Chagall*, 99.
103 Kafka, *Diaries, 1914–1923*, January 18, 1922, 203.
104 Utitz, *Psychologie života*, 59.
105 Adler, *Theresienstadt*, 1:li.
106 Fallada, *Alone in Berlin*, 113.
107 Cabet, *Travels in Icaria*, 79, 89.
108 More, *Utopia*, 92.
109 Adler, *Theresienstadt*, 2:529.
110 Bondy, *Elder of the Jews*, 337, 273.
111 Bondy, *Elder of the Jews*, 335.
112 In May 1944, for instance, 15 percent of the inmates declared themselves not Jewish by religion. Shortly before the liberation this percentage had risen to 36 percent. Bondy, *Elder of the Jews*, 15.
113 Bondy, *Elder of the Jews*, 15.
114 Makarova, *University*, 111.
115 Adler, *Theresienstadt*, 2:611.
116 Pavel Weiner, *Boy in Terezín*, 210.
117 Adler, *Theresienstadt*, 2:308.
118 Adler, *Theresienstadt*, 2:609.
119 Pavel Weiner, *Boy in Terezín*, 37.
120 Redlich, *Terezín Diary*, 156, 154–55.
121 Kaufmann, "Introduction," 18.
122 Emmanuel Levinas, letter to Jacques Rolland, December 1981, in Levinas, *On Escape*, 1–2.
123 Levinas, *On Escape*, 19. "Nausea," a novel by Jean-Paul Sartre, was published in 1938, three years after Levinas's essay.
124 Levinas, *On Escape*, 22, 24, 26.
125 Levinas, *On Escape*, 66.
126 Levinas, *On Escape*, 67.
127 Levinas, *On Escape*, 69.
128 Nancy, *Pleasure in Drawing*, 57.
129 Levinas, *On Escape*, 23.
130 Schoonheyt, *Boven-Digoel*, 26.

Chapter 16. Escape

1 Redlich, *Terezín Diary*, 3.
2 Karl Marx, in Benjamin, *Arcades Project*, 223.
3 Kafka, *Diaries, 1910–1913*, August 21, 1912, 26.
4 Céline, *Rigadoon*, 21.
5 Broch, *Sleepwalkers*, 482.

6   Rousseau, *Confessions*, 226–27.
7   Napier, *Age of Immunology*, 11.
8   Garrido, *On Time*, 69. Virilio, *Aesthetics*, 47.
9   Riis, *How the Other Half Lives*, 40.
10 Salim, *Vijftien jaar*, 112.
11 *Citra dan Perjuangan*, 97.
12 "Of Fog, Alexander's Campaign, and the Magnitude of the Yes," in Bloch, *Spirit of Utopia*, 167–68.
13 Barthes, *Neutral*, 43.
14 Poláček, *Posledni dopisy Doře*, 41.
15 Louis-Ferdinand Céline, in Kristeva, *Powers of Horror*, 171.
16 Bloch, *Traces*, 51. "From the Carefree Deficiency to the New Meaning," in Levinas, *Of God*, 51. "Transcendence and Evil," in Levinas, *Of God*, 125.
17 "Questions and Answers," in Levinas, *Of God*, 91.
18 "Ideology and Idealism," in Levinas, *Of God*, 11.
19 "On Death in the Thought of Ernst Bloch," in Levinas, *Of God*, 40; and Bloch, *Traces*, 11.
20 "On Death in the Thought of Ernst Bloch," in Levinas, *Of God*, 41.
21 Nemo, *Job and the Excess of Evil*, 106.
22 Heinrich Heine, in Presner, *Mobile Modernity*, 143.
23 Dostoyevsky, *House of the Dead*, 23.
24 A.K. Martynov, Dostoyevsky's fellow convict, quoted in Dostoyevsky, *House of the Dead*, xii.
25 Janouch, *Coversations with Kafka*, 16–17. For a more trustworthy account of something similar, see Kafka's own letter about trying to get out of Prague as "just a flapping of my completely unsuitable wings." Kafka, *Letters to Milena*, 234.
26 Broch, *Guiltless*, 261.
27 Broch, *Sleepwalkers*, 494.
28 Dostoyevsky, *House of the Dead*, 68.
29 Adler, *Die verheimlichte Wahrheit*, 252.
30 "Bevolking-Register der Geinterneerden," Boven Digoel, n.d., BDA 101.
31 Shiraishi, "Phantom World of Digoel," 106.
32 Schoonheyt, *Boven-Digoel*, 96.
33 "Memorie van Overgave van Aftredende Gouverneur den Molukken J. T. Tideman," ARA Mr. 699x/30, 107.
34 "Memorie van Overgave," 107. See "Justitia: Register," 1937, Boven Digoel, BDA 168.
35 "Justitia: Register," 1937.
36 Harney and Moten, *Undercommons*, 17.
37 Mawengkang, *Boven Digoel*, 84.
38 Mawengkang, *Boven Digoel*, 88.
39 Shiraishi, "Phantom World of Digoel," 103.
40 "Politie Dagboek," BDA 212.
41 Abdoel 'lXarim M.s. "*Pandu Anak Buangan*," 117–18.
42 Mas Marco, *Pergaulan Orang Buangan*, 120.

43 Salim, *Vijftien jaa*, 305.
44 "Rapport van het lid van de Raad van Nederlandsch-Indië, W. P. Hillen, over de interneeringskampen aan de Bovel-Digoel," July 22, 1930, ARA Vb. 1 Nov. 1930 lr. K24, 14.
45 Salim, *Vijftien jaar*, 303. Petrik Matanasi reports finding a grave at the Boven Digoel cemetery with the name Thomas Najoan. Matanasi, *Thomas Najoan*, 71.
46 "Pewarta Deli," March 13, 1930, IPO 1930.
47 "Kamponghoofd Kampongbestuur," Boven Digoel, March 1, 1932, BDA 264.
48 Abdoel 'lXarim M.s. "*Pandu Anak Buangan*," 116–17.
49 Balzac, *Treatise on Elegant Living*, 40.
50 "Nietzsche's Burst of Laughter," in Deleuze, *Desert Islands*, 130.
51 Barthes, *Neutral*, 150.
52 Barthes, *Neutral*, 90–91.
53 Krauss and Hollier, "Preface," in Barthes, *Neutral*, xv.
54 Céline, *Rigadoon*, 173.
55 Heidegger, *Being and Time*, 171.
56 Heidegger, *Being and Time*, 221, 234, 255.
57 Dostoyevsky, *House of the Dead*, 96.
58 Žižek, *Tarrying with the Negative*, 167–68. Georges Bataille's "Preface" to Jules Michelet's *La sorcière* (1946), in Barthes, *Michelet*, 220.
59 Redlich, *Terezín Diary*, 4. Also: "Escape . . . or attempts at . . . is punished by death." Adler, *Theresienstadt*, 2:317.
60 "Privileged until Further Notice," in Bondy, *Trapped*, 111.
61 Adler, *Die verheimlichte Wahrheit*, 122. According to Hilberg, "fled: 764; arrested by Gestapo and probably killed: 276"; Hilberg, *Destruction*, 2:455.
62 For instance "Vedem," in Křížková et al., *We Are Children*, 45.
63 Adler, *Theresienstadt*, 2:317.
64 Evžen Hilar, "Escape from the Ghetto," in Council of Jewish Communities, *Terezín*, 283–88.
65 Otto Kuhn, "An Escape from Terezín Ghetto," in *Council of Jewish Communities, Terezín*, 290–91.
66 Bondy, "*Elder of the Jews*," 261–62.
67 Adler, *Theresienstadt*, 1:145.
68 Pavel Weiner, *Boy in Terezín*, 22.
69 Pavel Weiner, *Boy in Terezín*, 96.
70 Lederer, *Ghetto Theresienstadt*, 159. Céline, *Rigadoon*, 173.
71 Lederer, *Ghetto Theresienstadt*, 159.
72 Dostoyevsky, *Crime and Punishment*, 55.
73 Makarova, *University*, 385.
74 See Barthes, *Michelet*, 92.
75 For a report of one Schoonheyt's such lecture, on New Guinea, "by a participant," see "NEFIS Brisbane geheim August 12, 1944," *Collectie van der Plas*, ARA 72.
76 "Louis Johan Alexander Schoonheyt, twice a victim of his times," in *Spotlight* (KITLV bulletin), 424. For "landverraders . . . potentieel gevaarlijken"

("traitors... potentially dangerous"), see van Kampen, *Een kwestie van macht*, 207–8.
77 Van Kampen, *Een kwestie van macht*, 208.
78 For "the so-called onverzoenlijke" referring to Dr. Schoonheyt and the group, see *Nieuwe Dag*, June 7, 1946, in *Archief Schoonheyt*, 5.
79 *Advocate Blad*, November 15, 1949, in *Archief Schoonheyt*, 5.
80 On article 37, Indische Staatsregeling to be used against the suspected Communists in 1926, see *Handelingen van den Volksraad*, December 4, 1926, 712.
81 Dr. Schoonheyt talking to van Kampen, in van Kampen, *Een kwestie van macht*, 172–73.
82 The postcard sent by Dr. Schoonheyt from the Tjipinang prison to his wife informing her about his situation, November 27, 1942, is in *Archief Schoonheyt*, 3.
83 Van Kampen, *Een kwestie van macht*, 180.
84 Van Kampen, *Een kwestie van macht*, 214.
85 Van Kampen, *Een kwestie van macht*, 168.
86 *Kritiek en Opbouw*, September 13, 1941.
87 Van Kampen, *Een kwestie van macht*, 206.
88 Van Kampen, *Een kwestie van macht*, 197–98.
89 Van Kampen, *Een kwestie van macht*, 193.
90 Van Kampen, *Een kwestie van macht*, 295.
91 Van Kampen, *Een kwestie van macht*, 314.
92 Van Kampen, *Een kwestie van macht*, 298.
93 Van Kampen, *Een kwestie van macht*, 298–99.
94 Van Kampen, *Een kwestie van macht*, 321.
95 On Becking's NSB. activity, including some letters, see "NSB Kring Soerabaja," Soerabaja, December 18, 1938, NIOD 123/2154, 18. Becking is here mentioned as De Gewestelijk Commissaris voor Java. See also Becking's exchange of letters with the Dutch pro-Nazi leader Mussert, NIOD 123/2202 and 123/393.
96 Van Kampen, *Een kwestie van macht*, 336.
97 E. van Blankenstein, *Dr. M. van Blankenstein*, 208–9, 231–32.
98 E. van Blankenstein, *Dr. M. van Blankenstein*, 245–56.
99 E. van Blankenstein, *Dr. M. van Blankenstein*, 257.
100 E. van Blankenstein, *Dr. M. van Blankenstein*, 276.
101 E. van Blankenstein, *Dr. M. van Blankenstein*, 288. The last thing, which is kind of relevant, to van Blankenstein is a report from 1947 about him writing a letter on the behalf of his friend, David Cohen, the former head of the Jewish Council in Amsterdam and then a "prominent" internee in Theresienstadt. David Cohen, wrote M. van Blankenstein, was a good man, and it could not be imagined that he would collaborate with the Nazis. E. van Blankenstein, *Dr. M. van Blankenstein*, 304.
102 Loebis, *Orang Indonesia*, 45.
103 Loebis, *Orang Indonesia*, 46.
104 Loebis, *Orang Indonesia*, 50.
105 Loebis, *Orang Indonesia*, 57.
106 Loebis, *Orang Indonesia*, 78.

107 The letter by "Perhimoenan Indonesia" is in ARA Vb. 12 Jan. 1939: Mr. 1964x/1930.
108 Loebis, *Orang Indonesia*, 116.
109 Loebis, *Orang Indonesia*, 133.
110 Loebis, *Orang Indonesia*, 139.
111 On Charles Welter and Boven Digoel, see Shiraishi, "Phantom World of Digoel," 102.
112 Loebis, *Orang Indonesia*, 137.
113 Loebis, *Orang Indonesia*, 194, 152.
114 Loebis, *Orang Indonesia*, 153.
115 Loebis, *Orang Indonesia*, 142. There were brothels in the camp. Loebis says, "Once I was there.... Only Aryans [*bangsa Arya*] were allowed in, which is Dutch, Dannish, Norwegians, Swedes, Belgians, and Luxemburgers." Loebis, *Orang Indonesia*, 201–2.
116 Loebis, *Orang Indonesia*, 153–54.
117 Loebis, *Orang Indonesia*, 185.
118 Loebis, *Orang Indonesia*, 189–90.
119 Loebis, *Orang Indonesia*, 208.
120 Loebis, *Orang Indonesia*, 164–65.
121 Loebis, *Orang Indonesia*, 212.
122 Loebis, *Orang Indonesia*, 165–66.
123 Loebis, *Orang Indonesia*, 99.
124 "Buchenwalder Geiseln," The Hague, August 8, 1942, NIOD 77/1322.
125 Rijshouwer and Wermeskerken, *Vier Jaar Indisch Gijzelaar*, 212.
126 For ter Haar's obituary, see "S" "Prof. Mr. B. ter Haar," in *De Fakkel* (Bandoeng), June 8, 1941.
127 Rijshouwer and Wermeskerken, *Vier Jaar Indisch Gijzelaar*, 261.
128 "Overzicht van de periode De Ruwenberg, 29 October, 1942 t/m 29 October 1943," in Rijshouwer and Wermeskerken, *Vier Jaar Indisch Gijzelaar*, 273.
129 "Van huis van bewaring te Utrecht naar Buchenwald, 23 Maart," in Rijshouwer and Wermeskerken, *Vier Jaar Indisch Gijzelaar*, 83.
130 "Rapport van het kamp Amersfort," in Rijshouwer and Wermeskerken, *Vier Jaar Indisch Gijzelaar*, 333.
131 "Overzicht van de periode De Ruwenberg, 29 October 1942," in Rijshouwer and Wermeskerken, *Vier Jaar Indisch Gijzelaar*, 282, 313.
132 "Van huis van bewaring te Utrecht naar Buchenwald," in Rijshouwer and Wermeskerken, *Vier Jaar Indisch Gijzelaar*, 52.
133 Rijshouwer and Wermeskerken, *Vier Jaar Indisch Gijzelaar*, 80.
134 Testimony by Catharine van den Berg, December 2, 1998, YVA 03/11.
135 Testimony by Ziegfried de Lima, Nov 18, 1987, YVA 033C/614.
136 Testimony by Yvonne Bouwer né Beynon, "Verhältnissen während der Kriegszeit in Indonesia," YVA 02/811.
137 Hillesum, *Interrupted Life*, 363. Etty Hillesum perished in Auschwitz on November 30, 1943.
138 Wertheim, *Vier Wendingen*, 162.

139 Wertheim, "Harry J. Benda (1919–1971)," *Bijdragen tot de taal-, land en volkenkunde* 128 (March 5, 1972), 214.
140 Kafka, *Letters to Milena*, 190–91.
141 Demetz, *Prague in Danger*, 20.
142 Demetz, *Prague in Danger*, 77.
143 Anderson, *Considerations on Western Marxism*, 23.
144 Milena Jesenská, in Demetz, *Prague in Danger*, 132. After the concession of the European democracies to Hitler in Munich in the fall of 1938, the still-unoccupied parts of Europe were overwhelmed, and so was Jesenská:"'It is not our fault. . . . As long as our home stood firm, we were hospitable and kinderhearted. Now all we can do is to wish them a new and good life somewhere far away." Milena Jesenská, in Rothkirchen, *Jews of Bohemia and Moravia*, 78.
145 *Moderne auf der Flucht*, 58.
146 Roth, *Life in Letters*, 364.
147 *Moderne auf der Flucht*, 27, 61, 61. Werfel's and Mahler's house sat directly in the immediate vicinity of the beach and had a small tower where there was a study with windows all around, some of it facing the sea. "There were blackouts. One night Werfel was looking for some manuscript with a flashlight. Immediately the French police arrived suspecting that the German was signaling to the enemy." *Moderne auf der Flucht*, 64.
148 *Moderne auf der Flucht*, 60.
149 Tucholsky, *Berlin!*, 14, 19.
150 Roth, *Life in Letters*, 229.
151 Roth, *Hotel Years*, 145.
152 "After my return to Berlin I would like to try (Leo) Baeck myself if things [his trip to Palestine] cannot be set in motion any other way." Benjamin to Scholem (1928), in Scholem, *Walter Benjamin*, 194. In 1934, already on the run, Benjamin made a note about a dream he just had: "There is an unrest in Berlin. The Nazis are threatening to storm the café where we have met; in feverish consultations, we survey all the other cafés, but none appear to offer protection. So we make an expedition into the desert. There it is night; tents are erected; lions are close by. "The Knower" (1934), in Benjamin, *Storyteller*, 40.
153 Benjamin's friends spoke of finding an apartment for him in proximity to Central Park in New York. See Benjamin, *Selected Writings*, 4:191n1.
154 Koestler, *Invisible Writing*, 513.
155 "Americans Poems, 1941–1947," in Brecht, *Poems*, 363.
156 *Moderne auf der Flucht*, 58–59.
157 "Ein Reisefilm unter Führung von Erika Mann," *Moderne auf der Flucht*, 51.
158 *Moderne auf der Flucht*, 52. For the Nazi press, Erika Mann by that time became a "flat-footed peace hyena" and "Zuhälterin der jüdischen Sklavenhalter." *Moderne auf der Flucht*, 55.
159 *Moderne auf der Flucht*, 171–72.
160 Lilly Joss Reich, "Einheimische und Emigranten," "Locals and emigrants," in *Moderne auf der Flucht*, 186.
161 "One-Way Street," in Benjamin, *Selected Writings*, 1:484.

162 "Jüdisches Nachrichtenblatt," January 5, 1940, in "The History of the Closing Gates," in Bondy, *Trapped*, 33.
163 "Jüdisches Nachrichtenblatt," November and December 1939, and August 1940, in "History of the Closing Gates," 21. "Jüdisches Nachrichtenblatt," April 21, 1940, in "History of the Closing Gates," 33.
164 "Jüdisches Nachrichtenblatt," November 1, 1940, in "History of the Closing Gates," 34.
165 Rothkirchen, *Jews of Bohemia and Moravia*, 117.
166 "Preface to the new edition" (1937), in Roth, *Wandering Jews*, 125.
167 "Preface to the new edition," 126.
168 "Jüdisches Nachrichtenblatt," December 13, 1940, in "History of the Closing Gates," 35.
169 Lanzmann, *Murmelstein*, 39–40.
170 Hoffer, *Utitz Legacy*, 161.
171 Hoffer, *Utitz Legacy*, 161.
172 Makarova, *Boarding Pass*, 34.
173 Makarova, *Boarding Pass*, 46.
174 Makarova, *Boarding Pass*, 46.
175 Bondy, "*Elder of the Jews*," 196.
176 "History of the Closing Gates," 37.
177 Segev, *One Palestine*, 439n.
178 Boas, *Boulevard des Misères*, 27.
179 "This was the only agreement of this type the German ever observed." Lederer, *Ghetto Theresienstadt*, 147.
180 Hyndráková et al., *Prominenti v ghettu*, 52.
181 Hans de Vries, "Židé z Holandska do Terezína," in Kárný and Blodig, *Terezín v konečném řešeni*, 57–58.
182 Hyndráková et al., *Prominenti v ghettu*, 168, 253. There was an exchange of letters between Wertheim, who was a professor of the law school in Batavia at the time, and Emanuel Moresco at his office in The Hague on a possible way for the Indies Jewish refugees, "around 1,000 of Jewish families," to escape and settle in Borneo and better, to New Guinea, Portuguese Timor, Suriname, or Rhhodesia. See "Collection Wertheim," 40, in *11ss*. On indirect (tangential) connection of Mr. Moresco and Boven Digoel see also Shiraishi, "Phantom World of Digoel," 94.
183 Makarova, *University*, 511.
184 Italie, *Het oorlogsdagboek*, April 7, 1943, 361, 361n43.

Chapter 17. Dust, or Memory

"Joy," in Singer, *Gimpel the Fool*, 125–26.

1 Félix Guattari, in "On Capitalism and Desire," in Deleuze, *Desert Islands*, 270.
2 Riis, *How the Other Half Lives*, 147, 149, 151.

3   Prokofiev, *Soviet Diary*, 137.
4   Wittgenstein, *On Certainty*, 40.
5   Wittgenstein, *On Certainty*, 58.
6   Chekhov, *Sakhalin Island*, 226.
7   Chekhov, *Sakhalin Island*, 273.
8   Chekhov, *Sakhalin Island*, 308.
9   Kwon, *Ghosts of War*, 10, 7, 86.
10 Kwon, *Ghosts of War*, 72.
11 Kwon, *Ghosts of War*, 17. Perhaps, "in 1965–66, in Hardjonegaran [Central Java] at the time of the massacres, only one person was abducted from the village. He is said to 'be still away,' though it is obvious he was killed." Siegel, *Naming the Witch*, 181.
12 Bloch, *Traces*, 119.
13 Napier, *Age of Immunology*, 38.
14 Schweitzer, *Out of My Life*, 83.
15 Baron Haussmann, in Benjamin, *Arcades Project*, 129. Francois Guizot, in Benjamin, *Arcades Project*, 147.
16 Lüdtke, "Organizational Order of *Eigensinn*?," 315–16. Lukács, *Makarenko*, 209.
17 Lüdtke, "Organizational Order of *Eigensinn*?," 316.
18 "The People," in Roth, *Report from a Parisian Paradise*, 139.
19 Dwork and van Pelt, *Auschwitz*, 102. The successful implementation of the Nazi Four-Year Plan of 1936 presupposed the inclusion, in Reinhard Heydrich's words, of "gypsies and persons traveling in gypsy fashion who have shown no desire for regular work or have violated the law" as well as "all male Jews with previous criminal records." Dwork and van Pelt, *Auschwitz*, 103.
20 Dwork and van Pelt, *Auschwitz*, 103.
21 Dwork and van Pelt, *Auschwitz*, 101.
22 Distel and Jakusch, *Concentration Camp Dachau*, 39.
23 "Sinar Sumatra," February 28, 1930, *IPO* 1930.
24 Salim, *Vijftien jaar*, 173–74. Also Burhanuddin [Boerhanoeddin], "Sjahrir yang saya kenal," 63.
25 Matanasi, *Thomas Najoan*, 54.
26 Amichai, *Poems of Jerusalem*, 39.
27 Walter Benjamin, in Presner, *Mobile Modernity*, 17.
28 Žižek, *Violence*, 24.
29 "One-Way Street," in Benjamin, *Selected Writings*, 1:480.
30 Kafka, *Diaries, 1914–1923*, January 24, 1922, 210.
31 Mehring, *Kein Weg Zurück*, 96.
32 Redlich, *Terezín Diary*, 95.
33 Pérez-Oramas, *Tangled Alphabets*, 35.
34 Thales, an Ionic philosopher, astronomer, and mathematician, according to Dante, ended up in Hell. See Dante, *Hell*, 341.
35 McNab, *Ghost Ships*, 108.
36 Makarova, *University*, 214.
37 Perec, *W, or The Memory of Childhood*, 68.

38 The children's art from Friedl Dicker-Brandeis's classes is now in the Jewish Museum in Prague.
39 "The Miracle of the Loaves," in Bondy, *Trapped*, 138.
40 "The Miracle of the Loaves," 145–46.
41 Roth in a letter to Stefan Zweig, March 28, 1936, in Roth, *Life in Letters*, 447n.
42 Roth, *Life in Letters*, 293n.
43 Roth, *Life in Letters*, 459n.
44 Roth, *Life in Letters*, 398n.
45 Roth, *Life in Letters*, 530–31.
46 Roth, *Life in Letters*, 196n.
47 Hannah Arendt, in Scholem, *Correspondence*, 268.
48 Paul Éluard, in McNab, *Ghost Ships*, 14, 22.
49 Paul Éluard, in McNab, *Ghost Ships*, 21.
50 McNab, *Ghost Ships*, 78.
51 McNab, *Ghost Ships*, 137.
52 McNab, *Ghost Ships*, 107.
53 Gaudy, *Une Île, Une Forteresse*, 197–202.
54 Kwon, *Ghosts of War*, 78.
55 Ronell, *Stupidity*, 200.
56 Testimony by Jacqueline Philips, July 9, 1993, YVA 015/726.
57 Spier, *Dat alles*, 88.
58 Testimony by Leontine Fels–de Jong, 1995, YVA 093/16753.
59 Loebis, *Orang Indonesia*, 220.
60 Loebis, *Orang Indonesia*, 220.
61 Robert Smithson, in Holt, *Writing of Robert Smithson*, 330n152.
62 Lumley, *Arte Povera*, 64.
63 Gertrud Koch, "Boris Lurie's NO!art and the Canon," in Kugelmann, *No Compromises!*, 140.
64 Makarova, *University*, 388.
65 Segev, *Seventh Million*, 117.
66 Segev, *Seventh Million*, 117.
67 Segev, *Seventh Million*, 159.
68 Paul Weiner, *Terezín Remembered*, 1. "I carry its stigma around with me and hide it like a character fault. I will not volunteer that I am a survivor, that I was in a concentration camp. I try to pretend that it did not happen, that it doesn't matter any more. But it is seared into my soul. . . . I understand why Bruno Bettelheim and Primo Levi committed suicide after long lives of professional achievement. As rabbi Weiss of the Yale chapter of Hillel once said to me. . . . If you cannot believe, than all that is left is despair. But I don't believe. Is that what makes life so hard?" Eva Benda, "From Prague to Theresienstadt," 251–52.
69 Segev, *Seventh Million*. 161.
70 Segev, *Seventh Million*, 161.
71 "The Miracle of the Loaves," in Bondy, *Trapped*, 118.
72 Scholem, *From Berlin to Jerusalem*, 157.
73 For example, "'*yekke*' means 'a German,'" in Grossman, *See under: Love*, 458.

74 Oz, *Tale of Love and Darkness*, 195.
75 Oz, *Tale of Love and Darkness*, 287.
76 Oz, *Tale of Love and Darkness*, 418.
77 Oz, *Tale of Love and Darkness*, 452.
78 Oz, *Tale of Love and Darkness*, 60.
79 Oz, *Tale of Love and Darkness*, 148, 149.
80 Amichai, *Poems of Jerusalem*, 47.
81 Plato, *Republic*, 2:109, 111.
82 "The Changing Image of the Theresienstadt Ghetto," in Bondy, *Trapped*, 10.
83 "The Changing Image of the Theresienstadt Ghetto," in Bondy, *Trapped*, 10.
84 Bauer, *Rethinking Holocaust*, 253.
85 "The refuges, the survivors, whom we generally treated with compassion and a certain revulsion, miserable wretches, was it our fault that they chose to sit and wait for Hitler instead of coming here while there was still time? . . . And if only they'd stop muttering on . . . , and stop telling us about all the things that were done to them over there, because all that didn't reflect too well on them or on us for that matter. . . . Survivors like Mr. Licht, . . . the local kids called 'Million *Kinder*'. . . . 'A million *Kinder* they killed! Kiddie like you! Slaughtered them!'" Oz, *Tale of Love and Darkness*, 13.
86 Cilly Kugelmann, "I would have loved to make pretty pictures . . . ," in Kugelmann, *No Compromises!*, 115.
87 Testimony by ex-internee Petr Lang, in Hájková, *Die fabelhaften Jungs aus Theresienstadt*, 133.
88 "From Songs of Zion the Beautiful," in Amichai, *Selected Poetry*, 108–10.
89 "From Songs of Zion the Beautiful," 155.
90 Interview with Chava Pressburger, Omer, Israel, July 16, 2013.
91 "Keng Po," July 11, 1928, *IPO* 1928.
92 B. Anderson, *Java in a Time of Revolution*, 354n43.
93 B. Anderson, *Java in a Time of Revolution*, 418.
94 B. Anderson, *Java in a Time of Revolution*, 448.
95 B. Anderson, *Java in a Time of Revolution*, 431–32.
96 Mrázek, *Sjahrir*, 283–90.
97 Salim, *Vijftien jaar* (1973 edition), 364, 244.
98 Salim, *Vijftien jaar* (1973 edition), 364–65.
99 Interview with Trikoyo, Tangerang, January 27, 2008.
100 Ramidjo, *Kisah-Kisah*, 195–96.
101 Heidegger, *Being and Time*, 253.
102 Interview with Trikoyo, Tangerang, January 27, 2008.
103 Interview with Bangun Topo, Jakarta, May 15, 2011.
104 Interview with Yudo Widiyastono, Depok, May 15, 2011.
105 Interview with Chamsinah Nasoetion, Jakarta, May 9, 2011.
106 Lukman, *Panta Rhei*, vii.
107 Interview with Tatiana Lukman, Utrecht, June 30, 2011.
108 Lukman, *Panta Rhei*, 182–85.
109 Le Clézio, *Desert*, 63.

110 Interview with Moedakir, Serang, May 8, 2014.
111 Ramidjo, *Kisah-Kisah*, 192.
112 Lockwood, *Black Armada*, 150, 166.
113 Céline, *Normance*, 323.
114 Perec, *W, or The Memory of Childhood*, 68.
115 "Roll Call," in Bondy, *Trapped*, 223.
116 Rothkirchen, *Jews of Bohemia and Moravia*, 213–14.
117 Žižek, *Violence*, 52.
118 Mirjam Wenzel, "From Display to Lust: The Deconstruction of Photographs in Boris Lurie's Collages," in Kugelmann, *Boris Lurie*, 50.
119 Kentridge, *Six Drawing Lessons*, 80.
120 "Central Park" (1938/1939), in Benjamin, *Selected Writings*, 4:173.
121 "Roll Call," in Bondy, *Trapped*, 178.
122 The wall was "completed" in 1959. "Roll Call," in Bondy, *Trapped*, 226. This is not to deny the effect of such "lists." In 2012, Nieuwe Amsterdam Uitgevers published *In Memoriam:* Addendum; *gedeporteerde Joodse, Roma en Sinta kinderen, 1942–45*. On 960 pages of the book there are just names of the Jewish, Roma, and Sinta children murdered in the camps, alphabetically ordered, name, number of transport, date of death. My friend Tom de Boer told me a story of his grandmother, a teacher in Amsterdam, who in 1942 lost courage and, as ordered, gave the names of her Jewish students to the authorities. Tom, in his mid-eighties when he brought the book for me to see, pointed to three or four names on the list with his finger and cried.
123 For documents on the film shooting, see Adler, *Die verheimlichte Wahrheit*, 229–33.
124 Florida, *Living in a Time of Madness*, 20–21.
125 Nancy, *Philosophical Chronicles*, 57.
126 Amichai, *Poems of Jerusalem*, 135.
127 Dwork and van Pelt, *Auschwitz*, 363. "The management of the Polish Auschwitz-Birkenau state museum has allowed the wooden hut of the children's barracks with its brick chimneys to crumble, and in camp B/2/b only its foundations remain today—a rectangular concrete frame. The electric fence behind the hut is corroded with rust." "Games in the Shadow of the Crematoria," in Bondy, *Trapped*, 176.
128 Koolhaas and Foster, *Junkspace*, 34.
129 https://cs.wikipedia.org/wiki/Druhá_světová_válka.
130 Salim, *Vijftien jaar*, 143.
131 Salim, *Vijftien jaar*, 9.
132 Hasjimy, *Tanah Merah*, 143.
133 "Karl Marx, Death, and the Apocalypse," in Bloch, *Spirit of Utopia*, 257.
134 Kafka, *Metamorphosis*, 85.
135 "Letter to editor Der Jüngste Tag (Doomsday)," in Kafka, *Metamorphosis*, 113–14.
136 Dostoyevsky, *Idiot*, 66.
137 Jeremiah 18:6.

138 Deva Group Utrecht, The Netherlands, info@devagroup.nl.
139 Koolhaas, "Singapore," 1015.
140 Blodig, *Terezín*, 7.
141 Blodig, *Terezín*, 7.
142 Interview with Greta Kingsberg, Jerusalem, May 14, 2015.
143 Sebald, *Austerlitz*, 189.
144 Lanzmann, *Benjamin Murmelstein*, 301.
145 Alton L. Becker and Ronit Ricci, "What Happens When You Really Listen: On Translating the Old Javanese Rāmāyaṇa; Rāmāyaṇa Kakwain, Sargah 26, Translation and Essay," *Indonesia* 85 (April 2008): 1.
146 Interview with Tobi Siregar, Jakarta, January 30, 2008.
147 Kentridge, *Six Drawing Lessons*, 187.
148 Job 4:19.
149 Heidegger, *Being and Time*, 372.
150 Interview with Trikoyo, Tangerang, January 30, 2012.
151 Deleuze, "Desert Islands," in Deleuze, *Desert Islands*, 10–11.
152 "Beyond Memory," in Levinas, *In the Time of the Nations*, 70.
153 Gilles Deleuze cited in Žižek, *Violence*, 48.

BIBLIOGRAPHY

Archives

ARA Algemeen Rijksarchief (General State Archives), The Hague (*Mr* or *Mailrapport* was a file in which documents were sent from the Indies; *Vb* or *Verbaal* was a folder in which several files were collected)
- *Collectie van der Plas*
- *Memorie van overgave*

BDA Boven Digoel Archief, Arsip Nasional Republic Indonesia, Jakarta
- "Politie Dagboek van het Interneeringskamp, 1934–1940"

IISH International Institute of Social History, Amsterdam
- *Collectie Wertheim*

JMP Jewish Museum, Prague

KITLV Koninklijk Instituut voor Taal- Land- en Volkenkunde, Leiden
- *Archief Schoonheyt*
- Leo Baeck Institute, New York

MGI Mondelinge Geschiedenis Indonesië, Leiden

NIOD   Nederlands Instituut voor Oorlogsdocumentatie, Amsterdam
·   Steven Spielberg Visual History Archives, Los Angeles and Jerusalem
·   Theresienstadt Memorial, Terezín
·   Wiener Library, London
YVA   Yad Vashem Archives, Jerusalem
YVAF   Yad Vashem Foto Archives, Jerusalem

Series and Newspapers

Handelingen van den Volksraad, Batavia
Indonesia, Ithaca
IPO *Overzicht van de Inlandsche en Maleisch-chineesche pers*, Batavia
Šalom na pátek, Terezín, YVA
Theresienstädter Studien und Dokumente, Terezín
Vedem, časopis domova L 417, Theresienstadt

Interviews

Bacon, Jehuda. Jerusalem, May 15, 2013.
Benedictus. Boven Digoel, July 5, 2013.
Boerhanoeddin. Jakarta, August 23, 1983.
Bondy, Ruth. Tel Aviv, October 15, 2012.
Duchâteau-Sjahrir, Maria. Lorques, France, February 13, 1988.
Kingsberg, Greta. Jerusalem, May 14, 2015.
Lukman, Tatiana. Utrecht, June 30, 2011.
Mawengkang, Joesoef. Jakarta, August 16, 1998.
Moedakir, Serang. May 8, 2014.
Moerad. Jakarta, September 15, 1983.
Moerwoto. Jakarta, July 23, 1985.
Nasoetion, Chamsinah. Jakarta, May 8 and 9, 2011.
Pressburger, Chava. Omer, Israel, July 16, 2013.
Schiller, Alisah. Givat Hain (Ihud), Israel, July 5, 2013.
Siregar, Tobi. Jakarta, January 30, 2008.
Tejo. Jakarta, May 11, 2011.
Topo, Bangun. Jakarta, August 11, 2008, and May 15, 2011.
Trikoyo [Tri Ramidjo]. Tangerang, January 27, July 7, and July 28, 2008; July 5, 2010; May 11 and 17, 2011; January 30, 2012.
Weingarten, Chava. Tel Aviv, October 17, 2012.
Wertheimer, Hannah. Tel Aviv, July 30, 2012.
Widayasih. Jakarta, January 23, 2009.

Widiyastono, Yudo. Depok, May 15, 2011.
Zakaria. Jakarta, May 10, 2011.

Diaries, Memoirs, Correspondence

Baker, Leonard. *Days of Sorrow and Pain: Leo Baeck and the Berlin Jews*. New York: Macmillan, 1978.
Biran, Misback Yusa. *Kenang-Kenangan Orang Bandel*. Jakarta: Komunitas bambu, 2009.
Boas, Jacob. *Boulevard des Misères: The Story of Transit Camp Westerbork*. Hamden, CT: Archon Books, 1985.
Bondan, Mohamad. *Memoar Seorang Eks-Digulis: Totalitas Sebuah Perjuangan*. Jakarta: Kompas, 2011.
Brenner-Wonschick, Hannelore, ed. *Die Mädchen von Zimmer 28: Freundschaft, Hoffnung, und Überleben in Theresienstadt*. Munich, Germany: Droemer, 2004.
Demetz, Peter. *Prague in Danger: The Years of German Occupation, 1939–1945: Memories and History, Terror and Resistance, Theater and Jazz, Film and Poetry, Politics and War*. New York: Ferrar, Straus and Giroux, 2008.
Djati, Arief W., and Ben Anderson, eds. *Menjadi Tjamboek Berdoeri: Memoar Kwee Thiam Tjing*. Pengantar James Siegel. Jakarta: Komunitas bambu, 2010.
du Perron, Charles Edgar. *Country of Origin*. Translated by Francis Bulhof and Elizabeth Daverman. Amherst: University of Massachusetts Press, 1984.
Durlacher, G. L. *Quarantaine*. Amsterdam: Meulenhoff, 1993.
Edgcomb, Gabrielle Simon. *From Swastika to Jim Crow: Refugee Scholars at Black Colleges*. Malabar, FL: Krieger, 1993.
Fest, Joachim. *Die unbeantwortbaren Fragen: Notizen über Gespräche mit Albert Speer zwischen Ende 1966 und 1981*. Hamburg, Germany: Rowohlt Verlag, 2005.
Haffner, Sebastian. *Defying Hitler: A Memoir*. Translated by Oliver Pretzel. New York: Farrar, Straus and Giroux, 2002.
Hatta, Mohammad. *Berjuang dan Dibuang: Untuk Negeriku: Sebuah Otobiografi*. Jakarta: Kompas, 2011.
Hillesum, Etty. *An Interrupted Life: The Diaries, 1941–1943, and Letters from Westerbork*. Translated by Arnold J. Romevans. New York: Henry Holt, 1996.
Hillesum, Etty. *Twee brieven uit Westerbork*. Amsterdam: Balans, 2013.
Italie, Gabriel. *Het Oorlogsdagboek, 1940–1945*. Amsterdam: Olympus, 2009.
Kafka, Franz. *Diaries, 1910–1913*. Translated by Joseph Kresh. New York: Schocken, 1965.
Kafka, Franz. *Diaries, 1914–1923*. Translated by Martin Greenberg, with the cooperation of Hannah Arendt. New York: Schocken, 1965.
Kafka, Franz. *Letters to Felice*. Translated by James Stern and Elisabeth Duckworth. New York: Schocken, 1973.

Kafka, Franz. *Letters to Friends, Family, and Editors*. Translated by Richard Winston and Clara Winston. New York: Schocken, 1977.

Kafka, Franz. *Letters to Milena*. Translated by Philip Boehm. New York: Schocken Books, 1990.

Kandinsky, Nina. *Kandinsky und Ich*. Munich, Germany: Kindler Verlag, 1976.

Kartodikromo. See Mas Marco.

Kertész, Imre. *Fatelessness*. Translated by Tim Wilkinson. New York: Vintage Books, 2004.

Koestler, Arthur. *The Invisible Writing: The Second Volume of an Autobiography, 1932–40*. New York: Stein and Day, 1984.

Lederer, Zdeněk. *Ghetto Theresienstadt*. London: Edward Goldston, 1953.

Levi, Primo. *The Drowned and the Saved*. Translated by Raymond Rosentahl. London: Abacus, 1979.

Loebis, Parlindoengan. *Orang Indonesia di Kamp Konsentrasi Nazi: Autobiografi*. Jakarta: Komunitas bambu, 2006.

Lukman, Tatiana. *Panta Rhei: Tidak Ada Pengorbanan yang Sia-Sia: Air Sungai Digul Mengalir Terus*. Jakarta: Pustaka Sempu, 2008.

Manes, Philipp. *Als ob's ein Leben wär: Tatsachenbericht Theresienstadt, 1942–1944*. Berlin: Ullstein, 2005.

Mas Marco Kartodikromo. *Pergaulan Orang Buangan di Boven-Digoel*. Jakarta: Gramedia, 2002.

Mawengkang, Joesoef. *Boven Digoel: Sebuah Cerita anak buangan*. Jakarta: unpublished typescript, 1996.

Mechanicus, Philip. *Waiting for Death: A Diary*. Translated by Irene R. Gibbons. London: Calder and Boyars, 1968.

Mehring, Walter. *Kein Weg Zurück*. New York: Samuel Curl, 1944.

Mehring, Walter. *The Lost Library: The Autobiography of a Culture*. Translated by Richard Winston and Clara Winston. Indianapolis: Bobbs-Merrill, 1951.

Nasoetion, Jahja Malik. *Perdjuanganku*. Jakarta: unpublished typescript, n.d.

Perec, Georges. *W, or The Memory of Childhood*. Translated by David Bellos. Boston, MA: Godine, 1988.

Poláček, Karel. *Poslední dopisy Doře*. Toronto: Sixty-Eight, 1983.

Pressburger, Chava, ed. *The Diary of Petr Ginz, 1941–1942*. Translated by Elena Lappin. New York: Grove Press, 2008.

Prokofiev, Sergei. *Soviet Diary 1927 and Other Writings*. Translated by Oleg Prokofiev. London: Faber and Faber, 1991.

Ramidjo, Tri [Trikoyo]. *Kisah-Kisah dari Tanah Merah (Boven Digoel): Cerita Digul Baru*. Bandung: Ultimus, 2009.

Redlich, Gonda. *The Terezín Diary of Gonda Redlich*. Translated by Laurence Kutler. Lexington: University of Kentucky Press, 1992.

Riedmann, Bettina. *Ich bin Jude, Österreicher, Deutscher*. Tübingen, Germany: Max Niemeyer Verlag, 2002.

Rijshouwer, J. A. H., and H. Van Wermeskerken, eds. *Vier Jaar Indisch Gijzelaar: Buchenwald-Haaren-St. Michielsgestel-Vught-Amersfoort*. The Hague: W. van Hoeve, 1946.

Roth, Joseph. *The Hotel Years*. Translated by Michael Hofmann. New York: New Directions Books, 2015.

Roth, Joseph. *Report from a Parisian Paradise: Essays from France, 1925–1939*. Translated by Michael Hofmann. New York: W. W. Norton, 2004.

Rousseau, Jean-Jacques. *The Confessions*. Translated by J. M. Cohen. London: Penguin Books, 1953.

Salim, Ignatius Franciscus Michael. *Vijftien jaar Boven-Digoel: Concentratiekamp in Nieuw-Guinea*, 2nd expanded edition. Hengelo, Netherlands: Smit, [1973] 1980.

Scholem, Gershom, ed. *The Correspondence of Walter Benjamin and Gershom Scholem, 1932–1940*. Translated by Gary Smith and André Lefevere. New York: Schocken Books, 1989.

Scholem, Gershom. *From Berlin to Jerusalem: Memories of My Youth*. Translated by Harry Zohn. New York: Schocken Books, 1980.

Scholem, Gershom. *Walter Benjamin: The Story of a Friendship*. Translated by Harry Zohn. New York: New York Review Books, 2003.

Schoonheyt, Louis Johan Alexander. *Boven-Digoel*. Batavia: De Unie, 1936.

Schoonheyt, Louis Johan Alexander. *Boven-Digoel: Het Land van Communisten en Kannibalen*. Amsterdam: G. Kolff, 1940.

Schweitzer, Albert. *Out of My Life and Thought*. Translated by Antje Bultmann Lemke. Baltimore, MD: Johns Hopkins University Press, 1990.

Shean, Nava [Vlasta (Vava) Schönová]. *To Be an Actress*. Tranlsated by Michelle Fram Cohen. Lanham, MD: Hamilton Books, 2010.

Sjahrir, Soetan (Sjahrazad). *Indonesische Opverpeinzingen*. Amsterdam: De Bezige Bij, 1945.

Sjahrir, Soetan. Letters to Maria Duchâteau-Sjahrir from Boven Digoel, February 21, 1935, to February 11, 1936. Courtesy of Maria Duchâteau-Sjahrir.

Spier, Jo. *Dat alles heeft mijn oog gezien: Herinneringen aan het concentratiekamp Theresienstadt*. Amsterdam: Elsevier, 1978.

Spies, Gerty. *My Years in Theresienstadt: How One Woman Survived the Holocaust*. Translated by Jutta R. Tragnitz. Amherst, NY: Prometheus Books, 1997.

Trikoyo. See Ramidjo, Tri.

Vondráčková, Jaroslava. *Mrazilo-tálo: O Jiřím Weilovi*. Prague: Torst, 2014.

Vuyk, Beb. *Kampdagboeken: Drie verhalen, dagboeken en aantekeningen*. Utrecht, Netherlands: Veen uitgevers, 1989.

Wechsberg, Joseph. *Sweet and Sour*. Boston, MA: Houghton Mifflin. 1948

Weil, Jiří. *Colors*. Translated by Rachel Harrell. Ann Arbor: Michigan Slavic Publications, 2002.

Weil, Jiří. *Life with a Star*. Translated by Rita Klímová, with Roslyn Schloss. London: Penguin Books, 1991.

Weiner, Pavel. *A Boy in Terezín: The Private Diary of Pavel Weiner, April 1944– April 1945*. Translated by Paul (Pavel) Weiner. Evanston, IL: Northwestern University Press, 2012.

Weiner, Paul [Pavel]. *Terezín Remembered*. Unpublished typescript of a talk at the Univerity of North Carolina Humanities Program Seminar, Chapel Hill, North Carolina, May 10, 2005.

Weiner, Valy. *Recollections*. Translated by Paul Weiner. Unpublished typescript, 1945.
Weiss, Otto. *And God Saw That It Was Bad: A Story from the Terezín Ghetto*. Translated by Iris Urwin. Jerusalem: Yad Vashem, 2010.
Wertheim, Wim, and Hetty Wertheim-Gijs Weenink. *Vier Wendingen in Ons Bestaan: Indië verloren-Indonesië geboren*. Breda, Netherlands: De Geus, 1991.
Whiteley, Suzanne Mehler. *Appel Is Forever: A Child's Memoirs*. Detroit, MI: Wayne State University, 1999.
Widayasih. *Masa kanak-kanak*. Vols. 1–2. Unpublished manuscript. Jakarta, 1990–2009.

History, Literature, Theory

Abdoel 'lXarim M.s. "Pandu Anak Buangan." In *Cerita dari Digul*, edited by Pramoedya Ananta Toer, 81–156. Jakarta: Gramedia, 2001. Reprint of Abdoel 'lXarim M.s. *Pandoe Anak Boeangan*. Medan, Indonesia: Aneka, n.d. [1933?].
Abidin, Kusno. *The Appearance of Memory: Mnemonic Practices of Architecture and Urban Form in Indonesia*. Durham, NC: Duke University Press, 2010.
Adler, Hans Günther. *Die verheimlichte Wahrheit: Theresienstädter Dokumente*. Tübingen, Germany: J. C. B. Mohr (Paul Siebeck), 1958.
Adler, Hans Günther. *Theresienstadt: Das Antlitz einer Zwangsgemeinschaft*. Vols. 1–3. Göttingen, Germany: Wallstein Verlag, 2003. Reprint of 2nd ed. of 1960.
Adorno, Theodor W. *Aesthetic Theory*. Translated by C. Lenhardt. London: Routledge and Kegan Paul, 1984.
Adorno, Theodor W. *The Jargon of Authenticity*. Translated by Knut Tarnowski and Frederic Will. Evanston, IL: Northwestern University Press, 1973.
Agamben, Giorgio. *Remnants of Auschwitz: The Witness and the Archive*. Translated by Daniel Heller-Roazen. New York: Zone Books, 2002.
Amichai, Yehuda. *Poems of Jerusalem and Love Poems*. Translated by Chana Bloch and Stephen Mitchell. Riverdale-on-Hudson, NY: Sheep Meadow Press, 1988.
Amichai, Yehuda. *The Selected Poetry*. Translated by Chana Bloch and Stephen Mitchell. Berkeley: University of California Press, 1996.
Anderson, Benedict. *Java in a Time of Revolution: Occupation and Resistance, 1944–1946*. Ithaca, NY: Cornell University Press, 1972.
Anderson, Benedict. "*The Suluk Gatoloco*, Part One." *Indonesia* 32 (October 1981): 109–150.
Anderson, Benedict. "*The Suluk Gatoloco*, Part Two." *Indonesia* 33 (April 1982): 31–88.
Anderson, Perry. *Considerations on Western Marxism*. London: Verso, 1987.
Appelfeld, Aharon. *Badenheim 1939*. Translated by Dalya Bilu. Boston, MA: Verba Mundi, 1980.
Arendt, Hannah. *Eichmann in Jerusalem: A Report on the Banality of Evil*. New York: Viking Press, 1963.
Artaud, Antonin. *The Theater and Its Double*. Translated by Mary Caroline Richards. New York: Grove Press, 1958.

Atlan, Henri. *Selected Writings on Self-Organization, Philosophy, Bioethics, and Judaism*. New York: Fordham University Press, 2011.
Augé, Marc. *In the Metro*. Translated by Tom Conley. Minneapolis: University of Minnesota Press, 2002.
Augé, Marc. *Paris, annés 30: Roger-Viollet*. Paris: Hazan, 1997.
Balzac, Honoré de. *My Journey from Paris to Java*. Translated by Barry Winkelman. Singapore: Mainland Press, 2010.
Balzac, Honoré de. *Treatise on Elegant Living*. Translated by Napoleon Jeffries. Cambridge, MA: Wakefield Press, 2010.
Barthes, Rolland. *The Fashion System*. Translated by Matthew Ward and Richard Howard. Berkeley: University of California Press, 1990.
Barthes, Roland. *Michelet*. Translated by Richard Howard. New York: Hill and Wang, 1987.
Barthes, Roland. *The Neutral: Lecture Course at the Collège de France (1977–1978)*. Translated by Rosalind E. Krauss and Denis Hollier. New York: Columbia University Press, 2005.
Barthes, Roland. *What Is Sport?* Translated by Richard Howard. New Haven, CT: Yale University Press, 2007.
Baudrillard, Jean. *Simulacra and Simulation*. Translated by Shella Glaser. Ann Arbor: University of Michigan Press, 1994.
Bauer, Yehuda. *Rethinking the Holocaust*. New Haven, CT: Yale University Press, 2002.
Bauman, Zygmunt. *Modernity and the Holocaust*. Ithaca, NY: Cornell University Press, 2000.
Becking. L. Th. "Reisverslag van [kapitein L. Th.] Becking, gezaghebber te Boven-Digoel op zijn tourneé van de Digoel-rivier naar de Ok Terrie (Alice-rivier) van 3 tot en met 30 Juni j.l." Unpublished typescript. Boven Digoel, July 16, 1927: KITLV 53 1992, 4.
Beckett, Samuel. *The Letters of Samuel Beckett, 2009–2016*. Edited by George Craig, Martha Dow Fehsenfeld, Dan Gunn, and Lois More Overbeck. Cambridge, UK: Cambridge University Press, 2014.
Bellow, Saul. *Mr. Sammler's Planet*. London: Penguin Books, 1977.
Benda, Eva. "From Prague to Theresienstadt and Back." In *And Life Is Changed Forever: Holocaust Childhood Remembered*, edited by Martin Ira Glassner and Robert Krell, 251–75. Detroit, MI: Wayne State University Press, 2006.
Benda, Harry J., and Ruth T. McVey, eds. *The Communist Uprisings of 1926–1927 in Indonesia. Key Documents*. Ithaca, NY: Cornell University Southeast Asia Program, 1960.
Benjamin, Walter. *The Arcades Project*. Cambridge, MA: Harvard University Press, 1999.
Benjamin, Walter. *Selected Writings*. Vol. 1, *1913–1926*. Cambridge, MA: Harvard University Press, 1996.
Benjamin, Walter. *Selected Writings*. Vol. 2, *1927–1934*. Cambridge, MA: Harvard University Press, 1999.
Benjamin, Walter. *Selected Writings*. Vol. 3, *1935–1938*. Cambridge, MA: Harvard University Press, 2002.

Benjamin, Walter. *Selected Writings*. Vol. 4, *1938–1940*. Cambridge, MA: Harvard University Press, 2003.
Benjamin, Walter. *The Storyteller*. London: Verso, 2016.
Birdsall, Carolyn. *Nazi Soundscapes: Sound, Technology, and Urban Space in Germany, 1933–1945*. Amsterdam: Amsterdam University Press, 2012.
Blanchot, Maurice. *The Space of Literature*. Translated by Ann Smock. Lincoln: University of Nebraska Press, 1989.
Blanchot, Maurice. *The Step Not Beyond*. Translated by Lycette Nelson. New York: SUNY Press, 1992.
Blaufuks, Daniel. *Terezín*. Göttingen, Germany: Seidl, 2010.
Bloch, Ernst. *The Spirit of Utopia*. Translated by Anthony A. Nassar. Stanford, CA: Stanford University Press, 2000.
Bloch, Ernst. *Traces*. Translated by Anthony A. Nassar. Stanford, CA: Stanford University Press, 2006.
Blodig, Vojtěch, et al. *Kultura proti smrti: Stálá expozice Památníku Terezín*. Prague: Oswald, 2002.
Blodig, Vojtěch. *Terezín Í' v 'konečném řešeni židovské otázky, 1941–1945*. Prague: Oswald, 2003.
Blodig, Vojtěch, et al. *Perpetrators of Crimes: The SS Repressive Staff in Terezín and Litoměřice, 1940–1945*. Terezín, Czech Republic: Terezín Memorial, 2013.
Boelaars, Jan H. *Papoea's aan Mappi*. Utrecht, Netherlands: De Fontein, 1957.
Bondy, Ruth. *"Elder of the Jews" Jacob Edelstein of Theresienstadt*. Translated by Evelyn Abel. New York: Grove Press, 1989.
Bondy, Ruth. "Šalom na pátek=Schalom zum Freitag: Die Theresienstädter humoristische Zeitung." In *Theresienstädter Studien und Dokumente*, edited by Miroslav Kárný et al., 184–211. Prague: Theresienstädter Initiative, 1994.
Bondy, Ruth. "The Theresienstadt Ghetto: Its Charactristics and Perspective." In *The Nazi Concentration Camps: Proceedings of the Fourth Yad Vashem International Historical Conference*, 84–304. Jerusalem: Yad Vashem, 1984.
Bondy, Ruth. *Trapped: Essays on the History of the Czech Jews, 1939–1943*. Jerusalem: Yad Vashem, 2008.
Brecht, Bertolt. *Poems, 1913–1956*. New York: Routledge, 1987.
Broch, Hermann. *The Guiltless*. Translated by Ralph Manheim. Evanston, IL: Northwestern University Press, 2000.
Broch, Hermann. *The Sleepwalkers*. Translated by Willa and Edwin Muir. New York: Vintage International, 1996.
Budgen, Sebastian, Stathis Kouvelakis, and Slavoj Žižek, eds. *Lenin Reloaded: Toward a Politics of Truth*. Durham, NC: Duke University Press, 2007.
Cabet, Étienne. *Travels in Icaria*. Translated by Leslie J. Roberts. Syracuse, NY: Syracuse University Press, 2003.
Caduff, Carlo. *The Pandemic Perhaps: Dramatic Events in a Public Culture of Danger*. Oakland: University of California Press, 2015.
Cage, John. *Silence*. Middletown, CT: Wesleyan University Press, 2011.
Canetti, Elias. *Crowds and Power*. Translated by Carol Stewart. New York: Farrar, Straus and Giroux, 1984.

Céline, Louis-Ferdinand. *Death on the Installment Plan*. Translated by Ralph Manheim. New York: New Directions Books, 1971.
Céline, Louis-Ferdinand. *Journey to the End of the Night*. Translated by Ralph Manheim. New York: New Directions Books, 2006.
Céline, Louis-Ferdinand. *Mea Culpa*. Translated by Simon Gree. Céline Blogspot .com, 2008.
Céline, Louis-Ferdinand. *Normance*. Translated by Marlow Jones. Champaign, IL: Dalkey Archive Press, 2009.
Céline, Louis-Ferdinand. *Rigadoon*. Translated by Ralph Manheim. Champaign, IL: Dalkey Archive Press, 2008.
Chekhov, Anton. *Sakhalin Island*. Translated by Brian Reeve. London: Oneworld Classics, 2007.
Chernyshevsky, Nikolai. *What Is to Be Done?* Translated by Michael B. Katz. Ithaca, NY: Cornell University Press, 1983.
Citra dan Perjuangan Perintis Kemerdekaan Seri Perjuangan Ex Digul. Jakarta: Direktorat Jenderal Bantuan Sosial, 1977.
Council of Jewish Communities. *Terezín*. Prague: Council of Jewish Communities of the Czech Lands, 1965.
Couperus, Louis. *The Hidden Force*. Translated by Alexander Teixeira de Mattos. Amherst: University of Massachusetts Press, 1985.
d'Amour, Monsieur [pseud. of Nioo Cheong Seng]. *Taufan Gila: Bung DaEng Mentjari Kiamat: Oleh-oleh dari Perantauan*. Jakarta: Tjilik Romans, 1950.
Dante Alighieri. *The Comedy: I: Hell*. Translated by Dorothy L. Sayers. London: Penguin Books, 1949.
Dante Alighieri. *The Comedy: II: Purgatory*. Translated by Dorothy L. Sayers. London: Penguin Books, 1976.
Deleuze, Gilles. *Desert Islands and Other Texts, 1953–1974*. Translated by Michael Taormina. Paris: Semiotext(e), 2002.
De Witte, Willy. *Kaja-Kaja: Eerste prentenalbum voor de jeugd uit de reeks M.S.C. over de wereld*. Borgerhout, Belgium: Missionarissen van het Heilig Hart, n.d.
Digoelschandaal: Het Nederlandsche volk in zijn geheel is mede aansprakelijk! Amsterdam: International Red Aid [Internationale Rode Hulp], 1927.
Distel, Barbara, and Ruth Jakusch, eds. *Concentration Camp Dachau*. Brussels: Comité International de Dachau, 1978.
Dostoyevsky, Fyodor. *Crime and Punishment*. Translated by Jessie Coulson. New York: Modern Library, 1994.
Dostoyevsky, Fyodor. *Demons*. Translated by Robert A. Maguire. London: Penguin Classics, 2008.
Dostoyevsky, Fyodor. *The Idiot*. Translated by Constance Garnett and Anna Brailovsky. New York: Modern Library, 2003.
Dostoyevsky, Fyodor. *Memoirs from the House of the Dead*. Translated by Jessie Coulson. Oxford: Oxford University Press, 1965.
Drewes, G. W. J., ed. *An Early Javanese Code of Muslim Ethics*. Translated by G. W. J. Drewes. The Hague: Martinus Nijhoff, 1978.

Dwork, Debórah, and Robert Jan van Pelt. *Auschwitz: 1270 to the Present*. New York: Norton, 1996.
Eiland, Howard, and Michael W. Jennings, eds. *Walter Benjamin: A Critical Life*. Cambridge, MA: Belknap Press, 2014.
Eisenschmidt, Alexander, and Jonathan Mekinda, eds. *Chicagoisms: The City as Catalyst for Architectural Speculation*. Zurich: Park Books, 2013.
Elon, Amos. *The Pity of It All: A Portrait of the German-Jewish Epoch, 1743–1933*. New York: Picador, 2002.
Ewen, F. *Bertolt Brecht: His Life, His Art, His Time*. New York: Citadel Press, 1992.
Fallada, Hans. *Alone in Berlin*. Translated by Michael Hofmann. London: Penguin Books, 2009.
Faulkner, William. *A Fable*. New York: Vintage International, 2011.
Fenves, Peter. *Arresting Language: From Leibniz to Benjamin*. Stanford, CA: Stanford University Press, 2001.
Flaubert, Gustave. *Sentimental Education*. Translated by Robert Baldick and Geoffrey Wall. London: Penguin Books, 2004.
Florida, Nancy K. *Living in a Time of Madness: Last Days of Java's Prophetic Prophet*. Unpublished working draft, Ann Arbor, 2010.
Foucault, Michel. *Discipline and Punish: The Birth of the Prison*. Translated by Alan Sheridan. New York: Vintage Books, 1979.
Furman, Erna. *Ways of Growing Up*. Rotterdam, Netherlands: Stichting Kunstenaarsverzet, [1942–45], 2007.
Garrido, Juan Manuel. *On Time, Being, and Hunger: Challenging the Traditional Way of Thinking Life*. New York: Fordham University Press, 2012.
Gaudy, Hélène. *Une île, une forteresse: Sur Terezín*. Paris: Dernière marge, 2015.
Geertz, Clifford. "The Impact of the Concept of Culture on the Concept of Man." In *The Interpretation of Cultures*, 33–54. New York: Basic Books, 1973.
Gilbert, Shirli. *Music in the Holocaust: Confronting Life in the Nazi Ghettos and Camps*. Oxford: Oxford University Press, 2005.
Gilman, Sander. *Jewish Frontiers: Essays on Bodies, Histories, and Identities*. New York: Palgrave, 2003.
Gilman, Sander. *The Jew's Body*. New York: Routledge, 1991.
Gladkov, Fyodor Vasilievich. *Cement*. Translated by A. S. Arthur and C. Ashleigh. Evanston, IL: Northwestern University Press, 1994.
Goethe, Johann Wolfgang von. *Faust*. Vols. 1–2. Translated by Stuart Atkins. Princeton, NJ: Princeton University Press, 1994.
Goodman, Tumarkin Susan, et al. *Chagall and the Artists of the Russian Jewish Theater*. New York: The Jewish Museum, 2008.
Green, Gerald. *The Artists of Terezín*. New York: Hawthorn Books, 1978.
Grossman, David. *See Under: Love*. Translated by Betsy Rosenberg. New York: Farrar, Straus and Giroux, 1989.
Hájková, Anna. *Die fabelhaften Jungs aus Theresienstadt: Junge tschechische Männer als dominant soziale Elite in Theresienstadter Ghetto*. Typescript, n.d.
Harney, Stefano, and Fred Moten. *The Undercommons: Fugitive Planning and Black Study*. Wivenhoe, NY: Minor Compositions, 2013.

Hasjimy, Ali. *Tanah Merah: Digul bumi pahlawan kemerdekaan Indonesia*. Jakarta: Bulan Bintang, 1976.

Hatta, Mohammad. *Alam Pikiran Junani*. Jakarta: Tintamas, 1961.

Hatta, Mohammad. *Pengantar ke Djalan Ilmu dan Pengetahuan*. Jakarta: Pembangunan, 1964.

Hatta, Mohammad. *Verspreide Geschriften*. Jakarta: C. P. J. van der Peet, 1952.

Heidegger, Martin. *Being and Time*. Translated by Joan Stambaugh and Dennis J. Schmidt. Albany: SUNY Press, 2010.

Heidegger, Martin. *Hegel's Concept of Experience, with a section from Hegel's Phenomenology of Spirit*. Translated by Kenley Royce Dove. New York: Harper, 1989.

Heukäufer, Margarethe. *Und es Gibt so wenig Menschen: Das kurze Leben des Künstlers Peter Kien*. Prague: Verlagshaus, 2009.

Hilberg, Raul. *The Destruction of the European Jews*. Vols. 1–3. New Haven, CT: Yale University Press, 2003.

Ho Chi Minh. *Prison Diary*. Translated by Aileen Palmer. Hanoi: Foreign Languages Publishing House, 1965.

Hofmann, Michael, ed. *Joseph Roth: A Life in Letters*. Translated by Michael Hofmann. New York: W. W. Norton, 2012.

Holt, Nancy, ed. *The Writing of Robert Smithson*. New York: New York University Press, 1979.

Horkheimer, Max, and Theodor W. Adorno. *Dialectic of Enlightenment: Philosophical Fragments*. Translated by Edmund Jephcott. Stanford, CA: Stanford University Press, 2002.

Huelsenbeck, Richard, ed. *Dada Almanac Berlin 1920*. Channel Islands: Guernsey Press, 1993.

Husserl, Edmund. *The Crisis of European Sciences and Transcendental Phenomenology*. Tranlated by David Carr. Evanston, IL: Northwestern University Press, 1970.

Hyndráková, Anna, et al. *Prominenti v ghettu Terezín*. Prague: Ústav pro soudobé dějiny, 1996.

Irigaray, Luce. *The Way of Love*. Translated by Heidi Bostic and Stephan Pluhácek. London: Continuum, 2002.

Janouch, Gustav. *Conversations with Kafka*. Translated by Goronwy Rees. New York: New Directions Books, 1968.

Juhasz, Esther, ed. *The Jewish Wardrobe: From the Collection of The Israel Museum, Jerusalem*. Milan, Italy: Continental Editions, 2012.

Kafka, Franz. *Amerika*. Translated by Willa and Edwin Muir. New York: Schocken Books, 1962.

Kafka, Franz. *The Castle*. Translated by Max Brod. New York: Schocken Books, 1974.

Kafka, Franz. "In the Penal Colony." In *The Metamorphosis, The Penal Colony, and Other Stories*. New York: Schocken, 1988.

Kafka, Franz. *The Trial*. Translated by Willa and Edwin Muir. New York: Schocken Books, 1983.

Karmi, Ghada. *Return: A Palestinian Memoir*. London: Verso, 2015.
Kárný, Miroslav, and Vojtěch Blodig, eds. *Terezín v konečném řesšení židovské otázky*. Prague: Logos, 1962.
Kárný, Miroslav, et al. *Theresienstädter Studien und Dokumente*. Prague: Theresienstädter Initiative, 1994.
Kárný, Miroslav, et al. *Theresienstädter Studien und Dokumente*. Prague: Theresienstädter Initiative, 1996.
Kartomi, Margaret. *The Gamelan Digul*. Rochester, NY: University of Rochester Press, 2002.
Kasperová, Dana. *Výchova a vzděláváni židovských dětí v Protektorátu a v ghettu Terezín*. Prague: Humanitas, 2010.
Kaufmann, Walter. Introduction to *Judaism and Christianity*, by Leo Baeck. Philadelphia, PA: Jewish Publication Society, 1958.
Kentridge, William. *Six Drawing Lessons*. Cambridge, MA: Harvard University Press, 2014.
Kentridge, William, and Rosalind C. Morris. *That Which Is Not Drawn: Conversations*. London: Seagull Books, 2014.
Kierkegaard, Søren. *The Concept of Irony with Continual Reference to Socrates*. Translated by Howard V. Hong and Edna Hong. Princeton, NJ: Princeton University Press, 1989.
Kleeblatt, Norman L., ed. *Mirroring Evil: Nazi Imagery/Recent Art*. New Brunswick, NJ: Rutgers University Press, 2002.
Koolhaas, Rem. *Delirious New York: A Retroactive Manifesto for Manhattan*. New York: Monacelli Press, 1994.
Koolhaas, Rem. "Singapore. Portrait of a Potemkin Metropolis, Songlines—or Thirty Years of Tabula Rasa." In s,m,l,xl, by Rem Koolaas and Bruce Mau, 1008–89. New York: Monacelli Press, 1995.
Koolhaas, Rem, and Hal Foster. *Junkspace with Running Room*. London: Notting Hill, 2013.
The Koran. Translated by J. M. Rodwell. London: J. M. Dent and Sons, 1953.
Kracauer, Siegfried. *Jacques Offenbach and the Paris of His Time*. Translated by Gertrud Koch. New York: Zone Books, 2016.
Kracauer, Siegfried. *The Salaried Masses: Duty and Distraction in Weimar Germany*. Translated by Quintin Hoare. London: Verso, 1998.
Kraus, Chris, and Sylvère Lotringer, eds. *Hatred of Capitalism: A Semiotext(e) Reader*. Los Angeles, CA: Semiotext(e), 2001.
Kristeva, Julia. *Powers of Horror: An Essay on Abjection*. Translated by Leon S. Roudiez. New York: Columbia University Press, 1982.
Křížková, Marie Rút, et al. *We Are Children Just the Same: "Vedem," the Secret Magazine by the Boys of Terezín*. Translated by Elizabeth Novak. Lincoln: University of Nebraska Press, 2012.
Kugelmann, Cilly, ed. *No Compromises! The Art of Boris Lurie*. Bielefeld, Germany: Kerber Verlag, 2016.
Kuna, Milan. *Hudba na hranici života*. Prague: Naše vojsko, 1990.

Kwantes, R. C., ed. *De Ontwikkeling van de Nationalistische Beweging in Nederlandsch-Indië*. Vol. 2, *August 1923 tot 1928*. Groningen, Netherlands: Wolters-Noordhoff Bouma's Boekhuis, 1978.

Kwantes, R. C., ed. *De Ontwikkeling van de Nationalistische Beweging in Nederlandsch-Indië*. Vol. 4, *August 1931 tot 1942*. Groningen, Netherlands: Wolters-Noordhoff Bouma's Boekhuis, 1982.

Kwee, Tek Hoay. *Drama di Boven Digul*. Jakarta: Gramedia, 2001. Originally published in 1928–32.

Kwon, Heonik. *Ghosts of War in Vietnam*. Cambridge, UK: Cambridge University Press, 2008.

Lanzmann, Claude, ed. *Benjamin Murmelstein: Transcript of the Shoah Interview*. Rome, September 2009 to October 2010. Translated by Lotti Eichorn. https://www.scribd.com/.

Lanzmann, Claude, ed. *Maurice Rossel: Transcript of the Shoah Interview*. January to March 2009. Translated by Lotti Eichorn. https://www.yumpu.com/.

Le Clézio. J. M. G. *Desert*. Translated by C. Dickson. Boston, MA: David R. Godine, 2009.

Le Clézio. J. M. G. *The Interrogation*. Translated by Daphne Woodward. London: Penguin, 2008.

Le Corbusier. *Towards a New Architecture*. New York: Dover, 1986.

Levinas, Emmanuel. *In the Time of the Nations*. Translated by Michael B. Smith. London: Continuum, 2007.

Levinas, Emmanuel. *Of God Who Comes to Mind*. Translated by Bettina Bergo. Stanford, CA: Stanford University Press, 1998.

Levinas, Emmanuel. *On Escape/De l'évasion*. Translated by Bettina Bergo. Stanford, CA: Stanford University Press, 2003.

Lipovetsky, Gilles. *The Empire of Fashion: Dressing Modern Democracy*. Translated by Catherine Porter. Princeton, NJ: Princeton University Press, 1994.

Lockwood, Rupert. *Black Armada*. Sydney: Australasian Book Society, 1975.

Lüdtke, Alf. "Organizational Order of *Eigensinn*?" In *Rites of Power: Symbolism, Ritual, and Politics since the Middle Ages*, edited by Sean Wilentz, 303–33. Philadelphia: University of Pennsylvania Press, 1985.

Lukács, Georg. "Makarenko, der Weg ins Leben." In *Russische Literatur, Russische Revolution*, 191–236. Munich, Germany: Rowohlt, 1969.

Lumley, Robert. *Arte Povera*. London: Tate, 2004.

Lyotard, Jean-François. *Heidegger and "the Jews."* Translated by Andreas Michel and Mark Roberts. Minneapolis: University of Minnesota Press, 1990.

Makarova, Elena. *Boarding Pass to Paradise: Peretz Beda Mayer and Fritz Haendel*. Jerusalem: Verba, 2005.

Makarova, Elena. *Friedl Dicker-Brandeis: Vienna 1898–Auschwitz 1944*. Los Angeles, CA: Tallfellow Press, 2001.

Makarova, Elena, et al. *University over the Abyss: The Story behind 520 Lecturers and 2,430 Lectures in KZ Theresienstandt, 1942–1945*. Jerusalem: Verba, 2004.

Malkin, Jeanette R., and Freddie Rokem, eds. *Jews and the Making of Modern German Theatre*. Iowa City: University of Iowa Press, 2010.
Marchetti, Luca, and Emanuele Quinz. *Dysfashional*. Jakarta: Galeri Nasional, 2011.
Matanasi, Petrik. *Thomas Najoan: Si Raja Pelarian Dalam Pembuangan*. Bandung, Indonesia: Ultimus, 2013.
Matu Mona. *Pacar Merah Indonesia*. Vol. 1. Leiden, Netherlands: Jendela, 2001.
McNab, Robert. *Ghost Ships: A Surrealist Love Triangle*. New Haven, CT: Yale University Press, 2004.
McVey, Ruth T. *The Rise of Indonesian Communism*. Ithaca, NY: Cornell University Press, 1965.
Melville, Herman. *Moby Dick; or, The Whale*. London: Penguin Books, 2001.
Mertins, Detlef, ed. *The Presence of Mies*. New York: Princeton Architectural Press, 1994.
Moderne auf der Flucht: Österreichische Künstlerilnnen in Frankreich, 1938–1945. Vienna: Verlag Turia+Kant, 2008.
More, Thomas. *Utopia*. London: Penguin Books, 2012.
Mrázek, Rudolf. "Beneath Literature, Beyond Empire: Imprisonment, Universal Humanism, and (Post)Colonial Mimesis in Boven Digoel, the Jodensavanne and Scheveningen." In *Shifting the Compass: Pluricontinental Connections in Dutch Colonial and Postcolonial Literature*, edited by Jeroen Dewulf, Olf Praamstra, and Michiel van Kempen, 37–55. Newcastle, UK: Cambridge Scholars, 2013.
Mrázek, Rudolf. "Boven Digoel and Terezín: Camps at the Time of Triumphant Technology." *East Asian Science, Technology and Society* 3, no. 2 (2009): 287–314.
Mrázek, Rudolf. "Healing in Digoel." *Indonesia* 95 (April 2013): 47–72.
Mrázek, Rudolf. "Lenin of the Camps: Radical Translation in Colonial Digoel and Nazi Terezín." *boundary 2* 43, no. 3 (2016): 133–57.
Mrázek, Rudolf. "Say Cheese: Photography." In *Camera Ethica*, edited by Susie Protschky, 255–80. Amsterdam: Amsterdam University Press, 2013.
Mrázek, Rudolf. *Sjahrir: Politics and Exile in Indonesia, 1906–1966*. Ithaca, NY: Studies in Southeast Asia, 1994.
Murto, Kari. *Towards the Well-Functioning Community: The Development of Anton Makarenko and Maxwell Jones Communities*. Jyväskylä, Finland: Jyväskylä University Press, 1991.
Nancy, Jean-Luc. *Corpus*. Translated by Richard A. Rand. New York: Fordham University Press, 2008.
Nancy, Jean-Luc. *Listening*. Translated by Charlotte Mandell. New York: Fordham University Press, 2007.
Nancy, Jean-Luc. *Noli me tangere: On the Raising of the Body*. Translated by Sarah Clift, Pascale-Anne Brault, and Michael Naas. New York: Fordham University Press, 2008.
Nancy, Jean-Luc. *Philosophical Chronicles*. Translated by Franson Manjali. New York: Fordham University Press, 2008.
Nancy, Jean-Luc. *The Pleasure in Drawing*. Translated by Philip Armstrong. New York: Fordham University Press, 2013.

Napier, A. David. *The Age of Immunology: Conceiving a Future in an Alienating World*. Chicago, IL: Univerity of Chicago Press, 2003.

Nemo, Philippe. *Job and the Excess of Evil*. Translated by Michael Kigel. Pittsburgh, PA: Duquesne University Press, 1998.

Nielsen, Aage Krarup. *In het Land van Kannibalen en Paradijsvogels*. Amsterdam: Querido, 1930.

Nietzsche, Friedrich. *Thus Spoke Zarathustra: A Book for All and None*. In *Complete Works of Friedrich Nitzsche*, translated by Thomas Common. Hastings, East Sussex: Delphi Classics, 2015.

Nioo Cheong Seng. See d'Amour, Monsieur.

Noonan, Pat. "Merdeka in Mackay. The Indonesian Evacuees and Internees in Mackay, June 1943-February 1946." In *Pramoedya Ananta Toer 70 Tahun: Essays to Honour Pramoedya Ananta Toer's 70th Year*, edited by Bob Hering, 273–93. Sulating Maphilindo: Edisi Sastra Kabar Seberang, 1995.

Oen, Bo Tik. *Darah dan Aer-Mata di Boven Digoel*. Bandoeng, Indonesia: Boelan Poernama, n.d.

Orwell, George. *Why I Write*. London: Penguin Books, 2005.

Oz, Amos. *A Tale of Love and Darkness*. Translated by Nicholas de Lange. London: Vintage, 2004.

Perec, Georges. *Species of Spaces and Other Pieces*. Translated by John Sturrock. London: Penguin Classics, 2008.

Pérez-Oramas, Luis, ed. *León Ferrari and Mira Schendel: Tangled Alphabets, with Essays by Andrea Guinta and Rodrigo Naves*. New York: Museum of Modern Art, 2009.

Peschel, Lisa, ed. *Divadelní texty z terezínského ghetta, 1941–1945*. Prague: Akropolis, 2008.

Picabia, Francis. *I Am a Beautiful Monster: Poetry, Prose, and Provocation*. Translated by Marc Lowenthal. Cambridge, MA: MIT Press, 2007.

Plaček, Max. *Double Signature*. Jerusalem: Yad Vashem, 1994.

Plato. *Republic II*. Translated by Chris Emlyn-Jones and William Preddy. Cambridge, MA: Harvard University Press, 2013.

Poeze, Harry A. "From Foe to Partner to Foe Again: The Strange Alliance of the Dutch Authorities and Digoel Exiles in Australia, 1943–1945." *Indonesia* 94 (October 2012): 57–84.

Poláček, Karel. *Povídky, Sloupky, Fejetony*. Prague: Nakladatelství Franze Kafky, 2001.

Presner, Todd Samuel. *Mobile Modernity: Germans, Jews, Trains*. New York: Columbia University Press, 2007.

Presser, Jacob. *Ashes in the Wind: The Destruction of Dutch Jewry*. Translated by Arnold Pomerans. Detroit, MI: Wayne State University Press, 1988.

Riis, Jacob A. *How the Other Half Lives*. London: Penguin Books, 1997.

Rilke, Rainer Maria. *The Notebooks of Malte Laurids Brigge*. Translated by M. D. Herter Norton. New York: Norton, 1992.

Riyadi, Dedi Ahimsa. *Hatta: Hikayat Cinta dan Kemerdekaan*. Bandung, Indonesia: Edelweiss, 2010.

Robson, Stuart, ed. *The Wédhatama: An English Translation*. Translated by Stuart Robson. Leiden, Netherlands: KITLV Press, 1990.

Ronell, Avital. *Finitude's Score: Essays for the End of the Millennium*. Lincoln: University of Nebraska Press, 1994.

Ronell, Avital. *Stupidity*. Chicago, IL: University of Illinois Press, 2002.

Ronell, Avital. *The Telephone Book: Technology-Schizophrenia-Electric Speech*. Lincoln: University of Nebraska Press, 1989.

Ronell, Avital. *The Test Drive*. Chicago, IL: University of Illinois Press, 2005.

Roth, Joseph. *The Wandering Jews*. Translated by Michael Hofmann. New York: W. W. Norton, 2000.

Roth, Philip. *Operation Shylock: A Confession*. New York: Vintage International, 1994.

Rothkirchen, Livia. *The Jews of Bohemia and Moravia: Facing the Holocaust*. Lincoln: University of Nebraska Press, 2006.

Rutherford, Danilyn. *Raiding the Land of the Foreigners*. Princeton, NJ: Princeton University Press, 2003.

Sander, August. *Photographs of an Epoch, 1904–1959*. New York: Aperture, 1980.

Sartre, Jean-Paul. *Baudelaire*. Translated by Martin Turnell. New York: New Directions Books, 1967.

Sartre, Jean-Paul. *The Wall*. Translated by Lloyd Alexander. New York: James Laughlin, 1975.

Schmitt, Carl. *The Concept of the Political*. Translated by George Schwab. Chicago, IL: University of Chicago Press, 2007.

Scholem, Gershom. *Kabbalah and Counter-History*. Cambridge, MA: Harvard University Press, 1982.

Scholem, Gershom, ed. *Zohar. The Book of Splendor: Basic Reading from the Kabbalah*. New York: Schocken Books, 2003.

Sebald, W. G. *Austerlitz*. Translated by Anthea Bell. New York: Modern Library, 2011.

Segev, Tom. *1949: The First Israelis*. Translated by Arlen N. Weinstein. New York: Henry Holt, 1998.

Segev, Tom. *One Palestine, Complete: Jews and Arabs under the British Mandate*. Translated by Haim Watzman. New York: Henry Holt, 2000.

Segev, Tom. *The Seventh Million: The Israelis and the Holocaust*. Translated by Haim Watzman. New York: Henry Holt, 1993.

Service, Robert. *Stalin: A Biography*. Cambridge, MA: Harvard University Press, 2004.

Shiraishi, Takashi. "The Phantom World of Digoel." *Indonesia* 61 (April 1996): 93–118.

Siegel, James. *Naming the Witch*. Stanford, CA: Stanford University Press, 2006.

Singer, Isaac Bashevis. *Gimpel the Fool and Other Stories*. New York: Farrar, Straus and Giroux, 2006.

Slavický, Milan. *Gideon Klein: Torzo života a díla*. Prague: Helvetica-Tempora, 1996.

Šormová, Eva. *Divadlo v Terezíné, 1941/1945*. Ústí nad Labem, Czech Republic: Severočeské nakladatelví, 1973.

Steenbrink, Karel (with the cooperation of Paule Maas). *Catholics in Indonesia, 1808–1942: A Documented History.* Vol. 2, *1903–1942.* Leiden, Netherlands: KITLV Press, 2007.

Suwardi, Purnama. *Koloni Pengucilan Boven Digoel.* Jakarta: Agung Hikmatnya, 2003.

Tanizaki, Junichiro. *In Praise of Shadows.* Translated by Thomas J. Harper and Edward G. Seidensticker. London: Vintage Books, 2001.

Tanpa Nama. "Minggat dari Digul." In *Cerita dari Digul,* edited by Pramoedya Ananta Toer, 221–314. Jakarta: Gramedia, 2001. Originally published by Solo: Boekhandel Soeleman, n.d.

Tan Tjio Siang. *Antara Hidoep dan Mati: Atawa Boeron dari Boven-Digoel.* Bandoeng, Indonesia: Boelan Poernama, 1931.

Tarkovsky, Andrei. *Sculpting in Time.* Translated by Kitty Hunter-Blair. Austin: University of Texas Press, 2003.

Toer, Koesalah Soebagyo. *Tanah Merah Yang Merah: Sebuah Catatan Sejarah.* Bandung, Indonesia: Ultimus, 2010.

Tolstoy, Leo. *Resurrection.* Translated by Rosemary Edmonds. London: Penguin Books, 1966.

Toul Sleng Genocide Museum. Phnom Penh: Toul Sleng Genocide Museum, n.d.

Tucholsky, Kurt. *Berlin! Berlin! Dispatches from the Weimar Republic, 1907–1932.* Translated by Cindy Opitz. New York: Berlinica, 2013.

Tydlitát, Jan, ed. *Karel Poláček a divadlo, terezínské období, vzpomínky, poláčkovské kalendárium.* Rychnov nad Kněžnou, Czech Republic: Albert, 2002.

Utitz, Emil. *Psychologie života v Terezínském koncentračním táboře.* Prague: Dělnické nakladatelství, 1947.

Vaihinger, Hans. *The Philosophy of "As If": A System of the Theoretical, Practical, and Religious Fictions of Mankind.* London: Routledge and Kegan Paul, 1935. Originally published in 1911.

van Blankenstein, Elisabeth. *Dr. M. van Blankenstein: Een Nederlands dagbladdiplomaat, 1988–1964.* The Hague: SDU Uitgevers, 1999.

van Blankenstein, Marcus. "Het verbanningsoord aan den Boven Digoel." *Nieuwe Rotterdamsche Courant,* September 8, 11, 13, 1928.

van Eechoud, Jan. *Vergeten Aarde.* Amsterdam: C. de Boer, 1951.

van Kampen, Anthony. *Een kwestie van macht: Het bewogen leven van de arts dr. L. J. A. Schoonheyt in het vormalige Nederlandsch-Indië, Nieuw Guinea, Suriname en Nederland.* Bussum, Netherlands: Van Holkema en Warendorf, 1975.

van Kampen, Anthony. *Jungle Pimpernel.* Amsterdam: C. de Boer Jr., 1951.

van Kampen, Anthony. *Wijkende Wildernis: Onder Kannibalen en Christen-Papoeas.* Amsterdam: C. de Boer Jr., 1956.

van Pelt, Robert Jan, and Carroll William Westfall. *Architectural Principles in the Age of Historicism.* New Haven, CT: Yale University Press, 1991.

Vančura, Vladislav. *Rodina Horvátova.* Prague: ELK, 1939.

Virilio, Paul. *The Aesthetics of Disappearance.* Translated by Philip Beitchman. New York: Semiotext(e), 2009.

Virilio, Paul. *Bunker Archeology*. Translated by George Collins. New York: Princeton Architectural Press, 2008.

Virilio, Paul. *Speed and Politics*. Translated by Mark Polizzotti. Cambridge, MA: MIT Press, 1986.

Virilio, Paul. *War and Cinema: The Logistics of Perception*. Translated by Patrick Camiller. London: Verso, 1989.

von Hofmannsthal, Hugo. *The Lord Chandos Letter and Other Writings*. Translated by Joel Rotenberg. New York: New York Review of Books, 2005.

Weber, Samuel. *Theatricality as Medium*. New York: Fordham University Press, 2004.

Wittgenstein, Ludwig. *On Certainty*. New York: Harper Torchbooks, 1972.

Wittgenstein, Ludwig. *Philosophical Investigations*, revised 4th edition. Edited by P. M. S. Hacker and Joachim Schulte. Translated by G. E. M. Anscome, P. M. S. Hacker, and Joachim Schulte. Oxford: Basil Blackwell, 2003.

Wittgenstein, Ludwig. *Remarks on Colour*. Berkeley: University of California Press, 1978.

Wix, Linney. *Through a Narrow Window: Friedl Dicker-Brandeis and Her Terezín Students*. Albuquerque: University of New Mexico Press, 2010.

Wolff, Kurt H., ed. *Sociology of Georg Simmel*. Translated by Kurt H. Wolff. New York: Free Press, 1950.

Žižek, Slavoj, ed. *Revolution at the Gates: A Selection of Writings from February to October 1917 by V. I. Lenin*. London: Verso, 2002.

Žižek, Slavoj. *Tarrying with the Negative: Kant, Hegel, and the Critique of Ideology*. Durham, NC: Duke University Press, 1993.

Žižek, Slavoj. *Violence: Six Sideways Reflections*. London: Profile Books, 2008.

INDEX

Page locators in italics indicate photographs

Abdoel 'lXarim, 106, 110
abstraction, 230, 237, 263, 286
"Absturz" (the plunge), 326
Adorno, Theodor, 4, 169, 203, 291;
  Works: *Dialectic of Enlightenment*,
  116, 251, 280; *The Jargon of Authenticity*, 53
Agamben, Giorgio, 271
Aliarcham, 19, *43*, 60, *143*, 250, 304
ambulances, 278
Amichai, Yehuda, 353, 362, 363, 373
Anderson, Benedict, 191
Angelus Novus (Klee), 321
Aragon, Louis, 357
"*Arbeit Macht Frei*" sign ("Work
  Makes You Free"), 153, 351, 408n148

Arcades Project (Benjamin), 241, 245,
  256, 293
Archipenko, Alexander, 234
architectonics, 227, 230
Arendt, Hannah, 169, 342, 356, 369,
  389n98
Artaud, Antonin, 190, 194, 259
"as if," 192, 228, 231, 327
Asphalt Rundown (Smithson), 359
Augé, Marc, 201, 207–8, 244, 274, 293
Auschwitz, 2, 23, 63, 96, 430n77;
  "*Arbeit Macht Frei*" sign, 153, 351,
  408n148; architectural plans, 215;
  communist underground, 435n12;
  "family camp," 195–96; layout of,
  214; lines in, 258; as "the murder,"
  4; music in, 114; paintings in, 202;
  rail access to, 271; rumors about,
  126–27; teeth of Jews, 45; theater in,

Auschwitz (cont.)
195–96; two- and three-story beds,
232–33; vegetation, 163; visitors to,
373; voice in, 99–100
Aussenberg, Adolf (painter), 131, 202
Austerlitz (Sebald), 219, 313–14,
376–77
Austrian socialists, 340
Autobahns, 274, 430n7
avant-garde, 2, 190, 194, 200, 234–35
Al-Azhar University (Cairo), 172

Badenheim (Appelfeld), 201
Baeck, Leo, 242, 286, 317, 356
Balzac, Honoré de, 12, 23, 30, 50,
286; *Treatise on Elegant Living*, 40
banknotes (*Ghettokronen*), 32, 384n43
Barnevelders ("privileged" Dutch
Jews), 347–48
barracks, 101; attics, 231; at Boven Digoel, 144, 212; "pleasure barracks" of
Berlin, 249; Theresienstadt, 151–52,
183–84, 221
Barthes, Roland, 23, 38, 42, 79, 118, 325;
on silence, 100, 101
Bataille, Georges, 326
Batavia, 187, 221, 257, 329
Baudelaire, Charles, 34, 158, 202, 328
Baudrillard, Jean, 204
Bauman, Zygmunt, 121, 259, 260, 286
"beautification," 229
beauty spots, 27–42, 158; armbands,
plaquettes, and patches, 36–38,
282–83; badges, 36–37; chains,
38–39; faces, 31–33; hats and caps,
29–30; jewelry and trinkets, 35–36,
71; Jewish star as accessory, 39–42;
makeup and cosmetics, 34; medals,
37; penholders, pencils, little books,
38; perfume, 34–35. *See also* bodies;
clothes; fashion
Beckett, Samuel, 4, 266
being-in-the-world, 127–29, 144
Beit Theresienstadt, Israel, 75

belongings, 4, 11, 227–28, 281–82
Benda, Harry, 339
Benjamin, Walter, 443n152; on
backdrops, 202; on basements,
236; on ciphers, 291; on fashion,
23, 29, 31, 36–37, 44, 57; on "goods
on display," 372; grave of, 356, 369;
on greenhouses, 159; on movies,
203; on music, 112; on seeing, 5;
on silence, 101; suicide of, 342–43;
Works: *Arcades Project*, 241, 245,
256, 293; *One-Way Street*, 282, 345;
Reflections, 21; "The Return of the
Flâneur," 267; *Travel Souvenirs*, 67
Bergen-Belsen, 410n12
Berlin, 249, 256, 267–68
Beyond Memory (Levinas), 378
Bialik, Hayim Nahman, 101
Biran, Misbach Yusa, 111, 154
birds, 83–84
birds of paradise, 35, 201
Birkenau, 126, 272–73, 290, 435n12
Blanchot, Maurice, 100, 125–26, 261,
293, 308
Blankenstein, Marcus van, 18, 332–33
Bloch, Ernst, 88, 102, 153, 202, 213; on
area, 236; on concrete, 246; on darkness, 160; on escape, 350; lavatoriality, 52–53, 55, 255; on schooling, 188;
on speed, 305–6; on "unpresent," 374;
Works: "The Philosophy of Music,"
116; *The Spirit of Utopia*, 320–21
blocks/geometry, 211–38, 289, 305;
architecture of camps, 258; area of
living spaces, 225–26, 228, 231; belongings, 227–30; in Boven Digoel,
216–19, 221–22, 225–26; cemeteries of camp people, 373; circles,
216–17, 219; cities, 222–23; clearing,
222; correctness, 214; cubism, 234;
fences, 218; forms, writing on, 213–
14; geometry, 212–16; "hacienda,"
232; "kumbálek," 232; lines, 218–19,
237–38, 256–57; "mansard," 231–32;

miniaturization, 224, 231–33; police as circle, 216–17; "quartier"/quarter, 224; rectangles, 213, 223, 233–34, 237; Salemba prison sleeping space, 234; subdivision/partitioning, 224–31; surfaces, 215–16, 234–37; tangential, 258–59; technical-statistical-geometric drawings, 215; telephone lines, 219; in Theresienstadt, *211*, 212–16, 219–21, 227–32; trains of people, 243; trunks, 223

"blood," 316

Boccioni, Umberto, 234

bodies, 43–71, 213; as accessories, 44; deaths by natural causes, 60–61; dental care, 45; epidemics and, 50–51; families at camps, 56–61; as fashion, 44, 125; food, 64–70; Heidegger on "taking care of," 44, 45, 47; hygiene, 51–55; *Läusedoktor* (lice physician), 50–51; malaria examinations, 47–49; medical care of, 44–51; neigbourlessness, 259; "pink," 44, 52, 55; postmodern, 125; pregnancy and abortion, 61–62; prone-to-be-polluted order, 51–52; rapture and vulnerability, 321; sport spirit, 73; table manners, 66–67, 70; "taking care of," 44, 45, 47, 63; teenagers, 62–63; toilets and bath, 51, 52–54; vermin and, 49–51. *See also* beauty spots; clothes

Boedisoetjitro, 25

Bois de Boulogne (Paris), 159, 343

Bolshevik Revolution, 285

Bolsheviks, 413n123

Bonaparte, Napoleon, III, 159

"Bonkes" (rumors), 128, 129, 343

books, 173–77, 288

Bourdieu, Pierre, 262

bourgeois order, 31, 55–56, 61, 112, 177, 311–12, 351–52; equivalence, 280; music and, 116; sympathy, ineffectual, 121–22

Boven Digoel (1927–43): agriculture, 150–51, 156–58, 236, 266; animals in, 84–86; barber trade, 28; barracks, 144, 212; belongings permitted, 4, 13–14; blocks/geometry in, 216–19, 221–22, 225–26; books in, 173, 176–77; Burger-Societeit (The Club), 107; clearing land for, 144–45, 150–51, 235; clothing stores, 16; "Committee-of-Welcome" ceremony, 110, 153; deaths and burials, 63–64; demonstrations in, 302–3; Dutch flag, 146, 216, 219; escape attempts, 322–25, 352–53; families at, 56–59; fences, 218, 301; food, 64–67, 282; former internees, fate of, 365–71; Goedang Arang camp, 154–55; gramophones in, 137–39; graves, *143*, 250, 304, 374; gutter network, 255–56; houses, 153–54, 158, 159, 202–3, 212–13; interrogations, 102–3; isolation from the world, 2, 6, 120–21, 127; jewelry and trinkets, 35–36; landscaping, 156–57; lists in, 288–89, 290; mail censored, 92–93; male to female ratio, 58; medical care, 46–51, 160; mentally ill in, 308–10; as model settlement, 221; Moluccan and Ambonese soldiers, 24; mosque construction, 154; movies in, 203; music in, 105–6, 110–16; naming conventions, 283; 1943 evacuation of, 364; noise in, 84–86, 89–90; non-Jews in, 2; perfume, use of, 34–35; planning for, 120; professions of internees, 28, 148; prominent people in, 172–73; radio in, 132–34, 136; raft, 253–54; religion in, 111–12; resistance in, 302–5, 306; Saminists (Oeripists), 306–7, 326; as "sanatorium," 56; schools, 180–83, 185–87; soil conditions, 150–51, 236; speed of construction, 268–69; spelling conventions, 6–7; spies

Boven Digoel (cont.)
in, 123; sport, 75–78, 237; status and schools, 185–87; tact of police, 260–61; Tanah Tinggi section, 247, 307, 309–13, 322, 324, 368; telephone lines, 219; theater in, 190–91, 196–98; tourism to, 375; as "town," 265; twilight, 160; varied population of, 31; vehicles, lack of, 269–70; *warungs* (roadside cafés), 160–61; "wild schools," 182–83, 302; work ethic in, 153–55; zinc in, 249–51. *See also* Kaja-Kaja people

Boven Digoel, current town, 373–74

Boven Digoel Heroes Cemetery, 374

Braille, 95

Brecht, Bertolt, 31, 135, 274, 287, 342

Breton, André, 356–57

Broch, Hermann, 27–28, 226, 243, 305

Brod, Otto, 13, 109

Buchenwald, 274, 335; Dutch "hostages," 335–37, 339; "Goethe Oak," 163, 335

Burian, Emil František, 299–300

Buru camp, 366–67, 370–71, 373, 378

Cabet, Étienne, 213, 222, 255, 315

Caduff, Carlo, 125

cafés, 166

Cage, John, 94, 116–17, 134

Cambodia, prison and camp, 119–20

camp: as apparatus, 125, 127, 129, 213; as-if-life, 192; as capital, 293; cave-like (Plato's cave), 88–89, 118, 125, 127, 191, 362; culture, relationship with, 268–69; definitions, 238, 271; as enlightenment, 188; as epitome of the world, 249; expansion of, 333, 337–41; as ghetto, 261; as "heavily made up," 34; music and establishment of, 116–18; opening of space for, 144; as partial system, 305; as site of modern, 2–3; as stage, 190, 196–97, 229, 266; as suburb, 265–66, 337, 361; supermodern ideal of, 213, 230; as theater, 190; as "toward death," 23; world as, 357

Canetti, Elias, 4

Capital (Marx), 297

capitalism, 23, 114, 191, 305–6, 359

Carpi, Aldo, 199

The Castle (Kafka), 263, 308

Céline, Louis-Ferdinand, 237, 258, 267, 305, 370; on escape, 326, 328; **Works:** *Journey to the End of the Night*, 321; *Rigadoon*, 126–27, 209

Cement (Gladkov), 235, 249

chains, 38–39

Chekhov, Anton, 119, 283–84, 350, 414n37

Chernyshevsky, Nikolai, 255

Chevalier, Michel, 241

children: art made by, 354–55; crying, 102; drawings made by, 62, 185, 202; homeless, 350; murdered in camps, 447n85, 448n122, 448n127; parents, restricted access to, 257; resistance by, 302–3

Churchill, Winston, 24, 126

city, 209. *See also* blocks/geometry; streets; suburbs

clearing, 143–68, 222, 304–5, 317; "civilized landscape," 165–66; clothes and, 159; Construction Commando, 145, 148–49; deforestation, 146, 235; electricity, 162; evacuation as, 145; gardens, 157–59; gardens and public order, 159; as glitter, 151; internees as light bearers, 147–49; Israel and, 361–62; of land for camps, 144–46, 150–51, 235; *Lichtung,* Heidegger on, 144, 170; as modern, 146–47, 160; neatness, 157–58

clothes, 11–26; brightness of, 159; "cloud and shroud," 12–14; of dead, 16; decisions about, 11–12; fashion as violence, 23–24; hats and caps, 29–30; heightened sense of fashion,

19–20; Nazi uniforms, 24; sent by relatives, 16–17; sewing machines and materials, 17–18; sports-related, 72–73, 79; stores, 15–16; uniforms, 14, 24–26, 79, 385n73
colonialism, 169–70
Columbia space shuttle, 364
"command pedagogics," 188, 413n123
commodities, 39–40, 151, 191, 288
Communists: Dutch, 334–35; Indonesian, 13, 19, 364; in Theresienstadt, 135, 297
compass, image of, 305
concentration: of acoustics, 87; clearing and, 145; of food, 68; geometry, 219; gramophones, 136; houses, size of, 226; in letters, 94–95; of light, 146; of medical records, 51; as metaphor for packing, 12–13; by military regime, 233–34; of will, 150
"Concentration Camp Set" (Lego blocks) (Libera), 223–24
concrete, 246–49, 254, 374
confiscation of Jewish belongings, 137, 145, 227–28, 292
conformist consciousness, 169
Construction Commando (*Aufbaukommando*), 145, 148–49
Council of the Elders (Theresienstadt), 24–25, 26, 75, 92, 263; electricity and, 167; music and, 137; "Talmud Commando," 288
Couperus, Louis, 160
Crime and Punishment (Dostoyevsky), 81, 121, 222, 328
The Crisis of European Science (Husserl), 212
Crusades, 349–50
Czech folk tales essay (anonymous), 298–99
Czech gendarmes, 97, 122, 130, 243, 274–75
Czech National Theater, 194
Czech Philharmonic, 115, 122

Dachau, 351–52
Dada, 356–57
dandyism, 428n15; bodies and, 55, 57; clothes, 40; pentjak (pencak), 77; in sport, 73, 75–76, 78
Darah dan Aer-Mata [Blood and Tears] (Oen), 58, 87, 154
Dasein, 261, 318, 367
David, Jacques-Louis (artist), 202
"The Dead of the Desert" (Bialik), 101
death, in camps, 60–61, 63
death camps, 55, 286
dedistancing, 261
Deleuze, Gilles, 292, 325, 378
Delirious New York (Koolhaas), 78
Demetz, Peter, 20–21, 34
deportatio in insulam (deportation to an island), 119
Der neue Tag (Nazi newspaper), 96–97
De Ruwenberg (camp in Netherlands), 336
Desert Islands (Deleuze), 292, 378
Desnos, Robert, 357
The Destruction of the European Jews (Hilberg), 273
Devil's Island of Cayenne, 14–15, 155
de Vries, Hans, 347
Dialectic of Enlightenment (Horkheimer and Adorno), 116, 251, 280
Diaries (Kafka), 141
Dicker-Brandeis, Friedl, 185, 213, 328, 354
Dieses Volk: Jüdische Existenz [This People: Jewish Existence] (Baeck), 317
Diogel River, 19–20, 35, 66, 77, 84–85, 269, 374
discipline, 53, 224–25, 257
displaced-persons camps, 360
Djamaluddin Tamin (revolutionary), 133

Dostoyevsky, Fyodor, 24; on escape, 326; funeral, 39; on Tsarist camps, 27, 29, 38, 307–8; **Works:** *Crime and Punishment*, 81, 121, 222, 328; *Demons*, 239; *The Idiot*, 287, 357, 375; *Memoirs from the House of the Dead*, 280, 307–8
"Drama in Boven Digoel" (Kwee Tek Hoay), 270
Dr. Mabuse, der Spieler (Jacques), 176
dust, or memory, 349–78; Dada and surrealism, 356–57; escapees, fear of, 349–50; former Boven Digoel internees, fate of, 365–71; former Theresienstadt internees, fate of, 357–64; liberation of camps, 358–59; Nazi plans for Jewish museums, 371–72; stars, references to, 353–54; vagrants, 350–51; Yad Vashem interviews with survivors, 357–58
Dutch: Buchenwald "Dutch hostages," 335–37, 339; music and, 115–16
Dutch Indies, 13, 55–56. *See also* Boven Digoel (1927–43)
Dutch New Guinea, 13
Dwork, Debórah, 352, 373

"Eastern fatalism," 306
education: "command pedagogics," 188, 413n123; schools, 179–87; status and, 185–86
Eichmann, Adolf, 115, 145, 241–42, 262, 346, 389n98, 408n148; trial of, 241
Eijkman, Christiaan, 66
Einsatzstab Reichsleiter Rosenberg (The Task Force Rosenberg), 137
embellishment, 229
The Empire of Fashion (Lipovetsky), 237
Empire State Building, 234, 268
enlightenment, 169–88, 212, 251, 280; books, 173–77; cultural circles, 178–79; diaries, 178; letters, 177–78; magazines, 178; "people of the book," 173; poetry, 178; "prominence," 170–73, 186; public readings, 178; schools, 180–87; status and education, 186–87; testing, 187–88
Enlightenment, 169, 212, 251
Entfernung (removal of Jews), 121
Ernst, Max, 357
error, fear of, 279–82, card index, 282–84; cataloguing and categorization, 282–90; coding, 284–85, 288–91; lists, 288–90; numbers assigned to people, 285–86
escape, 319–48; anguish/despair, 320–21; anti-Semitism and, 328; attempts, 103, 322; Boven Digoel attempts, 322–25, 352–53; camps expanding to world, 337–41; as "desertion," 326, 352; distance and, 326–28; fear of escapees, 349–50; games of chance, 321–22; insanity as "reason," 324–26; NSB-ers, attempts at, 329–32; running, 339–48, 353–54; by suicide, 342–43
Esther, Book of, 94–95; play based on, 299–300
evil, banality of, 169
exile from inside, 2
expectation, 261

Face of Our Time (Sander), 152
faces, 31–33, 383n41; as accessories, 31–33; makeup, 34; noses, 32–33; Stockjude face, 32. *See also* bodies
factories, 257–58
Fallada, Hans, 315
families, 56–57; Auschwitz "family camp," 195–96; children, 59–60; marriages and divorces, 57–59, 61; pregnancy and abortion, 61–62
Farinelli (Italian castrato), 117
fascism, 169
fashion: bodies as, 44, 125; catwalk concept, 19, 22, 49, 67, 76, 86, 110, 341; dandies, 40, 55; faces as, 31–33;

heightened sense of, 19–20; love and, 57; music as, 116; shame and, 37–38; skin as, 27–28; spas/hot springs, 55–56, 289n100; as violence, 23–24. *See also* beauty spots; bodies; clothes; sport
The Fashion System (Barthes), 23, 38, 42
Ferdinand, Archduke Franz, 313
Ferrari, León, 95, 354
final solution, mentioned, 2, 6, 114, 273
flâneurism, 19, 23–24, 177, 256, 267
Flaubert, Gustave, 146, 159, 311
food, 64–70; Boven Digoel, 64–67, 282; coffee, tea, cigarettes, opium, 70–71, 392n209; packages from outside, 68–69; ration cards, 280–81; sublime and, 69–70; Theresienstadt, 67–68, 280–81; vitamins, 66, 68
"Fortress B" ("Little Fortress"), 254, 289, 313–14, 357
Foucault, Michel, 188, 257
Frankensteinová-Volavková, Hana (museum director), 372
Frederik Hendrik Island (Yos Sudarso Island), 144
French empire, 14–15
French Revolution, 116, 133, 245–46
Freud, Sigmund, 117, 171
Friedmann, Hugo (librarian), 204–5, 219–20, 224, 288
Fritta, Bedřich, 215
fronts/queues, 257–58
fugitive analysis, 4
The Führer Bestows a City upon the Jews (Nazi propaganda film), *104*, 207, 372

Galanterieladen (thread and needle shops), 35
games of chance, 321–22
Geertz, Clifford, 124–25
Geitel and Co., the Berlin Flag Factory, 40

"General Order of the Jewish Self-Government" (Theresienstadt), 54, 130
geometry. *See* blocks/geometry
Gerron, Kurt, 207
Gestapo, 313
Geuzen (beggars), 352
ghetto, definitions of, 6, 261
Ghettowache (Theresienstadt camp police), 25–26, 101
Gilbert, Shirli, 114
Gimpel the Fool (Singer), 349
Giraudoux, Jean, 151
Gladkov, Fyodor Vasilievich, 235, 249
Godard, Jean-Luc, 207
Goebbels, Joseph, 137, 174
Goedang Arang (Coal Storage) camp, 154–55
Goethe, Johann Wolfgang von, 108, 163, 177, 179–80, 192, 194, 284, 336
Gogol, Nikolai, 194, 207, 414n37
Good Soldier Švejk (Hašek), 178, 287
Göring, Hermann, 40
Gorky, Maxim, 246, 320–21
gramophones, 136–37
greeting, order to give (*Grüßpflicht*), 31

Haas, Pavel, 105–6
The Happy End of Franz Kafka's Amerika (Kippenberger), 422n183
hardness, 38, 40, 236, 245–53; of belongings, 251–52; bricks, 256; concrete, 246–49; crystal, 251; floors, 252–53; piles, 253; tools, 252; zinc, 249–51, 256. *See also* streets
Hašek, Jaroslav, 171, 287
Hatta, Mohammad (former vice president of Indonesia), 88, 172–73, 176–77, 186–87, 226, 244, 334, 365
Haussmann, Georges-Eugène, 229
hearses, 278
Hegel, Georg Wilhelm Friedrich, 96, 279–80, 308, 372

INDEX 475

Heidegger, Martin, 1, 26, 308, 323, 366, 378; on being-in-the-world, 144, 328–29; *Dasein* as distancing, 261, 318, 328; on hardness and touching, 236; on hearsay as being-in-the-world, 127, 128; on human as "humus," 237; on *Lichtung*/clearing, 144, 170; Nazis, support for, 318; on "taking care of," 44, 45, 47, 63, 170; on thingness, 248–49; on time, 274, 276

Heine, Heinrich, 321

Heonik, Kwon, 357, 365

Heydrich, Reinhard, 40, 114–15, 220, 419n52, 429n64, 445n19; assassination of, 122; confiscation of Jewish belongings, 227–28

The Hidden Force (Couperus), 160

Hilberg, Raul, 273

Hillen, W. P. (Dutch official), 120, 310–11, 324

Hillesum, Etty, 11–12, 41, 73, 230–31, 338–39, 346

Himmler, Heinrich, 33, 240–41, 262, 271, 284, 346, 351

Hitler, Adolf, 71, 114, 167, 200, 274, 341, 403n92

Ho Chi Minh, 162–63, 408n147

Holan, Emil, 171, 178, 410n17

holidays, Jewish, 65, 89, 166, 299–300, 316

Holocaust, 337

Holocaust museums, 15, 99, 200, 202, 289, 291

horizon, 320

Horkheimer, Max, 116, 169, 280

Höss, Rudolf, 153, 271, 351

Husserl, Edmund, 212, 214–15, 305, 381n58

hygiene, 52–55

Icaria (Cabet), 213, 222, 255, 315

The Idiot (Dostoyevsky), 287, 357, 375

indexes, 282–84, 372, 433n196

Indies Staat van Oorlog en Beleg, SOB (State of War and Seige), 330

indifference, 260–64

Indonesia, 1927 rebellion, 2, 31, 144, 306

Indonesian Revolution (1945), 365–66; "Communist *putsch*" (1965), 366, 367

Indonesia Raya [Great Indonesia] (national anthem), 139

informational forms, 125

In Praise of Cosmetics (Baudelaire), 34

insanity, 308–13; escape attempts as, 324–26

In Search of Lost Time (Proust), 124

instantness, 125–26, 130, 134–35

Institute for the Holocaust and Genocide Studies (Amsterdam), 347

intensity, 108, 158

"interiors-as-cockpits," 230

"Internationale" (song), 113, 302–3

International Red Cross, visits to Theresienstadt, 21, 50, 68, 71, 94, 199, 208, 229, 265–66, 278, 298

interrogation, 92, 102–3

The Interrogation (Le Clézio), 130

In the Penal Colony (Kafka), 100, 213, 215, 253, 259–60, 275

isolation, 2, 6, 120–21, 127–28

Israel: Palestinians, 361–62; Six-Day War, 363; as suburb of camps, 361; Theresienstadt people in, 360–62

Jakarta, 221. *See also* Batavia

Janáček, Leoš, 106

Jan Kalista Hockeyista (Holan), 171

Japanese, 128, 135, 136, 345–46, 364

The Jargon of Authenticity (Adorno), 53

Jesenská, Milena, 340, 443n144

Jewish Museum in New York, 223

Jewish Museum in Prague, 232, 372, 398n10, 399n31

Jewish star, 26, 39–42, *104*, 118, 259, 335; on sports uniforms, 74, 79
Jewish War of Independence, 361
jews (lowercase j), 1–4
Job (Roth), 355–56
Job, Book of, 147, 237, 378
Joodse Savannah (Suriname), 331–32
Journey to the End of the Night (Céline), 321
Jüdische Presse-Agentur (JPA), 128
Jüdisches Nachrichtenblatt (Prague paper), 345
"Junkspace," 34, 281

Kafka, Franz, 9, 12–13, 109, 340, 384n48, 422n183, 439n25; on escape, 320; on fearlessness, 314; sisters of, 171, 179; on steadfastness, 353; on writing, 94; **Works:** *Amerika*, 208, 293; *The Castle*, 263, 308; *Diaries*, 141; *In the Penal Colony*, 100, 213, 215, 253, 259–60, 275; *The Metamorphosis*, 267, 374–75; *Nature Theatre of Oklahoma*, 36; *The Trial*, 31, 281
Der Kaiser von Atlantis (Ullmann opera), 108, 109, 131, 134, 137, 213
Kaja-Kaja people, 19–20, 49, 51, 52, 259, 323; food supplies brought by, 65; movies and, 203–4; noise made by, 89–90; sports clothes, 80; in twenty-first century, 373–74
Kampen, Anthony van, 328
Kandinsky, Wassily, 248
Kant, Immanuel, 153, 326
Karmi, Ghada, 191
Kartodikromo, Marco (Mas Marco): on Aliarcham, 19; death of, 285; on escapees, 324; on houses, 212; on music, 113, 115; on resistant behaviors, 301; on rumors, 128–29; on sounds, 85, 93, 100; on spies, 123; on theater, 196–97
Kentridge, William, 189–90, 237, 372, 377–78

Kertész, Imre, 72, 258, 274, 286
Kien, Peter, 109, 122, 137, 215
Klee, Paul, 321
Klein, Franz Eugen, 106
Klimt, Gustav, 44, 51, 386n2
Koestler, Arthur, 342
Koolhaas, Rem, 34, 78, 102, 215, 223, 281, 373; on flatness, 235, 236; on Singapore, 233, 235, 251
Koran, 147, 286
Koussevitzky, Serge, 105
Kracauer, Siegfried, 33, 234, 241, 249
Krása, Hans, 105
Kromoblanda (Tillema), 222
Kwee Tek Hoay, 270

Labe (Elbe) river, 84, 254
Lang, Fritz, 176
Lanzmann, Claude, 175, 208, 229, 262, 298, 377
lavatoriality, 53, 55, 255
laws and decrees, Boven Diogel: Article 37 of penal code, 334; fences, 218, 301; "wild schools," 182–83
laws and decrees, Nazi: against contact with outside world, 109–10; clearing of Theresienstadt, 145; food, Theresienstadt, 67–68; "General Regulations for Jewish Self-Government," 54, 149, 326; hygiene-related, 54; on isolation, 121; mail regulations, 93–94; music-related, 109, 129; naming of Jews, 284; on noise, 103; smoking prohibition, 71; suicide and self-mutilation, 315–16
leaking, 254–55
Le Clézio, Jean-Marie Gustave, 130, 369
Le Corbusier, 213–14, 218, 221, 223, 225, 234, 246, 248; on concrete piles, 254; on "house-machine," 272; on "regulating line," 256–57; on speed, 268; on tubes, 256
Leibniz, Gottfried, 100, 285, 432n169

Lenin, Vladimir, 173, 255, 283, 285, 353
Leo Baeck Institute of Jewish Studies (New York), 356
Lessing, Gotthold Ephraim, 194
Lessing, Theodor, 299
letters: censorship of, 92–93; concentration in, 94–95; enlightenment, 177–78; sent to the dead, 95–96
Levi, Primo, 233
The Leviathan (Roth), 355
Levinas, Emmanuel, 94, 98, 317–18, 321, 323, 378; "On Escape," 304
Libera, Zbigniew, 223
Lichtdom (Nazi light "cathedrals"), 167
Lichtung (clearing), 144, 155, 170
light, 141; bright houses in Boven Diogel, 158, 159; as contraband, 147; of culture, 171; electricity, 162, 165; hard-on-the-eye, 146, 147, 149; *Lichtsperre* (ban on light), 168; as modern, 146–47; restrictions on, 147–48; twilight, 160; types of, 147, 161–62, 174, 191; vegetation as, 150–51, 156–58, 163–65; windows, 165; work ethic as, 149–55. *See also* clearing; enlightenment; limelight
limelight, 189–208; backdrops, 201–2; movies, 203–6; painting, 198–201; photography, 207–8; theater, 189–98; walls as concept, 200–204
lines, 218–19, 237–38, 266; as regulatory, 256–57
Lipovetsky, Gilles, 23, 237
Liszt, Franz, 105
Litoměřice (Czech town), 204, 327
"Little Fortress" ("Fortress B"), 254, 289, 313–14, 357
Loebis, Parlindoengan (medical student), 333–35, 359
Loekman, M. H., 60, 182, 368–69
logic, 237, 284–85
Long, Richard (artist), 237, 242
"The Long, The Fat, and The Keen-Sighted" (Czech fable), 298–99

Lukács, Georg, 351
Lukman, Tatiana, 368–69
Luna Park (Coney Island), 246–47
Lurie, Boris, 201, 360, 363
Lyotard, Jean-François, 1–2

Maccabi Zionist Youth, 135
The Magic Flute (Mozart), 189–90
Maginot Line, 248
Makarova, Elena, 206, 346, 376
Maki, Fumihiko, 271
Manes, Philipp, 16, 22, 26, 29, 33, 36, 63, 75, 83, 89, 93–94, 102, 107, 123, 125, 128, 130, 134–35, 147, 149, 152, 163–64, 165, 167, 175, 204, 228, 233, 235–36, 239, 242, 243, 259, 262, 275, 279, 281, 284, 286, 288; the Manes Group, 192, 194, 195
Mann, Erika, 344–45, 443n158
The Marriage (Gogol), 194
Martaya (deathless void), 372
Marx, Karl, 297, 320
Masaryk, Tomáš, 285, 328, 335
The Mass Ornament (Kracauer), 234
Mauritius, 346
Má vlast (Smetana), 122
May Day, 302
Mechanicus, Philip, 15, 239, 248, 252, 277
medical care, 44–51; Boven Digoel, 46–51, 160; Theresienstadt, 44–46
Mehring, Walter, 189, 353–54
Melville, Herman, 212, 216
Memoirs from the House of the Dead (Dostoyevsky), 280
memory: aging of, 4–5; of voices, 91–92. *See also* dust, or memory
The Memory of Childhood (Perec), 371
Mephistopheles, 61
The Metamorphosis (Kafka), 267, 374–75
Michelet, Jules, 245–46, 328
Minggat dari Digul [Escape from Digoel] (Tanpa Nama), 78

miniaturization, 224, 231–33
Mirroring Evil (Holocaust exhibition), 223–24
Mischling (mixed-blood Jew), 20–21
Moby-Dick (Melville), 212, 216
modern: "being on the road," 243–44; camps as site of, 2–3; clearing as, 146–47, 160; concentrated, 341; culture of, 192; emergence from darkness to light, 160; in food, 69; geometry, 219; hardness of, 245–46, 252–53; instantness, 125–26; light as, 146–47; "modern human types," 152; monotony, 117; music and, 112, 117, 118; in Paris, 246; rumor and, 128; sport and, 72–73; supermodern, 213, 230; technology, sounds of, 87; theater as culmination of, 189–90; utility, 248–49, 252, 273, 289
Modernity and the Holocaust (Bauman), 121, 160
moratorium, 259–60
More, Thomas, 315–16
Moresco, Emanuel, 347–48
music, 104–18; applause, 118; in Auschwitz, 114; in Boven Digoel, 105–6, 110–16; camp intensity and, 108; communist (Red) songs, 113–14; composers and compositions, 108–9, 116–17; at De Ruwenberg, 336–37; gamelan, 105, 106, 110–11, 250; kroncong orchestra, 105, 110, 112, 115, 302, 336–37; marches, 113; modern and, 112, 117, 118; "muziek," 110, 111; Nazi interest in, 114–15; opera, 109; opera, Malay, 112; order and, 116–17, 118; religious, 111–12; *schlagers* (hits), 109, 112, 192; in Theresienstadt, 104–10
Music in the Holocaust (Gilbert), 114
Musil, Robert, 186
Muslims, 13, 124–25, 172
Mussolini, Benito, 346–47
Musulmans, 315, 335

My Journey from Paris to Java (Balzac), 30

Najoan, Thomas (internee), 19, 353–54
naming conventions, 283–84
Nancy, Jean-Luc, 88, 92, 169, 204, 213, 259; "Listening," 115
Napier, David, 350–51
Nathan the Wise (Lessing), 194
National-Socialist Bond (NSB), 329–32
National Library (Jakarta), 79
Nature Theatre of Oklahoma (Kafka), 36
nausea, 297–318; core of camp, 310, 314, 329; "insanity," 308–15; passivity/fatalism, 298, 306; "recalcitrance," 307–8; religion, 316–17; resistance, 299–302; revolt/return, 317–18; suicides, 315–16; withdrawal, 308
Nazi Four-Year Plan of 1936, 445n19
Nazis, 430n70; confiscation of items, 137, 145; Generalplan Ost (General Plan East), 163; "parasitic Jew" stereotype, 148; propaganda films, 74, 75, *104*, 118, 167, 199, 206–7, 372
neigbourlessness, 259
Nemo, Philippe, 321
neomania, 23
Netherlands Institute for War Documentation (Amsterdam), 347
newspapers, 96–99, 125, 155
New York City, 222–23, 224, 268–69, 305; "Street Arabs," 350
Nietzsche, Friedrich, 169, 190, 192, 234, 266
noise, 83–90; absence of familiar sounds, 85; of animals, 84–86; of birds, 83–84; of bombing, 89; of church bells, 88–89; concentrated acoustics, 87; echoes from outside, 88–90; of insects, 85; of rain, 84; of rivers, 84; of trees, 83–84; of trumpets, 86–87, 89; of typewriters, 87–88, 89

Les odeurs de Paris (Veuillot), 293
Ohře (Eger) river, 84, 254
Olympic Games, 74, 75
One-Way Street (Benjamin), 282, 345
Ordnerwache (Order Watch) (Jewish police section), 235
Oświęcim, 268. *See also* Auschwitz
overcrowding, as miniaturization, 233
Oz, Amos, 173, 361

Pacar Merah "[The Red Darling"], 133–34, 343
Palestine, 355, 361–62
Palestinian Memoir (Karmi), 191
The Pandemic Perhaps (Caduff), 125
Pandoe story (anonymous), 324–25
papier-mâché, 246
Paris, 229, 237, 241, 267, 293
Paris, années 30 (Augé), 207–8
Pascal, Blaise, 268
Patton, George S., 22–23
Pearl Harbor, 128
"people of the book," 173, 320
Perec, Georges, 23, 94, 201, 254, 271, 282–83, 289; post-war drawings, 354–55; **Works:** *W, or The Memory of Childhood*, 73, 371
perintah halus (a gentle order from above), 262
petitions, 300–301; requests to leave, 58, 61, 154, 186
phatic communion, 102
Philippson, Alfred (scholar), 170–71
Philip V, King of Spain, 116
The Philosophy of "As If" (Vaihinger), 192
"The Philosophy of Music" (Bloch), 116
Picabia, Francis, 236, 286, 306
Pinkas Synagogue (Prague), 371–73
Plato's cave, 88–89, 125, 191, 362
Poláček, Karel, 171, 232, 258, 314, 320
police: as "circle," 216–17; *Ghettowache*, 25–26, 101; Jewish police, 36, 37, 42, 89; Rust en Orde Bewaarders, ROB, 15, 19, 25, 37–38; tact of, 260–61

Pontjopangrawit (musician), 71, 105, 108, 111, 113, 250
pop-ups, 246
Potemkin villages, 2, 15
Prague, 5, 122; Jewish Museum, 232, 372, 398n10, 399n31; Pinkas Synagogue, 371–73
Prague Linguistic Circle, 298
precision, 280
Princip, Gavrilo, 313
Prison Diary (Ho Chi Minh), 162–63
Production Workshop (Theresienstadt), 199, 214–15
Prokofiev, Sergei, 350
"prominence," 170–73, 186, 196, 228–29, 358
Propaganda Ministry, 137
Proust, Marcel, 124
Psychology of Life in Theresienstadt Concentration Camp (Utitz), 126
Purim, 299

Querido, Emanuel, 355
queues, 257

radio, 129–31, 403n92; bodies molded by, 125; in *Der Kaiser von Atlantis*, 131–32. *See also* rumors
Rahm, Karl, 25, 229, 298
Ramon, Ilan, 364
Ranggawarsita (Javanese poet), 127
rapture, 321
Rathenau, Walther, 171
ration cards, 280–81
The Realist (Broch), 227
"recalcitrance," 307–8, 329–30, 334, 341, 360–61; post–Boven Diogel, 367, 368
Recitation of Gatuloco (Javanese), 127
Red Army, 23
Reflections (Benjamin), 21
"Reflections on the Art of Walking with a Bowl of Soup" (Poláček), 258
Reich, Lilly Joss, 344–45

Reichssicherheitshauptamt (Nazi office for security), 241–42
religion, 316–17
Remnants of Auschwitz (Agamben), 271
representation, 3, 5
resistance, 299–303; movement, refusal of, 301, 306, 308, 312–15. *See also* escape; nausea
"The Return of the Flâneur" (Benjamin), 267
Riefenstahl, Leni, 167
Rigadoon (Céline), 127, 209
Riis, Jacob, 222, 224, 305, 320, 350
Rilke, Rainer Maria, 70, 100, 108
rococo style, 219
Romans, 119
Rommel, Erwin, 248
Ronell, Avital, 279
Roosevelt, Franklin D., 346–47
Roth, Joseph, 40, 124, 223, 232, 246–47, 251, 280, 282; on numbers, 285, 286; on the run from Nazis, 341–42, 344, 345, 351, 355; **Works:** *Job*, 355–56; *The Leviathan*, 355
Rousseau, Jean-Jacques, 129, 320
Royal Dutch Indies Army, 105
rumors, 125–28; "Bonkes," 128, 129, 343; "cooking," 128–29; *Mundfunk*, 135–36. *See also* radio
Russian Army (Red Army), 359
Russian-Jewish emigrants, 340
Rust en Orde Bewaarders, ROB (Calm and Order Guards), 15, 19, 25; plaquettes and patches, 37–38

Saint Petersburg, 290–91
Sakhalin penal colony, 283–84, 350, 414n37
Salemba prison, 234
Saminists (Oeripists), 306–7, 326
Sammelstellen ("collecting sites"), 240
Sander, August, 152
Sartre, Jean-Paul, 261, 308, 317
sawahs (wet or irrigated rice fields), 156

Scarlet Pimpernel, 133
scattering, 295. *See also* dust, or memory; escape; nausea
Schendel, Mira, 95–96, 354
Scholem, Gershom, 173, 227, 267–68
Schönberg, Arnold, 105
Schorsch, Gustav, 194–95
Schoonheyt, Dr. L. J. A., 198, 304, 329–31
Schreibturnus (writing rotation), 94
Schweitzer, Albert, 351
Schwitters, Kurt, 267, 269
Sebald, W. G., 219, 224, 313–14, 376–77
Segev, Tom, 360, 362–63
Sentimental Education (Flaubert), 159, 311
Serat Wēdhatama [The Supreme Wisdom] (Javanese text), 153
shame, fashion and, 37–38
Shean, Nava, 12, 192, 194, 252
shroud, concept of, 12, 14–15, 20, 27, 29, 102–3, 147, 203
Siech (ailing or infirm person), 315, 335
silence, 1–2; music and, 116; voice and, 94, 100, 101
Silence (Cage), 94, 116, 134
silhouettes, 125, 215, 225
Simmel, Georg, 38
Singapore, 233, 235, 251, 271
Singer, Isaac Bashevis, 4, 349
Sjahrir, Soetan (former prime minister of Indonesia), 59, 88, 200, 330; on houses, 226–27, 251, 253; as intellectual, 150, 172–74, 177–78, 186–87; partitions, memories of, 223, 226, 244–45; as prime minister, 17, 172, 365; on sport, 78, 80
skin, 27–29, 32, 35, 38, 50
Smetana, Bedřich, 122
Smithson, Robert, 359–60
Soekarno (former president of Indonesia), 365–66, 375
Soekarno (internee), 368

Soewigno, Mahmud Siswo (painter), 17, 68, 198, 415n64
The Song of Love and Death (Rilke), 100
sound, 81; acoustic isolation, 120–21, 124, 127–28; barriers to, 119–20; cave-like (Plato's cave), 88–89, 118, 125, 127, 191, 362; church bells, 88–89, 119; as frame, 116; listening, 130; music as organization of, 116; rumors, 125–28; spies and, 122–24. *See also* noise; radio; voice
Soviet Union, 240–41
space, opening of, 144
Spain, rebellion against, 352
spas/hot springs, 55–56, 289n100
spectral analysis, 68–69
speed, 268–74, 305–6; pseudo-activity, 308
Speer, Albert, 167, 274
Spielberg Foundation, 358
Spier, Josef "Jo," 199, 200, 202, 277, 358
spies, 122–24, 301, 303
spirit of the time, 1–2
The Spirit of Utopia (Bloch), 320–21
sport, 72–80, 279; athletics, 78; basketball, 75; boxing, 78–79; dandyism of, 73; English as language of, 77; gymnastics, 75, 78; handball, 75; self-defense arts, 77; soccer, 74–80, 237, 336; tennis, 77–78, 159
SS (Schutzstaffel), 262–63; "character" of, 33; clothing and, 16, 21, 24, 26, 29, 31, 34–35; "housecleaners" for, 123; medical issues and, 44–45, 50, 54; music and, 107; uniforms, 24
Stalin, Joseph, 135, 173, 353
Stanislavsky, Konstantin, 194
stars, references to, 353–54
Steinherz, Samuel, 171
Strauss, Richard, 105
streets, 239–64, 373; Autobahns, 274, 430n7; "being on the road," 243–44; canals, water supply, and drainage, 255; ditches, 255–56; fronts/queues, 257; indifference and, 260–63; leaking, 254–55; as lines, 266; rails and rail connections, 253; rivers as, 240; *Sammelstellen* (collecting sites), 240; smoothness, 254–56; suburbs, connection to, 266–67; transports and closing off of, 261–62; walking to camps, 12, 239–40. *See also* hardness
subdivision/partitioning, 224–31
sublime, 17, 69–70, 293
suburbs, 265–93; of camps, Czech towns as, 328; camps as, 265–66, 337, 361; gates, 292–93; streets leading to, 266–67
suicide, 315–16, 320, 342–43
surfaces/flatness, 215–16, 234–37, 246, 252–54; crystal, 251; height as modality of, 236
surrealism, 356–57
survivor, as term, 360

tact, 259–61
taedium vitae (world-weariness), 293
Tagesbefehl (Nazi news sheet), 97, 99
tali api (lights), 160–61
tallit (prayer shawl), 12, 13
"Talmud Commando," 288
Tanah Tinggi (Higher Ground) section, Boven Digoel, 247, 307, 309–13, 322, 324, 368
Tanizaki, Junichiro, 190
Tanjung Priok harbor (Batavia), 329
Tan Malaka (revolutionary), 133–34, 343
tattoos, 27, 259, 286–87
Taussig, Josef (writer), 22, 37, 51, 100, 131, 178, 287
telegraph, 132
temporality, 261, 275–76, 291; speed, 268–74; "tempo," 278; temporality, 261, 275–76, 291; temporariness of camps, 271–72; untimeliness, 325

Terezín (town). *See* Theresienstadt/Terezín (Czech town)
The Test Drive (Ronell), 279
Thälmann, Ernst (chairman of German Communist Party), 335
theater, 189–98; in Auschwitz, 195–96; in Boven Digoel, 190–91, 196–98; camps as, 190; of cruelty, 190, 194, 201, 259, 303; German repertory, 195; as "Jewified," 189; as medium, 205; opacity of, 205; spectacular, 193; in Theresienstadt, 192–95, 278, 299–300; Theresienstadt as, 206
The Theater of Cruelty (Artaud), 190, 259
Theresienstadt (1942–45): acoustics of, 130; "Aryans" in, 61; barracks, 151–52, 183–84, 221; black-out curtains, 165, 166; blocks/geometry in, *211*, 212–16, 219–21, 224, 227–32, 289; Blocksperre punishment, 224; books and library in, 174–76, 288; cabarets and cabaret songs, 179, 192, 205, 220, 273, 279, 289; café, 166; clearing of town, 145–46; clothing stores, 15–16; Communists in, 135, 297; construction and organization, 214–15; Construction Commando (*Aufbaukommando*), 145, 148–49; curfew, 110, 165; deaths and burials, 63–64; dormitories, 232; elderly as *Überaltert* (overage), 63; electricity, 165–67; escape attempts, 103; Esther story as play in, 299–300; families at, 61–62; as film, 206; food, 67–68, 280–81; former internees, fate of, 357–64; "Fortress B," 254, 289, 313–14, 357; as "ghetto," 2, 6; *Ghettowache* uniforms, 25–26; gramophones in, 136; greeting, order to give (*Grüßflicht*), 31; houses, 163; Indies present in, 347–48; "insane" people in, 314–15; isolation from world, 121–27; jewelry and trinkets, 35, 71; last days and hours of, 126; latrines, 51, 53, 257, 285–86; liberation of, 274–75, 298, 358; light in, 146, 165–68; mail censored, 92–94; male to female ratio, 62; "mansard," 231–32; medical care, 44–46; as model settlement, 21, 220–21; movies and, 205–6; music at, 104–10; Nazi flag, 146; Nazi propaganda films, 74, 75, *104*, 118, 199, 206–7; noise at, 83–89; Order Section, 276–77; paintings in, 198–200; Paradeplatz, 83, 101, 107; Production Workshop, 199, 214–15; professions of internees, 148–49; prominent Jews in, 170–71, 228–29; protocols, 263; radio in, 135; "Ramparts II," 204; ration cards, 280–81; readings and lectures, 108, 131, 178, 354; schools, 183–85, 187; Sluice Gate, 292–93; soccer, 74–75; as "spa," 56; spelling conventions, 6–7; spies in, 122–23; sport in, 74–75, 279; as stage, 190, 229, 266; streets, 88, 289, 373; technical-statistical-geometric drawings, 214–15; as temporary, 272–73; theater in, 192–95, 278, 299–300; theft in, 264; as toward Auschwitz, 233; traffic, 279; trees and flowers, 163–65; varied population of, 31; vehicles in, 277–78; vermin in, 49–51; violence, lack of, among Jews, 264; walls of, 88, 200–204, 238; water service, 254–55, 257, 292; work ethic in, 149–50
Theresienstadt Memorial, 99, 135, 376
Theresienstadt people, in Palestine, 361–62
Theresienstadt/Terezín (Czech town), 83–84, 265, 373; as fortress, 130, 219–20; geometry, 219; schools, 183–84
thingness, 248–49, 288
Third Army, United States, 22–23
Thompson, Dorothy, 355

Threepenny Opera (Brecht), 31
Tillema, Hendrik Freerk (amateur geometer), 221–22
Torah, 120
total system, 305
touch, 129, 204–5, 334; avoidance of, 259–60; forbidden, 204, 258–59; indifference, 260–63; surface and, 236–37; violence, 262–63; walls and, 204, 372
tourism, 375–76
Towards a New Architecture (Le Corbusier), 213–14, 225, 256
Traces (Bloch), 202
trajectory/progress/*Immergleich*, 4
transports, 239–41; to Boven Diogel, 240, 244–45; calculation of, 241–42; closing off of streets and windows, 261–62; *Laufschritt* (run-walk), 274; lists, 288–89; ship, 13–14, 56–57, 127–28, 144, 245; to Theresienstadt, 241–44; trains, disguised, 242–43
Travel Souvenirs (Benjamin), 67
Treatise on Elegant Living (Balzac), 40
The Trial (Kafka), 31
Tucholsky, Kurt, 121–22, 341
Tuol Sleng (Cambodia), 119–20

Ukraine, Soviet, 350
Ullmann, Viktor, 105, 108, 109, 131, 134, 137, 213
Ulyanov, Alexander, 255
Utitz, Emil, 37, 126, 175, 178, 315, 354
utopia, 52–53, 116, 249, 315–16, 325
Utopia (More), 315–16

vagrants, 350–51
Vaihinger, Hans, 192
Vančura, Vladislav, 280
van der Plas, Charles O., 321
van Pelt, Robert Jan, 215, 352, 373
Vauban, Marquis de, 227
vehicles, 269–70, 277–78
Versailles Peace Treaty, 334

Vienna University, 44
Vietnam, 350, 365
violence, 262–63, 304; fashion as, 23–24
Violence (Žižek), 308
Virilio, Paul, 137, 204, 260, 268, 273–74
visitors, 92
voice, 91–103; in Auschwitz, 99–100; Book of Esther, 94–95; Braille, 95; censorship of materials, 92–93, 96–97; colportage, 102; human and divine incomplete without, 91; interrogation, 92, 102–3; letters sent to dead, 95–96; literacy, 95; memory of, 91–92; newspapers, 96–99; outbursts, 100–101; of paper, 92; readings in Auschwitz, 100; silence, 100; visitors, 99; written, 92
Vostell, Wolf, 372
vulnerability, 321

W, or The Memory of Childhood (Perec), 73
Wagner, Richard, 105, 114, 284, 432n63
Wallace Line, 84, 395n12
walls, 88, 200–204, 238, 322, 350–51, 372; *Schanzen*, 205, 322
Wannsee Conference (1942), 273
warungs (roadside cafés), 160–61, 336
wayang kulit (shadow-puppet play), 190–91, 197–98
Weber, Samuel, 205
Weil, Jiří, 116, 242–43
Wertheim, Willem, 290–91, 339
Westerbork (camp), 15, 97, 248, 252, 265, 277, 417n118; Barnevelders in, 347
What Is to Be Done? (Chernyshevsky), 255
"wild schools," 182–83, 302
Wilhelmina Ziekenhuis (hospital, Boven Diogel), 46–47, 159, 162
Wittgenstein, Ludwig, 3, 214, 233, 280, 285, 350

World War I, 246
World War II, 329

Yad Vashem Holocaust Memorial,
 Jerusalem: archives, 15, 99, 200, 289,
 291; interviews, 357–58
yekehs, 361

Zelenka, František, 194–95, 207
Zemlinsky, Alexander, 105
zinc, 249–51
Zionists, 297, 360
Žižek, Slavoj, 102, 308
Zweig, Stefan, 285, 341

www.ingramcontent.com/pod-product-compliance
Lightning Source LLC
Chambersburg PA
CBHW051843300426
44117CB00006B/247